John Ackerson
"Holding Ground"
Boston

31 August, 1962.

THE HOUSE BUILT ON SAND

THE HOUSE
BUILT ON SAND

The Conflicts of German Policy in Russia
1939 - 1945

GERALD REITLINGER

THE VIKING PRESS
NEW YORK · 1960

Published in 1960 by The Viking Press, Inc.
625 Madison Avenue, New York 22, N.Y.

Library of Congress Catalog Card No. 60-9628

PRINTED IN GREAT BRITAIN

CONTENTS

PART TWO—POLITICAL CRUSADE

MAPS *(between pages 396 and 397)*

The Eastern Front showing limits of occupation at various dates and principal partisan areas

The Eastern Front: German zones of authority

NOTE

THIS BOOK is in no sense a history of the military campaigns in Russia. It treats of plans and problems, to which the battlefront provided only a background and which can be said to have begun with the German negotiations for a pact of friendship in 1939. The plans end ironically with a German-sponsored Russian Liberation movement, desperately conceived in the last months of Hitler's Reich.

I should have liked to treat the story with all the dramatic unity of a five-act tragedy, but this has not proved possible, because of the interlocked and conflicting nature of German purposes. Therefore, at the risk of some chronological seesawing, I have decided to treat such subjects as civil-government policy, the Partisan problem, the treatment of the prisoners of war and the 'Eastern Workers' as separate entities. The Russian Liberation Movement, forming as it does an antithesis to the prevailing German policies in these matters, is treated in the second part of the book.

For the assistance of the reader, who finds the time sequence thus disturbed, a chronological table is provided. Although the incidents of the military campaign are referred to only in terms of the background of other events, they will be found in this table, since they serve conveniently to correlate the general picture.

It is usual in a book of this sort to sum up the evidence and conclusions in a sort of epitome at the end. Contrary to this practice, I have summed up in an introductory chapter, because the events are so little known to the general reader that the outline can conveniently precede the detailed picture.

Beckley, Sussex, 1958

INTRODUCTION

Grab-War or Political Crusade?

IN THE DAYS when the history of the twentieth century can be written as a whole, it may be found that one single event dominated it, namely Hitler's invasion of Russia. This prodigious plan and its failure transformed the Russian State from the condition of a timid Asiatic country, still licking the twenty-year-old wounds of civil war, to the military power that dominated Europe from the Elbe to the Adriatic. Indirectly it brought down in impotence and shame the old balances of power in the Near and Far East. Perhaps too it will be found that the military failure of a man who rejected civilization, caused the destruction of civilization itself. Yet when the causes of that single act of folly are studied, no reasonable explanation can be found.

Hitler spoke frequently of his war as a colonial war. He entertained several projects for dividing conquered Russia, for removing the population from great parts of it by hunger and economic pressure and for replacing them with Germans or north Europeans. These extravagances were not simply due to the intoxication of military success. They were already to be inferred in the famous fourteenth chapter of Hitler's *Mein Kampf*, as published in 1926. Though it can hardly be said that during the subsequent fifteen years Hitler acted consistently in accordance with the views which he had stated in *Mein Kampf*, on one subject at least he never withdrew his original standpoint. Germany's economic salvation, he would always argue, lay not in the recovery of her lost African colonies but in her traditional historic field of expansion, the plain of eastern Europe.

In the past, German colonies, some of them scattered as far east as the Urals and the Caucasus, had been a source of strength to the Russian Empire. In Hitler's scheme of 1941 they were to be increased to form a constrictive girdle round the homeland of Russian imperialism. But, though this was his purpose in invading Russia, even Hitler did not believe that the land-mass of the Soviet Union could be held for ever by foreigners. In March 1941, he admitted to his army commanders that, after the defeat of Russia, independent states would have

9

to be tolerated on the soil of the former Soviet Union. German policy would keep them disunited and militarily weak. German colonies would to some extent keep them apart.

Such was the very sketchy picture which Hitler drew for his generals.* In the next few days he allowed Alfred Rosenberg, his expert on Russia, to draft and later to amend a complicated plan for German administrative areas which were to provide the pattern for the future separatist states. And, after the first bout of conquest, which took his armies to the fringe of Leningrad, Moscow and the Caucasus, Hitler expressed his approval of several schemes for German and north European colonization. But, one may ask, did Hitler seriously believe in his 'separatist socialist states,' artificially limited by cunning German officials both in their intelligence and in their natural assets? Could any human being have believed in them? The order of Hitler's planning is significant. Between July 1940 and March 1941 it was exclusively military. Economic planning was scarcely considered before May 1941, civilian administration not before April, while it was more than two months after the opening of the campaign that the shape and character of the civil governments was decided. This suggests that, so far from having kept a colonization plan tucked away in his mind since the publication of *Mein Kampf*, Hitler approached the subject empirically. Until the last few weeks of the war Hitler was not an obsessed lunatic. Behind the ebullitions of a primitive, one-track mind there would occasionally gleam the realism of a horse-trading peasant. It was a mind that saw present alternatives clearly, but could never perceive anything beyond the successful achievement of the next move. Thus the colonialism, with which Hitler was associated and which he had to abandon in the face of defeat and the opposition of his own chiefs, was never thought out at all, because he saw nothing beyond a Germany that had been made the dominating power of the western hemisphere through the defeat of the one rival.

In November 1941 it must have become clear to Hitler that for the first time in his military career the next move had not been successfully achieved. So far from abandoning his original crude colonialist propaganda in favour of more concrete plans, he had to keep it up in its unchanged form as the stimulus for another campaign. In Hitler's own expressed view the anti-Bolshevik crusade was not enough to justify the sacrifices demanded from the German soldier.** At no time had

* See pp. 66–9
** See particularly pp. 341–2

Hitler offered the Germans National Socialist programmes that carried no material bait. Now, more even than before, the crusade against Bolshevism had to be made attractive with promises of a national standard of living, increased at the expense of the conquered; with promises of land and plunder taken from Slavs and Jews. Hitler was never able to retract this policy. It was a web which imprisoned him to the last and it is remarkable that, even in 1945, Party leaders could not offer the public the prospect of an honourable peace in the east, but only the mixture as before, a German *Lebensraum* extending as far as the Bug, the Dnieper or the Volga according to taste.

Behind this flight from reality, which must—by the most reticent of computations—have cost from fifteen to seventeen million lives, lurks the enigma not of one man but of a nation. All historical inquests, which assess this catastrophe in terms of power politics alone or worse still of the party politics within the power politics, are a self-delusion. Dictatorship and the double-talk life that goes on beneath it account for much, but they cannot account for everything. No one can explain in terms of the arrogance of one man the greatest of all wars, a war designed for the political annihilation of the most populous nation in Europe and the reduction of its best territory to colonies inhabited by an alien race. How did it happen that the German generals—and generals are normally the people least anxious for war—together with the German cabinet ministers, the civil service, the captains of industry, the party leaders and the economic experts—failed to record one single open protest?

The succession of 'Barbarossa' orders were communicated to a select few, but none of the classes named could have failed to notice what was being prepared. The rescinding of the demobilization orders, which Hitler issued after the fall of France, the massing of men and materials on the eastern border, the purpose underlying the invasion of the Balkans, were all common knowledge. Even if the German people in June 1941 were helplessly and passively inured to war, this does not explain why the High Command reacted so differently to Hitler's plans in 1941 from the way they reacted in 1939.

Perhaps it will be answered that the generals were persuaded that Russia was an easy prey; that the prospect of the downfall of Bolshevism and world communism appealed to most Germans. But the first supposition is untrue and the second only half true. Very few of the men who prepared the invasion of Russia shared Hitler's professions of optimism. The spirit in which they embarked on this adventure

seems to have been a sinister impulsion overcoming a profound misgiving. In some cases it was misgiving, drowned in a sort of drunken
frenzy as in the case of the once Russophil governor of the Ukraine,
Erich Koch. The vicious common factor in the speeches of Erich Koch and
of other men who shared the task of governing and exploiting Russia,
such as Goering, Sauckel, Rosenberg and Backe, was not merely a
lip-service to the style of Adolf Hitler, but a drugging of their own senses.

How was this drug compounded? Fear and hatred of Marxism
have been no less in evidence among the victor nations since the
war than they were at Hitler's court. An intervention in Korea,
a rearming of Western Germany that no one, not even the Germans,
desired, and an economic barrier across Europe have been some of the
results. But there has been no serious demand for a crusading war, no
demand for the political extinction of the Soviet Union. The notion of
races, inferior to west Europeans though of the same colour and
civilization, seems as incongruous in the present century as the companion notion that they can be displaced. Nor can it be paralleled in
history, except perhaps among the Mongols of the early thirteenth
century, who held the nomad way of life to be divinely ordained and
the dwellers in cities to be doomed to destruction.

The state of mind that could encompass such an idea undoubtedly
existed and it existed in our time. It must be tracked back a great deal
further in the present century than Hitler's wartime table talk, Martin
Bormann's admonitions and Erich Koch's speeches in the Ukraine. The
background of these utterances must be perceived clearly, for they
were not just wartime extravagances but systematic and to their
auditors not intolerable.

We in England in the Second World War were subjected to a
ceaseless flow of exhortations by ministers of this and that. So were the
Germans. And, like ourselves, the Germans were promised pie in the
sky—but it was a different pie. We remember the weekend orations
and the mixed metaphors of the men who bade us tighten our belts, put
our backs to the wall, our noses to the grindstone and our cabbages in
the asparagus bed. We also remember that they kept sugaring the pill
and that the sugar was sometimes thick, for the National Government
rested uneasily on the pillow of the party truce. Much was done even in
the great crises of the war to keep the socialists content. The tremendous defeat of the Germans at Stalingrad was less noticed in Britain in
February 1943, than the British Government's White Paper on the
Beveridge social insurance plan.

To the Germans, government speakers offered not the millennium of the Welfare State but the fruits of predatory war. A people, who had certainly not welcomed war in 1939 as they had welcomed it in 1914, were told that this was an exceptional war which would pay dividends. Literally they were told—and told repeatedly by almost every party leader—that they would fatten off the victims. Russians could go hungry because they were used to it. Germans came first and so it would remain, apparently for ever and ever.

Many German officials and soldiers expressed their distaste for these utterances in a flood of candid memoranda, but it never occurred to the authors to suggest that the speakers, whom they criticized, were mad. It may be said too that this was not so remarkable, for British cabinet ministers were not considered mad or even in need of the services of a psychiatrist, when they prophesied a rich and leisured future under Socialist planning to a small island which was spending fourteen millions a day on pure destruction. In their respective ways both Goering and Sir Stafford Cripps said the things that appealed to majority-audiences. Why then did they have to appeal so differently to secure the same end?

One reason was that the Germans had lost the last war, whereas the British had won it. The First World War had been not a twentieth century war but the last of the nineteenth century wars, a war of dynastic and imperial ambitions, not a war for an ideology or for an economic plan, but a war for King and Country. At the end, the surviving soldiers of both sides came home in a state of bitter disillusionment towards that simple conception. Most disillusioned of all were the young officers. In England many of them believed that the generation of very old men, who had stuffed their young heads with Greek Iambics, had done so only to sacrifice them from the age of eighteen on the altars of the Somme and Paschendael, waving them into action with their cracked voices and their shooting-sticks, their faces as red as the bands round their hats. It was a drift towards pacifism that began in literature and extended into politics. Not only the British Cabinet but the High Command itself entered the Second World War, resolved to avoid battles of attrition, resolved to avoid the reckless waste of young life.

Germany too had rebelled since 1918 against the old and against the conceptions of the old regarding duty and tradition. But it was a very different sort of rebellion. *Their* generals had not kept up the King and Country concept through thick and thin. They had capitulated to the

Allies over the heads of the *Reichstag* and they had forced their Kaiser to abdicate. If Hitler and the new race of politicians disliked old men and generals, it was not because they had sacrificed the young on their battlefields, but because they had not sacrificed them enough. The mood that was to prevail was not sentimentality about dead schoolboys and Flanders poppies but savage resentment, not against war but against civilization. The laureate of these Germans was not Erich Remarque of *All Quiet on the Western Front* but Ernst von Salomon of *The Outlaws*. Against that background Hitler bewitched his crowds. Against that background he created a National Socialist language, adaptable to all circumstances. In 1941 it easily embraced the concept of the sub-human Slav, as easily as it had always embraced the unending demands of German living space. The keys to this language were the words *Diktat* and *Entkreisung*, dictate and encirclement. They were the words with which Hitler's first backers described the Versailles treaty of 1919.

By 1941 a new generation had reached manhood, yet encirclement neurosis was stronger in Germany than it had ever been before. For many years Germans had been taught that the natural exchange of natural resources could only be achieved through a privileged position and that this position could only be attained through war. Yet paradoxically Hitler went to war with Russia precisely at the moment when this privileged position had been achieved without war at all and when the largest exchange of commodities between nations, that had ever been arranged in history, was functioning perfectly well. During the war with Russia there were even critics who pointed out that Germany could never hope to draw more out of Russia than Russia had been due to provide under the February 1940 trade agreement. But just as in the eighteen-forties it had been an axiom of faith among the anti-corn-law leaguers that free trade would one day abolish war, so now it was believed that the existence of one free trade loophole must provoke war.

Thus Hitler told his generals that England would only make peace when Germany became master of the entire continent. To Alfred Jodl in August 1940, Hitler expanded this idea even further. England, he said, had refused his peace offers, even after Dunkirk, because she had concluded a secret agreement with Russia.[1] Hitler, who had seen the supineness of the Soviet Union, when Czechoslovakia and Poland had been overrun, could not have believed what he said in any seriousness, but he needed this excuse just as he calculated that Jodl would need it.

Psychologically National Socialist thought, with its brooding insistence on the self-contained economy and the continuous land-mass could no longer tolerate upon the same continent the coexistence of the strong and the independent. All the National Socialist emphasis on autarchy and on freedom from the manipulations of international finance had been concentrated on the Four-Year-Plan of 1936 and that plan had failed. It had never been considered as an alternative that Germany with her special resources was peculiarly well fitted to embark on industrial investment in undeveloped countries. It had never been considered that such investment might provide far more true internal wealth for Germany than a system of European economic satellites, geared to a Four-Year-Plan. Instead the belief was fostered that Germany was poor and disinherited. Hitler, who was poor and disinherited himself, became the natural figurehead of the idea.

Thus the German people identified itself with its leader and perhaps subconsciously shared his state of mind. When the Germans read in their morning papers that they were at war with last night's ally, the shock was doubtless mitigated by the fact that they could not write to the papers about it. But to the overwhelming majority there was no shock at all. A traumic identification of their hopes and fears with the person of their Fuehrer had long made them immune to shock. At the Nuremberg trials it was a state of mind which had to be probed by lawyers and criminologists who grew daily more round-eyed and puzzled. The Russian lawyers, subject themselves to traumic identifications or at any rate accustomed to exploiting them, opted breezily (like the Red Queen) for death penalties all round. The Westerners departed, worried and dissenting and so shaken that there was never an international tribunal again. Four and a half million words had been read out in court from the documents and the evidence, but they provided no answer to the riddle of seventy million people who had identified themselves with one common little man; no answer to the question, can another seventy millions or perhaps 500 millions make themselves as accident-prone as the German people in 1941?

The phenomenon becomes harder still to accept when it is realized that Hitler in June 1941, was fulfilling no long-standing promise, was discharging no vow, was carrying out no programme which he had consistently advocated. Party leaders were quick to refer to the prophetic passages in the fourteenth chapter of *Mein Kampf*, but prudence forbade them to notice how unprophetic these had already proved. In 1926 Hitler had found Russia a 'putrid state corpse' and

England and Italy the only worthwhile allies.[2] A treaty with Russia would mean that Germany would have to support her in a war with the West. It would be the annihilation of Germany. Had Bismarck lived in 1926, he would not have allied himself with a nation in such decline. Yet Hitler advocated no 'Alexandrian campaign' against Russia, but rather a progressive occupation, as the Russian state continued to decompose 'through the influence of Jewry and the collapse of the old German leadership of the country.' And behind this leisured march of German arms would follow the German plough.[3]

In fact what Hitler envisaged in 1926 was, like most historic prophecies, a retrospect. The image was simply that of Russia in February 1918 after the negotiations at Brest-Litovsk. And what Hitler did in the Second World War was just what he had warned Germany against. He concluded a treaty with Russia—though such things had once meant the annihilation of Germany—and he planned an 'Alexandrian campaign'.

Furthermore Hitler, though he had regarded Russia in 1926 as a putrid state corpse, entertained no such illusions after 1933 when he came to power. Had Hitler remained in 1938 so convinced of Russia's weakness, he would certainly not have challenged the West over Austria and Czechoslovakia but built up his strength in another quarter. It is remarkable that on 5th November 1937, when he discussed his war plans with the service chiefs, Hitler spoke for four hours and a quarter without mentioning Russia. Even at a date when the first of Stalin's massed treason trials must have reminded him that the 'state corpse' was still putrefying, Hitler was looking for living space in the south and not in the great Eastern plains.[4]

Nevertheless, after the fall of France, Hitler persistently ignored the advice, both of his embassy staff in Moscow and of his military intelligence officers, who reported on the potential strength of Russian armament. He had now convinced himself that Russia was weak, just as he had convinced himself in 1925–6. Stalin's failure to provide a military guarantee to the Czechs in 1938 and his support of the German annexation of western Poland in 1939 in exchange for a squalid territorial deal, had both been proofs of weakness. Hitler could not comprehend that a great and strong power might desire peace so passionately as to perform degrading sacrifices of her integrity—or her pride—like the British nation in the shade of Chamberlain's umbrella. To Hitler's primitive mentality the fear of war was the same thing as inability to fight. Given this mentality, it was inevitable that Hitler

should have made the first overt admission of his intention to attack
Russia, almost immediately after the fall of France. The intimation
was passed on to Hitler's generals on 29th July and it should be noticed
that this was a moment when the preparations for the invasion of
England were still being taken seriously by Hitler's High Command and
when they had not passed into the later stage of camouflage or bluff.

There was not the least reason to suppose on 29th July 1940 that
the Russians were planning some military action because Hitler was
getting too powerful. In the following November, when his original
orders were nearly four months old, Hitler tried to justify the preparations he had begun by citing Russian behaviour in south east Europe,
where Stalin had increased the territorial demands on Rumania which
he had made originally in accordance with the Molotov-Ribbentrop
Pact. The additional land-grab was little more than a tit-for-tat to
balance the German control of the Rumanian oilfields and it was part
of a re-alignment of frontiers and interest-spheres, which had been
determined in principle between the two powers in August 1939.
Sinister as it was, there was nothing in it that Germany had not
bargained for. That Russia was preparing for war at this moment was
true only in the sense that she sought to strengthen her defences. The
tone of Russian diplomatic correspondence continued to be amiable.
The Russian grain deliveries under the Moscow Pact were faithfully on
their way on the day of the German invasion and the Russian forces,
deployed behind the frontier, were in no posture of defence—as several
German commanders have testified. It was no Judas kiss that Stalin
planted on the bristling cheeks of the German military attaché, Hans
Krebs, at the Jaroslavl terminus on the 13th April 1941, but the real
article. It expressed friendship—in Stalin's own guttural German 'auf
ieden Fall'.[5]

In the last stages of preparation, some criticisms were voiced and
several prophets of woe were dismissed—like General Koestring—
from Hitler's presence, only to emerge later with adequate promotion.
But, like the Foreign Office, the High Command accepted the great
gamble with something more than mere fatalism. Comparison with
earlier occasions is illuminating. In September 1938, shortly before the
Munich Agreement, Ludwig Beck had resigned his post of Chief of
Staff. Certain generals discussed a military Putsch against Hitler and
tried to convey their intentions to the British government. In August
1939, even Goering tried to act behind the scenes through the intermediary of a Swede, Mr Berger Dahlerus. After the conquest of

Poland almost the whole of the High Command were united against trying conclusions with the West. But not even the survivors of the 'Resistance Circle' claim that any Putsch was planned in June 1941. The High Command showed no reluctance towards a campaign for which they had been engaged in plans of detail since December 1940. There had been grave complications. A change of heart in Yugoslavia against a German alliance in April 1941 involved an unbudgeted military campaign and a two months' postponement of the invasion date. Even this did not divide Hitler from his High Command. Captain Liddell Hart, professionally kind to generals, prefers to think that they were not wrong-headed and dishonest but just unworldly. They were, he says, like so many specialists, rather naive outside their own sphere. Hitler overcame their doubts with the use of political information which convinced them of the necessity of the attack.[6]

But were German generals always so easy to convince? The most significant landmarks in his war with Russia were Hitler's quarrels with the High Command, quarrels that lost him his best Chief of Staff, Franz Halder, and his best field generals, Guderian, Rundstedt and von Manstein. In December 1941, these quarrels led him to commit his second most catastrophic folly, when he assumed the personal direction of the war. No general resigned in June 1941, but during the following years many generals were glad to have their resignations accepted. Some have written their memoirs and all maintain that the plans which they prepared for Hitler could have been carried out and the war won.

Very slowly the opposition to Hitler extended from strategy to political warfare, where the conflict became sharply defined. In pursuance of Hitler's directions, a horde of officials, chosen for their standing in the party, carried out the policies of colonialism and reckless exploitation. They worked for Rosenberg's Eastern Ministry as civil governors, for Goering's Four-Year-Plan Office as collectors of produce and booty, and for the Plenipotentiary for Labour, Fritz Sauckel, as slave raiders. Since more than half the occupied territory was ruled not by civilians, but by military rear-area commanders and their staffs, clashes of policy with the army were constant. The High Command of the Armed Forces under Hitler's faithful mouthpiece, Wilhelm Keitel, in principle forbade criticism, because Hitler ruled that the armed forces should not interfere in politics. Yet there was a horde of civilian-minded military government officers whose whole business was politics. So long as the organizations, which were controlled by Goering and Sauckel, operated in territory under military government, a ban such as Keitel tried to impose was unworkable. Criticism was constant and on certain occasions effective.

The power of such criticism was limited by the self-chosen status of the German High Command. The Commanders of Army Groups and armies, who signed for Hitler's invasion orders, also signed by implication for his political plans, particularly for the outright murder of Soviet officials and the massacre of the Jewish population. Having for many months tolerated both these horrors with only the barest murmur of dissension, their protests in 1942 over the stepping-up of the produce-drives and man-hunts lost the force they should have had. Moreover it was only when they realized that they were not fighting a *Blitzkrieg*, that the problems of political warfare and the appeasement of the local population began to worry the great Army Group Commanders such as von Kluge, von Kuechler, von Manstein and von Kleist. It was left on the whole to minor departments of the policy-making staffs at General Headquarters to conduct the struggle against the hard Nazi inner core, which comprised Hitler, Bormann, Himmler and Keitel. Such were the eastern section in the Armed Forces Propaganda Office, the Organization Section and Military Government section of the Operational Staff and the intelligence section known as 'Foreign Armies East'. A great deal could be done by such agencies, so long as it was not necessary to obtain a decision from Hitler. In the army at least the rebel exponents of liberal *Ostpolitik* could sometimes expect the support of the querulous Chief of Staff, Franz Halder, and of his more severely professional successor, Kurt Zeitzler. Much more rarely they could count on the blunt, remote and quizzical rival Chief of Staff, the head of the Operational Section of the High Command, Alfred Jodl. But access to Hitler was barred by the pompous, insufferable Keitel, not a Minister for War but a mouthpiece of the Fuehrer.

Yet occasionally Hitler made a concession, though he never openly changed his attitude towards an enemy whom he regarded, not as an armed rival but as an *Untermensch*, a sub-human. Hitler's attitude was in fact, in contrast with the mixed and tortuous motives of many of the rebels, extremely simple. His directions for the political treatment of the country, which he had first announced in March 1941, postulated a war that would end in six weeks and at the latest before the winter set in. The political problem would therefore exist almost from the beginning. When Hitler realized that he was in for a second campaign, the political problem ceased to be urgent. Henceforward the decisions which he made on the subject were no decisions at all. He merely shelved the problem, refusing to believe that there had ever been a friendly attitude among sections of the Soviet population or that he had created new enemies. Finally, when he realized that no significant part of the Soviet Union was likely to remain in German hands, Hitler forgot the original directions altogether. It no longer mattered what his military and civilian politicians played at. A Russian liberation army, a future head of a Russian State, national committees for future secessionist states, all these were tolerated with a shrug of the shoulders.

Having started with a cruel, repellent policy, Hitler had no faith in schemes for liberal revision. A war of brute force and of purely land-grabbing purpose could not be changed by any idealistic 'Proclamation for the East' into a liberation crusade. Hitler was much more realistic than the rebels, who pursued their chimera to the very end through defeat and chaos. What had begun as the half-treasonable notion of a few cranks became at the end of the war a popular form of wishful thinking. It was the notion that the Russian soul was anti-Bolshevik and that the awakening of the Russian soul would destroy the Marxist system. As a few people already believed in 1941 and as everybody knew in 1943, Russia could not be destroyed as a state and as a nation. But, said the rebel *Ostpolitiker*, Russia could be destroyed as a centre of world revolution. E en in 1945 it might not be too late to create a great Russian national army, recruited from the two million Russian prisoners who had not died of hunger. The apparition of such hordes of fellow-countrymen, the propaganda slogans which they would carry, might still nullify Stalin's huge superiority in weapons and equipment.

While no army commander had believed at the time of the invasion that Russian prisoners would fight for the Germans, no army commander could doubt it at the end of the first campaign. But there were always misgivings as to the level to which Russian leadership could be permitted to extend. In December 1942, for instance, Field Marshal von Kluge took fright and demanded the removal of a pure Russian brigade under Russian commanders from his Army Group Rear Area.* Eventually such objections were overcome, but the independent 'Russian national army' only came into being during the last desperate months of the war, when there was no limit to the meaningless prestige concessions which could be offered in order to persuade Russian prisoners to change their allegiance.

The *Ostpolitiker*, who planned to make the Russian people the allies of Germany, allowed themselves to be carried away by three pheno-

* See pp. 325–6.

mena of the first weeks of the invasion. They had seen entire Soviet regiments which, so far from fighting to the end in the encirclement *Kesseln*, had marched in column to the German lines. They had seen German tanks, bedecked with flowers by Ukrainian villagers. They had seen Red Army prisoners, who not only did useful chores in return for a bowl of soup, but were quite happy to pick up a rifle and shoot at their own countrymen.

Now all these three phenomena could be interpreted in more ways than one, but in each case there was an unglamorous explanation as well as a glamorous one. Ukrainian peasants in 1941 would have welcomed any invading army, but, however generously they behaved, the invaders could never have reconciled themselves with the diverse aspirations of Ukrainian leaders—any more than the relatively well-conducted Germans and Austrians had been able to do in 1918 when they had been invited into the country. As to the second phenomenon, masses of surrounded troops who gave themselves up without a fight were no novelty in 1941, apart from their huge numbers. Armoured warfare had produced the same terror and despair in France in 1940 and the Germans themselves were to fall victim to it on the central Russian front in June 1944, when those who gave themselves up had nothing to expect but slavery. As to the Russian prisoner who handled a rifle against his own country, there was little extraordinary about him. Regarded practically as a deserter by the Stalin government, doomed to slow death by hunger or typhus if he got as far as the German prisoner of war cages, starving already and often a foreigner fighting in a Russian formation, it was small wonder that he offered to change sides. The only surprise was the small number who did so. At the beginning of 1942 the Germans had taken 3,900,000 prisoners, of whom barely 200,000 had volunteered to serve with the Germans and of these only a small fraction could be trusted with a rifle. Eventually some 800,000 men out of more than five and a half million prisoners or deserters served with the Germans. No German official source would publish the proportion of those who could be counted as pure Russians, but it was unquestionably small. Overwhelmingly the men who changed sides, belonged to the minority races, White Russians, Balts, Ukrainians, Cossacks, Caucasians and Asiatics.

German army group commanders, who have written their memoirs, tend to agree that Hitler could have won his *Blitzkrieg* in 1941, as planned, had he not dissipated his strength by withdrawing troops from the Moscow front in order to secure the Ukraine. Thereby the main assault on Moscow was fatally delayed and a second campaign was rendered necessary after the Russians had been given breathing space. Hitler, however, in more than one passage in his Table Talk tried to justify the Ukrainian diversion.[7] He explained that the General Staff were incapable of understanding economic questions. They could not see that it would be fatal to make the final onslaught on the strongest part of the front, while the Russians still possessed the resources of the Ukraine. Hitler had already forgotten that Moscow had been intended to fall so quickly that the Russians would not have had time to draw on these resources. But the *Ostpolitiker* had another explanation for Hitler's failure and, while this explanation tends to become very popular today among German writers, it must be noted that it was contemporary. In a famous memorandum, which he drew up for his chief, Alfred Rosenberg, on 25th October 1942, Otto Braeutigam, wrote that the war could have been won long ago, had it been fought against Bolshevism and in order to split Russia. The trouble was that there had been a third aim, colonization. Had the Germans brought with them to Russia something like President Wilson's Fourteen Points of 1918, Russia would have disintegrated just as Germany had done then.[8]*

Following this argument, Hitler need never have diverted his armies from Moscow in order to secure the Ukraine, since the Ukrainians would have offered it to him. At this long distance of seventeen years such discussions seem academic. Whether or not Hitler could have won his war by being more humane and liberal or by listening to the advice of professional soldiers, in fact he lost it. The question seems less academic when one sees Braeutigam's claim repeated in the books, now so popular in Germany, of Erich Dwinger and Juergen Thorwald; still less academic when it is realized that the Russian section of the Bonn Foreign Office is directed by Herr Braeutigam, who once believed that Bolshevism could be so easily mastered and Russia so easily split.

But it has been left to writers outside Germany to exhort the nations of NATO to emulate Hitler's *Ostpolitiker* and to seek Russian deserters for the political campaign that Hitler never fought. It would be hard to imagine a more searching and objective work on the subject of German rule in Russia than Mr Alexander Dallin's. Yet throughout this huge book there are constant references to an article in the magazine *Life*, which can hardly have appealed to Mr Dallin's discernment because of its scholarship. There must be other reasons for calling

* See p. 202

attention to this bizarre product of the trigger-happy year, 1949, when Mr Wallace Carroll, former director of the London Office of the US Office of War Information, took the American public by storm.[9]

According to Mr Carroll, Hitler was able to get as far as Stalingrad only because the Germans had 'millions of eager accomplices in Russia.' That he got no further and that he was driven out of Russia was because he ignored these accomplices. From such premises Mr Carroll argued that the destruction of Russia would require no atomic war. Even if it succeeded, such a war must make the Americans the most disliked people in the world. What was needed was not nuclear but 'psychological' fission. Stalin could be beaten, Marxism could be overcome if all the tricks of Hitler's thwarted *Ostpolitiker* were repeated; propaganda on a scale that the Germans never knew, fifth columns such as Canaris never dreamed of and anti-Stalinist Partisans, handling weapons such as had never been seen in history.

This in the present author's submission is bunkum, but it is bunkum that offers a very useful challenge. For what, one may ask, would have happened if Hitler had done all the right things? Let us suppose for instance that Hitler had proclaimed himself at war not with the Russian people but with Marxism, just as Stalin was later to declare himself at war not with the German people but with Fascism. Had Hitler done this, it is possible that Stalin's appeal to the Russian people to continue the war behind the German lines, an appeal that was made within four weeks of the invasion, might not have met with so much response. At a considerably later period it was observed that, every time there was a German drive for forced labour, the Partisans would show an increase both in their numbers and their activities.* Hence a simple deduction; no mistreatment, no Partisans. But to suppose that Partisan warfare could have been avoided is unrealistic. An appeal by Stalin for a patriotic war was not even necessary and in fact it meant very little. So long as the Russians were able to parachute leaders and weapons behind the German lines, Partisan groups with considerable nuisance value were inevitable. There were areas of swamp and forest, where a German soldier would not be encountered for hundreds of miles. Fanatical Partisan leaders were not likely to be deflected by the claim that the Germans were only fighting Marxism. Nor did they need the loyalty of the villages, whose inhabitants were remorselessly terrorized by both sides. Partisan warfare was the result of peculiar campaigning conditions, which were due to the scale of the battlefield and the lack

* See pp. 373–4

of communications. Even the pure of heart could not have by-passed that.

But, said the *Ostpolitiker*, it need not have come to this. Hitler could have taken Moscow and dictated peace in 1941. It seems to have been very widely believed that there would have been no fight left in the Red Army after the fall of the Kremlin. Yet, when one considers the resilience of the Red Army in the winter of 1941 and again in the winter of 1942, in both cases after incredible losses in men and territory, one wonders what difference the loss of Moscow would have made. Let us suppose a different strategic decision, as a result of which Hitler held Moscow before the winter of 1941 with time to spare to mop up the Ukraine and Crimea. Let us suppose promises, duly fulfilled according to the advice of the most respectable *Ostpolitiker*, autonomies functioning in Reval, Riga, Kaunas, Smolensk and Kiev and a hand-picked Russian socialist administration in Moscow, instead of the most disreputable party notorieties who had been proposed as *Generalkommissars* for Great Russia.* Stalin in Kuibishev would still have ruled nearly a hundred million people, would still have retained the industries of the Urals and Siberia.

According to Hitler, even this eventuality was of no consequence. On 20th March 1942, when he had had the opportunity to study all the implications of another winter campaign, Hitler made a curious fore-cast in conversation with Goebbels. Assuming that the Caucasus, Leningrad and Moscow would be occupied by the following October, Hitler declared that he would then allow the eastern campaign to come to rest along a gigantic defence line. It might mean a 'hundred years' war' in the east, but not a war to worry about. The position of the Germans in relation to the rest of Russia would be like that of the British towards India.[10]

The heights of Hitler's lack of realism are shown in this talk of a gigantic defence line in a country where the Germans had never possessed the resources to create a closed front. Had Hitler won every-one of his objectives in 1942, he would still not have been able to ignore Stalin's remaining power, except by keeping more than three million men permanently holding a 2,000-mile frontier. Sooner or later the strain of this position would have forced Hitler to advance on the Urals. And, even if the Russians had had to land their lease-lend supplies at the mouth of the Ob, there would have been another Stalingrad for the Germans.

* See p. 142

The inability to appreciate this was shared equally by Hitler and by those who believed that victory could be achieved through granting autonomy to the vanquished Soviet nations. All the more surprising, therefore, is the realistic forecast which was made as far back as 28th April 1941, by the Permanent State Secretary of the Foreign Office, Ernst von Weiszaecker:

> I do not see in the Russian State any effective opposition, capable of succeeding the communist system and uniting with us and being of service to us. We would therefore probably have to reckon with a continuation of the Stalin system in Eastern Russia and Siberia and with a renewed outbreak of hostilities in the spring of 1942.[11]

Perhaps, however, the best way to judge the countless wartime memoranda of the *Ostpolitiker* and the case they have made out for themselves subsequently is to suppose that the war could have been won on the lines which they suggested. Of all the problems of war, victory is the most awkward. In one of Max Beerbohm's cartoons the great Dr Jowitt remarks to Dante Gabriel Rossetti, 'And what were they going to do with the Holy Grail when they found it?' Most of the *Ostpolitiker* had become by 1942 fascinated with the slogan 'only Russians can defeat Stalin'. It led them to abandon their separatist tactics and to support a Russian liberation army with a Russian leader, destined for some sort of federalist Russian State. Their hatred of Hitler's policy and their faith in the Russian deserters had got them into a paradoxical situation. Some of the *Ostpolitiker* took part in the plot against Hitler. Stauffenberg, von Tresckow, Wagner, Schulenburg, von Roenne and Freytag-Loringhoven lost their lives. It seems that, having got rid of Hitler in order to win the war their own way, they were going to create another Stalin.

Those who know of Hitler's occupation of Russia only through the picture, true as far as it goes, of oppression, murder and misery as presented by the documents of the international Nuremberg Trials, will be surprised that there should have been so much sentimentality and romanticism about the Russians in the German Wehrmacht. They will be surprised at the hero-worshipping cult that still surrounds the person of Andrei Vlasov, 'The Russian de Gaulle', and still more surprised that Vlasov owed his belated recognition to Heinrich Himmler, chief of the SS and one-time whipping-master of the subjected Russian population.

The story of the Russian liberation army is not simply tragic, it is wildly crazy. It was the outcome of a long conflict between sets of people who were completely lacking in realism. On the one side there were the party bosses, large and small, yesterday's booking clerks and café-waiters, lording it with a riding whip among the *Untermenschen*, who were sub-human because they did not scrub the kitchen-dresser every morning and because they slept on the stove. On the other side they were dedicated souls, who fell for the mystique of the Slav and who saw in a dim autocratic Russian soldier the Christ-like features of a national redeemer. Fundamentally they were the same sort of people. The German is oblique in his approaches to foreign ways of life. Clogged with incomprehension, he fears or he worships. His fear is cruel, his worship quixotic. But, to complicate this picture, it has to be added that some of Hitler's leading exponents of colonialism and on the other side the greater part of the *Ostpolitiker*, civil and military, had been born in Russia and had been brought up as Russians, many of them serving in the Russian Imperial Army and the White armies of the civil war. Some of them, like Alfred Rosenberg, the head of the Eastern Ministry, and Ernst Koestring, the General of the Eastern troops, came from humble German colonist families. Most of them, however, belonged to the Baltic aristocracy, which had been closely allied with the Russian nobility. Having emigrated to Germany after the revolution, these 'Baltic barons' maintained close contact with the Russian emigrant colony and still thought partly in Russian.

The war found them entrenched in key positions in the military bureaucracy because of their bilingual education and their experience. They were not objects of suspicion to the National Socialist Party, which Rosenberg, born in Reval and educated in Riga and Moscow, had helped largely to form. Hitler himself owed his lifelong antagonism to 'International Jewry' to the White Russian extremists in Munich, but he owed little else and for Tsarist aspirations he had no use at all. It became a fashion at Hitler's court to denounce the obscure machinations of the Russian born *Ostpolitiker* in the military bureaucracy as Tsarist, but this was an over-simplification. Inasmuch as they were German professional soldiers, they had shared in the veneration for the Soviet military system which derived from the Rapallo treaty of 1922 and the Seeckt-Tukhachevsky protocols of 1926. The latter had enabled the army of the Weimar Republic to by-pass the Versailles Treaty and to acquire experience of aeroplanes and heavy weapons on Russian soil. Hitler had passively allowed this arrangement to end, because it was inconsistent with party doctrine, but only eight and a half years separated his accession to power from the invasion of Russia. It was a very short time for the Red Army, who had made Hitler's much-loved Minister for Defence, von Blomberg, 'almost a Bolshevik',[12] to turn themselves into Asiatic hordes and sub-humans.

Hitler might preach of the destiny of the eastern lands as the living space of the German people and Himmler might preach of Germany's historic rôle as the bulwark of Europe against Asiatic barbarism. The only historic truth that Hitler's actions confirmed was the fact that Germany's relations with her eastern neighbour had always been dictated by momentary expediency. In 1812, for instance, the Prussians had turned against their alliance with Napoleon, whose retreat from Moscow stimulated the Prussian King to meet the Tsar at Tauroggen. So it became the fashion to invoke the spirit of Tauroggen, whenever similar flirtations were in the air, for instance, in 1922 and 1939. The links between the Prussian and Imperial Russian military castes were genuine and it was not difficult to renew them at any time, seeing that the Red Army was the least revolutionary part of the Soviet system. Hitler's contempt for the Slav on the other hand was not at all Prussian or military, but characteristically Austrian and lower middle class at that, a form of jingoism which fed on the concessions that were made by the declining Habsburg monarchy to its Slav subjects. It was not shared by the Prussian landowning class which formed the backbone of the German officer corps. One factor, which may have made the generals amenable to Hitler's invasion plans, was the belief that a rebellious pro-German faction existed among Stalin's military leadership. While it was inadvisable to take too seriously the 'confessions', made in open court, of the seven generals who were tried in Moscow in 1937, it was nevertheless a fact that these generals had had links with the German High Command in the days of the Seeckt-Tukhachevsky protocols and that they were charged with seeking German aid. It was believed that at least two of Stalin's army commanders in 1941, Tolbukhin and Rokossovski, had been imprisoned at the time of the trials and subsequently amnestied.

The impact of the Moscow treason trials on the German High Command explains not only the readiness of the generals to gamble along with Hitler but also the readiness of many of them to accept a Russian soldier as an ally when they were confronted with a protracted war. Although General Vlasov only fell into German hands in July 1942, the Russian-born experts in the German military bureaucracy were already dreaming of such a person before the war had even begun. Rumours circulated concerning the counter-revolutionary propensities of this or that Soviet Marshal. In Berlin the military *Ostpolitiker* encouraged a peculiarly shabby political group of Russian emigrés, the 'Solidarity Party' or NTS of Victor Baidalakov who modelled their programme on National Socialism.[13] The NTS people expected a national Messiah, a Russian Napoleon, and each captured Russian general was watched like a future Dalai Lama for the magic signs.

In June 1943, when there was still some hope of victory in the east, Hitler was urged by Keitel to stop the activities in the direction of a Russian liberation army. Vlasov was shelved for some fifteen months, the volunteers who might have served under him were dispersed to the western and Balkan fronts. It was a complete victory for the Austrian Hitler and for the Bavarians, Bormann, Himmler and Alfred Jodl, against a characteristic manifestation of Prussian military thought. Hitler's opinions, given on 8th June and 1st July 1943 have survived.* It is clear however that Hitler was uneasy in his mind. For a man who had talked two years previously of exterminating all Russian political leadership, the language was singularly moderate. It is to be noted too that until some of them plotted to kill him, Hitler left his Russian-born *Ostpolitiker* in peace. In a land where the Gestapo filled the concentration camps with listeners to English broadcasts or grumblers in trams, the *Ostpolitiker* distributed their memoranda, attacking the highest leadership in hundreds of copies, and the worst they suffered was temporary retirement to private life.

Hitler was in a difficult position. Under his schemes for splitting up the land-mass of Russia and partly colonizing it, there was no room for Russian military juntas which would in their turn create either Stalins or Tsars. On the other hand Hitler could not reject the services of professed Russian anti-Bolsheviks, so long as he had to employ Russian units to fight the Partisans, and German political officers to secure the collaboration of the civil population and the deserters. As a result of his dilemma, Hitler could neither eliminate his *Ostpolitiker* nor take their proposals seriously. Hitler's errors had been made in 1941 and could not be unmade in 1943. With just a little more realism than his critics, Hitler perceived that no spiritual conversion could change a thoroughly destructive undertaking into something quite different. How could it profit a German to know that Stalin could be overcome only by Russians? The greatest handicap for any Russian adversary of

* See pp. 325-6

Stalin would be the assistance of Germany. If the aim of all this talk was the arming of two million Russian prisoners, Hitler's High Command would tell him that the arms just were not there, nor ever could be there. Even the 800,000 'Eastern Troops' who eventually served in one way or another were never provided with the equipment of average fighting divisions.

These 'Eastern Troops', contemptuously named and contemptuously treated, owed no debt to the *Ostpolitiker* for their exhortations and their plans and in the end their lack of discipline showed it. The man who had handled a German rifle in return for a bowl of soup in 1941 faced a grim future in 1945. What could the promises of a captive Russian general matter to him, promises of a liberal property-respecting Russia, when the Red Army had overflowed East Prussia and Pomerania and when the news had reached him that the Western Allies handed over ex-Red Army captives to the Soviet Union?

What the fate of the volunteers was nobody knows. At the present moment the Soviet government is engaged in returning to their homes the collaborationist tribes of the northern Causasus, whom they deported to south Siberia fifteen years ago. Their fate may have been mild in comparison with the fate of the Red Army men in German uniform, whom the British, French and Americans surrendered so casually in 1944 and 1945. The era of Palmerstonism and Victorian knight-errantry had passed and the era of political appeasement was in full sway. Worse things have been done in its name since then.

But cruel as was the fate of most of the collaborationists, there are other aspects of their rôle that must not be forgotten. Many of them gave their services for some pretty nasty things. From Latvia, Lithuania and Galicia came the *Askaris*, auxiliary companies of the German Security Police, whose task it was to rout out the ghettoes and to operate the camps for the gassing of Jews. In the Ukraine the Germans used a native militia to press-gang the villagers for deportation and forced labour. During the Warsaw rebellion of 1944, the private White Russian army of the collaborator, Bronislav Kaminsky, had to be withdrawn from action because of its excesses. It was indeed an easy matter to make savages of men whose life was forcibly primitive. Of this the German public were reminded in 1945, when the Red Army let loose its least disciplined divisions in East Prussia, Pomerania, Mecklenburg and Silesia. It was rather late to complain of the hordes of Asia and the sub-humans for behaving like hordes of Asia and sub-humans, at a time when some 800,000 of them wore German uniform.

Yet in theory the Germans should have been the last people to think unrealistically about Russia, particularly the Germans of the north who shared the same flat living-space. Dotted like drops of spray as far as the Urals and Caucasus were colonies of their own countrymen. Numerous Russian towns once had German names, all had German-looking buildings. The youth of Russia still passed through an educational system and a military service system that were essentially German. Part of the German failure to think realistically sprang from the cult of 'geo-politics'. The German military mind had got into the habit of reasoning that the loss of so much territory or so much population meant the loss of wars. It forgot that Russian frontiers were so fluid that for Russians even access to the sea was a novelty not much more than two centuries old. It would have been better to have regarded Russia, as Americans are said to regard Boston, not as a place but as a state of mind. The revolution had demonstrated that it was easy to carve separate national states out of the Russian perimeter, but, so long as the kernel remained, it was only a matter of time before they became Russian again. In the summer of 1919 the Russia of Lenin and Trotsky had been much smaller than the territory that was left to Stalin in the Autumn of 1942 and yet it had survived.

Evidently the Ukrainians, who scattered flowers before the German tanks in the summer of 1941, were not patriotic Soviet citizens, but circumstances soon made many of them so. The pro-Russians in the Wehrmacht said it was all the fault of the vulgar brute, Erich Koch. But Koch was seldom in the Ukraine and his officials created not government but anarchy, which was no novelty in that unhappy land. What changed the Ukrainians was the certainty that the Red Army was coming back. Starry-eyed German soldier-writers, to whom everything is either passionate loyalty or hideous *Verrat*, are sometimes strangely reluctant to admit this. It is a relief to discover the humane common-sense of the Austrian field surgeon, Kurt Emmerich. In the hospital which he had established in Sevastopol he found his 'collaborationist' Russian assistants quite unperturbed at the approach of the Red Army. They told him that the Red Army too appreciated trained surgeons. But Emmerich guessed that the surgeons had already made contact with the Partisans and he did not blame them.[14]

Despite Mr Wallace Carroll, it may be doubted whether the conflicts of German policy in Russia have any lesson for the future except a warning not to do it again. And it is indeed hard to believe that it will again happen that a modern industrial country will invade the territory of a rival with the intention of extinguishing its spirit of common nationality and replacing much of its population with foreigners. One may doubt it in spite of the maps in the Sunday papers with their estimates of the range of rockets and their arrows pointing into the heart of the Soviet Union.

Part One

COLONIALISM

CHAPTER ONE

BACKGROUND TO INVASION

(a) The Moscow Pact

THERE IS A temptation to regard Hitler's accession to power as the end of an era in Germany's relations with Soviet Russia. Still commonly accepted are two contrasted mental pictures. In the first we see the works of the Weimar Republic, the treaties of Rapallo and Berlin, the secret Germano-Russian military exchanges of training and the German economic concessions which were granted on Russian soil. In the second picture we see the results of Hitler. The German communists, who had once been supported by Russian gold, are outlawed and imprisoned, the training agreements have lapsed, and the German staff officers, who had been responsible for them, are under the suspicion of Heydrich's security service. The trading agreements have lapsed too and for the first time Poland is courted in order to spite Moscow. And so it continued for more than six years; according to this picture, the Ribbentrop-Molotov pact of 1939 was a bolt from the blue.

In actual fact the relations of the Weimar Republic with Soviet Russia were never as simple as this. Both sides played a double game, each one seeking the economic and military support of the other in the struggle with the Versailles powers, while at the same time they respectively encouraged anti-communist elements in Russia and communist elements in Germany. The weaker Weimar became internally, the more precarious were its relations with the Holy See of the Comintern. Between 1919 and 1933 there were a number of crises, each so severe that the complete end of diplomatic relations was narrowly averted. No such crises occurred under Hitler's rule between 1933 and 1939, though the anti-communist crusade was preached daily and a copy of *Mein Kampf* lay in every German home. The policy that Hitler conducted towards Russia was not so much hostile as neutralist. If the old, wobbly pacts and military agreements were not renewed, neither were their inevitable accompaniments of cross-accusation and chicane.

Diplomatically Hitler treated Russia neither as a friend nor as an enemy. Nevertheless he retained as Minister of War the old General Werner von Blomberg, who had declared in 1927 that he had returned from a visit to Russia 'not far short of a complete Bolshevik'.[1] There was no conflict between Hitler and his once Russophile generals. This same Blomberg became his devoted admirer, his 'rubber-lion' or *Hitlerjunge*. Two successive commanders-in-chief of the 'hundred thousand army' of the Weimar Republic openly entered into negotiation with Karl Radek, the old guard Bolshevik. Yet neither von Seeckt nor von Hammerstein were converted into Bolsheviks by the visits of this bearded and Rabbinic Galician Jew. It was mainly through Karl Radek that these generals created German establishments, where the forbidden fruits of Versailles, the coveted instruction in aerial and armoured warfare, could be tasted over a period of years. The strange romance of Karl Radek and the generals showed only that defeat, reparations, inflation and the threat of world communism could lead the Prussian military mind into devious and murky channels. But in victory that mind spoke a simpler language, common alike to the heirs of Clausewitz and the Austrian corporal:

> Separate peace with France and Belgium, on the basis of the *status quo ante*. Then all land forces against Russia. Conquest of ten thousand miles, expelling the population, except of course Germans. Russia has a lot of room for them, particularly in magnificent south Siberia ... once there are two hundred millions of healthy and mostly German people on 200,000 square miles of soil, say in the year 2,000, we shall at least be somewhat secure against this immense Russia that may one day give birth to another Peter the Great ... against this what does it mean to expel a lot of riff-raff of Jews, Poles, Masurians, Lithuanians, Latvians, Estonians etc? We have the power to do it; and we have been plunged into conditions, which in terms of blood and destruction leave the *Voelkerwanderung* far behind; therefore let us behave according to the customs of the *Voelkerwanderung* period.*

From this passage it will be observed that, as regards Russia, the difference between Hitler and his policy-making predecessors was narrowed to something not very large or tangible. But the greatest

---

* This is not a quotation from *Hitler's Table Talk* of 1941–2, from Himmler's famous bloodthirsty Posen and Bad Schachen speeches or from Erich Koch's pep-talks to his staff in the Ukraine. It is a memorandum by the 'Russophil' Hans von Seeckt, written in the year of victories 1915 (quoted by Hilger and Meyer, *The Incompatible Allies*, New York, 1953, pp. 191–2).

irony in the career of the man who tried to destroy Soviet Russia, lies in the fact that in February 1940, he brought about the ideal economic exchange between Germany and Russia, which twenty years of Weimar hesitations and Moscow incompetence and ill will had failed to achieve. Trade had reached bed-rock in 1929, the year of the great economic slump.[2] Having ruined Russian agriculture at the expense of industry during the first Five-Year-Plan, Stalin had lost Russia her exportable surplus of raw produce. With her 180 million population Russia took less German goods than Denmark.[3] Ten years later, in 1939, Hitler boldly took advantage of the restoration of balance in the Russian economic system. Some months after the Moscow Pact, the exchange of German machinery and manufactures against Russian produce was brought to its most perfect pitch. But now the conflict between material expediency and political fanaticism also reached an intensity far exceeding any previous conflicts of the 'incompatible allies'. Impelled by his Daemon, Hitler went to war for something that virtually he had already achieved.

To understand Hitler's success in the trade negotiations of 1939–41 it must be realized that the war-scare of Hitler's advent to power in 1933 did not in the following six years change the character of Soviet foreign policy with its schizophrenic cleavage between peaceful co-existence and Comintern agitation. The period 1933–9 was nevertheless the Litvinov era, in which a Soviet Foreign Minister with Western affiliations sought the military alliance of Europe against a Germany, in whom he recognized not merely a striving against the fetters of the Versailles Settlement, but a future *Drang nach Osten*.

Such a reversal of the treaty of Rapallo was alien to the tradition of the early revolution. At no time would Lenin have approved of an alliance with the West in order to prevent a revision of the Versailles Treaty or in order to save the middle-class republics of Czechoslovakia and Poland. On the contrary, he would have approved the approaches to Germany which Stalin made in 1939, but he would have made them earlier. Long before 1939, he would have exploited the fact that Hitler's attitude to Russia was not one of provocation but of studied indifference. Had Hitler made one gesture, a repudiation for instance of the notorious passages in the fourteenth chapter of *Mein Kampf*, the ascendancy of the Western minded Maxim Litvinov in Russian foreign policy would have been even briefer than it was. For while the Litvinov policy was an experiment among the rulers of Russia, the thing that kept it alive was fear. And of all things that were fearful in

Hitler it was his silences that ranked highest. Thus in 1933 Hitler did not bother to end the anomaly of German military training stations on Russian soil, even when the round-up of the German communists had been completed. It was the Russians themselves who terminated these memories of the Seeckt-Tukhachevsky agreement and in 1937 they went even further and shot Tukhachevsky himself.

Perhaps no incident in modern history has attracted so many different interpretations as the Moscow Trial of the five generals in June 1937 and the purge of the Red Army officer corps which succeeded it. These incidents were generally interpreted as a sign of a Russian shift from friendship with the German General Staff towards security pacts with France and England. On the other hand, plausible attempts have been made since the war by German authors to show that Hitler actually contrived to bring these trials about, that he tried to weaken Stalin's military leadership by providing forged evidence of the guilt of the generals.[4] Perhaps it is wisest to believe the simplest explanation of all, namely that the Red Army High Command planned to get rid of the rule of the Communist Party in Russia. Gustav Hilger has noticed that Tukhachevsky, the most important of the condemned military leaders, wrote an embittered attack on Hitler in *Pravda* as late as March 1935, and that Voroshilov and Kaganovitch, who emerged so strong after the purge, had been as much involved in planning with the German General Staff as Tukhachevsky himself.[5] Gustav Hilger, who had known the Russian leaders since the very first days of the October revolution, seems to think that most of them, including Stalin, had some admiration for Hitler. The cynicism of the cleavage between the ideology and the self-interest of the Soviet government had never been so unblushing as it was in 1933–9. Litvinov himself was alleged to have said that he did not mind if the Germans shot their communists,[6] while Karl Radek, who had been a member of the German Social Democratic Party, is reported to have used the following words in 1934: 'There are magnificent lads in the SA and SS. You'll see, the day will come when they will be throwing hand-grenades for us.'[7]*

The fact is that totalitarian called to totalitarian. Stalin admired Hitler as long as he was successful and only spoke of him with contempt when Hitler was losing the war. Hitler, however, went on admiring Stalin till the very end, because Stalin did not lose.** That

* See p. 182
** In *Hitler's Table Talk*, op. cit., Stalin is: 'that cunning Caucasian, half giant, half beast', 'a devil of a fellow', 'a beast on a gigantic scale'. He is never a figure of contempt.

the Russians should make overtures for a military alliance with Germany became inevitable, when the Munich Agreement revealed the weakness among the partners of collective security in the West. It is a fact that the Munich Agreement was followed shortly by the Russian renunciation of press and foreign radio attacks on the Nazi government. Similarly the German march into Prague in March 1939 was followed in May by the fall of Litvinov, the champion of collective security with the West.

Between the two events there was a small attempt at a revival of Russo-German trade relations, which had unlooked-for consequences. In 1934, Stalin's collectivization programme had at last yielded tangible results, though at terrible cost. The Ukraine famine was at an end and some of the worst mistakes which had brought it about had been remedied. For the first time since the revolution, the traditional export-surplus of Russian agriculture was again on the market and at a time when Germany in the first stages of economic recovery could use a great deal of Russian wheat against manufactured goods. Hjalmar Schacht, the president of the Reichsbank, had a plan at the end of 1935 for a 500 million mark credit to Russia, in order to finance a ten-year exchange of products. It was a pitifully modest affair compared with the agreements of 1940 and 1941. Yet even this had to be withdrawn when a premature disclosure by Molotov threatened to bring down the anger of Hitler, who could never separate his economics from his political prejudices.[8] Unlike the Weimar politicians, who pursued such economic exchanges even when diplomatic relations were at their worst, Hitler consistently refused to discuss trade till there was a political truce. Thus even in January 1939, months after the Munich surrender had demonstrated Russia's unwillingness to put Litvinov's collective security plans into operation, another premature disclosure forced Ribbentrop, in terror of Hitler, to withdraw a new German trade delegation which was on its way to Russia.

This time, however, the Russians played on Hitler's inactivism with some skill, leading Hitler to what he described in retrospect to Mussolini in 1941 as 'a break with my whole origin, my concept and my former obligations'.[9] The story that follows has been pieced together from a chain of documents which the Washington State Department released to the world in March 1948, but in this chain of documents one thing is lacking, namely the personal reactions of the principal figure in the drama.

On 15th March 1939, Hitler marched his armies into Czechoslovakia and seized Prague. It is doubtful whether Hitler knew at that moment that, just five days earlier, Stalin had announced unmistakably what his attitude would be in the next crisis. Stalin had declared at the Eighteenth Party Congress: 'It looks very much as if this suspicious noise is designed to incense the Soviet Union against Germany, to poison the atmosphere and to provoke a conflict with Germany without any visible grounds . . . the Soviet Union is not willing to pull chestnuts out of the fire for anyone else.'*

It was probably not till 10th May, when he received Gustav Hilger's report, that Hitler knew the details of this speech. Nevertheless, at the signing of the Moscow Pact on 23rd August, Molotov toasted Stalin with a pointed compliment to the man, 'who through his speech of March of this year, which had been well understood in Germany, had brought about the reversal in political relations'.[10]

Evidently Molotov connected his own accession to Litvinov's former position on 3rd May with Stalin's Party Congress Speech. On the very day before his fall Litvinov had given an audience to the British Ambassador, so it seems that Stalin made a snap decision in the middle of a negotiation. What lay behind Stalin's decision was scarcely revealed when Molotov had his first audience with the German Ambassador on the 20th. Werner von der Schulenburg rapidly introduced the matter of the new trade pact, about which the Russians had been eagerly inquiring in Berlin. To his great surprise Molotov accused the Germans of allowing trade negotiations to be conducted as 'a tactical game which had then faded out'. The trade negotiation, Molotov said, could only be resumed by the Russian government, 'when the necessary basis had been constructed'.[11] What these political bases were, Molotov would not say, except that both governments would have to think about them.

Ribbentrop was slow in drawing the right inference from this conversation, for in his report to Hitler he stressed that the Russians were still apparently intriguing with the British for the encirclement of Germany. When Georgei Astakhov, the Russian chargé d'affaires in Berlin, saw the Baron von Weiszaecker on 30th May, this reproach was made openly to him during the discussion of so small a thing as a Soviet commercial agency in Prague. Astakhov did not deny the accusation, but with considerable subtlety he suggested that Hitler's policies were no bar to Russian neutrality.[12] A more astute tactician than the Ambas-

---

* Hilger, *The Incompatible Allies*, p. 90. The 'suspicious noise' was a reference to Allied accusations that Germany was aiming to create an independent Ukrainian State

sador Dekanosov, Astakhov made his next move through a third party. On 14th June, he called on the Bulgarian Minister and in the most casual way mentioned that his government would prefer a non-aggression pact with Germany to a pact with France and England, provided the misgivings created by the famous chapter of *Mein Kampf* could be allayed.*

Even Molotov was now a little less enigmatic. On 3rd July he asked Schulenburg whether he considered the 1926 treaty of Berlin still to be in force. Fortified by such favourable omens, Kurt Schnurre, the German Foreign Trade expert, dined Astakhov handsomely on the night of the 26th and, after some flattering references to the integrity of Russian foreign policy, got from the Russian Chargé d'affaires the admission that Danzig would return to the Reich one way or another and that the 'corridor question' would have to be solved in favour of Germany. It was time for Ribbentrop himself to step in. He received Astakhov on the night of 2nd August and wrote next day to Schulenburg, bubbling with pride at the way he had handled the situation: 'I conducted the whole conversation in an even tone . . . I conducted the conversation without showing any haste.' Despite all this high-bred reticence, Ribbentrop conveyed to Astakhov that in case of any provocation from Poland, Germany would settle matters with that country in the space of a week: 'I dropped a gentle hint at coming to an agreement with Russia on the fate of Poland.' Gentle hints, even when they were the size of brickbats, were still not enough for Astakhov. He wanted to pin the conversation down to more concrete terms. Ribbentrop said he could have something concrete 'when the Soviet government expressed its fundamental desire for a new relationship'.[13]

This, Molotov was expected to do when he saw Schulenburg on 3rd August, but it seemed that Molotov still baulked at the 'Pact of Steel', which had been signed by Hitler and Mussolini on 22nd May and which Japan was expected to join to the detriment of Russia. Schulenburg, however, knew that Molotov had reserved his famous icy negative behaviour for the British mission, whereas he had been quite exceptionally forthcoming when talking to a German. On the 14th, Schulenburg reported that 'this remarkable man and difficult character' had become accustomed to him and he begged, therefore, to be excused from attending the Nuremberg party rally, for which he would have to order a grey uniform.[14]

Next day Schulenberg learnt that he would not have to see his

* See pp. 15–16 (Introduction).

tailor. Hitler, who had received the reports concerning Molotov with diffidence and who had even at one moment ordered the trade negotiation to be called off, made up his mind abruptly. Within twelve days he proposed to march against Poland, defying the Anglo-French guarantee of protection. The neutrality of Russia was absolutely essential. Schulenburg must see Molotov and arrange for a meeting between Ribbentrop and Stalin. He was to give Molotov this message: 'the period of opposition in foreign policy can be brought to an end once and for all and the way lies open for a new sort for future for both countries . . . the decisions with respect to policy, to be made in the immediate future in Berlin and Moscow, will be of decisive importance for the state of relationships between the German people and the peoples of the USSR for generations.'

Molotov, who saw Schulenburg on the evening of the 15th, was friendly, but he used far less enthusiastic language than that contained in Ribbentrop's note. He made no immediate contact with Stalin and he harped severely on the pact with Japan, though he was too polite to call it, 'the Anti-Comintern Pact'.[15] Ribbentrop, however, telegraphed at once that he was ready to come as soon as the 18th and that Hitler wanted to make the non-aggression pact binding for twenty-five years.

Schulenburg and his Counsellor of Legation, Gustav Hilger, saw Molotov on the night of the 17th.[16] Molotov was as usual evasive and would not negotiate independently, but he promised very emphatically to obtain his government's ruling. Half an hour later he recalled the envoys in order to communicate a draft which Stalin had just telephoned him. Germany, Stalin declared, must show her good intentions by completing the trade agreement first; the treaty must come afterwards and, while appreciating the honour of a visit by the Foreign Minister, the Russian government was not in favour of the publicity it would attract.[17]

Ribbentrop's instructions now became frantic in tone. The conflict with Poland might break out at any moment. Hitler, so Ribbentrop said, considered immediate clarification to be necessary, 'if only to be able to consider Russia's interests in the event of such a conflict'. To this Molotov answered that if the trade agreement were concluded next day, Ribbentrop could be received as early as 26th August.

The stiff cogs of diplomacy now rotated with inconceivable haste. The trade agreement, which had hung fire since 11th January, was signed next day and by it Russia received a 200 million mark credit for her purchases in Germany. Molotov for his part produced a draft agreement for the non-aggression pact, which was accepted by Hitler in a personal telegram which he sent Stalin. In this telegram Hitler begged that, 'in view of the intolerable tension between Germany and Poland', Ribbentrop be received on the 22nd or the 23rd.

On the evening of the 21st, Stalin telegraphed Hitler his personal reply. Ribbentrop could come on the 23rd. Walter Hewel, who handed Hitler the telegram, said that Hitler shouted, 'now I have the world in my pocket.'[18] Early the following morning Ribbentrop left Berchtesgaden for Moscow, while Hitler spent the day receiving his military commanders, to whom he delivered two long lectures on the forthcoming conflict, the famous but debatable 'Jenghiz Khan' tirade being among them. 'Our enemies are little worms. I saw them in Munich. I was convinced that Stalin would never accept the English offer. . . . Four days ago I took a special step. . . . The day after tomorrow Ribbentrop will conclude the treaty. Now Poland is in the position in which I wanted her.'*

With the exception of a last-minute demand by the Russians for the inclusion of Libau and Windau in their sphere of influence, a demand which had to be telephoned to Hitler during the conference, the meeting in the Kremlin on the night of the 23rd only ratified what had been decided already. Nevertheless it will always rank as one of the most sinister moments in history. Stalin was completely cynical and quite self-possessed, his adversary totally humourless, as nervous as a cat and as tactful as a ton load of rubble.[19]

> The Reich Foreign Minister observed that the Anti-Comintern Pact was basically directed not against the Soviet Union but against the Western Democracies. He knew and was able to infer from the tone of the Russian press, that the Soviet government fully recognized this fact.
>
> Herr Stalin interposed that the Anti-Comintern Pact had in fact frightened principally the City of London and the small British merchants.
>
> The Reich Minister concurred and remarked jokingly that Herr Stalin was surely less frightened by the Anti-Comintern Pact than the City of London and the small British merchants. What the German people thought of the matter was evident from a

---

* *Nuremberg Document*, PS 798, Hellmuth Greiner, *Die oberste Wehrmachtfuehrung*, p. 38. There are other versions of the conference. Greiner's, which was taken down from the notes of Admiral Canaris, commands most credit.

joke which had originated with the Berliners, well known for their wit and humour, and which had been going the rounds for several months, namely, 'Stalin will yet join the Anti-Comintern Pact'.

Had it been only a matter of the seven articles of the Non-Aggression Pact, a little German effort might have obtained these even at the height of the period of Litvinov diplomacy. The whole point of the agreement of 23rd August 1939 was the secret protocol which made it quite simply an aggression pact. This declared that 'in the event of territorial or political rearrangement', the frontier between the German and Russian spheres of influence was to be the northern boundary of Lithuania and the line of the Narev, San and Vistula rivers. In the south, Russia declared an interest in Bessarabia, while Germany declared herself disinterested. It was a division of the cake the whole way from the Gulf of Riga to the Black Sea.

Nevertheless the Russians were at first reluctant to reveal this protocol to the world by openly taking advantage of it. Five days after the Germans had marched into Poland, Molotov told Ribbentrop that an excessive haste in sending Russian troops would injure his country's name. On 10th September he proposed to Schulenburg a formula, according to which Russia was compelled to come to the aid of Ukrainians and White Russians who had been threatened by Germany.[20] Ribbentrop countered with a formula that omitted any reference to Germany, but alleged intolerable conditions which had been created by the complete collapse of previous forms of government. Molotov, however, grimly insisted on adding his second reason, namely that a third party might profit from the chaos. The idiotic and unedifying brawl ended at midnight on the 17th, when Stalin briefly communicated his own decision, which Hitler found so brilliantly worded that he asked who had written it.[21] A joint communiqué was to announce that it was the duty of the two powers to restore peace and order and 'to bring about a new order by the creation of new frontiers and viable economic organizations'. It was not for nothing that Stalin had once studied theology in a seminary.

No sooner had the 'eighteen days war' ended when Molotov sent for Schulenburg to propose negotiations concerning the final frontiers. Molotov also hinted that Stalin was no longer interested in creating a residual independent Poland. There was more in this than showed on the surface. It is hardly likely that Stalin was frightened lest Hitler should revive Poland's aspirations. It was, however, a fact that since the final partition of Czechoslovakia in September 1938, the German Foreign Office had encouraged the idea of a small independent Ukrainian State, fashioned from the former Habsburg possessions, and the nucleus of something that was to become bigger.* Stalin had remarked in his party congress speech in March 1939 that the Allied press had used this to stir ill-feeling between Russia and Germany. What Russia now feared was a German Quisling government in Lwow as well as in Warsaw; Ribbentrop's exaggerated eagerness to come to Moscow augmented Stalin's misgiving. In an interview which he gave Schulenburg on 25th September, Stalin proposed a sweeping change in the terms of the secret protocol. He now wanted the Russian sphere of influence to include the entire Baltic coast down to the German-Lithuanian border. In return, the Germans could keep the Polish provinces which extended to the rivers Bug and San. The Germans would gain Lublin, Warsaw was not to be made a frontier town, but Lwow would pass to Russia.[22]

Ribbentrop's second mission to Moscow was less dramatic than his first. Hitler was prepared to hand Stalin the coastline of the Baltic States, provided that Germany retained Memel which she had already annexed. Stalin was able to draw his blue pencil almost straight down the map.[23] On the second evening of the conference, 28th September, while the delegates were enjoying the ballet *Lac des Cygnes*, Stalin dealt with the wretched Lithuanians and was so kind as to contrive a bit of their territory, the Suwalki district, for Hitler. Significantly two new secret protocols emerged from the conference. Both sides pledged themselves not to tolerate Polish agitation at the expense of the other party; both sides promised to permit the repatriation of their racial brethren, the Germans to permit the emigration of Ukrainians and White Russians, the Russians to permit the emigration of racial Germans.

It was a one-sided pact. Apart from the Jews, who were not included in it, few inhabitants of Poland, west of the San and Bug, wanted to live in the Soviet Union.** Eastwards, however, there were hundreds of thousands of Baltic, Volhynian and Bessarabian *Volksdeutsche*, who wanted to escape the Soviet embrace. Both the two secret protocols betrayed the uneasiness of the negotiating Russians. If Stalin parted

* See pp. 164-5
** According to Mr John Armstrong, only 3,500 Ukrainians moved from Poland to the USSR.

so easily with these valuable subjects, it was because he visualized the
demarcation line as a potential war area, rather than as a peaceful
frontier.

It was not a promising foundation and in the month of October the
German diplomats were filled with misgivings, both at the Russian
demands on Finland and at the Russian proposals for a mutual assistance pact with Bulgaria. But on 19th October, in approving the proposed draft of a speech by Ribbentrop, Stalin authorized a declaration,
which went far beyond neutrality and which amounted to a threat of
pressure on England and France.[24] 'The Soviet Union cannot give its
approval to the Western Powers creating conditions which would
weaken Germany and place her in a difficult position. Therein lies the
community of interests between Germany and the Soviet Union.'

The moment was ripe for negotiating a new and immensely bigger
exchange of trade, since this had been agreed in principle on 28th
August. With the Germans it was a question of nothing less than
replacing the overseas imports, which had been lost through the
British blockade. The price could only be the rearmament of Russia.
Hitler was placed in a dilemma. On the one hand he made the Foreign
Office drop their pro-Finn attitude and invent plausible justifications
for Stalin's 'Winter War', even though Finland had been permitted to
receive German arms. On the other hand Goering, Keitel and Admiral
Raeder protested at the volume of weapons and armaments demanded
by Russia under the terms of the trade pact. Consequently the negotiations, which were begun at the end of September, were not completed
till 11th February 1940. In the end, Germany's absolute need of
Russian grain and oil got the better of Hitler's reluctance to provide
Russia with weapons. The new purchasing credit was to be 650 million
marks. Germany was to get a million tons of grain stuffs from a single
harvest, a heavy burden on the Russian standard of living, and Germany was to build the Russians a battle-cruiser. Russia was allowed
eighteen months to complete her deliveries. Germany, having to pay
entirely in machinery and weapons, was allowed twenty-seven months,
but Stalin insisted on the right to terminate, if the six-monthly balances
were not achieved.[25]

Stalin had fallen into a singular trap. By proving his country's
ability to meet these demands and, in 1941, even to exceed them, he
persuaded Hitler that Russia was an immeasurable farming estate
which could be colonized by Germans. Effectively he revived the
dreams of 1925 which Hitler had recorded in *Mein Kampf.* Very

quickly Stalin came to regard the February 1940 agreement as no source of economic strength to Russia, but rather as a payment of *Danegeld*, which it was prudent to increase when Germany advanced from strength to strength, but which he could suspend when the strength seemed to be on the side of the Allies. Thus at the end of March, when the 'Winter War' had been broken off through the fear of Allied intervention in Finland, Schulenburg observed that a speech by Molotov conciliatory to the West was timed to coincide with a suspension of the wheat and grain shipments to Germany.[26] On 9th April, however, it was Schulenburg's duty to report the German landings in Norway and Denmark. All honey, Molotov now blamed the suspension of the deliveries on the excessive zeal of subordinate agencies, though Mikoyan, the villain of the piece, was almost as important a person as himself. Schulenburg believed that Stalin had been afraid of British and French landings in the far north. Stalin's fear of being involved with war in the West was now removed.

The conquest of France and the Low Countries should by the same reasoning have been a source of relief to Stalin, but the reasoning no longer applied, now that Germany had advanced to a strength that was altogether excessive. So henceforward, side by side with the payment of *Danegeld*, went that imprudent jockeying for positions in eastern Europe, which, though in the end it extended Russian political domination to the Elbe and Adriatic, cost Russia many millions of lives and retarded her present economic recovery by at least ten years. Thus on 18th June, when Molotov visited Schulenburg to congratulate Hitler on the French petition for an armistice, he coupled it with the news of the first stages of the incorporation of the Baltic States in the Soviet Union.[27] Stalin, however, cleverly sugared the pill. He personally wrote the *Tass* Agency communiqué which appeared on the 24th. This declared 'in the face of mischievous Allied rumours' that the dispatch of 'no more than eighteen to twenty divisions' to the Baltic States was not intended as a measure of pressure on the Germans, but as 'a guarantee for the execution of the mutual assistance pacts between the USSR and these countries'. The advantages of a theological training were again clearly demonstrated.[28]

But Stalin's sugar was meant for another pill, which was not wholly in the prescription of the secret protocol. Stalin proposed to use force, if necessary, on behalf of the suffering Ukrainians in Rumanian Bessarabia and Bukovina. In the famous secret protocol of 23rd August, Ribbentrop had explicitly renounced Germany's political interest in this area, but, as he rather lamely wrote to Schulenburg, he thought that he had made a verbal reservation concerning Germany's purely economic interests. There was now a danger that Rumania would resist and by doing so lose to Russia the famous oilwells at Ploesti, on which Germany depended.

Hitler must have been very worried, even at this supreme moment of his triumph over the Versailles powers. In fact his worry had begun as early as 24th May, before the British re-embarkation from Dunkirk, when Admiral Canaris had reported that thirty Russian divisions were massing against Bessarabia.[29] Hitler proceeded with the utmost delicacy; he made Ribbentrop prepare the note for Molotov, which was not a protest at the lack of consultation but in fact a condonement of Russia's action. Germany pledged herself to advise Rumania to accept the Russian demands. Only concerning the inclusion of the Rumanian province of Bukovina, which had never been Russian territory and which was not named in the secret protocol, was there a ghost of a protest.[30]

The Russians entered Bessarabia and northern Bukovina on 28th June, but that was only the beginning of the troubles. Hungary and Bulgaria were stimulated into presenting revisionist claims on Rumania dating from the end of the First World War, when Rumania had carved herself an empire from the ruins of the old Austrian and Russian imperial systems. On 25th August, after the negotiations had broken down at Turnu Severin, Hungary was on the point of invading Rumania. Hitler learnt through Canaris, who had built up a secret plain-clothes security police on the spot, that the Russians would use this as a pretext for crossing the Pruth so as to restore order at the Ploesti oilfields, though these were a German and by no means a Russian economic interest. Hitler immediately ordered the dispatch of two armoured divisions to the south east corner of Poland in order to forestall the Russians if necessary. But at this point Mussolini played the rôle of peacemaker. Four days later, Ribbentrop met the Italian, Rumanian and Hungarian plenipotentiaries in Vienna, at the Belvedere Palace. There Rumania was persuaded to give up an area containing 2,400,000 people in exchange for a German guarantee of her now much restricted territories. It was a thoroughly bad solution, but war between Hungary and Rumania was averted.[31]

Hitler maintained that Russia's action in occupying Bessarabia and northern Bukovina had been provoked by England. For months after this event he would constantly talk to Alfred Jodl, the chief of the operational section of the High Command, of the real reason why

England had not stopped the war after the evacuation at Dunkirk. It was because of 'private or undercover agreements' with Russia that she should either crush Germany politically or attack her.[32] Yet Hitler had no reason to think any such thing. On 13th July, Molotov actually handed Schulenburg a memorandum, describing Sir Stafford Cripps' interview with Stalin. The British Ambassador had told Stalin that 'his government believed that it was rightly the task of the Soviet Union to maintain the unification and leadership of the Balkan countries'. That sweet indiscretion, so picturesque in its historic irony today, was answered by Stalin very sharply indeed. He did not admit that there was any danger of Germany establishing a hegemony in eastern Europe. He knew several German statesmen well and he had not discovered any desire on their part to engulf European countries. No power had the right to an exclusive rôle in the consolidation and leadership of Balkan countries. The Soviet Union did not claim such a mission either, although she was interested in Balkan affairs.[33]

Evidently Hitler did not believe a word of this significant conversation. He was more impressed by the proclamation, in the latter part of July, of Soviet Republics in the three Baltic States, a thing for which he had bargained and for which he could only blame himself. And so it was that while on 16th July 1940 he had signed the first directive for the invasion of England, thirteen days later Hitler discussed plans with Halder and Jodl for the invasion of Russia in the event of the invasion of England not taking place.

(b) 'Barbarossa'

WHEN TWO POWERS are as frightened and suspicious of each other as were Germany and Russia after Hitler's conquest of the West, armed conflict would seem inevitable. Yet there was nothing that Russia undertook in July 1940 that was not completely to be anticipated under the secret protocol of 23rd August, 1939. That July 1940, was the moment when Hitler announced his decision to attack Russia was due to two things. Firstly it was due to his inland-peasant reluctance to proceed with the plans of his commanders for a water-borne invasion of England, something without parallel since the discovery of gunpowder. There was even a minor staff officer who translated passages from Julius Caesar as the only available historical model.[34]

Secondly it was due to the belief that had been confirmed in Hitler's mind by the success of the Russian trade pact the belief that he who was master of European Russia, possessed natural resources without limit. Possession would cancel out a British blockade or even a joint Anglo-American blockade of the Continent. The capitulation of Russia meant an easy deal with Anglo-American sea-power. Hitler scarcely took 'Operation Sea Lion' seriously, except as a bluff manœuvre. According to the official diarist of the High Command, Helmuth Greiner, Hitler said openly at a staff conference on 21st July that the invasion instructions were only for the case where all else had failed and that personally he believed that England would come to terms the moment Russia was no longer a threat to Germany.[35] According to Franz Halder, Hitler asked his Commander-in-Chief during this conference how many divisions would be needed for the conquest of Russia and Walter von Brauchitsch had optimistically replied 'eighty to a hundred'.[36]

A week later, on the 29th, Hitler abruptly asked Jodl whether he could not start concentrating these troops at once so that the assault on Russia could begin in the autumn. Jodl replied that such a concentration was impossible in less than four months and by that time winter would be upon them.[37] So Jodl returned to his special train, which was waiting at Reichenhall near Berchtesgaden, and told his deputy, Walter Warlimont, that he thought that he had argued Hitler out of a war with Russia.[38] In fact, as Warlimont heard from Hitler very shortly afterwards, the decision had only been postponed.[39] Two days after seeing Jodl, on 31st July, Hitler repeated all his arguments to Franz Halder, terminating with the statement, 'if we start in May 1941, we shall have five months in which to finish the job'.[40]

From this point on, the plans to occupy the Rumanian oilfields and the long-term planning for a general invasion of Russia were conducted concurrently, the former by Jodl of the Operations Section at Berchtesgaden and Berlin, the latter by Halder, the Chief of the General Staff, at Fontainebleau. Virtually these two men were rival and independent chiefs of staff. Till well into October the High Command were expected to believe that the invasion of England was still intended. Halder's Russian plan was therefore known at first only to a very restricted circle of staff officers. For instance on 8th August, Halder warned General Ernst Koestring, the military attaché in Moscow, to keep his eyes open, since he would have to answer a lot of questions soon.[41]

An outline plan for the attack on Russia was in existence by 3rd September. As described at Nuremberg by Field Marshal Friedrich Paulus, who was then Halder's deputy and Quartermaster General, it appears to have been basically the plan that was finally adopted. It required the use of Rumanian and Finn territory as well as East Prussia and Poland and it involved the deployment of 130 to 140 divisions. The aim was to destroy the Russian forces in the western part of the country by encirclements so complete that no large formations could escape into the interior. By this means it was expected before the winter to reach the 'AA Line', a front extending from Archangel to Astrakhan, well east of Moscow and near the Urals. It was a line from which peace might be concluded, because at this distance it was considered that Germany could no longer be attacked from the air. Further details of the process of armoured thrusts and battles of encirclement were worked out in two war-games which were played early in November at Fontainebleau with the connivance of a number of high staff officers.[42]

It may be argued in some quarters that Paulus had been put up to say this by the Russians, who used him as a hostile witness against the High Command; but Paulus's story of an operation-study is fully confirmed by the High Command archivist Helmuth Greiner.[43] Nevertheless the pretences of Autumn 1940, that the massing of German troops along the eastern border was not intended for an attack on Russia, were repeated even in the Nuremberg witness box. During the campaign in France the entire strength of the German army in the east had been reduced from seven divisions to five.[44] At the beginning of September 1940, however, ten divisions were transferred from the west to Poland, in addition to the two armoured divisions on the Rumanian border. Such numbers hardly constituted a striking force, but they were the vanguard of a movement ten times as big. And these twelve divisions should have been infinitely precious in the west, where the service chiefs still expected to launch an invasion operation across the Channel.

Halder's explanation at the High Command Trial of 1948 was ingenious. It was as follows; in order to stop the intensive smuggling which went on between German-occupied Poland and Russia, Himmler had been authorized to construct a fortified frontier, the 'Otto Line'. The work was done by conscripted Jews from Poland and, in order to guard them, Himmler demanded an enormously increased recruitment of 'Death's Head' battalions of the SS. So, to prevent the expansion of

the SS 'who were a kind of antithesis of the army in their conception
of military matters', Halder moved up ten infantry divisions of the
Wehrmacht, a remarkable force it might be thought for the guarding
of a few thousand docile Jewish labourers or the prevention of
smuggling.[45]

From now on Hitler played for time. Between the verbal directions
of 31st July 1940, and the publication of the first operational orders,
four and a half months elapsed. Wilhelm Keitel, the Chief of the High
Command, said that on this as on many other equally dubious occasions he sent Hitler a remonstrance. However he was grateful to learn
in October that no further written orders would be given, while a
further discussion with the Russians was still pending.[46] It was not
that Hitler expected anything from these discussions. History has
shown that he was almost incapable of unmaking his mind. But Hitler
was still not convinced of the proper order of priorities. Between
August and December 1940, other prospects danced before him, an
England eliminated from the war by bombing and blockade alone, a
spectacular campaign to secure the whole Mediterranean basin and
the Near East with the aid of Spain, Italy and the Vichy French. In the
meantime Russia could buy Hitler off with grain and oil.

But to keep the trade pact operating, Hitler had to take some notice
of the Russian government's profound resentment towards his Vienna
award. The Russian leaders believed, probably quite sincerely, that
they were entitled to reoccupy Bessarabia under the secret protocol.
They regarded the additional land-snatch in northern Bukovina as no
more than a *douceur* for giving the Germans a bit of Lithuania during
the performance of *Lac des Cygnes*. It was different with Hitler's
Vienna award, which guaranteed military aid to Rumania in recom-
pense for her loss of territory. That was regarded in Moscow as contrary to the secret protocol of 23rd August 1949, which renounced
any German interest in south eastern Europe. So, on 21st September
1940, Molotov presented Schulenburg with a long angry note, terminating with a declaration that his government was prepared to
negotiate for the deletion of Rule 3 of the treaty. Since this rule provided for joint consultation and exchanges of information, it was
equivalent to a threat to end the pact.[47]

There was a further deterioration of relations in October. Molotov
insisted that there was a secret military treaty between Germany and
Finland. Moreover Rumania had begun to admit German troops, a
so-called training mission which grew into a field division. Ribbentrop

explained that it was to protect the oilfields against the plots of the British, but Molotov told Schulenburg with a smile that the British now had other worries and ought to be glad to save their own lives.[48] The German trade mission in the meanwhile reported that Hitler's new rearmament programme made it impossible to keep up with the Russian demand for weapons. The Russians had become so suspicious of the future of the pact that they were now only willing to order German machinery which could be delivered at short date. The Russians had supplied the million-ton quota of grain stuffs in full, but if the deliveries were to be discontinued, Germany would face the year 1941 without any national grain reserve.[49] Against this background, Ribbentrop passionately repeated his request for a Russian mission to Berlin, a mission headed by Molotov himself. The request was sent on 13th October, but Stalin did not accept till the 27th.

Molotov's three-day visit to Berlin began on 12th November. The official purpose of the visit was to discuss a treaty admitting Russia as a partner in the Tripartite Pact which included Germany, Italy and Japan. However, on the first day of the talks Hitler circulated a secret directive among the High Command, known as *Weisung Nr. 18*. It declared that, irrespective of the discussions with Molotov, all preparations for the east which had been ordered verbally, must be continued and that the operations plan would be communicated as soon as it had Hitler's approval.[50]

Unlike the eager Ribbentrop who wanted to play the rôle of Bismarck, Hitler was not in the least interested in the proposed treaty. To him Molotov's behaviour at the conference and afterwards was to be a test of Russian strength. Molotov might refuse to accept Ribbentrop's bland assurances that the invasion of England was imminent and that the British Empire was approaching total eclipse. He might refuse the offer of a share of the British estate in bankruptcy, which the treaty would give him in the company of Italy and Japan. Molotov might also refuse to accept Hitler's assurances of his purely economic and non-political interests in Finland and south east Europe and he might openly throw in his lot with England who, following Mussolini's latest aggression on 28th October, had already landed a military mission in Greece. On the other hand Molotov might accept all the German assurances and by doing so he would reveal that the Soviet Union was ripe for the killing. If, however, Molotov gave any hint of Anglo-American alliances or guarantees, he would show that Stalin was doing at last what he should have done at the time of the Munich and Prague crises. It would be playing a very strong hand indeed.

In fact Molotov took neither course. He was certainly not impressed by gibes against England and America. Hitler told him that the English retaliatory measures were ridiculous, as he could see for himself from the unbombed state of Berlin,[51] and yet Molotov had to spend the last evening in Ribbentrop's air-raid shelter. Before he left, he remarked slyly that he did not regret experiencing a British air-raid because it was to this that he owed such an exhaustive conversation with the Reich Foreign Minister.[52] Hitler himself treated Molotov to one of his interminable lectures which had to be translated, sentence by sentence, through an interpreter. Molotov replied with compliments, among which reproaches were soon mixed. It has been said that this was something to which Hitler was quite unused and that it left him nursing a grievance, but for this he had little cause. Molotov, it is true, made it clear that he was not convinced of the collapse of the British Empire, that he was not satisfied with the Germans' explanations of their rôle in Rumania or of their treaty with Finland. On the other hand, Molotov dropped not the slightest hint that Russia would support an Anglo-Saxon *bloc*.

And therein lay the revelation of Russia's weakness. On the one hand the Christmas pantomime, staged by Mussolini's army in Greece, was the last thing to impress the hard Russian nature, the worst possible advertisement for a future treaty partner who was to help share out the British Empire. On the other hand, Stalin and the great men of the Politburo could not forget that Churchill had supported the intervention of British troops in the civil war, could not forget that the statesmen of Versailles had made both Germany and Russia victim nations. If Germany and Russia were bickering now, it was in Russian eyes a family quarrel. And this, which Hitler could easily read in Molotov's questions and answers, was just what he wanted. He knew that the Russians would continue the payment of *Danegeld* to Germany, disguised as an unbalanced trade treaty, in the hope that Hitler would annexe no more countries.

Stalin's reply to the treaty proposal was delivered by Molotov to Schulenburg on 26th November. Russia would join the Three Power Pact, provided that the Germans withdrew their volunteers from Finland, provided that Russia was allowed to act as protecting power over Bulgaria, provided that Russia was allowed to lease naval bases from Bulgaria and Turkey which would control the Bosphorus and Dardanelles.[53] The terms were unacceptable and were meant to be. The treaty plan now simply went to sleep.

Nine days later Hitler received Brauchitsch, Keitel, Halder and Jodl at the Reich Chancellery to inform them that he was about to issue the operation orders which he had suspended during Molotov's visit. Hitler had decided to change the code-name from 'Fritz' to 'Barbarossa'. If 'the old Fritz', Frederick the Great, had made Prussia a nation, what was that compared with the Emperor Barbarossa who had united all the German states and had marched them against the ancient east? Hitler was susceptible to historical omens and during the advance on Moscow he forbade his staff officers to read Caulaincourt. This makes it all the more strange that Hitler should have chosen the name of the great Barbarossa, who, as everyone who had been through a German schooling knew, had drowned in a brook. It was the sort of thing that made old soldiers shake their heads and Hitler, who had soldiered in the ranks for five years, should have known better. Already the famous *Gefuehl* was at fault.

Franz Halder had been responsible for the strategic plan, including the game of *Kriegsspiel* which had been played at Fontainebleau. In the light of this game, Halder demanded 105 infantry and 32 armoured divisions, the most powerful army in history. It seems from Greiner's notes that Halder did not altogether share Hitler's confidence in the rapid success of the first encirclement battles, but he soon learnt to parrot Hitler's opinions.[54] Early in the following May, Halder addressed the staff of the 17th Army at Rjeszow in Poland. Halder declared that the initial battles would produce a Russian collapse after a few weeks, but one of the witnesses saw his lips tremble.[55] Yet Halder went through with it, though in September 1938 he had toyed with a plot against Hitler and in November 1939 he had opposed the invasion of the western countries. In 1943, after his dismissal, Halder was again linked with the resistance circle and was arrested after the plot of 30th July 1944 on account of an intercepted correspondence with the exiled Chancellor, Josef Wirth. Halder was no 'devil's general'. The proofs were weak, he was never charged and he was liberated by the Allies. Torn in two directions, the case of Franz Halder might almost be called the case of the German High Command.

Directive number 21, the Barbarossa Order, was issued on 18th December, the day after President Roosevelt had promised lease-lend supplies to Britain. It was the plan on which Paulus had worked in

September, the plan which envisaged reaching the line Archangel-Astrakhan. The date was fixed at 15th May 1941. The aid of Rumania and Finland was assumed, but not as yet that of Hungary and Italy.[55] To many of the army group and army commanders it must have been the first intimation that Hitler was not planning for emergencies but for outright aggression. However, during the following month, there were several staff conferences with Hitler and at none of them were any moral objections made. The army group commanders, von Leeb, von Bock and von Rundstedt put forward, as Halder had done before them, a number of technical objections against destroying the Russian armies so near the western frontier, but Hitler assured them that on the first German successes the whole Russian political system would collapse.[57] Von Leeb, an old school general who had been ennobled by the Kaiser in the First World War, proved the most difficult to convince. He argued with Brauchitsch, his Commander in Chief, that England had withdrawn her armies from Dunkirk intact and that Germany would be faced with a war on two fronts. Nevertheless three days later he was happily discussing armoured warfare plans with his expert, General Hoth.[58]

Hitler did, however, describe his orders as 'precautionary in the case of a change of attitude by the Russians'. The real reason for this reservation was the storm-cloud brewing in the Balkans. During the latter part of January the Russians were exercised by the increased flow of German reinforcements through Hungary into Rumania. Molotov learnt that they now numbered 200,000 and that it was intended to march through Bulgaria in order to attack the British in Thrace. Molotov objected that the violation of Bulgaria would bring Turkey into the war on the British side in defence of the Straits—and he reaffirmed that Bulgaria was exclusively in Russia's sphere of interest.[59] Nevertheless German troops entered Bulgaria on 28th February and three days later Bulgaria joined the Tripartite Pact. The German forces in Rumania had in the meanwhile grown to 700,000 men.

When Hitler addressed his generals again on 9th January, the emphasis was mainly on the Balkan campaign, but he accused the British of relying on Russian intervention, and he declared that Stalin was a cold-blooded blackmailer who would repudiate any treaty.[60] Hitler now spoke of successes so vast that even the industrial resources of Baku and Sverdlovsk would be destroyed.[61]

At the end of the month, Halder and Rundstedt directed another *Kriegsspiel* at St Germain. This was to test the possibilities of an envelopment battle round Kiev with the Rumanians advancing into Russia from the south. The German High Command was certainly unlucky in the turn of fortune's wheel, by which certain of its members fell into Russian hands. The story of the war games at Fontainebleau was betrayed by Field Marshal Paulus, who surrendered at Stalingrad. The story of the war games at St Germain was betrayed by General Vinzenz Mueller, the deputy Commander of the 4th Army, who surrendered in the great disaster of June 1944 on the Central Russian front.[62]

Hitler studied the results of these strategic games with care, but in fact they had been designed to tell him what he most wanted to hear. He was obsessed with the rottenness of the Russian 'State corpse' which nearly sixteen years ago had inspired the fourteenth chapter of *Mein Kampf*; he was obsessed with the poor showing of the Red Army in the Winter War with Finland, obsessed with the conflicts between the Politburo and the General Staff, as revealed in the 1937-8 Trials. Through historical ignorance or through wishful thinking, Hitler forgot the astonishing number of executions of French generals that had paved the way to the first military victories of the French Revolution and eventually to Napoleon. Above all Hitler was obsessed with his easy victory in France and the Lowlands. He wanted to fight alone without sharing the spoils. Rumania and Finland he had to enlist in order to strike from their territories, but Mussolini he deliberately deceived even at the friendly meeting of 20th January and Japan he deliberately deterred so as to egg her on to the attack on Singapore and the dismemberment of the British Empire.[63]

At the Fuehrer conference of 3rd February Halder brought Hitler news that he did not want to hear. He had ascertained that the Russians had massed in the west 100 infantry divisions, twenty-five cavalry divisions and thirty mechanized divisions, a force even larger than the army which Hitler had planned on 18th December.[64] Moreover Hitler had allowed eight weeks' notice for the deployment of his forces and Jodl declared that not even fourteen weeks would suffice.[65] Hitler dismissed Halder's figures as preposterous. He still maintained his belief in a *Blitzkrieg* and this was clearly the basis of his instructions regarding the political preparations for a peacetime administration. These plans, which were divulged to a wide circle on 30th March, will be studied in the next chapter. They were founded on Hitler's conception that the best parts of Russia were to be colonized by foreigners and the remainder left as weak separate socialist states.

It was this special character of Hitler's campaign that predestined it not merely to failure, which was surely inevitable, but to absolute national suicide. And the basis for this special character is to be found not in *Mein Kampf* but in an event which had occurred on 10th January. Incredibly, at a time when Molotov's objections to the nature of Hitler's forthcoming Balkan campaign had not been answered, the trade pact, which had hung fire since October, was signed. The Russians were to deliver 1,400,000 tons of grain from the 1941 harvest and the delivery was to be completed in September.[66] It was a bigger harvest than that which was to have rescued the Hapsburg monarchy from starvation in 1918, when the entire Ukraine was occupied. If that could be done by blackmail alone, what could be achieved by ruthless colonization?* More than three months passed before this idea took concrete shape in the notorious 'Green File', but the germs were there. And to stimulate the deliveries Hitler used a form of blackmail on the Russians which showed clearly that what he wanted was war.

On 25th March, the Japanese Foreign Minister, Yosuke Matsuoka, arrived in Berlin. It was known officially that on his passage through Moscow Matsuoka had been in negotiation for a neutrality pact with Russia. All the resources of Hitler and Ribbentrop were therefore used to persuade the Japanese statesman that now was the moment in centuries for an attack on Singapore. There was no question of making Japan a partner in the invasion of Russian possessions. On the contrary the Russo-Japanese neutrality pact was much desired by Hitler in order to turn Japan's aspirations towards the British Empire. That in the outcome Japan should attack the USA as well was something for which Hitler did not bargain and which he did not welcome. But, in the knowledge that Matsuoka would again be seeing Molotov and perhaps Stalin, Hitler and Ribbentrop used him for their purposes. Hitler told Matsuoka that both England and the USA hoped to align Russia against Germany, but there was a practical guarantee against this contingency which was much more weighty than the existing treaties. In the case of danger, Germany would not hesitate to use 160 to 180 divisions against Russia—but Hitler did not think that the danger would arise.[67]

Ribbentrop was much more explicit. If the Russians were not entirely convinced that they were to be the next victims, here was all the proof they wanted and Matsuoka could be trusted to tell them. Having described in detail the recent deterioration of the alliance

* See p. 190

between the two countries, omitting nothing, the 'second Bismarck' went on to say that it was known that Russia was cultivating relatively open ties with England. Ribbentrop did not suppose from what he had seen of Stalin that he was 'inclined to adventure', but one could not be sure. The Fuehrer was convinced that, in the case of action against the Soviet Union, there would in a few months be no more great power in Russia. Ribbentrop did not think that Stalin would pursue an unwise policy, but in any case the Fuehrer relied on the Wehrmacht more than on the existing treaties.[68]

On 28th March Ribbentrop rubbed this in a bit harder. In reply to Matsuoka's questions, he said that Hitler had never considered an alliance of Russia with both Germany and Japan. It was as impossible as the union of fire and water. Since Russia had made impossible conditions for joining the Tripartite Pact, the whole matter was being handled in a quite dilatory manner and Russia was being watched closely. The Fuehrer would crush Russia if Stalin was 'not in harmony with what Hitler considered right'.[69] Matsuoka stayed in Berlin as late as 4th April and altogether between Hitler and Ribbentrop the threat against Russia was repeated four times.

In the face of so many open threats, the question whether later the Russians were warned with reliable military intelligence from the British government is academic. It must have been obvious from the treatment of Poland and Czechoslovakia that no government could be in harmony with what Hitler considered right, that it would require no act of war on the part of the Russians for Hitler to blow the whistle. Why then were the Russians caught unprepared on 22nd June 1941? The present Russian fashion is to declare that Stalin committed grievous errors, that Stalin obstinately refused to listen to his best military advisers; that Stalin was in the hands of Beria and the NKVD, who were the enemies of the High Command and all good Russians. Previously it was the fashion to say that Stalin had kept faith and had expected the Germans to do the same, that as a result Russia was treacherously attacked at a moment when she was practically unarmed and when no attack was to be expected. It was of course Stalin's genius that saved the situation.

What is the truth? That in spite of her huge mobilization, Russia was caught unprepared admits of no doubt. Gustav Hilger is probably right in attributing the crushing defeats of 1941 to the lack of clear orders from the top, to the inborn Slav dislike of responsibility and to the long indoctrination of officers and officials in the post-Lenin period which forbade them to take any initiative. The backwoodsman individualist warfare of the Partisans came late in the day in the Second World War and it flourished on the blissful difficulty of direct communication with Moscow. Nevertheless much of the catastrophe of 1941 must be laid at Stalin's door. If at home he was a ruthless dictator who was driven power-mad and ended as a sort of Tiberius, trusting no one, abroad Stalin was the weakest of politicians. It was outright folly to believe that those German encroachments in eastern Europe, which Stalin did not underestimate, could be stalemated without either a Russian alliance with the West or a trial of arms with the Germans.

It was still worse folly to believe that a sound defence system could be built up by moving incredible masses of men to the border, while the country was being pumped dry to fulfill the appeasing trade pacts with Germany. After the return of Matsuoka to Moscow and the report of his interviews, Stalin became that pathetic figure who embraced Colonel Krebs at the Jaroslavl Terminal a week later, a man hoping against all his deepest instincts as an old revolutionary that by doing nothing wrong he could avert the trap into which he had fallen. Just as Hitler ignored the pessimistic reports, which came to him from his *Abwehr* services and from the Moscow Embassy, so Stalin ignored his own military intelligence. Since this service was based on communist political cells that had long been established in every European country, it must have been one of the best military intelligence services in the world.

Soon after Matsuoka's visit came Stalin's weakest action. On 27th March, while Matsuoka was left to suck his teeth in an adjoining apartment, Hitler learnt that the latest recruit to the Tripartite Pact had deserted. The young King of Yugoslavia had rebelled against his pro-German uncle, the Regent Prince Paul. The treaty which Ribbentrop had signed in Vienna only two days previously, the treaty which obliged the Yugoslavs to fight against Greece, would in all probability be set aside by the new Belgrade government. The Yugoslavs, isolated among Germany's latest allies, appealed to Russia for a guarantee of protection. Stalin would not involve himself as much as this. So far from lending the huge weight of Russia against the Germans at a moment when they had been caught off their guard, he seems to have believed that the Yugoslavs would keep the Germans heavily committed in their difficult mountainous country and that their sacrifices would gain precious time for him.[70] So all that Molotov proposed to the Yugoslav Minister on 4th April, after faithfully informing the

Germans, was a pact of non-aggression. Much good did it do to Yugoslavia.[71]

Hitler attacked Yugoslavia on 6th April. It was a brilliant *Blitzkrieg*, culminating in another British withdrawal from the continent of Europe and the occupation of everything down to southern Greece and Crete. But the date for 'Barbarossa' had to be postponed from 15th May to 22nd June, sacrificing six out of the fourteen fair campaigning weeks in Russia. The Yugoslav *coup d'état* against the Regent Prince Paul may have been a Ruritanian little drama; the landing and re-embarkation of two British divisions may have been a very small military adventure, but these two events saved Russia from even worse calamities than were to befall her.

Hitler's rage expended itself in the senseless bombing of Belgrade and in privately abusing Stalin, even if Stalin on this truly wicked occasion had not emitted the least whisper of a protest. Schulenburg, who was sent for on 28th April, tried to persuade Hitler that Stalin's pact with Yugoslavia was nothing but 'a declaration of his interests'. He pointed out that the unfortunate Yugoslav Minister in Moscow had not been able to get any aid for his country. But Hitler would not believe that the Russians had signed a pact purely as an instrument of peace. What devil, he asked, had possessed the Russians? They were as much behind the Belgrade Palace coup as the British.[72] They had forced him to attack 'poor little Greece too, that small plucky nation'. Schulenburg told Hitler the truth, that Stalin was literally terrified of Germany, that even after the Yugoslav Pact the Russian Foreign Office had kept Sir Stafford Cripps waiting six entire days for an audience with a quite subordinate official; that Stalin had loyally told Matsuoka that there was no question of his co-operating with England and France and that, when Matsuoka's train left the Jaroslavl Terminal, Stalin had made an unrehearsed public appearance at the side of the train in order to be seen greeting the German delegation. Stalin had put his arm round Schulenburg's shoulder and he had gone up to the acting Military attaché, Colonel Hans Krebs, crying 'ah, a German officer. We will stay friends with you under all conditions (*auf jeden Fall*).'[73] Other reports say that Krebs, who was to become the last Chief of Staff of Hitler's armies and the General who tried to negotiate the surrender of Berlin, received the great Stalin moustache, full volley, on both cheeks.

Schulenburg believed that Stalin was ready for further concessions. It had even been intimated that Russia could provide Germany with five million tons of grain by 1942, a quantity which at that time Hitler thought impracticable. Unfortunately it was the only part of Schulenburg's report that Hitler grasped. It was no coincidence that next day the economic counterpart of the Barbarossa orders was issued to the military bureaucracy under the name of the Oldenburg Plan. The record of General Thomas's conference of 29th April is not very exciting reading, but it must be unique among peacetime military instructions in that it is concerned entirely with the seizure of produce.[74] On 15th May, the Schnurre mission produced a quite staggering account of the way the trade pact had been working since Matsuoka had conveyed the warnings of Hitler and Ribbentrop to Moscow. During March the deliveries had gone up by leaps and bounds. The Russians had committed themselves to the delivery of three million tons of grain by 1st August 1942. By the end of the month they were expected to exceed enormously the April delivery of 208,000 tons,[75] though their punctuality imposed a heavy strain on their economy. This report too had quick repercussions. A week later, on 22nd May, Goering's Four-Year-Plan Office circulated the first secret instructions which were to form the basis of the 'Green File' of 1st June, among them the instruction that order was only to be restored in invaded regions which possessed a surplus of agricultural products or crude oil. As to the industrial areas:[76]

> Many tens of millions of people in the industrial areas will become redundant and will either die or will have to emigrate to Siberia. Any attempts to save the population in these parts from death by starvation through the import of surpluses from the Black Earth Zone would be at the expense of supplies to Europe. It would reduce Germany's staying power in the war and would undermine Germany's and Europe's power to resist the blockade. This must be clearly and absolutely understood.

It is possible that this document or its forerunner of 29th April, may have reached the Russians, though the witness, Colonel Kyril Kalinov, is perhaps suspect, since he deserted from the Russian Military Staff in Berlin in 1949. According to Kalinov, the Russian intelligence service knew about the document before June, when a copy was procured through Switzerland. It appears, however, that Dekanosov, the Russian Ambassador in Berlin, regarded it as a decoy which had been planted on the Russians to persuade them to step-up their oil deliveries. Dekanosov based his view on the report of another agent who had actually spoken to Goering. This agent, a former friend of Karl Radek, had learnt that there would soon be 150 German divisions on the Russian border, in Goering's words the greatest blackmail undertaking in history. A little ultimatum would do the trick, but it would only be a matter of some harmless petrol and raw materials. This story from a gossipy book must be taken for what it is worth,[77] but at least it illustrates a basic truth namely that, in spite of his intelligence network, Stalin preferred to believe what he wanted to hear. His faith that the Germans, in spite of all their threats, would do nothing so long as the Russians supplied the goods, became a pitiful obsession. Thus, on the night of 21st June, as German assault troops waited for zero hour on the San River at Przemysl, the Russian oil trains continued to thunder over the bridge into German territory.[78]

On 28th April, when he sent for von Schulenburg, Hitler had still not fixed a date for the postponed opening of 'Barbarossa'. Many German divisions were still on their way north from the Balkan front and some would be committed in those difficult regions for an indefinite period. But if a date were not fixed soon, then the whole Russian enterprise must be postponed till 1942. It suited Hitler well that the permanent Military Attaché in Moscow, General Ernst Koestring, was on leave.[79] His place was occupied by Colonel Hans Krebs. Whether in spite of Stalin's embraces at the Jaroslavl railway station or because of them, Krebs reported to Halder on 5th May that he found the Russian higher leadership decidedly bad. Compared with the year 1933, the impression was strikingly negative. According to Krebs, it would take Russia twenty years to reach the quality of leadership, which she had known before the time of the military purges.[80]

A week later, the date of 22nd June was fixed for the postponed 'Barbarossa' invasion. The decision was taken just two days after Rudolf Hess, the chief of the Party Chancellery and Hitler's nominal deputy, made his ill-starred flight from Bavaria to Scotland. Hess hoped to conclude a separate peace with Britain, but, after the war, his first interrogators were to declare that Hess had brought no positive warning of Hitler's intention to invade Russia.[81] It is indeed improbable that Hitler confided the timetable of 'Barbarossa' to the virtually discarded Rudolf Hess. It is much more likely that the timetable was known to Hess's mentor, Albrecht Haushofer, who chose the moment for Hess's flight accordingly. Hitler's reaction was simple. The fact that the British treated Hess as a prisoner and blazoned his escapade instead of sending him back as a secret intermediary, meant that British neutrality was not to be bought at any price. Since the dove had not returned to the ark, Stalin, who had seen this, must not be given time to exploit the situation. So, two days after the British announcement, Hitler fixed the date for 'Barbarossa'.

During the remaining six weeks Hitler offered every provocation and Stalin remained sunk in his exaggerated neutralism. Hitler now completed his arrangements with Finland, Rumania and Hungary, so that the Russian Secret Service could hardly fail to draw the right inference from the mobilization and troop movements of these countries. The only ally of Germany who was not kept in the picture was Italy, but this treatment had now become traditional. The one occasion during the war when Hitler did not demonstrate Mussolini's unimportance to his own face was when he rescued him from his kidnappers.

Even at the meeting between Hitler and Mussolini on the Brenner Pass on 2nd June, Ribbentrop produced no more than the now commonplace threat of what *could* happen to Russia. The Italians were nevertheless well informed. On 14th May, the Italian Secret Service learnt in Budapest that the date was to be 15th June. Mussolini himself spoke of the imminent invasion on 4th June and hoped that the Germans 'would lose many feathers' in Russia. When, however, it came to actualities, he was frantic to secure a share of the spoils by providing military assistance.[82]

On 14th June, Hitler summoned his generals for a final briefing, of which only the invitation and general programme have survived.[83] It seems that Hitler spoke for an hour and a half on the necessity of a preventive war, and he described graphically the futility of his discussions with Molotov in the previous November. This lecture was the climax to a day of conferences, during which forty-five generals and admirals crossed the threshold of the Reich Chancellery. Fortified by a late lunch, the service chiefs were bewitched. Fritz Hoth found the lecture impressive. He was told by his fellow armoured-warfare general, Erich Hoepner, who was destined to play a part in the 'July plot' which was not distinguished by brightness, 'and now I am really convinced that the war against Russia is necessary'.[84] Keitel too deposed that the lecture contained 'new and very impressive ideas and they affected us deeply'.[85] But Keitel at his trial at least called things by their own name. The lecture, he said, had demonstrated not only the necessity of attacking Russia but also the necessity of abandoning the recognized restraints of warfare and of adopting the peculiar savagery required by a conflict between ideologies.

On the same day the Russian official *Tass* Agency denied to the world with extreme candour that the German troop movements from the Balkans were directed against Russia or that the Russian summer manoeuvres in the west were directed against Germany. The despatch contained Stalin's solemn declaration that Russia intended to abide by the non-aggression pact and it publicly absolved Germany of any war-like designs. The text was handed by Molotov to Schulenburg without comment.[86] But against what a background of provocation had this document been composed? As Molotov pointed out to Schulenburg on the night before the invasion, there had been eighty German military flights, reported over Russian territory in the three weeks to 18th April, and there had been 180 in the next seven weeks. The Luftwaffe had penetrated a hundred miles into Russian territory and one machine had force-landed at Rowné with its photographic equipment. When one considers how in this blessed age every half-baked little country reserves to itself the right to shoot at foreign aircraft, even obvious passenger liners, should they violate its precious air space by a mile or two, this incredible forbearance of the easily provoked Russians will be appreciated.[87] Marshal Timoshenko, the Commissar for Defence, was forbidden to order any shooting at these planes. The Germans made their air survey in peace, and as a result over 3,000 Russian machines were destroyed on the ground in the first hour of attack, uncamouflaged and unprotected by artillery.[88]

If any further proof were needed that the Russians were leaning backwards to avoid a war, the conversation between Molotov and Schulenburg on the night of 21st June would be enough. Molotov sent for the Ambassador, solely to find out what was amiss, why the Germans had not published the *Tass* declaration, why the reconnaissance flights continued. Schulenburg could tell him nothing. In the morning he had the nasty duty of communicating to Molotov the declaration of war which Ribbentrop had made to Dekanosov in Berlin at 4 am. The whistle had blown.

CHAPTER TWO

'LEAVING THE COURTS AT HOME'
THE COMMISSAR ORDER AND THE 'BARBAROSSA' JURISDICTION ORDER

(a) The Rôle of Himmler and Heydrich

ACCORDING TO HIS generals, Hitler's plans for the invasion of Russia contained, as late as March 1941, no departure from the accepted rules of warfare. This is not surprising, since the 'Barbarossa' plan was limited to strategy and military organization. Matters concerning the treatment of civilians and prisoners belonged to the general problem of occupying the country and this Hitler did not begin to approach till a very late hour, if indeed he can be said to have approached it at all.

It must, however, have been realized from the beginning that Himmler, who was Chief of Police, not only in Germany but in all occupied territories, would exercise his powers in Russia and that he would make every effort to keep these powers outside the competence of the High Command. Nearly all the generals who took part in the staff-talks with Hitler concerning the 'Barbarossa' plan had been present at a much earlier conference at Berchtesgaden on 22nd August 1939. There Hitler had described what were to be the duties of Himmler's police units in occupied Poland.[1] Admiral Canaris in particular must have recollected an occasion on Hitler's special railway train on 12th September 1939 when Keitel had warned him of the dangers of military interference with these special duties. Keitel had threatened that, if the generals disassociated themselves from the measures of Himmler's police, they would find that at the side of each military commander a corresponding SS police official had been appointed.[2] And the threat was altogether vain. A few weeks later, General Blaskowitz, the military governor in occupied Poland, was relieved of his post after grumbling about the SS, who lived outside the law and over whom he had no authority except in cases of mutiny. And Blaskowitz was replaced by Hans Frank, who, even if he quarrelled with SS leaders, did not as a civilian object to SS methods. Moreover the generals, who were building up their future armies and army groups along the eastern border, the so-called Otto line, could have had no illusions about the conditions in the rear areas in the Poland of 1940–1. Indignation they might profess at Hitler's language in describing Himmler's new powers in Russia. Surprised they could never be.

On 13th March 1941, Keitel circulated a memorandum in terms which are recorded by the High Command archivist, Helmuth Greiner, though the memorandum itself has been lost. It was based on a private talk which Keitel had had with Hitler on the 3rd.[3] Much of it was to be repeated on the 30th, when Hitler addressed the High Command, for the wording in Halder's diary is often the same as Greiner's.[4] Between the two versions a very clear picture may be had of the theory underlying Hitler's special orders for the political treatment of occupied Russia. For the first time Hitler envisaged Russia after defeat and after the collapse of the central government. Hitler's theory assumed that an alien sword could not govern everywhere and forever. Germany would have to permit a number of separatist states, whose government would have to be socialist. The reason for this was that socialism provided the only way of life the Russians understood, but it would be socialism without any politically trained minds. 'A primitive socialist intelligentsia is all that is necessary'.

Somehow these Russian separatist states with only minor military potential and with only minor intelligence at the helm would have to be launched and leaders found for them—but where? Not among the exiled leaders of pre-revolutionary Russia, Hitler said, because they were enemies of Germany and he trusted them no more than he trusted the Jewish Bolshevist intelligentsia of the Soviet Union. The leaders would have to be found in Russia itself, but no German military governors could be trusted with their selection and their training. For that purpose civilian *Reichskommissars* would have to be appointed. But, before the new leadership could be picked for the dismembered Russian states, all trace of Bolshevist rule must disappear. In Greiner's version Hitler seems to demand the liquidation, not merely of commissars but even of 'Bolshevik Headmen'. For that purpose it might be necessary to 'establish organs of the SS alongside the Secret Field Police of the Wehrmacht, right up to the front itself'. With these organs Himmler would have to undertake special tasks in order to prepare a political administration; and by special tasks Hitler meant not just political purging but 'the extermination of entire grades of society'. This would be entirely in Himmler's hands as Chief of Police and the Wehrmacht courts would have no competence in Russia, except where Wehrmacht subjects were concerned.

In the version circulated by Keitel on 13th March it seems that the Wehrmacht were mentioned purely negatively, but on the 30th the High Command heard from Hitler personally that the rôle of the Wehrmacht in the so-called political preparations for the new Russia was not to be negative after all. Hitler addressed his generals in the Berlin Reich Chancellery. Since all the army and army group commanders brought their chiefs of staffs and since Keitel, Jodl, Wagner, Halder, Warlimont and Brauchitsch were present too, there must have been an audience of at least thirty.[5] In a speech lasting two hours and a half, Hitler told them that every individual commander would have to be fully conversant with the political preparations. The elimination of the present Russian leadership would be in their hands as much as in the hands of Himmler and his police units. These measures were not a matter for military courts. The troops would be expected to strike towards the rear with the same methods that they used in attacking the enemy in the field. Commissars and GPU men were criminals and must be treated as such.

It appears, though there is no mention in Halder's account, that at this point Hitler must have embroidered on the theme of the Commissars and GPU men. According to General Hans Reinhardt[6] Hitler described atrocities that had been ordered by the *Politruks* or party indoctrination officials, who had been attached to units of company strength during the Russian war in Finland. Hitler declared that he had learnt through his intelligence service that the Russians were not going to treat German prisoners in the conventional way, especially members of the SS and police. Even so, he did not expect the German Officer Corps to understand his orders but he demanded that they obey them unconditionally.[7]

It did not mean, Hitler continued, that the troops could be allowed to get out of hand. That need not happen if the commanders gave orders that appealed to the general impulse of their people. Above all they would have to forget the conception of comradeship between soldiers, because a communist was a comrade neither before nor after a battle. If the commanders failed to grasp the fact that this was a war of extermination, they would again have to fight the communist enemy thirty years hence. Therefore the commanders must make up their minds to the sacrifice of overcoming their scruples. At that point, according to Halder's diary, Hitler broke off, leaving his audience, one would imagine, loosening their choker collars and gasping like so many fish. Little Halder's next sentence reads, 'Noon—all invited to lunch.[8]

If one is to draw any conclusion from these minutes of Greiner's and Halder's it is perhaps this. With perfect realism Hitler pictured the situation of Russia after defeat in a *Blitzkrieg*. With perfect realism he calculated that a reactionary government by Tsarist emigrés would not work. But when, after nine months of purely military planning, Hitler tried to imagine a political system which the Germans could leave behind them, the result was pure raving lunacy. No human mind can register the picture of a country of 180 million people, in which every person capable of quoting a sentence of Marxist dialectic and every responsible leader down to the lowest village headman or *starost* had been murdered. No imagination can conceive of that large portion of the earth's surface, coming to life afterwards under a handpicked socialist leadership of strictly limited intelligence. Hitler himself became aware of the inconsistency between his plans for exterminating Russian leadership and his plans for Russian self-government. Four months later, Hitler made it evident at his Angerburg conference that the independence of the separatist states would be only nominal. The gap created by the flight or murder of the old bureaucracy would be filled by Germans.* There was therefore no mitigation of the original instructions. The decrees, which Hitler had had prepared before the campaign began, were not repealed even when the campaign was clearly lost. It was then that Hitler became even more attached to them than ever, because there was no longer a political regime to be prepared for Russia, but only the maximum of devastation to be inflicted in the wake of the retreating Wehrmacht. Although the Germans were not in Russia long enough to exterminate all adherents of Marxist doctrine or to set up satellite states of limited intelligence, Hitler's address of 30th March 1941, remained the guiding principle of German rule, though this meant anarchy in the occupied territories and opposition in most branches of German leadership.

It may be that in March 1941 Hitler hoped to enslave the High Command to his will by incriminating them in something which would make it impossible for them to sue for peace over his head, if the campaign failed. That is in fact what happened to the High Command,

* See p. 140

but it is hard to believe that Hitler planned it as a second contingency at a time when he did not consider the possibility of a long war. As the invasion date approached, Hitler's plans became more rigid. Hence the profound change in the overall conception of the address of 30th March, compared with that of the 13th. Between the two dates Hitler became much more certain of the totality and swiftness of the Russian collapse. This can be seen from Hitler's remark to Halder on the 17th that the ideological ties of the Russian people were not strong enough to survive. They would break up with the elimination of the Bolshevik functionaries.[9] It would seem that Hitler was more afraid of nationalist than of communist movements. For some reason he told Halder that he thought the White Russians would welcome the Germans with open arms, but that the Ukrainians and Cossacks were dubious, which was the very reverse of the truth.

What happened to the generals after Hitler had launched his bomb-shell on 30th March? Several of them survived to describe their experiences at Nuremberg, either as witnesses or defendants. Not one was prepared to admit that he had found himself in agreement with Hitler. Yet if they had all come back after lunch and declared that they would not go on with it, there would have been no Commissar Order and probably no invasion of Russia either. That, however, is not a realistic view of history. Alfred Jodl, who was a very realistic man, told a wide-eyed American lawyer in cross-examination that German generals do not make revolutions. He believed that the nearest they had ever come to it was in 1848, when the Prussian generals struck the ground with their sabres. So, instead of saying anything to Hitler, some of the generals persuaded each other that they could kill the thing when the time came, by issuing their own orders.

Such at least was the explanation both of Hitler's Commander-in-Chief and of his Chief of Staff. Neither of these generals had to stand trial at the hands of the Allies. On 8th August 1948 in the course of the American 'High Command' Trial, Brauchitsch was moved from an internment camp at Bridgend in Glamorganshire to Munsterlager in Germany. It was proposed to try Brauchitsch, Manstein and Rundstedt in Hamburg before a British court. But Rundstedt was declared to be too old and ill and Brauchitsch died before the end of the year. So in 1949 only Manstein was tried. As to Halder, who was also a British captive, it was apparently considered that Hitler had punished him enough already. He was therefore allowed to give evidence on behalf of generals who had come under his authority.

Brauchitsch and Halder did not appear as witnesses in the same trial, because in 1948 the former's evidence was no longer admissible under British procedure. Moreover, Halder's evidence of 1948 did not tally with Brauchitsch's evidence of 1946, when he had committed perjury. So the two accounts do not help very much to solve a many-sided problem of human behaviour. In any case to understand the inaction of these two generals in March 1941, one must realize that this was not the first time that they had been asked to treat the enemy as second-class human beings. That had been going on in Poland since September 1939. On the 19th of that month, the generals Eugen Mueller and Eduard Wagner had reported to Halder on a conference with Heydrich concerning a forthcoming housecleaning of Jews, intelligentsia, nobles and clergy. Halder had noted in his diary that this housecleaning would have to be deferred till the beginning of December, when the Wehrmacht would have handed over its responsibilities in Poland to a civilian administration[10]. This became the aim both of Halder and Brauchitsch. They were concerned only in getting the Wehrmacht disassociated from Heydrich's measures. They formed the theory that, if they offered to resign and if they succeeded in doing so against Hitler's wishes, resignation would mean disgraceful dismissal or a still worse punishment. This, they argued, would be a useless sacrifice, because their places would be filled by others who were less humane than themselves.

Brauchitsch gave evidence at Nuremberg on 9th August 1946. He was sixty-five years old, had held no military command of any kind for nearly five years and he was going blind. The cross-examination by Brigadier General Telford Taylor was extremely brief and quite superficial. Brauchitsch described how, after Hitler's long lecture on 30th March 1941, the three army group commanders, the Field Marshals von Rundstedt, von Bock and von Leeb, together with some of the army commanders, came to him in a state of great excitement, because such a way of waging war was intolerable to them. Brauchitsch promised that, as far as the High Command of the armies in the field was concerned, he would see to it that no such orders were issued but he would have to think things over. It was no use speaking to Hitler, because he knew that once Hitler had made his decision public nothing could dissuade him. So in due course he issued an order for the maintenance of discipline 'along the lines and regulations that applied in the past'.[11]

Brauchitsch did not remember any of the sentences in this order and it was by no means clear how such an order could nullify Hitler's whole principle of waging war in Russia. A much puzzled American prosecutor, Telford Taylor then put these questions:[12]

> *Question* You stated that you had cancelled Hitler's decree about the shooting of captured Soviet Commissars. Did I understand you right?
> *Answer* Yes.
> *Question* What was Hitler's reaction to your disregarding this decree?
> *Answer* He never said anything to me about it. I do not know. He never reacted.
> *Question* And you never notified Hitler that you were suspending his decree?
> *Answer* No.
> *Question* How did it happen that actually the decree was carried out, as a great many Soviet Commissars were annihilated by the German forces?
> *Answer* I am not in a position to answer that because I never received a report about it. I only received a report that the order had not been carried out.

Pressed on this point again by Lord Oaksey, the President of the Court, Brauchitsch declared, 'Mr President, I am not trying to tell stories. I am merely telling the truth when I say that I did not receive any reports on it. I only received the information that the order was not being carried out'.[13]

This was the version that was allowed to stand at the first Nuremberg Trial in 1946. Two years later, at the time of the High Command Case, several more documents had been discovered and were in the hands of the Tribunal. They showed that all Brauchitsch's answers had been untrue. His own decrees, implementing Hitler's instructions, had been discovered, decrees that had been signed and forwarded to an impressive circulation-list of generals. They had also traced Brauchitsch's order for the maintenance of discipline, a vague innocuous thing that could never have been cited against the Commissar Order. And, so far from receiving no reports concerning the execution of Political Commissars, it was shown that all three army group commanders had called Brauchitsch's attention to such reports and that he had been persuaded to forward a memorandum to Hitler.

Halder's evidence at the High Command Trial was more circumspect than this and he told a story that could neither be proved nor disproved. He admitted that he had been the first to learn of the special rôle of Himmler's police units and he had recorded it in his diary as early as 5th March 1941, but he claimed that he failed to grasp the implications even after Keitel's circular of the 13th, albeit filled with mistrust.[14] After the meeting on the 30th, Halder approached Brauchitsch and suggested that he demand that Hitler should dismiss both of them.[15] Brauchitsch refused because of his responsibilities towards his troops. He still hoped to enlist the aid of Keitel in killing the new orders. At this point Brauchitsch appealed to Halder's devotion. He recalled the last occasion when Halder had wanted to resign. That was before the Polish campaign and Brauchitsch had talked him out of it all night, finally making him promise never to leave his side in the common struggle against Hitler. So, after eighteen months, Halder had to keep his promise. 'This was my reason for not offering to resign. I had promised not to do so.'

Halder kept that promise so well that, though Brauchitsch was dismissed in December 1941, he himself contrived to stay on as Hitler's Chief of Staff in Russia till the following September. But to turn to the three army group commanders who attended the meeting of 30th March 1941; Leeb and Rundstedt confirmed at the Nuremberg Trials that they too had protested to Brauchitsch. But they gave this evidence perfunctorily and without angling for much credit. Neither Field Marshal asserted that he had done anything so spectacular as to offer to resign.[16] But on behalf of von Bock, who was dead before the Nuremberg Trials began, much more picturesque claims have been made. It seems that von Bock told his troubles to his chief of staff, Major General Henning von Tresckow, who was to become famous as a conspirator against Hitler.* Von Tresckow had a plan for the three army group commanders. They were to fly to Berlin and demand to see Hitler again. This time they would refuse to carry out the Commissar Order. But von Bock said that it could not be done, so he sent his protest in writing to Hitler who ignored it. This candid story seems to have acquired some less candid snowball elements. It has even been alleged that through von Tresckow the three army group commanders stopped Hitler from extending the blanket execution order, from applying the commissar definition to all captured Red Army officers,[17] political or otherwise.

In reality the whittling down of Hitler's orders was very slight and it

* See pp. 311-12

was achieved, not by Commanders-in-Chief with the rank of Field Marshal, but by the army bureaucracy. And the impulse was practical rather than moral, because in the transmission of a Fuehrer order the devolution of military authority needed a great deal of protocol. Only a very few days after the lecture in the Reich Chancellery, Brauchitsch sent Eduard Wagner, the Quartermaster General of the forces, to arrange with Heydrich, as head of the Reich Main Security Office (RSHA),* the terms of authority of the SS Security Police units in Russia and the limits of the army's competence. Although he was the most feared man in Germany, Reinhard Heydrich was technically subordinate to Himmler, who was the supreme authority over the German police system, as well as over the SS in its other ramifications. But at this period, when he had not weakened his position by undertaking the additional task of governing Bohemia-Moravia, Heydrich was in practice all but independent of Himmler and had direct access to Hitler, who had a high opinion of him, mingled with distrust.

Heydrich had a special interest in the security arrangements behind the future Russian front. For the past seven years he had been constructing his own military intelligence organization. Although this rival SS body was bound by a series of rules to co-operate with the Intelligence Service of the Wehrmacht, the *Abwehr* of Admiral Canaris, it was generally believed that Heydrich was trying to supplant Canaris. In this way he would win a further position for the SS and encroach on the supreme direction of the war. Hitler, however, did not encourage such ambitions in SS leaders and at this period of the war he was reluctant to irritate a General Staff that had given him so little trouble. But Hitler had a weakness for reports on the same subject from different and competing agencies. He let both military intelligence organizations continue their work and he believed the reports of neither.

It was through this doubling of military intelligence duties that the High Command had a chance to control the wholesale thuggery behind the front, as Hitler had outlined it on 30th March. The performance of this thuggery would be in the hands of the Action Groups (*Einsatz-gruppen*) and special Commandos (*Sonderkommando*) of the Security

---

* RSHA was nothing but a new name, coined in 1939, for the SD or Security Service, an eight-year-old branch of Himmler's SS, which had swallowed up the Criminal and Political Police Bureaux. In the RSHA organization the investigating branch was the *Gestapo* and the executive branch the *Sipo* or Security Police. Officers of both branches bore the title of commanders of the *Sipo* and SD. In the language of the Wehrmacht, commandos of the Security Police were always referred to as the SD, chiefly to distinguish them from their own Secret Field Gendarmerie units. It has been found convenient to use the term SD in this sense in this book.

Service and the Security Police, and these were not only the executive arm of the Gestapo, but also Heydrich's intelligence service. Such a combination of duties was implicit in Hitler's instructions that these units should prepare the way for the new political administration. But, even in peacetime, the Gestapo had been able to encroach on military preserves, because, since Hitler's seizure of power, Gestapo agents had been allowed to collect political intelligence abroad as well as at home. Such confusions between police spying and military spying are common to states that employ a political police force. The same state of affairs existed on the other side of the hill, where the NKVD doubled the functions of the *Rasviedupr* or Military Intelligence Corps. In Germany this rivalry was toned down by the good relations which subsisted between Canaris and Heydrich who had served under him in the navy. Moreover the two men were compelled to co-operate, because the *Abwehr* had no power in peacetime to make arrests. For that purpose it had to request the services of the 'political bureaux' of the police in the different German States and these political bureaux had been absorbed by the Gestapo.

The relations between the rival intelligence services were still governed in April 1941 by an agreement, known as the 'Ten Commandments', which had been made in January 1937.[18] This was the trump card of the High Command, because it required Heydrich's SD and its intelligence services to pass on to the *Abwehr* any information it possessed. As an intelligence service, the SD was obliged to report what it had been doing as a secret police force.

It was therefore Heinrich Mueller, the head of the Gestapo, who had to regulate the competence of the Security Police units of the SD with the Quartermaster General of the Wehrmacht. Heinrich Mueller had the reputation of the hardest, cruellest man in Germany. He seems also to have been one of the most stupid. The reputed 'Grand Inquisitor' of Europe was a Bavarian policeman, accustomed only to interview suspects. His method was to tease his adversary with hints of a secret dossier concerning him, and then to proceed through threats to abuse.[19] Wagner, however, was not a meek subject. He was a small red-faced, impatient, harassed general who hated everything that was not military and did not much like what was. The interview was a grizzly failure.*

The draft agreement which met finally with approval, both from

---

* *The Schellenberg Memoirs*, p. 210. Wagner, who was 45-years-old, had succeeded Eugen Mueller as Quartermaster General in August 1940.

Heydrich and Wagner, was the work of a young SS man, called Walter Schellenberg, who served in Heydrich's foreign intelligence section, bureau VI of RSHA. Schellenberg was already Heydrich's counter-espionage expert and he was destined before the end of the war to succeed Admiral Canaris as Chief of Intelligence for the entire Reich. In spite of the immaturity and superficiality of the memoirs which purport to be his, Schellenberg possessed one advantage. Having only joined the Party in 1933, his education had not consisted exclusively of street fighting and he was a qualified lawyer.

The document which emerged from Schellenberg's drafting was produced for the first time in 1948 at the High Command Trial. It had been circulated by Brauchitsch, the man who knew nothing, on 28th April 1941, that is four weeks after Hitler's lecture in the Reich Chancellery. It is a curious document. The army appears from it to have kept far more control of Heydrich's police units than the evidence at the first Nuremberg Trial suggested. Walter Schellenberg himself has described the meeting between Heydrich and Wagner as very amicable.[20] Foreseeing perhaps that the generals would not take the trouble to interfere even when given the opportunity, Heydrich made few difficulties. Under the terms of the protocol, the control of each army commander was left unimpaired in his own area of operations. A representative of the Security Police had to be stationed at each Army Headquarters and it was his duty to report all the instructions he received from Heydrich's office. Whatever they might be, the army commander's operation orders took precedence. The Security Police units were also dependent on the army commander for food, transport and quarters. In accordance with the 1937 agreement they had further-more to maintain a liaison officer with the Ic or Chief of Intelligence of the army command and report all intelligence matters.

If fulfilment had been correctly exacted by all army commanders, these provisions would have cancelled the Commissar Order. They were a complete contradiction of the section which declared that measures against the civilian population were the responsibility of the Action Groups of the Security Police alone. Moreover these provisions applied not only to the combat zone but also to a deep stretch of country behind the front, which each army commander controlled through his Army Rear Area Commander or *Korueck*. It meant that in a large portion of occupied Russia the *Koruecks* could exercise their authority over the Security Police of the SD in the same manner as could the Commanders-in-Chief in the field. Only in areas which had been handed over to the German civilian government would the Wehrmacht lose all rights of control. There the police commanders were in no wise subordinate to the civilian Commissars of Rosenberg's ministry, except for a duty to consult them. There Heydrich's authority would be unchallenged.[21]

(b) The Drafting of the Decrees

IN THE INSTRUCTIONS circulated by Keitel on 13th March 1941 Hitler had declared his wish that the freedom of Himmler, Heydrich and the Security Service should extend to the front line. This, as Hitler knew at heart, was an absurdity. Even Heydrich, who hated the High Command because they regarded him as a sort of untouchable, is said to have declared before his meeting with Wagner, 'we can't have wild irresponsible hordes being allowed to run about the front line'. Unlike Mueller, he was willing to restrict the Action Groups in the operational area to the rôle of tactical auxiliaries.[22] But he expected in return that the High Command would equip his men as motorized units.

On its own, this basic statute of the future *Einsatzgruppen* was not enough to secure the compliance of the Wehrmacht. Two more decrees were required to bring into action the terms of Hitler's address of 30th March. The first must govern the treatment of prisoners. It must provide the instrument by which Commissars and party officials could be selected for execution. The second decree must provide full indemnity for German soldiers who were expected to 'attack towards the rear with the same methods they used in attacking the enemy in the field'; full indemnity too for officers who gave orders 'that appealed to the general impulse of their people'. Such were the so-called 'Commissar Order' and military Jurisdiction Order that had now to be drafted. The person responsible for the first order was Walter Warlimont, head of the National Defence Office and deputy to Alfred Jodl, the head of the Operation Section of the High Command. Warlimont did not like his responsibility, although everyone thought him a Nazi General. At the beginning of May he tried to get the order drafted by Colonel Rudolf Lehmann, head of the legal section of the High Command. Warlimont also tried to persuade his close friend, Eduard Wagner, to issue the order orally without any written decree. Wagner said he could not do this, because if he failed to produce a formal decree for him, Hitler would repudiate Wagner's recent agreement with Heydrich and so give the Security Service full powers in the combat zone. Wagner declared that it had cost him the greatest of efforts to prevent the Security Service giving the army orders in the front line itself.

So Warlimont had to produce his decree. On him descended the burden of deciding what was a Commissar. If Hitler's expressed wishes were to be taken literally, the order for summary execution must apply to anyone who took any orders whatever from the Soviet government and to anyone who had shown the least activity in the Communist Party. Warlimont proceeded cautiously. On 12th May he issued under his own name a document which was described as 'the OKH presentation of the instructions of 30th March'.[23] Following the terms of Hitler's lecture, Warlimont wrote that identification as a political functionary was to provide sufficient grounds for execution at the orders of any German officer who possessed disciplinary powers. The German officer would have to consult with two other members of the Wehrmacht, but only one of them had to be of commissioned rank. The term 'political functionary' was to include the *Politruks* or political education officers who were believed to accompany all Red Army units of company strength and over—and who wore uniform. On the other hand the 'presentation' embodied a suggestion which had come from Alfred Rosenberg and which limited the definition of a political functionary. Rosenberg proposed simply that Russian officials, who stayed at their posts without offering any resistance to the invader, should not be molested for the present.

At the High Command Trial Warlimont explained why he had quoted Rosenberg. He had believed that Hitler would be impressed with the views of such an old party leader. Considering Hitler's real estimate of Rosenberg it is nothing less than astonishing that this proposal found its way into the final decree. But, though innumerable Russian local government officials were saved from death, the definition of a Commissar was never determined at all. The decree created no principles to guide the SD in making selections and it offered no checks to their power when so engaged.[24]

An attempt to clear the matter up was made by Rudolf Lehmann, who in his capacity of legal expert to the High Command was already concerned with the second decree, the decree indemnifying the German soldier. Lehmann received a sharp reprimand from Keitel.

'*Herr Ministerialdirektor*, we are talking about jurisdiction here. The Commissars have nothing at all to do with jurisdiction.'[25] It was nevertheless to Lehmann that Warlimont sent his final draft of the Commissar Order, which included the rules for execution by any officer with disciplinary powers. Lehmann was chiefly concerned not to get the Wehrmacht courts into disrepute, so he slipped in a final paragraph which received Hitler's approval. It stated that military courts must not be charged with 'the measures indicated under I and II.'[26]

This was in line with Lehmann's handling of his own assignment, the jurisdiction order, a handling that brought him no credit. Still less did it help the reputation of Alfred Jodl. Although, like all the others, Jodl claimed to have been outraged by Hitler's demands, he slipped a comment into the margin of Warlimont's text. It was a suggestion that the shooting of Commissars be presented as a reprisal. And, as a ground for reprisals in a war that had not even begun, Jodl added this: 'one must count on retaliations on German flyers.'[27] In that way, it seems, the risk of disobeying Hitler was to be avoided and at the same time the good name of the Wehrmacht kept pure.

That was on 12th May. With no changes of substance Warlimont's notes were circulated by Brauchitsch as a decree on 8th June, after he had presided in person at a conference which determined the rules by which Russian prisoners were handed over to the Security Service.[28] The sentences, which bore Brauchitsch's signature, scarcely differed from Hitler's own:[29]

> When fighting Bolshevism, one cannot count on the enemy acting in accordance with the principles of humanity or International Law. In particular it must be expected that the treatment of our prisoners by the political Commissars of all types, who are the true pillars of resistance will be cruel, inhuman and dictated by hate.

The order to kill Commissars would, therefore, apply to Commissars of every type and position, even if instigation to sabotage and resistance were merely matters of suspicion. If recognized as Commissars, they were to be shot at sight. Apparently Brauchitsch thought they would be accommodating enough to fall into German hands, wearing a red star with an inwoven golden hammer and sickle on their sleeves. At the end came Warlimont's saving clause; in effect all it said was that the peaceful administrators would not be shot at sight; a decision would be taken later whether to hand them over to the

Security Service. 'On principle the personal impression of the Commissar's attitude is of more importance than the facts of the case, for which proof may not exist.'

The rules for execution of the captured men, who were not shot at sight, but turned over to the Security Service, still remained to be drafted in agreement with Heydrich; but they had already settled the position of the German soldier, who, if he got an order like this, might shoot everything down to a postman or refuse-collector. His position was covered by the basic decree of the Jurisdiction Order, which had been circulated by Keitel on 14th May. It was a difficult decree to draft and Colonel Lehmann, who was charged with the work, proved obstructive. He knew what was coming before 3rd April, when he received his brief from Keitel. Months before this, Lehmann had learnt from Colonel Rudolf Schmundt, Hitler's adjutant with the High Command, that in the next campaign the Fuehrer was going to 'leave the courts at home'. That was Lehmann's greatest fear. His plan was to make the whole thing unworkable by taking Hitler entirely at his word. So he designed an absurd decree, recalling all army legal officers to their fighting units and nominating only inexperienced officers to attend courts-martial. Keitel, now completely exasperated, summoned Lehmann to Berchtesgaden and again threatened this professorial person (who was heard conversing in ancient Greek in an American internment camp) with the severest disciplinary consequences.[30] Fortunately, Lehmann said, Jodl was present and calmed Keitel down. So Lehmann was allowed to go off and prepare a new decree which left the military courts a vestige of competence in cases of Russian civilian resistance.[31]

That was Lehmann's story, but the evidence at the High Command Trial showed that he had been so intimidated by his interview at Berchtesgaden that he left the courts no competence at all. Both Franz Halder and Eugen Mueller, Brauchitsch's general for special assignments, tried to persuade Lehmann to draft a clause which at least left the courts power to decide in cases which had not been obvious at first sight. But Lehmann refused. He declared that, if Russian civilians were acquitted by military courts, it would have to be recorded and that such cases might attract Hitler's notice, as had happened on some occasions during the Polish campaign. Another such intervention by Hitler might mean the end of the military courts, so, to protect their existence, Lehmann gave them no say in the matter. In the judgment of the American Nuremberg Tribunal, Lehmann sacrificed innocent lives to

save the military courts from Hitler's criticism. He was sentenced to seven
years imprisonment which in fact meant his release at the end of 1950.[32]

Lehmann's draft was circulated as a decree by Keitel on 14th May.
Twenty-three copies, signed by the learned military historian Kurt von
Tippelskirch, reached the department heads, including Admiral
Canaris and Colonel Hasso von Wedel, the chief of armed forces
propaganda. Though the decree suspended the military courts indefinitely as regards civilian offences in Russia, it envisaged the
eventual setting-up of civil courts. In the meantime suspects were on
no account to be detained in order to await legal proceedings, whether
civilian or military. Courts-martial were not to be wasted on Russian
civilians or guerillas, whose fate could be decided by any German
officer who held a rank equivalent to battalion commander. These
officers could order collective measures against entire communities. On
the other hand they were not obliged to proceed against their own men
for offences against civilians and they were to call courts-martial only
when the offence threatened discipline.*

> When judging offences of this kind, it must be borne in mind
> that Bolshevist influence was responsible for all Germany's
> troubles since the collapse of 1918. Judges should be severe when
> the offences are a symptom of mutiny, but less severe when it is
> only a question of senseless destruction of property which may be
> to the disadvantage of the unit.[33]

At Angerburg on 16th July, in conference with Goering, Keitel,
Rosenberg, Lammers and Bormann, Hitler declared that Stalin had
ordered Partisan warfare behind the German front. 'This Partisan warfare again has some advantage for us. It enables us to wipe out everyone
who opposes us.[34]** So, six days later, Hitler ordered Keitel to circulate
the 'Barbarossa' Jurisdiction Order to a still wider list, adding a strong
rider. Commanders were not to apply to the Security Service for
assistance. They must take 'suitable draconian measures' themselves.
On the 27th however Keitel had doubts and ordered that all but army
commanders must destroy their copies of the order, which, however,
remained valid.[35]

In fact the 'Barbarossa' Jurisdiction Order remained valid throughout the war. It became the German soldier's charter for anti-Partisan

---

* This part of the order was strengthened by Keitel's decree of 29th December 1942,
which forbade the confirmation of any court-martial sentence which had been passed in
connection with acts against Partisans (Document NOKW 2961 and see p. 393)

** See p. 238

warfare. The decree was approved by Hitler at a time when the campaign was expected to last six weeks and when organized resistance was not envisaged behind the lines. Hitler never imagined a state of affairs in which Russian units of division and even army corps strength hid in the great forests behind the front. But it was to these and to their civilian helpers that the 'Barbarossa' Jurisdiction Orders were to apply. In the chapter dealing with the Partisans something will be seen of the fate of these civilian helpers, in most cases villagers who had been forced to feed and shelter Russian armed bands. Under the decree they could be killed *en masse* at the order of any officer of battalion-commander rank. Numerous operational reports as late as June 1943 show that they were indeed killed in this way, often many thousands at a time.* The Commissar Order has achieved world renown as the expression of a new code of barbarism in war. The Commissar Order became an excuse for the wholesale murder of prisoners of war, but the 'Barbarossa' Jurisdiction Order justified the extermination of the civilian population.

As we have seen, Keitel issued the original 'Barbarossa' jurisdiction decree on 14th May 1941, while Brauchitsch issued the Commissar Order on 8th June. During the interval, on 24th May, Brauchitsch made the gesture which, as he alleged, fulfilled his promise to the army commanders by nullifying Hitler's directions. The gesture took the form of an annexe to the Jurisdiction Order and it bore the title, 'maintenance of discipline'.[36] Distributed together with Keitel's original order to no less than 340 commands, this so-called order for the maintenance of discipline was presented as a commentary on the Fuehrer's wishes, the purpose being to avoid wasting combatant troops on mopping-up operations. It was stressed that Hitler's directions really concerned serious cases of rebellion and it was most important that troops should not be allowed to become unmanageable—Hitler's own words. The individual soldier must not act as he personally thought proper towards the civilian population. He must be bound by the orders of his officers.

Since the officers had already been told quite specifically that they could shoot whom they pleased, it is difficult to see how Brauchitsch's insistence on normal unit discipline could affect Hitler's orders in the very slightest degree. In fact, by coupling the issue of the Jurisdiction Order to no less than 340 commanders with instructions to impose normal field penalties on minor delinquents, Brauchitsch appeared to be

* See especially p. 242

suggesting that minor delinquency meant going a little beyond the letter of the order. So at least it was interpreted by one of the commanders, Karl von Roques of the Southern Army Group rear area. Von Roques thought that the Maintenance of Discipline Order entitled him to decide that soldiers who shot Jews on their own initiative should get the customary sixty days for insubordination.[37]

It will be remembered that Brauchitsch swore at Nuremberg that he had cancelled the Commissar Order. Yet the maintenance of Discipline Order expressly mentioned that instructions would shortly be given for the treatment of political dignitaries—as indeed they were under Brauchitsch's own signature on 8th June. Finally it may be observed that, while the 'Barbarossa' Jurisdiction Order was re-issued repeatedly by Keitel, Brauchitsch's annexe, for what it was worth, was not issued again. But, having completely foxed the field commanders by his contradictory instructions, Brauchitsch found it necessary to clarify the situation. Just as Keitel had his General Reinecke to look after administrative questions at OKW, so Brauchitsch had his Eugen Mueller as General for Special Assignments.* At Nuremberg this rather shadowy character was a crown witness against Reinecke, who in return deposed that Mueller used to spy on him on behalf of the party.[38] On 11th June 1941 Mueller demonstrated that, as a political general, he could do just as well as Reinecke. He collected an audience of intelligence officers and judge-advocates from each of the army commands and addressed them at Warsaw. His speech was in fact a defence of the Commissar Order.[39] 'One of two enemies must die. Do not spare the bearer of enemy ideology but kill him.' As to the Jurisdiction Order, on which there now existed such a pretty state of confusion, Mueller had a suggestion of his own. Minor cases of disobedience by Russian civilians need not be punished by shooting. The civilians could be flogged; the Russians themselves had done it when they occupied a bit of East Prussia in 1914. There indeed was a precedent and straight out of twentieth century warfare at that.

It is easy to see why Brauchitsch's Eugen Mueller had to brief the 'Ics'. These were the men with whom the special commandos of the Security Police and SD would have to keep the most constant touch under the terms of the Heydrich-Wagner protocol. Given the will, the Ics were in a position to prevent the activities of the special commandos offending decency. They could do so by constantly reporting on them

---

* Eugen Mueller had been Commandant of the War Academy till 1939 and Wagner's predecessor as Quartermaster General till April 1940.

to their army commanders and rear area commanders. About a week before Eugen Mueller's address to them, the Ics had been in the Bendlerstrasse, the old War Office, where the agreement was explained through Wagner, Heydrich and their own chief, Canaris. Schellenberg, who was present, deposed at Nuremberg that even divisional Ics were summoned to this conference and that the army command Ics stayed mysteriously behind for a few days. Schellenberg believed that this was in order to communicate to them the most secret order of all, the unwritten order by which the Security Police were to be allowed to massacre the Jewish population of Russia without hindrance from the Wehrmacht.[40] Schellenberg also believed that it was through the Ics that the army group and army commanders were notified of the unwritten order.

In spite of the astonishing passivity of these commanders during the massacres of the Jews in Russia, Schellenberg's story is open to doubt. Although acquitted on this count in 1949, the charge of complicity in the massacres of Jews hung over Schellenberg himself when he signed this affidavit. In Schellenberg's purported posthumous memoirs it is hinted that the unwritten order had been communicated to Wagner at his meeting with Heydrich in April 1941—but only after the innocent Schellenberg had left the room, from which, half an hour later, he saw Wagner emerge, even redder in the face than usual.[41] If Heydrich told Wagner the truth so early in the day, there was surely a pledge of secrecy. On the whole, the army commanders may be believed, when they state that they only learnt about the orders to kill Jews after the massacres had begun.

Yet there was a singular failure on the part of the Ics to exploit their advantage under the Heydrich-Wagner accord, though we are told repeatedly how constantly the *Abwehr* opposed the Party extremists. The Ics were in a position to demand a complete 'activities report' from the extermination commandos, which functioned in their area. Masses of such reports have survived in addition to parts of a dossier concerning the massacres which was compiled for Admiral Canaris. Yet not one massacre of Jews in the rear areas under military government was prevented by the intervention, either of Canaris in person or of the Ic officers of his *Abwehr* organization.

It is true that Canaris has been credited with some vague form of opposition, for instance by Fabian von Schlabrendorff.[42] On the other hand there is very positive evidence that the Security Police acknowledged the co-operation in this matter of Canaris's own police arm, the

Secret Field Gendarmerie. It seems that the Secret Field Gendarmerie co-operated both in the Commissar Order and the unwritten racial murder order.* It must be concluded that the Ics were indifferent to the doings of the *Einsatzgruppen*, so long as they caused no disturbance in the combat areas. There was no reason why they should think any differently from the High Command. Halder himself was asked at Nuremberg whether he did not consider the massacre of thousands of people a disturbance sufficient to warrant a commander-in-chief invoking his powers to interfere under the Wagner-Heydrich agreement. Halder replied, 'I cannot quite imagine that it would constitute a disturbance in the operational meaning'.[43]

So too thought the three army group commanders, who had attended Hitler's lecture on 30th March. At the end of October 1941, it seems that von Bock was entreated by his staff officers, some of them weeping tears of indignation, to remove the *Einsatzgruppe* from his rear area after the massacre of 7,000 Jews in Borissov, a town which was quite close to his own headquarters. The massacre, by no means the largest of its kind, had been elaborately studied by the *Abwehr*, whose reports were referred to von Bock's staff. But against the entreaties of his officers, von Bock retorted that it was virtually civil war to employ force against a unit of the SS. The most he would undertake was the dispatch of a memorandum to Hitler, concerning 'these unheard of crimes'.[44] Yet von Bock's successor, von Kluge, had no hesitation in ordering this same *Einsatzgruppe* out of the combat area in May 1942, when a report from the 4th Army declared them to be a menace to security.[45]

The indifference of staff officers and intelligence officers was therefore not universal and it could be less paralysing when military operations were involved, but behind it there were nine years of party terrorism, from which the officer corps had not been immune. Thus there can be no question that Admiral Canaris was horrified by these matters, just as he was horrified by the murder of prisoners of war, who were dragged from the army's camps by the Security Police under the vague terms of the Commissar Decree and the Wagner-Heydrich protocols. But on the massacres of Jews Canaris kept on compiling his dossier and doing nothing about it, while on the murder of prisoners his intervention was half-hearted and inadequate.

* See p. 175 The habitual co-operation of the Secret Field Gendarmerie is confirmed by Braeutigam (*Ueberblick, etc.*, p. 61). A flagrant case of a Divisional Ic, supervising an execution under the Commissar Order is cited with adverse comments by Major General Hermann Tescke, *Die Silbernen Spiegel*, Heidelberg, 1952.

(c) The Orders in Practice

IF WE ARE to credit his chief biographer, Canaris warned the intelligence officers soon after the first circulation of the Commissar Order that the screening order was a trap to involve the Wehrmacht in the hateful policies of the SS and so make all future resistance to the SS impossible.[46] This was no false estimate of the situation. Yet Canaris did nothing for at least two months, in fact not till the middle of July. Before a pretext could be found for intervening, thousands of Asiatic prisoners, principally Crimean Tartars captured on the Black Sea front, had been dragged out of the prisoner camps and murdered by the screening commandos on the pretext that they were circumcized Jews. This error offered a loophole in the defences of the screening order, inasmuch as Hitler himself had ordered that minority races should receive preferential treatment—though not of this kind. The initiative in sorting out the confusion came, however, not from Canaris, but from the General Wehrmacht Office (AWA) where Major General Hermann Reinecke dealt with everything that concerned prisoners of war.

By 15th July 1941, three months had passed since the agreement between Heydrich and Wagner, yet no screening rules had been issued. In this matter the military intelligence section of the SD was obliged to act in combination with the *Abwehr*. Canaris had therefore to be brought into the picture and Reinecke invited him to his office in order to confer with 'Gestapo' Mueller. It is a fact, not flattering to the memory of Canaris, that he did not go in person but sent as his deputy the Austrian Brigadier, Erwin Lahousen, head of the department *Abwehr II*. Abshagen says that it was because of Canaris's intense dislike of Reinecke, the little party man, and of Heinrich Mueller, the odious policeman. Personal dislike is a bad excuse for refraining from personal action. Abshagen, however, not only dilates a great deal on Mueller's sinister personality but admits outright that his hero was afraid of him.[47] Lahousen, when questioned at Nuremberg, was more oblique about it. He described a different reason that Canaris had given him for not meeting Mueller.* 'As a department chief he could be by no means as outspoken as I, who, thanks to my subordinate position, could use much stronger language.' According to this remarkable logic it

* For Lahousen, see p. 165, and *IMT*, I, p. 279.

would have been still better to send Mueller the office charwoman, but exponents of the great Canaris legend, like Abshagen and Lahousen, see in such reasoning a subtlety far deeper than anything that lurks in the normal Nordic cranium.

Lahousen arrived at Reinecke's office, briefed with two lines of argument which were intended to provide Reinecke with a 'golden bridge' to overcome Mueller's objections. Evidence had been collected to show that already, less than four weeks after the first attack on Russia, German troops had become demoralized by the spectacle of the public mass-execution of Jews and suspects. Evidence had also been obtained that the Russians knew about the screening of the prisoner camps and that this was increasing their will to resist. The latter unfortunately was not a strong argument, because on 15th July 1941 there were certainly no signs that Russians were reluctant to surrender. Hundreds of thousands of Red Army men had surrendered already and nearly four millions were to do so by the end of the year. Mueller therefore overcame this objection with ease. As regards public executions, he offered to issue an order ensuring that they should take place in remote spots, an order easy to fulfil in a country like Russia. As to Reinecke, he rejected the 'golden bridge'. Throughout the conference he acted as Mueller's echo, declaring that German staff officers still lived in the Ice Age and not in the present age of National Socialism. Reinecke also outlined orders which he intended shortly to issue for the special treatment of Russian prisoners, stressing the importance of whips and the need for the constant use of firearms.* Neither Mueller nor Reinecke would clarify the rules for selective murder. The Security Police commandos were to be guided solely by a Jewish appearance or by evidence of superior intelligence in determining the two main classes for execution. Lahousen turned to Mueller and asked, 'Tell me, according to what principles does this selection take place? Do you determine it by the height of a person or by the size of his shoes.'**

Of Mueller we have already spoken. If he was a less than gifted man, enlarged by an unnatural office, the same holds true of Hermann Reinecke. This person was to become lord and master of five and a half million Red Army prisoners and close on four million of them died, a fair proportion through his own malevolence. Yet Reinecke was no chewer of broken glass or drinker from skulls, but, in the summer of 1941, a desk-born Major General with the dullest of service records.

* See p. 109
** See p. 123

Had Reinecke spent his war, as he might well have done, in the army clothing department, he would not have ended in a war criminal's prison at Landsberg, from which he emerged in 1957 as almost the last incumbent.*

It all began in 1938, when at the age of fifty Reinecke found himself a Colonel on the reserve list with nothing more exciting to occupy him than the direction of an Ibero-American institute in Berlin. The Czechoslovak crisis revived his hopes of becoming a general, but Munich with its fallacious promise of world peace seemed to end them for ever. There was, however, one hope even for a soldier so lacking in glamour as Reinecke. The military revolution of February 1938 had created the organization known as OKW to replace the old War Office. Instead of von Blomberg, a popular Minister Field Marshal, there was now a Wilhelm Keitel who existed only to take Hitler's orders. Under Keitel's rule OKW became a caste apart from the army, a caste in which military reputation counted little. Reinecke now accepted the virtues of the National Socialist Party, which he had ignored in the days when they offered no key to military advancement. Shortly after the Munich Agreement, in November 1938, he delivered a lecture outlining a plan for compulsory political indoctrination courses throughout the services.[49] It is true that Reinecke's ideas were not adopted till December 1943, when he became Chief National Socialist Leadership Officer to the armed forces; but these ideas appealed greatly to Keitel and, within a few weeks of his lecture, Reinecke was taken into the OKW bureaucracy. He had charge of the General Armed Forces Office (AWA), a maid-of-all-work department handling everything that did not relate to field operations. AWA dealt with army orphanages, pensions, veteran's welfare associations and the like. Unfortunately AWA also included the prisoner of war department.[50]

It was a dreary post and at his trial Reinecke explained how frequently he had tried to resign. His real ambitions lay elsewhere. It was no coincidence of history but part of its essential malice that this man, who played a part second only to Heydrich and Mueller in exterminating Soviet political leadership among the captured Red Army men, should have worked at the same time to create the Political Commissar system in the German army. Till December 1943 Reinecke was called the 'little Keitel' but henceforward he became the *Oberpolitruk*. His party activities had given him a reputation far above that

* The prison was finally closed in June 1958.

of a desk-born general. He liked to sit as an assessor on the People's Court Tribunals, where the Wehrmacht had the right to send a representative. There he would help pass death sentences on people who gossiped in trams and the inconspicuous figure of General Reinecke can be perceived in the famous film of the trial of the conspirators of July 1944. From the beginning of his new career Reinecke threw in his lot with Martin Bormann, who planned throughout the war to make the office of the Party a more potent weapon than the SS and its Gestapo, and who in the end succeeded when it was too late to matter. Reinecke's National Socialist Leadership Officers became in practice the agents of Bormann, the only truly Commissar-like figure in the Nazi hierarchy, while Bormann's patronage made Reinecke a man of influence, so much so that the novelist Erich Dwinger, who made great efforts to meet him at a cocktail party in August 1942, believed that 'Reinecke Fuchs' saw Hitler every day.[51] In fact Reinecke only spoke to Hitler once in his life, but in July 1944, when the NSFO office was regarded as the last hope for the drooping morale of the Wehrmacht, he became a Lieutenant General.

Lahousen must have left Reinecke's office in the Schoernberger Strasse on that July day of 1941 with the feeling that the lives of uncountable hordes of men were now committed to the hands of this mediocre and repellent person. He had many more discussions with Mueller and Reinecke on the same subject and at one of them it seems that the branding of prisoners was discussed.[52] But Mueller kept his word, so far as it went. In the long instruction which he sent off on 17th July 1941, it was laid down that executions must take place at least 600 yards from the prisoner camps. The great importance of this instruction, of which 340 copies were sent, was that it relieved the camp commanders of the responsibility for screening prisoners. It informed them that the Security Police were specially trained for this task. The commandos could use the services of trustworthy prisoners, for instance Volga Germans.

Apparently it did not matter whether the informers were communists or not, though henceforward a single informer was no longer to be considered sufficient for the denunciation of 'political, criminal or in some way undesirable elements'. In late September or October, when the screening operations were extended to prisoner camps in Germany, Mueller was even more considerate than in his original undertaking. Rules were drafted for the transfer of the screened prisoners to concentration camps, well out of military jurisdiction.

Here everything was regularized and the executions only took place after warrants had been duly signed at the Gestapo main office.[53]*

On 8th September 1941 Reinecke finally circulated the code of rules which was to govern the treatment of Russian prisoners of war, and here the instructions concerning methods of screening were repeated. They spurred Canaris to the second and last of his tepid interventions. On the 15th he sent Keitel a memorandum, which had been drafted by James Helmuth von Moltke, the *Abwehr's* expert on international law. This was the heroic young Moltke, great-nephew of the famous Field Marshal, who was executed after the failure of the July 1944 plot against Hitler. With Moltke's memorandum Canaris enclosed two supplements. These comprised both Reinecke's rules and the latest Russian regulations, concerning prisoners of war, which had been published as recently as July 1941. The memorandum then set out to show that the accepted usages of war concerning prisoners could not be considered as superseded merely because Russia had not been a party to the Geneva Conventions of 1929. There followed an argument that was clearly meant to appeal to Hitler. It postulated that neither the Germans nor the Russians were likely to act at the front according to their respective decrees. The decrees were meant in both cases for home consumption. If Russian propaganda could point out that the Russian rules, governing prisoners of war, were more humane than the German rules, German prestige would be destroyed among likely Russian collaborationists. It would also be impossible to protest at the ill-treatment of German prisoners by the Russians.[54]

Keitel, according to his own story, expressed immediate agreement. At the same time he proposed to Hitler that the part of the Reinecke rules, which concerned the screening of unreliable elements by the SD should be rescinded. It must be borne in mind that at this moment, the middle of September, the number of executions under the screening rules had already reached five figures in Germany alone.** But Keitel was not able to persuade Hitler. As Keitel put it, 'the Fuehrer said that we could not expect that German prisoners of war would be treated according to the Geneva Convention or international law and that we had no way of investigating the matter.'[55] So the order remained in force and Canaris received his memorandum back with Keitel's marginal comments.

It is astonishing that Keitel should have told this story, knowing that his own written comments were in the possession of the court. Next day they were read out by the Russian prosecutor and they were the very reverse of the comments of a man who had approved the Canaris memorandum. Against Canaris's objections that the directions for screening had not been sent to any Wehrmacht establishments, he had written the words 'highly expedient'; and to the observation that the results of the screening could not be checked he had added 'not at all'. Finally he had scribbled a postscript:

> These objections arise from the military conception of chivalrous warfare. We are dealing here with destruction of a world philosophy and therefore I approve such measures and sanction them. Keitel.[56]

Of course Keitel explained that he only wrote what Hitler had told him to write, but the explanation lost its force when he disclosed that an order for mass-reprisals, which he had issued on the very day after he had presented Canaris's memorandum, was justified by the discovery of the murder of German prisoners at Lwow.[57] The Canaris document was perhaps the most damning in the entire dossier that brought Keitel to the gallows and it left Canaris with the posthumous laurels of a hero. But what had Canaris done about it after he received his memorandum back?

The struggle against the Commissar Order, such as it was, now passed to the three Field Marshals who commanded army groups in Russia. It seems that von Leeb had been rather more active about it than von Bock, whose chief interest in the memorandum, which had been prepared for him by von Tresckow, was to tone it down before it reached Hitler.[58] Sixty-four years old and ennobled by the Kaiser in the First World War, Friedrich Ritter von Leeb was regarded as a general of the old school.* Ulrich von Hassell had once considered him a possible member of the military conspiracy against Hitler. But it was in this month of September 1941 that von Hassell wrote off Leeb as 'fossilized'. By his own admission during the High Command Trial of 1948 Leeb had been absolutely terrified of Hitler, whom he regarded as 'a demon, a devil'. Leeb had been convinced that if Hitler had been in any way thwarted after the famous lecture of 30th March, both he, Rundstedt, von Bock and Brauchitsch would have gone into a concentration camp.[59] Nevertheless during July and September Leeb was

* He was released at the end of the High Command Trial in October 1948, being deemed to have served his sentence of three years' imprisonment. He died in May 1956, aged 79.

visited in his headquarters near Kovno, once by Brauchitsch and twice
by Keitel, and he was able to persuade them to place a further memorandum before Hitler, which was signed by all three army group
commanders. The memorandum was drawn up by Eugen Mueller and
produced at Hitler's daily military conference or *Lagebesprechung* on
25th September. A new argument was added, namely that the power of
the political Commissars in the Red Army would not be nearly as
strong if such men did not face the certainty of execution after
surrender.[60] Not only was the memorandum rejected by Hitler but
apparently Brauchitsch was compelled to issue further instructions to
his field commanders, confirming the rules for screening prisoners. It
was this circular, as sent off under Wagner's signature on 7th October,
which contained 'Gestapo' Mueller's revised rules for executions. The
High Command confirmed that executions were to be carried out
inconspicuously and as far away from the prisoner camps as possible.
But in every other respect it was the same prescription as before.[61]

There was no reason to expect that Hitler would change his mind on
25th September, when the memorandum was submitted to him. His
armies had surrounded Leningrad and were about to enter Kiev. Within a matter of days the final assault on Moscow was to begin and the
Blitzkrieg was to be won before the winter. Hitler held well over a
million Russian prisoners, but Stalin held only a few thousand
Germans. Neither reprisal nor Nemesis were therefore serious considerations. So the screening and execution of Russian prisoners
continued and it was applied now to sick and disabled men, simply
because they were sick and disabled: a dispensation that was no part of
the original Commissar Order.

Since 8th June, when the original order had been circulated by
Brauchitsch as a decree, there had been no less than three orders con-
cerning the rules for screening prisoners. 'Gestapo' Mueller's on 17th
July, Reinecke's on 8th September and a confirmation of both under
Brauchitsch's signature on 7th October. Yet utter chaos reigned in the
prisoner camps. At the end of August, when a 'scrutiny' by the Security
Service in a camp, which had been established in the town prison of
Minsk, resulted in 615 people being dragged off, no clearer description
could be found for the victims than 'racially inferior elements'.[62] It was
not suggested that they were Jews or communists. On 15th November
eighty-three more victims from Mogilev labour camp were described
in the same way.[63] At about the same time the Tartar prisoners in
Nikolaiev camp narrowly avoided the same fate and this was the very

moment when the Tartars in the Crimea were welcoming German troops. At the Eastern Ministry, Otto Braeutigam commented bitterly in a long memorial which he sent to Rosenberg in the following February. In May 1942, Rosenberg most miraculously brought himself to speak to Hitler on the subject. But by this time the policy had been clarified. Only Jews were to be killed off on racial grounds alone.[64]

It was in the officer camps, where party officials were most likely to be found, that absolute inferno reigned under the Mueller-Reinecke rules. The largest officer camp was at Hammelburg in Bavaria. At this time, when most of the Red Army prisoners were still held in occupied Russia, Hammelburg was partly reserved for captive generals and notable persons, such as Major Jacob Dzhugashvili, Stalin's son by his first marriage. In November the Nuremberg Gestapo office installed a civilian inspector in Hammelburg. This man, Paul Ohler, testified after the war that he had found hordes of so-called confidential agents among the prisoners. According to his own estimate, Ohler examined 15,000 captured officers. About 500 were segregated and later taken in lorries to Dachau concentration camp, where they were shot on the rifle range.[65] Among some of the captured generals there grew into being a diabolical cabal. A captured Red Army judge advocate, named Mal'zev, formed a 'Russian Socialist People's Party'. Adopting a party programme that had once been devised by Russian emigrés at Kharbin in Manchuria, the cabal had the backing of the Gestapo who used it to ferret out Jews and active communists.*[66] Eventually two generals, Trukhin and Blagovestshensky, seceded from this terrorist group and, under the protection of the Wehrmacht Propaganda Section, helped to form the National Liberation Army.** But if the overwhelming majority of the senior officers in Hammelburg refused freedom at this price, it was because of their experience of camp government by delation and murder under the Mueller-Reinecke rules.[67]

Eventually the delators were murdered too. Whether they served the military intelligence service of the SD or merely its murder squads, they got to know too much. Many confidential agents were chosen by the screening teams for sabotage work behind the Russian front, an enterprise known as 'operation Zeppelin'. It was a hobby of Walter Schellenberg and it was to prove his undoing, for the untimely fate of some of his Russian agents was the cause of the one conviction that could be secured against the author of the Heydrich-Wagner protocols.[68]

* See p. 555
** For Trukhin, see Chapter Ten, p. 309. Both generals were hanged in July 1946.

On one pretext or another, the executions that followed the process of screening reached gigantic proportions and only a small portion of the victims were in any sense implicated in Soviet politics. The list which was made out in Reinecke's office on 1st May 1944, mentions 473,000 men *exterminated* while in the custody of OKW in Germany and Poland. An unspecified portion of a further half-million missing men were written off as *exterminated* in the custody of the Field High Command (OKH) in occupied Soviet territory.[69] It is evident, however, that wholesale execution after screening virtually ceased in February 1942, when Goering's demands for Russian labour and the Wehrmacht's demands for field auxiliaries made themselves felt, in spite of the opposition of Himmler and Heydrich. Finally the Commissar Order became a dead letter, when Hitler himself endorsed the plans for a Russian liberation army, but it was still on the statute book. In June 1943 Kurt Zeitzler, who had succeeded Halder as Chief of Staff nine months previously, became a somewhat tepid and unreliable advocate of the recruitment of Russian deserters. Zeitzler regarded the Commissar Order as a very serious obstacle but, possibly because it was dangerous to admit that the order had ever existed, he failed to persuade Hitler to revoke it.[70]

Till the end of the war the SD never lost the right to pull anyone they liked out of the prisoner camps. Although this right was exercised after February 1942, only at the request of the camp commanders, the latter were frequently zealous collaborators, more so than front line commanders whose degree of connivance with the extermination commandos remains a vexed question, clouded with political recriminations and *esprit de corps* writing.

Brauchitsch declared that he knew of no case of Wehrmacht members carrying out the Commissar Order. On this subject we know that Brauchitsch told lies, but many will be tempted to dismiss the subject as academic and the comparison with the SD as valueless. Firstly because the greatest slaughter under the Commissar Order was carried out, not in military areas at all but in the German concentration camps, to which hundreds of thousands of condemned Russian prisoners were sent by the civilian German Gestapo offices.* Secondly because it was the Wehrmacht and none but the Wehrmacht, who were responsible for a slaughter of prisoners many times greater than the total of victims under the Commissar Order and the screening rules, namely through their failure to keep four million prisoners alive. Yet it

* See p. 126

was precisely this failure which arose from the state of mind that produced the Commissar Order and its attendant decrees: a state of mind unknown in any other war. The history of the screening operations derived from the general mentality which regarded Russian prisoners as less than human beings and watched them die like flies. The Field Marshals, who believed on 30th March 1941 that they could scotch the order without committing themselves on paper, failed to estimate the true strength of many years of National Socialist indoctrination on the rank and file.

Nor is it clear that any army or army group commander took open steps to stop the Commissar Decree working, beyond the drafting of protests for OKW. The case of Ritter von Leeb, the most liberal-minded and humane among the three army group commanders, offers the best illustration of what happened. It is a fact that among the documents, which were in evidence at the High Command Trial at Nuremberg in 1948, there were more reports on the shooting of political Commissars from Leeb's Northern Army Group than from any other. In this group there was Hoepner's 4th Panzer Army which claimed the liquidation of 172 Commissars in the first four weeks. More modestly the 16th and 18th Armies on Leeb's front claimed to have shot ninety-six Commissars by December 1941.[71] Leeb argued that this was really a very small proportion, because 4,250 political Commissars had been captured on the front of these two armies alone. But it came out in cross-examination that 4,250 was only a hypothetical figure. The 16th and 18th Armies had taken 340,000 prisoners. Leeb supposed that in the Red Army there must be a *Politruk* to every eighty men—a grotesque notion—so this would mean 4,250 captured Commissars. To have shot only ninety-six of them implied a most successful sabotage of Hitler's orders.

This argument with all its ingenuity did not appeal to Hans Reinhardt who had commanded a corps in the 4th Panzer Army, the army that had shot far more Commissars than the others. Reinhardt described the figures as fictitious from end to end. His chief was Erich Hoepner, whom the world knows better as a leader of the conspiracy of July 1944. According to Reinhardt, the figures were used by Hoepner in order to silence the hierarchy at OKW and make them believe that the order was being carried out.*[72] Von Manstein, who also commanded a corps under Hoepner, says that Hoepner intended to

---

* Sentenced to fifteen years' imprisonment, Reinhardt was released in 1955, see p. 278

protest to Alfred Jodl, as chief of the Operations Staff.[73] Nevertheless, in a report of his activities, the infamous Franz Stahlecker, who commanded an *Einsatzgruppe* of the Security Police on Leeb's front, wrote to Heydrich that he had found Hoepner's co-operation 'close and almost cordial'.*[74]

Brauchitsch, when questioned, was at first inclined to call this a monstrous falsehood against a general whom Hitler had after all dismissed and later on hanged. Afterwards Brauchitsch changed his mind and said that the passage referred to co-operation at the front, where the *Einsatzgruppe* had to fight side by side with the army. Brauchitsch was not the man to give things their right names. If generals like Hoepner were embarrassed with testimonials of this kind, who was more responsible for that situation than Brauchitsch?[75]

Nor was it possible for the German soldier in the field to be any more accurate in his assessment of what constituted a Political Commissar than were the screening teams in the camps. The Viennese journalist, Erich Kern, who served in the Adolf Hitler SS division, describes the case of an arrested woman who had cooked for the Commissars of a small town in the Ukraine. She was denounced as a disguised Commissar by some fellow-prisoners and executed. Her clothes were given to a peasant woman who extracted from them 100,000 roubles and some marked military maps, which she handed over. It seems that the denunciators had not lied.** But one wonders how many genuine Commissar's cooks may not have been executed on similar evidence. When the prisons of the French Revolution were emptied after Thermidor, it was found that there were hardly any *ci-devants*, foreign agents or priests left. Nearly all, who were waiting to be guillotined, were ordinary peasants with their smocks, shawls and bundles. They had been denounced by their neighbours.

The final ridicule of the Commissar Order appears in the report which the Intelligence Officer or Ic of the XXVIIIth Corps sent to 18th Army Headquarters on 27th September 1941. A railway protection battalion of elderly Russian reservists had been encircled and captured. Among them a white-haired academic gentleman was found asleep on the bank of a river. He was discovered to be Professor Kanaiev, author of a history of Russian literature. It seems that the Professor had

---

* For Stahlecker, see p. 233
** Erich Kern, *Der Grosse Rausch*. More recently Peter Neumann, who served in the same division, has described far more summary executions of supposed political commissars, but the credentials of this book, which appeared in French and not in German, are not very strong (*SS!*, Paris, 1958).

emerged from beleaguered Leningrad in order to run a cinema-van for
these veterans—rather like a WVS lady and her bun-wagon. But, since
Kanaiev was the secretary of the Literary Institute of the Academy of
Sciences and therefore an official of the Soviet State, he was classed as a
Political Commissar and shot. On the same grounds they might have
picked a member of the British Council or a stage-manager from
ENSA or a lecturer on the British Way and Purpose.[76]

> *Anjou* Who have we here?
> *Retes* 'Tis Ramus, the King's Professor of logic.
> *Guise* Stab him.
> *Ramus* O good my lord,
>   wherein hath Ramus been so offensious?
> *Guise* Marry Sir, in having a smack in all.
>   And didst never sound anything to the depth.
>
> (Christopher Marlowe, *The Massacre in Paris*).

CHAPTER THREE

THE PRISONERS OF WAR

(a) The Aftermath of the Encirclement Battles

THE DEATH OF nearly four million Russian prisoners of war was not part of Hitler's plans for a new type of warfare, which was intended to destroy a political system and a way of thought. It was, however, the logical and inescapable consequence of these plans and it can only be studied against that background. It was the least publicized of the fruits of the Commissar and 'Barbarossa' Jurisdiction Orders, because it was underplayed not only by the Germans but by the Russians as well.

The presentation of the Russian case during the international Nuremberg Trials in February 1946 must have been a ponderous ordeal for those who had to sit through it. It went on for sixteen days, an interminable reading of gruesome excerpts, interspersed with the hearing of a few Russian witnesses and some testy arguments on procedure. It fills 540 pages of the British printed transcript, yet only a tenth of this space is occupied with the charges concerning the treatment of Red Army prisoners of war. The proportion is an odd contrast with the figures, admitted by the Germans themselves, which show that at least 3,700,000 Russian prisoners died in their hands.* Apart from the incredible slaughter on the battlefields, this must have been the greatest loss of life in the Soviet Union, far greater than the massacre of Jews, the shooting of supposed Partisans or the losses through deportation, greater even perhaps than the deaths through famine, as each retreating army scorched the land behind it.

As one ploughs through the mass of individual atrocities, as one tries to swallow the unsteady and sometimes purely rhetorical statistics in the Russian prosecution brief, one begins to wonder whether human life meant anything at all to the minds that assembled all this matter, whether indignation was not an abstract end in itself without any refer-

---

* *Trials of War Criminals*, X, p. 132. Alexander Dallin, *German Rule in Russia*, p. 427, gives an elaborate statistical table. See Appendix Three, p. 446 at end of this book.

ence to scale. Such a conclusion is almost forced on one, when the same amount of space is devoted to a camp, where 130,000 men are said to have perished, and to the room in a house in Kaluga, where some German soldiers practised with their revolvers on the portrait of a professor of aeronautics.[1]

But it is not a simple lack of a sense of proportion which has caused the fate of the prisoners of war to be underplayed. One may search this section of the Nuremberg proceedings in vain for any acknowledgement that in the campaign of 1941, 3,800,000 members of the Red Army had surrendered to the Germans; that by the end of the war the Germans had counted more than five and a half million prisoners from the eastern front; that while nearly four million of them were dead, 800,000 had become deserters and had put on German uniform. Since the huge number of surrenders and desertions had never been admitted in Russia, the fate of the prisoners was obscured at Nuremberg by the casual manner with which the Russian prosecution stated its case. Only one representative prisoner of war gave evidence, the medical officer Eugene Kivelisha, who had been captured in the Ukraine in August 1941. It was significant of the Russian attitude that this witness was not a propagandist, speaking in the rich Byzantine style of a *Pravda* leader-writer like so many of the Russian witnesses, but a soldier speaking the common language of all soldiers. There was not a word in Kivelisha's testimony that could not have been confirmed a dozen times over in captured German documents. It was modest, it was dignified and it was soon over. And with that, Lieutenant Kivelisha vanished from the court and from the pages of history, sole spokesman for five million muted tongues.

For in peace as in war the Russians did not want to draw attention to their soldiers who had surrendered. In July 1929, Stalin had refused to sign the Geneva agreement by which captured Red Army men would be entitled to inspection by the International Red Cross. It would have meant a corresponding right of inspection by a protecting power in the Soviet Union. This refusal, as we have seen, was exploited by Hitler in the political arguments with which he sought to convince his general staff. In Hitler's view, the Russian refusal to work with the International Red Cross meant that they would also refuse to honour the unwritten safeguards of warfare, which had been in use for two centuries. Hitler chose deliberately to overlook the fact that the Russians had never repudiated The Hague conventions of 1907.* In this

* See p. 90

way Russian secretiveness in the matter of foreign rights of inspection
was made to look something even more sinister than it was.

Some of the generals, as we have seen, were persuaded by these
arguments. They were tempted to believe that it would be a war in
which Political Commissars and NKVD men butchered prisoners on
general principle. Jodl for instance was unwise enough to suggest that
the Commissar and 'Barbarossa' Jurisdiction Orders could be presented
as a reprisal measure.* But even generals like Reichenau, who vied with
Hitler in callousness towards prisoners, must have seen the idiocy of
making assumptions ahead. If the Russians should be the first to
murder prisoners on principle, general reprisal-orders by the Germans
would justify them in continuing the practice. And if the Germans did
it first, the Russians would need no justification. Though he never
repudiated the Commissar and 'Barbarossa' Jurisdiction Orders, there
was a moment when Hitler was not opposed to a reciprocal agreement
on the treatment of ordinary prisoners of war. It was with this prospect
in view that Hermann Reinecke invited Professor Carl Burckhardt,
the President of the International Red Cross organization, to inspect
one of the German prisoner camps behind the eastern front. Reinecke
also claims that he approached the American chargé d'affaires in
Berlin, Mr Jefferson Patterson, and he had lists of the names of Russian
prisoners drawn up in case there should be a Red Cross agreement.
Reinecke did this, he says, without the knowledge of Keitel, who had
already censured him severely for a critical report on prisoner camp
conditions in Riga.[2]

Since Keitel had been executed nearly two years before the High
Command Trial and since Reinecke failed to secure for his defence
affidavits from Professor Burckhardt and Mr Patterson, some doubts
must be cast on his testimony in the dock. But it seems that there had
been some authority for all this from Hitler. Apparently Hitler told
Baur, the Captain of his escort flight, that Stalin had replied to a
request for an exchange of postal arrangements for prisoners of war.
Stalin's words had put an end to the inquiry:**

* See p. 79
** Hans Baur, *Ich flog Maechtige der Erde*, p. 223. The experiences of the International
Red Cross fully confirm this impression. The German High Command agreed on 30th
August 1941, that the Red Cross might distribute food parcels to Russian prisoners, but a
detailed scheme for collecting food parcels from neutral countries was turned down by
Molotov on 16th February 1942 because the Soviet government would not agree to
transfer any currency. Similarly an offer of vitamins for Russian prisoners by the Canadian
Red Cross was turned down by the German government because the Russians would not
permit a Red Cross delegate to inspect German prisoner camps in Russia. (*Report of Red
Cross Activities during the Second World War* ,Vol III, Geneva 1948, pp. 54–5.)

There are no Russian prisoners of war. The Russian soldier fights on till death. If he chooses to become a prisoner, he is automatically excluded from the Russian community. We are not interested in a postal service only for Germans.

Whatever the truth of this story, it expresses Stalin's views on the subject of prisoners. After the allied landings in Normandy, when great numbers of former Red Army soldiers fell into allied hands, the Russian Government demanded the repatriation of their subjects and showed the greatest concern for them. But it was a concern lest ignorant and bewildered men, who had turned traitor to avoid a slow death from hunger, should again escape punishment for not having died. For them repatriation meant the labour camps. It was the first occasion that the Russian government showed any interest in captured soldiers after years of torture and murder. The Russian lawyers, who presented the case for the prisoners of war at Nuremberg, had it on their consciences that their government shared at least part of the blame for the death of millions of men.

For the loss of about 3,700,000 prisoners of war, a figure so unearthly that it becomes utterly unintelligible, there was not one cause but three quite distinct causes. In the first place there were the incredible encirclement battles of June to October 1941. After these battles from 100,000 to 700,000 men would be found in a quite small area of country. They would be corralled in the open on the ground on which they had fought; swamp, forest or steppe. There would be starvation already before their surrender. Nothing had been anticipated by Hitler's eager military planners, there was no food, there were no medical supplies and most of the Russians were too weak to stand the long marches to the rear.

To make these conditions still more disastrous, there existed between July and November 1941, an order which forbade the evacuation of Russian prisoners to Germany, even though camps had been prepared for them. The first influx of supposedly communist prisoners had so terrified local Nazi officials that Hitler was persuaded to issue this order. So the prisoners in Russia starved—not that their chances of survival would have been any better in Germany, where the screening teams removed hundreds of thousands for execution in the concentration camps during this short period.

There was a third reason for the appalling death roll of 1941. It was to be found in the instructions which were issued to the Economic

Staff East, three weeks before the invasion; instructions that no food was to be wasted on those who did not work for Germany, because produce was to be pumped from Russia more vigorously than from any other occupied area, and that even those whose work mattered should not be fed well. It was an instruction which continued to operate in Russian prisoner camps till the end of the war, as many allied prisoners could witness for themselves. Its great exponent was one of the less-known tyrants, Herbert Backe, who was at first Ministry Director in Walter Darré's Food Ministry and after May 1942, the undisputed controller of German food supplies. It was Backe's instructions which were responsible for the deaths of half a million prisoners between November 1941 and February 1942, a time when there were no encirclement victories, when the German army was on the defensive and when far fewer prisoners were being taken.[3]

Even the calamities that followed the encirclement battles cannot be written off as entirely accidental or inevitable. Staffs who could plan the envelopment of whole army groups, should have been capable of making some provision for feeding them. It was a warning—a first warning to be repeated four years later at Hiroshima—that the power of modern weapons had outstripped man's capacity for organization.

In the First World War the problem of mass-capitulation, involving whole armies and even army groups, hardly existed, although it was said that the Germans and Austrians took three million Russian prisoners. It is true that on the western front in 1918 armoured warfare had already created great penetrations in depth, but the speed was never so great that something could not be organized for the prisoners. Still less had the problem arisen in the classical battles of the Napoleonic and American Civil Wars. In these battles the surrender of 20,000 men was something quite exceptional. But on one occasion in the nineteenth century a German General Staff had to look after a captive army on the modern scale, an army that had suddenly become an additional burden on their supplies. In September 1870, the Prussian army and its allies captured the entire French Army of Sedan, 104,000 men. A month later a very much bigger army, 173,000 men, capitulated in the fortress town of Metz. But while Metz contained provisions for a much longer siege, the Army of Sedan was herded without resources of its own in the narrow peninsula of Iges in the bend of the river Meuse till evacuation could be organized. The French prisoners lay in the open in torrential rain, practically without food and surrounded by floating corpses, for anything up to a fortnight. What happened has been described by

Emile Zola in *Le Débacle*, a narrative which conveys something of the fate of the Russian prisoners in 1941. But terrifying as Zola's description of the *camp de misère* of 1870 may seem, it was nothing to the fate of the victims of the Kiev and Viasma encirclements. The scale was so much vaster, the country in most cases so much poorer and the attitude of the victors, after nine years of frenzied popular nationalism, so much more callous than that of the Prussian army in the Bismarck era.

The figures may be judged from the news bulletins of the High Command. The first great victory, the double encirclement of the armies round Bialystok and Minsk, yielded 328,878 prisoners. This was on 11th July, only nineteen days after the opening of the campaign. On 5th August 103,000 prisoners were claimed, following the rout of the Russian Budyeny offensive at Pervomaisk and Uman. On 24th August there were 78,000 more prisoners in White Russia. On 26th September the huge envelopment action, which took Kiev, ended with the surrender of the greater part of a Russian army group, 655,000 men. On 13th October similar figures were announced from the White Russian front, when the envelopment of Viasma brought in 663,000 prisoners.

Viasma was the most terrible case of all. The surrounded divisions had been without supplies for eight or ten days and were already reduced to living off leaves and the bark of trees. The railways in this area had been destroyed and there was no way of getting the men out of the dense forests. As at Sedan, heavy rainfall descended.[4] An attempt to move some of the prisoners back from Viasma to Smolensk, from one concentrated murder-trap to another, seems to have resulted in a death-march, in which everyone lost his head, and there were massed shootings all along the route. In the rear area camps, conditions were no better than in the Transit Camps or *Dulags*. On 14th November, Hitler's Chief of Staff, Franz Halder, was at Molodechno, where he saw a camp in which 20,000 men were doomed to die of typhus, as well as two other camps where they died of hunger, but 'no improvement seems possible at the moment.' On the same day Halder saw 'scenes of prisoner of war misery' in Minsk.[5] It was here that at the very start of the campaign 100,000 captured soldiers and 40,000 civilians had been reported as living in the open in 'an area the size of the Wilhelmsplatz'. Four months had passed and the same things were going on as had been reported then. The huddled masses of men had to relieve nature on the spot. Only one company of German troops was available for guard duties. 'The only possible language for a small detachment, which remains on duty day and night without being relieved, is the firearm of which ruthless use is made.'[6]

This it may be said was White Russia, a miserable land of swamp, heath and forest, where even the sparse inhabitants lived badly at the best of times, but the same thing had been going on in the famous black earth region of the Ukraine, a land so rich that, as Goering noticed on his first visit, untold quantities of butter and eggs could be bought in exchange for an empty jam-jar or cigar-box.[7] But the pathetic peasant women with their children, who implored to be allowed to feed the prisoners, were prevented by the Barbarossa decrees from even going near them. If they did, they were shot.

The man who ordered these things permitted himself to be shown them once and then it was only to make a vain Caesar-like gesture that had no basis in reality. This was on 30th August 1941, when Hitler flew with Mussolini to Uman. Round this place more than 100,000 men had been captured two or three weeks previously. After an open-air luncheon among his soldiers, Hitler came under the more benign influence of Mussolini and ordered the release of all the Ukrainian prisoners. The illustrious visitors went to inspect them in an old clay and brick works some miles away. It was such a jolly party that Hitler, feeling no doubt like Napoleon, had a conversation with a captive Russian doctor—an *Untermensch*.[8]

This Uman brickworks was notorious. Kivelisha, the solitary Nuremberg witness for the Russian prisoners, had passed through it a fortnight earlier, spending some days among the mass of men who lay there in the open, because the sheds had become choked with excrement; waiting for the chance of a bowl of lentil soup, for which men fought and died or risked the rifles of the sentries.[9]

At Nuremberg in February 1946, the Russians produced the recent affidavit of a German company commander who had been on duty at the Uman brickfield. On 14th August 1941, he had actually taken two photographs of the place. It then housed 74,000 men, but the kitchens could produce hot food for 2,000 men at most and sixty to seventy died every day, mostly in the struggle to get food. 'The truncheon was inevitably the foundation of all things.' It may be that the numbers had been reduced a fortnight later when Hitler arrived, but those who know their war from the soldier's end, will conclude that the inspection was confined to one corner of the camp, cleaned up in the way that all things are cleaned up for the visits of the great.[10]

Much worse was to come. After the mopping up of 655,000 Red Army prisoners round Kiev at the end of September, the conditions which existed at Uman became commonplace all over the Ukraine. If a little camouflage had been managed on 30th August, it was now out of the question. The few dusty earth roads in the rear areas were blocked with endless columns of scarecrows, marching five deep, the weary and dehumanized German pickets, often over-aged men, hanging on to their flanks at close intervals. There was shooting all the time, shooting when ranks were broken, shooting when civilians tried to throw loaves of bread, shooting when men dropped with exhaustion and shooting when they failed to get up after the periodic rests. On 10th October a lieutenant on the intelligence staff of Rundstedt's Southern Army Group at Uman, reported that a devastating effect was being produced, because often the stragglers were shot down in the very middle of friendly Ukrainian villages.[11]

Five days later Rundstedt himself received an amplification of this report from the commander of his Army Group Rear Area, Colonel General Karl von Roques. In a single operation of removing prisoners to permanent camps, a thousand men had died. Von Roques was a fairly typical *Korueck*. He was sixty-one years old, a dug-out who had been retired in 1933 and who had begun the war organizing Civil Defence in Berlin.* Apparently he saw nothing extraordinary in these losses, for on the 26th he signed an order, commending the 24th Division for their conduct on the march. Later there was talk of a court of inquiry into the conduct of this division but nothing happened till the High Command Trial of 1948, when a whole dossier was produced.[12] The commander of the 24th Division, Hans von Tettau, then declared that the number of men who had been shot was not excessive, seeing that the Division had removed 200,000 prisoners.[13] He described how he had bustled up and down in his staff-car. He had seen to it that the march was limited to twelve or fifteen miles a day with frequent rests. He had organized transport for the sick and wounded and given orders that the men who fell out through exhaustion should be taken to neighbouring camps. But von Tettau admitted that there was often shooting during the rest-periods, when men tried to sneak off, and he thought that many of the stragglers were too weak to survive, even when picked up.

That is how a divisional commander saw it. But the American

---

* Von Roques died in Landsberg prison hospital, close on seventy years of age, on Christmas day 1949. He was serving a twenty year sentence passed in October 1948.

Tribunal unearthed two more witnesses, a German medical officer and a Red Army Jewish prisoner, both from the camp at Khorol from which something between 12,000 and 20,000 men had been evacuated on this very march to Kremenchug. The medical officer declared that he had been told to pick out the sick men, who would not be able to stand this sixty-mile march. Later he learnt that the camp commander had turned them all in to the Security Police of the SD, together with fifty Jewish prisoners, many of them his own medical assistants. All had been shot. One Jewish prisoner, who survived the march, described the way in which the screened categories of prisoners, the Jews, Commissars and supposed communists, were placed in front of the column, where the Security Police dealt with them according to the Commissar Order. Both witnesses agreed in their description of a roadside littered with bodies.[14]

That was what it meant to transfer prisoners in October 1941, far from the front and among a peaceably disposed population. But the miseries of the marches from the transit camps to the permanent camps were repeated till heavy rain put a stop to using the roads and the prisoners died on the spot instead.

By 25th November, matters in the Ukraine had not improved in the least. A report by the Chief Quartermaster of the 17th Army, which at this time was fighting a desperate defensive battle along the Donetz river, showed that this army had captured and sent to the rear 366,540 Russian prisoners. Many of these had been taken in the Kiev battle without boots or underwear. No shelter could be provided and the death-rate had worked out at one per cent every day. When men had died or had been shot by the guards, their clothing was distributed among the others. In not one single case could the scale of rations, as laid down by the Quartermaster General of the armed forces, be honoured.* Only occasionally was there bread. Like so many canaries, the prisoners were fed on lentils, peas and sunflower seeds. The Quartermaster seemed to think that it was the fault of the prisoners themselves, because when they surrendered they did not bring their field kitchens with them.[15]

But the worst conditions probably existed at the other end of the huge front, where von Kuechler's 18th Army and Hoepner's 4th Armoured Group besieged Leningrad. 'All the inmates of Camp East' says the war diary of the 4th Armoured Group on 28th November, 'will have died within six months at the latest. In the camp at Pskov,

* For the actual scale, see p. 118

where there are 20,000 men, a thousand die from extreme weakness every week.'[16]

These were the prisoners, taken by the Hoepner Armoured Group, in which von Manstein commanded the 56th Corps. At his trial at Hamburg in October 1950, Manstein described the occasion when he had sent for a divisional commander and reprimanded him. This was none other than Theodor Eicke who had led the Death's Head Division of the SS into Russia. Eicke, as the Bonn trial recalled in May 1957, had murdered Ernst Roehm in his prison cell in 1934. Subsequently Eicke had become the overlord of the German concentration camp system and in 1940 he had stopped his division holding a court of inquiry into the massacre of the men of the Royal Norfolks at Le Paradis. More than a year after the affair of Le Paradis, Manstein found it peculiar that Eicke's division were still taking very few prisoners. He told this thug, whom he described as a former policeman who knew nothing of the duties of a divisional commander, to conduct himself henceforward according to military rules.[17] But what was the sense of reading lectures to SS men, if the best that most of these old style Junker generals could do was to be too busy to notice the deaths of a few hundred thousand prisoners, whose existence had been merely overlooked? There were even merits in Eicke's way of doing things by comparison with this.

(b) Terror by Hunger—the Backe and Reinecke Rules

ENOUGH INSTANCES HAVE been produced to show what happened after the great encirclement battles between July and November 1941, but in fact the conditions continued with only here and there a local change for the better till at least as late as February 1942. For this situation neither genuine food shortages nor labour and transport deficiencies were to blame, but causes that must be traced back to the days of the Commissar and 'Barbarossa' Jurisdiction Orders. It had been intended at that time to remove the prisoners to Germany. Each *Wehrkreis* or military area, corresponding in peacetime to an army corps, was notified of the quota it was to take through its chief of prisoner of war affairs. The attitude of these officers differed widely. Some of them improved on the already appalling orders which issued from Reinecke's office, like the commander attached to *Wehrkreis VII*, who decreed that Russian prisoners should have no blankets but make their own from paper.[18] Others, particularly in the Bavarian area, behaved with a courage and decency that shamed the High Command. More than twenty of these officers were briefed by General Reinecke in Berlin as early as March 1941. They were told that they would not have time to erect enough buildings and shelters. They must prepare wired enclosures for great masses of men and they must be ready to shoot at the first signs of a breakout.[19] The orders applied to some eighteen camps, which, according to a circular issued by Walter Warlimont on 16th July 1941, had been cleared for the reception of Russian prisoners in eastern Germany and Poland. There was room for 790,000 men and this no doubt was a reasonable figure in a campaign which Hitler expected to last six weeks. That two million men should be captured in three months and close on four million by the end of a year was something not dreamed of.

Or had it been dreamed of? Was the whole plan countermanded because Hitler, remembering the fall of France, suddenly envisaged masses of men beyond all computation drifting back into the Reich? It is certain at least that on 16th June, when Warlimont issued his directions, the fear of Bolshevik contamination was running very high. Warlimont spoke of the treacherous Asiatics who might be expected to fill these camps, of the necessity of eliminating completely even passive forms of resistance. And already there was mention of the segregation of specially dangerous elements.[20]

Warlimont expressed the views of the party, the views of the Gauleiters of the German *Laender* and their close associates the Gestapo offices. In view of the reckless way in which the 'political' screening of Russian prisoners was practised in Germany, it seems likely that it was these people who put pressure on Hitler to issue through Brauchitsch an order which banned further evacuation of prisoners to Germany, hardly more than a month after the opening of the campaign.[21] At that time close on a million prisoners had been taken. Halder at once told Keitel that, if the ban was to be applied, the General Staff could no longer take charge of such large numbers. Cases of cannibalism had reached his notice.[22] Through the mediation of Eduard Wagner, the Quartermaster General, Keitel was eventually persuaded to agree to provide permanent prisoner camps in the OKW zone, the non-operational areas of occupied Russia, which were outside the responsibility of the General Staff, but there was a long time-lag. Everything had to be started from the beginning and well into 1942, when the German army was taking few prisoners, the original transit camps still contained Red Army men who had surrendered in the first encirclement battles.[23]

In the OKW zone as well as in Germany the prisoners came under the Reinecke rules. We have noticed the language which was used by Reinecke when he met Mueller and Lahousen in order to prepare these rules. That language was repeated in black and white in the circular which Reinecke issued on 8th September 1941.[24]* 'The Bolshevist soldier has therefore lost all claim to treatment as an honourable opponent in accordance with the Geneva Convention.' Any indulgence by German guards, any friendly disposition was to be punished with severity. The Russian camp police, who must be picked from reliable elements, were to be furnished with whips and sticks. Germans, however, were not to carry such things. They were to use their firearms as a more honourable weapon and insufficient energy in their handling was to be punished. Firearms were to be used at the slightest indication of disobedience. At places where prisoners were put to work, guards must maintain a distance sufficient to enable them to manipulate their weapons at once. Firearms would also be needed against civilians who tried to speak to prisoners. 'Never turn your back on a prisoner of war.'

In addition to rules for the screening of Jews, communists and party functionaries, there were rules for the release of likely collaborationists. These included racial Germans and members of the Baltic Nations, but not as yet Asiatics. It was not till the beginning of 1942 that Hitler agreed that they could be enlisted as soldiers without exciting political aspirations. This was largely due to the Foreign Office and its concern for the reactions of neutral Turkey.** In September 1941, Asiatics were considered rather more sub-human than the rest. On the other hand it was only ten days since Hitler's visit to Uman, so Ukrainians were to be released as a potentially friendly element. But very soon there were second thoughts about the Ukrainians. On 7th November, when issuing a new code of orders for the employment of Russian prisoners in Germany, Goering commented, 'Ukrainians have no special privileges. The Fuehrer has ordered that in future they shall not be released from war captivity.'[25]***

The Reinecke rules of 8th September were the work of a dyed-in-the-wool desk officer, who would have done anything to retain the support

* See p. 87
** See p. 291
*** See p. 174

of the Party that had made him a man of destiny. That real soldiers carried out these orders, and many documents show that they did carry them out, is less easy to understand. It must be pictured what sort of a man the commander of a *Stalag* or a *Dulag* was in Russia in 1941. He was an officer whose career had failed, a Captain or Major in late middle age who had been given an unpopular task because of his incompetence. With twenty or thirty thousand, sometimes even seventy thousand lives in his hands, with insufficient supplies, with insufficient guards, both on the march and in camp, he became inured to the incessant presence of death. The dead were more numerous than the living and generally less trouble. If any sensibility was still left him, he took to drink. Under such conditions his soldiers needed no telling. Their hands strayed seldom far from the trigger. And if a single Security Policeman was hindered in his murderous searches, if a Russian was so much as seen holding out a piece of bread to one of the prisoners on the march, the camp commander believed that the Security Service might report him for it.

Ignorance probably exaggerated his fear. Actually at this stage of the war Himmler, as Chief of Police, had no jurisdiction inside the Wehrmacht. Consequently the Security Police of the SD could not detain a member of the armed forces. Their duty was to surrender him at once to military jurisdiction. The commander of a prisoner camp could only be tried by the Army. If the sentence was dismissal, the SD could of course still catch up with him as a civilian and send him to a concentration camp, but it never happened. On the contrary the camp commander was more likely to be supported by his superiors. On 3rd November 1941, one of these tussles was mentioned by the *Einsatzgruppe* commander in the Ukraine in his daily report to Heydrich's office. It seems that at Vinnitsa, which had recently been Hitler's headquarters and where there was a large transit camp far behind the front, the camp commander had stopped the removal of 362 Jewish prisoners who had been picked out by a screening team. He had put his Second in Command on trial for assisting in this operation. There followed a duel between OKH, the Field High Command, who supported the camp commander, and OKW, the former War Office, who invoked the agreements with Heydrich. In the end OKW won; even so, no action was taken against the camp commander.[26]

However, in reporting this support of a small man by the highest agencies, the *Einsatzgruppe* bulletin of 3rd November 1941 mentioned something very ominous. 'Since the Reichenau Order of the Day of

10th October, better co-operation may be expected. With the Secret
Field Police there has never been any friction.' This sentence acknow-
ledges the fact that generals in the field had already begun to copy the
language of the Reinecke rules, generals who were ambitious of
promotion and generals who felt insecure in their posts. And the first
of the combatant generals who touted the ideas of the Party in this
way was Walter von Reichenau.

On 10th October Reichenau commanded the 6th Army which,
having swept through Kiev, was engaged in the assault of Kursk,
Bielgorod and Kharkov, the most easterly spray of the German wave.
Reichenau was an able General, but unpopular and furiously ambitious.
Since the birth of the Nazi State, he had made good contacts with
Himmler and the Party. In February 1938 Reichenau had been the
obvious candidate to succeed von Fritsch as Commander in Chief, yet
the job had gone to Brauchitsch. Disgruntled with his treatment,
Reichenau was foremost among the generals who opposed an invasion
of France in 1939. Hitler, who knew that Reichenau had composed a
memorial on the subject, avoided making him a Field Marshal in the
mass-promotions of June 1940. It was therefore urgent for Reichenau,
since the Russian campaign was expected to end so soon, to attract
Hitler's attention in some desperate fashion.

The Order of the Day which Reichenau distributed to the 6th
Army on 10th October 1941 had for background the mining of the
central part of Kiev at the end of September. A delayed action enterprise of the retreating Russians, this had caused huge loss of life,
particularly in the great buildings occupied by German military staffs.
With the agreement of Major General Eberhardt, the town commandant of Kiev, the commander of the *Einsatzgruppe* of the Security
Police arranged a tremendous retribution, nothing less than the
extermination of all the Jews who had stayed behind in Kiev. It is
unlikely that Eberhardt could have made such an agreement without
some reference to Reichenau. It was the greatest single massacre of the
entire war, since the execution of 33,780 people was completed in two
days. Astonishingly the shooting ground, the Babi Yar ravine, was
within earshot and almost within sight of the city centre.* Since news
spreads quickly among soldiers, most of the 6th Army, battling far to
the east of Kiev, must have learnt of the massacre, which was so little

* Reitlinger, *The Final Solution*, p. 233. Eberhardt, the former commander of the 60th
Infantry Division, was named at Nuremberg by Paul Blobel who had directed the
execution. (Case IX, transcript, p. 1571.)

concealed that it provided 137 truck-loads of the clothing of the dead
for the use of needy racial Germans, born in the Ukraine, as well as
enough blankets to stock a Waffen SS field hospital.[27] It was with such
things in his mind that Reichenau justified in his order 'a severe but
just revenge on sub-human Jewry'.

In the second instance the Reichenau Order was an attack on the
Russian prisoners, for whom German soldiers were much more likely
to feel sorry, given favourable circumstances and no responsibilities.[28]

> The combating of the enemy behind the front line is still not
> being taken seriously enough. Treacherous cruel partisans and
> unnatural women are still being made prisoners of war, while
> guerilla fighters, dressed partly in uniforms and partly in plain
> clothes, as well as vagabonds, are still being treated as proper
> soldiers and sent to prisoner of war camps. In fact captured
> Russian officers even speak with derision of Soviet agents, moving
> openly on the roads and very often eating at German field
> kitchens. Such an attitude of our troops can only be explained by
> complete thoughtlessness, so it is now high time for the com-
> manders to clarify the meaning of the present struggle.
>
> The feeding from our army kitchens of the natives and of
> prisoners of war, who are not working for the armed forces, is an
> humanitarian act just as much misunderstood as the giving of
> cigarettes and bread. Things which our people at home can only
> spare under great sacrifices and things that the Command can only
> bring up to the front under great difficulties, should not be given
> to the enemy by the soldier, not even when they are acquired from
> booty. They are an important part of our supply.

One gets the impression from this famous document, of which less
than a quarter has been quoted, that Reichenau knew what he was
talking about. He knew the irresponsible generosity of the front line
soldier and he knew the harassed security-ridden life of the commanders of rear formations, who were perpetually at the mercy of
ridiculous orders from the High Command. Reichenau's order was
addressed to the front line soldier, who believed that the rear area
swarmed, not only with privileged units living in gilded palaces, but
also with filthy murderers who dragged down the name of the army.
But above all it was addressed to Hitler—and Hitler responded. Within
a few days Hitler welcomed the Reichenau Order of the Day as a
model of the language which generals ought to use and he ordered

Brauchitsch to send copies to all other army commanders. Brauchitsch did so on 28th October, because it seems there was nothing whatever that Brauchitsch would not circulate. He even added his personal recommendation that the army commanders should each issue an order on the same lines.[29]

It is not known how many generals complied, but versions of this order circulated by von Kuechler of the 18th Army on the 16th and by von Manstein of the 11th Army on the 20th November, have survived.[30] Von Manstein's version is particularly interesting. He had more to say on the 'just punishment of Jewry' than von Reichenau, perhaps because his real name was Lewinsky. Nor was Manstein behindhand in condemning the wickedness of giving bread to starving Russians in almost the exact words used by Reichenau. But Manstein was an advocate of recruiting friendly prisoners. His own headquarters in the Crimea were guarded exclusively by Cossacks. So he toned down the original order by adding a set of instructions. These were intended to secure a just treatment of the non-Bolshevik section of the population, particularly the Tartars of the Crimea.* No officer, reading the manifesto of his revered army commander, could fail to notice the contradiction between the first and second parts. And if he was expected to carry out both, he might as well stand on his head.

So we approach the month of December 1941. The German army was now everywhere on the defensive. On the Moscow and Rostov fronts the situation had become perilous. The winter campaign, which no one had been allowed to mention in Hitler's presence, though most army commanders knew it was coming, was now a shattering reality. Many of the generals, who had attended Hitler's military conferences and who had allowed their better judgments to be overcome, were beginning to pay for it. Brauchitsch himself handed in his long-delayed resignation, which to his surprise Hitler accepted with delight. During that December and January all three army group commanders and more than half the army commanders were sent into retirement. Reichenau on the contrary had done the right thing at the right time, so he succeeded Rundstedt as Commander in Chief of the Southern Army Group. The field marshal's baton that had eluded him in 1940, was his. Reichenau held it only a few weeks. On 17th January he died of an infection that eluded all analysis, save that the ancient gods of

---

* R. T. Paget, *Manstein, his campaigns and trials*, London, 1951, p. 166. Mr Paget does not view the order in this light.

Russia had hit back. As to the deposed Rundstedt, he had the curious consolation of representing Hitler at Reichenau's funeral.[31]

The Kiev massacre, the outrageous order of the day and Reichenau's death, all these had happened inside four months. Perhaps the older soldiers shook their heads, as they had done when von Manstein slipped and fell into von Schobert's open grave so soon after the notorious massacre in Nikolaiev.[32] But, as to any improvement in the moral climate, the wrong generals had left the war. Throughout an avalanche of dismissals, Keitel, Jodl, Warlimont and Reinecke remained as steady as mountain tops. Under this immovable priesthood the prisoner problem solved itself only in death.

However, the disasters which affected the German supply system at the first touch of the Russian winter, induced a slight current of commonsense at Hitler's headquarters. It was realized that Germany could not afford to lose the Russian prisoners as a labour force. So on 31st October, Keitel obtained from Hitler leave to lift the ban which had been imposed on the removal of further prisoners to Germany.[33] There was a hint from high quarters that the fear of Bolshevist contamination was no longer to provide an excuse for the wholesale condemnation of Russian working prisoners by local Gestapo offices. Goering announced on 17th November, that the new Fuehrer order required the maximum employment of prisoner of war labour. Scruples were, therefore, of secondary importance.[34]* The disadvantage of having Bolsheviks in Germany would have to be the concern of the counter-espionage and Security Police services. For the moment this meant little. In the chaos that overtook the railways in November 1941 not many prisoners could be brought to Germany. The serious movement began only in the following February after a big reorganization of the Ministries of Labour and Armament.

So the disastrous state of affairs continued in the uncleared prisoner camps in Russia. On 14th December, Hitler himself learnt from Rosenberg that in the Ukraine 2,500 Russian prisoners died of hunger every day.[35] Six days later, a report, compiled by Colonel von Krosigk, Chief of Staff to Karl von Roques, showed that in the Southern Army Group zone there were 52,513 Russian prisoners who were still living in the three transit camps, Alexandrya, Novo Ukrainka and Stalino. The death-rate was running at 80 per cent a year. At a fourth but permanent camp the situation was the same. There were 22,776 inmates on 20th December and fifty died every day. Von Krosigk observed that

* See p. 260

if the releases of Ukrainians, which Hitler had stopped in November, were resumed, the 75,000 prisoners in the four camps could be reduced at once by 21,846.[36]

On 13th January, von Krosigk sent another report, this time to Eduard Wagner in his remote stronghold at Mauerwald in East Prussia. The situation in the four camps had become much worse and it was estimated that a third of the inmates would die before the end of March. Wagner was urged to send supplies and stop the employment of prisoners on heavy labour, 'otherwise all will be dead within a few months'.[37]

The most notorious was the camp at Stalino. A lieutenant, returning to the front, repeated some of the stories to Major Heinz Herre, the Chief of Staff at XXXIX Corps Headquarters. As a result, this Russian-speaking Major visited Stalino camp in person. It was his Damascus journey. The horrible experience drove Herre into the ranks of the rebel exponents of pro-Russian policy, among whom he was to play an important part.*

On 26th January, a fortnight after Krosigk's report to Wagner, Herre found the prisoners housed in the State High School of Stalino. He saw a lecture theatre, large well-lit class rooms and playgrounds, a typical shop-window of Marxist enlightenment, such as was shown to countless wearied tourists in pre-war Russia. But the playgrounds had been dug up for mass-graves and the rooms were filled with the living and the dead alike. There was an elderly reservist captain in command. In 1946 the Soviet prosecution read his name as Gaubel. Sitting in a dirty porter's lodge, this captain tried to oppose Herre's entry and warned him that he would die of typhus. But in the end the unwanted Brass Hat was taken round by a reluctant lieutenant, smelling of strong drink. They entered the first of three lecture theatres; it was intended for employable prisoners, who were out at work, and the place was empty. Herre noticed the icy cold and the fact that everywhere excrement and urine were frozen to the ground. The second lecture theatre was for the conditionally fit for duty. It was so full that most of the Russians could not sit, but had to prop each other up. Those who could stand no longer, slipped to the ground and were crushed under foot. Some in fact were dead. Even this was surpassed in the third section which was reserved for the unfit for duty. Herre saw the dead and the dying lying together on equal terms, piled between the long rows of children's desks. And everywhere he saw the Russian camp police with

* See p. 334

their heavy truncheons; the nerve-strung elderly German reservists, fingering their rifles, and the lieutenant with the Schnapps-laden breath.[38]

Who can tell how much longer these conditions continued at Stalino? Herre, like many German officers before him, wrote a memorandum. He was related through his wife to a reputedly influential person at OKW, the head of the Armed Forces Propaganda Section, Colonel Hasso von Wedel. In reality this was not a good avenue of approach to the powers. Wedel was not a dynamic figure. So Herre's memorandum was never answered, but Wedel, possibly to keep him quiet, got him transferred to the OKW bureaucracy. From April 1942 Herre worked under Colonel Gehlen in the important Intelligence Section known as 'Foreign Armies East'. And here we shall meet Herre again.*

Two Russian soldiers escaped from Stalino and their testimony was read at Nuremberg in February 1946. Except that they mentioned the burial of 25,000 men in the grounds, there is nothing in their description that will not be found in Herre's.[39] Unfortunately the detailed descriptions of murder-camps, as presented by the Russians at Nuremberg, must be believed in most cases, though they were occasionally distorted because of the habits of Marxist propaganda, which attaches the same value to mere rumour-mongers and professional propagandists as it does to genuine survivors and first-hand witnesses. It is, for instance, hard to recognize in the Russian prosecution brief the field hospital which was established in the Sevastopol prison-building by the Austrian surgeon, Kurt Emmerich, whose modest account of a brave enterprise can surely be trusted. Yet it is undoubtedly the same hospital.[40]

On one point, however, all accounts of the life of Russian prisoners, at least until February 1942 show a singular uniformity; and that is in the description of the food that was issued to them. The breakdown of transport and the hard conditions, under which the Russian civilian population** and occasionally the German soldiers too had to live, explained why the prisoners went hungry long after their removal from the battlefields. But they do not account for the fact that for months on end the Russian prisoners' diet was everywhere the same. A scale had in fact been laid down from the beginning and it was one that could not keep men alive more than a few weeks.

* See p. 334
** For the civilian food shortage in the Ukraine, see pp. 188-9

The bureaucracy, which dictated these conditions, was complicated. The German army lived largely on the country. Attached to each army rear area command was a branch of Goering's Economic Staff East, which was formed of military as well as civilian personnel. These staffs apportioned the Wehrmacht's share of the local produce in consultation with the staff of the rear area commander. But the feeding of the prisoners was dictated by the orders of a food controller, who was attached from the German food ministry to Goering's Economic Staff. The scales of feeding were published in orders by the Quartermaster General, Eduard Wagner, but they were dictated to him by the food controller, Herbert Backe.

This person was to become very powerful after May 1942, as the supreme food dictator of Germany at war. At the time of Goering's 'Green File' instructions, that is to say three weeks before the invasion, Backe was very much Goering's man. It was said that the instructions Goering gave him were concealed even from Backe's chief, the great exponent of Nazi land policy, Walter Darré.[41] Backe's contribution to the 'Green File' was an admonition to his future assistants in Russia, which he called his Twelve Commandments. It is an enlightening document. Among other things one reads that the Russian's stomach is elastic. 'Therefore have no pity on him.' And also 'don't ask how this will benefit the peasants, but how it will benefit Germany'.[42]

A civil servant, who used this not very pretty language, Backe had nevertheless been born in Russia: at Batum on the Black Sea. He was much in favour with the Russian-born Rosenberg, who wanted him to govern the Ukraine. Goering, however, had better uses for Backe and proposed in his place Erich Koch, the Gauleiter of East Prussia. As a civil servant Backe was inadaptable. Having absorbed the 'Green File' instructions, which were meant for the quick surrender of Russia, he could not see that they would be nullified by a long campaign. With Goering's support he continued throughout the war to discriminate in the rationing system against Russian workers and prisoners. This was in spite of the protests of all who had charge of Russian labour. At the end of the war Backe was unaware that he had become a war criminal. As a member of the Flensburg government of Admiral Doenitz, he officiously offered to handle the German rationing system for the Allied Control Commission, who put an aeroplane at his disposal to fetch him to Rheims. By the time the aeroplane landed, Backe's reputation had caught up with him and he was arrested. He was sent to a war criminals' camp, where in the autumn of 1947 he committed suicide, having just learnt that he was to be included in the mass-trial of the German civil service, the so-called 'Wilhelmstrasse Trial' of 1948 –9. Had Backe been able to foresee the future, he would not have done this, for he would certainly have fared no worse than his co-defendants, Hans Lammers and Gottlob Berger, who, though sentenced to twenty-five years imprisonment, were released at the end of 1951.[43]

The basis for the feeding of Russian prisoners of war was an order, circulated by the Supreme Command of the Army, the Armed Forces equipment office and the Replacement Army (*Ersatzheer*) on 6th August 1941. The preamble states that the Soviet Union had not subscribed to the Geneva Agreement of 27th July 1929, consequently there was no obligation to follow it at all. The proposed scale of rations was not up to the Geneva standard, but it was considered 'adequate according to medical findings'. A man was to receive six kilograms of bread in twenty-eight days. It requires no great exercise of calculation to perceive that this meant less than half a pound of bread a day. In the entire four weeks he was to get rather less than a pound of meat and a pound of fat, as well as a pound and a half of sugar. So, in addition to his half-pound of bread, the most a Russian prisoner could expect each day was a soup so thin as to be barely distinguishable from water and two or three cubes of sugar.

A prisoner, doing specially heavy labour, was to be allowed half as much again. So he would have three-quarters of a pound of bread, occasionally a soup which had a faint flavour of meat in it, and nearly an ounce of sugar. But these splendours were not guaranteed. It was provided that, if rations to non-Soviet prisoners had to be reduced, this scale would be reduced in proportion.[44]

However, it was decided that the feeding difficulties in occupied Russia were such that medical findings would have to be ignored. On 24th November 1941, Backe sent for Reinecke of the prisoners of war department and for Erwin Mansfeld, who was acting for the absent Dr Syrup in the Ministry of Labour.* Backe declared that there was great discrepancy between the health and medical authorities in estimating quantities, so, till a final decision was reached, there would be a seven days' régime of flour soup for everyone, whether at work or not,[45] a decision worthy of the great Dr Wackford Squeers. At the same conference some interesting light was thrown on the bread that was issued. Apparently there was nothing in it that could be dignified by the

* For Mansfeld, see p. 261

appellation of flour. Half of it was rye bran, the other half a useful mixture of cellulose, sugar-beet, straw and leaves. How the thing was to be baked was not described, but innumerable prisoners have testified to the digestive pains, skin-complaints and more serious disorders which it caused. The meat, which was to be in suspense for seven days, consisted of horse-flesh and any dead animals that had not passed through the slaughter-house. It was 'regretted' that the fat ration could not be other than 'good and edible because with the present technique of fat production, inferior fats no longer exist'.

That was the state of feeding among the Russian prisoners after five months fighting. It may be wondered whether any Russians, captured in the first two months of fighting, were still alive.*

A marginal note in a copy of the minutes of 24th November, shows that Backe had declared that something had got to be done. He was 'losing his nerve'. That nothing was done at all appears from a circular, issued by Martin Bormann's office on 17th December, instructing the Gauleiters' offices throughout Germany that the August 1941 rationing scales were still in force. Nevertheless some feelings had been roused and there was another approach towards a more generous treatment. The reason was provided by the Russian government. On 25th November, the day after Backe's loss of nerves, Molotov delivered one of his formidable notes to the embassies and legations of the allied and neutral world. It was the usual assembly of atrocity reports, to which German ministries were not generally very susceptible. But the note contained an exact account of the rationing scales of 6th August, though in Germany discussion, whether orally or in writing, had been forbidden because of the danger of enemy propaganda. The scales had in fact been published in the Allied press and the Swedish government had replied to an inquiry from the Soviet ambassador that, though the text had not been published in Germany, the version was correct.[46]

The name of Sweden was of such awesome respectability that it could be used to assail the most inaccessible quarters, such as Keitel, the dictator of OKW. It was also a fact that with the improvement in transport conditions in February 1942, trainloads of living skeletons were leaving Russia to work for Germany under Hitler's new dispensation. On 20th February, Erwin Mansfeld read a lecture to his staff in the Ministry of Labour; he declared roundly that the present

* Mr Alexander Dallin believes (p. 332) that Paul Koerner, head of the Four-Year-Plan Office, disagreed with Backe's decision of 24th November 1941, and that thereafter he opposed Backe's influence in Russian affairs. See also p. 191

labour crisis would not have arisen if it had been decided to employ
the Russians in Germany from the start, and he stated his belief that
only 1,100,000 Russian prisoners remained alive out of 3,900,000; that
half a million had died since November alone; that of the survivors
only 400,000 were immediately employable and that, even when the
typhus ceased to rage in the camps, not more than a further 150,000
able-bodied men need be expected. Also it was senseless to ship
Russians for several days on end in unheated box-cars only to unload
corpses at the destination.[47]

A week later a memorandum reached Keitel from Rosenberg's
ministry. It was a very bold document, but that was because it had not
been written by Rosenberg. The author was Otto Braeutigam, the
deputy head of Rosenberg's Political Department. Braeutigam's
memoranda were usually sardonic in tone, but seldom impractical.*
Braeutigam's memorandum of 25th February 1942, repeated Mansfeld's figures and the reports from the prisoner camps in Russia. He
demanded the issue of protection-cards to genuine Russian deserters.
He cited the leakage in Molotov's note of 25th November 1941, as an
example of Germany's disregard of propaganda possibilities.[48]

It is a fact that a new scale of Russian prisoner rations was announced
almost immediately but it was still far below that of other allied
prisoners. Yet Backe fought a long fight to impose the same scale on
the Russian workers who were supposed to have come voluntarily to
Germany. But a new personality now entered the struggle. At the
beginning of April 1942, Fritz Sauckel took over the duties of Plenipotentiary for Labour. He found that only 70,000 Russian prisoners
were employed in Germany. By agreement with Reinecke, they were
sent to farms, to be fattened up for three months. It was done at the
expense of the farmer, who received an assurance in return that he could
keep them at work till the end of the war.[49] So the prisoners arrived in
the German countryside, crawling out of the trains at the frequent stops
to chew blades of grass. But the promise was not kept; when the prisoners
had been fattened up, they were requisitioned for heavy industry.[50]

On 24th April, Goebbels recorded in his diary that the Russians had
recruited a corps of lecturers to the forces, composed exclusively of
men who had escaped from German hunger camps. Instructions had
therefore been issued for better treatment.[51] In fact very little was done
in spite of Goebbels's interest. Reinecke's instructions, as revised on
24th March 1942, differed little from the instructions of 8th September

* See p. 139

1941. Again it was emphasized that equality of rations among prisoners of war did not apply to Russians, for whom the scales had been decided in the previous month. And this was repeated even a year later after the disaster of Stalingrad.[52]

The instructions of 24th March 1942, repeat that the German soldier must remember that Russian prisoners are bearers of Bolshevism, but in general he is to avoid violence by keeping his distance.[53] Sticks are no longer to be used but there is the same emphasis on firearms. Insubordination is to be met with the bayonet, rifle-butt or bullet. Guards are still to be punished for not using weapons with alacrity and there must be no warning shot when aiming at suspected escapers.

This new Reinecke order of March 1942, admits that the prisoners are undernourished, 'partly as a result of recent events', but they are to be put to work just the same, even if full achievement cannot be expected. It is apparently still necessary to punish cases of cannibalism and the dead are to be buried without ceremony, neither shrouded nor coffined but wrapped in paper. A concession is, however, made for the non-Russian prisoners. Bona fide deserters will be issued with a protection certificate, while other members of minority races, who are still in prison camps, are to have a heated room in winter and they may be permitted to play on their balalaikas. Mohammedans are to have a room for religious worship, but Christians are to receive religious consolation only when dying.

In the following winter, the winter of Stalingrad, a serious effort was made to improve the lot of some 650,000 deserters, who had elected to serve the Germans. In the course of 1943 they were promoted to the status of ordinary German soldiers. But right up till the capitulation of Germany, it was the second edition of the Reinecke rules which governed the lives of some 800,000 surviving Red Army prisoners who would not change their allegiance. For them it was blows, hunger and cold till the very end.

(c) The Snowball Growth of the Commissar Order

THE TWO EDITIONS of the Reinecke rules, that of 8th September 1941, and that of 24th March 1942, share this in common, a scrupulous avoidance of trespassing on the preserves of 'Gestapo' Mueller. On 15th July 1941, when he had interviewed Reinecke and Mueller on behalf of Canaris, Erwin Lahousen could glean nothing concerning the screening rules; moreover Reinecke had made it clear that staff-officers from the Wehrmacht were not to interfere. This was made even clearer on 15th September, when Keitel sent back Canaris's memorandum with his comments. The only result of Canaris's intervention was that Mueller prudently altered his instructions so that the executions could take place in the veiled secrecy of concentration camps. This instruction seems to have been given almost simultaneously with the first issue of the Reinecke rules.*

The result was an absolute reign of terror. Mueller himself admitted on 10th October 1941, that 16,000 Russians had already been dealt with this way—out of 20,000 who had been screened. The Sachsenhausen camp guards, who were tried twice in 1947 and in October–December 1958, talked of 13,000 and 18,000 victims in two months in a single camp. They told how Theodor Eicke, the founder of the SS Death's Head Units, had taken a short leave from his command of a famous SS division on the Russian front in order to give them instruction in mass killing. After Eicke's visit, a measuring apparatus was evolved which efficiently put a bullet in the victim's neck, while he believed himself to be undergoing a medical examination. The sound of the shot was concealed from the waiting patients by gramophone records which were played in the room. The two Sachsenhausen guards, who had been repatriated from Russia in 1956 had every opportunity to withdraw the unconvincing confessions which they had made in 1947, but they only modified their estimate of the number, executed at Sachsenhausen, to 10,800.**

Such mass-execution took place in every German concentration camp, in Lublin, Buchenwald, Dachau, Auschwitz, Flossenburg and Gross Rosen. The practice ceased only in February 1942, when Goering's new instructions began to take effect. There had been one forlorn but creditable attempt at resistance on the part of a few, a very few of the prisoner of war inspectors, who were attached to the military area commands in the Reich. These officers belonged to an older generation who cared less about holding on to their jobs than their counterparts in the Russian rear areas. This attempt can be studied in detail in an astonishing file of Nuremberg trial documents, which were discovered in the Munich Gestapo office.

* See pp. 93–4
** Heinrich Toeplitz (editor), *SS in Einsatz* Berlin, 1957, pp. 217–18, 237–8. *The Times*, 21.10.58 and 18.12.58. The work was done after duty hours and the guards were rewarded with extra supplies of beer and fried potatoes.

It was on 12th September 1941, that the Munich Gestapo first concerned themselves with the case of 5,288 Russian prisoners who had arrived in a neighbouring Stalag at Moosburg. The camp was run by a certain Colonel Nepf, whom the Gestapo described as an 'ossified old officer', and it was under the inspection of Major Meinel, deputy for the area prisoner of war inspector, General von Saur. Against all three officers the Gestapo report was negative, particularly against Meinel who had been pensioned off as head of the Upper-Bavarian provincial police two years before the war, when Himmler became Chief of Police. It was stated that Meinel habitually mentioned 'God and not the Fuehrer in his orders of the day'.

Through the head office of the Gestapo in Berlin, contact was made with Reinecke's office to find out whether the terms of the Mueller-Reinecke accord had been applied.* Back came the answer. The screening of the prisoners at Moosburg had been only superficial. So, shortly before 15th November, the Security Service descended on Moosburg. Confidential agents were picked from among the minority races in the prison camps and with their aid 410 'intolerable persons' were weeded out. They included twenty-five Jews, who had been employed as interpreters by an officer who was attached from the *Abwehr*. There were also 147 'fanatical communists' and 47 incurably sick prisoners. Out of the 410 intolerable persons, 310 were taken to Dachau concentration camp for execution by shooting.

It seems that Meinel complained about the methods of screening to an officer called Woelzl, who represented the *Abwehr* in area VII. Unlike more publicized *Abwehr* officers, Woelzl was an ardent Nazi, a croney of Schurmer, the criminal investigator of the Munich Gestapo. On 24th November, Schurmer sent his deputy, a man called Schimmel, to see Meinel. Meinel was very open with Schimmel, declaring he would not be a party to such treatment of honourably captured soldiers. Schimmel replied that the SS men did not like it either. The hearts of some of the executioners had been near breaking point. Meinel then criticized Reinecke's agreements with the Reich Security Office and said that he was going to make an official complaint, because of the appalling results all this might have on the treatment of German prisoners by the Russians. Schimmel mumbled that no German prisoners were likely to return from Russia in any case and he went off to think it over. Nearly three weeks passed before he sent a letter to Berlin, to the grand inquisitor Heinrich Mueller. It seems from this

* See p. 90

letter that Schurmer had spoken to Friedrich Karl von Eberstein, the Higher SS and Police Leader for Bavaria. Eberstein talked of transferring Meinel elsewhere.

Mueller was in no hurry to deal with this unimportant matter, but Eberstein, a relic of 1928 when the SS had been baronial and quite respectable in relation to the hungry rowdy SA, made some inquiries. He was assured by Major General von Saur that he and his camp commanders supported Meinel's action. Schurmer and Schimmel— somehow these names seem to have been created by nature for two Gestapoists—switched their attack to von Saur. They discovered that of the 474 men at Moosburg, who had been screened, only 301 had been delivered for execution. Furthermore at a camp near Regensburg, which was also under von Saur's command, the Gestapo had received only thirty men out of 244 who had been screened as intolerable. On 23rd January 1942, Schimmel made a report to the deputy commander of the Security Service in Bavaria, enclosing a note from von Eberstein which declared that he saw no reason why these men should be screened a second time over, the implication being that the Security Service could dispose of them forthwith.

On 16th January, Meinel had actually refused to hand over any more men to the Regensburg Gestapo Office. He declared to the commissioner, whose name was Popp, that he had received instructions over the telephone from OKW, forbidding him to do so. Was this bluff or was Meinel really receiving some support against the Gestapo from his superiors? It was a fact that soon after the massive executions in the German concentration camps had began, Rosenberg had been induced to forward a protest to Keitel. As a result, on 10th October 1941, the heads of Rosenberg's Political Department, Leibbrandt and Braeutigam, were invited to meet Reinecke and Mueller. The Ministry of Labour, having some interest in the prisoners, sent a *Ministerialrat*, a certain Herr Letsch. None of these wartime civil servants belonged to an inner circle of SS secret-bearers, yet Mueller told them with the greatest frankness that he had already screened 20,000 Russian prisoners and that 16,000 had been executed. Nevertheless Reinecke declared in Mueller's presence that in future Russian prisoners, who were needed for special labour in Germany, would not have to be screened. This may explain why there was no ruling from Mueller's office after Schimmel's letter of 13th December.[54] But the sequel will show that the end of the reign of terror by the screening teams was not even within sight.

Twelve days after Meinel's bold action in Regensburg, on 28th January, Schurmer was still without instructions from the Gestapo head office in Berlin, so he wrote to Mueller that the number of Russian prisoners, whom Meinel was protecting, had risen to 400 and that Meinel had grouped them in labour detachments. There was still no answer from Berlin. On 9th February, Mueller's deputy, Colonel Panzinger, received a telephone call from von Eberstein. This time there was no pigeon-holing. Reinecke's instructions were issued three days later and on the same day von Saur reported both to the Munich Gestapo and to von Eberstein that the 400 men would be screened again by the Security Service. The tragedy ended on the 17th, when Panzinger instructed the Munich office to deliver all the men to Buchenwald camp for execution.

None of these documents was brought up against von Eberstein, the Nuremberg witness who pretended he had spent his war on the shelf as a dear old gentlemen, though all this happened when he was forty-seven years old. He was asked to explain a lot of things about which he knew nothing—that is why the SS chose him as their witness—but he was not asked about his own particular contribution, the death of 400 Russian prisoners of war.[55]

But let us revert for a moment to the Munich Gestapo report of 15th November 1941, and to that curt allusion to forty-seven incurably sick, who were screened as intolerable and ripe for execution. How did that come about? There was nothing in Hitler's original Commissar Order which authorized the execution of invalid prisoners. But then for that matter there was never any written decree, authorizing the massacre of Jews and Gipsies, the killing of the insane in German asylums and the liquidation of unproductive persons in the concentration camps. Theoretically all these practices could have been challenged at law, though they never were challenged.

In all these cases the device by which busybodies were kept at bay—and it was never the very high-placed who constituted themselves busybodies—was the pretence of an invisible decree. At a conference of prisoner of war officers in December 1941, General Graewitz, the head of the SS medical services and director of Himmler's infamous human guinea-pig experiments, declared that there ought to be an order, enabling medical officers to kill off incurable Russian prisoners. A member of Graewitz's audience believed that Reinecke's office issued instructions soon afterwards, authorizing murder by phenol injections,[56] but no written copy of such instructions has survived.

There was no need for Reinecke to issue such instructions. For months past, invalid Russians, whom the Wehrmacht could not be troubled to feed, had been dealt with in concentration camps by phenol injections, by the Sachsenhausen *Genickschuss* apparatus and by gassing. The first experimental use of the notorious cyanide gas, *ZyklonB*, had been made by Rudolf Hoess at Auschwitz on 15th September and the subjects had been 600 invalid Russian prisoners of war and some of the sick from the camp.[57] No decrees were needed for this sort of thing, since the High Command had utterly renounced the rights of the Wehrmacht in areas under civil government. Minor Gestapo officials in Germany could do what they liked with the hostages of the German soldier's famous *Ehre*.

Yet in other directions the powers of the Gestapo were singularly circumscribed. As several memoirs and biographies of members of the German 'Resistance' show, the Gestapo was often powerless or unwilling to proceed against the circle of high-placed German plotters. It was otherwise with the *Untermensch*, who could be turned over to the SS through a nod or a telephone call. These powers were used on Russians, even while the majority of the High Command supported an appeal for a National Russian Liberation Army. And at a time when every sort of political promise was being made to induce Russians to desert, the Gestapo in Russia was still murdering wounded prisoners.

The subject may be studied from a second captured file which tells a complete story. The time was the end of 1942, when General Vlasov had already been permitted to publish Russian political manifestos with the blessing of the commanders of German army groups. The place was Zhitomir in the Ukraine. The front was falling back but it was still hundreds of miles away. The commander of a local Stalag, an officer of the Wehrmacht not of the SS, had transferred seventy-eight disabled Russian prisoners to what was called an SS education camp, in reality a punishment camp for unmanageable prisoners of war. The court of inquiry could find no motive for this transfer, except for the fact that these men, all of whom had lost a limb and some of them two limbs, were not wanted by the camp commander. There was no communist record against any of them. They were employed in the 'education camp', in so far as it was possible to employ them, as hospital orderlies, but on 23rd December ten of them had already died.

The execution of the remaining sixty-eight men was ordered, not by the Security Service commander of the district but by his deputy and, but for the unforeseen event which followed, the deputy's action would presumably have been approved and no court of inquiry would have followed. The deputy, Captain Kallbach, had the men driven off in carts to a quiet spot outside the camp. Four NCOs of the SS were detailed to conduct the shooting. All four were experienced executioners, for they had taken part in the famous Kiev massacre of September 1941. One NCO, however, asked to be relieved of the task on the grounds that three men would be quite enough to handle the situation and Kallbach had relieved him. The first group of twenty men gave no trouble. They had no legs. But with the second group of twenty-eight, who could move after a fashion, it was different. It was thought that they had been warned by the Ukrainian cart-drivers. Somehow these pathetic Russians disarmed two of the SS men and shot them. The third SS man succeeded in killing six Russians, the rest got away.

Kopp, the Security Police Commander, had the last group of twenty shot on Christmas day. He believed that the fugitives had warned the Partisans, who were now very active and had even appeared on the once safe motor road between Berdichev and Zhitomir. So he took no chances. The unknown Stalag commander, the gentleman from the Wehrmacht, sent a guard of twenty men with light machine guns and the execution took place without incident.[58]

That was at the end of 1942 and yet most of the generals, who gave evidence at Nuremberg, maintained that the Commissar Order had become a dead-letter within a few months of the invasion, but, as we have seen, the scope of the order had been vastly extended on the initiative of mere subordinates. The reason why this happened must be understood properly, because Commissar Orders and their equivalents are not just a nightmare from the past, but a menace for the future. There are totalitarian states, where the Security Police may even now acquire too free a hand as guardians of a cast-iron ideology. At the same time it must not be forgotten that the Commissar and 'Barbarossa' Jurisdiction Orders were carried out in a state which hated the Commissar system so much that it could do even worse. Dictatorship had been chosen by the people of Germany in their fear of communism. It was by no means a watertight dictatorship. There were times when the very expression must have seemed the hollowest of mockeries in the chaos that went on. But, however ill-rooted it may be, dictatorship means the suspension, be it here be it there, of some of the safeguards of human existence. It is a bill that is commonly paid by the least articulate.

CHAPTER FOUR

THE EASTERN MINISTRY AND THE BALTIC STATES

(a) Rosenberg and his Ministry

As FAR BACK as March 1941, Hitler had intended that a large part of occupied Russia should be administered by civilian Commissars. Their duty was to create the political conditions for the new Russian separatist states, which were to be permitted after the *Blitzkrieg*.* It was not intended that the Commissars should remain in the country for any length of time. Himmler's police were to secure the territory from all forms of resistance, while the Commissars and their staffs carved out new constitutions. Then they would have to go.

During the next three months this conception changed radically. It was not that Hitler calculated on a longer war, but he wanted a longer period of thorough German occupation after the war in order to carry on his policies of exploitation and colonization. This new conception deprived the *Reichskommissars* of the independence of action which they would otherwise have had. Instead of being responsible to Hitler, they were made responsible to a special ministry with elaborate co-ordinating departments. Such was the origin of perhaps the least satisfactory of Hitler's wartime government departments, the Eastern Ministry or *Ostministerium*, known in abbreviation as OMI or derisively as the *Chaosministerium*. In July 1941, when the Ministry was formed, it was obvious that its head would be Alfred Rosenberg because from the beginning of April Hitler had given him the task of dividing Russia into Commissariats and preparing a draft plan for their government.

But why had Hitler chosen Rosenberg in the first place? No doubt Rosenberg liked to think that, as the head of the Foreign Political Section of the Party (APA), he was the leading expert on foreign policy, though unfortunately he remained outside the Foreign Office;

* See pp. 67–9

that as a Russian-born German he was the Party's expert on Russian affairs; that as the author of *The Myth of the Twentieth Century* he was the official exponent of National Socialist doctrine as applicable to all Europe. In reality Hitler chose Rosenberg because he was the one-time deputy leader of the Party and he owed him a job. Also, in the discredit into which Rosenberg had fallen, this was the least important job he could give him, and Hitler saw to it that it remained unimportant. No German minister was worse treated. From the beginning Rosenberg was not intended to play the part of a true Governor-General for Russia. His authority was clipped by the independence of Himmler's Security Police organization in occupied territory, by the large areas which were left to military government and by the detachment of the spheres of economic exploitation and manpower as an appanage of Goering's Four-Year-Plan Office, acting in conjunction with the Wehrmacht.

Nevertheless in his day Rosenberg had been second in importance in the Party only to Hitler and in 1924 he had taken over the Party management, when Hitler was in prison. In later years Hitler spoke of Rosenberg with undisguised contempt. He would speak of him as a half-Russian by origin, who wanted to be a Russian rather than a German. Yet in the early days Hitler owed much of his anti-communist zeal to Rosenberg's Russian-tinted influence. In physical appearance Rosenberg was almost completely Russian, though it would be hard to say why this was so. Rosenberg's memoirs are reticent on the subject of his mother's family. One gathers only that she had the German forename of Elfriede and that her father owned a dyeing works. Ernst Dwinger thought that she was Latvian.[1] Alfred Rosenberg's father, Woldemar Rosenberg, was a modest German tradesman of Reval in Estonia, where he himself was born in 1893. Reval had a more Russian atmosphere than most of the Baltic towns which owed their first colonization to Germans, but the class from which Rosenberg sprang—the Baltic Germans of the old Russian Empire—had a less Russian outlook than the Baltic German nobility, 'the Baltic Barons', who were allied by marriage with Russian noble families. The extreme aversion to Estonian, Latvian and Lithuanian home rule, which Rosenberg showed as Minister, was less typical of the Baltic Barons than of the Baltic German middle classes, who had not rid themselves of their colonist background. But Rosenberg's hatred of the rule of Moscow was something quite different. Like Hitler's, his nature was of a thwarted artistic kind. The very thin veneer of the arts, as practised in

Imperial Russia, had impressed him deeply as a student in Riga and Moscow. He saw the Bolsheviks as the destroyers of these arts.

A more unsuitable chief of occupation affairs cannot be imagined. On the one hand Rosenberg hated the pure Russians, whom in his belief the revolution had turned into Asiatics by destroying the Germanized upper crust. On the other hand he had a parochial dislike of the non-German races in those north-western parts of the Russian Empire which he knew from childhood. Only in the Ukraine, of which he knew very little, was he prepared to recognize an old culture, which had not been altogether extinguished by the revolution and which entitled the country to independence. But even if these prejudices were not sufficient in themselves to wreck Rosenberg's chances of producing a reasonable policy, his intellectual defects made it quite certain.

Alfred Rosenberg bequeathed his appearance to posterity without reticence, for he had the Nazi fondness for facing the camera. Generally he was photographed in an imitation military uniform, which created an incongruous effect. Although twenty-one years old at the outbreak of the First World War, Rosenberg had never soldiered in his life. From 1914 to 1918 he pursued his artistic and architectural studies in Riga and Moscow. After the war, Rosenberg came to Munich and settled down to be a German, but he was to make some acquaintance with international Bohemian life in Paris and he was not naturalized until 1923.[2] Rosenberg in later years may have ranked himself among the small and trying company of artists, revolutionary and militant, which had included David, Courbet and William Morris in the last century, D'Annunzio, Paderewski and Hitler in the present. Yet the pictures of the uniformed Rosenberg, posing before the camera in the days of power, suggest not a militarized Bohemian so much as a heavy-footed NCO, trying to hold down a desk-job for which he is not suited. There is a look of loutish bewilderment about him.

Between Rosenberg's physical appearance and his record as a minister there is a certain concordance and consistency. As the practical administrator, it was Rosenberg's task to mitigate the unworkable idiocies which were passed on to him, allegedly from the lips of Hitler, through the offices of Bormann and Lammers. Yet, had it depended on Rosenberg alone, he would never have mitigated them at all. Time and again Rosenberg simply parroted Hitler's original expressions. There would follow long appeals by officials of the Eastern Ministry to Rosenberg, the philosopher, the humanist and the student of ancient civilization. And then, painfully and reluctantly, Rosenberg would try to wriggle out of his position. He was not an absolute nonentity, but he would have been one if fate had not landed him in such an interesting position. To find Rosenberg's real character it is not necessary to linger among his so-called philosophical works. The memoirs, which he wrote in Nuremberg prison, are less burdensome to read. In 1955 a Goettingen publishing house brought out a complete undoctored text, which has all the charm of immeasurable silliness. Here will be found Rosenberg's meditations on Goths and Dolmens, on Catharians and the Albigensian heresy, meditations in the midst of total defeat.[3] Here will be found the biographies of dull little men, the Nazis with whom Rosenberg remained on speaking terms until the end, Meyer, Mutsch-mann, Uiberreither and Schickedanz, designated Satraps with the mentality of town clerks.

When one considers the unpromising situation of Rosenberg in November 1918, a refugee from Russia living among fellow refugees in Munich, one can imagine him very well fulfilling a different career, most of the time in a cheap Parisian Left Bank Hotel. East European and heavily overcoated in appearance, one sees him enjoying a café reputation, despite the dullness of his eyes, as a genius who will one day produce a book of monumental and world-shaking obscurity.

The trick of fate which made Rosenberg's career different was his acquaintance with Hitler. Shortly after the 1918 armistice, Rosenberg met, through his dancer wife, a romantic proto-fascist called Dietrich Eckart, who wrote poems that were not without merit and who ran a Munich anti-semitic journal, called *Auf gut' Deutsch*. Eckart gave this displaced Russo-German, this twenty-six-year old perpetual student, some articles to write and, though not until the end of 1919, introduced him at Hitler's meetings. In February 1923, when Eckart's magazine *Voelkische Beobachter* was expanded to become the Party's daily news-paper, Rosenberg became editor, supplanting and mortally offending the drink-sodden and fast sinking Eckart.

Rosenberg was also permitted the rôle of Party Theorist. He had to make a system out of Hitler's not very consistent antagonisms to Jews, landlords, cartels, freemasons, priests, pacifists and trade unions. But it was not until October 1930, that he produced *The Myth of the Twentieth Century*, the official Party Gospel which Hitler never troubled to read. In the early twenties, however, Rosenberg's literary works were purely anti-semitic and 'White Russian' in character. He even reprinted the famous forgery, popular in emigré Russian circles, which was known as the 'Protocols of the Elders of Zion'. At that time Rosenberg was the link between Hitler and the Munich Tsarist refugees. In 1923 Rosenberg and his fellow Baltic-German, Scheubner-Richter, introduced Hitler to the Hetman Skoropadsky, the former head of the German-sponsored Ukrainian State. Skoropadsky is said to have helped to finance *der Voelkische Beobachter*, the first Nazi Party newspaper, and this may have had much to do with Rosenberg's passionate support of Ukrainian nationalism in 1941.[4]

Although Hitler never rid himself of some of the ideas peddled by Rosenberg, anti-semitism in particular, his political course parted company with the east European mystical conservatism of Rosenberg and the Munich Russian set. Rosenberg remained a theorist and was soon excluded from the hard-headed manœuvres which led to the seizure of power. He had some part in the plot to kidnap and coerce the Bavarian government in 1923 and he marched with Hitler in the November *Putsch*. But having failed signally to keep the Party together during the year that Hitler subsequently spent in prison, he slipped back into his position as editor of the Party newspaper. But even this found a rival in 1925 in Goebbels's newspaper, *Der Angriff*. Seventeen years later, when he had made Rosenberg Minister for the Occupied Eastern territories, Hitler still reviled him for his inadequacy as an editor.[5] After Goebbels had robbed him of the control of the Party press, Rosenberg's only supporter was his sub-editor, Arno Schicke-danz, whom he later proposed as governor of the Caucasus.[6]

It is therefore not surprising that after the seizure of power Rosenberg's rewards were small. In April 1933, he was made head of the Party's Foreign Political Office (APA). In fact Rosenberg had been encouraged to believe that he would be made State Secretary of the Foreign Office and that eventually he would succeed von Neurath as Foreign Minister.[7] If this had taken place, history might have demonstrated that a worse Foreign Minister than Ribbentrop was not an impossibility. Rosenberg did not give up hope, so long as Neurath held precariously to this post. Consequently the appointment of Ribbentrop in February 1938 was a grievous disappointment to him. In the meantime APA lost rather than gained influence. It was meant to be a foreign propaganda office rather than a policy-making body. Rosenberg began with a friendly mission to London in May 1933, which was adversely received in so far as it was noticed at all. Thereafter he was busy forming friendship organizations for the nations of the world, organizations which were intended to sell National Socialism. Even in this field, Rosenberg suffered from the rivalry of Ernst

Bohle's *Auslandsorganization* and of Goebbels's ministry of Propaganda, while till 1937 Hitler retained as private Foreign Press Chief one of his early patrons, the Munich art publisher Ernst Hanfstaengl, who was a jealous and embittered competitor. On one occasion only was Rosenberg able to play a part in Hitler's grandiose plans. This was in June 1939, when, at a meeting of a Nordic Society in Luebeck, Rosenberg discovered the pro-German ambitions of Vidkun Quisling and so helped to build up the German fifth column in Norway.[8]

Rosenberg was also charged with the 'spiritual and ideological supervision of the Party', but he never succeeded in making good his claim to a monopoly. If it was a matter of indoctrination courses, Robert Ley, the head of the Labour Front, was able to do the same thing more effectively through his Strength Through Joy holidays and through his *Ordensbuerge*, the training seminaries for shop stewards of the Party who were sent to the works and factories. So complete was Ley's victory that, during the occupation of Russia, the Rosenberg ministry had to pick most of its minor officials from the *Ordensbuerge*, while even the uniform they wore was made of the yellow-brown Labour Front material.[9]

Another section of ideological education was lost by Rosenberg to Himmler, who stole Rosenberg's own ideas in order to establish 'racial-biological schools' under the banner of the SS.[10] This last was a particularly fantastic piece of nonsense, but since the Second World War the pursuit of subjects that are not knowledge has attained far larger proportions than anything of the kind in Hitler's Reich. Sociology, social science, social psychology, public relations, consumer reactions, there is no limit to the letters-patent that are available to the modern articled pedant in the old world and the new alike. Most of the things that seemed far-fetched or ludicrous to foreigners during Hitler's Reich, no longer sound even funny today. To the youngest generation the words Strength Through Joy, no longer sound like a music-hall joke. In such a world of spurious generalizations, false inferences and mass-slogans Rosenberg could have stayed, immured for life and reasonably happy, so long as there were no administrative responsibilities. Thus, on 28th March 1941, on the eve of his new mission, Rosenberg could hardly have been more congenially occupied. He was presiding at an international conference on the Jewish Question. This joyous bevy of mid-European and professorial anti-semites gathered daily at the Frankfurt *Buergersaal*, dreaming of the orgy of racial murder that was to come.[11]

On 31st March, while the Frankfurt conference was still in session, Hitler put Rosenberg in charge of a Political Office for the East, whose mission it was to draw up those civilian areas of government in Russia, which Hitler had mentioned to his generals on the previous day. On 20th April, the name of this office was changed to 'Central Department for the Treatment of Eastern Questions.' On 17th July, it became a Ministry.

Rosenberg only learnt of his first assignment on 2nd April, and he seems to have provided Hitler with an outline of his views on the same day.[12] This draft, 'memorandum no 1', was made at a moment when Rosenberg did not realize the proposed limitations of his own power and when it was purely a question of a theoretical plan, based on the assumed rapid conquest of all Russia.[13] Separatist States were outlined for White Russia, the Ukraine, the Cossack lands, the Caucasus and even Turkestan. An enormous area, comprising the Baltic States and the former Polish provinces, was reserved for colonization by Germans, Scandinavians, Dutchmen and Englishmen. The displaced population was to be received in a 'rump Russia' containing Moscow and the Urals, but even this area was to be smaller than the present Russian Soviet Republic. The White Russian or White Ruthenian State would reach as far east as Tver and the Cossack State as far as Saratov, though in both cases 'the awakening of a living state would be difficult and tedious.' The independent Ukraine would include the Crimea and parts of Kursk and Voronezh. The Ukraine would be allowed a greater degree of sovereign power than the other secession states. This would enable Germany to keep the balance of power, should the residual Russian State ever regain strength.

On 20th April, Hitler's birthday, Rosenberg was ordered to produce a far more detailed scheme for the future *Reichskommissariats*. On 9th May, he visited Hitler, armed with the final fruits of his various memoranda. The revised scheme was 'legitimist' in character, being based on Article 17 of the Soviet constitution of 5th December 1936, which gave the sixteen Soviet Republics the individual right to secede. Presumably Rosenberg thought this extremely ingenious, but he was not prepared for the change that had affected Hitler's outlook since his brief to the High Command on 30th March. Hitler no longer had any interest in the separatist states. There was no question of legitimizing new nations. The *Reichskommissariats* were a mere temporary device, pending the German colonization of the country.[14]

As a result of Hitler's objections, the Cossack State slipped out altogether, the Ukraine, though much increased in territory, was to be deprived of its links with Galicia and with Ukrainian Nationalism of the civil war period.[15] The Crimea and the Baku area were to be detached as German territory. With the Caucasus and its 'savage peoples' Rosenberg could do as he liked, but Turkestan, which was far beyond the Archangel-Astrakhan line as envisaged in the 'Barbarossa' plan, could be left in Hitler's view as a *cura posterior*.[16]

However deflated Rosenberg may have been by his reception on 9th May, the long discourse which he made to his staff on 20th June, two days before the invasion, shows that he still hoped to put his ideas into practice, particularly as regards the Ukraine.[17] Rosenberg declared that the freedom of the Ukrainian people must be a point in the political programme. The historical conscience of the Ukrainians must be revived with suitable literature, a German-approved university must be founded at Kiev and the Ukrainian language must be cultivated.[18]

The reason for this policy, which directly contradicted Hitler's words and which Hitler himself attacked four weeks later at Anger-burg, was explained by Rosenberg as follows. The nations of Russia had never produced their own leaders. Till 1917 the Russian Empire had been ruled by an aristocracy of Germans, who had been 'linguistic-ally slavized'. In Imperial times resistance against this class had pro-duced nothing but Nihilist or Liberal anarchy. As to the Soviet Revolution, it had replaced German leadership with a leadership that was Caucasian or Asiatic in character, and which had substituted world revolution for Pan-Slavism. The Ukrainians had in the past been incapable of achieving a nationality, but now they must be helped to do so, because only in this way was the Soviet 'Many Nations State' to be destroyed.

Peter Kleist, who listened to Rosenberg's address on 20th June, describes his Cloud Cuckoo Land proposals for the true Russians or Great Russians. They were to be evacuated eastwards, away from the Ukraine, White Russia, the Baltic States, the Crimea and Caucasus, a task which would require the strongest characters. 'Perhaps this decision may be approved by the future Russians in thirty or maybe a hundred years, because in the divided Russia of the past 200 years the Russians could find no outlet either east or west. If we close the west to the Russians, they may become conscious of their own inbred force and conscious of the area to which they belong. In hundreds of years' time a historian may see this apparent brutality in a different light from that of the Russians of today.'[19] And Rosenberg went on to say that the Germans were not enemies of the Russian people. The Russian could be very likeable and able to assimilate Western culture, but he lacked the force of character of the west European. 'Our fight for re-organization is conducted entirely in line with the right of national self-determination of peoples.'

More than any of his numerous speeches, Rosenberg's address of 20th June 1941, illustrates why he failed to impose any policy that could counteract the out-and-out nihilism of Adolf Hitler. The address reveals that the inhumanity of Rosenberg's ill-expressed ideas was hardly less total than the inhumanity of Hitler and Bormann. But Rosenberg remained an unimpressive person who might just as easily have stayed a shabby Bohemian character in an astrakhan collar, perpetually writing a book, whereas Hitler had possessed for more than twenty years a mesmeric faculty of creating fear, and Rosenberg was no match for him. Hitler was a bad talent-spotter, sometimes deliberately. Only two of his wartime ministers, Goebbels and Albert Speer, were men of outstanding ability. In most cases Hitler wanted men who feared violence as much as they loved the thought of it and who, even when Hitler refused to make a decision himself, would go to any length not to make a decision on their own.

Such men were Ribbentrop and Rosenberg, whom Hitler deliberately made great in order to hamstring them. When he created the Eastern Ministry, Hitler ensured that the future governers of Russia would be either loyal friends of Rosenberg, willing to take his orders and therefore nonentities, or they would be outsiders who would be in perpetual conflict with the minister. Nevertheless Rosenberg's original list for these appointments, dated 7th April 1941, was an attempt to compromise between the two alternatives.[20] For the future German-annexed province, which at this time Rosenberg still called the *Baltenland*, he proposed Heinrich Lohse. This was the Gauleiter of Schleswig-Holstein, who had presided over Rosenberg's Nordic Association and who was chosen because it was necessary to stress the historical Hanseatic background of the Baltic States.

This Lohse was the very essence of a Nazi small-town big shot, a gross, vain, silly man, whose walrus-like appearance explained what he was at first sight. For the Ukraine Rosenberg proposed his old sub-editor, Arno Schickedanz, because, as an official of APA, he had worked for twenty years in the 'Russian sphere'. Later Schickedanz was proposed for the Caucasus, while Herbert Backe, another Russian-born German, was substituted for the Ukraine.* For the Cossack State

* See pp. 296–9

which was to extend to the Volga, Rosenberg proposed the school-master Dietrich Klagges, author of numerous educational tracts and Minister President for Brunswick. For 'rump Russia' which was to include Leningrad as well as Moscow, he proposed the Gauleiter of East Prussia, Erich Koch, because an absolutely ruthless person was required. Out of this list, however, only Lohse and Koch were appointed.

How did Rosenberg come to put forward the name of his future bugbear, Erich Koch, of whose character he could be in no doubt? On 7th April no pressure had been put on Rosenberg by Hitler or by Koch's protector, Goering. Either Rosenberg regarded this appoint-ment as outside his sphere because he doubted that Moscow would be occupied, or he thought that the competence of his Ministry would not extend as far. At Angerburg, on 16th July, when it was a question of Koch governing either the Baltic States or the Ukraine, Rosenberg opposed the idea to the utmost.

Rosenberg wanted to be appointed 'Protector General' of the eastern territories and he wanted his administrators to be known as governors. But Hitler preferred to call Rosenberg a minister because the word 'protector' contained a suggestion of local liberties. As to the word 'governor', Hitler linked the German-adopted French word, *Gouverneur*, with a Russian term of Tsarist times, *Gouvernement*. The words *Reichskommissar*, *Generalkommissar*, *Landkommissar* and *Gebietskommissar* suggested the Bolshevik system; but this was not objectionable to Hitler, since the Commissar system was associated with fear and that was right because 'they ought to hate us like the plague'.[21]

Rosenberg estimated that he would need a staff of 5,000 and he wanted them to be given Field-Grey uniforms and military rank according to their duties, as members of an *Ostfuehrer Korps*. This too was turned down, because the High Command had already objected when Ribbentrop wanted to put the entire Foreign Office into Field-Grey.[22] Since there was a surplus of yellow-brown cloth which had been made for the Labour Front, this became the Eastern Ministry uniform, the garb of the 'golden pheasants' or *Goldfasanen*, as they were contemptuously known to the German soldier, the equivalent of the *Greenflies* in post-war occupied Germany. The yellow-brown uniform created a historical confusion. After the war, when the SA was indicted as a criminal organization, several witnesses from Russia testified in the Nuremberg witness-box to the brown-shirted appear-ance of their persecutors under the belief that the SA still functioned as an executive force, a thing it had not done since the murder of Roehm and his colleagues in June 1934.

In forming a policy-making staff in Berlin, Rosenberg met with the same difficulties as in recommending regional Commissars. For the higher grades he had to draw on the members of his own almost meaningless organization, the APA, or else embark in a competitive manhunt with Ribbentrop's Foreign Office, which had for some time ear-marked professorial experts for a Russian Committee of its own. In stealing a number of experts from Ribbentrop, Rosenberg gained one of his very few victories, but the personnel of his Eastern Ministry, first in the old Yugoslav Embassy in the Rauchstrasse and then in the Soviet Embassy on Unter den Linden, was not imposing. For his deputy, Rosenberg chose Alfred Meyer, Gauleiter of Westphalia, whose only merit seems to have been his love of ceremony. Meyer prided himself on having been the first Party Member to become an alderman.[23] At Muenster, his capital, Meyer kept a sort of court and waged an undignified fruitless struggle with a churchman of positively mediaeval determination, the Cardinal Archbishop Clemens von Galen. Meyer retained his position as Gauleiter, so that even in this second-rate figure Rosenberg only got half a man. Later on the pompous creature refused to accept the rank of Secretary of State as Rosenberg's deputy, because it was inferior to his own rank of *Reichstatthalter* for the little state of Lippe.[24]

Under Meyer there were four main departments with at least thirty subordinate offices. But only one department, the *Hauptabteilung Politik*, was important, because through its ten subdivisions it attempted to impose policy directions on the *Reichskommissars*. The resounding insuccess of this department will be studied later. Had Rosenberg's plans for his Ministry worked out properly, the Political Department would have governed occupied Russia by dictating the whole basis of relationship with the subjected population. But it was inevitable from the start that rule by theorists in Berlin would fail, irrespective of the disobedience of Commissars, whose courts were seven or eight hundred miles away. The organization of the Political Department belonged to the pre-campaign months when the future Ministry was still an advisory office. Turning it into an executive arm was a monstrosity.

Over the Political Department there hung a cloistral air of professorship and research. At its head was Georg Leibbrandt, who had returned to Germany in 1933 to direct an east European branch of APA. After studying in six universities of the Old World and the New, he had emerged a convinced National Socialist. But Leibbrandt was suspected as a person of cosmopolitan notions and was chased out of the Ministry in 1943.* During his two years with the Political Department he had never been the strong man of the office. It was Otto Braeutigam, Rosenberg's deputy and leader of Section I, who stood behind most of the memoranda and protests, which have attached a little credit to the memory of the helpless and in the end useless Political Department.

As a soldier at the time of the invasion, Otto Braeutigam was Rosenberg's Liaison Officer with the High Command. Previously he had held the office of German Consul in Kharkov, Batum and Tiflis. Braeutigam was not a professorial expert, but a forty-year-old reserve officer with a working knowledge of the Soviet system. His bitter sarcastic nature was not the kind to influence high policy, for that is a machinery which needs oil rather than vinegar. Nevertheless Braeutigam's wartime memoranda seem monuments of commonsense, even if their irony was misplaced at the time. His 'General View of the Occupied Eastern Territories', which has circulated in typescript since the war, is the most reliable work on the subject.[25] Braeutigam in 1941 adopted a position of liberal utilitarianism. He believed that, if the Germans announced themselves as liberators and not enslavers, the Russians would reject communism and set up some sort of pro-German government. He had no use whatever for the more romantic *Ostpolitiker*; neither future Russian Napoleons nor rival crusaders for Ukrainian nationalism were attractive to him.

Under Leibbrandt and Braeutigam there were ten group leaders in the Political Department, among whom two are worthy of notice. Peter Kleist, a former German sales agent in eastern Europe, had joined Ribbentrop's private Foreign Policy Bureau in 1936 and was one of Ribbentrop's appointments from the Party to the Foreign Office, from which he was released, together with his own staff, to take charge of the Baltic or *Ostland* section for Leibbrandt. An outspoken supporter of Baltic autonomy, Kleist claims to have been dismissed by Rosenberg. He returned to the bosom of Ribbentrop in 1943 and his book is partly concerned with a later diplomatic transaction with some alleged Russian peace agents in Stockholm.[26] As a liberal utilitarian with an unsentimental outlook, Kleist somewhat resembles Braeutigam, but his witty and waspish book is more tendentious and less accurate.

* See p. 217

The second group-leader worthy of notice is the Baltic German, Gerhard von Mende, who had charge of the section dealing with political directives for the Caucasus and the Russian Asiatic minorities. A Turcophile and a professor of philology, von Mende was one of the experts who were procured from the Foreign Office. Profiting from Hitler's fear of antagonizing Turkey, von Mende was able to create national committees and national legions for the minority races of the south. For a short time he gave some reality to the activities of the Political Department, but many quarters suspected him because of his friendships with emigrés from the Soviet Union. The military government officers of the High Command took good care to keep the professor out of the areas in which he was interested. Yet, even after these territories had been lost, von Mende's influence remained considerable. Till the end of the war he was a zealous champion of the eastern workers in Germany and a tireless opponent of the 'Great Russian' pretensions of the Vlasov committee.*

In their task of preparing instructions for the civil commissars in Russia, the members of the Political Department were hampered by their ignorance of Rosenberg's brief. The minister prepared several plans, had several interviews with Hitler between 2nd April and 22nd June 1941, but returned each time with curtailments of his original powers. When war broke out, Rosenberg still did not know the nature of the notorious 'Green File'. These instructions of the Economic Staff East, which were published on 1st June, meant that Goering had absolutely independent powers in Rosenberg's own area. On 22nd June, Braeutigam saw the orders on his first official visit to the headquarters of the General Staff at Mauerwald. On informing Rosenberg, he learnt that Hitler had not even bothered to tell him.[27] Effectively Hitler established Goering's position by decree on 29th June; on the other hand the powers of the police in occupied Russia were still an unknown quantity. The position of Himmler and Heydrich in relation to the Eastern Ministry was not established to the satisfaction of both sides till September.[28]

Under the final plan, the Eastern Ministry had no control over Himmler's SS Police Leaders or Heydrich's Commanders of the Security Police and SD. Here, however, the area of conflict of authority was very small. Like the Military governors, the *Reichskommissars* and the officials of the Eastern Ministry had no wish to be involved with the doings of the Security Police. Very early in the day the chief pre-

* See p. 293

occupation of the latter, the murder of Jews and suspected communists, had been clearly defined by Hitler. Rosenberg was no critic of the 'Final Solution of the Jewish Problem'. On the contrary he was the first laureate of the state of mind that inspired it. But he was glad to wash his hands of its practical application. He does not seem to have regarded the massacres and the state of uncertainty which they induced in the population as an obstacle to peaceful administration. Rosenberg never forwarded a single protest to Hitler on the subject, though there was some interference by Wilhelm Kube, the *Generalkommissar* for White Russia, whose appointment, strange to say, was made by Hitler against Rosenberg's wishes.*

It was not till four weeks after the opening of the campaign that Hitler decided to co-ordinate the various plans for an Eastern Ministry, while the decree establishing the first two *Reichskommissariats* was not issued till 20th August and even then it was not published. According to Braeutigam, Hitler originally wanted to give these appointments resonance by announcing the occupation of Leningrad and Moscow at the same time. The press announcement was therefore delayed till 17th November, while the stormy personalities of Lohse and Koch were only known to the newspaper-public a month later.[29]

Before his department was made a Ministry, Rosenberg was summoned to a conference in Hitler's special train at Angerburg on 16th July. The minutes were kept by Martin Bormann, a piquant document abounding with quotations and asides that were clearly not meant for the eye of posterity.[30] Since the conference lasted from three in the afternoon till eight, it must have been even more disputatious than the minutes suggest. In addition to Hitler and Rosenberg, Keitel, Goering, Lammers and Bormann were present.

Hitler began with a long pronouncement of policy which can be contrasted with his talk to Keitel four months earlier. Hitler had then described a Russia divided into militarily weak socialist states. Now, after the military successes of the first twenty-five days, it was no longer clear whether the Russians would be allowed any sovereignty at all. 'Every successor of the Fuehrer should know that security for the Reich exists only if there are no foreign military forces west of the Urals.' Yet though 'we ourselves must know clearly that we shall never leave those countries', the fact was not to be advertised to the world. The Germans should act as though they had a temporary mandate, simply to preserve order and security. Under cover of this pretence,

* See pp. 156–7 and Thorwald, p. 29

Hitler told his chiefs that they could proceed with 'the shooting and resettling, necessary for the final solution.' But no one should be able to recognize what this solution was to be. It seems that the British occupation of India, as Hitler saw it, was a possible model.* Certain territories were to become German immediately, the Baltic States, the Crimea, the Baku region, the German Volga Republic and the Kola peninsula. Leningrad was to be razed to the ground and the site given to Finland, Rumania would recover Bessarabia and gain a strip which included Odessa.

Rosenberg tried vainly to put his claim for favoured treatment for the Ukraine. That the Ukraine would lose Galicia and the Crimea he already knew, but now he became involved in an argument with Goering, who considered that the terms of his economic dictatorship entitled him to appoint *Reichskommissars* over Rosenberg's head. Although the appointment of Lohse for the Baltic States had already received Hitler's approval, Goering wanted the substitution of Erich Koch or, failing that, the appointment of Koch to the Ukraine, for which Rosenberg now proposed Gauleiter Sauckel of Thuringia. Finally Hitler decided on Lohse for the Baltic and Koch for the Ukraine. These were the only *Reichskommissars* ever to be appointed, though for future contingencies Hitler decided also on Siegfried Kasche for Moscow, Alfred Frauenfeld for the Crimea, Terboven for the Far North and Schickedanz for the Caucasus, the last being strongly opposed by Goering. A host of obscure and unworthy candidates—one of them was rejected as insane—were proposed for the *Generalkommissariats*, which would be at least the size of provinces. It was apparently thought that anyone would do for these.**

After the coffee-interval, Hitler remarked that Europe was nothing but a geographical term. In reality 'Asia extends to our previous frontiers'. On the strength of this pronouncement, with which no one was disposed to argue, it was decided to call the Baltic States the *Ostland* or Eastern Land, the proposal having come from Rosenberg, who was so anxious to obliterate the past that he substituted 'White Ruthenia' for White Russia and even 'Holmgard' for Novgorod.[31] The word 'Eastern' became in fact a substitute for 'Russian' or 'Soviet'. It is doubtful whether the word 'Eastern' had been previously more than faintly derogatory among Germans. As a nasty expression, equivalent

* Even after experiencing a first winter campaign in Russia, Hitler could still tell Goebbels in March 1942 that he expected to rule Russia as the British ruled India. See p. 24
** See p. 188

to 'sub-human', it derived from the parochial racialist movements which Hitler had known before the First World War in Vienna. The conference copied this expression with the same ease that it copied Hitler's personality. It is astonishing how often shooting was mentioned that afternoon. Hitler included shooting as a necessary measure and welcomed Partisan warfare as a means of wiping out 'all who are opposed to us'. Goering wanted to 'shoot anyone who even looked sideways'. Field Marshal Keitel, the faithful echo, said that the inhabitants would have to be shot if they did not perform their duties properly. The only one who did not propose shooting anyone at all was Hans Lammers, Chief of the Reich Chancellery. Possibly Lammers was too busy thinking out the appropriate decrees. Unlike the other five members of the conference, Lammers came to no violent end. Having spent six years in allied internment camps and prisons, he is still alive and rising eighty.

(b) The Ostland

AFTER THE CONFERENCE in his train at Angerburg, it may be said that Hitler dismissed the matter of governing Russia as something of little consequence, with which he would not be troubled, so long as he had a war on his hands. It was a matter of making a virtue of postponement. All sorts of offers and promises could be made to the native population, provided there was no interfering with government by martial law and no interfering with the maximum exploitation of the country.

From his civil-government officials Hitler kept himself in Purdah. Rosenberg himself was not able to see Hitler more than half a dozen times during the two years following the meeting at Angerburg, and after November 1943, when very little Soviet territory remained in German hands, not at all. For others concerned with the government of occupied territory, it was even more difficult. Erich Koch may have reported to Hitler once or twice in secret. Otherwise an appointment could only be secured through the good offices of the chiefs of the Party and Reich Chancelleries, Bormann and Lammers, and this bordered on the impossible. A very few were able to see Hitler personally through Hitler's favourite entertainer, Walter Hewel, whose position was peculiar. Hitler disliked the company of Ribbentrop, who held court twenty-five miles away at Mauerwald, but he liked to have about him the portly, genial ex-planter from Sumatra who acted as

Ribbentrop's messenger-boy. Sometimes Hewel used his position to influence High Policy in the direction of commonsense, but he was lazy and unambitious and he rarely tried to break the cordon of holiness, which Martin Bormann maintained round Hitler and which gave Hitler's East Prussian Headquarters the atmosphere of the Byzantine or Chinese Imperial courts.*

It was Bormann who opposed any kind of innovation in the handling of occupied Russia, since his own views were even cruder and more brutal than Hitler's.** He took care that no experts on Russia resided at the peculiar court which grew up in Hitler's wired compound. Rosenberg's permanent liaison officer, Dr Werner Koeppen, was no more than a titled postman who wanted to be relieved of his office, because he had nothing to do. The very experienced staff of Schulenburg's former embassy were not given even advisory posts after their return to Germany. When Hitler wanted to know the meaning of a caption beneath a picture in a Russian magazine, Bormann had to send over to Ribbentrop's headquarters for an expert.[32]

Hitler's Headquarters, known as the *Wolfsschanze* or Wolf's Lair, were near Rastenburg in East Prussia. They were something out of this world. Spiritually as well as physically the clearing in the deep Masurian forests, from which Hitler directed his war, was an inaccessible sanctuary; or rather it was a sanctuary within a sanctuary. For, after the dismissal of Franz Halder in September 1942, Hitler ate all his meals by himself and insisted on the presence of an army of stenographers when he spoke to members of the General Staff and High Command.[33] The camouflaging of the Wolf's Lair was made so efficient that the roofs created no shine, even when seen from an aeroplane flying at 200 feet, and Hitler owed it that he met the assassin's bomb of 20th July 1944 in a flimsy hut and not in a lethal crypt to the fact that the roof of his deep shelter, in which he practically lived, was being increased at the time from a thickness of four metres to seven.[34]

This was the mole-like Xanadu from which Hitler directed an empire which at one moment extended from the Pyrenees to the Caspian, from the North Cape to the Western Desert. Hitler was immersed in strategy. Apart from strategy, it was rarely that a question penetrated to the inner shrine of the oracle and more rarely still that a decision emerged.

* Peter Kleist, op. cit., pp. 221–4, describes how Hewel procured him an interview with Hitler in June 1943.
** For a dazzling specimen of Bormann's views, see p. 200

On 25th July 1941, the High Command handed over to Rosenberg's Ministry all Lithuania, as well as Latvia as far as the river Dvina. The great city of Riga was still excluded, but Gauleiter Lohse, who established his first capital in Kovno or Kaunas, sent his *General-kommissar* to Riga before the High Command were ready for him. Yet actually the High Command were glad to be relieved of the responsibility. Local commanders had encouraged local administrations without any regard to Hitler's sweeping plans and it was the Rosenberg Ministry's task to replace these administrations with Germans. And plenty would be needed.

Before moving off from Kovno to the Ukraine, the staff of General Karl von Roques, the Rear Area Commander, had an opportunity of watching the first descent of the *Goldfasanen*, whose appetite for offices and hotels, furniture, provisions and drink was to become as famous as Lohse's own passion for issuing trivial decrees.[35] The difficulties that lay ahead were far beyond the experience of this rubicund exponent of small-town politics. Under his rule there was to take place the Germanization of Lithuania, Latvia and Estonia; yet barely twelve months had passed since the three countries had made their last fight for a sovereignty that they had enjoyed for the past twenty years. Though they had lost their independence through Hitler's deal with Stalin, the three states still looked to Hitler's armies to restore it for them. Though using languages that did not belong to the European family, their political leaders were nevertheless nearer to the German way of life than to the Russian, and were in the majority not attracted to communism. Latvia and Estonia, if not Lithuania, would have made faithful military allies if left alone. Germanization, already an ancient process on this side of the Baltic, could well have been allowed to resume its course when the fortunes of war had been decided. In any event the three small republics would have stayed inexorably interlocked with Germany's fortunes.

But already, before Lohse's arrival in Kovno, the Wehrmacht had disbanded a new cabinet, formed by a former Lithuanian minister in Berlin.[36] This was in pursuance of Hitler's strict orders. Not only was there to be no return to native non-communist government, but even the restoration of private property was to be delayed, so long as the recently applied collectivism of the Russians offered a chance of getting more produce from the country than the growers could normally spare. Precisely as if these territories had always been Russian, they were to be treated according to the recipe of Goering's 'Green File', that is to say as objects of plunder. Eventually concessions had to be made, both on behalf of private property and regional autonomy, but at the moment of invasion, ministry policy was dominated by the fact that Rosenberg, a German, born in Estonian Reval, wanted to see the country part of Germany. With Rosenberg this was a form of sentimentalism, with Hitler it was pure cynicism. The Munich Agreement and the collapse of Czechoslovakia had convinced him that the day of the small buffer states had passed. In the secret protocols of August and September 1939, Hitler had readily concurred with Stalin's wishes that there should be no return to independence in Poland. Still more significantly Hitler had signed for the total Russianization and Sovietization of the Baltic States by permitting and virtually compelling the repatriation of the ancient German-speaking population to the Reich. This repatriation was still in progress on 22nd June 1941. Henceforward Hitler wanted to reverse the machinery. It was the Germans who were to come back and the Russians who were to leave. The purpose of the native Lithuanians, Latvians and Estonians was simply to be milked by both occupants in turn.

In fact the machinery was not reversed. If, compared with the Ukraine, the Baltic States got milder treatment at German hands, it was because it was too difficult under war conditions to bring back the resettled racial Germans, let alone bring in the north European immigrants with whom Hitler and Rosenberg wanted to repopulate the country. It was also too difficult to impose a uniform policy. The Estonians were found to be thoroughly pro-German and eager to fight the Red Army, the Latvians almost as eager though more penetrated by Russian influence, but Lithuania, though nearest to Germany, was on a different footing. Only a few towns, apart from Kovno, contained a strong pro-German element, while Vilna was mainly Polish in population and anti-German in sentiment. The Lithuanian middle class was largely Jewish, while the peasants were primitive small-holders with a well-grounded suspicion for both houses. Lithuania was comparable with White Russia, which Hitler included in the *Ostland* not because it was ripe for Germanization but because it was a poor, thinly populated region, which would serve as a dumping ground for those who were not worthy of assimilation.

During the first days of the German occupation, a nationalist group in Kovno assisted the German SD in organizing a pogrom of the Jews, only to find that, apart from such unexceptionable antics, outlets for nationalism were not encouraged.[37] Henceforward Lithuania provided police troops to deal with the ghettoes and the insurgent Poles, but it became no reservoir for the Wehrmacht. In the end Lithuania showed its essential difference from Latvia and Estonia by harbouring great numbers of Red Army Partisans.

With the occupation of all three capitals, even the staff collected by Lohse became insufficient for the completely German administration which was set up in Riga. Nor was Lohse able to do without the 'native administrations' which had been set up by the Wehrmacht. At the end of September 1941, Hitler himself gave a decision in their favour and they were permitted in some sort to remain, though there were exceptions.[38] In Lohse's own capital at Riga there were five competing German authorities. There was Lohse himself, the *Reichskommissar* of the entire *Ostland*, there was Herr Drexler, the *Generalkommissar* for Latvia; there was a *Gebietskommissar* for the province of Livonia and an *Oberbuergermeister* for the city of Riga, who was a German acquaintance of Rosenberg. There was also a German chairman of the City Council, and perhaps one should add, a German Ghetto Commissar for some 15,000 Jews who were permitted to survive till the summer of 1943.[39]

The *Oberbuergermeister* refused to work with the native administration, because he considered Riga to be a German town. In this matter he was supported by Rosenberg himself, who had studied architecture in Riga in 1917, when, most appropriately, he had won a diploma for designing a crematorium. The dispute was the cause of one of many fights between Lohse and the Political Department, which led to the dismissal of the Political Department's *Referent*, Peter Kleist, who opposed Lohse. Kleist argued that Riga could not be treated as a German town because, since the repatriation of the native Germans and the flight of the Russians, it had become a 100 per cent Latvian town.[40] To this, however, Lohse had a counter-argument. During the twelve months of Soviet rule the GPU had removed the official classes from the Baltic States, 'down to the village schoolmaster and postmaster.' Therefore only Germans could replace them.[41] Kleist has written a most entertaining book, but he seems to have lacked the tact for handling the new class of Satraps. He pointed out to the puffing, exploding, neckless Lohse that the Germans in the east must be occupying at least two million square kilometres and that, even if 20,000 German officials were imported, they would amount to no more than a girl-typist or washerwoman to every hundred square kilometres, who would have to avoid all contact with the population. 'You did not have to be a Talleyrand to arrive at that political multiplication table.'*

It seems that Lohse was no Talleyrand. Though the fate of the individual in the *Ostland* was only in a very slight degree less arbitrary than it was in the rival Satrapy of Koch's Ukraine, many more German officials were required. There were 170 in Kovno with its 100,000 inhabitants. To unpick the strands of Soviet nationalization and collectivism, 25,000 German and Latvian officials were needed in Latvia alone, 7,000 of them in Riga.⁴² Immediately after the Stalingrad disaster, a manpower-pruning commission arrived in Riga, the *Heldengreif* staff of General von Unruh. It was proposed that each *Generalkommissar* should reduce his staff to 200 and each *Gebietskommissar* to twenty. The commission accomplished nothing and Lohse continued to send personal memoranda on the use of ink and rubber-erasers, continued to issue personally signed warnings against smoking in picture theatres, continued to regulate the maximum prices by weight for artificial silk rags.** Not only in England was the Second World War Bureaucracy's finest hour. National Socialism was a true child of its age and, as trade once followed the flag, so forms and regulations followed the knuckleduster, though throughout his life Hitler made fun of the small bureaucrat, as personified by his own father, the customs inspector of Linz.

Yet sheer lack of German manpower made it necessary to give some statutory authority to the three National Directorates or Native Self-Governments, which had existed since the occupation. In a decree of 7th March 1942 Rosenberg explained that the native appointments had still to be confirmed by the *Generalkommissars* and that the Directorates could decide nothing without their consent.⁴³ On 8th May, on the eve of his departure for Kovno and Riga, Rosenberg told Hitler that his decree was not binding. It was 'a historic alibi', showing that 'we have met the Baltic Nations more than half-way'.⁴⁴ But Rosenberg's journey was exploited by the Political Department to press for real concessions. Through Kleist, Rosenberg was persuaded to meet the Directorates and listen to their complaints. Lohse was enraged, but he

---

* Kleist's hypothetical figure (p. 158) of one German employee to a hundred square kilometres seems to have been very close to the mark. In the Ukraine, for instance, the 43,500 square kilometres of the *Generalbezirk*, Nikolaiev contained 500 German officials. (John A. Armstrong, *Ukrainian Nationalism*, 1939–45, p. 212)

** Peter Kleist, pp. 161, 165, 169. Lohse was at least not a cruel man, though he was too idle and selfish to prevent cruelty. For a short time he ventured to criticize the massacre of Jews, of which he was meticulously informed. In August 1942 he criticized the methods of Partisan warfare because of the effect on the harvest. See p. 242

did not dare, like Erich Koch in the Ukraine, to sever connections with a Ministry which dictated over his head. There was, however, a drunken scene on Rosenberg's train, when Alfred Meyer tried to reproach Lohse with pursuing an independent and self-seeking policy. Lohse admitted outright that he was working towards a 'ducal coronet for his newly-born son'.[45]

Rosenberg travelled back from Kovno to Germany a day ahead of his programme in order to attend the funeral of one of his small-town Nazi friends, Gauleiter Roever of Oldenburg. Next day the train, which should have carried Rosenberg through the Lithuanian countryside, ran into a mine which had been placed by Partisans. It was an apt commentary on ducal crowns.[46] It was also an indication of what might be expected, if these former sovereign states were not permitted their own armies. At Angerburg Hitler had said that only the Germans should be allowed to bear arms, but this was now less rigidly interpreted. Under the influence of Gottlob Berger, his chief of recruitment, Himmler began during the course of 1942 to take an interest in small national legions, which had been enlisted for home duties in Estonia and Latvia. Young Nordic types with Scandinavian or Germanic features, they responded perfectly to the new conception of the pan-Germanic SS, which had recruited Scandinavian volunteers as far back as November 1940. In fact the Latvians and Estonians were destined to provide some of the best SS divisions. But at present Himmler was warned that a general mobilization was impossible, because, in the absence of any independent sovereignty in Latvia and Estonia, the Red Army could claim the legal right to shoot captured Baltic SS volunteers as traitors.[47]

To add force to this argument, it became widely known in the summer of 1942 that Mr Churchill had been to Moscow and that the British had renounced their former guarantees of Baltic independence. Here then were two powerful inducements that might force even Hitler to approve a true autonomy statute. And, with the great German retreat from the Volga and Caucasus and the isolation of Stalingrad, these inducements became even stronger so that, in December 1942, Lohse himself undersigned a memorandum to Hitler. If the memorandum did not ask for much more in the way of immediate autonomy, at least it demanded a propaganda statement on future political plans.[48] At about the same time, Lohse half-agreed in a moment of good humour to a so-called autonomy statute, which had been drawn up by Kleist and by Burmeister, an official of the Ministry for Interior. But in

January 1943 Kleist was dismissed by Rosenberg for a too candid memorandum on a police reprisal-affair in now largely rebellious Lithuania.[49] Rosenberg grumbled, 'their own flags—that means an Irish rebellion.' But in February he forwarded the plan under the persuasions of his latest strong man, Gottlob Berger, whose chief, Himmler, had drawn up conscription plans for Estonia and Latvia. Under the plan, the three territories would become Protectorates or 'state entities', each with severely limited rights, a German resident and no diplomatic standing.[50]

Stalingrad was too fresh a writing on the wall for Hitler to repeat the orders of July 1941. He only rejected the plan to the extent of sending Lammers to inform Rosenberg that outright autonomy could not be promised the Baltic States. In fact Hitler turned a blind eye and the year 1943 saw a slight drift towards autonomy at least in internal affairs. And in the meantime complete autonomy was strongly supported by the *Generalkommissar* for Estonia, Karl Litzmann, a fifty-year-old regular cavalry officer, the son of the victor of Lodz in the First World War and like his father an ardent Nazi. Litzmann tried to enlist the support of Himmler as well as the High Command and he also approached the Foreign Office. Under his rule Estonia suffered little from Partisan outbreaks, produced an SS division and in the final collapse organized a national defence of her own frontiers.* Since Estonia had from the beginning enjoyed a condominium status as a military rear area, though governed by a civilian *Generalkommissar*, it was easier for Litzmann to defy Lohse than it was for his colleagues in Riga and Kovno.

Yet Estonia was never declared even nominally a State. The autonomy statute was dragged up again on November 1943, when Rosenberg attended the last interview Hitler bothered to grant him. Seeing that Hitler's mood was unfriendly, Rosenberg did not hesitate to abuse the plan that had once had his personal blessing. Though he could expect no further support from Rosenberg, Litzmann enlisted allies for the autonomy plan against Lohse. He won over General Friedrich Braemer, the Wehrmacht representative for the *Ostland* who held a rival court in Riga. He also won over Himmler's police leader for the *Reichskommissariat*, the SS General Franz Jaeckeln, whom the Russians hanged in the former Riga ghetto in February 1946. Another war-criminal who came out all for the freedom of Estonia was the Security Police commander in Reval (and later in Verona), the former

---

* *Memoirs of Felix Kersten*, English text, 1956, pp. 223–5 (differs totally from New York edition, 1947).

extermination group leader, Martin Sandberger. Officials with original
ideas, who needed friends in Hitler's Reich, could not afford to be too
particular.*

The status of the former Baltic States was now no longer a test case
of Germany's true intentions in Europe, the model for the New Order.
It was the sport of politicians with Lohse clinging hard to his future
ducal coronet and enlisting the aid of Martin Bormann against Himmler, the 'Uncle Heini' of Bormann's letters whom Bormann in reality
wanted to destroy. With Hitler the more uncompromising school of
flatterers as usual prevailed and, since this was the winning faction, the
dithering figure of Rosenberg identified himself with it. In February
1944 the ancient fortified Hanseatic town of Narva was bravely
defended against the Russians by the 7th SS Volunteer Corps, by
Estonian SS men fighting alongside SS troops of almost every north
European country. In SS circles this struggle is still regarded as a
symbol of the New Order in Europe which was fated not to be.[51] But
it was nothing of the kind. The Estonians fought for a gaping void to
save themselves from another gaping void. And while they fought,
a parallel engagement of equal severity was waged on paper. Lohse
plotted to make the *Ostland* independent of the Ministry, while Rosenberg plotted to govern the *Ostland* in person without the intermediary
of Lohse.

Finally at the end of July 1944 the Russians broke right through to
the Baltic Sea, west of Riga, and Lohse deserted his capital, a broken-
down man as he has been ever since. Erich Koch, a monarch now without a kingdom, was ordered to take Lohse's place early in September,
but Koch never went to the Baltic States. Parts of it were held and
administered by the Wehrmacht, while a small pocket of the Latvian
coast round Libau survived to the very end of the war.

There also survived a number of national committees, which comprised former members of the National Directorates of the Baltic
States, who were evacuated from place to place across the fast shrinking
German Reich. The National Committee for Latvia was in session in
Dresden on the night of the terrible bombing raid of 13th February
1945. Even at this late hour the National Committees played some part
in the game of court intrigue, which had taken the place of politics
in Germany. The separatist hopes of the committees were still encouraged by the Rosenberg Ministry and the Foreign Office, while on

* Dallin, p. 196, says that Braemer had his ears boxed by Lohse in public. Braemer had
been an SS Gruppenfuehrer.

the other hand they were bludgeoned by OKW, the SS and the Party Chancellery into supporting an army of Red Army deserters, with whom the Baltic Nations could have nothing in common.*

Could the fate of the three former Baltic republics have been any different? It is hard to believe that peace terms, whether drafted in Moscow or Berlin or even in London or Washington, would have guaranteed their survival. Yet during the three years' emancipation from Soviet rule, the treatment of the republics by the officials of the Rosenberg Ministry need not have been so hard. As the prospects of total victory faded, so there faded the huge project of 1941, the Germanization of the country. And once this had been forgotten, the treatment of the individual should have improved. But there was something else that never faded out at all and which the exigencies of war made worse, namely the temptation to extract the utmost possible from the country, whether in labour or material.

It began, when the German liberators were still receiving bouquets of flowers, with a decree of Lohse's dated 19th August 1941, confiscating all USSR property. Though it was a provisional measure which envisaged an ultimate return to private ownership, it affected all large business enterprises.[52] The country was invaded by a host of German companies, acting as public trustees. Factory-owners were reduced to hired administrators and in Kleist's words the *Generalkommissars* completed what the Russians had only begun.

Under Rosenberg's Agrarian Decree of February 1942, some progress was made in unpicking the very recent structure of the Soviet collective farms, but industry was all the more centralized and Lohse's objection to autonomy sprang largely from his mania for controlling everything from Riga.** Though far less brutal than Erich Koch, he seems to have been insensitive to the rights of private owners in a struggle against Marxism, which was after all supposed to exist behind all the confusion and the shouting of the captains. Braeutigam put it to Rosenberg in his bitter sarcastic way: 'To the unbounded astonishment of the Baltic population, the German administration stepped in to play the rôle of receiver of the goods, stolen by the Bolsheviks'.[53] But none of these protests had much effect on Lohse. Most of the bothersome and inefficient machinery of state-control remained in his capital city till the last.

Yet the largest item in Hitler's original programme was all but

* Peter Kleist, pp. 169, 216–17. See p. 368
** For the decree, see p. 192 and Kleist, pp. 159–66

spared the *Ostland*, namely the dumping of Germans or Germanics and the expulsion of such natives as were deemed unsuitable for Germanization. What would have happened, if the war had been won, cannot be predicted, but, since the war dragged on and since its demands for transport could not be satisfied, not even Germans who had been expelled in 1940 were allowed to return to the Baltic States. Under the protocols of September 1939, more than half a million native Germans were moved from the Baltic States, as well as from Volhynia, Podolia, Bukovina and Bessarabia. Very few were given the chance to go back, though, apart from conscription for the forces, the problem of their housing and their employment was never solved. They were intended to receive new lands at the expense of evicted Polish peasants, a policy which was only carried out in a few localities. As late as August 1943, nearly 100,000 racial Germans were in western Poland, still living in camps. About 130,000 were removed from the Baltic States.[54] In May 1942 Rosenberg told Hitler that 30,000 Germans from Lithuania were neither provided for in their old country nor in their new one.[55] Braeutigam also complained that VOMI, the Resettlement Agency of the SS, would not agree to repatriate the Germans to their homes in the Baltic States, even when they were forced to live in refugee camps.[56]

When finally, at the end of 1942, 36,000 racial Germans were brought back to Lithuania, they were not allowed to resume their old homes, but were allotted farm-houses along the main communication roads between East Prussia and the Latvian border in order to protect these roads from Partisans. Frequently the homes of the resettled Germans were fired by Lithuanians.[57] But if the Partisan problem gave a special urge to the repatriation of the *Volksdeutsche* to Lithuania, in Latvia and Estonia there was less hurry about it. While Germans from the Reich made the laws and derived the profit from the country, the former German inhabitants of the Baltic lands were not considered. Even the laws, which restored the rights of private property, confirmed the titles of those who had stolen the possessions of the 'Baltic Barons' in 1919.

Elsewhere in the Soviet Union, in White Russia and the Ukraine, attempts to favour the *Volksdeutsche*, the descendants of German colonists, met with no success. Hitler, who shifted the native Germans from their homes as a result of his political bargains with Stalin and Mussolini, was never seriously interested in their welfare. In July 1942 he discussed a half-baked plan for moving the German-speaking South Tyrolese to the Crimea, as if all he had to do was to float them down the

Danube.[58]* The arbitrary shifting of populations commended itself to German officials with fatal ease, for they had long accustomed themselves to political doctrines which set no value by human life. In the severe winter of 1939 the repatriation movement had caused almost as much hardship to the resettled Germans as to the Poles whom they were to displace. But it set the precedent for worse displacements. Before the invasion of the Soviet Union and subsequently, some 700,000 German-speaking people were removed by Hitler's government. But this was a small thing compared with the flight of east Germans at the end of the war and the expulsions from Poland and Czechoslovakia, when the number of refugees exceeded eight millions. That was the door which was opened by the infamous Moscow protocols of 1939.

The still more grandiose plan to relieve over-population in England and western Europe by treating the Baltic lands as if they were another Canada hardly got beyond the blue-print stage. It was mentioned by Rosenberg in his first draft plan of 2nd April 1941.[59] A fortnight later at Hitler's headquarters for the Balkan campaign, Himmler told his masseur, Felix Kersten, that he meant to move most of the population of Holland, at least eight million people, to eastern Poland. Kersten claims that only his own persuasion stopped this actually happening, something which one may believe or not as one wishes, for this favourite of Himmler's is far from reticent in advancing his own credentials. But the plan was at least typical of Himmler, and some of the schemes which Himmler submitted to Hitler were hardly less fantastic.[60] In April 1941 Himmler seems to have spoken in a fit of ill-temper, because recently the Dutch had staged a strike in Amsterdam and Rotterdam, a unique event in occupied Europe. Hitler, however, admired the farming skill of the Dutch and reverted to the idea of Dutch settlements in Russia more than once.[61]

On 8th May 1942 Rosenberg submitted a scheme to Hitler which had been drafted by Seyss-Inquart, the *Reichskommissar* for Holland. Half a million hectares of land near Libau in Latvia were to be farmed by Dutchmen. Although Hitler declared that such settlements ought to be limited to a few thousand people at most, a Netherlands Eastern Company was launched in Holland on 11th June, which thought in terms of millions.[62] A special department was formed in the Rosenberg Ministry to deal with this enterprise and two Dutch co-operative dairies were actually formed from collective farms near Vilna.[63]

* See p. 185

In August 1942, Peter Kleist met a representative of a Dutch export firm at *Generalkommissar* Kube's dinner-table in Minsk, where he formed the conclusion that the unproductive land of White Russia was to replace Holland's lost East Indian markets.[64] All this was before Stalingrad. From the end of 1942 no more was heard of colonizing projects, which came under the censorship ban.[65] They still figured regularly in Himmler's long speeches, which till the end of the war remained the faithful echo of the sort of things Hitler used to say at the beginning of the Russian campaign.

(c) White Russia

A SMALL SECTION of this chapter covers a very large country. White Russia was included in the *Ostland* as an afterthought and it remained little more. From the winter of 1941 onwards most of the White Russian Soviet Republic remained in the hands of the Partisans till the return of the Red Army. The actual extent of territory, which the Germans controlled at any one moment, was so small and the degree to which civilian rulers were entrusted with it so slight, that the real history of the country under German occupation must be sought in the annals of Partisan warfare, of which White Russia remained the principal theatre throughout the German occupation.*

It is not clear how and when White Russia came to be included in Lohse's 'dukedom'. In Rosenberg's first draft of 2nd April 1941 it is described as one of the future independent states, rival to Moscow, with a frontier stretching as far east as Tver, though it is admitted that the sense of nationality is weak.[66] In Rosenberg's amended instructions of 8th May White Russia is considered more as a dumping ground for unruly elements than as a potential state, and there is a proposal that a belt of resettled Poles should separate it from Russia proper.[67] By the time of Hitler's Angerburg conference, it seems to have been agreed that White Russia was not worthy of a separate government. Yet it was a curiously haphazard arrangement to tag White Russia on to the highly Germanized Baltic States. Even on its own, the territory had no national entity. The western part had been Polish between the years 1919 and 1939, and in the remoter past a bone of contention between Polish and Lithuanian rulers. The eastern part had been under Moscow

* See particularly pp. 239 and 241-3

rule for centuries and had been completely Sovietized since the October Revolution.

White Russia lay behind the heavily contested front of the Central Army Group, where the Wehrmacht was extremely reluctant to diminish the area of military control. This area extended as much as 250 miles from the front and almost as far west as Minsk. In fact the civilian *Generalkommissariat* included very little that was not part of Poland before 1939, except the battle-ruined city of Minsk itself, the *Generalkommissar's* capital. The eastern districts, which were to be based on Smolensk, Mogilev and Vitebsk, were never taken over. These towns remained under the Rear Area Command of the Central Army Group and its chief, the controversial figure of General von Schenckendorff.* An unexplained result of the arrangement was that the Jewish population was liquidated far more rapidly and efficiently here under military tutelage than in the *Generalkommissariat*, where some communities survived till the autumn of 1943.**

As to the civilian area, it was regarded as a dustbin. As long as the Wehrmacht kept its supply lines open, no one minded much what happened there. The worst kind of official was normally posted to White Russia. A milk roundsman became a political adviser and a criminal sadist was *Gebietskommissar* at Slonim.[68] The German civil ruler of White Russia was himself a man in disgrace, though he kept up some pomp and circumstance in miserable crumbling Minsk with its murderous ghettoes and prisoner of war camps.

Generalkommissar Wilhelm Kube was an old Nazi, a bearer of the Blood Order of 1923 and, as Minister President for Brandenburg, renowned for his pompous speeches on all Party occasions. Hitler once said that Kube needed no loudspeaker because he had a voice like a rhinoceros. Hitler felt an affection for a man who had preached violent anti-Semitism in the days when he was still a student. But in 1936 he permitted Kube to be stripped of his appointments and sent for a short time to a concentration camp. It had been discovered that Kube was the author of an anonymous letter to Walter Buch, the President of the Party Tribunal, insinuating that Buch's wife, the grandmother of Martin Bormann's children, was partly Jewish.[69]

Coming, as it did, after many other unsavoury reports, Kube's rehabilitation was not welcomed by the Party notables. It was Himmler who recommended Kube to Hitler's notice, because he had cleared his

* See pp. 309–10
** See p. 255

name by volunteering in the ranks of the SS at the age of fifty-three. So at Angerburg Hitler proposed Kube as *Generalkommissar* for Moscow.* Rosenberg and Goering at once objected that he was too old. The post in White Russia was probably given him at the request of Lohse, an old colleague with whom Kube corresponded on the most intimate terms.

Kube was a peculiar *Generalkommissar*, yet on balance not untypical of this thwarted class of men. At Minsk his old reputation for promiscuity and loose morals pursued him and he was the subject of Gestapo reports throughout his two year's reign. On the other hand, Kube was appalled by the daily horrors of anti-Partisan warfare and the massacres of Jews, things that other people took in their stride. The value of Kube's protests was small, but he desired a reputation for humanity, even if most of his complaints against SS excesses concerned trespasses on his own authority. Kube might have got into trouble had he mattered more. After his assassination on 22nd September 1943, when a Russian woman Partisan, employed as a chambermaid, laid a bomb under his bed, Himmler declared that only this event had prevented him sending Kube back to a concentration camp. And Goebbels observed, after Rosenberg had delivered a long, flattering funeral oration for a man whose appointment he had opposed with the utmost spite, that 'there was really nothing one could find to praise in Kube's life.'[70]

Kube clashed with Rosenberg, not only in his attitude towards the Jews, but also in his support of White Russian nationalism. Rosenberg had abandoned his own plans for a White Russian national state very early in the day, if indeed he had ever intended them seriously. Kube did not advocate the plan openly, but, living in a little island in a sea of anarchy, he seems to have had some faith in native collaborationists as a weapon against the Partisans. Largely this meant employing White Russian emigrés or natives of the former Polish provinces to act as officials in the Soviet area. In June 1942 Kube installed at his Minsk headquarters a sort of native spokesman and adviser, a Dr Ivan Ermashenko who had been an officer in Wrangel's army and had fought the Bolsheviks in the civil war.[71] This action of Kube's was not approved by Himmler's Security Police Commanders, who were in most respects a law to themselves. Eduard Strauch, the Police

* *Nuremberg Document*, L. 221. According to Braeutigam (*Ueberblick*, etc., p. 16) Rosenberg afterwards wrote a formal objection against Kube, which was dismissed by Lammers. Kube took up office on 1st September 1941.

Commandant in Minsk, claimed that it took him a year to liquidate Dr Ermashenko.* That was in the spring of 1943 when Ermashenko was arrested for gold smuggling. It seems that he had gained Kube's confidence by providing him with the company of a pretty Russian woman doctor in the absence of Frau Kube.

The loss of Dr Ermashenko came at a critical moment for Kube. From the middle of May till the end of June 1943 there was a huge drive against the Partisans in the *Generalkommissariat* of White Russia, where the Germans had been deprived of the harvest within forty miles of Minsk. At first Kube co-operated with Himmler's police commander in 'Operation Cottbus', but soon he became disgusted with the butcheries, conducted by the SS and their Ukrainian, White Russian and Lithuanian auxiliaries. Although his complaints went unheeded,** Kube tried to rally the better class of White Russian collaborator against the Partisan menace. He created a *Rada*, an amorphous council of White Russian leaders and he recruited a White Russian Youth Movement. Hitherto, Kube had indulged his typically Nazi passion for collecting blond Aryan types, wherever they could be found, a passion that even led him to intercede for some of the German Jews who were deported to Minsk in 1941.*** But the White Russian boys who joined Kube's Youth Movement had little cause to thank him. Soon after his death, they were shipped to Germany as forced labour in the course of the famous *Aktion* Heu.****

Kube was assassinated at a moment of virtual civil war in Minsk, when even the capital offered no security to German officials. Smolensk fell to the Red Army three days later, on 25th September 1943, but the threat was premature, since Minsk was not lost till 2nd July 1944. At the time of Kube's death, Rosenberg was in the hands of his new director, Gottlob Berger, who, instead of appointing an Eastern Ministry man, such as Schickedanz, installed an SS government in Minsk under Major General von Gottberg, who had been Police Leader in Kube's day. Gottberg had been associated with the downright massacres of the 'Cottbus Operation' in the previous year.***** Yet he had to be even more conciliatory than Kube. At the end of 1943 Gottberg created a White Russian Central Council under yet another

* Reitlinger, op. cit., Document NO 2262. According to Braeutigam, Ermashenko was not liquidated, but exiled to Prague. (*Ueberblick*, etc., p. 16)
** See pp. 242–3
*** See p. 255
**** See pp. 282–4
***** See p. 241

White Russian professor from Poland, a certain Ostrovski who was destined to wander about Germany among the other dispossessed national minority leaders in the dissolving Reich of 1945.*

Gottberg was, however, successful in recruiting a fair number of White Russians for the Wehrmacht, since the threat of the return of the Red Army forced many collaborators to accept this course. There was even the beginning of a White Russian SS division, and on 1st April 1944 Hitler made Gottberg independent of Lohse and answerable only to Berlin.[72] But there were only three months to go. Minsk fell earlier than the capitals of the *Ostland*. It was overrun on 2nd July 1944 in the course of the most devastating penetration of the German front which the Red Army ever made. Thus ended three years of German rule in White Russia, but rule is too strong a term. If German rule in the Baltic States was too elaborate and in the Ukraine too brutal, in White Russia it was just the law of the jungle.

* See p. 368

CHAPTER FIVE

THE UKRAINE—
THE UNWANTED ALLY

(a) Intrigues and Projects

RETURNING FROM AN interview with Hitler on 17th March 1941, Franz Halder wrote in his diary that Hitler expected the inhabitants of White Russia to welcome the German troops with open arms, but he considered the Ukrainians and Don Cossacks dubious.[1] No sentence can explain better Hitler's failure to understand the true situation in Russia. It may be that there has been too much German romancing about Cossacks, offering bread and salt, and Ukrainian maidens, garlanding the invaders' tanks with flowers, but there was no such thing as this in White Russia. And whatever the final outcome of the war, an allied, autonomous Ukraine would certainly have been worth the Germans several field divisions of a sort.

Why did Hitler reject these possibilities? The answer lies deeper than in Hitler's superficial brutality. To listen to German writers of the *Ostpolitiker* school, one might suppose that an alliance with the Ukrainian people would have won them the war. That can be believed only by assuming that the Germans under National Socialism were capable of retaining their friends or by assuming that there were Germans capable of steering a sensible, intelligent course among the rivalries of Ukrainian politics—both singularly vain assumptions. Hitler was nearer to perceiving the realities of the situation in the Ukraine than Rosenberg and the pro-Ukrainians, in spite of his astonishing limitations. Most of Hitler's judgments on foreign affairs were based on the newspapers, which the corporal had read during the First World War. Hitler did not perceive any changing pattern in history. For him the situation was simple. The Ukrainians had proved themselves the worst of investments.

Hitler knew that in 1918 the German and Austrian Imperial High Commands had burnt their fingers in the Ukraine. Having tried to defend an autonomous regime, treating the Ukrainians with justice, though with a short-sightedness which bordered on stupidity, the German soldier had been forced to flee the country with brickbats about his ears, lucky to escape at all in an incomprehensible welter of anarchy. The High Command had been reluctant in accepting these allies and they were made to regret it. In February 1918, when the Bolsheviks sued for peace at Brest-Litovsk, the presence of an Ukrainian delegation was almost as displeasing to the Germans as it was to Lenin and Trotsky. And the chosen Ukrainian leaders drifted either towards Tsarism or towards Bolshevism. In both cases they became imperialist and anti-German. Finally, when the German-supported leaders were overthrown by their own countrymen, numerous Ukrainians fought Russians and Germans alike, each Hetman or Batkho carving out a world of plunder for himself.

Before the Revolution, the Ukrainian opposition to Russian rule had not been vigorous. On the contrary the Ukrainian subjects of the Habsburg monarchy had felt themselves close enough in blood to welcome the Russians as deliverers. In 1915, when the brief Russian occupation of Austrian Galicia ended, the Russian retreat was embarrassed by hordes of civilians who did not want to return to Habsburg rule. In Galicia itself the Austrian liberators were so little welcomed that they were impelled to set up concentration camps. In 1917 the Germans and Austrians held 700,000 Ukrainian prisoners of war. In marked contrast to the autumn of 1941, when tens of thousands of Ukrainian prisoners were released, many of them to act as German police troops, only 2,000 prisoners were recruited in the First World War to serve as a pro-German Ukrainian legion.[2] The Ukrainian *Rada* of 1918 were drawn to negotiate with the Germans and Austrians through fear of Bolshevism alone.

In 1918 German bayonets had failed to keep the *Rada* in power or to stop the penetration of the Bolsheviks. To Hitler with his contempt of the House of Habsburg, whom he believed to be half-Slav and entirely sold to Slav interests, this failure had a deep significance, since it was the Austrian Emperor and the Austrian Chancellor, Count Czernin, who had insisted on recognizing the Ukraine at the Brest-Litovsk negotiations. In those days the Dual Monarchy was threatened with famine and it was hoped to win from a friendly Ukraine a million tons of wheat. A million tons indeed! Hitler expected three millions in 1941, seven millions in 1942 and then perhaps ten or twelve millions in a year.[3] And how had the Austrian Slavophils been rewarded for their forbearance? The Ukrainians had murdered their greatest friend, the German Field Marshal Hermann von Eichorn.

Hitler never forgave this Ukrainian crime. It became such an obsession with him that as late as May 1943, Alfred Rosenberg was stirred into submitting a lengthy memorandum on the subject. This set out to show that the murder of 30th July 1918, had been the work of a Bolshevik agent, assisted by two Jews.[4] Ideologically perfect as this explanation was, it could not change Hitler's contempt for the Ukrainians. He could only recall that the Ukrainian peasants, having been despoiled by every sort of war-lord in turn, had welcomed the Bolsheviks. The Bolsheviks had shown their gratitude by according the Ukraine a special status, which in the early twenties included diplomatic representation abroad.

Hitler overlooked entirely the price which the Ukrainians had subsequently to pay for their failure to unite in 1918–20. The country was allowed to recover from the famine which the civil war left behind it in 1921, but in 1930 Stalin introduced the full weight of State Collectivization, the most bigoted, doctrinaire and desperately Russian thing that ever emerged from that great intellect in blinkers. Extortion, flight and expulsion were the daily order till in 1933–4 an artificial famine afflicted the Ukraine, fully equal to the earlier famine. In Izyum in 1934 a shopkeeper was tried for selling human flesh. She confessed that she had done the same in 1921.[5]

German intelligence reports on the depressed and embittered state of the Ukraine were not wanting, yet in 1941 Hitler failed to see what Stalin had done to the Ukraine. Under the last of the Tsars there had been nothing more formidable than a literary movement in the Ukrainian language, some professorial politicians and the cult of a few historical myths. Now there was a social resentment, strong enough to overcome the natural anarchy of the Ukrainians. Thus, on his visit to Melitopol in June 1943, Rosenberg was shown a monument which the elders of the town had erected to the memory of German soldiers who had once defended Ukrainian independence during the civil war. There, where nothing had been seen for more than twenty years except the conventional Marxist images, was this modest token. But the *Reichskommissar* Erich Koch only grumbled, 'No German soldier will ever die for that nigger people.'[6]

Hitler did not intend to create separatist states on Soviet territory till the last vestiges of Soviet rule had been eliminated. But he permitted the boundaries of the German-run Commissariats to indicate the

eventual form these states were to take. Even Hitler might have con-
ceded more, had he realized how popular German troops would be in
the Ukraine six years after the end of Stalin's collectivization programme. The gesture which he made at Uman on 30th August 1941
was already considerable.* But it was too late to expect from Hitler
anything more than a recognition that captured Ukrainian soldiers
were not very anti-German. For of Ukrainian politicians Hitler had
already seen enough since the invasion of Russia to justify his worst
fears and revive his worst recollections of 1918–19

Since 1933 Hitler's anti-Russian sentiments had given some hope to
the Ukrainian exiles in Germany but, so long as there was a treaty with
Poland, the arch-enemy of Ukrainian aspirations, the encouragement
of Ukrainian nationalism by the Nazi had to be clandestine. Still more
was this the case after the conquest of Poland, when the ally to be
placated was Russia. As a result, the Ukrainian nationalists were
surrounded by a peculiarly unsatisfactory atmosphere. These Ukrainians had their centre in what had been Austrian and was now Polish
Galicia, for the Ukrainians of the Soviet Union were barely accessible.
For some years they grouped themselves round the national figure of
Simon Petliura, the cab-driver's son, who had dethroned the German-
sponsored government of the Hetman Skoropadsky in November
1918. Petliura was killed in Paris in 1926 by a Jew, seeking to avenge
his race against this pogrom-raiser. The leadership of the exiles then
devolved on a rival Ukrainian leader of the civil war period, Colonel
Konovalets. As the representative of the National Ukrainian committee, OUN, Konovalets had some traffic with Admiral Canaris and
the *Abwehr* in 1938, when the Germans played with the notion of a
Ukrainian State in the Carpathians, rising out of the ruins of Czechoslovakia. In 1939, however it was the turn of Konovalets to be
murdered by presumed Soviet agents in a Rotterdam café.[7]

There were two candidates for the succession. On the one hand, the
aged Hetman Skoropadsky lived at Wannsee, a pensioner of Hinden-
burg who gave the Nazi government several worries in 1940.[8] On the
other hand, the true followers of Petliura accepted one of his colonels,
a former Austrian officer called Andrei Melnyk, who is still acknowledged by thousands of dispersed Ukrainians today. Hitler's pressure on
Poland had begun and Ribbentrop and Canaris could interest themselves in Melnyk more openly than in Konovalets. They were now
planning a Ukrainian state in Polish Galicia. But, in view of past

* See pp. 104

German experience, the plan was mainly required for nuisance value and it was highly doubtful that Hitler would allow it to come to fruition. Hitler had in fact already dealt a severe blow to Ukrainian aspirations.

It began with the Munich Agreement of September 1938, when the helpless Czech government was forced to grant autonomy to the tail-end of its long composite state, known as Carpathian Ruthenia. Here in the towns the population was largely Hungarian but in the country Ukrainian; yet, under the presidency of the Roman Catholic Father Voloshin, Carpathian Ruthenia was renamed Carpathian Ukraine. Members of OUN streamed in from Galicia and, with the blessing of Ribbentrop and Canaris, formed a Ukrainian army. But the policy of baiting Poland with Ukrainian irredentists from across the border ended dramatically in March 1939, when Hitler occupied Prague and Czechoslovakia was dismembered. As the price of her uneasy compliance, the Hungary of Admiral Horthy shared in the dismemberment and received Carpathian Ruthenia at Hitler's hands. There was some armed Ukrainian resistance to the Hungarians, but Hitler's action paid dividends. He had calmed the apprehensions of Hungary, Poland, Russia and Italy in a single gesture. As to the Ukrainians, they had their first glimpse of the two faces of German policy and they could expect more.[9]

Diligently Canaris tried to collect the pieces. Many of the followers of Father Voloshin found refuge in a Polish-Ukrainian battalion, which Canaris trained at Chiemsee and which took part in the invasion of Poland six months later. Not surprisingly, the Ukrainians in invaded Poland remembered Carpathian Ruthenia and they gave the Germans a far more dubious welcome in eastern Galicia than they were to receive later in the Soviet Ukraine. Not surprisingly, the more radical part of the secret forces of OUN, which had been fighting the Polish government since the early twenties, was ready to fight the Germans too. In any case the Germans were not long enough in eastern Galicia to come to terms with Ukrainian nationalism, because by the secret protocol, concluded between Ribbentrop and Molotov on 23rd August 1939, all Galicia, east of the river San, including the western Ukrainian metropolis of Lemberg or Lwow, had to be handed to the Russians.

Ribbentrop seems to have thought that the Russians would not demand the execution of the whole protocol and on 25th September, when Stalin demanded the surrender of Lwow, it was almost the deathblow to the Ukrainian schemes, which he shared with Admiral Canaris. Ribbentrop's hopes can be studied in the notes which were kept by Canaris of an interview between Ribbentrop and Keitel in Hitler's railway train at Illnau on 12th September. Russian troops had not yet marched into eastern Poland and Ribbentrop seems curiously to have under-estimated Molotov's toughness. In preparation for an Ukrainian independent state in Galicia, Ribbentrop was going to arrange with Melnyk and OUN for Ukrainian bands to burn all the farms of the Poles and kill off all the Jews, 'provided this arrangement is agreeable to the Soviet Union'.*

After the conference, Canaris was told by Keitel that he was actually going to transmit this half-baked proposal as a directive to the High Command. It seems, however, that at this moment Hitler entered the railway compartment and that the conversation which followed was not recorded, for Keitel's directive to the High Command, as approved by Hitler, was something very much milder. It authorized a radio proclamation to the Ukrainian people by the Wehrmacht Propaganda Section, but it was not a proclamation to urge them to murder and plunder. It was simply to tell them that the German Army had no hostile intentions towards the Ukrainian population of Poland.

The secret supplementary protocol to the Moscow Pact, which Ribbentrop had to sign in Moscow on 28th September 1939, obliged the German government to 'suppress all agitation in their territories which affected the territory of the other party'.[10] Ribbentrop accordingly dropped the official Foreign Office support of Melnyk and OUN and Canaris was forbidden to meddle, but Melnyk was permitted to stay in Berlin. For more than a year Ukrainian nationalist activities remained under the ban; but in the winter of 1940 the preparation of the 'Barbarossa' plan brought OUN well into the picture again. At Neuhammer near Liegnitz, Canaris was permitted to train a new battalion for his sabotage regiment, 'Brandenburg'. It was recruited from captured Polish soldiers of Ukrainian race and it bore the name 'Nachtigall'. The commander was the same intelligence officer whom Canaris was to send in July 1941, to interview Reinecke and Mueller, the Austrian Brigadier, Erwin Lahousen.** Originally it was intended to

---

* This is according to the notes taken by Erwin Lahousen and read out at the first Nuremberg Trial (D 421, *IMT*, I, p. 275). Melnyk, however, had a reputation among Ukrainians for moderation and it is most improbable that he would have countenanced such a thing.

** See p. 86

move the battalion ahead of the German troops so as to seize tunnels and bridges.[11] Other members of OUN, not in uniform, were to provoke resistance to the Russians among the Ukrainian population. For this purpose Canaris required a less static personality than Andrei Melnyk. He therefore encouraged a second and rival organization to the original OUN and a new leader. The Warsaw prisons were thrown open and the Galician hotheads released, among them a certain Captain Stepan Bandera, who had been locked up since 1934 for his part in the murder of the Polish Minister of the Interior.[12] As the secessionist party, OUN-B, Bandera's followers soon formed an opposition to Melnyk's policy of close collaboration with the Germans. During the occupation of the Soviet Ukraine, OUN-B fought OUN-M almost continuously. In fact they used their German weapons against German officials, Russian Partisans and their own compatriots alike.

Ribbentrop and Canaris might have reflected, when they opened Pandora's box, that history, when it repeats itself, is no more easy to come to terms with than before. Moreover even allies such as these could not be had without pledges, whereas neither the High Command who sponsored the adventure, nor the Foreign Office had any reason to suppose that Hitler would honour any pledges at all. And if they wanted the support of the Ukrainian population after the annexation of the country, it was not a good beginning to be forced to lock up its political leaders.

That, in fact, is what happened after the chaos which followed the German occupation of Lwow. The town was taken after eight days' hard fighting on the 1939 frontier. Brutal and stupid as German rule in the Soviet Ukraine was about to be, it could yield points to Russian rule in Galicia in 1939–41. Having begun by wooing the Ukrainians at the expense of the Poles, much as Ribbentrop had planned to do,[13] the Russians proceeded to remove the Ukrainian property-owning and intellectual classes—much no doubt as the Germans would have done. Moreover, as soon as the Germans crossed the border, some three or four thousand citizens of Lwow were seized by the NKVD in a round-up and lodged in the prisons. On 25th June, three days after the outbreak of war, when it was already apparent that the Russians would give up the town, an unsuccessful attempt was made to free the prisoners. The NKVD thereupon killed them all, leaving Lwow too quickly to remove the bodies from the prisons.

The Germans entered Lwow on 30th June with a special Commando of Heydrich's Security Police among the foremost units. The first concern of this Commando was the organization of a pogrom, which broke out on 2nd July. Photographs of bodies, which had been found in the prisons, were exhibited in shop-windows and the pogrom was presented as 'Aktion Petliura' in honour of one of the most dubious national heroes of all time, who had been assassinated by a Jew in 1926. Several members of Melnyk's Berlin committee accompanied Heydrich's commando,[14] while survivor narratives mention that Ukrainian patriots, wearing blue and yellow arm-bands, took a large part in the pogrom.[15] But this kind of legend-mongering is a delicate explosive, for soon the city was filled with the members of OUN-B who were determined not to be German collaborators. Under the command of Jaroslav Stetsko, they seized a radio station and proclaimed the 'Renewal of the Ukrainian State.'[16] An Austrian professor of theology, called Hans Koch, had entered Lwow as the *Abwehr's* expert on Ukrainian affairs. He was invited to a cultural gathering of the Ukrainian 'Prosvita' association, where the proceedings turned out to be nothing less than a declaration of independence.[17]

The Stetsko 'government' lasted nine days. It enjoyed the protection of Canaris's 'Nachtigall' battalion, which included several unofficially appointed members of OUN-B. Thus the chaplain of the battalion, profiting from the general ignorance both of German intentions and of the internal politics of OUN, obtained for the new state the all-important blessing of the Metropolitan Sheptytski. An octagenarian patriot, Constantin Levitsky, was proclaimed President of the Council, while liberationist committees sprang up in other east Galician towns besides Lwow. It was not till 9th July that Hitler's orders filtered through and the same SD commando that had arranged the pogrom, arrested Stetsko and some of his companions.[18]

Even now the negative nature of Hitler's future policy in the Ukraine was not fully grasped. The Stetsko cabinet, together with Bandera, who had been arrested in Cracow, were taken to Berlin for interrogation, but for the time being they were kept merely under a form of house-arrest and Stetsko was permitted to return to Cracow. The disarming of Ukrainian bands in other Galician towns took several weeks and in the confusion the Jews of Galicia escaped annihilation—or rather annihilation was postponed. In Lwow itself some 2,000 Jews, who had been rounded up in the Sports Stadium, were allowed to escape by the Security Police Commander.[19]

In the meantime, precisely as Canaris had intended, 'marching groups' both of OUN-M and OUN-B infiltrated the Soviet Ukraine in the wake of the Wehrmacht, while the nationalists in Lwow continued to broadcast words of encouragement, unaware that their head had been cut off. The military government officers of the Wehrmacht accepted their presence gladly. Some kind of provisional native administration was wanted, at any rate in the bigger towns, and these people were at least not communists. But the distinction between OUN-M and OUN-B was becoming all too apparent. At Zhitomir, at the end of August, two members of the Melnykist town council were murdered in the street by a member of OUN-B. At first the SD denounced the killing as the work of communists, but almost immediately they instigated a wave of executions which engulfed all the members of OUN-B that could be found, in Zhitomir, in Balta, in Nikolaiev, even at Yankoi in the Crimea.[20]

The dignified and moderate-natured Melnyk still lived in freedom in Berlin, while many of his adherents were attached to Wehrmacht units. After the OUN-B arrests it seemed that their moment had arrived. They were allowed to comb the prisoner-of-war camps for Ukrainians, who were to serve as a police force in Kiev; they were even allowed to form a town council after the occupation of the city. Under the still tolerant control of the Wehrmacht, a Melnykist from Galicia, Dr Kandyba, was allowed to direct propaganda; other missionaries from Galicia directed native police forces in Kiev, Vinnitsa and Dniepropetrovsk. In Kiev the Wehrmacht tolerated a mayor, the schoolmaster Bahazy, who made violent pro-Melnyk propaganda.[21]

But the honeymoon with Ukrainian nationalism, which had been begun by Ribbentrop and Canaris, had to end. Kiev had fallen under the rule of the violently anti-Ukrainian *Reichskommissar*, Erich Koch. In a much-changed climate Bahazy was denounced by his own countrymen for his boasts to foreign journalists and for his local administration, which was said to employ 20,000 people. The fact was that the Galician missionaries were disliked by most of the inhabitants of Kiev, a city which had become more Russianized than Rosenberg had supposed. These indifferent Ukrainians failed to understand the reverence for forgotten civil war heroes and the loyalty to unknown political eminences in Berlin and Cracow. And the more Sovietized and Russianized they had become, the more likely they were to be favoured by the Koch administration. The tide turned against the nationalists. In November 1941, there was a nasty mass-execution by the SD at Bazar, near Zhitomir. It seems that the nationalists had staged a celebration of the twentieth anniversary of the last stand by Ukrainians against the Bolsheviks. In February Bahazy was arrested at the instance of the *Generalkommissar*, Waldemar Magunia, and executed. Thenceforward both the OUN organizations were in opposition to the Germans, proscribed, frequently the object of arrests and sometimes of executions.[22]

The background to this feeble collapse of the plans of Ribbentrop and Canaris was the decision which Hitler took within a few days after the arrest of the 'Lwow government'. In Rosenberg's first plan, which he submitted to Hitler on 2nd April 1941, Galicia was to have been the kernel of the new Ukrainian state.* But on 16th July Hitler announced abruptly at the Angerburg conference that 'the former Austrian part of Galicia will become Reich territory.' Provisionally it would be governed by Hans Frank as part of the General Government of Poland.[23] Rosenberg tried to defend Hitler's decision, however much it hurt him. 'For the loss of a couple of square kilometres in the west, the Ukrainians would get hundreds of square kilometres in the east.'[24] To this the sardonic Peter Kleist claims to have replied that no one would expect to replace the square kilometre containing Cologne cathedral with even thousands of square kilometres in Poland.

If the Ukraine had lost Lwow, Rosenberg still expected a capital in Kiev, but there was to be no capital. On 29th September Hitler told Rosenberg that he would only agree to 'policy by postponement.' There must be no immediate public announcement on the future of the Ukraine and the Ukrainians must receive no treatment that might suggest they were a favoured race. Rosenberg was to lose the University of his dreams which was to spread Nazi ideology from Kiev.[25]

On 1st August the Wehrmacht handed Lwow over to Frank's Government General. Parts of the 'Roland' and 'Nachtigall' regiments mutinied in places as far east as Vinnitsa and Tiraspol. Thereupon the OUN-B officers and NCOs were interned in Sachsenhausen concentration camp in the company of Bandera. Most of them, however, were released in May 1943, when the SS began to recruit Ukrainians in Galicia.[26] While their leaders were in Sachsenhausen, the two battalions continued to serve the Germans as police-units in the White Russian area, fighting Partisans. But a great many former members of 'Roland' and 'Nachtigall' had joined the independent Ukrainian nationalist army, UPA.** Others went underground deep into the Soviet Ukraine.

In this way was dissipated the cadre of a potential allied army, but

* See p. 134
** For UPA, see pp. 246–8

it was not the worst consequence of Hitler's policy towards the Ukraine. Hitler separated Galicia from the *Reichskommissariat* Ukraine in order to defeat the activities of Ukrainian politicians, whose centre he correctly judged to be Lwow, not Kiev. Yet the result was the reverse of his intention. Under the rule of Hans Frank there were a dozen Polish resistance movements, whereas in Frank's new province of Galicia Ukrainians had always fought Poles. So Governor Frank favoured his Ukrainian subjects. They were permitted their own committees in Lwow and Cracow. At the head was professor Vladimir Kubiowych, with whom Frank himself, as he admitted at Nuremberg, kept constant touch.[27] Even before the invasion this Ukrainian professor had been entrusted with the secrets of the 'Barbarossa' plan. He was particularly friendly with Frank's Commissioner for Galicia, the Austrian SS man Otto Waechter, and it was through Kubiowych and Waechter that the mistimed notion of a Galician SS division came to fruition in 1943.[28*]

Across the former Soviet border, Erich Koch would declare that when he met an intelligent Ukrainian, he had to shoot him. Yet in Galicia the rule of Waechter and Kubiowych gave every encouragement, both to OUN-M and OUN-B. The former Soviet Ukrainians became in time more and more anti-German, the Galician Ukrainians, so long as the Germans had a chance of surviving, more pro-German—particularly in lonely parts of the Carpathians where they fought a civil war against the Polish resistance movement.** Moreover, Rosenberg, who had abandoned these subjects with reluctance, continued to beam on them. As a result, Ukrainian politicians from Galicia and from the Slovak and Hungarian parts of the Carpathians received the minister's permission to visit the former Soviet Ukraine, now known as the *Reichskommissariat*. Others filtered through without permission. When the Germans lost the goodwill of the population and, above all, when the return of the Red Army was imminent, agents of UPA and OUN infiltrated the German-controlled Ukrainian militia, who now made themselves independent, controlling large territories up to the edge of the towns. The blustering Erich Koch was powerless against this traffic, for Ukrainians were now looking to the heroes, who, once before in their history, had fought Germans and Russians at the same time.

* See also p. 372.
** The exception was in July 1943 when Soviet Partisans entered Galicia. The Galician followers of Bandera seem then to have fought the Germans and the Russians as well as the Poles. See p. 248

But on 16th July, when Hitler announced his intention of treating Galicia as part of occupied Poland and eventually as Reich territory, the Wehrmacht had already discovered the astonishing goodwill of the submerged Soviet Ukrainian population. Berdichev and Zhitomir were in German hands and practically all the territory between the Bug and Dniester, agriculturally the richest part of the Soviet Ukraine and indeed of the entire Soviet Union. It was in this region that the Germans got a better reception than in any part of Europe. At the entrances of the villages the victors were offered bread and salt as a token of hospitality and maidens covered their tanks with garlands of flowers.[29] It was something that the sentimental German soldier had never experienced. Yet it was the southern part of this friendly region which Hitler now handed over to Rumania, a country that had no valid ethnic or historical claims to it.

Already in May 1941, when Marshal Antonescu visited him in Munich, Hitler had promised that the Rumanians should administer south Russia up to the Dnieper.[30] In reality this was not Antonescu's price. His own preference was the return of the balance of the Transylvanian territories, which Rumania had ceded to Hungary under German compulsion on 29th August 1940. Antonescu thought that the Hungarians could be compensated with parts of Galicia that had been formerly Polish. Hitler, who wanted the alliance of Hungary, would not agree and Antonescu accepted the Soviet territory across the Dniester in the hope that he might do a bargain with it after the war.[31]*

So on 17th August 1941 Antonescu reminded Hitler of his promise. His letter declared that only the northern border remained to be clarified.[32] Two days later Hitler confirmed that the Rumanians would be responsible for administration as far as the Bug and for security as far as the Dnieper. Hitler's letter gave birth to a new name, 'Transdniestria' which existed on no map. It was a conception to which Rosenberg was completely opposed, though his political department had to draft the agreement. The chief anxiety of the department was not that Ukrainian nationalism would be outraged, but that the Rumanians might encourage Ukrainian nationalism in their territory while Hitler forbade it in Rosenberg's. On the 25th a conference was conducted at Vinnitsa under Eduard Wagner, the Quartermaster General of the Forces, in order to arrange the hand-over of the military government of the Southern Army Group to the civilian *Reichskommissariat* of the Ukraine. At this conference Colonel von Krosigk, Chief of Staff to the

* See also p. 30

Rear Area Commander, General Karl von Roques, reported that the flood of volunteer Ukrainian militiamen could safely be put under the orders of Major General Franz Jaeckeln, the Higher SS and Police Leader.[33] Since the minutes revealed that he was principally concerned with the liquidation of 11,000 Ruthenian Jews whom the Hungarian Army had put across the Dniester, Jaeckeln could no doubt find uses for Ukrainian militiamen.[34] But Krosigk was worried because, on 25th August, nearly two months after the trouble in Lwow, the illegal Banderist Militia had infiltrated from Galicia. And during the conference Dr Otto Braeutigam, the Political Department's representative, received a telephone call from Dr Werner Koeppen, Rosenberg's liaison man at Hitler's headquarters. It was a warning that the Rumanians might set up a Ukrainian committee west of the Bug.

On the 30th Braeutigam had to attend another conference in the town-hall of Tighina on the Dniester. Here the protocols were drawn up to decide the competence of the Rumanians in response to Antonescu's request of the 17th. Provisionally the Rumanian military zone was to extend as far north as the line, Uman-Cherkassy. East of the Bug and west of the Dnieper the Rumanians were to be responsible for the security arrangements, but not for the administration of the country. It was a cumbrous arrangement, made more cumbrous by the German retention of the port of Nikolaiev which was west of the Dnieper. Diplomatic decisions on the limits of Rumanian sovereignty were postponed till after the war. But Antonescu waited only for the fall of Odessa on 19th October to proclaim the formal annexation of all territory up to the Bug.

The protocols of 30th August left the Rumanians a long strip of territory which included the great city of Odessa, though this had not yet fallen.[35] And the fears of Colonel von Krosigk were justified, for though the Rumanians encouraged no Ukrainian separatism in their own territory, all sorts of people could pass through their long unguarded frontier, an unwelcome two-way traffic for the German High Command and civilian administration. In the low state of morale that prevailed in the autumn of 1943, when the Russians got across the Dnieper and cut off the Crimea, numerous German deserters escaped this way to live on the black market in Rumania.[36] Antonescu was reluctant to give up his rights. He refused to transfer the railway administration to the German Army or to surrender his jurisdiction in areas which were now very close to the front. In November 1943 there was an angry inconclusive correspondence between Antonescu and

Hitler, which was solved only by the Russian advance to the Dniester in the following April.[37]

But to the Ukrainians, who were forced to deliver their produce to Goering's Economic Staff East and their breadwinning population to Sauckel's labour organization, life under Rumanian rule was to have advantages during the next two years, for Rumania was a backward country, almost mediaeval. The calamities of a mediaeval bad government, as depicted in its idleness and corruption on the walls of the Siena *Podestá*, were quite mild compared with what could be done by a great military nation in the Century of the Common Man. And one of the typical un-thoroughnesses of Antonescu's government was that it got tired of killing off Jews and shipped them instead to Transdniestria. Whereas in the whole of the vast Ukraine the returning Red Army could hardly count the hidden Jews in more than hundreds even in huge cities like Kiev and Kharkov, a considerable community of Jews was still alive in 1944 between the Bug and Dniester.

Hitler himself took no pleasure in giving Rumania a slice of the Ukraine. Antonescu's hardness in bargaining had not been matched by the valour of his troops, nor was this action at all attractive to a more important ally, Mussolini. Ukrainian independence had long been a favourite project in Italian Fascist circles, because Italian ships had retained the largest share of the trade with South Russian ports since the Middle Ages. Thus Mussolini was 'saddened' by the Rumanian occupation of Odessa and would have preferred the emergence of the Ukraine as a third force in the combat between Hitler and Stalin.[38] Hitler's freeing of the Ukrainian prisoners of war on the occasion of his joint visit with Mussolini to Uman on 30th August must be understood against a larger background.* In 1939 Mussolini had opposed the extinction of self-government in German-occupied Poland. Later he pointed out that, had the Poles been treated properly, they would now be fighting Russia on the side of Germany. But of course the same idea had crossed Molotov's mind in September 1939, for it was he who insisted that Hitler should create no sovereign Polish state. The results of this could be seen in August 1941, as the train bearing the two dictators passed down the line from Brest-Litovsk to Lwow. The hostile appearance of the population explained the excessive military measures that had been taken to protect the track. Mussolini was able to read Hitler a moral lesson out of this and, he thought, effectively. By the time he had reached Uman, Mussolini expected Hitler to join him

* See p. 104

in a bilateral proclamation of a free Europe and a disavowal of colonialist aims.

Hitler may have toyed with the idea, but for quite opposite reasons
to Mussolini's. At Angerburg, on 16th July, he had stressed the
importance of concealing colonial aims till victory was assured. At that
time Hitler might well have welcomed a camouflage pronouncement,
such as he was to denounce so bitterly* on 1st July 1943. That the
story of the proposed proclamation was no mere invention of Filippo
Anfuso's seems to be borne out by Hitler's freeing of the Ukrainian
prisoners in Mussolini's presence. Yet by 7th November, the amnesty
for the Ukrainian prisoners had been revoked, while Anfuso's draft
for the joint declaration was whittled down in Ribbentrop's Foreign
Office to something quite meaningless which was never signed.
Filippo Anfuso, who went to Uman as Mussolini's Foreign Office
representative, believes that the last minute changes in the draft were
the result of German palace intrigues.[39]** It is more likely that Hitler
had only agreed in order to avoid an argument.

In the history of the Ukraine under German rule the abandonment
of the 'Free Europe' manifesto marks the end of an era. Two days
before the visit to the Uman brickfield, Erich Koch had taken up his
post in Rowné. And, with the arrival of Erich Koch as *Reichskommissar*
for the Ukraine, all dreams of Ukrainian independence and of Ukrainian collaboration against the Soviet Union were at an end.

(b) Erich Koch and his Kingdom

ERICH KOCH WAS a controversial figure even in party circles. At the
Angerburg conference on 16th July Goering had proposed that Koch
should be given either the Baltic States or the Ukraine and Rosenberg
had protested against this, because Koch had already announced freely
that he was not going to take Rosenberg's orders. Thereupon Goering
had blustered that Rosenberg should not keep his people in leading-
strings and Hitler himself had confirmed that Koch was undoubtedly
the man for the Ukraine.[40]*** Even so, Koch's appointment was not
officially published till 20th August. Goering in the meantime had

* See pp. 341–2
** See also p. 104
*** See also p. 142

fought Rosenberg with the argument that Koch had done marvels in rearing pigs in East Prussia, and he was supported by Martin Bormann —which was generally good enough.[41] So Koch was made *Reichs-kommissar* in addition to his duties of Gauleiter for East Prussia and Bialystok.

Koch was appointed for the single purpose of exacting huge quantities of wheat and cattle from the Ukraine. Not only the civil government but also the military operations were geared to this. Just as in 1918 the Austro-German High Command took on the dangerous adventure of policing the Ukraine against Moscow in order to win a million tons of wheat, so in 1941 Hitler gave the occupation of the Ukraine precedence over the assault on Moscow in order that in the third year of the war the Ukraine might feed Axis Europe.

For this task Koch was deemed quite remorseless, a virtue of which he himself reminded the public on many occasions. Koch made himself a symbol of Goering's dizzy-headed plans of exploitation and the living echo of Hitler's contempt and hatred of his Slav subjects. Stalin himself was said to have taken notice of Koch's peculiar oratory. Somewhere about July 1942, he was said to have expressed regret that he could no longer bestow the highest decoration in the Soviet Union, while Koch who deserved it most was not there to receive it. Koch was described by Stalin as the chief of those blockheads in Berlin who reminded every man in the Soviet Union every day what he had to fight against.[42]

Whether or not Stalin's gratitude lingered, it is a fact that in 1949, when the Polish government demanded Koch's extradition from Germany, there was no corresponding demand from Russia. The disinterestedness of the Russians completed the historic paradox, whereby the man whose indiscretions Stalin found so valuable had chosen the same victims as Stalin himself. For Koch's bitterest hate had been reserved for the Ukrainian nationalists, the favourites of Alfred Rosenberg and the pioneers of his anti-Soviet State. Behind all Koch's speeches on a 'nigger people' lurked the contempt of a man who had been almost a communist in his day for the flotsam and jetsam of the White Armies.

Many people found it convenient to blame Koch for the disastrous German policies in the Ukraine, but the truth is that Koch was put there because he allowed every other agency to run the country for him except Rosenberg's Ministry. He seldom visited the place, and, when he did so, it was chiefly in order to give hunting parties and to play the

Satrap. His capital was at Rowné and not historically speaking in the Ukraine at all. Situated till 1918 on the frontier of the Austrian Empire, Rowné had belonged to Poland between 1920 and 1939. In the Volhynian countryside, which surrounded the town, the farmers were still Polish as they had been for several centuries, though the big land-owners had disappeared in the twenty months of Soviet occupation. The peculiar choice of a seat of government was not Koch's. He had wanted to move the administration to Kiev, but Hitler would not permit this ancient centre of Slav civilization to preserve even the shadow of a capital city.*

This choice, which was intended to express Hitler's contempt for the Ukrainians, served ironically to emphasize Koch's remoteness from any real dominion over the country. The most significant things that were done in the Ukraine were the work of Goering's Economic Staff East, Sauckel's labour press-gangs and Himmler's murder-commandos. Koch did little more than provide staff, while signing for these policies and defending them in the noisiest possible way. Koch's real pre-occupation, when he gave the Ukraine his attention, was to fight the woolly and often contradictory orders of the Rosenberg Ministry and to compose memoranda against his chief.

As the mouthpiece of the pure racialist party-line, which was dictated to him by Martin Bormann from the shorthand notes of Hitler's conversations, Koch made his own position unnecessarily difficult, because it is always easy for a dictator to change his mind. Professor Theodor Oberlaender, 'the Lawrence of the Caucasus,' who was to become for a short time an intelligence officer serving on Koch's staff, saw Hitler in July 1941, after the troubles in Lwow. He was told, 'Russia is our Africa and the Russians are our Negroes.'[43] Thus already Hitler had begun to use the language which is found so frequently in his published Table Talk, where he even spoke of using beads as barter with the natives. Bormann not only had these remarks recorded, but sometimes used them as policy directives, with the result that Erich Koch, the former pro-Russian and pro-communist, now talked as though the steppes and forests were occupied by tribes as black as ink. And so it went on till the evening of 30th August 1942, when in the middle of one of his fireside monologues Hitler extolled the chastity of Ukrainian women, most of whom remained virgins till marriage.[44] The master-mind was moving on a new tack, as appeared

* Braeutigam, Ueberblick, etc., p. 19. Nevertheless, Kiev alone possessed a complete native administration which remained loyal to the Germans.

four days later when Fritz Sauckel arrived at his staff conference with the authentic words of a Fuehrer message.

> The Germans had spread like beer. Only the young had left, leaving the old behind. Hence we find hordes of blue-eyed blond-haired people, living north of the Black Sea, who must be Germanized. It is the Fuehrer's wish that in a hundred years time 250 million German-speaking people should live in Europe. He wants the greatest possible number of the Ukrainian workers to be Germanized and they must be selected for service for their suitability on that account.[45]*

This must have been a terrible blow for Erich Koch, coming from Sauckel of all persons. Koch had never supposed that the slave-drives, in which he had been so helpful, were intended to Germanize the Ukrainians—those nigger people with whom one bartered beads. Somehow Koch failed to keep up to date and, when in the following March he sent Hitler his famous fifty-two-page memorandum against Rosenberg, he harped on this point. Since he could not criticize Hitler, he dug up a so-called secret decree of Rosenberg's, dated July 1942, which declared that very many points of contact existed between the German and Ukrainian peoples. 'This decree demands not only correct but amiable manners in dealing with Ukrainians. One is no longer only surprised but astonished.'[46]

Clearly Koch was no statesman in spite of his considerable cunning. Nevertheless his career is interesting, if only to show the sort of hands into which power had fallen under party rule. Like Sauckel, with whom he worked in such close harmony, Koch was a man of the people. His career had begun as a railway booking-clerk in the Ruhr industrial town of Wuppertal. Yet, unlike Sauckel, who under a different dispensation might have terminated a successful career in the trade unions with a seat in the House of Lords, Koch could never have been anything outside Germany but a financial and political charlatan. Only in the atmosphere of bogus revolution which had prevailed in Germany since 1931 could Koch have achieved real power.

The son of a roaster of *Kornkaffee*, that vile synthetic product, Koch was born in Elberfeld (now Wuppertal) in 1896. He claims to have been converted to 'revolutionary socialism' at the age of twenty by a fellow-soldier serving with him in the trenches of the Russian front. But Koch's first flirtation with the Left must have been short, because in

* See p. 270

1921 he served in Silesia in the notorious 'Freikorps Rossbach', a violently chauvinist and anti-communist association. In the same year he joined the infant Nazi Party as its ninetieth member. The year 1923 found Koch engaged in sabotage activities against the French in the Ruhr.[47] In May he figured as one of the pall-bearers at the funeral of a fellow saboteur and member of the Rossbach corps. This was the so-called Nazi proto-martyr, Leo Schlageter. When the occupation crisis ended in the Ruhr, Koch's energy was diverted to more strictly Nazi activities, which brought him for the first time in close contact with Hitler. In 1926 these party activities lost Koch his livelihood as a booking-clerk on the State Railways. Hitler had to provide for him, but Koch was already a difficult subject. He had become drawn to the radical faction in the Nazi Party, the faction that had been formed in 1924 by the brothers Gregor and Otto Strasser during Hitler's imprisonment in Landsberg. In 1926 the Strasser faction sustained a serious defeat, when Goebbels, its most demagogic member, became suddenly converted to Hitler's new policy which was intended for the enticement of rich industrialists. Koch thereupon wrote an article in Gregor Strasser's magazine, called 'Some results of mixed racial breeding'. In covert language it compared the club-foot Goebbels to the club-foot Richard III and, more to the point, to the club-foot Talleyrand who had betrayed both the revolution and Napoleon.[48] Till the last minutes in the Reich Chancellery, Goebbels never forgave Erich Koch.

For a time Koch helped Gregor Strasser to run a sort of rival Party Office, known as 'Gau Ruhr', from which Hitler finally detached Koch in October 1928 by making him Party-organizer or Gauleiter in distant East Prussia—with the handsome stipend of ten pounds a month.[49] During the war years Hitler invented a more flattering interpretation of Koch's exile. He had appointed Koch to East Prussia in order to make sure that the great Junker estate owners did not make use of the Party for their own ends.[50] Koch did in fact dabble in socialist schemes of land-distribution through his 'Erich Koch Foundation', but his greatest success in East Prussia was in making himself a sort of absolute monarch, out of reach of Party discipline.

The choice of East Prussia meant even more for Erich Koch. It made him an obvious candidate for the Satrapies of the conquered east. Koch's capital was Koenigsberg, that placid, prosperous city, where Kant had spent eighty years without moving from the place and where the poplars were cut down to enable him to enjoy his evening view of a mediaeval tower. But the traveller by air gets an impression that will not be found in De Quincey's essay. The cosy agglomeration of red-tiled roofs is scarcely passed before the aeroplane is over a terrifying primaeval domain of forests, swamps and lakes, which seems to stretch without a break as far as Moscow. The situation of Koenigsberg before the Second World War resembled that of a Middle West town of the early nineteenth century, beyond which Red Indians and buffalos roamed for the next 2,000 miles. And if that had been Koenigsberg's position since Kant's day, it had been accentuated by the peace treaties of 1919. For East Prussia was made an island, separated from the Reich by the Polish Corridor. Its disgruntled citizens were fair game for any party that made the revision of the peace treaties its object. An extravagant fear and hatred of the Slav was engendered in the ancient university town, a sense of colour bar and *Apartheid* that had played no part in its former history. The Gau leadership of the large separated German community became a key-post in the Nazi hierarchy, comparable to the leadership over the Germans in the Danzig Free City.

In this way both Koch and Greiser were destined for the future *Drang nach Osten*, for which, when the time came, they furnished a staff of intolerant racialists. Since 1945 Koenigsberg has had to pay for this even more dearly than Danzig. Koenigsberg is now a Russian city, Kaliningrad. It is said to have been resettled with Russians who have been moved from the deep interior and, if a few German Communists remain in this depressed place, they certainly do not remain as *Herrenvolk*.

In Koenigsberg Koch tried to be a local government dictator. He quarrelled with everyone from Brauchitsch, the military area commander, to Bach-Zelewski, the regional SS and police leader. Yet Hitler's support of Koch was unremittent. Koch had gifts of a peculiar order. As Gisevius put it, 'Koch provided the Fuehrer with something novel at every interview, something extravagant, exorbitant and impressive[1]. Among Koch's discoveries were an alchemist who made gold, a chance to acquire the diamonds of the Negus of Abyssinia, and a friendly, boundlessly wealthy, Maharajah, things that had been the stock-in-trade of the eighteenth or early nineteenth century charlatan, rather than his successor of the twentieth.[51] In October 1958, when the haggard wreck of Erich Koch faced the Warsaw judges, there was a brief flash of this extravagance of the past. It was when Koch declared how, as a true socialist, he had fought the British monopoly of soap and margarine in the Germany of the thirties. He had been extradited by the British in 1950 because they could not forgive him.[52]

In those days Goering had been Koch's greatest supporter, because he was always proposing shady deals for the Four-Year-Plan Office. If today the childishness of the rulers of Hitler's Reich seems almost beyond belief, it must be remembered that the first symptoms of revolution, even of bogus revolution as this was, are the loss of a sense of proportion with which a sense of humour is identical.

Koch endeared himself also to the respectable and to the allegedly hard-headed. The SS leader, Bach-Zelewski, claimed in his Nuremberg evidence that he had walked out of the hall during the *Ostmesse* celebrations at Koenigsberg in 1935 when the director of the Reichsbank, the famous Hjalmar Schacht, began to sing the praises of the Gauleiter whom he, Bach-Zelewski, had tried to get dismissed for corrupt practices.[53] Since Nuremberg, Schacht has declared that he had not been singing Koch's praises at the *Ostmesse*, but attacking the persecution of the Jews. Yet Schacht admits that Koch sat next to him and patted him on the head afterwards. In those days Koch had not acquired either his wartime subservience to Hitler and Bormann, or his open condonement of savagery. He seems at no time to have preached anti-Semitism. Schacht was not the only member of the future 'Resistance Circle' to whom Koch appealed. At the height of Koch's extravagances in the Ukraine the highly fastidious ex-ambassador, Ulrich von Hassell, was to write that Koch had once been considered as 'half-way decent'.[54]

Koch's dislike of interference by the SS in his kingdom of East Prussia persisted. During the war, as governor of part of Poland and the Ukraine, he liked to obstruct Himmler's impracticable racial-settlement policies. But he did not dare to obstruct the arrests of the Gestapo or the extermination measures of the Security Police, even when his own authority was encroached. It was for this omission that the Poles tried him in 1958. Koch's contempt of Himmler did not extend to the apparatus which Himmler commanded, and for this there was good cause. Koch had maintained a correspondence with the Strasser brothers as late as 1933, if not 1934. At least one member of the Gestapo seems to have believed that Heydrich had been employed in Koch's office in 1931 and that he had obtained this correspondence as blackmail material.[55] This had put Koch in mortal peril on the notorious 30th June 1934. In the document entitled 'Political Sketch of My Struggle,' which Koch composed in 1950 and which he read out at his trial in 1958, Koch wrote that Goering had withdrawn his protection at the time of the murder of Roehm, Gregor Strasser and their followers. The great Gauleiter had to hide in Koenigsberg in the house of Mueller, the evangelical 'Reich bishop', while Goering had Koch's house and office searched. As late as April 1936 Koch told Hans Gisevius that he expected to be murdered in the next proscription. It was not only Himmler who would be after his blood, but Hitler himself, for he 'knew the perfidy of the Habsburgs'.[56]

This memorable conversation goes far to explain Koch's conduct in office in occupied eastern Europe and above all his squalid lip-service to a side of Hitler's ideology which he had never shared. Till the invasion of Russia, Koch did not profess the contempt of the Slav and Jew which had been fostered in Hitler's mind during his guttersnipe days in Vienna and which was accentuated by Hitler's own sensitivity to his obscure origins and questionable facial appearance. Koch never suffered from that, for he looked like a pink pig. And he was the last man to rail at the Soviet system. As late as 1939 Koch had a conversation with Professor Carl Burckhardt, the League of Nations High Commissioner in Danzig, whom he met in the castle of Podangen. After lamenting the leaderless plight of German youth before the advent of National Socialism, Koch admitted that only Hitler had saved him from being an out-and-out Communist.[57]

As *Reichskommissar* for the Ukraine, it was from Hitler that Koch borrowed his jibes at 'Nigger Peoples'. No such feelings beset the railway clerk from the Ruhr in the 1920's when he entered his future East Prussian kingdom, scarcely knowing what a Slav looked like. The proximity of Koenigsberg to the Soviet Union tended to increase Koch's radicalism rather than his German nationalism. In 1934 he published a small book called *Aufbau im Osten*. Printed in a peculiarly mediaeval black-letter type, it contains a number of pretentious historic comparisons, which were said to have been written for him by a certain Weber-Krohse.[58] It also contains some of Koch's speeches. Whatever Koch's share in the authorship, the book at least shows the sort of thing to which Koch lent his name, for instance the theory that German youth should throw in its lot with the hardened classless youth of the Soviet Union, rather than with the decadent youth of the capitalist West; the theory that the great land spaces of the east were not, as he was later to preach, a place from which the natives should be evicted like Red Indians in order to create a grain belt, but the home of German and Russian pioneers living happily together.

Still more significant was Koch's friendship with the Russophile professor from Koenigsberg University, Theodor Oberlaender, who was to work under Koch for a short time in the Ukraine. In the year of the publication of his book, Koch had been a party to a secret discussion between Oberlaender and the Old Guard Bolshevik Karl Radek, a Galician Jew. Both Oberlaender and Radek opposed the hostile drifting of their governments. Radek, a strange figure indeed, showed himself an admirer of the SS and SA.[59]* This, above all things, Koch had to live down after his Ukrainian appointment. It was known that he had welcomed the Moscow Pact and that he had been disillusioned by the 'Barbarossa' Plan. When Oberlaender became attached to the Ukraine government as an *Abwehr* officer, straight from the calamitous involvements of Lwow, Koch got rid of this reminder of his past almost immediately.

It seems that there was a hidden idealist in Erich Koch. If so, it was very well hidden, even though one so fastidious as Ulrich von Hassell could find him 'half-way decent'.[60] In August 1941, Koch was forty-five years old. His figure was small and bull-necked, his face large and red, not quite humourless even though adorned with a ridiculous Hitler moustache. In this music-hall appearance the keynote is certainly aggressiveness. Photographs of Koch accord perfectly with the vulgarity and brutality of his speeches, for which he set the tone from the very beginning. It is illuminating to discover what Koch was doing on 25th August 1941, the day when his deputy Paul Dargel met Eduard Wagner at Vinnitsa to accept the first portion of the Ukraine from military government. It seems that Koch himself was at the Rosenberg Ministry in Berlin. He was received by a certain Major Crantz of the Luftwaffe, head of the section 'Information and Press'. According to a colleague, Anatol von der Milwe, Crantz greeted Koch as follows: 'Herr *Reichskommissar*, may I congratulate you on the interesting and fruitful assignment you have just undertaken.'

Koch: What assignment?

Crantz: I mean the undertaking to bring back a sense of nationality to so strong and valuable a race as the Ukrainians.

Koch: My dear sir, you must have read that in some local newspaper. Let me tell you one thing. The Ukrainians will be handled with cheap tobacco-stalks for them to smoke, with vodka and the whip (*Machorka, vodka und Nogaika*) while you are sitting in the same place, discovering the Slav soul.[61]

* See p. 38

As Koch left the building after his interview with Rosenberg, he suddenly turned round and, pushing his face into Crantz's, he shouted, 'I don't need your blessings and I don't need your money. I'll have only one advance payment. That advance will be returned to this office in a year's time and then we shall be quit for ever.'

Koch did not forget Crantz. In the summer of 1943 he forced Rosenberg to dismiss him because he had censored for foreign publication a part of one of his own bloodcurdling speeches.[62]

Three days after his visit to Rosenberg, the Satrap arrived in his new Capital at Rowné. The report of Koch's inaugural speech was such that Rosenberg is alleged to have remarked, 'These gone-mad parvenus from Posemuckel (a legendary provincial town akin to Pudsey or Podunk) will bring us all to the grave.'[63] Therein Rosenberg was more prophetic than he supposed, for somehow these speeches, though delivered to a select and alien audience who scarcely left the office without an armed police escort, were known in detail among Ukrainians and even reached the Allied side long before they were cited as Rosenberg's death-warrant at Nuremberg. 'Gentlemen', said Koch, 'I am known as a brutal dog; for that reason I have been appointed *Reichskommissar* for the Ukraine. There is no free Ukraine. We must aim at making the Ukrainians work for Germany and not at making the people happy.'[64] And Koch proceeded to explain that Hitler's demands on the Ukraine were not for the million tons of wheat which the Germans and Austrians had expected in vain in 1918, but for three million tons from a single harvest, to be more than doubled in the following year.

In all this Koch was not speaking for himself but for Goering. We have already noticed language of this kind in the 'Green File' of the Economic Staff East, distributed secretly on 23rd May and openly on 1st July. We have also noticed it in Herbert Backe's 'twelve commandments'. Koch simply regarded himself as a collecting agency for the Economic Staff East, unaware perhaps that there was already a conflict within that staff as to how far the 'Green File' should be applied. Koch made sure that his own very large staff at Rowné understood their duties in this respect and then he left them. At the end of September he paid a brief visit to the newly captured city of Kiev and resumed his reign in his true capital at Koenigsberg.

(c) The Land—Repartition and Settlement

THE REICHSKOMMISSARIAT UKRAINE had now been organized as
a German area of exploitation, theoretically without the faintest flicker
of autonomy. But the great encirclement battle for Kiev was not concluded till 19th September so that, during Koch's first visit to Rowné,
most of the Soviet Ukraine republic was either under German military
rule or still in the possession of the enemy. Only three of the projected
six *Generalbezirke* could be set up and these were based on Rowné,
Zhitomir and Nikolaiev, to be followed at the end of the year by Kiev.
Dniepropetrovsk and Melitopol became the capitals of *Generalbezirke* in
the course of 1942 but were handed back to the military early in 1943.
A further three districts, Stalino, Kharkov and the Crimea, were never
surrendered by the Wehrmacht.

However, a decree, which was signed by Hitler on 15th August 1941,
ensured for Koch a personal empire which extended (at any rate on
paper) from the Baltic to the Black Sea. It was a product of the Moscow
Pacts of 1939, which had left Russia in possession of the entire Grodno
province of the old Poland as far as the rivers Narev and Bug. The
province included the by no means White Russian cities of Bialystok,
Grodno and Brest. By all the rules the territory should have been
treated as Polish and added to the Government General of Hans Frank
after the Germans had conquered it, but Koch contrived that the
greater part should be subordinated to his Gau of East Prussia and the
remainder made part of the *Reichskommissariat* Ukraine. According to
his 'Political Sketch of My Struggle' which was produced at the
Warsaw Trial, Koch had been extremely ingenious. He had learnt that
Goering had asked Hitler to reserve the entire province for him as a
hunting estate, the inhabitants to be removed mostly to the Ukraine.
Hitler had agreed with Koch that deportation on such a scale was
impracticable, but he considered that incorporation in the Government
General would ensure that this would not happen. Koch remonstrated
that Frank would be no match for Goering and that it would be better
to allow him to administer the territory himself.

Goering could not have resisted for long, for his support of Koch
is clearly recorded in the Angerburg minutes.[65] But Koch's inspiration
was unfortunate. It is doubtful whether the Poles would have asked
for his extradition in 1949 in respect of the districts of Mlawa and
Ciechanow alone.

In the south, Koch failed to round off his empire, because the Wehrmacht held on to the Crimea even in the winter of 1942 when the front was more than 600 miles away. Koch was so bitter about his lost inheritance that, if one may trust Peter Kleist, he tried to blockade the country by stopping the shipment of Ukrainian wheat. The Crimea was saved by the action of the *Generalkommissar* for Taurida (Meli-topol), the Viennese playwright Alfred Frauenfeld, a mercurial and somewhat inconsistent person who defied Koch on many other occasions too.[66]

The background to the separation of the Crimea from the Ukraine was Hitler's plan, announced at Angerburg on 16th July 1941, to colonize it with Germans.[67] After the fall of Sevastopol on 1st July 1942 Hitler proceeded with this plan, the only case in which he was prepared to carry out his colonization proposals under war conditions. In a sense it was a strategic decision, because Hitler did not possess the sea-power to guarantee the Crimea against Russian landings, moreover the European part of the population was Russian and not Ukrainian. During the long siege of Sevastopol, when several landings were attempted across the Straits of Kertch, the Red Army had been aided by the Crimean Russians with courage and fanaticism, whereas the Tartars had collaborated with the Germans. As usual, however, Hitler was unable to keep a strategic decision out of the domain of racialist bally-hoo. The Crimea was the home of the Goths and must therefore become German soil. At one moment Hitler visualized an *Autobahn* to connect Germany with the Crimea via Brest and Moscow and it would be lined with German farmhouses on either side.[68] Today the first part of that materialist dream has been fulfilled, but no one told the privileged British tourists who drove along it in 1957 that the *Autobahn* was built by the slave-labour of German prisoners and not, as was first proposed, by Russian prisoners. The adventurous motorists little knew that it had been intended to make the whole thing look like Bavaria.

Actually, at the time of the fall of Sevastopol, Hitler was interested in another plan. On 2nd July 1942 he received the proposals of Alfred Frauenfeld that the Crimea should be settled with Mussolini's German-speaking subjects, the South Tyrolese. All that these unfortunately placed people had to do, according to Hitler, was to sail down a single German river, the Danube, and there they were.[69]* In order to make room for the Tyrolese, several hundred thousands of Russians were to

* See p. 153

be marched by land almost at once from the Crimea into the Ukraine. The consequences of this deportation were viewed with equal concern both by the High Command and the Rosenberg Ministry. Neither, however, was called upon to carry out the operation. That was Himmler's task. Himmler's agencies, RUSHA and VOMI, had had some experience of this sort of thing in 1939–40 with the settlement of racial Germans in the newly annexed Polish territory, and the experience had been an almost unmitigated disaster. Himmler told Frauenfeld on 10th July that the Crimean plan was a phantasy that must be postponed. During the subsequent delaying action, however, Hitler became restive. On the 27th the gossipy Walter Hewel came into the tea room at Vinnitsa with a report that all sorts of Russian refugees from Leningrad were in the neighbourhood on the way to the climatic delights of the Crimea. Hitler exploded. Here was the army issuing passes for Russians, just when he was trying to empty the Crimea. It is not clear how Himmler succeeded, but by September the orders were withdrawn and the mistake of a full-scale racial resettlement was not repeated in wartime. The Crimea was made part neither of Germany nor the Ukraine. It was ruled as a naval base by an admiral.[70]

Much more important than the Crimea to the political entity of Koch's *Reichskommissariat* Ukraine was Kharkov, which with 833,400 inhabitants was the chief industrial city of the Soviet Union. It was the obvious capital for the Ukraine, if Kiev was ruled out. But till the end (though with a short Soviet interruption in March 1943) the Wehrmacht ran Kharkov as a rival capital to Rowné during their whole period of possession between October 1941 and August 1943. When Kharkov was finally lost, the whole structure of civil government in the Ukraine became a shadow and soon afterwards Koch's territory was reduced to what it had been in the beginning. It had never embraced even half of the Ukrainian Soviet Republic, which in 1939 was reputed to have thirty-one million inhabitants. It was none the less a sizeable empire for the small-town boss of Koenigsberg, officially 16,910,008 inhabitants on 21st February 1943, when all six General Districts were functioning.[71] But from this one must deduct the whole of the forest and swamp belt along the northern border of the steppes which remained in Partisan hands.

It is a mistake to assume, though many German authors imply it, that the army's share of the Ukraine got better government than Koch's share. In April 1943 Goebbels recorded with some glee that, since the retreat from Stalingrad to Kharkov, the Field Marshals Manstein and von Kleist had modified the severity of the measures that Koch had failed to execute.[72]* It was certainly a fact that, since the beginning of the year, von Kleist had ignored the Economic Staff East and introduced his own economic system in Taurida and Crimea, but he did so at a moment when everything had to be done to placate a population that might aid the advancing Red Army.[73] During the year 1942, when the exactions of the Economic Staff East, the slave-raids of the Sauckel organization and the mass-shootings of Jews and prisoners of war by the SS raged continuously in the Ukraine, the military government in Kharkov did considerably less to stop these things than some of Koch's own officials. Military government officers, however, refrained from making the sort of idiotic speeches, for which Koch was famous, and a few of them composed well intentioned memoranda. Since the military governers were anxious to recruit auxiliary troops and loyal militiamen, these memoranda were fairly numerous, but it must be added in fairness that two of Koch's *Generalkommissars*, Ernst Leyser at Zhitomir and Alfred Frauenfeld at Melitopol composed equally humane memoranda for the impotent Rosenberg.**

The system of administration in the Ukraine owed nothing to Erich Koch. It had been drawn up in the Ministry after Hitler had rejected most of Rosenberg's original proposals. Each of the six *General-bezirke* under its *Generalkommissar* was to contain about twenty *Kreisgebiete*, which were at least equivalent to an English county, under the rule of a *Gebietskommissar*. All these officials were to be Germans. In practice it turned out that a surprisingly large portion of the administrators had lived in Koenigsberg, where they had excelled themselves in Koch's Gau office, making patriotic speeches, collecting subscriptions and denouncing their neighbours. The best posts in the Ukraine went to some of these Party heroes. Particularly favoured young Koenigsbergers were Joachim Paltzo, the propaganda chief of the new kingdom, and Koch's deputies Ferdinand Grossherr and Paul Dargel. Three of the six huge *Generalbezirke* went to the older Koenigs-berg Party officials, Nikolaiev to Ewald Opermann, a building con-tractor, Kiev to Waldemar Magunia, a master-baker, and Volhynia-Podolia to the Koenigsberg chief of police, Heinrich Schoene.[74] So far as experience went, it was like sending the members of a countrified Urban District Council to take over Mexico, but experience was the last thing that Koch or, for that matter, Hitler wanted in a civil

* See also p. 461
** See p. 349

governor. The Angerburg minutes of 16th July 1941 show, for instance, that Hitler particularly desired Karl Holz to be a *General-kommissar*. He was to govern part of the *Reichskommissariat* Moscow, the huge unit which was to replace the Russian Soviet Republic proper. The chief merits of Karl Holz were his editorship of the anti-Semitic rag *Der Stuermer* for Julius Streicher, besides twenty political convictions including five terms of imprisonment.[75] When Rosenberg proposed another drivelling anti-Semitic journalist, Arno Schickedanz, as governor of the entire territory between the Black Sea and Caspian, Hitler made no objection. Only one candidate of Rosenberg's encountered at Angerburg what Bormann called 'General consternation, general rejection', and that was the former SA leader, Captain Petersdorff, whom both Hitler and Goering pronounced to be insane. If that was all, Petersdorff seems to have been unfairly treated.[76]

Practical men might, however, sometimes find their way into the lower administrative grades, if only because a few such were inevitable, where numbers were so large. In February 1943 the Ukraine contained 114 German *Gebietskommissars*.[77] Below the *Gebiet* the next unit was the *Rayon* or group of villages and here the *Rayon-chefs* were native Ukrainians. Still lower were the village headmen and small-town Starosts and the Councils of Elders.

Such in theory were the limits of native self-government in the German occupied Ukraine. Here, however, theory could not be reconciled with realities. The whole Soviet apparatus of State collecting-centres for produce had collapsed with the retreat of the Red Army. Thus a great part of the 1941 harvest was deliberately destroyed or allowed to rot, while what was left was earmarked for the Wehrmacht. No immediate attempt was made to replace the Soviet marketing system, which meant that the great industrial Ukrainian towns were virtually left to starve. This had been quite implicit in Goering's 'Green File' orders.* The survivors of the urban populations, still very numerous, had to bargain as best they could on a free black market. If the Germans washed their hands of the problem, they also washed their hands of the activities of the bargainers. Consequently the Ukrainian towns, filled with misery though they were in the first winter of the campaign, achieved a degree of self-government that was not in the book of rules.

This was thoroughly consistent with German policy in eastern Europe. The Ukrainian towns were treated in the same way that the Germans had been treating the Polish ghettoes since 1940. Only a

* See p. 62

highly organized black market could keep the immense closed ghettoes of Lodz and Warsaw alive. Within the ghetto walls a Jewish administration worked this market and distributed its products as a completely independent power. The same principle, when applied to Russian cities, was the very reverse of what Hitler called his 'political preparations', but it was the only principle that worked.[78]

According to Hitler's address to the generals of 30th March 1941, a good many of the Ukrainian local government officials should have been murdered long ago as bearers of Soviet indoctrination, for it is inconceivable that enough anti-Bolsheviks could have been found competent to fill these thousands of posts. The first function of the *Rayon-chef* was to satisfy the demands of an endless stream of visiting German officials, looking for produce, slaves or suspected Partisans. Later on, as the Germans carried out the Scorched Earth Order, the *Rayon-chef's* duty was to destroy the crops, mills and livestock on which the community lived. Thus the native administration had the agreeable choice of being shot either by the Germans or by the young men of their race who had taken to the woods. In the Ukraine however, where such a choice was no novelty, there were mysterious survival properties. No physical calamity has yet destroyed the communal sense of man. Witness the strange case of *Vucoopspilka*, an Ukrainian co-operative marketing association, which, according to Otto Braeutigam, survived Stalin's all-out attack on the Ukrainian peasant in 1929–34. It also survived Erich Koch who tried to confiscate its assets and Himmler's Security Service who murdered its chiefs. It survived the avenging Red Army in 1943–4 and it survives today.[79]

Not all Ukrainian local government bodies were faced with the choice of 'kill or be killed', but it is certain at least that those who worked closely with the Germans had lost all credit with the population long before the Germans were forced to abandon Ukrainian territory. The era of the bread and salt of hospitality and of German tanks, garlanded with flowers, was a very short one. Disillusionment came with the separation of Transdniestria, with the imprisonment or execution of members of OUN and UPA, with the callous abandonment of the prisoners in the Ukrainian Stalags and Dulags and the consequent uncertainty whether racial extermination was reserved for the Jews alone. It came with the exorbitant demands for produce by civilians and soldiers alike, with Sauckel's press-gangs and the antics of Erich Koch. Yet the sum total of these errors was surpassed by the German land policy. Possibly the Ukrainians would have put up with all the other misfortunes, if they had been allowed to believe that the Germans would relieve them of the Marxist system. But, just as had happened in the Baltic States, the Germans retained the collective farms and State farms because they assured the delivery of more produce. In the Baltic States Soviet rule had lasted scarcely more than a year and the Germans became heirs only to very patchy collectivization and nationalization. But in the Ukraine collectivization had been carried out in four years of coercion and resistance which were a recent memory. That alone had been responsible for the extravagant welcome of July 1941.

The minutest instructions were issued through Goering's Four-Year-Plan Office to the *Lafuehrer* or district agricultural leaders of the Economic Staff East. The instructions, which were contained in the first draft of the 'Green File' as issued on 23rd May 1941, were for preserving, intact and unchanged, both the collective farms or *Kolkhozi* and the State farms or *Sovkhozi*. Any attempts by German agencies to dissolve the *Kolkhozi* were to be fought with the severest measures. Herbert Backe, the arch-bureaucrat who was responsible for these ninety-four pages of instructions, was said to have declared that, if the *Kolkhozi* had not existed already, the Germans would have had to invent them.[80] Hitler himself was able to reconcile his avowed intention to destroy everyone and everything, connected with Moscow rule, with this perpetuation of the king-pin of the Marxist system. There was, he was reported to have said to Seyss-Inquart on 26th September 1941, no alternative to collective farms, because 'the Russian intelligentsia must be considered destroyed'.[81] Thus Hitler could imagine nothing better than a system of which Stalin had made a gross failure. Yet this same system was expected to extract three million tons of Ukrainian wheat in the first harvest alone and seven millions in 1942.

This expectation became still more grotesque when peasants were dragged from their small-holdings to work large estates, from which the Russians had removed the tractors and draught-cattle. Koch himself complained that fields of unworkable size were being ploughed by hand.[82] So in the chaos of this first Russian winter German officialdom had to achieve some flexibility. On 29th January, Goebbels's Diary noted with unusual approval that Rosenberg's office had drafted an agrarian plan for the Ukraine, which aimed at a gradual return to the private ownership of land.[83] But it was not Rosenberg who had earned Goebbels's approval. He indeed had played little part in this revolution of policy.

On their very first encounter with the collective farm system in the Soviet Ukraine, military government officers had reported in favour of abolition. But Herbert Backe objected to this with that faith in rigid State Control which afflicts all civil servants in wartime and which attests the strength of their secret passion. Backe's Agricultural Leaders even seized the cow which had been granted in the collectivization plan to every household serving the *Kolkhoẓi*—the famous Stalin cow which had here and there survived the devastation measures of the retreating Red Army. Backe, however, was too far away to control the Economic Staff East. On 15th September 1941 his aides, Hans Riecke and General Georg Thomas, took it upon themselves to restore the statutory hectare and a cow and even to double them.[84]

Complete restitution was not to be undertaken so light-heartedly. Parcelling out tens of thousands of collective farms could not be done without interrupting the order of production. In the case of the State farms or *Sovkhoẓi*, of which there were 2,000 in the Ukraine, the question of restoration was associated in the peasants' mind with the Pomestchiks, the former landlords of these estates in imperial times. In Podolia-Volhynia it was no idle fear, since the big Polish landlords had been in residence not two years since. But, after a journey to the Ukraine, Backe reported against further changes and on 8th November under Backe's guidance Goering re-issued the original instructions of the 'Green File'.[85]

But the campaign to undermine Backe continued. A plan was produced by Otto Schiller, Riecke's delegate to the Rosenberg Ministry. As an agronomic professor, Schiller had been economic attaché in Moscow and was reputed to know the terrain. Schiller sent a memorandum to Goering on 14th September advocating a progressive abolition of the *Kolkhoẓi* with a continuance of compulsory labour, because of 'the absence of incentives for free enterprise'. For this plan the support of Paul Koerner, head of the Four-Year-Plan Office, was enlisted against Backe.* Even Goering no longer defended the original 'Green File' rules. His interest in State Control was not fanatical, unless it was a matter of obtaining remunerative seats on nationalized boards. Finally Backe himself ceased to argue and a joint recommendation from the *Ostministerium* and the Economic Staff East was sent to Hitler on 16th December. The last objector was Erich Koch. He proposed that, in return for putting up with the hated Soviet collective system, the Ukrainians would be adequately recompensed if they were

* See p. 119

allowed to elect their own village councils. This, as Rosenberg glee-
fully recalled, was laughed off by Hitler as 'Koch's House of Lords'.
Hitler approved Schiller's draft on 5th February 1942.[86]

Published as a decree of the *Ostministerium* on the 26th, the new
Agrarerlass showed a German change of heart rather than a practical
amelioration of the lot of the Ukrainian peasants. In theory all Soviet
legislation concerning collective farms was abolished. The name was
therefore changed from 'collective farms' to 'communal farms'
(*Gemeinwirtschaften*).[87] Though the labour of the members of the co-
operative remained compulsory, the land became their own property,
free of tax, and, if they chose to work harder, they could apply for
a larger share. Thus the happy subjects of Utopia had within their
reach the advantages which had been achieved by the villeins in the
late fourteenth century. To advance beyond the fourteenth century
was less easy. If these semi-collective farms should fulfil the delivery of
the enormous quantities of export produce which were demanded by
the German authorities, then these authorities would permit the dissolution of the collective structure. The component parts would revert
to private farms as in the west. But any kind of bad report against a
farmer, whether it concerned his work or his political opinions, would
disqualify him from independence.

But what advantage was there in such independence? Once again
Braeutigam's study demonstrates the hollowness of the new policy.[88]
Under the Soviet system each member of the family on a *Kolkhoz* was
entitled to sixteen monthly kilograms of bread-stuffs. Under the
German decree it was only ten, a starvation ration. It meant that grain
had to be concealed or exchanged on the black market.

Nevertheless Riecke was proud of his work. As a Nuremberg witness
in 1946, he declared that the decree had proved a success. In the
Kharkov basin, for instance, the 1942 spring planting had given a
70 per cent yield as against 30 per cent under Soviet collectivism.[89]
This conflicts with Braeutigam's memorial of 25th October 1942,
which alleged universal failure both in Koch's Ukraine and the
Wehrmacht's Ukraine. Braeutigam had learnt from Paul Koerner that
only a quarter of the farms had been decollectivized by that date,
though the process was to have been completed by 1st August.[90]
Apart from physical difficulties, it had been held up by the feuds of
Rosenberg and Koch, of Riecke and Backe. Koch had his own 'Head
Office for food and agriculture' at Rowné, which was directed most
confusingly by another Koerner, Major General Helmuth Koerner of

the SS, bull-necked and scar-faced.[91] This office made it a policy to register as many farms as possible as *Sovkhozi* or State farms, which had no co-operative basis. These remained under German management even under the terms of the new decree. Like the former Soviet tractor depots, they were not even affected by Rosenberg's final decollectivization decree of 3rd June 1943. They remained German strong-points in an increasingly hostile land.

This policy of Koch's was in line with some of Hitler's pronouncements which he studied so carefully. On 17th October 1941, Hitler repeated the threat, which he had made at Angerburg, that the Ukraine should be colonized by foreigners. He envisaged twenty million foreign inhabitants in twenty years' time.[92] Hardly had Hitler approved the Agrarian Decree when he received the 'General Plan East' of Professor Meyer-Hetling. The professor was an adviser to Himmler— which was appropriate since Himmler had a monopoly of resettlement matters—and the way he looked at it was this. The German and western European colonies should be placed in a wide semicircle, extending from Kherson on the Black Sea to the Pripet Marshes. In this way the Poles would be isolated from the eastern Slav world. But the settlement of twenty million west Europeans was incompatible with the progressive return of the land to the Ukrainian peasants, even if Hitler believed that the Ukrainian humus was ten metres thick.[93] It was, however, the colonization plan and not the reinstatement of the Ukrainian peasants that slipped out of the picture; so once more Koch found himself a move behind his Fuehrer, because he had not the sense to see that the solution, which guaranteed immediate food supplies, would be preferred.

But if Hitler's change of mind saved the German occupation of Russia from being totally unproductive, production could still not be maintained at a fraction of the scale which he demanded. Nor could the policies of his unco-ordinated ministries produce consistency, even where sheer naked exploitation was concerned. In 1942, the year that was to see the harvest increased through decollectivization, more than 700,000 able-bodied workers were shipped from the Ukraine to Germany by the Sauckel organization. The resultant loss of farm man-power was great, but even more damaging was the flight of young men to the Partisans, as Sauckel's press-gangs got to work.* Koch lent his administrative staff to Sauckel as generously as he lent them to Backe and enjoyed doing so even more, because it annoyed Rosenberg. The

* See p. 267

final balance sheet is eloquent of what happened. Pleased though he was with the first results of the Agrarian Decree, Riecke at Nuremberg had no illusions about what had been the final outcome. The Germans, he declared, had never throughout their occupation achieved the production figures of the ill-functioning and unpopular Soviet system. As for Hitler's dream of a surplus, sufficient to feed twenty or thirty million people, there was not even a tenth of it. Fifteen per cent of the food of the Reich at war came from occupied countries. In 1944, when the entire Russian harvest was lost, the figure fell to 10 per cent. So the best land of European Russia had not sufficed to grow 5 per cent of Germany's annual food consumption.*

But it is in the mines and heavy industries of the Ukraine that one may read the true failure of Hitler's predatory war, the end of an Austrian corporal's dream of a campaign, involving millions of men but fought solely at the expense of the enemy. The first proposals of the 'Green File' and the 'Brown File' were influenced not so much by the desire to destroy Russian industry as by the belief that it could be left out of the calculation.** The trade agreement of February 1940 had broken down on the German side because the Russians refused to take consumer goods and would only exchange their raw products for the munitions of war. In May 1941, however, it was envisaged that any consumer goods would do to attract the flow of Russian raw produce, because the restraints of the Soviet economic system had been removed. The war would be short and therefore the Germans would not require the use of Russian industrial plant. Where plant had been destroyed, it was a mistaken notion to re-establish order and economic life. The Economic Staff East was to concern itself only with areas which had an agricultural surplus or which produced oil.[94]

In September 1941 Hitler still cited these pre-invasion instructions as the basis of the peacetime economy which he proposed for conquered Russia. And even a year later he declared that he would not copy the British in India, who had ruined themselves by permitting

* *IMT*, XI, p. 90. *Hitler's Europe*, I, p. 215. The proposition can be stated better in the figures which were supplied up to 31st March 1944 by the *Handelsgesellschaft Ost*, the marketing board of the Four-Year-Plan Office. They show that, first to last, the Greater Reich received no more than 1,160,187 tons of grain and breadstuffs. The armed forces in Russia received five times as much, 5,650,000 tons, and the population of occupied Russia, 2,341,000 tons. The armed forces figure is so huge that it must include stocks exported to Germany by Wehrmacht agencies as well as the stocks which were destroyed to avoid capture by the enemy, a very considerable item. Even so the figures are nowhere near the quotas of which Hitler commonly spoke, and perhaps not even as high as the despised Austro-German quota of 1918. Braeutigam, *Ueberblick* etc., p. 40

** *Nuremberg Document*, EC 126, quoted on p. 62

industrialization. Only such machinery need be left in Russia as would be wanted for the absolute necessities of the country's future German and West European occupants.[95]

That was in August 1942, before the shadow of Stalingrad clouded Hitler's daydream. The prospect of a long war altered the picture. Within a few weeks Hitler not only praised Stalin's industrial achievements, but planned to get some use from them by repairing the damages of war.[96] This had in fact been going on for some time in a quiet way; now it received priority. The great Dnieperstroi dam, blown up by the Russians in September 1941, was to be rebuilt—and by the end of 1942 Hitler expected the power stations of the Ukraine to be working and German munitions to be manufactured in the Donetz basin. Something in this direction was certainly achieved, but the start was made too late. Barely a year after the mines started working, the tide of war swung back to the Donetz basin. The Dnieperstroi dam, repaired in January 1943, had to be blown up for the second time in the following September. The Donetz basin, after swallowing up German money, yielded less than a tenth of its annual production under Stalin.[97]

CHAPTER SIX

THE UKRAINE—THE ILLFARE STATE

(a) Rosenberg versus Koch

THE AGRARIAN DECREE and the plans for deporting Russian labour to the Reich made the month of February 1942 the beginning of Rosenberg's trial of strength with Erich Koch. Previously Rosenberg had enjoyed some favour with Hitler, even if he had been appointed only because Hitler did not think that the civil administration of Russia mattered very much. On his second report to Hitler on 19th December 1941, Rosenberg had found the Fuehrer sympathetic when he complained that Koch claimed to be acting directly under Hitler's orders. Hitler went so far as to promise not to receive Koch except in Rosenberg's presence. In February 1942, when Koch stated his claims formally, Hitler sent him a rap on the knuckles through Hans Lammers, declaring that he had adopted an untenable position.[1]

This did not stop Erich Koch who in the end was to win a barren legal victory. His claim to be acting under Hitler's direct orders had some justification. In Norway, Holland and Poland, *Reichskommissars* governed without the interference of a Ministry. They were Ministers in their own right, responsible only to Hitler. In Russia Koch and Lohse were second class *Reichskommissars*,[2] and their position was made more infuriating by the claims of the *Hauptabteilung Politik* to prepare lines of policy for them. The decisions which Hitler announced at Angerburg on 16th July 1941 were illogical. He had made Rosenberg his adviser on matters concerning Russia, and Rosenberg had drawn-up occupation plans in time of peace. With the creation of *Reichskommissars*, Rosenberg's function should have ended or it should have remained purely advisory. Two motives impelled Hitler to give Rosenberg the powers of a Minister over the *Reichskommissars*. One was his curious loyalty to old colleagues of well-tried incapacity and the other was his wish that there should be no strong rulers in Russia, while he was himself so uncertain of the future disposition of the conquered territory.

Encouraged by his reception of 19th December 1941, Rosenberg made some first attempts to assert his authority in Koch's own domain. Impressed by the policy of the Rear Area Commanders, who re-opened churches and permitted the installation of ecclesiastics, Rosenberg sent Seraphim, the Metropolitan of the exiled Russian Church in Germany, on a visit to the Ukraine. On 29th January prayers for German victory were offered by Seraphim in the cathedral of Rowné. Koch was incensed that this political gesture in his own capital should be the work of the author of the atheistic *Myth of the Twentieth Century*, the declared enemy of the churches in Germany. 'You are not the Rosenberg I used to know', he wrote, 'but a man in the hands of *émigrés*'.[3] Goebbels too thought it extremely funny when Rosenberg wrote to him at this time concerning his religious toleration policy. 'Now, when we are in a tight place, everyone poses as the champion who fights against the very things that he has started'.[4]

The Agrarian Decree and the visit of the Metropolitan brought Koch out of his winter quarters in Koenigsberg. Rosenberg complained that Koch had been to Rowné only twice since September,[5] but he soon gave up that sort of complaint, because in Rowné Koch was a much worse nuisance than in Koenigsberg. In March Koch announced his own rules for the conduct of his German officials. Since they were in line with Hitler's observations concerning niggers and strings of beads, Rosenberg was rash in making an official complaint to Hitler, as he did through Hans Lammers on the 16th, and rasher still in attacking Hitler's own assessment of Koch. It was wrong, according to Rosenberg, to compare Koch's policy with the British in India. The British at least did not advertise their attitude. They kept silent about their harshness and only talked about the blessings they had conferred on the Indians.[6]

Since Hitler did not intervene, Koch enlivened the month of April with three more addresses to his staff on the treatment of 'niggers'. It was reported to Rosenberg that one of these addresses had inspired an ordinary *Kreisleiter* to testify that he would shoot anyone in his area who showed signs of intelligence.[7] At the same time Koch sought external support. On 2nd May he sent a memorandum to Goebbels. The bearer was a young man called Joachim Paltzo, who had been a sort of ambassador of Goebbels's Ministry at Koch's court. Paltzo complained of Rosenberg's ineptitude and then added tenderly that the work of the Goebbels Ministry was the only thing that had so far helped Koch's difficult task in the Ukraine. That, of course, as the amiable and pink-cheeked ambassador well knew, was the one and only way to talk to Goebbels. Through the lines of his *Diary*, Goebbels can be heard purring and, after this embassy, he had no difficulty in believing that Rosenberg was lost in plans for the millennium and that the Wehrmacht had eaten up all the food in the Ukraine.[8]

Rosenberg was received by Hitler a few days later, on 8th May, but he was too afraid to mention Koch's speeches. It was safer to attack the 'Adloniada', Ribbentrop's elaborate attempt to stake a claim in occupation politics in Russia.[9]* With the cold eyes of Bormann and Lammers upon him, Rosenberg did not dare to refer to his unanswered memorandum of 16th March.

After the audience Rosenberg left for Riga, but all that he could not say to Hitler was put on paper in the form of a long bill of indictment against Koch. Copies were also sent to Koch's own subordinate officials, who were designated as responsible to Rosenberg for carrying out the rules he had laid down. In particular Rosenberg warned them against administering corporal punishment, of which there had been several complaints. To these laborious charges Koch replied equally laboriously in his involved German style, for Koch had never set himself the ideal of the strong man of few words.[10] Koch admitted that he knew of cases of whipping, but he had forbidden the practice. A year later he modified this statement. In the worst case of whipping he would have preferred outright shooting.[11] Whipping, however, was not the crux of the matter. By circularizing his own officials against him, Rosenberg had made Koch's position intolerable. Koch had no alternative but to appeal to Hitler.

By the middle of July four entire months had passed since the offensive instructions, which Koch had issued to his staff on his return to Rowné, and still there was no decision from Hitler. It is uncertain how many memoranda had been sent to the Fuehrer's headquarters on both sides. Mr Dallin mentions another appeal to Hitler by Koch on 29th June, while Peter Kleist describes a most elaborate document which the Political Department prepared for Rosenberg and which was put before Hitler about the same date, the so-called Grosse Denkschrift.** The area of complaint had been expanded to include Koch's refusal to reopen the Ukrainian technical schools and the questionable methods used by Koch's officials in assisting Sauckel's labour deportation plan.

* See p. 292
** See p. 268, Kleist, p. 206, and Dallin, p. 141

Hitler's ruling, when at last it came, was disconcerting for Rosenberg but not altogether without precedent, for it was another of those occasions when Hitler permitted his fireside musings to be transmitted through Martin Bormann as a policy directive. It seems that, on the night of 22nd July, Bormann came into the tearoom at Hitler's head-quarters at Vinnitsa, weary, jack-booted and beetling with gloom after a long motor drive through the Ukrainian countryside. He was oppressed with the numbers of blue-eyed and chubby-faced Ukrainian babies that he had encountered. Since Hitler fell in with Bormann's mood, the conversation bore a marked resemblance to that of the Walrus and the Carpenter, to whom the parties bore a physical resemblance as well. Bormann lamented that the Ukraine was multiply-ing too fast. German colonization could never keep up with it.[12]*

'If seven maids with seven mops
Swept it for half a year,
Do you suppose,' the Walrus said
'That they could get it clear?'
'I doubt it', said the Carpenter,
And shed a bitter tear.

Hitler, however, mixed the bitter tear with some suggestions of his own—or rather some suggestions which he had read in a plan for Poland, which Himmler had sent him in May 1940.[13] Hitler told Bormann that both education and health services would be a great mistake in the Ukraine. The Ukrainians should be taught that Berlin was the capital of Germany and they should be able to read the German road signs—no more than that. They should not be regimented, but rather the reverse. The Ukrainians could be left to crowd into their kraals outside the handsome new German towns, where the Jews could sell them contraceptives and where their fear of vaccination could be liberally encouraged.

At the end of this tirade Hitler remembered that he was expected to decide between Rosenberg and Koch, that since the middle of March the whole status of Rosenberg's Ministry had been in question. Forgetting that he himself had created this superfluous Ministry, but recollecting with the pride of an individualist that he had once stopped a government department in Berlin from forbidding dog-breeding, Hitler came down heavily against centralization.

As regards the eastern territories, therefore, I wish only broad instructions to be issued from Berlin; the settlement of day-to-day

* See p. 144

issues can safely be left in the hands of the respective Regional Commissars. I propose, therefore, to reduce the danger of regimentation in the eastern territories by reducing the German administrative machinery in them to an absolute minimum and seeing that the Regional Commissars deal with and through the local mayors. I do not, of course, intend that out of this should grow anything in the nature of a Ukrainian Civil Service.[14]

Next morning the substance of Hitler's remarks was conveyed by Bormann to Rosenberg in the form of 'Eight principles for the government of the Eastern Territories'.[15] As summarized in the *Hauptabteilung Politik*, the first part reads like this:

The Slavs are to work for us. Insofar as we don't need them, they may die. Therefore compulsory vaccination and German health services are superfluous. The fertility of the Slavs is undesirable. They may use contraceptives and practice abortion, the more the better. Education is dangerous. It is sufficient if they can count up to a hundred. At best an education is admissible which produces useful servants for us. Every educated person is a future enemy. Religion we leave to them as a means of diversion. As to food, they are not to get more than necessary. We are the masters, we come first.[16]

Rosenberg had received no answer to his complaint of 16th March concerning Koch's speeches, and now he was confronted with something more extreme than any of them, delivered to him apparently under the orders of the all-highest. Rosenberg described his state of panic in his Nuremberg evidence. He described how, on receiving Bormann's 'eight principles', he had expected an attack on himself from the Fuehrer's headquarters or at the very least a rigid Fuehrer decree on the same lines. Faithful to his Russian past, Rosenberg at first did nothing whatever. And the wisdom of that course was proved five days later, when, instead of a sharp reminder, Hitler sugared Bormann's pill with a splendidly worded piece of meaninglessness, appointing Rosenberg 'sole delegate of the Reich government in matters of policy relating to all peoples of the former Soviet Union'.[17]

There was only one thing for Rosenberg to do and that was to show that he was pleased. So, on 11th August, he wrote to Hitler that not only did he approve the eight principles, but that in the course of the past year he had already put them into practice, particularly as regards simplifying the administration and reducing staff. As to 'maintaining the protection of German rule against the pressure of the Slav race', he had done that too by issuing instructions that the increase of the Ukrainian population was not to be encouraged. Vaccination was rather different, because epidemics among Ukrainians might become a danger to German personnel.[18]

Rosenberg's assertion was untrue. He had in reality created a Health Department in the Ministry, which sent well-intentioned people to lecture to Ukrainian physicians. Koch, however, took good care to see that they did not amount to a National Health Service for Ukrainians. The hospitals were banned to all but Germans and those who worked for them.[19] But, if henceforward Rosenberg proposed to march in step with Bormann's principles, then the medical jurisprudence of National Socialism would surely find a way to deal summarily with epidemics. Among the Rear Area Commanders of the Wehrmacht, who were as correct in their dealings with the Security Service as the hooks of their collars, such things were taken for granted. For instance, in October 1941, there had been a shortage of milk in the three military hospitals at Poltava. So the Security Police shot 599 lunatics in the neighbouring asylum and the hospitals received the milk from the asylum farm and the lunatics' bedding as well.[20] Far more recently, at Mariupol in the same military area, a commando of *Einsatzgruppe D*, which was attached to the 17th Army, had expeditiously gassed all the syphilitic patients at an institute, whereupon, in anticipation of further hygienic measures, an entire TB clinic had taken to the woods.[21]

Such incidents explain the consternation that was felt in the *Hauptab-teilung Politik*, when Rosenberg's letter to Hitler was read out by Job Zimmermann of the Propaganda Section. It was believed that Rosenberg was about to issue Bormann's Eight Principles as an instruction to the *Generalkommissars* and *Gebietskommissars* and that these men, 80 per cent of whom were said to oppose Koch's methods, would be ordered to follow them implicity. A remonstrance was drawn up by Dr Markull of the Legal Section and sent to Rosenberg through Leibbrandt. It was urged that Rosenberg could not possibly issue the Eight Principles in their present form, whatever he had promised Hitler in his letter.[22] The language, it was said, was not in keeping with the importance of the historical problem involved. Of course no one dreamt of questioning the sincerity of Herr Bormann, but a phrase like 'a brisk trade in contraceptives' had better not be brought into connection with the name of the Fuehrer.

After all this hullabaloo in the Rauchstrasse, which caused him no harm at the time but a great deal at Nuremberg four years later, Rosenberg continued to do nothing or next to nothing. A Hitler order to simplify the administration was another stick with which to beat Erich Koch. On 21st August Rosenberg circulated an order which forbade members of Koch's staff to send any direct communications to Hitler's headquarters.[23] Koch realized now that Bormann's heavy guns had misfired and that no real decision had been made in his favour. So he issued a challenge; either Rosenberg should inform him that there was no longer a *Reichskommissariat* Ukraine or he should send him the sort of orders that enabled him to govern the country.[24]

At this time, the tide seemed to be turning for Rosenberg. On 6th August Koch attended a gigantic conference in the Berlin Air Ministry, where, before a horde of Gauleiters and occupation authorities, Goering openly snubbed him. Koch had given the figures of the numbers of workers shipped to Germany from the Ukraine. 'Your miserable half-million,' Goering shouted. 'How many has Sauckel brought in? Nearly two millions. Where did he get the others?'[25] Koch was now under attack both for his ruthlessness and his lack of it. Hitler demanded another 225,000 workers for Germany from the Ukraine by the end of the year. On 5th October Sauckel complained to Rosenberg that Koch would not even answer letters on the subject. Where was this *Reichskommissar*, who flitted between an office in the Ottokarstrasse in Koenigsberg, a hunting lodge near Rowné and the Adlon Bar in Berlin? Could Rosenberg tell him where Koch was to be found? On leave in Vienna from the Russian front, the journalist Erich Kern learnt from one of the highest of the 'Bonzes', Gauleiter Josef Buerckel, that the Party wanted to get rid of Koch.[26]

It was time for another memorandum from Rosenberg's Political Department and this time Otto Braeutigam did not mince matters. The memorandum of 25th October 1942 was an attack, not only on colonialism but on Rosenberg's own separatist plans. It was a plea for a declaration to the peoples of Russia on the lines of President Woodrow Wilson's fourteen points of 1918. Koch and Sauckel were both under fire. If the Ukrainians were to be treated for ever as second class whites, the Partisan movement would eliminate their country as a source of food for the Reich. Koch had alienated forty million [*sic*] friendly Ukrainians. The lower administrative chiefs in most cases meant well, but in Koch's kingdom they were 'frightened by the policy of the higher echelons'.[27]

Stimulated but not altogether convinced by the suggestions of the dynamic Braeutigam, Rosenberg was persuaded to meet the Rear Area Commanders of the Wehrmacht, who ruled more territory than did the Ministry. To his horror, Rosenberg learnt that these remotely cloistered brass-hats believed him to be an influential Old Party Fighter, who could persuade Hitler to change his entire Russian policy.* Rosenberg, however, did no more than forward the minutes of the meeting to Hitler without demanding personally either the removal of Koch or the promise of future autonomy to the Russian peoples. As to Koch, he was not depressed by his setbacks. On 28th October he had issued a decree without consulting Rosenberg. As a war economy measure in line with Germany, all trade and technical schools in the Ukraine were to be closed.[28] Since Koch might argue that this was a Fuehrer order, Rosenberg did not challenge it outright but only urged the importance of the schools for the prosecution of the war. Thus Rosenberg's homily to Koch lacked both tact and force. As sent off on 14th December 1942, it reads like the Rescript of some shadowy fifth century Roman Emperor.[29]

> By appropriate bearing and deeds one becomes master, but not by insolent shocking manners. One does not lead people by insolent talk and one does not gain authority by exhibiting contempt for others.

The reactions to this pompous sniff were quicker than usual, since Koch was no farther away than the Adlon Bar. Next day he arrived in Rosenberg's new office, the former Soviet Embassy on Unter den Linden. While Koch pushed his way into Rosenberg's room, his deputy, Paul Dargel, sought Anatol von der Milwe in the Culture Section. It was this section that had infuriated Koch by debiting the *Reichskommissariat* 2,300,000 Marks for new school-books, printed in Ukrainian—and this in June 1942, when there were not enough school-books for German children.[30]

Paul Dargel was a timber-merchant from Elbing, whose entire experience of administration had been acquired in the Gau office of his home-town. After the conquest of Poland, Koch had made this sympathetic East Prussian blusterer, *Regierungspraesident* for the annexed district Zichenow (Ciechanow) and in August 1941 his deputy and virtual governor of the Ukraine during his absences. Dargel was thirty-eight years old, had the cauliflower-ears and thick jaw of a prize-fighter and a juvenile crest of blond hair that made him

* See p. 323

look like a barnyard rooster.[31] The apparition burst into von der Milwe's room without knocking and, after an exchange of acerbities, launched forth with a tirade, declaring that the Ministry's Culture Section was trying to recreate an Ukrainian educated class, while 'we want to destroy the Ukrainians'. When von der Milwe told him that one could not exterminate forty million Ukrainians, Dargel answered, 'You can let that be our trouble. Do you live on the other side of the Moon? It should be known to you that the Fuehrer wishes the Ukraine to be made a settlement land for German peasants.' Pressed on this point, Dargel explained that, on the achievement of victory, the Ukrainians would be expelled beyond the Volga, leaving behind a Helot class to work the mines.

After ten minutes of Paul Dargel, von der Milwe had to deal with Koch, whom he found upstairs, pounding up and down the room before a very scared Rosenberg. Koch came straight to the point. He showed von der Milwe his fist with a massive gold ring on it. 'Look at that,' he said. 'I once pushed that ring in the face of a civil servant who interfered in my affairs.'

Von de Milwe. Then you certainly did right if the civil servant wasn't polite to you.

Rosenberg. Koch, calm yourself. I am not used to that sort of language.

Koch. You can't stand any forthright manly language.

Rosenberg. In my Ministry I alone decide the language. You wanted Herr von der Milwe to come up here. What have you to say to him?

Koch. There won't be any judgment of my actions here. I told you, Rosenberg, that you and your Ministry have got to keep your fingers off planning schools for my Ukrainians. What happens in the Ukraine and what happens to Ukrainians I alone decide in agreement with the Fuehrer. If von der Milwe or any other of your education artists shows himself in the Ukraine, I'll arrest him as soon as he sets foot across my border. That's what I have got to say to von der Milwe.

Rosenberg. I won't have such language used in my house.

Von der Milwe withdrew, but as he left the room the storm was still raging and Koch's voice continued to boom, 'In my Ukraine I alone decide.'

Koch was as good as his word. Not only was no member of the Ministry allowed henceforward in the Ukraine, but Koch also forbade his own staff to visit the Ministry when on leave. This happened, moreover, at a moment when Rosenberg's stock was lower than ever at Hitler's court. A week later Rosenberg received Hitler's bitter comments on the conference with the Rear Area Commanders. On that occasion even Hitler's reputed confidant, Alfred Jodl, had consented to consult the Ministry's views, but, if Rosenberg believed that he had the might of the Wehrmacht behind him, he was disappointed, since the Wehrmacht received another stern admonition against meddling in politics.* As for Koch, he tried to repair his lost position in the Party, remembering the criticisms of Goering and Sauckel. It was a struggle, in which he could hold his own only by delivering something material. So it was that, on 13th December, a whole trainload of Ukrainian food, including symbolically a great deal of butter, reached Berlin as a personal compliment to Goebbels as Gauleiter. Goebbels took care to give Koch no public credit for it. He distributed the food to needy cases as a 'gift from the Party'.[32]

Hundreds of miles beyond the border of the *Reichskommissariat*, this month of December 1942 brought peril to an entire German Army Group. Russian reinforcements crossed the Don and cut off Stalingrad. The Wehrmacht needed all the transport it could lay hands on to the detriment of the Sauckel Organization and the slave-trains. Even this situation Koch exploited to his own advantage and his ingenuity helps to explain the riddle of his present survival. As the leave-trains passed through the *Reichskommissariat*, the soldiers were offered 'Fuehrer parcels' to take home, parcels as big as they could carry. In this way some of the rotting food surplus of the Ukraine was shifted by the very Wehrmacht that had commandeered the rolling stock. And of course the soldiers blessed the name of Erich Koch. Unfortunately, once the principle of Fuehrer parcels had been established, similar parcels had to be given to men going on leave from White Russia and the Baltic States, where there was no food surplus.[33]

Rosenberg was now virtually cut off by Koch from communication with the Ukraine. On 23rd February 1943 he tried to issue a formal decree, reopening the elementary and technical schools. Ten days later Koch summoned his civil government officers to his presence at Kiev and said all that he wanted to say about such decrees. It took two months before Rosenberg learnt by a very roundabout route of Koch's contumelious utterances. Koch had declared that each official should get a rubber stamp and use it to print the words 'not essential for the war' on anything from the Ministry that he did not like. The rest of Koch's speech was in his usual strain, 'I will draw the very last

* See p. 323

from this country. I have not come to spread bliss. I have come to help the Fuehrer.'[34]

Thus Koch had orated for the past eighteen months. Only now the Red Army held Kharkov and their patrols were not two hundred miles from Koch's audience in Kiev, where the population speculated on an immediate return of the Red Army. More important but hardly more realistic was Koch's boast that he had reduced his staff at Rowné from 800 to 250. Without public health, transport or education services to look after, with nothing to do but sign for the manhunts and exactions of the other Ministries, the Rowné government could never be understaffed.

In March 1943 Rosenberg knew nothing about this speech, but he knew that Koch had ordered the use of still more savage press-gangs to assist Sauckel in fulfilling his 1943 labour-quota of another million workers from occupied Russia. On the 13th Rosenberg distributed orders to the commissars in the Ukraine, forbidding them to follow Koch's circular. Koch called in the order and re-issued it with part cut out. Even so, Koch felt far from sure of his own position. In spite of that heavy gold ring, he was always very much a man of words and he now composed an enormous open letter to Rosenberg to be circulated to all Gauleiters, to Gottlob Berger for submission to Himmler and to Martin Bormann for submission to Hitler. The memorandum of 16th March 1943 is as large as a thick notebook and it occupies fifty-two pages of foolscap in the stencilled Nuremberg Trial text.[35]

In this memorandum Koch listed all the most petty interferences of the *Ostministerium*, together with their dates, and all the decrees which Rosenberg had forbidden Koch to circulate or which Rosenberg had circulated over Koch's head. So far as we have followed it, the history of the Rosenberg-Koch feud derives largely from this document, 'PS 192'. The most important part, however, is where Koch restates his claim to be directly responsible to Hitler.

As an old Gauleiter, I am accustomed to go to my Fuehrer directly with all my problems and requests. In my capacity of *Oberpraesident*, this right has never been denied me even by my superior Minister. By decree 1 c-b, 470w, I was ordered to report to you [Rosenberg] on matters where the Fuehrer's wishes were to be consulted, since the forwarding of the Fuehrer's communications was your affair exclusively. I must state here

that in my position as an old Gauleiter, the Fuehrer has frequently
given me political directives himself. If one takes away or curtails
the position of the *Reichskommissars* in relation to the Fuehrer,
then very little remains that is in keeping with the position of a
Reichskommissar . . . my position has been encroached on by
you so often in the past three weeks that it can only be re-
established by the Fuehrer.[36]

Rosenberg retaliated by sending Hans Lammers a file of documents
covering the entire dispute.[37] Then, as the inevitable silence followed
from Hitler's headquarters, he petitioned formally for Koch's dismissal.
This was on 15th April. Quoting from the unpublished file of Himmler's correspondence in the Library of Congress, Mr Dallin records
that on the same date Koch had a three-hour talk with Martin Bormann
who promised him 'full cover'.[38] Rosenberg searched desperately for
more ammunition. Brutality and insubordination were worthless
charges, when Koch made a virtue of both. There remained his
notorious corruption, but Koch's record on this count had been
surprisingly clear since he had become a *Reichskommissar*. His Satrap
style of living was apparently no more spectacular than that of other
Reichskommissars, such as Hans Frank in Poland or Hans Terboven
in Norway. Nor did corruption count very much among Party
eminences.

The exception to this easy-going attitude was Himmler, who had
tried since 1929 to give his SS organization the asceticism and inacces-
sibility of a religious order, not a very hopeful goal when so many of
the duties of the SS had to be handled by convicted felons and criminal
sadists. Himmler, however, affected not to notice the inconsistency and
remained personally a monument of incorruptibility. So it was to
Himmler that Rosenberg addressed himself, recollecting how the SS
had denounced Koch's corruption in the middle 'thirties. A subject of
complaint had not been easy to find, because Koch's officials were too
scared of him to talk. The 'Tsuman scandal' was in fact unearthed for
Rosenberg by a prospective candidate for the post of *Landkommissar*.

Tsuman was an enormous forest domain, not far from Rowné in
the direction of Luck. It had been a hunting estate of the Radziwill
family, the great Polish landlords of Volhynia. In late Tsarist times it
had been famous for hunting-parties of a feudal magnificence that,
but for the incidence of Edwardian dress, must have come straight out
of the *Très riches heures de Jean, duc de Berry*.

Koch, it was declared, wanted nothing less than to hunt like a Radziwill in this forest, which, under the Polish republic and the brief Soviet occupation had become a government estate for the production of resin. Koch was alleged to have admitted it openly. He had seized the domain, because he needed a place where his guests could hunt when they came to Rowné. He claimed to have done it with the knowledge of Alfred Meyer, Rosenberg's deputy and *chef de protocol*. The evacuation of the Tsuman region had begun as long ago as December 1942, but it was not till 2nd April 1943, a fortnight after Koch's monstrous great circular, that Rosenberg sent the papers to the same circulation list. Gottlob Berger was expected to lay the Tsuman papers before Himmler and Lammers was to submit them to Hitler.[39]

According to the indictment, Koch had removed hundreds of people from their homes in the depth of winter. They were taken overnight a distance of forty miles. Hundreds more of these forest-dwellers had been shot as Partisan agents by a police company of the SS. But no Ukrainian had believed the tale about Partisans and even Germans had noticed that no such anti-Partisan measures had been required in other parts of the Ukraine. Enclosed with Rosenberg's memorandum was the report of a chief forestry adviser of the Ministry of Agriculture. The report showed that the evacuated families had now to be transported twenty-five miles by lorry in order to carry out their daily work. In the hunting domain itself Koch had banned all resin-tapping. Three hundred thousand resin taps were out of action, tar factories had stopped working for the Wehrmacht and the saw-mills had been closed at Klewan.

Recalling that Himmler had once at Posen listened to him sympathetically, when he had tried to explain 'Koch's so-called policy', Rosenberg requested Himmler to investigate the charge through Hans Pruetzmann, his Police Leader for the Ukraine. But this was a particularly vain hope of satisfaction; for if the facts were confirmed, Pruetzmann himself would be implicated in a massacre which had been conducted, not for exemplary racialist motives, like that balance sheet of 363,111 murdered Jews which Pruetzmann had sent Himmler for Christmas,[40] but simply to find favour with the former railway clerk from Wuppertal.

On 29th April, having heard nothing from Himmler, Rosenberg again reminded Lammers of the Tsuman file, but it was not till 19th May that Rosenberg and Koch were summoned to Hitler's presence.

In the meantime Koch had dug up a report from his 'Chief of Population Affairs', which contradicted the chief forestry adviser. It seems
that the Tsuman domain had to be cleared in order to provide railway
sleepers. The mopping-up of Partisans in the forest had been necessary,
because the timber-cutters had to be protected. Koch claimed that he
had been thanked by the resettled forest-dwellers, for whom he had
provided better land in another forest.[41]* After hearing this explanation
Hitler shrugged his shoulders and said that, though he was obliged
to accept the forestry adviser's report, he found the matter too difficult
to decide and would leave it alone.

And now Hitler turned to the two huge files of charges and counter-
charges that had waited his decision for the past two months. It seems
that Hitler knew at least of some of the matters which they contained.
At first Hitler seemed prepared to put some of the blame on Koch, in
spite of the prejudiced manner in which Lammers and Bormann had
presented the material. Basically, however, Hitler supported Koch's
views on governing the Ukraine, where he would not tolerate any
liberalization. 'If we were to apply gentle treatment for a spell, it would
become impossible to ship labour to the Reich and the export of food
to the Reich would cease.' Then, bolstered by some provocative
interpellations from Bormann, Hitler launched an attack on the
'sentimentality' of Rosenberg and some members of the General Staff.
And so to Hitler's favourite theme, the treachery of the Ukrainians
as allies in 1918, and their murder of their greatest friend, Field Marshal
von Eichhorn.

It seems that Hitler then left the room, abandoning to Bormann and
Lammers the task of making the Minister and *Reichskommissar* shake
hands, a task in which they failed. Hitler had avoided making any
decisions. The questions of the Ukrainian schools, of the right of
Rosenberg to give instructions to Koch's subordinates, of Koch's
right of complaint over Rosenberg's head, of the right of the Ministry
staff to visit the *Reichskommissariats*, all remained equally unsolved.
It was not till June that Lammers sent Rosenberg a document which
purported to be Hitler's ruling. In fact the long-delayed judgment of
Solomon ran true to form. Hitler simply stated his cast-iron general
views, disdaining to pay serious attention to any mere Koch or
Rosenberg.[42]

But Lammers recalled at Nuremberg that, though there was no
settlement of the differences of opinion and though no agreement was

* It was not long before the Partisans were back in the Tsuman Forest, see pp. 247–8

reached, 'the unwise decision was made that these two gentlemen should meet once a month and co-operate'.[43] There is no evidence that this part of Hitler's instructions was carried out. Rosenberg shortly afterwards visited the Ukraine in person, probably at Hitler's behest, but after that sinister visit the two men met publicly only once. This was soon after Rosenberg's return, on 13th July 1943, when Koch attended a conference of ministries in Rosenberg's office, the subject being labour in the east.[44]

While Rosenberg could not have hoped that a journey to the Ukraine would re-establish his authority over Erich Koch, the journey at least gave him an excuse for avoiding the onerous rôle which the Area Commanders had cast for him. Shortly before the interview with Hitler, Rosenberg had been visited by General Hellmich, Inspector of the Eastern Troops, that is to say the prisoner of war volunteers, a not very political soldier who had been put up to demand the dismissal of Erich Koch.* Hellmich had returned from the interview, declaring that Rosenberg was 'not a man but a dishcloth'.[45] Worse still were the importunings of General Eduard Wagner, who was now more than ever convinced that only a proclamation of liberation for the Russian people could win another campaign in Russia. On 25th May a delegation, which was led by Braeutigam, met members of Wagner's staff at Mauerwald. Once again Rosenberg was told that the military government officers looked to him to persuade Hitler to make this proclamation by forcing his way to Hitler's presence past the barriers of Keitel and Jodl.** Now, however, Rosenberg could tell Wagner that the interview with Hitler must be postponed, unless Hitler consented to see him before 3rd June, the date of his departure for the Ukraine. So Werner Koeppen, the elderly messenger-boy who alone represented the Ministry at the Fuehrer's headquarters, was ordered to arrange an appointment through Keitel and of course no appointment was possible till after 3rd June.[46]

There was a further motive for Rosenberg's Ukrainian tour and that was pure vanity. The visit was timed to coincide with the publication of Rosenberg's decree freeing the *Kolkhozi*. Not only would Rosenberg's presence instil confidence in the lesser commissars, who were loyal to the Ministry, but it would rejoice the Ukrainians who would hail him as a liberator. The Private Property Decree had been approved by Hitler with singularly little obstruction from any quarter. The

* See p. 326
** See p. 335

exception was Erich Koch. In the previous March, when Koch was making his ridiculous Kiev speech, only the hurried despatch of three armoured divisions of the SS from France had prevented the loss of the entire Ukraine. For a time the Red Army had been back in Kharkov, yet here was Koch still fussing about the danger that the peasants would inherit the *Kolkhozi*. The *Erbhof* or ancestral farm was something, he said, for the German colonists of the future and not for the helot race.[47] More to the point, Koch argued in his memorandum for Hitler that the establishment of land titles for the shared-out *Kolkhozi* would need tens of thousands of surveyors.[48] Where could they be found? Koch might have added, 'How much time?' For by the end of the year almost every *Kolkhoz* in the Ukraine was back in Soviet hands. And, within three months of Rosenberg's tour, the Economic Staff East had abandoned all attempts to implement the decree, though Koch went on disputing the principle.

So Rosenberg set out on his ghostly triumph through Rowné, Vinnitsa and Kiev, through the eastern Ukrainian cities, Poltava, Dniepropetrovsk, Zaporozhe and Melitopol to the Crimea. In 1924–5, when Hitler was in prison, Rosenberg had taken the Fuehrer's place. Now, eighteen years later, he was absolutely friendless in high Party circles. If Rosenberg had been able to travel in the company of a Goebbels or a Himmler, even in the company of a Robert Ley or a noisy aggressive Gauleiter like Josef Buerckel or Paul Giesler, he might have frightened Koch. But nowadays no one who expected to achieve the higher leadership wanted to be seen in the company of the discredited author of *The Myth of the Twentieth Century*.

Rosenberg took with him his chief of information services and propaganda, Job Zimmermann, and his ministerial director for Ukrainian affairs, Dr Kinkelin. This physician and SS Major-general had formerly been employed by Himmler in resettling racial Germans from Volhynia under the terms of the Moscow Agreement of 23rd September 1939. Neither Zimmermann nor Kinkelin would have been allowed into the *Reichskommissariat* by Koch, had it not been for Rosenberg's state visit. Rosenberg also took with him the Gauleiters of Steyermark and Mainfranken, Messrs Uiberreither and Helmuth. They were the least aggressive sort of Gauleiter, the one a small town lawyer and treasurer of the sick fund in Graz, the other a Wuerzburg dentist of anti-clerical leanings.[49]

Publicly at any rate the eighteen days' tour began with decorum, for in Rowné Koch actually consented to meet Rosenberg at the airport and to drive with him to his baronial castle. It may be thought that Tsuman was not a dinner-table topic, but the evening did not end on the same polite note; for Zimmermann was present when Koch announced his position. If Rosenberg took advantage of his tour to issue decrees or to introduce his theories into the administration, Koch would go to the Fuehrer.[50] Henceforward Koch tried to prevent Rosenberg speaking with any Ukrainian. Trouble began at Vinnitsa on the very next day, when Otto Schiller demonstrated on the spot the method by which a *Kolkhoz* could be partitioned. Koch declared that this was sabotage of Hitler's orders and he indulged in a long attack on his chief in the presence of a number of Ukrainians.[51]

And so it went on. At Kiev Rosenberg wanted to ask some Ukrainian professors to lunch, to which Koch observed that, if the guests were important enough to lunch with him, he would have to shoot them. At Nikolaiev Koch left ostentatiously, when the *Generalkommissar*, the Koenigsberg building contractor, Ewald Opermann, introduced folk dancers for Rosenberg's entertainment.[52]

Outwardly all was pomp and circumstance. Rosenberg and Koch were photographed for the press, riding together in a *Kaleske*, drawn like a royal coach across the flat Volhynian landscape by four splendid greys. They were shown surrounded by their staffs, Koch's tubby figure in a shockingly ill-fitting white military raincoat and Rosenberg in the uniform of a cinema commissionaire. There was no need to emphasize their permanent proximity. Even in the areas of military government Koch still dogged Rosenberg's heels. Only in the Crimea, which, it will be recollected, was ruled by the navy, Koch decided to leave Rosenberg in peace. For a few days Rosenberg could dream among the palaces of Livadia and Bakhtcheserai, and among the gardens of Simeis, where in the year 1917 he had honeymooned with his first wife, a young Russo-German, unconscious of what destiny was already preparing for him. Still more unconscious was Rosenberg amid the distinctly crumbling shell of June 1943. The place, that was soon to be the scene of the partition of Germany, called from him only speculations on the home of the Goths.[53]

In the lost *Commissariats*, where the Wehrmacht ruled, Rosenberg had a chance to meet Koch on equal terms, but even that chance was missed. At Dniepropetrovsk he accompanied Koch to the Head-quarters of Field Marshal Ewald von Kleist. Many years after the war, von Kleist was tried by the Russians as a war criminal, who had been extradited to Moscow by the Yugoslavs. He died in a prison camp in

1955 at the age of seventy-five years. Koch on the other hand is still alive, a sinister irony of fate for a man like Kleist, who thought himself the very opposite of Koch and what Koch stood for.

In Koch's presence Kleist delivered a deliberate lecture for Rosenberg, terminating with these words, 'Unfortunately it has been our experience as soldiers to defend positions that are already lost, unless there is a change of policy in the Ukraine.' This was no place for Koch to display his jewelled fist, but he delivered some acid comments on the Field Marshal's ill-judged pessimism. Yet, even with this opportunity, Rosenberg dared not support von Kleist, who briskly terminated an uncomfortable conversation, to which Rosenberg had contributed nothing.[54] It was the same at von Manstein's headquarters in Melitopol. Manstein remembered that Koch had spoken of labour-recruiting in the Ukraine, denying that it was forcible. He had no recollection that Rosenberg had said anything at all.[55]

But even Koch's presence could not prevent Rosenberg learning the truth from one of his *Generalkommissars*. Ernst Leyser, the *Generalkommissar* of the Zhitomir region, was a former State Railways official and a severely practical man, who had been deputy Gauleiter in the Saar. It is astonishing how Koch came to approve such an appointment, unless it was due to his respect as a former railway booking-clerk for a *Staatsbahnrat*. The sort of official whom Koch preferred, was Paul Dargel or *Kreisleiter* Knuth of Kiev against whom there were the 'gravest accusations',[56] and who declared that Kiev ought to be destroyed through epidemics. Rosenberg saw Leyser at Zhitomir on 17th June, his last day in the Ukraine. It is not quite clear from the memorandum of the conference, which Leyser sent to the Ministry, whether all of it was delivered verbally by Leyser in Koch's presence, but the man who could write such a paper evidently did not fear the consequences for himself.[57]

According to the memorandum, the Partisans were now collecting 60 per cent of the produce in the *Generalbezirk* Zhitomir and even supplying the peasants with seed to grow it. So great were their inroads on live-stock that only 28 per cent of the sheep went to the Germans' share. In only five of Leyser's eighteen *Gebiete* were the German Agricultural Leaders able to operate. In the remaining thirteen *Gebiete* they were forced to barricade themselves in the former Soviet tractor depots, which were garrisoned as strong-points by German police troops.

Apart from these depots, the Germans had lost most of the collecting places for produce, because of the lack of troops to guard them. The Partisans held most of the forests, so that in the Vinnitsa region, which was free of Partisans, the timber had been overcut. The Partisans swarmed so freely that there was only one road in the *Generalbezirk* Zhitomir, which could be used without convoy-protection—and that was the eighty miles of road separating Hitler's summer headquarters at Vinnitsa from Himmler's headquarters, the former Soviet military academy at the *Volksdeutsche* colony of Hegewald near Zhitomir. In fighting the Partisans of Leyser's *Generalbezirk*, some 4,500 police, Ukrainian militiamen and German civilians had died in a year. Leyser, a much decorated veteran of the First World War, commented that, though there always seemed to be plenty of troops in places behind the front, the military Rear Area Commanders invariably protested that they could not spare men for campaigns against Partisans.

In rather more guarded language, Leyser went on to connect this state of affairs with the deportation of labourers to Germany. This had been intensified since April 1943, when Sauckel himself had visited the Ukraine.* No doubt Rosenberg listened to this too in that state of dumb wretchedness which was habitual to him when under Koch's choleric eye. In Leyser's report he could read the total failure of all that Hitler's 'colonialism' had tried to achieve, for the subject was the richest and most populous part of agricultural Russia and also the part that had welcomed the Germans with flowers less than two years ago. But at least it could be said that in some parts of the Zhitomir district there was government of a kind. Northwards and still further north-wards into White Russia and Lithuania there was no government at all, except in certain towns on the German supply lines.

The struggle between the Minister and the *Reichskommissar* had become a phantom struggle between men without substance. It was none the less bitter and it was taken seriously by many German senti-mentalists, who thought there was still time to turn an utterly immoral war into a Russian people's crusade for liberty under the Swastika banner. Such men could still rejoice at the victory of a Rosenberg over a Koch, as if the two poor creatures meant anything any longer.

Koch had been busy with his complaints to Lammers, even while Rosenberg was with him in the Ukraine. The subject was once again Rosenberg's decree of 23rd February 1943, re-opening the elementary and technical schools in the Ukraine. Koch now advanced a line of argument, which was calculated to appeal to Hitler. In the Ukraine he

* See p. 275

had 'lost half a million Jews'. As a result there were no skilled trades-
men left. One could not even get boots mended. 'Which is the more
important? That I train Ukrainians to make boots or that I send them
to High Schools so that they can build the Ukrainian State?'[58]

It was a reminder to Hitler that he had not announced his decision
after his arbitration between Koch and Rosenberg on 19th May. So, on
22nd June, when he returned to his office in Berlin, Rosenberg found a
Fuehrer Directive which had been waiting for him well over a week.
According to Rosenberg's own recollection of it, he was to be 'limited
by basic principles as far as legislation was concerned and not to
interest himself too much in the details of the administration of the
eastern territories.'[59] The actual text of Lammer's note shows that it
was worse than that. Koch was to have the right to submit counter-
proposals and Lammers and Bormann were to be the arbitrators, if
there was no agreement. In effect Koch was now independent, because
Lammers and Bormann were sure to support him.[60] Rosenberg concealed the humiliation from his staff, but the *Hauptabteilung Politik*
knew the truth and advised Rosenberg to tender his resignation.
Rosenberg replied that this was not possible in an authoritarian state.[61]

But though Hitler had given a decision favourable to Koch, he
would not decide personally on any specific issue. When Koch
continued to memorialize against the Private Property Decree,
Lammers wrote in September that he was not to bother the Fuehrer
any more about it.[62] And the question of the Ukrainian schools
remained unsolved. Not that either schools or *Kolkhozi* mattered in
September 1943, the month of the German Scorched Earth Order in
the Ukraine, for few indeed were the farms where a German *Lafuehrer*
dared show himself, and few the towns where a German official could
either open schools or shut them.

Rosenberg received through Keitel another Fuehrer directive, which
could afford him only relief. A teleprinted message, dated 8th June,
informed him that Hitler had banned all discussion of Russian liberation movements and that Rosenberg's proposed meeting with Jodl and
Keitel was now superfluous.[63] So Rosenberg was spared that much
dreaded journey to Rastenburg.

Rosenberg had realized for some time that the Ministry could only
rule over the Satraps in the east if some high Party personality, of
whom Koch and Lohse were equally afraid, could be induced to serve
in it. But there was no such personality who could want to work with
Rosenberg, unless he was allowed to give him orders. There was

indeed an organization which was always ready to take over posts in every Ministry, but which was seldom invited to do so, and that was the SS. To ask a very high up SS leader to take over the *Hauptabteilung Politik* would weaken Rosenberg's authority still further, but there was this to be said for it. While the SS acted in Russia almost independently of Rosenberg, SS activities were chiefly directed against Jews, Partisans and prisoners of war. In these matters Rosenberg did not quarrel with the SS, as he quarrelled with Goering, Sauckel and his own *Reichskommissars*. A point in favour of appointing an SS man was that Koch was jealous of Himmler's encroachments, both in East Prussia and the Ukraine, and that now he might show himself still more so. On the other hand Rosenberg had no love for Himmler, because he had dragged the Party indoctrination schools out of his hands and generally replaced him as an ideological expert. It was otherwise with Himmler's mentor and reputed good fairy, Gottlob Berger, who from the SS Leadership Head Office (SSFHA) directed the domestic affairs of fifteen SS field divisions. With Berger, Rosenberg was on good terms.

Forty-seven years old, bushy-eyebrowed and somewhat Slav in appearance, Gottlob Berger, the former village schoolmaster of Waldstetten and director of the Wuerttemburg gymnastics institute, was not a pronounced Slav-hater in spite of the fact that it was Berger's office which had sponsored the notorious *Untermensch* illustrated brochure. Since 1940 Berger had recruited natives of Finland, Scandinavia and the Low Countries for the fighting SS on the principle that any Aryan type could be considered Germanic. Berger had gone further than that. He had decided that all fighting tribes were basically Germanic too, for the SS now included Bosnians and Albanians of Moslem stock, as well as the beginnings of a Ukrainian division from Galicia.[64]*

As head of the SS, Himmler was still obliged to imitate Hitler in describing the Ukrainians as an inferior race, but for a long time racialist mumbo-jumbo had been losing the battle within the SS against the hunt for cannon fodder. Even in June 1941, the intelligence service of the SS had competed with Admiral Canaris for the services of Ukrainian terrorist groups. At the moment of Rosenberg's return from the Ukraine, Berger was trying to get some of these terrorists out of the concentration camps to serve in his Galician SS division.

Berger was not only opposed to Koch's view of the Ukrainians, but was half in Rosenberg's Ministry already. Since July 1942, shortly

* See also p. 355

after Heydrich's death from a Czech patriot's bomb, Berger had added
to his appointments the position of liaison man between Himmler and
Rosenberg. Almost at once he had intrigued to get possession of the
Hauptabteilung Politik. By January 1943 Rosenberg was willing, but
he encountered opposition from his deputy, Alfred Meyer, and strong
opposition from within the *Hauptabteilung Politik* itself. This situation
changed considerably in April, when Himmler supported the plans of
the *Hauptabteilung Politik* for Baltic autonomy, the motive being the
recruitment of SS divisions by Gottlob Berger.* Berger even pretended
to support Rosenberg in the Tsuman affair.

For Rosenberg the removal of the head of the *Hauptabteilung Politik*
entailed no difficulties, since the dynamic force had been not Georg
Leibbrandt but his deputy Otto Braeutigam, who was well supported
in the Wehrmacht bureaucracy. But Rosenberg could not afford to
jettison Leibbrandt, if his action should be interpreted as an appeasement of Erich Koch. It was better to let the SS provide the motive as
well as the successor, and it was fortunate that Leibbrandt had been in
the bad books of the Main Security Office from the start. Everything
was against him. He had been born a Russian subject in a German
settlement near Odessa, he had lived in the US. As a Rockefeller
scholar he had studied at not less than six universities, and one of them
had been London. Moreover, in the days before the *Ostministerium*,
Leibbrandt had cultivated numerous Russian emigrants on behalf of
Rosenberg's APA. Some of his protégés had been picked up by the
Gestapo, the moment Hitler invaded Russia. By October 1942, when a
genuine large scale communist conspiracy, the *Rote Kapelle*, had been
unearthed, Leibbrandt became severely under fire. He retained his
post, more through the exertions of his colleagues than through the
loyalty of Rosenberg.[65]

Rosenberg probably decided to drop Leibbrandt after the interview
with Hitler and Koch on 19th May 1943. Four weeks later, while still in
the Ukraine, Rosenberg sent Leibbrandt on sick-leave to enable him to
undergo a cure at Karlsbad (Karlovy Vary). To a Nazi official this
prim spot was a certain harbinger of disaster, the *Baiae* of the Third
Reich. At Karlsbad Leibbrandt learnt not only that he had been dismissed but that he had been called up in the ranks of the SS as well. As
a former *Gruppenfuehrer* of the SA, Leibbrandt contrived to avoid this
ignominy. On 10th August, at the age of forty, he enlisted in the
German Navy as an ordinary seaman. In 1949 he was discovered as a

* See p. 150 and Dallin, pp. 172–4

forgotten man, lecturing to an American cultural institute in Munich.*

But Gottlob Berger stepped into Leibbrandt's shoes too late to effect any policy change in the Ukraine, since the *Reichskommissariat* had only a few months to live. Rosenberg failed to see the true end which Berger's appointment was to serve, namely the emergence of Himmler as a champion of Russian liberation. Berger became far too concerned with these matters of high policy to bother himself over the office affairs of the *Hauptabteilung Politik*, which was now renamed 'The Political Operations Staff'. At first he paid a daily visit to Rosenberg's deputy, Alfred Meyer, but he occupied no desk and signed no papers. Eventually it was contrived that an adjutant, one Brandenburg, should sign for him. In the summer of 1944, when he had not been near the Ministry for weeks, Berger proposed to Rosenberg that the Political Operations Staff be transferred to the SS Head Office. When Rosenberg refused, Berger built up a parallel organization of SS men.[66]

Thus Berger completed the paralysis of Rosenberg's powers. Even those who had showered good advice on Rosenberg for two years sent their reports to the SS. It is true that, for the first time, the Ministry had ambassadors at the courts of Koch and Lohse, but this hardly affected the situation that then existed. In the Ukraine the *Referenten* were afraid of Koch and reported in his favour. In the *Ostland* they were not afraid to report against Lohse.[67] Consequently, when there was no longer a *Reichskommissariat* Ukraine for him to govern, Koch was ordered to the *Ostland* to supersede Lohse. But slowly and very steadily the curtain was coming down on the Rosenberg-Koch tragi-comedy.

(b) The Scorched Earth

ON 5TH JULY 1943, a fortnight before Rosenberg's return from the Ukraine, Hitler opened his third Russian summer campaign. 'Operation Citadel' was not a bid to end the war, but an attempt to forestall the Russian initiative by pinching off the Kursk salient. The attempt failed and a month later the Russians used the salient to launch a deep relentless armoured thrust towards Kiev and the river Dnieper.

* Charges against Georg Leibbrandt and Otto Braeutigam, *Nuremberg-Fuerth Landgericht*, 18.1.50. A few months later this court absolved both men of all charges without bringing the case to trial.

Kharkov was lost for the second and last time in the middle of August. There followed a strategic and, for the time being, controlled withdrawal of the Southern Army Group and Army Group A. By the beginning of October all the Ukraine east of the Dnieper was abandoned, except for part of the Nogai steppe covering the Crimea. A month later Kiev fell and by the end of December the Russians had broken the Dnieper line. The Crimea was now isolated from the German front except by sea. Russian pressure continued till the middle of April, by which time the Red Army had reached the Dniester and the Carpathians. On 5th February 1944, Koch's capital, Rowné, was in Russian hands. By the middle of March the *Reichskommissariat* Ukraine was only a name.

That all this would happen within a few months must have been apparent to realists in the High Command even in August 1943. Civil and Military government officers lived, however, in a dream world. The fall of Kharkov found them obsessed with trivialities. The sardonic Braeutigam, who had a good eye for such things, mentions a Ukrainian grammar for elementary schools which came out that very month. Issued by the *Ostministerium* but banned by Koch, it was printed in Roman type which the Ukrainian children could not read.[68] Then there was the conference between the Ministry and the High Command to discuss the settlement of German soldiers, who, like Roman legionaries, were to colonize the Ukraine. The Wehrmacht were anxious that the Minister should remember their share before he returned the *Kolkhozi* to the peasants. But the problem was not as grave as it looked. There were perhaps three million German soldiers in Russia, but, according to the settlement officer, less than 200 had volunteered for the Ukrainian *Limes*. More difficult were the babies, the only mementos the Wehrmacht were likely to leave. Should they be left to grow up little Slavs? The Racial Political Office of the Party ruled that, if they exhibited Germanic characteristics, they must be taken to Germany. But how to tell which were Marxists and which were National Socialists, when even the elders of that community had scarcely attained fourteen months of age? There was but one solution. The babies stayed.[69]

During eight months of continuous retreat there were problems of a more pressing nature. Some could have been simplified, had the Wehrmacht been permitted to take over the rest of the *Reichskommissariat*. But Koch and Bormann obtained a decree from Hitler that the Wehrmacht could only take over from the Civil Government as much territory as it had abandoned to the enemy. When the retreat grew too fast to afford time for such land-surveying, it was laid down that military government extended only ten kilometres behind the front. When there was no front at all, this too became unworkable so that the soldiers found themselves fighting in areas where the authority, if such it could be called, was civil and not military. Reports concerning the retreat show that the German soldier was not impressed by this authority.[70]

But to speak of civilian and military authority was a euphemism. The faint borderline had disappeared between Hitler's Exploitation-State and promiscuous plundering by all and sundry. Largely that had been brought about by the Scorched Earth Order which the Russians themselves had initiated in 1941–2, when it had been their turn to retreat. The Germans introduced their Scorched Earth Order into the Ukraine before the retreat had reached the Dnieper, for Himmler's instructions to Pruetzmann's police units and Goering's instructions to the Economic Staff East were issued on 7th September 1943, the day after Stalin's announcement of the recovery of Stalino and the Donetz basin.[71] Himmler's order reads as follows.

> Not a human being, not a single head of cattle, not a hundredweight of crops and not a railway line is to remain behind. Not a house is to remain standing, not a mine is to be available which is not destroyed for years to come and not a well which is not poisoned.

There is a world of difference between precept and practice. If that were not so, most of the population of Asia would have disappeared in the time of Jenghiz Khan. There were infinite obstacles to the execution of the Scorched Earth Order, though one may doubt the claim of some soldier-authors that it was always the Wehrmacht who opposed it and always the civilians who carried it out. It was for instance the military Rear Area Commander who informed the *Gebietskommissar* at Kazatin on Christmas day 1943 that the entire male population between the ages of fifteen and sixty-five were to be shipped back with the cattle behind a given line.[72] Four days previously the *Berliner Boersenzeitung* had reported that eighty evacuation trains were operated daily in this particular menaced sector, where 400,000 head of cattle had been driven back.[73]

But in most places it must have been impossible to enforce any part of the Scorched Earth Order. Not only did the Partisans control most of the countryside between the German-garrisoned towns, but the bulk of the police forces which were available to the Germans were Ukrainian and unreliable. At first these Ukrainian units had been employed congenially in the massacre of Jews. Later they had fought Partisans and, while they believed that the Red Army was not coming back, they had even assisted the German man-hunts for the labour deportations in their own villages.[74] But what inducement was there to carry out German orders in the autumn of 1943? Koch had already noticed a revival of the activities of OUN in his great memorandum of 16th March, when he had reported the arrest of some of their agents in the *Reichskommissariat*.[75] At that moment the UPA bands of Taras Borovets had detached most of Volhynia-Podolia from the *Reichskommissariat*.* In May Warlimont received a report from the Southern Army Group, recommending that an attempt should be made to enlist these bands as an anti-Partisan force. The report admitted that German civilian officials had been assaulted by members of UPA, but suggested that these members might prove more tractable if the *Reichskommissariat* was brought under military rule. General Hellmich, the Inspector of the eastern troops was then told by Warlimont that it would be better to kill off UPA and 'any other so-called volunteers who gave trouble.' Karl Michel, who accompanied Hellmich on this occasion, thought that he had headed off Warlimont by pointing out that it would be better if they were killed off in battle. But, after the Scorched Earth Order of 7th September 1943, such a recommendation could only be feasible if the volunteers fought on some totally different front. Five weeks later Hitler decided to remove all the volunteers to the west coast of Europe, Italy and the Balkans.[76]**

Even the removal of the volunteers could not prevent the growth of a third force in the Ukraine, at war with Russia and Germany at the same time—just as it had been in 1918. The third force drew its strength more than ever from Galicia, where the government of Hans Frank still tolerated UPA-controlled groups as a counterpoise to the Polish resistance movements. In Galicia the 'Benderovce' existed openly, though their leader, Stepan Bandera, languished in Sachsenhausen concentration camp. When the German retreat reached Galicia, the third force took the field. At the end of July 1944, when Lwow fell into Russian hands, there occurred a dramatic sequel to the declaration of independence of July 1941. As the remnants of the German XIVth

* See p. 248
** See also p. 345

corps crossed the Carpathians into Hungary, they were accompanied by 3,000 survivors of Himmler's locally recruited SS division which was named *Galizien*. The passes were held by the Benderovce who relieved the Germans of their weapons, sparing their own country-men.[77] These weapons were for use against any future occupying power in the Ukraine, whether Germany, Russia or Poland.

These, the last of the Partisans, were certainly still active as late as September 1947, when former members of the Benderovce and the SS division *Galizien* were reported to be crossing from Poland to Slovakia. Many of these fugitives reached Germany, where they were interned in the American zone. It seems that they operated on both sides of the Russo-Polish demarcation line.[78] Since those days the Benderovce have disappeared from the meagre trickle of news that comes from Soviet-annexed Galicia. It would be unwise to suppose that they have disappeared from history. Bearing in mind the re-emergence in 1942 of the Cossack leaders, who had laid hidden since the Civil War of 1918–21, one should not forget that peculiar brand of Ukrainian individualism which survived Stalin's rule of force in 1930–4 and Erich Koch's in 1941–3.

While pro-Moscow Partisans and anti-Moscow nationalists alike saved great areas of the Ukraine from the effects of the Scorched Earth Order, the dissensions and indiscipline of the Germans were also helpful. After months of demoralizing rear-guard actions and retreats, the legend of Prussian discipline took some hard knocks. It was said that the German troops who were left behind in the evacuation of the Crimea in May 1944 opened fire on the departing boats before surrendering to the Russians.[79] That was but one glimpse of the riotous confusion of human destiny which makes war so unlike the *Kriegsspiel* of the staff colleges. There were also the Rumanians, ruling a strip of Russia, sovereign, independent and undisturbed by Armageddon. In November 1943, Rumanian-held Odessa was a fabulous spot where German deserters lived unmolested and where the black market found customers both in German field commanders and Russian Partisans.[80]

In many Ukrainian towns German soldiers looted the warehouses and collection-centres which for the past two years had served the policy of territorial exploitation. The German officials who were in charge had either run away or were left helpless by the breakdown of the Rowné administration. The soldiers for their part were not actively discouraged from taking that which they had the duty to destroy, if it could not be removed. It was the last harvest of the

'Barbarossa' Jurisdiction Decree, which had been circulated under
Keitel's signature on 14th May 1941 and repeated on later dates.*

On 3rd November 1943, the Russians began their great attack on
Kiev which fell on the 6th. By the 11th there was a menacing armoured
wedge which threatened Koch's last two *Generalbezirke*, Volhynia-
Podolia and Zhitomir. The town of Zhitomir itself was already in
Russian hands, but on the 20th it was retaken by the 4th Panzer Army
in the last German counter-offensive on the eastern front. For another
five weeks there was actually a stable Ukrainian front. When the crisis
had passed, the *Gebietskommissar* for Zhitomir sent a report to the outspoken Ernst Leyser. He accused the retreating German troops of
looting the houses and offices of German officials before the administration had even left. There was little looting in the town during the
nine days of Soviet occupation, but it began again when the Germans
came back.[81] A similar report was sent from Korostyshev, where non-
combatant troops stole the stores of grain and seed. Here on 10th
November in the middle of the town the Ukrainian population had the
pleasure of seeing German soldiers raiding a German co-operative
store, soldiers of an appalling appearance, loaded with pigs and geese
like heroes of the Thirty Years War. At Kazatin the *Gebietskommissar*
was made to surrender the grain-store to a corporal at the pistol point.

In these scenes of anarchy the Scorched Earth Order foundered, but
Rosenberg had a remedy after his fashion. It was to detach the officials
of the Economic Staff East from the dual control of Goering and the
Wehrmacht and to subordinate them to his own Ministry. On the day
that Zhitomir was retaken, Rosenberg sent a detailed memorandum to
Koerner at the Four-Year-Plan Office.[82] In December, when the
Wehrmacht showed clearly that the retreat was not going to deprive
them of their share of the plunder, Rosenberg composed a second
memorandum. Finally, on 24th January 1944, he wrote to Goering
personally, demanding the liquidation of the Economic Staff East.
Goering waited till Rowné had fallen and so was able to reply on 14th
February in negative terms. Goering informed Rosenberg that the
conference on future economic administration must be postponed,
because the *Reichskommissariat* Ukraine was now almost entirely under
military rule. Goering might have specified that the military rule was
that of the Red Army.

Undeterred, Rosenberg transferred his claims from the Ukraine to
White Russia, where some vestige of civilian rule remained till the

* See p. 82

following June. The correspondence continued during March and April, Goering refusing to give way and Rosenberg helpless in spite of the strong SS man in his office. Appropriately the curtain fell on German rule in Russia with Rosenberg engaged in another meaningless struggle for precedence, this time with Goering in place of Erich Koch, who had returned to Koenigsberg many months ago.

Koch's final adventures must complete the story of this epic quarrel, even if they took place far from the Ukraine. On 18th July 1944, two days before the plot to kill Hitler, Koch was at the Wolfsschanze, reporting on his plans for the defence of East Prussia, whose border the Russians had reached at one point. When Field Marshal Model attacked these plans as amateurish, Hitler defended Koch who belonged to the infinitely small band whom he still trusted.[83] As defence commissioner for East Prussia Koch recruited his own home guard levy. It was the model for the future *Volkssturm*, but such a nuisance that in October Model's successor, General Hans Reinhardt, complained that the ammunition trains of the Central Army Group had been diverted by Koch for his own private army.[84]

Such was Koch's credit with Hitler that, in addition to the defence of East Prussia, he was given another *Reichskommissariat*. On 8th September 1944, Keitel circulated a teletype message which stated that Hitler had entrusted Gauleiter Koch with the utilization of local resources in the parts of the *Reichskommissariat Ostland* which were occupied by the troops of the Central Army Group. Koch was to take particular care of the confiscation of economic resources and for that purpose all German administrative authorities were to be subordinated to him.[85] It was an evacuation order, for in the middle of July the Russians had all but split the front by reaching the sea west of Riga. The days of the *Ostland* were numbered, but Koch's oratory remained true to form. He was alleged to have said that he would exterminate any *Ostidiote* who tried to negotiate with Latvians, Lithuanians and Estonians as independent nations. He would impose 'the tried and tested methods of the *Reichskommissariat* Ukraine'.[86]

But Koch did no such thing. Within a week of his appointment, the Russians attacked again and by the beginning of October all Estonia had been given up, together with most of Latvia. Riga and Kurland became isolated far behind the Russian front, which stretched from the mouth of the Memel along the East Prussian border. Before the end of the month the loss of Riga reduced the pocket to an area round the port of Libau which Hitler insisted on defending till the capitulation of

Germany, because of its alleged importance as a submarine base. As to Koch, he never went near the *Ostland*. From the beginning of November, when the Russians were established in his own Gau of East Prussia, even Koenigsberg was too near the front and Koch kept to the Adlon Hotel in Berlin as much as possible. At the end of January, when Koenigsberg was cut off from the Reich, Koch set up his headquarters at Pillau on the Baltic, swearing to Hitler that he would defend East Prussia if need be with the *Volkssturm* alone. Koch openly accused the army commanders, Hossbach and Reinhardt, of plotting surrender to the Western allies. But he had brought about the downfall of these generals and he would do the same to all who abandoned a yard of East Prussia.[87]

On 9th April General Lasch capitulated and the Koenigsberg of Immanuel Kant began its career as the Russian town, Kaliningrad, a sad agglomeration which is not recommended to adventurous tourists even by novelty-hunting Sunday columnists. During the death throes of German Koenigsberg, Koch had not been near the place, but he sent Hitler another telegram to say that Lasch had taken advantage of his brief absence to commit treachery. Again Koch saw Hitler in his bunker and departed for Pillau, weeping copious tears and vowing to defend the place to the last. On 23rd April Pillau was burning and the Russians were closing in. The removal of Erich Koch, his staff and his possessions occupied an entire icebreaker steamer, the *Ostpreussen*, from which all refugees were excluded. The *Ostpreussen* cruised the Baltic for eight days till, off Copenhagen, Koch learnt of Hitler's death. Knowing that no one would protect him now, he sneaked ashore at Flensburg, armed with the forged identity papers of Major Rolf Berger. Under this name Koch spent nearly a year in a camp for East Prussian refugees at Segeberg in Schleswig. He grew a moustache of enormous dimensions and passed as a dispossessed landowner from Gumbinnen. He emerged early in 1946 to establish himself at Haasemoor, seventeen miles from Hamburg. Koch worked as a day-labourer, renting a room in a cottage where he kept backyard fowls for the black market.

Koch abused a camouflage that was almost miraculous to attend local gatherings of East Prussian refugees, where, in the character of Rolf Berger, he would state his opinion that the *Ostpreussen* with Erich Koch on board had been bombed and sunk by the Russians, believing that he had established the demise of a person whom all the refugees clearly execrated. But, one day in 1949, an army officer from

Koenigsberg spoke to him, staring very hard. This officer had once asked Koch's permission to evacuate his wife and daughter. This request, like all others of its kind, had been refused and the women had perished without trace in the final headlong flight. A few days after this meeting Koch was in the hands of the Hamburg police.*

The British occupation authorities wanted to leave Koch to the German courts. When the Polish government demanded Koch's extradition, it was pointed out that the time-limit had elapsed under the Allied Control Statute. On 8th June the Soviet newspaper *New Times* demanded indignantly that Koch be tried in Russia. But the article was not followed up by a demand for extradition. There was less mystery in this than appeared. In Moscow there was nothing against Koch's treatment of the Ukrainian nationalists, but there was very much against publicity for Koch's victims.

The Poles persevered with their demand. When success was in sight, the doomed man began a fruitless hunger-strike in Duesseldorf prison. In February 1950 Koch was flown to Warsaw and then began a gap in Koch's life of nearly nine years. In the first months of his confinement in Mokotow prison he composed the 'political sketch' of his life which he was to read out at his trial. It created a rumour in west Germany that he had been released in order to write a book incriminating Allied statesmen. Two further rumours appeared; in March 1952 that he had been extradited to Russia and, in September 1956, that the Poles had dropped their charges and were sending him to west Germany. No official news of the solitary captive of Mokotow was released till the beginning of 1957, when the trial of Erich Koch was announced for 28th January. It was postponed *sine die* on account of Koch's state of health.

When, at the end of September 1958, Koch faced his accusers, there began a new record of his life, which has nothing to do with the career of the *Reichskommissar* of the Ukraine, as we know it. The charges were restricted to Koch's rule of the Bialystok *Generalbezirk* and of the incorporated Polish districts. In this part of the old Poland nameless things had been done in the disguise of racial resettlement and anti-Partisan warfare. That 72,000 Poles and 210,000 Jews had perished was probably no exaggeration at all. But Koch had not interfered in SS measures of this kind. Few of the witnesses had even seen him in that part of the world. After a few weeks of a scrupulously fair and open trial it became evident that neither volumes of evidence nor strings of

* *Giessener Freie Presse*, 22.11.58.

witnesses could establish Koch's share of responsibility. The trial became a theatrical piece, beautifully staged in order to show the West that Polish justice in Gomulka's Poland had rid itself of Stalinism. And though the death sentence was pronounced in March 1959, it does not seem to have been carried out.

Still more theatrical was the last public appearance of the haggard, prematurely aged Gauleiter, at sixty-four years a dying man. He was photographed, carried in the arms of burly policemen and rolling a febrile eye at the dainty little Polish hospital nurses who attended him in the dock. A trace, a minute trace of the quality that had dazzled Hitler and Goering was apparent even now. But the mystery remained overriding. How could such a pitiful exhibitionist maniac have reached such heights. Had it been to establish *this* that Hitler had fought half the world?

CHAPTER SEVEN

THE OUTLAWS — THE PARTISANS AND THE JEWS

(a) The Partisans

THIS CHAPTER IS concerned with the two classes whom Hitler's orders had put outside the law before the campaign had even begun, the opponents of the German occupation and the Jews. After the prisoners of war these were the largest groups to be affected by Hitler's threat to 'leave the courts at home'.* Their treatment never varied; they were outlaws first to last.

At present the Partisan movement has proved too vast and confused to attract the precise labours of military historians, though there is a large Russian patriotic literature on the subject. From Russia there may one day emerge a monumental work of research, for this aspect of the 'patriotic war' must, in spite of its unspeakable horror, remain for Russians the most popular and romantic. Until then it must be a matter of assembling bits and pieces from which general conclusions are not easily drawn.

Though the Partisans received the same treatment as the Jews, the German attitude towards them was less simple and less decided. There was never any dispute how the Jews were to be treated. At first civil government officers would inquire whether 'economic considerations' were to apply in exterminating the sources of skilled labour. They received brisk answers and that was generally the end. On the question of Partisans, however, there was continuous conflict. While the liquidation of Jews proceeded smoothly, the liquidation of Partisans meant costly operations and generally the liquidation of the wrong people. For this state of affairs every agency blamed every other agency so that a school of thought grew up which considered that Hitler alone had invented the Partisan movement.

The subject has been bedevilled both by Germans and Russians.

* See p. 80

The Russians show a disposition to underestimate the sheer physical odds that doomed the Germans to failure. They claim that the pro-digious come-back of the Red Army in the winters of 1941 and 1942 was not the result of these physical odds, but of the patriotism of the Russian people, particularly of that portion which was engulfed by the German conquests. On the German side there is a disposition, which I have discussed in the Introduction, to treat Partisan warfare as if it were simply a product of the crassness of Hitler's occupation methods; a tendency to regard it as an additional and unnecessary hazard which could have been avoided had due attention been paid to the anti-Communist leanings of the Russian people. This was the thesis of Hitler's dissident officials, men like Schenckendorff and Braeutigam who wrote frequent memoranda, associating Partisan outbreaks with this or that slave-raiding or wheat-raising campaign.

The connection is of course undeniable. But, even if the German occupation had been a monument of liberal conduct, there would still have been Partisan warfare, increasing in violence as German prospects of victory receded. The physical nature of the war area—for front it can scarcely be called—made warfare behind the German lines inevit-able. Nor was the grouping of the Partisan bases in any sense related to the areas where German misrule was at its worst. In the flat unwooded southern and eastern Ukraine, where the population had most to complain of in the way of slave-raiding and confiscation, Partisan warfare achieved very little till the German retreat through the country late in 1943. On the other hand the Partisans were strongest in wild, thinly populated districts which the Germans had never occupied at all. Partisan warfare, fanning out from the free districts, thrived on the abuses of German rule elsewhere, but basically it was a product of the anarchy that had been left behind when the too elaborate Russian State apparatus quitted. Peter Kleist claims that he once told Martin Bormann to his face how little he understood the *Untermensch*. The Russian people had a splendid tradition of rebellion behind them. They were the heirs of Stenka Razin, Mazeppa and Pugachev. In that sense Kleist's boast that the first Partisans were anti-Stalinist was not far-fetched.[1] Where there was a non-Russian tradition of self-government, as in Estonia, Partisan warfare arrived only at the very end in spite of the suitability of the country. Here the population hoped to the last for the restoration of full self-government by the Germans.

Above all, Partisan warfare is associated with White Russia and the rear areas behind the Central Army Group front. Here in July 1943

Partisan warfare may have proved the decisive factor in ruining the last German attempt to launch a general offensive. 'May have been' rather than 'was', because among German military historians, as opposed to writers on political affairs, the Partisans are never regarded as a decisive factor but treated at most as an inevitable nuisance. In July 1943 the situation on the Central Army Group front was none the less incredible. The Partisans had the strength of several divisions and in many cases the equipment and professional leadership of first-class troops. Moreover every small town contained a clandestine Partisan group which was built up by former Party officials in hiding, an underground sabotage movement distinct from the bodies of Partisan troops, which moved about in the open and which controlled their own territory.

Airborne forces, living behind the enemy's lines, were a phenomenon not confined to the Russian front in the Second World War, but Russia rather than Burma or the Balkans was their classical soil. The Russian High Command kept contact with every sort of Partisan group. It might be a handful of young men who had taken to the woods to avoid a labour draft, or it might be a group of picked parachute troops of the regular army. A group might arm itself with improvised Molotov cocktails or it might possess an airfield, a radio station and numerous guns and tanks. A Partisan group might include prominent local officials, who would establish a government which sometimes proclaimed itself a constituent republic of the Soviet Union. A Partisan leader might, as in the case of the famous Sidor Kovpak, conduct a snowball force on an expedition 700 miles into German-occupied territory.

So far from being identified with strong local loyalties to the reigning party, Partisan movements tended to flourish in places where the population had always opposed authority of any kind, places where taking to the woods was an ancient established tradition and the natural response to unfair terms of existence. The Robin Hood impulse and the ardent Communist impulse were not at all identical. In the forest south of Briansk, one of the worst Partisan areas, the picturesque habit of holding up the Moscow-Kiev express dated back to Tsarist times.[2] In such places the Russian High Command exploited a native love of banditry rather than any affection for communism. With this form of partisanship the sedentary town-dweller tended to be out or sympathy. Yet many towns were lost to the German occupation zone, because it was easier for the forest-dwellers to occupy them than it was for the Germans to protect them. Between the violence and extortion of both occupants there was little to choose.

It was truly an extraordinary war. On the German side a smaller number of soldiers held a line more than twice the length of the Russian front as it had been in the First World War, when a patrol could not have penetrated the enemy's front without crossing trenches and barbed wire or making their presence known to enemy sentries. In the Second World War a huge noisy armoured column could pass between the scattered foremost posts and travel fifty or a hundred miles before the Germans knew of its existence. Often the front was an imaginary line like the Equator. There were times during the winter when the Germans could keep no troops in the open, when their foremost positions consisted of log cabins or *isbas*, many miles apart, in which the men crowded helplessly together to prevent themselves freezing to death. There were times when a conquered village could not be occupied, because the retreating enemy had blown up the stoves.[3]

Why then no German-organized Partisan movement behind the Russian front? The total and permanent absence of such a thing suggests that, even if the Russian Partisans relied on terrorism, they must have possessed something which the Germans had not got. It suggests that the patriotism of the population counted for more than the Germans cared to admit.

Truth, however, is not so simple; the matter was never put to the test. Even in the victorious summer of 1942 the Germans did not possess the manpower and the mastery of the air necessary for the launching of Partisan operations beyond the Don or Volga. Soon the Germans were so short of aircraft that in the spring of 1943 Russian fliers supplied the Partisans virtually without molestation. And after Stalingrad the time for German Partisan operations had passed. The belief that the main forces of one's friends are on the way is a prerequisite of successful Partisan warfare. For this reason Stalin's appeal to the civilian population to continue the war behind the German front, as made on 3rd July 1941, met with little immediate response. The response came when the Red Army had launched a winter offensive and recovered tracts of country from the Germans.

This response by bands of dispossessed and unoccupied young men became a death sentence to many thousands of peasant families, seeking a miserable subsistence from the soil. Such peasants might choose to receive arms from the Germans to defend their harvest from the Partisans or they could receive arms from the Partisans and in some

cases even grain for sowing. In either case they risked being shot when
the area changed hands. Peasants who were believed to have benefited
from German decollectivization were not popular with the Soviet
government. Even when the Germans were in full retreat, dragging
back with them an enslaved and dispossessed population, to hide and
remain behind in one's village might invite denunciation as a former
collaborator.

These, the real implications of Partisan warfare, were something for
which the German High Command were unprepared and to meet
which they could offer nothing but makeshifts. The 'Barbarossa'
Jurisdiction Order foresaw organized resistance in occupied territory,
but its terms suggest that Hitler regarded it as a problem of local
administration, rather than of general strategy. The unlimited powers
which the order gave officers in the field, the rejection of judicial
proceedings even of the most summary kind, remained, however, the
basic charter for Partisan warfare till the end.* Hitler professed himself
quite pleased that Stalin's broadcast of 3rd July 1941 had urged guerilla
warfare and the Scorched Earth Policy, the all-out effort of every
individual Soviet subject. 'The Russians', Hitler declared two weeks
later, 'have now ordered Partisan warfare behind our front. This
Partisan warfare has some advantage for us; it enables us to wipe out
everyone who opposes us.'** Thereafter Hitler's references to the
Partisans were rare; he did not complain overmuch, for they were part
of the kind of warfare he advocated. But on his visits to Russia, as for
instance his visit to Smolensk on 13th March 1943, Hitler took the
greatest care that his own person was adequately guarded.⁴

The first serious outbreak of Partisan activity seems to have been
in the particularly wild country south of Leningrad. A commando of
the Security Police, attached to Hoepner's 14th Armoured Group
reported on 29th September 1941, that Partisans had appeared north
of Pskov and between lakes Peipus and Ilmen. According to this
report the Wehrmacht had 'adopted the new methods of the Security
Police' and the familiar pattern of burnt villages and mass shootings
had already taken shape.⁵ It need scarcely be recalled that on all
such occasions the army commander had complete operational
control.

Keitel had already strengthened the 'Barbarossa' Jurisdiction Order
on 16th September by ordering the execution of fifty to a hundred

* See p. 82
** See p. 143, Document L 221

Communists for every German soldier killed. 'Communist sources are to be suspected, regardless of what the individual circumstances are.'[6] The wording of this most incriminating order suggests that only isolated attacks were expected, but soon more elaborate counter-measures were needed. Before the end of the year most of the exter-mination group, *Einsatzgruppe A*, was diverted from the liquidation of the Jews of the Baltic States in order to tackle Partisans on the Leningrad front. On 26th March 1942 the commander of the group, Franz Stahlecker, was killed by Partisans outside his own headquarters at Krasnovardeisk, not, however, before he had sent a report to Heydrich in which he boasted of the execution of 221,000 Jews.[7] Like other extermination group commanders, Stahlecker, who was a Russian-born German, was foremost a politician and a somewhat intellectual sort of butcher. As a former head of Heydrich's military intelligence section, he had once entertained foreign office ambitions and Ribbentrop had considered him for his Russia Committee.[8]

The classical country for Partisan activity, the forest of Briansk, which lay behind the German sector facing Moscow, scarcely became significant before December 1941, when the Germans withdrew from their forward positions at Tula and Orel. It was too large a thing to be passed on by the Wehrmacht to the rough-and-ready methods of the Security Police commandos. There was consequently an element of imaginative handling, when the soldier politicians of the Central Army Group stepped in. The plan was to contain the Partisan forces with a reliable militia, recruited from Russian prisoners. A Cossack battalion was formed and a pro-German Russian self-government area was set up on the fringe of the Briansk forest, the so-called Lokot government of Bronislav Kaminsky. These measures, described in Chapter Ten, led to the far more significant development of a Russian liberation army, but they were ineffective in crushing the Partisans.* It was decided to use Hungarian troops, who were regarded for front-line purposes as second-class material. Yet, in May 1942, Hitler declared that the Hungarians were useless even for Partisan warfare.[9] In the same month Goebbels made an entry in his *Diary* which told a story that was to be familiar for the next two years.

> *19th May 1942.* Partisans blasted the railway tracks on the central front between Briansk and Rosslavl at five points, a further proof of their extremely discomfiting activities. South of

* See pp. 309–10

this region Hungarian elements are fighting under great difficulties. They must now capture one village after another and
pacify it, a thing that has not proved exactly a constructive
process. For when the Hungarians report that they have pacified
a village, this usually means that not a single inhabitant is left.
In consequence we can hardly get any agricultural work done in
these regions.[10]

By contrast with the wild lands along the pre-1939 Soviet borders,
which were systematically ravaged by the Germans in 1942–3 till they
could support no more life, the Briansk forest and the neighbouring
forests were never cleared of Partisans even by the methods which
Goebbels described. The front lay too close and the liaison with the
Red Army was too strong. Though German front-line troops were
never far away, it was seldom that they could be spared for Partisan
warfare.

Five hundred miles and more behind the German front, Partisan
activities were carried out on a scale that was equally large, because
here the Germans possessed virtually no trained troops at all. They had
to rely on mercenary police companies, an extremely inferior material,
composed largely of Latvians and Lithuanians who were too savage,
and Ukrainians, whose loyalty was too uncertain.

During the encirclement battles of the first few months, groups of
Red Army men succeeded in escaping the lingering death of the
prisoner of war cages. At first their only concern was food, but looting
expeditions led to attacks on the Germans and in the winter of 1941
contact was made with Moscow and the attacks became co-ordinated.
The civilian area of the *Generalkommissariat* White Russia was the
worst affected. In Minsk itself, the German capital, a conspiracy was
discovered which aimed at killing the *Generalkommissar* and poisoning
the water supply. The Minsk Partisan leader, Stolyarevich, was
executed at the end of February,[11] but the pattern of Partisan warfare
had now taken shape. When a number of groups could link together,
make contact with the Russian side, and receive arms, they would
constitute themselves a Republic. Thus at the end of April 1942 there
was mention of a guerilla republic at Usakino, south-west of Minsk,
near the pre-1939 frontier railway station of Negoroloje, whose
magnificent waiting-room with the gold inscriptions was once familiar
to tourists.

To reduce this stronghold, a battalion of German convicted

criminals, genteelly described as poachers, was produced from Cracow. It was to become notorious as the Dierlewanger SS Regiment. It enjoyed the protection of Gottlob Berger at the SS Main Office and it attracted the interest both of Hitler and Goering. The speciality of Oskar Dierlewanger, an ex-convict who became a major general, was to march the women and children, who had been left behind in the villages, over the mine-fields which protected Partisan hideouts.[12] In this way Dierlewanger improved on the standard Wehrmacht practice of employing Russian prisoners, covering them with rifles to see that they stepped over the entire ground.[31]

By the spring of 1942 this warfare had achieved a standard of barbarism on both sides which recalled the Thirty Years War, or the Chouans of the Vendée, except that the scale was many times bigger. Only in the area close to the front was an effort made to stem the tide of horror. In May 1942, for instance, Gotthard Heinrici of the 4th Army persuaded von Kluge to keep the Security Police units out of the entire Army Group combat zone. Heinrici also defied the 'Barbarossa' Jurisdiction Order by refusing to hand captured Partisans over to the SD. General Hans Roettiger, Heinrici's Chief of Staff, claimed some success from these methods. In March 1943 the 4th Army had to evacuate Viasma, the nearest German strongpoint to Moscow, but at the same time they were able to liquidate a Partisan group, which for many months past had constituted a second front, extending a hundred miles back. This was partly achieved through radio appeals to the women to 'get their men back from the forests'.[14]

But it would be drawing a false inference to suppose that massacres and village-burnings only took place where SS leaders were in command or where SD units were used. In the rear areas, as opposed to the civil government areas, these leaders and units were strictly under the control of the *Korueck* or Rear Area Commander of the Wehrmacht.* Some of the *Korueck* despatches on anti-Partisan warfare, which were produced at the Nuremberg 'High Command' Trial, are absolutely indistinguishable in their cold-blooded horror from the *Einsatzgruppen* despatches, which were edited by the SD for Heydrich. It was only in the civil government area that the 'Barbarossa' Jurisdiction Order could work the other way round and that the Higher Leaders of the SS and Police (HSSPF) could request the services of the Wehrmacht. Even then there was a rule-of-thumb arrangement between Himmler and the High Command that the commander with the most troops

* See p. 76

should take over the operation, whether he was an SS leader or a Wehrmacht officer.[15]

The result was an administrative chaos, particularly in White Russia. The German offensive towards the Caucasus, which began towards the end of June 1942, denuded the rear areas of troops. At the very moment when the Germans were taking a look at the Caspian Sea and planting a Swastika banner on Mount Elburz, they lost control over a sector where the Russians were supposedly on the defensive. At Goering's high level conference on food production on 6th August, *Reichskommissar* Lohse declared that the Partisans would certainly prevent the removal of half the White Russian harvest that year. 'I have been crying out for help for four months.' Goering said he had known Lohse a long time and that Lohse had a very vivid imagination; 'I never imagine anything', shouted Lohse indignantly.[16]

But something had to be done. A single anti-Partisan command, which transcended regional authority, had become essential. Yet Hitler's next instructions on anti-Partisan warfare, the Direction No 46, which was issued by Keitel twelve days later, only reaffirmed and defined the old separate zones of competence.[17] Common sense demanded that a unified control should be in the hands of the General Staff. Hitler, however, wanted a different form of unification. Partly because he believed that the High Command were too soft and partly because he needed a prominent Party personality on the spot, Hitler extended Himmler's powers to cover the whole of Partisan warfare. Like Stalin, Hitler considered that security matters behind the front concerned the police and not the military.

Himmler was not expected to command the operations in person, though in the summer months he had a field headquarters at Hegewald near Zhitomir and received operational reports. Himmler appointed an SS General to deputize for him. By his own admission von dem Bach-Zelewski volunteered his services and his letter to Himmler is dated very shortly after the issue of Direction No 46.[18] His application was supported by the Wehrmacht commander under whom he was serving, von Schenckendorff of the Central Army Group rear area.[19]

Bach-Zelewski is a figure of controversy. In his many Nuremberg depositions he claims to have been a friend of the Jews and Himmler's good angel, who sought constantly to humanize the conditions of Partisan warfare. He was accused of having both Slav blood and Jewish marriage-connections and he says that Himmler kept a dossier about him.[20] Such is his self-portrait, but in several Nazi memoirs, particularly those of Peter Kleist, Otto Skorzeny, Rudolf Rahn and Walter Schellenberg, he is denounced as a brutal policeman, responsible for all sorts of unimaginative errors and a bad commander of troops. That he was so hated springs from the fact that Bach-Zelewski was a prosecution witness at Nuremberg, where Goering shouted the word 'Schweinehund' at him, and that he avoided his own trial and punishment by giving evidence at other war trials, even going to Poland with complete immunity to testify against the Governor of Warsaw, Albert Fischer. Against Bach-Zelewski's account of himself must be offset the fact that the war against Partisans reached its most ruthless stage after his appointment as Chief of Anti-Partisan Units on 23rd October 1942. On more than one occasion Bach-Zelewski was commended by Hitler[21] and he seems, in spite of his malicious stories about Himmler, to have owed his many preferments to Himmler's favour. It is a remarkable fact that while the most hair-raising reports were sent to Bach-Zelewski concerning anti-Partisan operations, nothing has survived which records his disapproval.

Another factor which stepped up the savagery of Partisan warfare was the blundering interference of Goering, who resented the retort he had received from Lohse at the Food Production Conference. On 24th September Goering inquired of the Ministry for Justice whether the Dierlewanger regiment could be brought to strength by the committal, not only of convicted poachers but also of armed gangs of smugglers and perhaps other sorts of criminals as well.[22] By 27th October, soon after Bach-Zelewski's appointment, Goering had his own plan ready which he submitted to Keitel. Goering proposed to remove all cattle and food-stores from the pacified Partisan areas and to round up all the surviving inhabitants into camps, from which the adults would be separated from their children and shipped to Germany for labour.[23]

In practice this meant that the police troops killed off all the villagers, not excepting the children, to save themselves the trouble of having to move them or look after them. Goering was nevertheless very pleased with his plan, describing it to Mussolini on his state visit to the Palazzo Venezia. To Mussolini, who found the realities of German warfare invariably distasteful, Goering depicted the practices of anti-Partisan fighting.[24]

Wherever attacks occurred, the entire male population of the villagers were lined up on one side and the women on the other.

The women were told that the men would be shot unless they
pointed out which men did not belong to the village. In order to
save their men, the women always pointed out the non-residents.
Germany had found that, generally speaking, it was not easy to
get soldiers to carry out such measures. Members of the Party
discharged this task much more harshly and efficiently.

Goering's plan was officially adopted, but, as usual, Alfred Jodl
showed himself more cautious than Keitel over the introduction of
abnormal measures. For instance, on 11th November, he issued an
order forbidding the burning down of villages as a reprisal measure.
When challenged by Hitler at the staff conference of 1st December,
Jodl declared that even Himmler felt doubtful about reprisals when
they were taken 'after the battle'. Such things might drive the whole
population to join the Partisans. Pretending as usual to have missed the
point, Hitler argued back that one must not tie a soldier's hands while
fighting. 'The poor devil cannot think about it. He is fighting for his
life, his very existence.' In his blunt, disrespectful manner Jodl tried to
get back to the point. 'My Fuehrer, what people do in battle does not
come into this instruction at all. As far as I am concerned, you can
quarter them or hang them upside down.'

It was unfortunate for Alfred Jodl that, out of the 200,000 sheets of
minutes of Hitler's staff conferences which were destroyed after the
capitulation at Hintersee, only 800 were recovered intact when the
smouldering pit was searched by Mr George Allen. But of course
Jodl's ill-tempered remark just had to be among them. And to what
purpose? The unlucky Jodl had been forced to withdraw his humane
order.[25]

The operations were no longer known as anti-Partisan warfare, but
as 'anti-band warfare', a denial of combatant status which had been
decided as early as 4th September, when it was also ruled by at least
one army command that captured people who had fought in civilian
dress should be hanged and not shot.[26] Keitel used the expression
'anti-band warfare' in an order of 29th December which suffered from
none of Jodl's inhibitions. There had been complaints that soldiers
were held accountable for their actions in anti-band warfare. 'That was
wrong; they were justified in taking any measures even against women
and children.' Reaffirming the original 'Barbarossa' Jurisdiction Order
of 14th May 1941, Keitel ruled that no soldier, so engaged, could be
brought before a court-martial, and that no sentences passed in con-

nection with actions during anti-band warfare would in future be confirmed by OKW.[27]*

It was no idle threat. In the next two months six large-scale operations were carried out against Partisan strongholds, which winter had made more accessible by freezing the swamps. The brief summaries, which were sent to Himmler, are illuminating. The first operation, called *Erntefeste* was a combing out of the Cherven-Osipavichi area, west of Bobruisk, one of the oldest hideouts. More than eleven police battalions took part. They killed 805 men in battle, executed 1,165 people for taking sides with the Partisans and took only thirty-four prisoners, who were probably Red Army men in uniform. Then there was the 'Hamburg' operation in the Slonim area, far to the west in former Poland. Here it was possible to capture four tanks and eight field guns, 500 miles behind the front. In addition to 1,676 men killed in action and 1,510 people shot as suspects, 2,658 fugitive Jews from the ghettoes of Slonim and other White Russian towns were discovered, probably living in the so-called 'family camps' in the Partisan protection area. These of course were executed.[28] In a further clean-up in former eastern Poland, known as 'Operation Altona', the Germans executed 786 suspects and 126 Jews in the course of an affair in which there was not a single German casualty. February saw the 'Hornung' operation in the previously immune Pripet Marshes, east of Pinsk, where the redoubtable cavalry raider, Sidor Kovpak, had taken refuge from the western Ukraine. This was the largest operation to date. 2,219 Partisans were said to have been killed in action, but, if that was truly the case, it was remarkable that the Germans suffered only twenty-nine casualties and captured only 172 rifles. Admittedly executed were 7,378 people, who had harboured the Partisans, and another 3,300 fugitive Jews. Before the month of February 1943, was over, another 4,000 such murders were carried out, where the Russian Partisans had penetrated the Latgale region of Latvia. Here only seven Germans were killed.[29]

These methods fulfilled neither Goering's plan for bringing the Partisans to Germany as slave-labourers, nor the plans, at total variance with his own, of his agricultural experts, such as Hermann Riecke, who wanted to save the harvest. One report, which reached Riecke's office on 29th June 1943, asserted that a single anti-Partisan operation in the previous November had lost Germany the produce of 115,000 hectares.[30] Even Erich Koch, in whose territory the *Hornung*

* See also p. 82

operation took place, joined the ranks of the remonstrants. He was alleged to have criticized the wholesale destruction of villages and the removal of their inhabitants. Himmler's police leader in the Ukraine, Max Thomas, demanded an explanation from Koch who acted true to form by denying everything. Koch telegraphed Himmler on 25th February, declaring that he had always been in favour of emptying a huge zone to either side of the Brest-Gomel railway, which ran through the Partisan-infested Pripet Marshes.[31]

A more persistent objector was Fritz Sauckel, though his own conscription methods had helped to recruit the Partisans. In March 1943 Sauckel achieved an agreement with the Security Office whereby the police commanders put as many Partisan prisoners as possible at the disposal of the labour offices in Germany, sparing the population for this purpose, when they fired the villages. Executions were to be reduced and even the Commissar Order was to be suspended. 'Generally speaking, no more children are to be shot.'[32]

These instructions, as passed on by the commander of *Einsatzgruppe D* on 19th March 1943, were already out of date, for, five days previously, General Warlimont had ruled that the population, which had been rounded up in this way, should be sent in large groupings to the concentration camps of Germany and Poland.

The origin of Warlimont's order was a conference with Eduard Wagner, who had wanted to confine the incriminated villagers in labour camps in their own area instead of shipping them to Germany. This had been in keeping with the wishes of Riecke and the Agricultura Leaders. As was often the case, the fire-eating Warlimont had disagreed with Wagner. The villagers ought to be more adequately punished. So, in his new instruction, Warlimont pointed out that Himmler was already empowered to send prisoners of the SS to German concentration camps. If the villagers, who were suspected of aiding the Partisans, were transferred by the Wehrmacht to the SS and Police Leader, competent for the area, they too could be sent to concentration camps. This must be done in future and it must be made plain to the Russian population that there was a sharp distinction between punitive labour and ordinary labour-conscription for Germany.[33]

After Warlimont's instructions of 14th March 1943, it was possible to pick up almost anyone for the concentration camps. In September and October, about 3,000 villagers were shipped from Vitebsk to Lublin and Auschwitz, where their survival could be reckoned in weeks or in months at the best.* From Dniepropetrovsk in the Ukraine trainloads of men and women, picked at random, were sent in August straight to Buchenwald and Ravensbrueck.[34] In this case there was no question of Partisan involvements.

After the issue of Warlimont's order there was a new wave of memoranda. Wagner and the military government officers lined up with the Rosenberg Ministry, with officials of the Economic Staff East and even with the Sauckel organization. Hitler was expected to amend these latest rules for anti-Partisan warfare, but on 24th May Martin Bormann reported that no change was contemplated. It had been established that the Partisans were always worst, where 'politically smart' generals commanded against them.[35]

Already a new operation had been launched against the Partisans of the former borderlands. Under the name of 'Operation Cottbus' it proved to be the most savage of them all. It was directed against the 'Republic of Lake Pelik' which had been formed out of two large Partisan groups before December 1942. At the southern end, the republic approached to within twenty miles of the trunk railway from Minsk to Moscow in the neighbourhood of Borisov. Northwards it reached almost to Polotsk on the Moscow-Riga line, covering an intricate roadless area of lakes and swamps which can best be appreciated from the air. Since in theory the area belonged to the *Reichskommissariat*, the command was entrusted to an SS man, Major General von Gottberg, the future *Generalkommissar* in Minsk. Operations lasted from the middle of May to the end of June 1943, involving the use of 16,662 men on the German side, mostly police units from the Baltic States or Russian volunteer battalions, but there was also a civilian emergency force which included ninety members of the administration in Minsk.[36] On the Partisan side there were tanks and field-guns, an air-strip and troop-carrier gliders, all under the command of a Brigadier of the Red Army. It was admitted in Bach-Zelewski's despatches to Himmler that the Luftwaffe had to bomb towns, hundreds of miles behind their own front, where recently Germans had been living quite peaceably.[37]

Operation Cottbus was completed only a few weeks before the Russians launched the great offensive of 1943, which was to recover most of the Partisan area before the end of the year. It far exceeded any of its predecessors in ruthlessness. Bach-Zelewski reported in his final despatch that 15,000 Partisans had been wiped out. But of this total

* See p. 279

only 6,042 were listed as killed in action; nearly 5,000, including many women and children, were executed as suspects while the remainder died, 'spotting mines'. That is to say, the estimable Dierlewanger had driven them into the mine-fields. The Sauckel organization obtained 5,500 labour conscripts but these perforce were all women. The German losses were 127 killed and again there was a mysteriously low figure for captured weapons, only 1,100 rifles and 326 small arms.[38]

For once the realities behind all these horrifying statistics emerged in the reports of a hostile and critical witness. *Generalkommissar* Kube forwarded four of them to Lohse and in July they were passed to Berger at the SS Head Office by Braeutigam in Rosenberg's Political Department, with caustic strictures of his own attached to them.[39] In these reports Kube described how he had tried to win the villagers from the Partisans in order that the harvest within forty miles of Minsk should not be abandoned. At the beginning of the operation he sent his chief of propaganda, one Lauch, with a loudspeaker-van to follow the troops. Lauch set off as if he were launching a war-savings appeal. His first brush with reality was the discovery of a queer smell. It came from a burnt-out barn, where the bodies of presumed Partisans had been half-roasted and then eaten by pigs. Three days later, on 27th May, Lauch took his van back to Minsk, because a Colonel of the SS had begun to burn the very villages to whom he was trying to appeal. Kube also heard from Borisov that some of the people who had been left for dead after the mass-executions, had turned up at the town hospital for treatment. Lohse added his own observations which were not quite as strong as Braeutigam's. The 'special treatment' of the Jews, he thought, needed no comment but the affair of the pigs in the barn was likely to 'damage our reputation'. 'What is Katyn to this?'[40]

Berger in his new rôle as manager for Rosenberg was not sympathetic either to Lohse, Kube or Braeutigam. Kube, he declared, ought to have seen von Gottberg about it in the first place. Berger was extremely angry at the attacks on his First World War comrade, Oskar Dierlewanger, whose men were not to blame. They were all former Party members who had been 'punished for poaching or some stupid action'. In the following month Dierlewanger, an ex-convict and now a Brigadier General, received the German Cross of Gold from Hitler.*

Berger added that he had asked Alfred Meyer to administer a severe

* Case XI, Transcript, pp. 284–94. The discovery of mass-graves containing the bodies of Polish officers, allegedly murdered by the Russians, had been published on 17th April 1943. This was the Katyn affair.

caution to Kube during his forthcoming visit to Minsk. That, however, was not destined to happen. In September a Partisan conspiracy
was discovered in a street in Minsk itself. It was followed by the usual
indiscriminate round-up and there was a mass-execution of 300 members of neighbouring families.[41] On the 22nd Kube was blown up in
his bed. The White Russian chambermaid who laid the bomb, had been
employed by him for many months and had incurred no suspicion.*

It is likely that along the pre-1939 Soviet border alone more than
100,000 people had been exterminated in so-called anti-Partisan warfare
since the winter of 1941. And so it would have continued, had not the
northern front come under heavy enemy pressure soon after 'Operation
Cottbus'. The mass of anti-Partisan troops were moved eastwards
from the pre-1939 border in order to fill the gaps. On 6th October
1943, when the Red Army broke through at Nevel, east of the Latvian
border, Bach-Zelewski had to organize all his available police units
into two army corps in order to establish a new front between Polotsk
and Idriza.[42] The same thing was happening 300 miles to the south-
east, where the classical Partisan area of the Briansk forest was thrown
open by the Red Army, as the deep thrust to Kiev and the Dnieper left
a huge gap in the German front. Briansk fell on 14th September. It was
the climax of an immense number of Partisan attacks on the railway
system leading to the Central Army Group front.** Rapidly the
Partisans themselves were swept up in the advance of the Red Army,
some of them none too willingly.

The front from the Baltic to the Black Sea was not stabilized till well
into April 1944. It then ran southwards along the Estonian and Latvian
borders and across the western part of White Russia. At the Pripet
Marshes it swung due west in a prodigious salient which penetrated
Volhynia, Galicia, Bukovina and Bessarabia. Except in White Russia,
the whole front lay in non-Russian territories that awaited complete
occupation by the Red Army with certainty but without enthusiasm.
Only in White Russia the Germans retained a hinterland which had
been part of the pre-1939 Soviet Union. From Mogilev on the Dnieper,
westwards to Minsk, it exceeded a hundred miles in depth. It was still
the most disturbed part of Hitler's Europe, but the situation had
improved since July 1943. It was no longer necessary to send expeditions of 10,000 to 17,000 men at a time against regions that were
supposed to be in German occupation.

* See p. 158
** See p. 343

Several causes contributed to this reduction in the scale of anti-Partisan warfare during the last twelve months that the Germans were in White Russia. Firstly the systematic depopulation and the ruin of the harvest in their former hide-outs had stopped the Partisans returning to them. It is probable that many places remain uninhabited to this day. Secondly the Red Army was pre-occupied elsewhere and thirdly the German retreat had brought back a great number of collaborators, whose fate was now linked with Germany. I suspect there was also another cause. The Germans were inconceivably brutal but there were not enough of them, whereas the power that stepped into their place in White Russia, was destined to be everywhere and all the time. No lakes or swamps or forests would repel *them*. As the campaign of 1944 approached, the Russian Robin Hoods, the heirs of Mazeppa, Stenka Razin and Pugachev, had something new to think about.

(b) The Partisans of the Third Force

To TURN TO the vastly different story of Partisan warfare in the Ukraine, it appears that as early as the spring of 1942 a pilot of Hitler's escort flight was ambushed and murdered not far from Hitler's own headquarters at Vinnitsa. Later a man was captured, wearing the pilot's decorations.[43] The security experts were perplexed. Was this Partisan a Communist? In the Ukraine it was not just a matter of collaboration with the Germans or with the Red Army. In the Ukraine there was a third force, the followers of Melnyk and Bandera, who, though divided against each other, were united against the Red Army and finally united against the Germans too.

For the Partisans of Soviet rule, warfare in the Ukraine was generally restricted to the immensely long northern border, a belt of swamp, scrubland, heath and forest, which separated the steppes from the huge forests of White Russia. The steppes themselves, whether grassland or wheat, provided neither cover for troop movements nor hide-outs for groups of men of any size. Thus in the industrial Donetz basin Partisan warfare did not exist, except for some political activities of UPA and OUN in the larger towns and some organized sabotage by the Great-Russian industrial workers. Where open Partisan warfare was possible, the conditions closely resembled Yugoslavia. In that country the Croat nationalists under Pavelic, as well as the Bosnian

Moslems, worked with the Germans, while the Serbs were divided between the German collaborationists under Nedic and the true nationalists under Mihailovitch who fought between the lines. At the same time all areas provided Partisans who fought the Germans under Tito, ostensibly as Communists.

The confusion of motives makes the history of the civil war, both in Yugoslavia and the Ukraine, very difficult reading. In the latter country the Germans never understood what was going on and there was always uncertainty whether a band, which occupied an area of country, was composed of Ukrainian nationalists from one of the recognized groups or whether it had been organized by contact men from the Soviet side. By June 1943, when in theory the Germans still held most of the Soviet Ukraine, very little of the countryside between the garrisoned towns remained at the disposal of the Germans, north of the line, Kremenets-Rowné-Kiev-Kharkov. This was the time of the Leyser memorandum to Rosenberg, which disclosed that more than half of the *Generalkommissariat* Zhitomir was virtually in the hands of Red Army Partisans.* Yet this memorandum did not even mention the fact that the territory to the west was largely in the hands of the Ukrainian nationalists.[44]

Originally bands of Red Army Partisans, formed of men who had cut their way out of the great encirclement battles, operated in the steppes, in the marshes of the lower Dnieper below Nikopol and also west of Kharkov. These were fairly soon disposed of and all through 1942 and the first half of 1943 the German lines of communication in the steppe regions remained much more secure than in other areas behind the front. There remained three Ukrainian areas which were never cleared of Red Army Partisans throughout the German occupation. They were in the scrubland belt, north of Chernigov, Sumy and Putivl. The Wehrmacht in its rapid march to the Donetz basin never troubled to clean up these unprofitable northern regions which became a sort of no-man's land between two Army Groups. But the Russians made rapid use of them and it is said that the Partisan groups in these areas were the creation of Nikita Khrushchev, then first secretary of the Communist Party in the Ukraine.[45]

Another no-man's land lay considerably to the west, near the old Polish border, in the forests north-west of Zhitomir and north-east of Rowné, known as Polesia. Here Partisans of a different kind were in control. Taras Borovets, the owner of a stone quarry in Kostopol, had

* See p. 213

planned to create a *Sich* or republic, soon after the Soviet occupation of Volhynia in September 1939. In August 1941, he came out in the open, driving the Red Army stragglers out of an area between Pinsk, Mozyr and Olevsk, where he declared the Ukrainian republic of Polesia. The Wehrmacht was at first relieved of the trouble of clearing this difficult area, but with the creation of the *Reichskommissariat*, the Wehrmacht no longer had the first say. In November Borovets was required to withdraw and for a time he kept his men quietly disposed at Liudivpol. Early in the following year, finding that the Wehrmacht did not interfere, Borovets built up the Polesian *Sich* again with the aid of agents from both OUN groups.

The trouble began in the summer of 1942. The Red Army Partisans were very weak in Polesia and long protracted Soviet negotiations took place in order to persuade Borovets to attack the Germans. Borovets claimed that his own forces were also too weak, with the result that Stalin himself decided to give the Ukrainian nationalists a lesson. At a time when the front was still 500 miles away from Borovets's centre at Olevsk, a Partisan leader was ordered to conduct a march through the entire forest region west of the Dnieper. The chosen commander was a Ukrainian, who had fought in the traditional Cossack cavalry style during the civil war, but on the side of the Red Army. Major General Sidor Kovpak had hitherto directed Partisan operations in the Sumy region, using a mixture of Ukrainian and Great-Russian troops. In October 1942 Kovpak left Sumy and marched through the northern fringe of the Ukraine to Lelchitsy, some 400 miles to the west, where he captured the administration centre of a German *Gebietskommissar*. Then he moved south, driving Borovets from Olevsk, but the German anti-Partisan forces were closing on him and he had to quit the Ukraine, wintering among the White Russian Partisans in the Pripet Marshes, where he formed an airfield on a frozen lake, which the Luftwaffe destroyed by bombing the ice.[46]

In February von dem Bach-Zelewski launched the 'Hornung' Operation against the Partisans in the Pripet Marshes. The operation was carried out with great thoroughness, but Kovpak escaped with a large band of men and headed south again. Once more skirting the northern edges of the Ukraine, he was back at his starting point in May 1943.

The effect of the first of the two great Kovpak marches was to re-animate the forces of Ukrainian nationalism, which, militarily speaking, had lain dormant since the revolt in Lwow in July 1941, and the arrest of the Galician leaders. Kovpak's march brought down upon it large German anti-Partisan forces, not only Latvians and Lithuanians but also Ukrainian militia and police companies. The latter soon became disgusted by the atrocities they were expected to commit against their own countrymen. Many of these men deserted and joined the fugitive Borovets in Volhynia. This was the westernmost *Generalkommissariat*, which had been Polish until September 1939 and which consequently was a far less favourable terrain for Red Army Partisans. Moreover it bordered on eastern Galicia, where the activities of UPA and OUN were openly tolerated by Governor Waechter. By March 1943, the country surrounding all the big towns, Rowné, Luck, Kovel, Dubno, Kremenets, was in the hands of the nationalists.[47] It can truly be said that this state of affairs was the result of Hitler's decision to separate Galicia from the Ukraine.

Erich Koch was menaced in his own capital. His complaints were vociferous. The remedy, proposed by the military government chiefs of the Southern Army Group, was that they should relieve Erich Koch of all the remaining *Generalkommissariats* as far back as the Polish border. The Ukrainian militia, they said, would be more amenable to the persuasion of soldiers. The *Roland* and *Nachtigall* battalions, which had mutinied at Lwow in July 1941, were now fighting the Partisans in White Russia, though their own officers were in German concentration camps. Consequently the Eastern Troops Office regarded the return of the rebellious Ukrainian militia men as quite feasible and militarily important. In April General Hellmich, Inspector of the eastern troops, was sent to Hitler's headquarters at Berchtesgaden to report on the situation. Hellmich would move the 'political units' to almost any front where they could be used up in battle, whereas Warlimont wanted to liquidate them outright on the spot.* But the problem far transcended German military genius. The Nationalist militia controlled Volhynia till it was overrun by the Red Army and to a lesser extent long afterwards.

And scarcely had Kovpak got back to his swampy hide-out at Putivl on 12th June 1943, when he received his marching orders again, this time to cut right through the recruiting grounds of the Banderists, through Galicia to the Carpathians. After a march, exceeding 700 miles in the rear of the enemy's front, he was to attack the oil-wells at Drohobicz. By July, Kovpak's gypsyish band of riders were back in Volhynia. The Tsuman forest, which had been cleared by Erich Koch

See p. 335 Carl Michel, *Ost und West*, pp. 145-9

at the end of 1942, only to be occupied by Borovets in the following March, was now cleared again on behalf of the Red Army. So much for Koch's hunting domain, if such it was. Heading south along the old Russo-Polish border, Kovpak entered Galicia at Tarnopol, having apparently ridden his force well over 600 miles in twenty-five days. But in Galicia the underground Ukrainian armed forces were brought into the open and Kovpak found himself between them and the Germans. He destroyed a minor oil refinery near Tarnopol, but he failed to reach Drohobicz, though part of his force got to the foot of the Carpathians and even to the river Pruth at Delatyn, some ten months ahead of the main forces of the Red Army. Kovpak escaped with difficulty. In the western Ukraine he had to dodge one of the few German divisions which had been specially trained for cavalry warfare. The entire 1st SS Cavalry Division, 'Florian Geyer', formerly commanded by the show rider Hermann Fegelein who was to become Hitler's adjutant for the SS, was diverted from the front to deal with Kovpak's raid.[48]

On 1st September, when Kovpak reached the security of the Pripet Marshes, he had only 300 men left, yet he survived the war. In 1946 his memoirs, edited for him by a professional journalist, became a Russian best-seller. Kovpak, now a very old man, has probably conducted the longest guerilla raid in the rear of an enemy in the recorded annals of warfare. Even the best achievements of bearded unconventional warriors on the Western Allied side look small when compared with this episode, worthy of medieval Nomadic Asia.*

The second Kovpak march left the Ukrainian nationalists in control of their former areas, which they extended to the east into the former Soviet Ukraine Republic. After a kind of civil war among the nationalists themselves, in which the followers of Bandera triumphed over the followers of the moderate Melnyk, a semblance of a State was set up with its headquarters east of Rowné and an army which was reputed to muster at least 40,000 men.** Late in November 1943, when the Red Army had already appeared a hundred miles to the east, the Banderist Partisans penetrated the centre of Rowné and shot some of Erich Koch's officials.

* I have to confess that I am not able to read *Vid Putivlia do Karpat*, but I have derived critical comments on it from Mr Armstrong's sixth chapter and an unusual aspect from Solomon M. Schwarz, *Jews in the Soviet Union*.
**Armstrong, op. cit., p. 156. Among the feats of the UPA Army in the summer of 1943 was the assassination of two bishops of the Uniate church, allegedly collaborators with Germany. (Ibid., pp. 203–5.)

The situation called for diplomacy, because the Germans were still recruiting Ukrainians for their 14th SS Division. It was decided to arrest the leaders under guise of negotiation. Thus in the same month Borovets at last fell into German hands. He was not shot, but sent to join Bandera in the privileged 'political bunker' of Sachsenhausen concentration camp. The capture of Borovets was followed in January by the long-delayed arrest of the non-belligerent Melnyk, which took place in Berlin. All of the Ukrainian nationalists were, however, released in the autumn of 1944.[49] Borovets volunteered to form a parachute unit for Partisan work behind the Red Army front. Remarkably enough he is alive today.[50]

Three months after the arrest of Borovets and his chiefs, the whole of Volhynia was in Soviet hands. Henceforward the struggles of OUN and UPA, of Melnykists and Banderists, were directed against the NKVD companies and other police troops in the wake of the Red Army. More than three years elapsed before law and order finally returned to Galicia and the western Ukraine.

In the plight in which they found themselves in the winter of 1943–4, the Germans lost some of the temptation to use the mailed fist. Compared with the general standards of Partisan warfare, the treatment of the Ukrainian nationalist leaders seems mild indeed. But in all their dealings with the Ukraine the Wehrmacht had a sense of shame and guilt. On 16th July 1941, Hitler had declared, 'Only the Germans shall bear arms.' Had the High Command countered these words effectively, the militarily despised Ukrainians would long ago have been merged into brigades and divisions, trained on German lines and strictly disciplined to a war in which there were only two sides.

(c) The Jews

THIS SECTION CONTAINS only a brief reference to the extermination of the Jews of the Soviet Union. A chronological history will be found in two chapters of my book, *The Final Solution*, while the controversial rôles of the SS and Wehrmacht are discussed in *The SS: Alibi of a Nation*. The subject has still to be integrated in the general background of conflicting war aims, of the struggle between Party fanatics and liberalizing opponents. But to speak of conflict in the matter of the treatment of the Jews is like re-writing that chapter on the snakes of Ireland, which Dr Johnson could repeat in full because it consisted of a single sentence.* The truth is that the extermination of the Jews of the Soviet Union, in which by the most rigorously modest computation three-quarters of a million people perished, played no part whatever in the conflict of aims. Among the opponents of Hitler's Russian policy there was no objection to the exterminations, apart from some delaying tactics by the Wehrmacht Transport Command in the first weeks, some discreetly circulated expressions of disapproval and a few individual acts of protection.**

It is incredible that this should have been the case in occupied Russia, where there was no curtain of secrecy such as surrounded the deportations of Jews from western Europe. In the Baltic States, White Russia and the Ukraine, extermination was practised so openly that in 1941 at any rate every soldier must have known what was going on. While there were plenty of high-placed soldiers and civilians who made it their business to criticize the methods of occupation, the same people washed their hands of the Jews in Russia. The answer to this riddle lies perhaps in the 'service mentality' which was common to both sides in the Second World War. The German *Ostpolitiker* were concerned with ending the war advantageously and swiftly. With this purpose in view, they believed that the sympathies of the Russian population must be regained, that Russian political aspirations must be placated in order to destroy Stalin's government. They were opportunists, concerning themselves only with what seemed essential to that end and nothing else. The rescue of the Jews had nothing to do with winning the war against Stalin. In the flattening phraseology of the period it was not essential to the war effort.

Partly this was due to the Russians themselves. If the Western Allies failed to back words with action, failed for instance to show that the United Nations Declaration of 17th December 1942, was sincere, the Russians for their part soon ceased even to admit that the Jews were being singled out for extermination. For the Russian case, as presented at Nuremberg, the prosecution did, it is true, produce a few Jewish survivors as witnesses. But very seldom in the long prosecution brief were the Jews mentioned. The mass murders were mass murders of 'Soviet citizens'. Even the incredible execution of 33,000 Jews at Kiev was presented in this way. It has been said that the instructions of the Politburo were fundamentally humane, that the expression 'Soviet

* 'There are no snakes to be met with throughout the whole island.'
** For instance See p. 87

citizen' was used to show that, while to the Germans the Jews were sub-human, in the Soviet Union all races and tribes were equal. It is, however, more probable that in a country where anti-Semitism had so long a history Stalin was afraid of making the Germans popular among some sections of the population by drawing attention to measures which the Germans reserved for the Jews alone. Mr Solomon Schwarz believes that Stalin encouraged the expression 'Soviet citizen' so that no German propaganda could accuse him of fighting a Jewish war.[51] Thus in Molotov's note to the Allies of 6th January 1942, a number of massacres were described as directed against 'unarmed defenceless Jewish working people'. But at the time of the second Molotov note, 17th April 1942, there was already a change of policy. It is easy to identify the massacres which Molotov named, but the fact that the victims were Jews was not mentioned at all.

I do not follow Mr Schwarz in his further conclusions that the Soviet government hindered the escape of Jews and that all stories of attempts to evacuate them in time were concocted for foreign consumption. The statistics of the *Einsatzgruppen* reports certainly suggest that at least two thirds of the Jews must have been evacuated in time, along with the working Soviet population.[52] Nevertheless the policy of anonymity had disastrous consequences. Soviet loyalists, who listened to home propaganda, received no guidance how to behave at a time when an enormous number of collaborators assisted the Germans in these atrocities, undenounced by Moscow. As Himmler's chief Intelligence Officer, Walter Schellenberg claimed that he had obtained captured Russian reports which showed that many of the collaborators had been actually briefed by the NKVD to encourage the Germans in unpopular courses. There is of course no limit to what people with the Secret Service mentality will believe. It is hardly surprising that Himmler and Heydrich failed to be impressed with Schellenberg's story.[53]

There is, however, no reason to doubt that there were members of the Russian Communist Party who had not lost the taste for pogroms. There exists a report, which was sent to Admiral Canaris by a sergeant-interpreter, employed by one of the military intelligence staffs in White Russia. It concerns the massacre of 7,620 Jews in Borisov in October 1941, which was carried out entirely by the local administration as appointed by the Germans, with the aid of the local White Russian Security Police. The latter, in Sergeant Soennicken's opinion, were mostly former communists, while the assistant to the White Russian mayor was a former regular policeman, who recalled the pogroms of the pre-revolutionary period with satisfaction.[54]* This, however, happened as early as October 1941. In 1942 and 1943 the complete extermination of the Jews in White Russia had to be carried out by Germans and foreigners.

This absence of propaganda-value may account for the indifference of the liberalizing opponents of Hitler's policy towards the activities of the *Einsatzgruppen* and other units under SD control. Even in the self-government areas, which were created by von Kleist and Koestring in the north Caucasus late in 1942, no efforts were made by the military government officers to hinder the activities of an *Einsatzgruppe*, which murdered Jews as well as lunatics and hospital cases.** In Sevastopol, at about the same time, Jews were taken out daily to be gassed from a building which housed a Wehrmacht field hospital.[55] Kharkov offers perhaps the most astonishing case of this willing compliance. Re-taken from the Russians on 15th March 1943, it was finally lost on 16th August. During these five months Kharkov was a front line city where the army commander reigned supreme. Yet in June some 3,000 Jews, who had survived previous massacres, were rounded up and shot by the SD, because it was alleged that they had welcomed the Red Army troops during those few days in March that the Russians were back in the city.[56]

The excessive compliance of military government officers owed much to party indoctrination, from which very few of the *Ostpolitiker* were immune after nine years and more of national socialism. Their compliance was also encouraged by the virtual silence of Russian propaganda, which created an impression that there was no sympathy for Jews in the Soviet Union. This impression was incorrect. The growth of the Partisan movement in White Russia was greatly stimulated by the fear and uncertainty as to whose turn it would be next to be massacred on the latest ideological grounds. It is likely indeed that the local population helped in the Borisov pogrom in October 1941, but a change of attitude occurred when the first organized Partisan centres were established. Goebbels detected the hand of Jewry in the increased Partisan activity of March 1942.[57] In the same month an *Einsatzgruppe* bulletin uttered a clear warning. The massacres, it declared, had created a feeling of insecurity and even anxiety in the population of White Russia. Educated circles professed themselves unused to such procedure and doubtful of its outcome. The

* See p. 132
** See p. 509

subject of this warning was the mass-killing of fugitive Jews, who had found their way to Partisan areas at Rakow, west of Minsk, and at Cherven, west of Bobruisk.[58]

Reports by Jewish survivors on the subject of the attitude of the White Russian Partisans vary a great deal.[59] It may be the case that helpless wandering communities of entire Jewish families were not given much protection in the forest hide-outs, but able-bodied men who escaped from the ghettoes were certainly welcomed. The German practice of gradually reducing the large ghettoes, which had survived the holocaust of 1941, was therefore doubly idiotic. It deprived the Wehrmacht of its last exempted Jewish workshops and it stimulated Partisan recruitment. It is all the more astonishing that the outspoken memoranda of men like Gehlen, Schenckendorff, Braeutigam and Oberlaender never emphasized the connection between the massacres of the Jews and the Partisan movement. The connection seems to have eluded utilitarians and idealists alike, though both schools condemned the destruction of skilled labour. In December 1942, Professor Peter Seraphim, the author of a popular Nazi encyclopaedia of anti-Semitism, wrote a report on the loss of skilled labour in the Ukraine. Writing to General Thomas at the Armaments Office at OKW, Seraphim pointed out the results of the massacres in dramatic language.[60] The most rudimentary repairs could no longer be made. Even Erich Koch, whose speeches are curiously lacking in anti-Semitic pronouncements, complained in June 1943, that, since he had lost half a million Jews, no one could get a pair of boots mended.*

In the Wehrmacht there were rare outbursts of emotion at Staff Conferences. There was for instance that dramatic scene, described by Fabian von Schlabrendorff, at von Bock's headquarters in Smolensk, when the reports concerning the Borisov massacre were read.[61] Nothing came of this outburst. Actual military intervention was confined to little more than local resistance by officers on behalf of Jewish workshops. For that matter minor SS leaders, who made a good thing out of these workshops, frequently tried to get them spared. In such incidents there may sometimes have been an element of sentiment, but a real stand on behalf of the laws of humanity did not come into the matter. If asked to intervene, the higher military bureaucracy would declare themselves bound by a Fuehrer order which had been circulated by Keitel on 12th September 1941. In those early days the Transport Command and the Armament Office could still obstruct Himmler and

* See p. 215

Heydrich in their plans to 're-settle' the Jews of the Baltic States, whom the Wehrmacht employed without paying them. It was therefore decreed that Jews, whether working for the Wehrmacht or for civilians, must remain in the sole keeping of the SS. Henceforward the Wehrmacht could issue no employment certificates to Jews.[62]

As to the civilian *Ostpolitiker*, a liberalization of their policy was unlikely to embrace the renunciation of anti-Semitism, because, had they not given some proof of anti-Semitism, they would not have been accepted by the Rosenberg Ministry in the first place. Rosenberg was almost the forefather of National Socialist anti-Semitism. He might give way on Baltic autonomy, he might pester Hitler with his own plans, but on this subject he did not disagree with Hitler. Even in June 1944, when there was precious little for a Minister for the Occupied East to do, Rosenberg was occupied after his own heart, just as he had been occupied in March 1941. Rosenberg was preparing the invitations for an international anti-Jewish congress which was to meet in Cracow. The delegates were to swear an oath to help remove all Jewry from Europe. Bormann, always delighted to deliver a snub, wrote to the dim-eyed creature that, when the great destinies of the nation were at stake, his conference might 'by every evidence pass unnoticed'. The Fuehrer therefore wished Rosenberg to refrain from calling the conference till further orders.[63]

Such was Rosenberg. His personal favourites, Meyer, Schickedanz and Lohse, who had worked with his Foreign Political Office, were not less anti-Semitic than himself; even the more practical men, whom Rosenberg obtained for his Political Department from Ribbentrop's Russia Committee, had passed the Party test. In the days before Keitel's edict, when some branches of the Wehrmacht still impeded the mass-slaughter in the Baltic States, when even Lohse wrote an alarmed, almost hysterical letter after the massacre at Libau, the liberal-minded Otto Braeutigam coldly observed the protocols. The Jewish question in the *Ostland*, he told Lohse, 'had been solved in verbal discussions'. On principle, economic considerations were not to apply at all. Such matters should in any case be settled with the Higher SS and Police Leaders.[64]

Even the bête-noir of Bormann and Koch, Georg Leibbrandt, could hardly have been assailed on the count of failing to be anti-Semitic, though in 1942–3 he was accused of being pro-British, a leftist and perhaps a Russian spy as well.* Leibbrandt attended Heydrich's con-

* See p. 217

ference at Wannsee, where the significance of the word 're-settlement' was openly explained. But that was no news to Leibbrandt in January 1942. In his own Political Department there was a section-chief for racial affairs called Erwin Wetzel, who had written to Lohse on 25th October 1941, a detailed description of the gassing camps which were intended for the Jewish population of the Baltic States. A fortnight later Leibbrandt not only discussed this letter with Rosenberg, but on Rosenberg's instructions had a copy sent to Erich Koch.*

With such a background not much could be expected from the most dissident of Rosenberg's officials, but there was one exception. After the particularly savage pogroms that reduced the Jewish population of White Russia to a manageable size in the summer of 1942, Wilhelm Kube became the protector of a small remnant of the 8,700 Jews who had been deported to Minsk from Germany in November 1941. In this case it was more than a utilitarian interest. Kube risked the adverse reports of the Gestapo out of softness of heart. It must be added that he had not a scrap of this to spare for the White Russian Jews, for on more than one occasion Kube recorded his approval of the measures he had witnessed. But, rather late in life, he decided that the Jews from Germany were 'people from our own circles of culture'. His interest had been awakened at the time of the first deportations to Minsk, when he had discovered some pretty Aryan-looking girls and also a number of ex-service men who had been decorated in the First World War. There was even a naval ADC of the Crown Prince Wilhelm, with whom Kube believed himself connected by marriage.[65] A year later Kube's first indignation had developed into a genuine affection for this dwindling company, Germans like himself in a hostile land. He forgot his own lifelong frenzied anti-Semitism, to which he had given expression as long ago as 1909, when he had founded a racialist student fraternity in Berlin. Surrounded in war-battered Minsk by savageries that were almost unbelievable, his own feeble attempts at conciliation defeated by the resentment of the oppressed population, Kube found an island of civilization in the depopulated and doomed German ghetto.

Kube's sympathy, though it made him notorious, was of no value in the end to the Jews. The last of them left Minsk in September 1943, a day or two before his own assassination—in the gassing-vans. As

---

* *Trials*, etc., I, pp. 803, 870, 888. NO 365. Erwin Wetzel also composed plans for the expulsion of Poles and Russians and had a part in the 'General Plan, East' of May 1942. He is one of the missing men, last seen in a Russian internment camp at the end of the war. See p. 173

Generalkommissar for White Russia, Kube was nevertheless the one high official in Russia, civil or military, who for any length of time obstructed the path of racial murder. Pathetic and ineffective, fat and libidinous, this elderly man did for many months what no member of the much-vaunted opposition to Hitler dared to do.[66]

To the very end of the war the *Ostpolitiker* cherished the illusion that anti-Semitism still offered a bait for Russian opposition movements against Stalin. The Baltic German background, the long Party in-doctrination and the connection with Tsarist emigré circles, all helped to keep the illusion alive, even in 1944, when General Vlasov was permitted his own national committee and national army. Vlasov him-self seems to have kept his own speeches free of anti-Semitic senti-ments, but to most of the collaborationist Russian generals they came naturally, while Vlasovite Russian news-sheets abounded with them.[67] Moreover some of the most relentless mass-executioners of Jewry were attracted, as by a magnet, to Vlasov's cause. Among them were Kaltenbrunner, Ohlendorff and Radetzky and even the head of the 'Reinhardt programme', Odilo Globocnik, the man with two million murders on his conscience.* Many members of extermination com-mandos hid themselves in the ranks of the liberation army. Almost any educated Russian prisoner, who could reel off the National Socialist anti-Semitic patter, was assured of a job in the growing army of propagandists. The High Command was to regret this irresponsible activity, when the propagandists were permitted to speak their own mind in their own language to Russian units serving in the west. The way to German hearts had been too easy.** Vlasov himself told Wilfried von Oven in March 1945, that Stalin had instructed Russian agents, who were about to cross the German lines, in the following memorable words. 'Always say *Jawohl* and abuse the Jews roundly.'[68]

* See p. 392
** See p. 346

CHAPTER EIGHT

THE EASTERN WORKERS

(a) The Sauckel Organization and its Chief

CLOSELY BOUND UP with some features of Partisan warfare was the vast press-gang organization which tapped the labour resources of occupied Russia. Through the record of conferences and decrees, of constant improvisations to meet the growing shadow of defeat, flits the ill-defined figure of the Plenipotentiary for Labour Recruitment, Fritz Sauckel. Like that of so many wartime Nazi ministers, Sauckel's rôle was ambivalent and perplexed. Almost everyone held him responsible for the spread of the Partisan movement, yet he tried frequently to mitigate the horrors of its repression in the hope of exploiting the situation as a source of slave labour.

Sauckel's immense demands for human beings, which fell largely on the food-producing Ukraine, brought him also in conflict with the 'agricultural leaders' of the Economic Staff East, who were engaged in obtaining the enormous grain deliveries which Hitler continued to demand. Thus, while in the main the history of German rule in Russia is that of a conflict between the extreme Hitler loyalists and the liberalizing groups of *Ostpolitiker*, the history of Sauckel's eastern workers is one of conflict among the Hitler loyalists themselves.

It is not easy to steer a course between the existing black and white presentations of the same story. To the Russian and Polish workers, labour-conscription and deportation to the Reich were a form of slavery with the concentration camp constantly in the background. It was mitigated only by the fact that conditions of life and labour in Germany were sometimes no worse than in their own ravaged homes. Yet to the German civilian population this form of labour seemed a privilege. Germans were exhorted to believe that they conferred a blessing on the poor barbarians by giving them German rations and clothing and teaching them German ways of life. The Nazi attitude was that of the early Victorian governing classes towards the relief of poverty, long working hours, washed faces and dull insufficient food being regarded as wholesome benefits in themselves. Some of the reports on the conditions of the *Ostarbeiter* and the attempts to alleviate them read like a sociological novel by Charles Reade or Charles Kingsley.

What was behind this extraordinary anachronism? At the great Nuremberg Trial, Goering, Speer and Sauckel, who rightly bore the brunt of the slave-labour indictments, pleaded that they were impelled by necessity. The demands of total warfare were insatiable. Even the millions of foreign workers in Germany were never sufficient. Already, before the invasion of Russia had begun, they numbered three millions and a half and of these two million were civilians. Once it was realized that the Russian campaign was no *Blitzkrieg*, that it would swallow up more men and material than any campaign in the history of the world, the conscription of the Russian population became, so they said, inevitable. Nevertheless this plea of inevitability was an over-simplification. In proportion as the German occupation depressed their standards of living, so were the inhabitants of the occupied countries disposed to accept employment in Germany. Thus employment in Germany was more tempting for Frenchmen and Italians than it was for Danes or Belgians. For Russians such employment could have been made very tempting indeed. Huge as were the numbers of conscripted workers from the Soviet Union, an impressive number could have been obtained voluntarily. And the value of the volunteers' work would have been greater, just because it was voluntary. It was a fact that the German war economy, geared to a form of convict labour, gave a lower yield per head than the British war economy. In spite of labour conscription, the British worker greatly increased his earnings under war conditions. Though restrictions on wages negotiation and on the right to strike existed in theory, they were not applied. However harmful the post-war effects have been in the form of monetary inflation, the policy justified itself in wartime. Compared with Germany, more was obtained from the individual.

The truth is that German policy towards Russian labour was dictated not by the inevitability of conscription but by three fatal misjudgments. The first was the fear of the spread of Marxist propaganda. In 1941 it caused the wastage of 2,800,000 Russian lives in the starving Stalags and Dulags behind the front, at a time when camps and food were available in Germany and Poland for a very large proportion of the prisoners of war.* Later it caused the imprisonment and isolation

* See p. 120

of the eastern workers in guarded camps and barracks or in strict house arrest on farms, even when they had volunteered to go to Germany. It was a fatuous anxiety. Given better wages than they earned at home and an opportunity to experience western European life in a state of freedom, very few of the eastern workers would have remained evangelists for Karl Marx. Even if some skilled workers and professional men and women had done so, they could hardly have caused more harm than the swarms of voluntary agents of communism in Hitler's Europe, who were described by the general name of *Rote Kappelle*. On the other hand, the return to Russia in 1945 of millions of Soviet subjects, had they been treated better than ever before, could have changed the whole of European post-war history in a very surprising way.

The second fatal misjudgment was the application of the *Untermensch* theory towards the eastern workers. The conviction that the Slavs were low-grade human beings, who responded only to shouts and kicks and beatings, seems to have been very widely spread among the Nazi small fry who acted as overseers, even though most German farmers were by the nature of their calling too hard-headed to be influenced by this lunacy. The numerous directives from Party offices, which have survived, are written in a language that is scarcely credible. Yet the Germans should have been the very last people in Europe to accept this language. There must have been two or three million Germans and Austrians who had served in Russia in 1914–18 and who had seen that Russian soldiers were much like themselves. Hundreds of thousands had been prisoners of war, making their way home after the Revolution. These middle-aged and elderly men had acquired a knowledge of Russian life, much less superficial than that of the hordes of tourists of the years between the wars. They had real contacts with the Russian outlook, such as the Western Allies badly lacked. Large numbers of these veterans were employed in occupied Russia or were put in charge of eastern workers in Germany. Yet their influence on policy was negligible. The *Untermensch* mentality, as spread by small-town political bosses and their toadies, proved too strong for them.

The third and the most fatal misjudgment of all was due to the temptation to get something for nothing. Till the very end there was a strong discrimination against the eastern workers, as compared with workers from other European countries. Till quite late in the war it was an article of faith that they would do the same work for less money, that they needed less food, that the comforts of the German home were wasted on them, that they would be satisfied with their lot, if the low standards of living of their homeland were kept rigorously pegged. The Germans had a funny way with their friends, perhaps because, in the suspicious inhibited way of life which Party rule had imposed on them, they could no longer distinguish who their friends were. Friendly and ingratiating behaviour towards Germany induced only a deep psychotic repulsion, so that everyone was savaged—and the more so when it was easiest. The determination to get the utmost from the *Ostarbeiter* without offering anything in return was part of the general decline in human relationships under Nazi rule. But the subject is a delicate one, for the example which the Germans set was followed with enthusiasm and all the Allies retained their prisoners as slaves for years after the war, the Russians for ten years and more in some cases. But it was left for the Germans alone to use civilians as slave labour at a time when, both practically and politically, it served their own interest least.

The conscription of the civilian population in occupied Russia for labour behind the lines had been part of Goering's original 'Green File' instructions of 23rd May 1941, but the 'Green File' contained no authority to deport civilians to Germany. It was only after the failure before Moscow that such a step was contemplated. At a conference of the Four-Year-Plan Office on 17th November 1941, Goering made the first proposals.* Having announced that Russian prisoners of war would have to work in Germany, he added that a certain amount of civilians would be taken on too. Goering gave the rather sheepish explanation that it was intended to employ fewer German women, whose place was in the home, and fewer foreigners from the west, who worked too little and ate too much. The Russians would be treated in the same way as the prisoners o war. Their labour would be sold by the State to the employers and they would be allowed only a little pocket-money.[1]

For the moment very little more was done about it. During the next ten weeks no trains were available from Russia, except for troop movements. But the Russians, as usual, were wonderfully well informed about German plans. Molotov's note to the Allies of 6th January 1942, did not fail to accuse the Germans of deporting civilians, pretending that they were prisoners of war and including them in their exaggerated victory statistics.[2]

At the beginning of February, when the first labourers arrived in Germany from Russia, Hitler lost a man who could have prevented

* See p. 114

some of the mistakes that were to follow. On the 8th, the Minister for
Armaments and Munitions, Dr Fritz Todt, was killed in a passenger
airliner which burst in the sky over Hitler's headquarters in East
Prussia. It was said that Dr Todt had leant against a button which
detonated a time-bomb under one of the seats, a device intended for
occasions when it might be necessary to destroy the machine on the
ground.[3] Todt was the founder of the OT or Todt Organization, which
had built the *Autobahnen* and the Siegfried Line and which was to
construct all Germany's wartime defence systems. Although intimate
with Hitler, Todt was not a demagogue but an astonishing organizer.
Unlike his successor, Albert Speer, he was content to do the work with
the manpower as made available to him. Todt did not try to be
Minister for Labour and Minister for Munitions at the same time.
Albert Speer, however, was not satisfied with this arrangement and
took personal decisions concerning labour conscription, as the reports
of his Staff Conferences testify. He was much younger but more remote
from life than the amiable Todt. To Speer human beings were just
units in a machine and his personal cold-bloodedness dominated the
entire labour programme.

One of the defects of Hitler's wartime administration was a failure
to allow ministers sufficient independence for special tasks. Todt himself had served under three successive masters, the Ministry for
Economic Affairs, the Armaments Office of the Wehrmacht, and
finally Goering's Four-Year-Plan Office. Not only Todt but also Dr
Friedrich Syrop, the Head of the Labour Office, was subordinated to
Goering and the Four-Year-Plan. A fortnight after Todt's death Syrop
retired owing to ill-health and for the next six weeks the labour office
was run by Dr Erwin Mansfeld, a subordinate official. Mansfeld was
far too humane to conduct the gigantic slave-raiding operation which
Hitler had planned with Albert Speer, although the instructions which
he issued at his Staff Conferences on 20th and 24th February, envisaged
the recruitment of 627,000 Russian workers almost at once.[4] Mansfeld
was highly critical of the methods that had already been used in Russia
and hoped desperately to obtain these numbers without using conscription, without crimping and without recruiting by false promises.*

A permanent plenipotentiary for employment had therefore to be
discovered urgently in order to replace the too gentle Mansfeld. Speer
proposed a Party diehard of the most proven brutality, Gauleiter
Hanke of Breslau. The reason for this odd choice, which Speer gave at

* See pp. 118-19

his trial, was that the permanent officials of the Labour Office were non-political and that the Gauleiters therefore had it their own way and refused to co-operate in labour allocation plans. So Speer suggested a forceful Gauleiter to be Plenipotentiary for Employment. Goering agreed, but the nomination of Gauleiter Hanke meant a reference to Martin Bormann, chief of the Party Office. Bormann proposed Fritz Sauckel, the Gauleiter of Thuringia, whom he preferred to Hanke. Hitler as usual listened to Bormann and so made the appointment. Although Goering had had nothing to do with the choice of Sauckel, a legal fiction was permitted to continue that Sauckel was under Goering's orders at the Central Planning Board. In fact Goering was too enraged to attend the Central Planning Board any further and Sauckel remained undisputedly Speer's man.[5]

So there came into being another Erich Koch situation. Goering's officials of the Economic Staff East worked against Sauckel's officials, to prevent them removing all their sources of labour. Goering himself became a more placid Rosenberg, not so much unable as unwilling to intervene. Though very jealous of Koch, Sauckel sometimes joined forces with him against both Rosenberg and the Economic Staff East. Where a fine balance should have been struck between the labour force for food-growing on the spot and the labour force for Germany, there developed instead a war of office precedences. Sauckel, like Koch, became involved in acrimonious correspondence and sometimes he used the same language, for he was a Party man who felt himself to be at loggerheads with the experts, the professional bureaucrats and the officer caste.

There, however, the resemblance between Sauckel and Erich Koch ceased. Sauckel had been a demagogue, but not outrageously so. Forty-seven years old at the time of his appointment, Sauckel was born at Nassfurt near Bamburg, the only child of a postman. During his youth he had spent five years as a seaman, starting as a five-shillings a week cabin boy and serving mainly under sail; in 1914, when twenty years old, he had been captured by the French, while outward bound on a sailing ship for Australia. After his return to Germany from captivity in 1919, Sauckel was too poor to take the examination for a mate's certificate, so he worked near his home at the Fischer ball-bearing works at Schweinfurt. It was a centre of red radicalism and the politics of his fellow workmen drove him into the arms of the National Socialist Party. Sauckel was a genuine working man, which was a rare thing indeed among the band of Nazi agitators who became Hitler's ministers. In 1923, when he joined the Party, he married the daughter of a fellow workman who remained a Social Democrat and a Trade Unionist. Remarkably enough, Sauckel found time for politics, although he had to work at the factory to maintain a family of ten children. In 1927 Hitler made him Party Gauleiter for Thuringia and in 1932 he was one of the first Nazis to become a minister in the Federal States, being appointed Minister for the Interior in this same Thuringia.[6]

Thus, Sauckel, like Erich Koch, came from a Trade Unionist background and belonged to the left wing of the Party. Unlike Koch, Sauckel was not corrupted by office. In October 1944, when he accepted a cheque from Hitler on his fiftieth birthday, his salary was 30,000 marks, a purchasing power hardly exceeding a thousand pounds a year, but it is unlikely that these were his only resources, for in 1935 Sauckel had been made administrator of two factories in his Gau, which came under Party control.[7]

Sauckel was not considered an important person. To remain Gauleiter of Thuringia in wartime was as good as being shelved, for the *Gauleiterschaft* consisted largely of once important Party personalities, who were not deemed worthy of cabinet posts. Sauckel knew that he had outlasted his usefulness on 16th July 1941, when Rosenberg proposed him as *Reichskommissar* for the Ukraine in place of Herbert Backe who had refused to stand. It does not appear from the minutes that the proposition was even discussed. Goering had already determined to secure Erich Koch's candidature. Mortified by his failure, Sauckel arranged to get himself smuggled on to a submarine as an unofficial seaman, but Admiral Doenitz gave orders that Captain Salmann was to put the Gauleiter aboard the first homeward-bound ship.[8]

From this short record two impressions emerge. One is that of a simple, hard-working, patriotic man, the other that of an over-ambitious small-town boss, a nonentity who owed his position only to the fact that he had personified National Socialism in an area that was once considered Red. Goebbels called Sauckel the dullest of the dull, long-winded, pedantic and neurotic. And from the same source one learns that Hitler found Sauckel too weak.[9] Sauckel perished by the hangman's noose, because he carried out a bad assignment uncritically. He died for being a yes-man, whereas Albert Speer, who fixed the labour quotas which Sauckel had to fulfil, escaped with life imprisonment. Behind his ranting, Sauckel showed himself in his memoranda to be acutely conscious of the things that make a man's labour tolerable and for which he himself had fought in his day. But he too was obsessed with the concept of different grades of races. As a quite uneducated man, he admired what National Socialists were expected to admire and one of his unfulfilled ambitions was the creation of a Nietzsche Research Institute in Weimar.[10]

Sauckel's new position was curious. When Hitler's decree of 21st March made him General Plenipotentiary for the Employment of Labour (briefly the GBA), he possessed neither staff nor office. He was not a successor to the temporary plenipotentiary, Erwin Mansfeld, from whom he took over no files,[11] nor did his new office replace the permanent Ministry of Labour under Franz Seldte—nor for that matter the Labour Front under Robert Ley nor the Reich Labour Service under Konstantin Hierl. Sauckel had to borrow his staff where he could; in Germany from the regional labour offices and the Labour Front, in Russia from the Rosenberg Ministry and the military and civilian staffs of the Economic Administration. There was never any ministry building. Sauckel remained in his own Berlin office, the Thuringiahaus, which he maintained as 'Regent for Thuringia'. His officials were housed in the Ministry of Labour in the Saarlandstrasse. Sauckel made a little too much of this, for so far as actual conscription was concerned, the only veto on his actions was the inactive authority of Goering's Four-Year-Plan Office, whereas under Hitler's personal brief Sauckel could use any methods of compulsion that he liked.[12]

On 21st March 1942 Sauckel arrived at the Reich Chancellery with his own plans, which were grandiloquent enough for so early a stage in the war, since they envisaged a *levée en masse* of German women and of adolescents of both sexes. This Hitler at once corrected by pointing out that he had not got the time to train such people. He must have experienced labourers available at once. In rhetorical language Hitler described the first Russian winter, which had put almost every piece of German machinery, including tanks and locomotives, out of action. If the battle for new weapons were not won now, Stalin would be at the Channel by next winter. Hitler said that he had freed half the captured French Army, most of the Belgian and all of the Dutch Armies. He could recall them to captivity and to forced labour and indeed might have to do so one day, but at present the fight against Bolshevism demanded a united European front. Therefore the bulk of the new labour force must come from the east. Hitler quieted Sauckel's legalistic anxieties by declaring that Russia had not subscribed to the

Geneva Convention. Furthermore Stalin had applied labour conscription in occupied Bessarabia and Bukovina and had 'some three
million Chinese working in Soviet Russia'.[13]

So much for Sauckel's Nuremberg recollections more than four
years after the event. Peter Kleist, however, says that he attended a
Staff Conference at the Rosenberg Ministry, which Sauckel addressed
immediately after his interview with Hitler. The address lasted a whole
hour and, according to Kleist, the conference was as one-sided as a
Reichstag session. If there had been any conflict of ideas between
Sauckel and Hitler, it did not appear now. Sauckel declared that, since
it was not proposed to restore any of the industries of the Soviet
Union, there would be an infinite pool of labour, cheap and easy to
feed and not politically dangerous, if segregated and supervised.
Kleist contrived to make his point that all this emphasis on compulsion
was unnecessary. Most Russians craved for nothing more than a
posting abroad. The Russian *wanderlust* should be encouraged through
kindness and fair inducements. Sauckel's reply, however, was in the
authentic Erich Koch tradition.

> What you say is all well and good, and if people from the east
> want to come voluntarily, they can do so. But I have neither time
> nor inclination to occupy myself with the tastiness of Russian
> cooking or with the spiritual life of the Moujiks. I have received
> my instructions from Adolf Hitler, and I will bring millions of
> eastern workers to Germany without consideration for their likes
> and dislikes, whether they want to or not.

Kleist also says that Sauckel told his conference the reason why
Hitler would not imitate the example of Britain and call up German
girls for the factories. Hitler remembered the hardships and the moral
dangers to which girls of good family had been subjected in the
factories of the First World War. If German girls were allowed once
again to succumb to these moral dangers, it would be an insult to
fighting men, returning from the front; and the thought of what their
women were doing might damage their fighting morale.[14]

This was not a jovial invention of Kleist's, for, a month later,
Sauckel himself wrote down in a memorandum for the Rosenberg
Ministry Hitler's objections on behalf of the mothers of the nation and
his fear that they might come to moral or mental harm.[15]

Thus Hitler's fateful decision to create a slave trade in place of a
German call-up was prompted by a peasant prudishness, which he

must have inherited from his forebears in the Austrian *Waldviertel*. But even in making a decision so momentous and so dangerous as this, Hitler could not be consistent. By 3rd September he was already demanding the importation of half a million tough Ukrainian women in order to free German girls from housekeeping—so that they could fulfil their duty-year in the Women's Labour Service.[16]

(b) The Slave Trade at its Height

HAVING MADE HIS tough speech on 21st March, Sauckel had to face chaos. While his commissioners in Russia were successful in collecting their quota of heads, so many offices and agencies became involved in the subsequent process of moving these people and putting them to work that the apparatus broke down from the beginning. Sauckel was concerned with recruitment and no more. He could not dictate for instance to Dorpmueller, the head of the Railway Administration, to Backe, the Food Minister, or to Heydrich, the Chief of Security. Sauckel was always promising an improvement in the eastern workers' rations or else boasting publicly that they received the same food as Germans. In fact Herbert Backe, now food dictator of the Reich, refused to budge from the scale which he had laid down on 4th April 1942. In the following August and September Backe demanded that no increase in the eastern workers' ration, such as had been advocated by Sauckel, should be granted till the general food situation had improved.[17] At Goering's conference of 6th August, Backe went so far as to demand that the importation of eastern workers should be limited to the surplus food available.[18] But it was the food which was withheld and not the workers. A memorandum from Sauckel's welfare section, dated 30th September, asserted that the workers from Russia were still being worse fed than the Polish workers in Germany. Their bread was still being made from turnips and there was a prevalence of hunger oedema.[19]*

With Himmler and Heydrich the whole question of security, which had been so lightly baulked by Goering at his conference on 17th November 1941, had to be re-opened.[20]** The new rules were circulated under Himmler's signature on 20th February 1942. As a result, Sauckel,

* See pp. 118–19
** See p. 114

who in the first few weeks had to deal with volunteers as much as with conscripts, found that he was sending these people virtually to a concentration camp. The Gestapo was to be their only judicial authority. Hanging was the penalty for almost every offence they could commit. If no death penalty was passed, Himmler could demand to see the prosecution papers. The undisciplined could be sent to a true concentration camp on the report of any guard. Hangings would take place in the camp itself and in public.[21]

Within a few weeks of his appointment Sauckel had to tackle Heydrich on the subject. Heydrich after his habit did not hesitate to criticize Hitler's orders. He found the *Ostarbeiter* programme fantastic and he declared that Sauckel was making his work more difficult.[22] He refused to remove the barbed wire or the armed guards or the derogatory badges, which were designed to prevent German racial contamination. A few weeks after this interview Heydrich was assassinated, but a long time was to pass before any noticeable alterations were made in the rules. Only a small part of the strict penal discipline under the original Himmler order was relaxed in the camps. Provided that he did not go near any eating place or house of entertainment or use any public transport, the happy Soviet explorer of the western Utopia might be allowed to run about without a lead for an hour or two each week.

From Russia the complaints of military government officials, of Riecke's agricultural leaders, of the civilian commissars, came rolling into Rosenberg's Ministry. On 8th May Rosenberg had his last truly favourable interview with Hitler, at which most of his complaints were heard sympathetically, even those against Erich Koch.* Rosenberg complained that Sauckel's agents ignored the orders of his *Generalkommissars*, that the young Russians were taking to the woods and that the deportees jumped the trains, which later reached the Polish border half empty.[23] Rosenberg declined to bear any further responsibility for the share of his own officials in the matter, if Sauckel continued to take instructions from Albert Speer. Hitler promised to get this sorted out. Lammers must draft a decree, defining the respective spheres of Rosenberg's Ministry and Speer's. But nothing was heard from Lammers, and in the following month Rosenberg forwarded to Hitler the so-called *Grosse Denkschrift*, an immense tabulation of charges against Koch and Sauckel which had been drawn up in the Political Department. An ominous silence followed, and Rosenberg withdrew

* See p. 198

his endorsement of the *Denkschrift*.* In fact Lammers never drew up the defining decree and to the very end Lohse and Koch allowed Sauckel a free hand.

Sauckel was at last induced to pay a visit to Russia. In June or July he got as far as Smolensk, where Field Marshal von Kluge supported the many complaints of his Rear Area Commander, von Schenckendorff.** From von Kluge Sauckel also learnt of a disturbing incident which was supposed to have occurred in Rowné, in Erich Koch's own capital. It seems that the entire audience at a cinema had been surrounded by armed men with waiting lorries and carried off to Germany with nothing but the clothes they had on them. It took, Sauckel said, three months for him to get at the truth. The audience had consisted of a labour-gang who were celebrating the completion of a contract. They had been carted off to a new assignment in the middle of the performance and the works manager had employed police to keep them moving.[24]

But it was not as easy as this for Sauckel to ward off the complaints of the appalling conditions in which his slaves travelled. On 20th July Sauckel himself sent a circular, pointing out the poor state of the rolling stock, old unheated French coaches with broken windows.[25] But the truth was a lot worse than that. The railways in the occupied territories, right up to the front, were operated by the staff of the German *Reichsbahn*, who wore a special blue uniform, but who were not under the Wehrmacht's jurisdiction or anyone else's. Short of rolling stock in Germany, still shorter in occupied Russia, the *Reichsbahn* had been neglected for ten years in favour of motor highways and it had become the Achilles heel of Hitler's Germany. Dorpmueller, the *Reichsbahn* Minister, was moribund, his assistants, Ganzenmueller and Kleinmueller—all these Muellers—were hidebound bureaucrats. The stipulations which Sauckel had made for uncrowded cars, for heating, feeding and water on the journey, were ignored.[26]

A few reports have survived concerning the incredible conditions of the trains from Russia, as they were running in the spring and probably also in the summer of 1942. In Rosenberg's Ministry Dr Otto Braeutigam had organized a central relief agency for the eastern workers, the *Zentralstelle Ost* or ZAVO of Dr Guttkelch. A report by Guttkelch, dated 30th September 1942, showed that habitually 5 per cent of the eastern workers had been arriving in Germany during the

* See p. 198 and Peter Kleist, p. 206.
** See p. 323

past six months in such a state that they had to go to a so-called 'Return Camp' at Berlin-Blankenfelde, from which they were shipped back to Russia as unfit. Soon after the deportation trains had started running, Guttkelch organized a visit to this camp by delegates from various ministries. It seems that in the course of the inspection a Russian inmate attempted to relieve nature on the ground and was at once shot and wounded by a guard. Education on the treatment of the *Untermensch* had now reached such heights of perfection that the president of the Brandenburg Employment Office watched the incident without saying a word. Soon afterwards, a number of inmates were shipped off to Russia, but in such frightening conditions that Guttkelch organized a party to overtake the train and detain it before it reached Brest-Litovsk. The volunteers succeeded in getting the worst cases off the train, but one of their number, a Frau Mueller, reported that she had found several dead bodies in the locked box-cars. Venereal and TB cases lay together without straw, women had thrown their dead babies out of the windows. A body was hurled on to an embankment in full view of another train, containing eastern workers on their way to Germany.[27]

Within a week a similar incident was reported to the Rosenberg Ministry by Lieutenant Theurer, a Labour Recruitment Officer in Kharkov. Sometimes a train, like the one described in these reports, would pull up for hours alongside a cheerful healthy transport of volunteer skilled workers. When loaded with sixty people to each box-car, a train might well contain two or three thousand passengers. And in this way it would travel for days on end, most of the time with the doors sealed and the windows wired, and with only three or four guards in attendance.

Theurer also enclosed the report of the commandant of the Kharkov collecting centre who had to return large numbers of workers to their villages because they had been brought to the centre in a state of destitution. The Ukrainian militia had dragged them from their homes without even a chance to pack a few possessions.[28] In his much-quoted memorandum of 25th October, Braeutigam estimated that the number, who had been returned to Russia as unfit, had already reached 100,000. Methods were being approved by Sauckel which recalled 'the blackest period of the slave trade'.*

Sauckel for his part claimed that, in the first six months of his office,

* PS 294. Guttkelch's estimate of 5 per cent suggests that fifty thousand was the more probable figure.

during which a million people had been shipped from Russia, he had not been idle on the eastern workers' behalf. He had given orders that Red Cross personnel should escort the returning train-loads of the unfit and he explained at his trial that the Theurer and Guttkelch memoranda only referred to the very first weeks of the programme. All had been put right by the summer of 1942.[29] As early as June Sauckel had increased the free pocket-money allowance of the eastern workers to nine marks a week.[30] He had made them better off than the Germans. And as to the sick, he had established a centre in his own Gau at Frankenhausen. Nevertheless Guttkelch had noticed that the camp at Frankenhausen was still in the planning stage six months after Sauckel's appointment. And at the end of the year 1942, Rosenberg could still complain that no sick camps were provided by the Regional Labour Offices.

In spite of the chaos and the poor results, Hitler demanded a second and still larger quota of eastern workers. At the end of August 1942, he made one of his unpredictable about-turns of which the first manifestations appeared in one of his fireside talks.[31]* In his instructions to Sauckel, Hitler expatiated on the Germanic strain in south Russia and on the chaste peasant virtues of Ukrainian women. He had exchanged one lunacy for another. Some brief moment of vision, while motoring in the outskirts of Vinnitsa, had recalled the laughing Austrian girls of his boyhood, haymaking in their long black skirts and gold plaits. Anyone could make Germans out of such women. Only a commission of right-thinking Party members was needed. The half-million strong Ukrainian girls would not only relieve German women of their household chores, they would be Germanized. But the course of Germanization must be hard. At his Staff Conference on 3rd September and in his subsequent written instructions, Sauckel laid it down that the recruitment was to be for an indefinite period, that there was to be no home leave and that three hours' time off a week, terminating at latest at eight pm, was the utmost that could be granted by the employers.[32]

Since it was to be a matter of racial selection, for which Himmler would take the necessary measures, the recruitment would have to be voluntary. And since the girls would have to receive the full German food ration, this was now accorded to all eastern workers. But it also seems that Hitler's decision was coupled with a plan to reduce the rations for west European workers when their output fell below the east European standard.[33] This, said Sauckel, was a plain Fuehrer order

* See p. 177

and Herbert Backe had had the temerity to dispute it. But Sauckel was not impressed when Backe insisted on the difficulty of getting the extra food. Sauckel would find ways and means, 'even if it meant collecting the Jews of Europe in a human chain to pass the food-parcels by hand all the way from the Ukraine to Germany.'

The inducements to the future Germanics were not overwhelming. The bitter Braeutigam noticed that they would not be allowed to go to the pictures, as the German newspapers had predicted for them.[34] In the following March Sauckel was reduced to offering contracts of two years in place of an undertaking to work in Germany indefinitely. But he admitted that the recruiting plan was a complete failure. Not more than 13,000 to 15,000 Ukrainian girls came to Germany as domestic servants from first to last.[35]

Quite apart from the half million girls, the Ukraine was expected to produce 450,000 labourers for the armaments industry. Sauckel's announcement to Rosenberg, dated 3rd October 1942, showed that the quota had to be obtained within the next four months as part of a drive for two million more foreign workers for Germany.[36] Rosenberg was expected to chase Erich Koch, who had apparently disappeared from view. The *Reichskommissar* must be told that the 450,000 labourers could only be obtained by 'the ruthless employment of every means'. Rosenberg was not at all inclined to intervene. He regarded the Sauckel mission as a lever to detach Koch from his authority. Early in November, after reading Braeutigam's memorandum, he attacked Sauckel openly at an address to Robert Ley's Labour Front Leaders. Millions of Russians trembling with fright, Rosenberg said, now regarded Germany as another Siberia. It was not right to bring them to Germany in a frozen condition.[37]

The millions of Russians would have had still more reason to tremble with fright, had they known of the agreement, concluded between Himmler and the Ministry of Justice on 18th September. Henceforward eastern workers could be delivered to the concentration camps on a general accusation that they were 'asocial types.'[38] The way was open to the mass-deportation of Russian civilians to Auschwitz and Buchenwald, which occurred during the 1943 retreats. The terms of the secret agreement mentioned *working to death* with the utmost frankness and it meant no less for tens of thousands of eastern workers. It put them on the same footing as the Jews and confirmed all the worst anxieties that had been created by the German massacres.

The background to this astounding agreement was the dispute

between Himmler and Speer, who opposed the right of the SS to manufacture their own armaments. In spite of Speer's objection Himmler made arms in the concentration camps. In order to get back this production under his own control, Speer arrived at a compromise. It was the result of a series of conferences between Speer, Himmler and Hitler, which were held in this same month, September 1942. It was agreed that the concentration camps should provide labour for civilian factories under Speer's control and that the SS should get a proportionate share of the arms thus produced.[39] Himmler had therefore to find some simplified machinery by which the concentration camps could be filled and expanded. Sauckel showed no reluctance to help Himmler out. For instance Himmler had plans to clear a large area of eastern Poland for German settlements. On 26th November Sauckel instructed the employment offices, telling them that the evicted Poles were to be separated from their families and sent to the Berlin armament factories. The criminal and asocial elements among these Poles would go straight to the concentration camps.[40] Three weeks later, on 17th December, another instruction went out to the employment offices, this time from Gestapo Mueller. In the course of the next six weeks all fugitives and absentees from among the workers from enemy states must be rounded up. By 1st February 1943, Himmler needed 35,000 fresh inmates for his establishments, where the death-rate now exceeded the replacement rate.[41] The official returns show that 12,000 were in fact obtained in the first fortnight.

At his trial Sauckel protested that the proportion of eastern workers, who had suffered legal penalties, was very small, not a tenth of one per cent.[42] Unfortunately that boast applied only to cases dealt with in the courts. At the end of the war, when the survivors in the concentration camps were liberated, it was obvious that many of them were utterly bewildered people, who had no notion how they came there in the first place. In the first six months of 1943, 193,000 foreign workers were committed to concentration camps, nominally for leaving their work, but genuine absentees and deserters could only have made up a fraction of this figure. It meant that the same rate of delivery to the concentration camps had been kept up since Mueller's circular of 17th December 1942. Finally in May 1944, Speer himself complained that his labour force of eastern workers was shrinking through these deliveries at the rate of 40,000 a month. Very reluctantly Himmler had to promise Speer that the short-sentence offenders would be set free at the expiration of their terms.[43]

It is not necessary to describe the meaning of commitment to a concentration camp. The implication of these figures is plain. A very large number of eastern workers who came to Germany, whether voluntarily or under compulsion, perhaps a hundred thousand of them, perhaps more, did not benefit by any of the reforms. They died in prison-labour camps of epidemics, overwork and plain starvation.

In December 1942, Rosenberg was again persuaded to take a hand in the campaign against Sauckel, which was led by Otto Braeutigam in the Political Department. As a result of a long letter of complaint, Rosenberg was invited to attend a meeting at Weimar, where Sauckel addressed 800 officials of the Rosenberg Ministry and of the Economic Staff East, who were brought home with great difficulty and expense from their task of labour recruitment in Russia. Sauckel announced a number of pious general principles among which it is interesting to read that 'anyone who works in Germany, may live in Germany even if he is a Bolshevist.'[44] The chief purpose of the gathering was to clear Sauckel's name, but protestations that Sauckel 'would not tolerate that human beings are treated badly' could be received by his audience only with a tongue in the cheek, when such gigantic quotas of labour were demanded.

A new difficulty was arising. After the fall of Stalingrad, the eastern part of the *Reichskommissariat* Ukraine came under military government. Field Marshal von Kleist needed all the available civilian labour to construct defence lines. Under the rule of the Rear Area Commander, Karl von Roques, Sauckel had had no more reason to complain of military government in the Ukraine than he had of Erich Koch. But now, for the first time, his labour-recruitment commissioners in the Ukraine encountered Wehrmacht opposition. Both von Kleist of Army Group A and Frederici of the Rear Area Command, Army Group South, forbade conscription in their territory.* On 10th March 1943, Sauckel sent Hitler a telegram, declaring that since the beginning of the year he had obtained no labour recruits from Russia, because the Wehrmacht had withheld railway transport. He had been told by Erich Koch that certain politically-minded army commanders opposed the recruiting. He asked Hitler to cancel all orders which obstructed the deportation of labour to Germany. The generals, Sauckel declared, were giving too much credence to the atrocity and propaganda campaign of the Partisans. As usual, Sauckel loaded his telegram with

* Alexander Dallin, p. 441. In the White Russian rear area labour conscription had been banned by Schenckendorff from the beginning.

pompous phrases that did not appeal. Hitler was not likely to be impressed with the statement that never before in the world had foreign workers been treated as correctly as in wartime Germany. Interference by generals was, however, a more serious matter. After some skirmishing between OKW and the Army Commanders, the ban on Sauckel's activities was withdrawn on Keitel's instructions.[45]

At home Sauckel's position was strengthened by Hitler's decree of 17th March which was probably a result of Goebbels's visit to Hitler's headquarters at Vinnitsa on the 9th.[46] For the first time Sauckel was granted absolute control over the regional offices of the Ministry of Labour. The interference of the Gauleiters was curtailed. Yet Franz Seldte, the Minister for Labour, continued to stay in office and he was an old *Stahlhelm* man and not even a true Nazi. It was a half-measure which Goebbels did not relish. He wrote in his diary, 'Here we have another case of a Ministry being done away with bit by bit without having its head removed.'[47] On the same day the new quota of eastern workers was announced in a memorandum from Sauckel to Rosenberg. It was for a million men and women in four months, 5,000 a day for the first fortnight and then 10,000. Two thirds and more were to be supplied from the Ukraine.[48]

Even Hitler was sufficiently awed by these numbers to consider a new treatment of the *Untermensch*. From Vinnitsa Goebbels telegraphed his under-secretary, Leopold Gutterer, that Hitler had entrusted him with the task of negotiating uniform treatment for all foreign workers, 'in view of the fact that the discrimination against the eastern workers was creating difficulties for the troops as well as diminishing production'. Very hastily a conference was held by Gutterer at the Propaganda Ministry on 12th March. Yet, except as Gauleiter for Berlin, Goebbels had no competence in these matters. Short-cut arrangements of this kind, when made with the Fuehrer in person, always caused resentment. So Goebbels's proposals were hotly contested. The Security Office and the Fuehrer's Chancellery both protested at the proposal that camp managers should be punished for beating or ill-treating the eastern workers. Backe's representative thought that the eastern workers had become too arrogant already. Even maternity wards for women workers were opposed by speakers at the conference, though it was pointed out that the return of pregnant women workers to Russia was bad propaganda.[49]

But Goebbels's star was in the ascendant. Five weeks later he had won most of his points. On 16th April Martin Bormann circulated a new code for the treatment of foreign workers, which had been agreed between the Security Office and the Ministry for Propaganda. It could not have given Bormann much pleasure to record the remark, 'No great accomplishments can be demanded from people who are described as beasts, barbarians and sub-humans.' A supplementary ruling to Himmler's decree of 20th February 1942, was to bring down the barbed wire surrounding the worker camps, though it was Sauckel's contention that he had seen to this a full year previously. The standard rations and the maternity wards were also confirmed. There were even to be books and entertainments for the camp inmates.[50]

There still remained the derogatory *Ost* Badge, the lack of leave and evening-passes and the prohibition against public transport and places of entertainment. An evening with an *Ostarbeiter* some months after Stalingrad, is humorously described by Carl Michel. He had brought with him to Berlin one of his Ukrainian volunteers, who wanted to meet his sweetheart, a voluntary worker stationed at Berlin-Mariendorf. Even as a Wehrmacht officer, Captain Michel had difficulty in penetrating this closely-guarded and sinister establishment, which adjoined a refuse-dump. The Director was an ex-prison warder, the overseer a Party fanatic who made his own rules. Much diplomacy was required to obtain an evening-pass. When at last the happy group set out, it proved impossible to sit down even in a worker's restaurant, though the owner obligingly supplied the *Herr Offizier* with a private room. An attempt to visit the cinema in the company of a labelled *Ostarbeiterin* was frustrated by the manager, though some of the audience showed themselves sympathetic.[51]

Sauckel had now to provide 10,000 workers a day from Russia. He had intended to send his deputy, *Staatsrat* Rudi Peuckert, to visit Russia, but the tremendous assignment demanded that he should go himself.[52] In fact Sauckel made three journeys in 1943. On the first he took in Rowné, Zhitomir, Kiev, Dniepropetrovsk, Zaporozhe, Simferopol, Minsk and Riga, all in the course of April. In June he paid a second visit to Poland and the Ukraine, taking in Melitopol as well.[53] During the first journey, on 20th April, Sauckel telegraphed a long manifesto to Hitler on the occasion of his birthday, while flying from Minsk to Riga. Sauckel was so pleased with his work that he had it printed and distributed in 150,000 copies. In platitudes and pomposity it exceeded anything that Sauckel had yet written. If Erich Koch always pretended to be a fierce man when he wrote, whereas Sauckel always pretended to be a mild man, they had at least this in common, a vapourish wordiness such as only twenty years of Party oratory could produce.

The main point of Sauckel's manifesto was the equality of all foreign workers and the uniformity of their treatment.[54] Sauckel was thus taking credit for a great deal that had been achieved by Goebbels. According to Sauckel, Goebbels objected when he printed the manifesto, because such a document could only be issued by the Fuehrer himself.[55] Goebbels's comments have survived in his own private *Diary*. The manifesto, he said, stank and it gave him a pain. Sauckel was suffering from megalomania and it was time his wings were clipped. He must be taught not to make an irresponsible use of words. There were seven to ten superlatives on every page.[56] Yet Sauckel did not suffer from Goebbels's jealousy. In fact he made his peace with him. By June 1944, Sauckel had become a member of Goebbels's 'Wednesday Group', who paid court to a future dictator to some purpose. For in August, when Goebbels was made Plenipotentiary for Total War, Sauckel retained his post.[57] Most people considered Sauckel to be the very archetype of the tactless, bad mannered, 'Old Party Member' sort of official. Yet no one was prepared to dislike him sufficiently to want to take his place.

(c) The Slave Trade in Decline

ON SAUCKEL'S SECOND visit to the Ukraine in June 1943, the great retreat had not begun and it was even expected to launch a German summer offensive, but it was clear that the new labour quotas were unobtainable. Even though the objections of the Army Commanders to the use of conscription had been overcome by a direct Fuehrer order, a million men and women could not be obtained within four months from the middle of March. Sauckel had declared at Riga on 21st April that Latvia and Estonia would be exempted from the labour quota, because of the bad effect that more deportations might have on the recruiting drive for the SS. But Lithuania must provide 40,000 and White Russia 130,000 workers, though the time limit was extended to the end of August.[58] On 28th June, while Sauckel was in the Ukraine, it was reported to Riecke of the Economic Staff East that in many areas of the White Russian Civil Commissariat the anti-Partisan campaign had left no population to till the harvest. Of the 183,000 workers who had been demanded by Sauckel and Lohse in April from White Russia and Lithuania, only 50,000 had been obtained and half the time had already elapsed. On 18th July, Sauckel was again in Kovno in Lithuania, urging that recruitment be speeded up and demanding 30,000 workers before the end of the year. But Lithuania was now as much a Partisan area as White Russia. On 2nd February 1944, the Town Commissar of Kovno reported that only 8,200 labour recruits had been netted in the past six months.[59]

Except in the Ukraine, all pretence at an orderly civilian call-up had long been abandoned. The quota, fixed in March 1943, was based on the forthcoming slave-raiding expeditions against the Partisans. As we have seen, the police commanders were instructed to secure the maximum of live heads.* Keitel's instructions of 5th July went even further. The Sauckel Commission was to take over all male prisoners between the ages of sixteen and fifty-five, who should be captured in anti-Partisan operations in Poland, the Balkans and the eastern *Commissariats*.[60] To this, five days later, Himmler added the amendment, which had been already proposed by General Warlimont; only the females should remain in the Sauckel organization. The males from the Partisan areas were to work in Germany 'under the same conditions as prisoners of war'.[61] That is to say, they were to go to concentration camps.

It was too late. Certain habits had become endemic to Partisan warfare. Invariably the male villagers were just murdered. The gain in labour recruits, mostly women, was ludicrously small in proportion to the moral effect of the methods. German civilian officials in Russia had no confidence that the system would work. *Generalkommissar* Leyser, reporting to Rosenberg on 17th June, declared that, since Sauckel's April visit, his own assistants had been compelled to carry out the severest measures. While he admitted that the labour problem could not be handled with kid gloves, he nevertheless deplored the deterioration in morale.[62]

Sauckel was sensitive over the recruiting failure of 1943. It was Goering's men, in particular the Agricultural Leaders of the Economic Staff East, who blamed him for the Partisan movement. His reply to his critics on 1st March 1944, was not, however, without ingenuity. In Kiev, where there had been no Partisans throughout the two years' German occupation, he had obtained 100,000 recruits. In Minsk, where he had not been allowed to recruit, the Partisan movement was so strong that the *Generalkommissar* himself had been murdered. So Sauckel

* See p. 240

suggested that there would have been more Partisans, if his methods had not 'relieved Russian unemployment'. Goering was not present at this meeting of the Central Planning Board, but unexpected support for Sauckel came from Goering's representative. As a Luftwaffe man, Field Marshal Erwin Milch could not help seeing that the escape of the labour conscripts was the fault of that refuge of incompetence, the army, who kept training-forces in every hole-and-corner town, but had not bothered to prevent this happening. The charge against Sauckel, Milch said, was idiotic.[63]

August 1943 saw the beginnings of the great retreat from the Don and Donetz to the line of the Pruth and the Carpathians. At this time, three weeks before the publication of the Scorched Earth Order, the policy of dragging back the adult population, along with the routed Wehrmacht, had already been set in motion by a simple extension of the Sauckel Programme. With the approval of Albert Speer, Sauckel ordered on 17th August that the military government officers in the area of Army Group South were to conscript all boys of sixteen and seventeen years of age. Enlistment must be completed by 30th September.[64]

The initiative in recruiting slave labour had, however, passed from Sauckel to the SS and the Wehrmacht. On 14th March Walter Warlimont had ruled that in Partisan areas the Wehrmacht could transfer civilians to the jurisdiction of the SS. They could then be sent automatically to the German concentration camps.* Not all army commanders liked this, but there were always ultra-Nazis among them, like Hans Reinhardt who commanded the Third Panzer Army at Vitebsk. In August Reinhardt rounded up all the active population near his headquarters and kept them in camps till transport for Germany could be obtained. In September the SD agreed to take them. The movement, which was called 'operation Heinrich' after Himmler, did not begin till 30th October, when Reinhardt himself signed the order that all persons fit for military duty should be shipped by the SD to Auschwitz and Lublin. Under no circumstances were they to be turned over for free labour in Germany. It was a matter of two to three thousand people.**

* See p. 240
** Reinhardt was dismissed by Hitler in January 1945, for abandoning east Prussia, rather than sacrifice the 2nd Army. It was said that Erich Koch had accused him of treason and that Hitler wanted to try him by court-martial. He was tried not by Hitler but by the Nuremberg American tribunal which sentenced him to fifteen years' imprisonment, mainly on the charge of recruiting slave-labour. Reinhardt was released in the autumn of 1952.

Somebody, either the SD commander or the chief of the labour group in the economic administration at Vitebsk, went beyond the Reinhardt order. Consequently the family dependants were sent too, wives, children and grandmothers. No one knows what was the ultimate fate of these families, against whom there was no complaint. For a short time at any rate babies and small children were seen in the horrible *Frauenlager* at Auschwitz, where hitherto no children had got past the gas-chamber. But for most people survival in that place was only a matter of months.[65]

Paradoxically, as the methods of recruiting grew worse in Russia, there was an improvement in Germany in the lot of the eastern workers, who were paid pocket-money, who possessed labour contracts and who by a legal fiction were supposed to be neither slaves nor prisoners. The new Charter of Rights, which had been circulated by Martin Bormann at the end of April 1943, was supplemented by the permission for eastern workers to marry Russian volunteers who served in German uniform. This stage could only be surmounted after a notable staff discussion on 8th June during which Hitler had shown himself indifferent. In July the office for the eastern troops was encouraged by Hitler's silence to draft a new and more liberal set of rules for Russian volunteer soldiers.* But one of the many objectors was Sauckel, who complained that the volunteers would be free to make his women workers pregnant and so lose them to German industry.[66]

On the question of the degrading badges, Himmler still remained adamant. If Sauckel had once declared that a Russian worker had a right to live in Germany even as a Bolshevist, Himmler was at least determined that anyone could pick him out in a crowd. During 1943 Gottlob Berger and even Keitel were won over by the critics of the *Ost* sign, but no change was made until early in 1944, when Himmler ordered that the large blue-bordered square sign, worn on the chest, could be changed for a choice of armlets, denoting the racial group of the bearer.[67] Thus the new badge had a suggestion of national colours, but it was not till the formation of the half-phantom Vlasov liberation army at the very end of 1944, that the armlets lost their demeaning character and became in theory a form of Allied uniform. Other interests beside national security were at stake. Believing that the demeaning character of the armlet would prevent their men walking out with eastern workers, the *Reichsfrauenfuehrung*, a strident opposite

* See p. 348

number of the British Housewives' League, demanded the retention of the armlet to the last.[68]

If there was still a substantial deportation of labour to Germany from Russia in 1944, it was because unit commanders of the Wehrmacht had greatly simplified the procedure. On the southern front the retreat of the Wehrmacht continued well into April, leaving only Lithuania and western White Russia as areas from which labour could still be obtained. Nevertheless, at a large conference in the Reich Chancellery on 11th July 1944, Sauckel reported that, though labour recruitment in occupied Europe as a whole had been a failure in the past six months, 420,000 of the total of 560,000 recruits had come from the eastern territories.[69]

At this conference Walter Warlimont, as fire-eating as ever, proposed that the Wehrmacht should increase its already considerable contribution by moving whole populations from big towns and cities and putting them to work. Warlimont said that the soldiers should not try to protect these people. They should copy the Bolsheviks, who put everyone to work wherever they went. Sauckel was grateful for this tip from the right quarter, this lesson learnt from the *Untermensch* himself. But the proposal was already meaningless, for on this very day Minsk and Vilna had fallen. In the next few days the last shreds of pre-war Soviet territory were lost and, nine days after Sauckel's conference, Stauffenberg's bomb plot failed and there was a tremendous General Post in the higher offices of the Reich. Such fragments of deported labour as could still be gleaned from Holland, Italy, Poland, Hungary and the western Balkans, were integrated in Goebbels's great schemes for total mobilization. Sauckel's position became obscure and almost redundant. Once again, he was little more than Gauleiter for Thuringia.

But before he was finished with the most disagreeable part of his assignment, Sauckel became involved in the serious charge of large-scale child kidnapping. Such are the workings of totalitarianism that the position in which Sauckel found himself was due in the first place to a philanthropic conception, like the mercy-killings of the insane which had provided the machinery for racial extermination. The problem of the children in the Partisan areas had come up in October 1942, when Goering had proposed the creation of children's camps.[70] Nothing was done about it during the anti-Partisan drive of the next eight months. Children were shot, simply to avoid the creation of responsibilities for the soldiers and police troops. There was indeed no limit to what members of Soviet minority races would do, when given German uniforms and a German example.

A new proposal for the children was not produced till 10th July 1943, when Himmler had a plan. Though it was perfectly idiotic, it could not have astonished his intimates. Himmler proposed to his Police Leaders and to Backe's Agricultural Leaders that the lands from which the Partisans had been evacuated should be cultivated with *Kok Sagys*, the Russian rubber-producing dandelion. This plant occurs in Himmler's memoranda and speeches as a peculiar obsession, dating from his agricultural student days. The children of the deported villagers, Himmler said, could be kept on the edge of the area in camps, ready to pick dandelions.[71] But the children could not be left, picking dandelions indefinitely, if other Partisans were moving into the area or if the German main forces were retreating, as they were on the Leningrad front on 21st September 1943. For such cases a better solution was proposed. The Rear Area Commander allowed Sauckel's representatives with the Army Group Economic Inspectorate to pick out the able-bodied labourers before the evacuations took place. Their solution of the children problem was, it is true, only a half-way one, but it was commendably simple. 'Children over ten are considered labourers.'[72]

Not only were they considered labourers but they were deported to Germany as labourers, though this was pre-eminently the privilege of the children of collaborators, who were ripe for Germanification. In Minsk *Generalkommissar* Wilhelm Kube had created an imitation of the Hitler Youth Movement, the White Russian *Jugendhilfe*. After Kube's death it was taken over by an SS man and former Hitler Youth Leader, Siegfried Nickel, who held the post of Chief of Youth Affairs in the Rosenberg Ministry. In March 1944, when the retreat in the Ukraine was at its height and Gottlob Berger of the SS was running Rosenberg's Political Department, the somewhat reluctant Nickel was told to provide boys, aged between fifteen and twenty years, to serve in Germany as auxiliaries in SS Training Centres and in anti-aircraft batteries. By 19th October 1944, Nickel was able to report the impressive figures of 28,117 children and adolescents, but 3,700 were girls and 6,700 were sent not to the SS and Luftwaffe, but to the hard-bombed German factories in the Ruhr.[73]

It was, said Rosenberg in his Nuremberg defence, a form of education, a glimpse of the west for the youth of the Soviet Union.[74] But, as the Nuremberg Trial developed, it came out that the youth who were to be re-educated in this summary fashion, were as young as ten years old, the age at which Sauckel's commissioners classed children as labourers.

The evidence is involved, but it seems that on 10th June 1944, Berger submitted to Rosenberg a plan to deport a further 40,000 to 50,000 boys, aged between ten and fifteen years. The plan was said to have originated with another soldierly person, the commander of the Ninth Army on the White Russian front, and the intention was to deprive Russia of future manpower. Rosenberg objected that ten-year-old boys were no asset to the enemy and that the world would consider this a matter of abduction. Rosenberg was then informed by Berger's representative at the Ministry that Sauckel had already passed the plan. The commander of the Ninth Army was ready to go ahead, whether Rosenberg approved or not, but feared that without the Ministry's assistance there would not be proper treatment for the children. Thereupon Rosenberg gave way, but on 23rd June the Russian summer offensive burst like a flood. The staff of the Central Army Group had to run for it. Nevertheless, on 11th July, Rosenberg informed Sauckel through Alfred Meyer that it was still the job of the Labour Recruitment Commando, formerly in Minsk, to 'conduct young people of ten to fourteen years of age to the Reich'.[75]

Berger had gone himself to the Army Group Area in Himmler's special train, *Gotenland*, from which he telegraphed Braeutigam on the same day that Nickel's Commando must continue its activities. The Commando with its boys had been evacuated from Minsk in time and was now in the Bialystok region. Bialystok fell and the children were sent to Germany. On 20th July Rosenberg wrote to Lammers that the children between the ages of ten and fourteen were being trained as apprentices for the German economy. The Ministry was co-operating with Sauckel on the lines of the well-known White Russian Youth Service.[76]

Rosenberg gave two distinct reasons for accepting a plan whose dangers for himself he had distinctly foreseen. At Nuremberg he declared that he had feared that the Ninth Army's proposals would not be carried out humanely without his co-operation.[77] But in his death-cell memoirs Rosenberg explained that he had done it to oblige an old friend, Field Marshal von Kluge. Actually von Kluge no longer commanded the Central Army Group in June 1944, but till his appointment as Commander in Chief in the west on 4th July, he used to frequent the Berchtesgaden daily Staff Conferences, where he advised Hitler unofficially. Putting the blame on Kluge had the added advantage at the time of Rosenberg's trial that Kluge was dead.[78]

In any case, Rosenberg declared, he had satisfied himself that the children had a wonderful time. He had been to a Children's Camp at Dessau where there were 4,500 of them. The White Russian women in charge had thanked him with tears in their eyes for the care that he had taken. As to Sauckel, he was more circumspect. He simply denied that he had seen any of the correspondence or that he knew anything about it.[79]

The month of November 1944, saw the curious farce of the despatch of representative eastern workers to Prague to attend Vlasov's National Liberation Committee as alleged worker's deputies, in reality agents, who had been picked out from the labour camps by the Gestapo. In Berlin there was a monster rally of eastern workers, who listened to the words of the liberator in the *Europahaus* near the Anhalter Railway Terminus.* These things were but a thin disguise of the fact that the status of the *Ostarbeiter* had changed only on paper. Those, who were not fortunate enough to live on farms, still returned from their work to gloomy comfortless camps, where discipline was still enforced with concentration camp sentences, with beatings, confinements and the deprivation of food; camps where the opportunities of going out were few and were productive of little satisfaction.

The eastern workers' mood of resentment was obvious and in the crumbling of the battle-fronts it filled Germany with fear. The numbers were formidable. Quite apart from the Poles, about 2,800,000 eastern workers from the Soviet Union were recruited from first to last. There were two and a quarter millions in Germany in October 1944, and nearly two millions at the end of the war.[80] Hitler himself is said to have been so impressed with the thought of a slave rebellion of eastern workers that he was persuaded by Admiral Canaris at the end of 1942 to issue the sealed orders, known as *Walkuere*. These orders, which were invoked by the rebel generals for their coup d'état against Hitler on 20th July 1944, had been designed for a quite different eventuality.[81]

After the failure of the plot, Himmler noted in his Posen speech that the rebels would have opened the concentration camps, thereby freeing 450,000 foreigners. 'It meant therefore that a half million of the most embittered political and criminal elements, political enemies of the Reich and criminal enemies of every human and social order, would be

* See p. 369

poured out all over all Germany.'[82] Naturally the fear which had created the *Walkuere* orders did not diminish. On 21st January 1945, when there was a false alarm that Russian tanks had crossed the Oder, Goebbels ordered the alarm signal, *Gneisenau*, to be given. On receipt of the signal, the Berlin Home Guard had to turn out to meet a possible *Ostarbeiter* rebellion.[83] In the last weeks of the war, German householders in lonely places or in small communities lived in permanent dread of roving bands of foreign workers, who had already begun to exploit chaos and to live on loot.

Where eastern workers with a long grievance joined forces with the Russian invaders, revenge took forms which, though they were ghastly and appalling, can scarcely have been unexpected. Yet quite large numbers, mostly on farms, stayed loyal to their employers. A great many tried to conceal their identity in order to avoid repatriation. Others, profiting by the special scale of rations which the occupation authorities allowed them, appeared to be in no hurry to leave the house of bondage. In the case of the Ukrainians there was something like a national diaspora. More than 120,000 registered themselves in the western zone as displaced persons on the grounds that they had been born in Poland and elsewhere and that they were not Soviet citizens. Mr George Fischer is probably right in believing that the majority were concealed Soviet subjects, due for repatriation.[84]

The DPs ceased to be martyrs and heroes when they became a burden on the occupation authorities. Already during the march into Germany at the beginning of April, a British military Government team opened fire on Russian looters in Osnabruck and a German auxiliary policeman set fire to a cellar, where some of the looters were hiding,[85] thereby provoking accusations from *Pravda*. Many months elapsed before looting was suppressed and still more before the Germans lost the habits which they had acquired in the treatment of the *Untermensch*. As late as the end of June 1945, a former German colonel was executed by the British in Kiel for shooting a freed Russian *Ostarbeiter* dead, because he was stealing a watch.[86] On the whole the memories of Allied soldiers, who once served in occupied Germany, are unfavourable to the former slave-workers. It would be a pity if this became the verdict of history. At any rate we know what lay behind the Saturnalia of 1945.

Part Two

POLITICAL CRUSADE

CHAPTER NINE

THE CAUCASUS ADVENTURE
AND THE NATIONAL LEGIONS

(a) Plans for the National Minorities

RUNNING THROUGH THE previous chapters there is a thread of a different colour. It marks the intrusions of German officers and officials who dissented from the official view. Some of them wanted to encourage collaborationists among the former enemy, so that in the end they created a Russian liberation army which defied Hitler's original scruples. This, however, only came about when Hitler had grown indifferent. The real conflict was not with Hitler but among the dissenters themselves, among whom there were two main groupings —and neither won.

By contrast with the dissenters, the Hitler loyalists were much more united, even when the extremism of some inflicted a heavy burden on the consciences of others. The ruthlessness and thoroughness with which Hitler's orders were carried out, when they concerned the outlawed categories of Jews, prisoners of war, Partisans and slave labourers, testify to the solidarity of the great bulk of officers and officials. No such solidarity will be found among the opponents, many of them very highly placed, of Hitler's policy.

From very early in the campaign there was the idea of a single national liberation army, composed of all the elements on Soviet territory, which were opposed to the Soviet system. The first support came from members of various Wehrmacht administrative staffs, who wanted to attract recruits from among the Red Army prisoners and deserters. When the recruits were so numerous as to require a unified inspectorate, the command of a Russian general was logically the next step, though slow and difficult. However, long before this formidable step could be attempted, several national liberation movements of a separatist character had achieved their own 'legions' which were recruited from Caucasian and Asiatic minority races. This movement was associated with Rosenberg's Political Department and with certain military government officers and it remained till the end of the war violently opposed to any form of 'Great Russian' revival.

Originally the two movements, 'Russian liberation' and 'national legions' belonged geographically to the North and the South, since the enormous number of non-Slav Red Army soldiers, whom the Germans recruited, were captured in the great encirclement battles on the Southern Army Group front and, later, in the advance to the Caucasus. But, by the end of 1942 there was no such geographic distinction, for on the northern front the SS were recruiting Latvians and Estonians who had never been in the Red Army. It was, however, the peculiar nature of the Caucasus that determined the course of the 'national legions' movement. Rosenberg approved of it because it fitted in with his theory that the hegemony of Moscow could be limited and even destroyed in future history. Soldiers like Eduard Wagner and Ewald von Kleist viewed the movement differently and from a very short-term and practical standpoint. In the creation of national legions, approved by Hitler, they saw a way to secure the territories beyond the Don for military rule; a way to avert the creation of another civilian *Reichskommissariat* like the Ukraine.

Supported in this way from opposite sides, the national legions received Hitler's approval some months before the advance to the Caucasus had begun. It was not, however, till December 1942 that Hitler sanctioned a unified inspectorate for all troops who had been recruited from Soviet subjects, the so-called *Osttruppen*. While this meant an improvement in the treatment of the legionaries, it was not a victory for their cause but a setback. The unified command meant the end of the political and separatist character of the legions. The *Osttruppen* inspectorate was established at a moment when the Germans were in full retreat from the Caucasus and it was an intimation to the legions that they would never return to their homes as the forces of independence. After Stalingrad, when the military government of the north Caucasus belonged to the past, Wagner and von Kleist had no further interest in separatist politics. The Foreign Office had been cold-shouldered from this field and there remained only Rosenberg and his Political Department who played with their national committees till the exceedingly bitter end.

Yet still less was the unified command of the *Osttruppen* a victory for the champions of united liberated Russia. Two more years were to elapse before General Andrei Vlasov received the status of a Russian de Gaulle and in the meantime Hitler removed the volunteers from Russia and was with difficulty restrained from taking their weapons and sending them to the mines. Such success as the supporters of General Vlasov achieved was due to Himmler and his personal military ambitions. But in this struggle the national legions had no interest at all. Till the very end, their political spokesmen refused to recognize Vlasov.

The Armenian, Georgian and Tartar prisoners who fell into the hands of the Allies on the Western Front in 1944, were not Vlasov soldiers, as many news-commentators supposed. They had put on German uniforms for far different purposes than defending the Atlantic Wall against Stalin's Western Allies. They were not interested in the future either of the German or the Russian states, but in 1942-3 they had hoped to recover the independence that half a dozen secessionist governments had enjoyed in 1918-21. Theirs was an unhappy lot, fighting enemies with whom they had no quarrel, 3,000 miles from their homes. Many mutinied, such as the Armenians at Lyons and the Georgians on Texel island. The very remoteness of these place-names conveys the bewilderment and the forlornness of their case.

Yet, compared with the gloomy story of the *Reichskommissariats*, the German occupation of the lands north of the Caucasus was probably as humane as could be expected of an army living entirely on the country. Were it not for the horrible activities of the Security Police, which they did next to nothing to restrain, history might accord some credit to the German Military Government Officers, who, for the very few months that they were in the country, contrived not to overstay their welcome. If the generals, Koestring and Ewald von Kleist, made no very disastrous mistakes, it was chiefly their good luck in keeping out of the country those who were most likely to involve them in such mistakes. I use the word 'good luck' advisedly, because it happened that Hitler was too little interested in the Caucasus to authorize large-scale civilian interference. He was far less suspicious of the genuinely non-Slav minorities of the Caucasus than he was of Ukrainians, Balts and White Russians.

The occupation of these lands may not have been such a ballet from *Prince Igor* as German writers pretend, but one shadow at least had almost gone. In the late summer and autumn of 1942 prisoners of war in general did not die of hunger and typhus and there was some moderation in applying the infamous Screening Order. In these lands, moreover, military government was less out of its depth than in the industrial eastern Ukraine. Primitive tribes have an irresistible appeal for the professional soldier. While it is the dream of Civil Servants to turn primitive tribes into urban communities, it is the professional soldier's dream to turn urbanized man into a primitive tribal society, a feat that is only made possible by conscription and war. Thus there emerged in the huge rear area of Army Group A something that resembled the native protectorates of South Africa. For the few weeks or months that they lasted, these little autonomies functioned without much friction. But it is inconceivable that they could have remained a soldier's Garden of Eden for long, even if the German soldier had been able to defend them. If Stalingrad had not fallen, if the great German winter retreat of 1942–3 had been postponed, there would have been time enough for the carpet-baggers, the staffs of Sauckel, Schickedanz and Backe to enter the country and do their worst.

In April 1941, Rosenberg's original plans for the lands beyond the Ukraine had boded little good for them. Remembering the rôle of the Cossack Atamans in the civil war of 1918–21, Rosenberg considered that the Cossacks of the Don would prove difficult to organize into a nationality, separate from Great Russia. Without speculating on a future Cossack State, Rosenberg sketched a *Reichskommissariat* for the Don-Volga area, which would extend as far east as Saratov. For a ruler he chose the Minister-President of Brunswick, a secondary school teacher called Dietrich Klagges, whose only qualifications were these. He was on the nationalized board of the Hermann Goering steelworks at Salzgitter and he was the only unassigned person at Rosenberg's disposal who could speak some Russian.[1]*

For the Caucasus area Rosenberg proposed originally Herbert Backe, because, in addition to being the virtual food controller of the Reich, he had been born in Batum. Later he reserved Backe for the Ukraine. But Backe was in the succession to Walter Darré as Minister for food and agriculture, a succession he had no wish to sacrifice for a satrapy in Russia. So in June 1941, Rosenberg had to look round for another *Reichskommissar* for the Caucasus. He chose Arno Schickedanz, a man of no standing in the Party but a Russian-born Baltic German like himself and a so-called expert on Russian affairs in Rosenberg's Foreign Political Office.

By 20th June 1941, Rosenberg had become so immersed in his greater Ukraine project that he had dropped the idea of a separate Cossack *Reichskommissariat*. His greater Ukraine was to reach the

* See p. 137

lower Volga and include Saratov and Tambov. Among the fifty-nine million inhabitants of this Greater Ukraine there would be pure Russians and Tartars as well as Cossacks, but the Russians would be pushed east to make way for German settlements. We have already seen how Rosenberg defended this mass-eviction,* but the whole project was swept away by Hitler at the Angerburg meeting of 16th July. Hitler wanted no Greater Ukraine but an immediate earmarking of the Crimea, the German Volga republic and the Baku region as Reich territory.[2] Hitler refused to consider the Soviet minority races in these future areas of conquest as possible allies. Very early in the minutes he damped down all discussion of the matter by declaring, 'Only the German may bear arms, not the Slav, not the Czech, not the Ukrainian and not the Cossack.'

To the champions of separatism there was a loophole in Hitler's definition, because he had left out the non-Slavs. But there was a sharp cleavage of opinion as to which non-Slav element should be most encouraged. There were Georgian emigrants in Germany who pursued a sort of irredentism, claiming themselves to be the historic leaders of a Caucasian hegemony. Through his verbose friend, Arno Schickedanz, and a Germanized Georgian named Nikuradze, Rosenberg leant somewhat towards this idea. In the SS Heydrich had his own Georgian protégé, one Akhmeteli. In the Foreign Office, however, the champions of regional autonomy were more interested in the Turkish-speaking Azerbaijanis and Crimean Tartars, because certain personalities in Turkey were beginning to show concern over Germany's Moslem prisoners and subjects. But, even in the Foreign Office, there was a cleavage of policy. Influenced by von Papen's reports from Ankara, Ribbentrop favoured independence for the Moslem races, whereas the former ambassador in Moscow, Werner von der Schulenberg, wanted a federal solution to the entire Russian problem and even, it was said, a restored Russian hegemony over all the minorities.[3]

Between the rival competences of the Foreign Office and the Eastern Ministry, between the doubts of the High Command and the hostility of Hitler, the chances of recognition for the Caucasian nations were very small. What was done for them was done furtively and under cover of the general confusion. The Foreign Office soon came to occupy an inferior position in the struggle, a struggle which Ribbentrop had already lost when, to his great disgust, Hitler created an Eastern Ministry. Ribbentrop was compelled to dissolve his 'Russland

* See p. 135

Gremium' and his experts on the minorities were dispersed, Leibbrandt and von Mende to Rosenberg's Political Department, Hans Koch and Oskar Niedermeyer to the Wehrmacht and Franz Stahlecker to Heydrich's extermination squads, the *Einsatzgruppen*.[4]

The month of April 1942, when Hitler began to prepare the invasion of the Caucasus, saw not only a revival of interest in the Caucasian volunteers from the prisoner-of-war camps, but an attempt by Ribbentrop to recover the position he had lost to Rosenberg. He authorized von der Schulenburg to collect some forty exiled champions of Caucasian nationalism for a conference in Berlin. Since the champions were housed at great expense in the Adlon Hotel, they became known as the *Adloniada*. Hitler was not likely to be impressed by these ex-princes and descendants of tribal heroes, who had assembled from Paris, Ankara and Switzerland, *balalaika* players from a dozen *boîtes de nuit* and sword dancers in embroidered shirts. When Rosenberg was received by Hitler on 8th May 1942, he had no difficulty in persuading him that the *Adloniada* was a nest of Allied agents and political leftists. So the Caucasian patriots were sent home and three months later Rosenberg obtained a ruling from Hans Lammers that the Foreign Office had no competence in occupied Soviet territory.*

To fight Ribbentrop's pretensions, Rosenberg used the arguments that most appealed to Hitler and Bormann. Yet he was doing the same thing himself and using the same agents as Ribbentrop had once hoped to use. Ribbentrop's game of placating the Turkish government had been pursued in Rosenberg's Political Department from the very beginning by the Riga-born philologist and Turcophil, Professor Gerhard von Mende. As early as September 1941 Mende's national committees were able to rescue some of their Crimean-Tartar, Turkestani and Turkish compatriots from the starvation camps and the attentions of the screening commandos. This could only be done through the connivance of the General Staff, more precisely through the Organization Section which came under the authority of Eduard Wagner. This general was by no means a lover of civilian interference, but in the Organization Section there was also a young major, whom the world knows best as the man who all but assassinated Hitler on 20th July 1944. Three years earlier, Major Stauffenberg canalized his great energy in the cause of the Soviet minorities, winning over the strictly military Eduard Wagner to this cause, just as in 1944 he was to win him over to the Resistance circle.[5]

* See p. 198. Document PS 1520 and Dallin, p. 137

At first von Mende was allowed only to sort Turcoman prisoners, because Turkestan was too far away to matter politically. He enrolled the services of two Turcoman exiles. Veli Khayum Khan claimed to be a descendant of Jenghiz Khan, having appeared mysteriously in the twenties as a student in Berlin. Mustafa Chokai had formed an anti-Bolshevik government in Khokand after the revolution and had been forced to escape to France in 1921. These two Turcomen had permission to comb the prisoner-of-war camps, but the permission arrived late. At Czestochowo in Poland, 30,000 Turcoman prisoners had died already of hunger and typhus. In December Chokai himself died of the infection.[6] Asiatic prisoners were still murdered by the screening teams of the Security Service as Jews. As late as November, a detachment of *Einsatzgruppe B* under the orders of the notorious Otto Ohlendorff appeared in the Transit Camp at Nikolaiev after massacring the Jews of the town. It took some time to convince the detachment-commander that the Fuehrer Order did not embrace all Asiatics as such. Eventually he headed off his herd of trained killer-sheep. Ironically Ohlendorff soon acquired an interest in the aspirations of the Crimean Tartars, that made this gifted mass-killer an opponent of Hitler's policy.[7]

In October 1941 von Mende made a start with two battalions of Moslem volunteers. Both had to be camouflaged as special duty units, working for the *Abwehr*, since it could not be admitted officially that Red Army men served in the German front-line. The first battalion was one of mixed Caucasian nationalities, the *Bergmann* or Mountain-eer battalion of Theodor Oberlaender, a militant professor of economics who had been involved in the tricky question of the Ukrainian nationalists.* The second battalion, composed of prisoners from Turkestani units from the Red Army, was intended for sabotage work in Central Asia under the command of a Major Meyer-Mader, who had been a military adviser to Chiang Kai Shek and was reputed to know Mongolia.

It was an obscure and fairly daft beginning to an important movement. It must have been a surprising project, even for a professor of economics from Koenigsberg, to drop saboteurs beyond the Caucasus and in Turkestan, when the Germans had not yet taken Kiev. It was something from that fairy-godmother side of the Second World War, which could rescue an interior decorator from a Bath and Laundry Company in Iceland and, after an appropriate course in Siamese, send him off to govern Elba or Stromboli. Yet the activities of von Mende,

* See pp. 166–8

Oberlaender and Meyer-Mader had their influence on high policy. By May 1942 both the Oberlaender and Meyer-Mader battalions were in service on the southern front.[8] It was the first step in Wagner's bid to save the Caucasus region from civilian government. If Hitler could be persuaded to regard the forthcoming campaign for the Caucasus as partly a recruiting drive, the territory might be preserved from the catastrophic fingers that were ruining the Ukraine. Already, on 20th April, Stauffenberg had been able to issue the order for the creation of separate national legions for the main Caucasian races.[9]

Some eighteen days later, Hitler appeared unmoved when Rosenberg proposed issuing appropriate banners to the legions. They were Armenian, Turkish and Tartar banners, banners for races that were not even Aryan. Yet Rosenberg produced the drawings for the flags at the same conference at which he condemned Ribbentrop's *Adloniada*. Seldom was he to find Hitler in such a receptive mood. The famous rabid National Socialist racialism, which was so slavishly parroted by Bormann and Koch, was indeed a frail thing.[10]

(b) The Germans in the Cossack lands and the Caucasus

ON 28TH JUNE 1942, Hitler opened the grand offensive of the southern front. By the middle of July, the Cossack steppe-lands, inside the great bend of the Don, were in German hands. But for the Cossacks Rosenberg had no national committees, since Hitler had stated that the Cossacks were not to bear arms. Rosenberg himself had warned his staff that the attitude of the Cossacks would be uncertain. And yet, neglected both by the Foreign Office and Rosenberg's Political Department, the Germans had in their hands a group of famous Cossack civil war leaders, whose recruiting value must have been considerable. There was an unofficial Central Cossack Office in Berlin which was directed by the famous Piotr Nikolaievich Krasnov, Ataman of the Don Cossacks. During the civil war Krasnov had at least two remarkable historical episodes to his credit. He had been offered the person of Lenin in exchange for Kerensky whom he was supposed to be protecting,[11] and he had been the first general to attempt the capture of Stalingrad—in the Autumn of 1918 when it was still called Tsaritsin —with weapons supplied by the Germans, which Krasnov 'purified by washing them in the clear waters of the Don.'[12] Then there was

Shkuro, who had recruited the notorious 'wolves' from the Terek and Kuban Cossacks in 1918. There was also living in Germany the famous Bicherakhov, a fantastic condottiere who had captured the Russian Caspian fleet for the British Navy and had tried to hold Baku against the Bolsheviks.[13] It was only in June 1943, when the organization of a Cossack army corps was taken seriously, that these three ageing Cossack leaders found employment as propagandists. They were opponents of the Vlasov movement and rumours reached the Allied press that Krasnov was to replace Vlasov as the German Quisling for Russia.[14*] It was a German change of heart towards the Cossacks that brought all three men to a Soviet gallows.

In July 1942, however, there was no question of any Central Cossack Office taking over the territory of the Don. It was left almost by chance to a member of Canaris's *Abwehr* to take the first step. Lt-Colonel Wessel, Freiherr von Loringhoven was Ic to Weichs's Army Group B, which attacked on the northern front of the German offensive towards the great eastern sweep of the Don between Voronezh and Lisichansk. Freytag-Loringhoven, like almost all the Russophile staff officers whose names occur so often in this book, was a Russian-born German from the nobility of the Baltic provinces. He had been brought up in St Petersburg and had fought in the Imperial Russian Army, in the counter-revolutionary forces and in the Latvian Army. He spoke not only the Russian and Latvian of his boyhood but also several south Russian dialects.[15] Freytag-Loringhoven had to work quickly. By the middle of November 1942, the Red Army was already swarming back into the Don Cossack country and a month later he himself was transferred to the Eastern Troops Office at Hitler's headquarters. The whole of his recruiting activities were compressed within five months.

At Army Group B headquarters in Poltava, Freytag-Loringhoven made surprising discoveries. There was the desertion of entire Cossack regiments, which Stalin had created quite recently in order to heal the old sore of Cossack antagonism to the Marxist state. There were the old Cossack soldiers, who had gone into hiding to avoid war service and who had even kept their Tsarist uniforms. The climax was the arrival in Poltava of the legless civil war leader, Ataman Kulakov, who was reputed to have driven himself a thousand miles in a sledge-wagon from a cliff village of the Terek, where he had hidden in an underground burrow since 1926.[16]

After this spectacular event, Freytag-Loringhoven established a

* See also p. 339

reception camp in a factory at Woienstroi Selestshina, where he appointed a commission to sift out the genuine Cossacks from the prisoners who reported to him, starved and ragged, from the transit camps. At the same time the Cossack militia of Ataman Domanov was formed through the rough and ready selections of the Rear Area Commander. Cossack self-government was not officially established by the Poltava authorities, but it was assumed to exist in so far as the local Hetmans assured the delivery of the surplus harvest to the Germans.[17]

More decisive steps were taken in the lands of the Kuban Cossacks, which formed the Rear Area of Army Group A. By an order of Wagner's office dated 1st October 1942, six *rayons* containing 160,000 inhabitants were made a self-governing district. This was extended still further in spite of the protests of Arno Schickedanz, whose *Reichs-kommissariat* was meant to reach as far north as the line Rostov-Astrakhan. On 10th November, Hitler himself approved a joint proclamation by Keitel and Rosenberg, promising the Cossacks limited property and autonomy rights.[18] But it was already too late to differentiate in this way between one sort of *Untermensch* and another. The entire honeymoon with the Don, Kuban and Terek Cossacks lasted less than six months. The only promise that the Germans could keep was that of creating a Cossack army. With the German Army there retreated 70,000 Cossack fighting men, enough to form at first a division and later an army corps.

With the Cossacks, National Socialism could have no quarrel since they were both warlike, anti-Bolshevik and anti-Semitic, while they possessed no oil or industries and little that was worth requisitioning. The situation became more delicate as the Germans entered the foot-hills of the Caucasus. It was hardly to be supposed in August 1942, that the *Goldfasanen* would keep their fingers off an area, which already included the oilfields and mines of the Terek basin and which might soon include Tiflis and Baku. Yet Eduard Wagner was determined to stop them. So he secured the appointment of a 'specially assigned general for the Caucasus' in the person of Colonel-General Ernst Koestring. It was not a perfect choice, for Koestring was sixty-six years old. On the other hand he possessed more real experience of Russia than any other general. Born in Moscow, Koestring had dealt with occupation problems as long ago as 1918, when he had led the German military mission at the court of Hetman Skoropadsky in Kiev. He had been military attaché in Moscow in 1927–30 and again in

1935–41. Koestring, as we have seen, had been deep in the secrets of the 'Barbarossa' plan.[19]* Nevertheless, in July 1941, when Koestring was repatriated under diplomatic immunity, Hitler took offence at his pessimistic attitude. Koestring was without official employment for the next year, but he busied himself. Just at this moment there was a complaint against him because he had accompanied his old chief, Werner von der Schulenburg, on a commission which selected volunteers from the prisoner-of-war camps.[20] Koestring had the charm which could survive most complaints. Although he was the son of a bookseller, his Red Army opposite numbers in Moscow used to call him 'the last Baron', because they retained their snobbery and Baltic barons were a class they appreciated.[21] In the German Army he was the 'Wise Marabu', since his great hooked nose and the many folds round his eyes gave him the appearance of one of the larger breeds of stork. In the British Army he would doubtless have been called the Adjutant bird.

Koestring reported to Wagner at Vinnitsa on 10th August 1942. Vinnitsa was then Hitler's headquarters and the seat of the Operations Section of the High Command. Wagner lived out of town and remote from this nest of hornets, but the demons of irony had housed the perspiring Quartermaster General, not merely beyond the Bug but positively in the former Soviet lunatic asylum. In these quarters, clinical but spacious, Wagner received Koestring and told him of the favourable omens for a workable administration beyond the Don. Koestring learnt that, in spite of Hitler's approval of Caucasian national legions, there was a danger that Caucasian regional autonomy would be opposed by the Four-Year-Plan Office. Koestring was to be the man on the spot 'who could distinguish sense from folly'. When, however, Koestring asked Wagner whether he thought the Caucasian homelands would ever be occupied, Wagner answered briefly 'No'.[22]

Till the middle of January, Kleist's Army Group A held the outer valleys of the northern Caucasus. By this time the Russian advance, west of the Don and into the Donetz basin, had left the army group as much isolated from the main front as Paulus's 6th Army was now isolated in Stalingrad. A retreat was ordered to a bridgehead position, east of the Straits of Kerch. Thus military rule in the area of Army Group A lasted no longer than in the area of Army Group B in the Cossack country. There was something feverish and unreal about the whole affair. The Germans had come so far that on the Terek river

* See p. 63

the stars were already out when the officers' watches, set by Berlin time, showed half past one in the afternoon. And a sinister *surréaliste* quality attached itself to the life of the soldiers. Mice in enormous quantities invaded their boots and pockets. The leave train took ten days to reach the German border and it was festooned with geese from the Caucasus, frozen in the locomotive steam.[23] The front was at least 1,200 miles from Hitler's headquarters in Vinnitsa, while beyond the bridgehead at Rostov there was not one railway track working for the Germans. The supply columns had to cover such enormous distances that lorries consumed their entire loads of petrol before they reached the front. Resource was had to the camel, an animal that consumed no petrol, but which did not figure in the Barbarossa Plan. On 5th August von Kleist sent his famous dispatch from the Kalmuck Steppe: 'No enemy in front of me and no reserves behind me.'[24]

It seems that Hitler had no permanent plans for this region. On 12th July, early in the campaign, Lammers was told to inform Ribbentrop that the Caucasus was outside the range of German settlement. While Ribbentrop was not to interfere with Rosenberg's competence, the possibility was envisaged of future sovereign states, with whom the Foreign Office would maintain relations.[25] It was therefore unlikely that the eager Arno Schickedanz would enter into his kingdom. But Wagner, Kleist and Koestring had to guard against an invasion of *Goldfasanen* and the best way was to have the like-minded deputy director of Rosenberg's Political Department there on the spot. So for the first time Otto Braeutigam descended from the critic's desk into the shoes of the criticized. While Shickedanz dreamt of a palace in Tiflis, Braeutigam had actually lived there, if only as a German Consul. But Rosenberg, who received so many outspoken memoranda from this down-to-earth assistant, was not anxious to promote him, believing that Schickedanz possessed every qualification. Had he not attended the Riga Technical High School with Rosenberg as a boy? Had he not marched with him in the 1923 Munich Putsch, had he not held a seat on the management board of Rosenberg's newspaper and directed the Russian section of his Foreign Information Service, the APA?[26] Still better, Schickedanz, who bore an odd physical resemblance to Goebbels, had written an anti-Semitic tract, 'Social Parasitism in the life of the Nation.' With such credentials Rosenberg would have sent him to govern China.

Somehow Wagner and Koestring had to keep Rosenberg's protégé out of their territory. Even if Hitler never listened when Rosenberg complained about Koch, he might be inclined to listen if Rosenberg complained about the army. The next choice, if Schickedanz could be kept away, was Rosenberg's Professor von Mende. Wagner feared that von Mende would flood the military government area with his various committees of Tsarist exiles from Berlin, another *Adloniada* of balalaika players and sword dancers. They would bring their political quarrels with them, Armenian, Georgian, Azerbaijani and Turcoman. Mende moreover was a philologist and not a soldier. Wagner would have preferred Theodor Oberlaender, the more adventurous professor who was actually serving with his men in Army Group A, but Oberlaender was not in Rosenberg's Ministry. So, when Mende himself agreed, the choice was reduced to Braeutigam.[27]

The proposal was put to Rosenberg, who objected that Schickedanz had already appointed one of his future *Generalkommissars* to administer the territories, conquered by Army Group A. Rosenberg would only release Braeutigam from Berlin, if it was agreed that Schickedanz's man should succeed him as soon as possible. Schickedanz had spent the past year in collecting a staff of no less than 1,200 persons. He had already arranged to govern the fair lands, south of the mountains, through two officials of APA, who had run a bureau to promote friendship with Sweden. Schickedanz would have nothing to do with Rosenberg's Political Department and chose his own staffs and committees for the different minorities of the Caucasus, independent of von Mende. It was, however, believed that in practice Schickedanz would prove a mere stand-in for Goering's Four-Year-Plan Office. Goering had opposed the candidature of Schickedanz and Rosenberg was only able to secure his appointment by a compromise.[28] It had been agreed that Schickedanz would take on as his economic administrator Goering's agent for the Balkans, an Austrian financier and former Mayor of Vienna, called Hermann Neubacher, who was reputed to have done wonders in the Rumanian oilfields.[29]* There was therefore all the makings of another government by exploitation and another Erich Koch situation.

Had Schickedanz been bold enough to claim his inheritance then and there, it would have been awkward for Kleist and Koestring. Fortunately the man was a ditherer and Wagner had time to put in his word with Hitler. One morning towards the end of August he reported at Hitler's daily *Lagebesprechung* at Vinnitsa. Since Hitler made no objection to the dispatch of Braeutigam from Berlin, Wagner was able

* Thorwald, p. 39. Neubacher's own memoirs are silent concerning this episode.

to tell Rosenberg that this was a Fuehrer Order.[29] Rosenberg was also persuaded by Wagner that Hitler had banned forced labour in the new military area and had ordered the dissolution of the collective farms.[30]

Wagner achieved even more. On 8th September he published a decree that native governments were to be created under the sole discretion of the Army Group Commander, while, five days later, von Stauffenberg worked out the details with Altenstadt and Braeutigam.[31] Accompanied by Otto Schiller as agricultural expert, Braeutigam proceeded to Kleist's headquarters at Stavropol, to a land where convoys and guards were not needed, where the names of Koch and Sauckel were not feared and where the only Partisans were those who had resumed the Civil War against the Bolsheviks. On the fringe of Asia the German Army re-lived the happy experiences of the first days in the Ukraine. The welcome of the Cossacks of the Kuban and Terek was repeated by a picturesque array of tribes, by the Circassians of Krasnodar, the Chechens, the Balkars and Kabardians and the Karachai.

In the Ordzonikhidse sector the front touched the territory of the Ingush and Ossetes. The latter were reputed to be the ancient Alans and, according to some authorities, their language contained elements of an early Germanic tongue, akin to Gothic. It was an opportunity which Himmler and the Dervishes of racialism sadly let slip. And where was Rosenberg, who had once proposed to Hitler that Sevastopol should be renamed Theodorichhafen as soon as it was taken? Either Rosenberg had forgotten about the Ossetes or Hitler's decision had mortified him so much that he could not think of Goths on this occasion.

But the Generals Kleist and Koestring were not worried overmuch by ethnology. The elders of the tribe came to pay their homage, offering cattle, remounts and the services of their young men. The generals then left them in peace to run their own self-governments, provided that they paid tribute in kind.

That was as far as the generals went, but there were other agencies at work from the beginning. Into an idyll, straight out of the Russian Ballet there marched four miserable special Commandos of the Security Police, the *Einsatzgruppe D* of Colonel Bierkamp. It seems that against these few hundred SS men and their renegade Russian helpers, no one could do anything, neither the Intelligence Officers, who had to report their activities to the Army Command Staffs, nor the good intentions of von Kleist and Ernst Koestring. The literary champions of the *Ostpolitiker* have little to say concerning the activities of Bierkamp's men, though they have been recorded elsewhere. In September 1942, shortly after the occupation of the town, they emptied the hospital at Stavropol and gassed all the patients.[32] Just before Christmas, they removed the tubercular children from a sanatorium at Teberda near Mikoyan Shakar—one case among several that were similar, for this extermination group seems to have taken special interest in children's homes.[33] Even in January, during the general evacuation, they were still gassing the inmates of Krasnodar Hospital in daily batches almost till the Russian capture of the town. Nor was the hygiene of the happy autonomies their only concern. On 29th September the occupation of the Caucasian watering places, Piatygorsk, Essentuki and Kislovodsk, was celebrated by a round-up and registration of all the Jews, including many members of the evacuated staff and students of Leningrad University. A few days later 2,000 Jews were shot in an anti-tank ditch at Mineralny Vody.[34]

As we have seen, Braeutigam had long ago renounced his interest in incidents of this kind.* But ethnology had a nasty trick in store for those who tried to reconcile racialist doctrine with the prudent support of tribal autonomy. Among the German forward positions, east of Nalchik, lived the first communities of the *Tats*, the mountain Jews of Daghestan, Mosaic in their observances, but Aryan by race according to the ethnologists and even pure Goths. What was to be done about them? Were they to be allowed their own self-government or were they to be massacred like the Tartar Jews of the Crimea? The problems of high policy became acute when the *Tats* brought their fears to the military government officers at Nalchik. For once, says Mr Dallin, the SD were forced to desist.[35] But were they? Erich Kern, then a corporal in the SS Viking Division, viewed the case more sardonically. 'The military developments,' he writes, 'deprived our theoreticians of any need to know, for we never got to Daghestan.'[36]

But of all the ape-man idiocies which the Security Police performed and the military government staffs lazily condoned, the liquidation of the insane and the sick created most moral damage. When one considers that among these ancient Asiatic peoples and among the Moslems in particular the protection of the insane and sick is a divine ordnance, one wonders what would have been the final verdict on the German occupation. In the restricted enclave in the Kuban, which the Germans still held in the summer of 1943, the military government officials tried to register the population. But, says Peter Bamm, 'we had every difficulty in making them believe that no ulterior motives were

* See p. 254

concealed behind the registration.'[37] It is an interesting admission that the implications of registration were not perceived only by the Jewish community.

One may also wonder how long these populations would have found satisfaction in exchanging one form of autonomy for another, both of them equally fictitious. Kabardin-Balkar and Karachaev had been autonomous divisions of the Soviet Union and Kleist and Koestring could not do less than recognize their status. The Moslem Karachai had formed an anti-Bolshevik committee a few days before the Germans arrived, and it seems that the elders were invited by Koestring to a Bairam feast at Kislovodsk on 11th October. Koestring was carried shoulder high in triumph, but even at this feast there was a skeleton.[38] It happened at this moment that the head of the Four-Year-Plan Office, Paul Koerner, was on an ominous mission in Stavropol. Some members of the mission attended the feast and one of them made a speech, telling the Karachai that liberation from Bolshevism did not mean they could do as they liked. It was no time for relaxation. Henceforward they must work for the Fuehrer. Braeutigam claims that he read out a totally different translation of this speech, in which he assured the Karachai that they would be left in peace.[39] But, as in the case of the Kuban Cossacks, the grants of autonomy to Karachai and Kabardin-Balkar alerted Schickedanz, who again complained that his appointment had been ignored. Though Hitler had done little more than shrug his shoulders when Rosenberg put forward his name, Schickedanz now had the support of Goering and Koerner and a seat on the board of the Continental Oil Company which was expected to take over the oil-wells of Grozny and Baku, making fabulous fortunes for Goering's friends. With such a stake in the country, Schickedanz was still a danger, so Koestring dispatched von Mende to clog his departure in red tape. Time favoured the *Reichskommissar* no more than it favoured the Wehrmacht. Schickedanz was not to see even the outskirts of his kingdom.

(c) Stalingrad and the Great Exodus

ALREADY ON 19th November the thrust of General Rokossovski's army across the Don had isolated Stalingrad. Thus the land communications between Army Group B in the north and Army Group A in the south were menaced, though they were not actually cut till ten weeks later. In early December Braeutigam learnt from Kleist himself that it was intended to bring back Army Group A behind the Don. In the absence of Koestring, who had gone sick, Braeutigam dared not bring up the question of evacuating the tribesmen-collaborators, who still had no doubt of German victory. On 28th December Kleist informed Braeutigam that Hitler had forbidden the escape not only of the 6th Army from Stalingrad but of Army Group A from the Kuban. In readiness for another campaign to recover the Caucasus, the Army Group was to hold a large enclave, east of the Black Sea and Sea of Azov, with a bridgehead across the Don at Rostov. In the following February, however, Russian pressure was so great that Rostov was given up and the enclave was only linked with the main German area of occupation by an ice-track across the Strait of Kerch to the Crimea.

Although the Exodus of hundreds of thousands of civilians hindered the army's retreat, Kleist permitted the evacuation of those who had exposed themselves to Russian reprisals. Braeutigam undertook that they would not use the roads.[40] A refugee staff was formed and by 30th January thousands of Cossacks and mountaineers were on the move with their wagons and cattle. Some crossed the frozen Kerch Straits to the Crimea and some the frozen Azov Sea to Taganrog and Mariupol. A large part of the Kuban Cossacks made their way north across the Don at Rostov before the army forbade the use of this last bottleneck communication with the main front, which was lost early in February. Braeutigam personally directed the march of the Cossacks from Taganrog into the western Ukraine.[41] Finally, before his recall to Berlin, he arranged their temporary encampment at Baranovice in White Russia. On the march through the *Reichskommissariat*, the requisitioning officers of Erich Koch took all the Cossacks' horses from them.

It was the fate of a great many of the resettled tribesmen to be over-taken by the Soviet advance in the Crimea, the Ukraine and elsewhere. Some of them never even reached the escape route over the frozen sea. Those who served in the uniform of the German Army were mostly handed over to the Russians by the Allies at the end of the war. Thus the honeymoon with the invaders, which began with banquets and jewelled gift-daggers, ended in nothing but tragedy for these tribesmen in flight from collectivization. Few indeed were destined to see their homes again. But specially miserable was the fate of one tribe which occupied the largest territory though the smallest in numbers.

The whole of the huge Steppe between the mouth of the Volga and the eastern Caucasus was inhabited in 1942 by the Kalmucks, a pure Mongol race which was reputed to have settled in Russia in the thirteenth century. The greater part of the tribe returned to Central Asia in 1771 and is to be found in several regions, thousands of miles apart, a small fur-capped species with a wide grin, perhaps the most unsettled and nomadic of all modern Mongols. Scarcely more than 60,000 in number and living in tents, the Kalmucks west of the Caspian had been made an autonomous division of the Soviet Union with a cluster of huts as a capital at Elistar. A beginning had been made with collectivization, education, sanitation, taxation and all the things with the same suffix that Nomads dislike. And, to cap this, the Russians removed most of the cattle on which the Kalmucks lived, when they mobilized the resources of war.

Over the immense Kalmuck Steppe there roamed between August 1942 and January 1943, a single motorized German division, the 16th, which assured the liaison between Army Groups A and B. On one occasion the division sent a motor patrol to the lonely salt lagoons of the Caspian. Attached to this division through the office of Freytag-Loringhoven in Poltava was a Russian interpreter who used the German name of Dr Doll. With the aid of the divisional intelligence officer, Dr Doll recruited sixteen squadrons of Kalmuck light cavalry, mounted on ponies. They were useful enough in heading off Russian patrols in this huge emptiness, but a doubtful investment anywhere else.[42] The Germans had difficulty in stopping the Kalmucks from murdering their prisoners, for which, it might be said, there was some precedent on the German side. So the Kalmucks too had to be taken along in the retreat to save them from reprisals. Guided by Dr Doll, the tribes with their remaining belongings crossed the Don and entered the eastern Ukraine, where the men were separated from their families and made to guard railway tracks. Soon they became mutinous and unreliable. They were moved from camp to camp and finally they ended up, a frightful apparition of wild independence in the vast slave workshop which Germany had become at the end of 1943. The most reliable Kalmucks were incorporated in the 162nd Turcoman Division which trained at Neuhammer in Silesia.[43] Some Kalmucks were taken prisoner in Italy by American soldiers who mistook them for Japanese. Their families lived in a huge Nomad encampment at Tolmezzo in the Dolomites, where they became a problem for Allied military government officials after the war.

Only the families of the volunteers left with the Germans. The others had to face the consequences. A few months after the Russian capture of Stalingrad, a decree of the Supreme Soviet terminated the autonomous divisions of the Chechens, Ingushes, Karachai, Balkar-Kabardin and Kalmucks. Not till 1957 was it admitted officially that the tribes had been removed from their homes for their rôle in welcoming the Germans. The decree of 11th February 1957, described the deportation as a gross violation of Leninist principles. It seems that a committee is to handle their repatriation from south Siberia and Kazakstan and that this will be completed by 1960. In the words of Mr Gorkin, Secretary of the Praesidium, the settlement will be costly and must be carried out in an orderly manner, because of the lack of housing and other amenities in their homelands. Consideration must also be given to the manner in which these national groups will earn a living.[44] Houses and amenities for the Kalmucks! One recognizes the colourless Welfare State language of the mid-twentieth century, but behind it lies all the obscure tragedy of simple-minded people, so simple-minded that they never wanted either a German or a Russian system, but hoped to be allowed to live in their own way, rejecting water-closets as a substitute for liberty.

The catastrophe of Stalingrad came too late to have any effect on the policy pursued by the Germans in the Ukraine, White Russia and the Baltic States. The exploitation-machinery of Sauckel and Backe could not be slowed down except by the resistance of the population, but Stalingrad and its consequences did teach the High Command the necessity either of dispensing with the volunteers altogether or of treating them on lines which differed from the speeches of Erich Koch. The numbers alone demanded careful attention. The Germans now disposed of 70,000 Cossack soldiers, 110,000 Turcomen, 110,000 Caucasians and 35,000 Crimean Tartars.[45] In victory these men could be flung into the line as cannon-fodder, but in retreat they had to be handled more delicately. The Babylonian conception of warfare had to be renounced.

The part played by the national legions in the invasion of the north Caucasus, had been slight and unsatisfactory. In the actual mountain area the small tribes, who were allowed autonomy, could contribute only light cavalry units and horse transport columns. On the other hand the three principal nations who lived mainly south of the mountains, the Armenians, Georgians and Turkish-speaking Azerbaijanis, were beyond the reach of the German advance. The great bulk of the prisoners who belonged to these races had been combed out of the cages after the first campaign with the aid of von Mende's national committees, but the method of training was stupid and unimaginative. Unfortunately it came under the jurisdiction of Walter Warlimont rather than the more liberal Eduard Wagner. The legions were not permitted their own officers. These were chosen haphazard among serving Germans without language qualifications. In some cases officers were posted to the legions as a punishment, for in modern times the very name 'legion' has acquired a derogatory sound. Once they had been selected, the legionaries lost all contact with their national committees and were given no idea what cause they were fighting for. Since they were trained in Poland, they learnt how the Germans treated conquered races without being told. They were also made to realize that inferior captured weapons were good enough for second-class troops like themselves.

Without knowing about these conditions, Koestring arranged for an Armenian battalion, a Georgian battalion and a mixed battalion of north Caucasian tribes to be sent to the front. Fighting in a region of Armenian villages and possibly finding fellow countrymen on the other side, most of the Armenian battalion deserted. A Georgian detachment went over to the enemy because a soldier had been tied to a gun for indiscipline.[46] Hitler was impressed by these incidents. On 18th August 1942, he forced Keitel to issue the directive No. 46 on Partisan warfare. Volunteers from the 'Soviet Nationalities' were henceforward only to be used as small anti-Partisan formations.[47] Later, Hitler relented to the extent that he was prepared to trust the purely Moslem units; but, after Directive No. 46, Koestring had to ask Stauffenberg, who was then at the Organization section of OKW at Mauerwald, to stop immediately the dispatch of any more legionaries to the Caucasus. He also demanded an inquiry into the conditions in the training area in Poland. Since Oberlaender's mixed mountaineer battalion had fought well on the Terek front, the human material might not be at fault. So a commander with fighting experience was sent to Poland to re-organize the legions.

During the days of the Seeckt-Tukhachevski honeymoon, Colonel Ralph von Heygendorff used to accompany Russian officers at army manoeuvres in Germany and, during Hitler's alliance with Stalin, he had been attached to the Russian Army in Poland. Heygendorff had served on the commission which drew up the new boundary with Russia and at the outbreak of war he was on Koestring's staff in

Moscow.[48] But he had had no experience of commanding foreign volunteers and he knew nothing of their conditions. The first awakening of Heygendorff was the sight of a notice on a train in Warsaw station. 'Poles, Jews and Legionaries—last coach.'

It was 23rd September 1942, and the training area of Rembartow had become a reception centre for the great numbers of prisoners and deserters who sought to get into the legions. The difficulty of giving orders must have been appalling, for only the Azerbaijan and Armenian Legions consisted of single racial entities. The Turkestan Legion included Usbeks, Kasaks, Kirgiz, Karalpaks and Tadjiks. The north Caucasian Legion included all the six nations who had welcomed the Germans. The Georgian Legion included at least five tribes with separate languages, fascinating ones like those of the south Ossetes, Svanetians and Adshars.

What Heygendorff found in the five legions was something far from the conditions of a volunteer army, which is prepared to live hard for the sake of a national cause. Rather were they penal conditions, which were little more than a half-way house from the wholesale murder of the prisoner camps. The shadow of Reinecke's rules and of the screening teams of the Security Police was everywhere. The camp for unreliable legionaries at Deblin, the so-called U-camp, was also used as the camp for unserviceable legionaries. Men who had been crippled in action shared the same treatment as those who had been awarded punishment. This, as we have already seen, was a common Wehrmacht practice towards Russian prisoners.* In the two independent Torki battalions, which had native officers, it was quite usual for the German Commander to address these officers, telling them that their duty was to avoid the shedding of more valuable German blood. And this same importance of German blood ensured that the hospitals for legionaries were deprived of equipment, lacking even wheelchairs and crutches, and that captured medical officers, who had volunteered for the legions, were employed on sanitary fatigues by a corporal.[49]

These are instances, taken from Heygendorff's report, and they are explicable in part by the fact that this was not the front line but the General Government of Poland, where the National Socialist creed of master-race and sub-humans was much in evidence. When Heygendorff complained to a civil government official about the legionaries in the Jim Crow coaches on the trains, he was assured that the British in India would never permit native troops to travel with their own

* See p. 126

soldiers. It may only have been an illustration of the lack of experience in a nation which had administered no colonial empire for twenty-four years. On the other hand this extraordinary attitude towards subject peoples owed still more to an article of faith in National Socialist teaching. It was the belief that Germany had been handicapped deliberately by the imperialist powers, who lived richly at home by ruthlessly exploiting their colonial subjects abroad. There was a long road for Nazi officials to travel from the colonial notions of Nebuchadnezzar to the healthier colonialism of the Roman Empire, but much less time in which to do it.

With the formation of an inspectorate of the *Osttruppen* or Eastern Troops, some two months after Heygendorff's arrival in Poland, there was a marked change in the conditions of service. The creation of this office owed more, however, to the recruiting campaigns of the Wehrmacht Propaganda Section than to the Caucasus adventure. It will be necessary to go backwards a year in order to find the origins of this parallel recruiting movement, which led not only to the creation of a unified inspectorate, but, eventually and vastly too late, to the recognition of a Russian liberation leader.

CHAPTER TEN

THE EASTERN TROOPS
AND THE LIBERATION ARMY

(a) The Ostpolitiker

IT IS IMPOSSIBLE to decide when and where German Army units first employed Russian prisoners and deserters as voluntary helpers. It was difficult to move prisoners to the rear and, when the prisoners showed so little hostility, it was a natural and obvious thing to make them work. In this way, it was said, more than 200,000 Russian prisoners became attached to German units in the course of the first campaign. As cooks, drivers, orderlies, stretcher-bearers, labourers or interpreters, there were a dozen chances for prisoners who were fortunate enough to be able to surrender in small groups and in quiet places. Occasionally they were given a German uniform and a rifle. Occasionally they distinguished themselves in battle, fighting on the German side. Since they did not exist, they could not be commended for their conduct by mention in dispatches. But that was a minor misfortune for it was better, far better, to live without an official existence than to disappear in the mass-graves of the Stalags and Dulags.

By the winter of 1941-2 it was the fate of many of these *Hilfsfreiwillige* or *Hiwis* to acquire a sort of combatant status. In December 1941, in the incredible forests of White Russia behind the front of the Central Army Group there appeared the first large-scale and co-ordinated formations of Russian Partisans. The Russian counter-Partisan force was the inspiration of Major von Kraewel, Chief of Staff to the Rear Area Commander, General Max, Graf von Schenckendorff. Kraewel authorized the formation of an anti-Partisan militia to be recruited from the *Hiwis*. It seems that the first complete battalion was formed in the town of Briansk under the command of a Major Weiss. There were soon six such battalions in Schenckendorff's area. Kraewel also armed a Cossack cavalry battalion under the command of a colonel Kononov who had deserted with part of his regiment. As a complete Cossack unit with its own officers, the Kononov battalion antedated the recruiting drive in Cossack territory by nine months. Kononov was in those early days the most important Russian deserter to offer to serve with the Germans. In 1944 he became a Major General in the Pannwitz corps and at the end of the war he was the 'supreme Ataman' of the Cossack troops in the Vlasov liberation army.[1]

Also in Schenckendorff's area but on a quite different footing from the Cossacks and *Hiwis*, was the private kingdom and army of Bronislav Kaminsky, a colourful adventurer who likewise became a Major General—in the SS! Kaminsky's case illustrates the extreme lattitude which army commanders could permit themselves in ignoring the Commissar Order when they chose. According to the strict letter of Hitler's order, a Soviet *Rayon-chef* or district administrator, who failed to escape with the Red Army, was doomed to destruction. Yet Kaminsky, the *Rayon-chef* of Lokot, continued in office in spite of the Fuehrer Order and the SD commandos. It suited those who found Kaminsky useful to accept the story he told, namely that his appointment under the Soviet government had been a form of forced domicile after his return from a Siberian labour camp.[2] The rayon of Lokot stood at the edge of the Partisan-infested forest of Briansk. When Kaminsky kept his rayon free of Partisans, this unofficial experiment of a certain Lieutenant von Veltheim attracted the notice of higher authorities. Through the action of General Rudolf Schmidt, commanding the 2nd Panzer Army, an action which must have been approved by Keitel, if not by Hitler himself, Kaminsky was given the rank of Brigadier General. His territory was recognized by the High Command as a self-governing area and he was permitted his own forces, which were named RONA or Russian People's Army, a precedent for the Russian initials ROA, which, when applied to the eastern troops, paved the way for the Vlasov Army. Kaminsky's RONA was equipped by the Germans with captured tanks and guns. Members of the Russian emigré political party which was most encouraged by Rosenberg, the Solidarity Party of Baidalakov or NTS, were sent to Lokot to help Kaminsky in creating a political administration in line with National Socialism.[3]

All this was strictly against Hitler's declared policy, yet Kaminsky was the one Russian collaborationist who earned Hitler's praises and these too in July 1943, at the very moment when Hitler wanted to disarm the Russian volunteers. Kaminsky retained his private army long after the volunteers had been dispersed to other fronts. It was the reward of his unscrupulous pro-Germanism, but it could not have happened, had not Kaminsky's case been too freakish to tie up with the wider-based Russian Liberation Movement. Kaminsky was not a soldier but a civilian, not a Russian but half a Pole with a background which was too shady for a national liberation figure. He was of no value to the exalted group of German officers who wanted a leader capable of heading a nationwide Russian appeal.* He was also too ruthless. Major General Hermann Tescke saw four former staff officers of Kaminsky hanging on a gallows outside his headquarters in March 1943.[4] Thus Kaminsky became an embarrassment. Though Himmler praised the capacity of Kaminsky's men to live on loot, he was obliged to liquidate him in the course of the Warsaw rebellion of 1944 when, as a police commander, Kaminsky brought German methods into too open and flagrant disrepute.[5]

The *Ostpolitiker* would certainly have been most ill-advised to sponsor such a small town war-lord as Kaminsky for their Russian national leader. Yet it is surprising that they did not repeat von Veltheim's experiment in other places. A number of Lokot governments might have made a better base for their plans than the unwise direct challenge to Hitler which was issued by the Central Army Group in the autumn of 1941. Much has been written concerning the highly controversial figure of Major General (then Colonel) Henning von Tresckow, who was Chief of Staff first to von Bock and then to von Kluge as commanders-in-chief of this Army Group. It was von Tresckow who devised the plan which was followed by Stauffenberg in July 1944, the plan for a military *coup d'état* in Berlin which was to accompany the assassination of Hitler. Yet the man who plotted so persistently to kill Hitler, had, as a young lieutenant in 1930, tried to convert the officers of the 9th Infantry Regiment to National Socialism.[6] The son-in-law of the famous von Falkenhayn, Chief of the General Staff in the First World War, von Tresckow belonged to a class which it is not easy to comprehend outside the framework of German history between the two wars, a class of Putsch-making officers, over-imaginative for their circumscribed trade. If a lack of allowance for the sheep-like characteristics of twentieth-century man wrecked the plan of 20th July 1944, just as it wrecked other plans of von Tresckow, it must be remembered that the most original of

---

* According to Karl Albrecht, Kaminsky was a Polish noble whom Schenckendorff befriended because he was also a noble. Judging from Kaminsky's role in the Warsaw rebellion, this would seem to be rubbish. (*Sie aber werden der Welt zerstoeren*, p. 295.)

staff-officers are but soldiers, a species of tram or train that functions ill when it leaves the rails.

It seems that late in September 1941, when any Russian prisoner who looked as if he could read and write, had a good chance of being shot under the Commissar Order, von Tresckow persuaded his chief, von Bock, to forward a memorial to Hitler. Purporting to come from the German-appointed City Council of Smolensk, it was drafted by the Deputy Mayor, Professor Boris Bazilevsky. It accompanied a peculiarly ill-omened gift, namely a cannon from the museum which Napoleon had left behind in 1812. The memorial was no mere profession of loyalty. It contained a proposal that Smolensk be made the self-government capital of the German-occupied territories and the recruiting centre for all who wanted to fight Stalin.[7] Here was a Russian collaborator, who had tried to make contact with Hitler himself, and it might be supposed that Professor Bazilevsky would be unusually high on the list of wanted Soviet war-criminals. But that would be underrating both the capacities of Russian double-agents and the value of a *volte-face* in a Communist country. Five years later the Professor appeared at Nuremberg with a great deal of extremely hearsay evidence concerning the German part in the massacre of Katyn.[8]

Someone, it seems, had the courage to submit the memorial of this *Untermensch* to Hitler who, instead of flying into a rage,[9] said something about exploiting such manifestations 'gradually'. Von Tresckow was emboldened to continue. In November 1941, he traced a plan with the aid of his Chief of Intelligence, Colonel Rudolf von Gersdorff, for a Russian Army of 200,000 men, the estimated strength of the *Hiwis*. Tresckow believed that he would be supported by Keitel at OKW, because of the acute manpower shortage in the face of Russian counter-attacks on this front. He went so far as to propose several complete Russian Army Corps, holding front-line sectors, with the safeguard of only one German division to every three Russian divisions. Von Bock was persuaded to send the plan to Brauchitsch, who put it before Hitler with his marginal approval. No reply came from Hitler's headquarters and in December Tresckow went there himself, only to receive a severe dressing-down from Keitel. Political questions, he was told, were no concern of the Wehrmacht. 'Such ideas are not discussible with the Fuehrer'.*

---

* Thorwald, pp. 80–83. Thorwald's source is possibly Braeutigam. The latter, however, states in his *Ueberblick* that Hitler did not definitely turn down the Tresckow plan till 15th February 1942 (p. 88)

Neither Keitel nor Hitler had any suspicion at this stage of the war what a nest of conspirators the staff of the Central Army Group was to become. That did not influence Hitler's decision. At this time, when a Blitz victory was still expected, Hitler had not modified his views on allowing 'the Slav' to bear arms and, moreover, even if Hitler's views had been more liberal, the project was fantastically dangerous. In December Tresckow's hopes receded further, when Hitler dismissed Brauchitsch and when von Bock was succeeded, first by von List and then by the more cautious von Kluge. The plans for the new divisions had now to be shelved altogether. During the winter of 1941-2 the only Russian units, which could be employed on the Central Army Group front, were the various anti-Partisan battalions of von Kraewel, Weiss and von Veltheim. This ambiguous situation did, however, eventually produce some recognition of the status of the *Hiwis*. In the revised rules, which Hermann Reinecke distributed from the General Wehrmacht Office on 24th March 1942 there was mention of certificates which guaranteed genuine deserters from internment.[10]* It was the response of OKW to an agitation, in which von Schenckendorff played the leading part. Schenckendorff pointed out the danger to *morale* in units, which had no proper uniform and whose officers were not recognized by the German soldier. In many of his battalions, as in the case of the *Osintorf* which subsequently mutinied, Russian officers had no alternative but to serve in the ranks.[11]

During the month of February, when Sauckel's slaving gangs began to operate, Schenckendorff found his task made more difficult by the rumours circulating among the ex-*Hiwi* battalions. He was stimulated into writing a memorial on Partisan warfare which owed something to the older Tresckow plan. He demanded that the goal of a National Russia, free from Bolshevism, should be put before the volunteers' eyes, even if that goal were only a sham one.[12] This document, dated 18th March 1942, must be one of the first in which this propaganda device is mentioned, but the initiative in the matter had passed into other hands. Lieutenant Wilfried Strik-Strikfeldt, the obscure Baltic-German interpreter who had drafted the details of the new Russian divisions for von Tresckow, now worked for the Wehrmacht Propaganda Section and it was in the remote *coulisses* of this branch of the military bureaucracy that the Vlasov movement was to be launched. Strik-Strikfeldt himself was destined to become the ADC and confidant of the liberator and even at times the architect of his fortunes.

* See p. 121

Henceforward the generals hesitated to repeat von Tresckow's mistake in seeking a direct ruling from Hitler, but Schenckendorff continued to be amazingly active in urging others to do so.*

Political warfare in Russia was carried out by several conflicting agencies, the Rosenberg Ministry, the Goebbels Propaganda Ministry and for a time by the Foreign Office, as well as the propaganda services of the Wehrmacht under Colonel Hasso von Wedel and of the *Abwehr* under Admiral Canaris. The fights for precedence, which consequently took place, are too complex and wearisome to be described. For the moment we are concerned only with the Wehrmacht agencies. Colonel Wedel himself was an unimpressive figure whose pronouncements show a time-serving nature. Under Wedel, however, there was a subsection directed by Colonel Hans Martin, who, as a former official of the Propaganda Ministry, acted as liaison-man with his old chief, Goebbels. Martin was in the habit of reporting to Goebbels in private and on one occasion he produced a whole dossier concerning defeatist officers in the bureaux of OKH and OKW. Although Martin had no great enthusiasm for the Russian liberation project, he was very useful to his subordinates as a man who understood the vanity of politicians and knew how to flatter Goebbels.[13]

Martin's department, 'Wehrmacht Propaganda IV' became the chief nest of pro-Russian intrigue and its immunity from attack owed much to Martin's position with Goebbels. Yet Goebbels gave it no open and positive support. As often happened in Goebbels's life, he found himself on both sides of the fence. His propaganda for the Germans had to pay lip-service to the *Untermensch* outlook, whereas he himself was in sympathy with nearly every aspect of the Bolshevik system. Faithful to his own leftish past, he permitted three former German Communists, Thaelmann, Kaspar and Albrecht, to use their dialectic powers in running a bogus Russian radio station. Pretending to be the mouthpiece of a secret Leninist party who spoke from Russia, the station was used to recruit the first pro-German propagandists from among the prisoners of war.[14] Yet openly and officially, Goebbels could not

* Schenckendorff died of heart failure in the summer of 1943. The imaginary remarks, attributed to him in Thorwald's book, may be somewhat flattering to his true rôle, which, though constantly urging liberal treatment for the occupied areas, was a strictly utilitarian one. In the light of Schenckendorff's memoranda, it is astonishing that Carl Albrecht, who interviewed Schenckendorff in his own capacity as Commander of a Russian construction unit, should identify him with the views of Hitler, Bormann and Erich Koch. This ex-communist author commands little confidence. In the same breath he praises the humanity of Gottlob Berger and Hermann Reinecke. *Sie aber werden der Welt zerstoeren*, p. 255–6

associate himself with offers of freedom for Russia, while officially he had to preach that conquest would be swift and absolute. Early in 1942 Goebbels believed that a new policy was needed, but a year was to pass before he dared ask Hitler to draft a proclamation of liberty for the Soviet peoples.

In March 1942, therefore, the newly organized Wehrmacht Propaganda Section IV had to look elsewhere than the Goebbels Ministry for support. But where? The whole of Wedel's organization was mistrusted by the close caste which comprised Keitel and the heads of the operational staff, Jodl and Warlimont. The plotters would have got nowhere, had it not been that almost every function in Hitler's military system had a double. Thus Franz Halder, the chief of the General Staff on the eastern front had his own intelligence office, doubling the functions of Canaris's *Abwehr*. The latter, as we have seen, was inextricably involved with the Security Service and its screening teams. Halder was forced to create an office for the interrogation of valuable and important prisoners, which would be immune from the attentions of the murder commandos. Thus there came into being the office 'Foreign Armies, East' of Lieutenant Colonel Reinhardt Gehlen. Within this office there was a section III, which was concerned only with the interrogation of the most important prisoners. It was run by Lieutenant Colonel Alexis von Roenne who of course was a Russian-born Baltic-German. Von Roenne's interrogation centre at the old castle of Boyen near Loetzen was separated from Hitler's sacred compound, the *Wolfsschanze*, but it was not far away.[15] It can be said that in the comfortable quarters of Schloss Boyen the Commissar Order and the Prisoner Screening Order were flouted right under Hitler's nose. Gehlen and von Roenne had good friends among Keitel's OKW staff. They were supported vigorously by Stauffenberg in the Organization Section and by Schmid von Altenstadt in the Military Government Section.[16] Less vigorously but usefully, they were supported by Eduard Wagner, the Quartermaster General. On a few occasions Gehlen's office was even able to influence Halder's severely military successor, Kurt Zeitzler.

The liaison between von Roenne's office and Martin's was in working order by March 1942. A few of the most spectacular prisoners had already been transferred from Boyen to Berlin, where Martin had taken over a villa in the Viktoriastrasse from the Propaganda Ministry. This villa had already housed Soviet prisoners of war, who worked for the Eastern Section of the Goebbels Ministry under Dr Taubert. To tidy up the situation, it ranked officially as part of the prisoner camp, Stalag IIId. The change, which took place in the villa in March 1942, though full of portent, was invisible on the surface. The establishment was directed henceforward by Hans Martin, assisted by two passionately 'liberationist' Russian-born Germans, Captain Nikolaus von Grote and Lieutenant Duerksen. They in turn were assisted by a naturalized Russian exile, called Kazantsev. Just as under the previous rule of the Goebbels Ministry, the Viktoriastrasse agency were outwardly engaged in training prisoners of war as propagandists. In secret they were sifting future Russian national leaders.

The rôle of Alexei Kazantsev was important. He belonged to the NTS or National Alliance of Russian Solidarists. This was the Young Guard of the Russian exiles, founded in Belgrade in 1930. It was not Tsarist but intensely nationalist, owing much to the example of Mussolini. The advent of Hitler to power and the growth of anti-Slav feeling in Germany had alienated NTS from the Nazis but the gap had been narrowed by the Moscow pact. From the beginning of the war Rosenberg defied Hitler's ban on Russian emigré organizations by appointing members of NTS as mentors for his native administration. At Wustrow Rosenberg established an indoctrination course under NTS instructors. Emissaries were sent from Wustrow to Kaminsky's government of Lokot and among the Wustrow pupils was the captured Major General, Fedor Trukhin, a Red Army officer with an aristocratic background[17] and Colonel Meandrov, the Chief of Staff of an army corps.

Trukhin was one of the first Russian converts of general rank and he was destined to became the leading propagandist of the National Liberation Movement,* but the Solidarists were looking for bigger fish. A Russian Mussolini or even a Napoleon was essential and Messianic hopes were directed towards several Soviet Marshals, whom the great military purge of 1937–8 had shaken but not finally displaced. Kazantsev would speak mysteriously in the Viktoriastrasse villa of this Russian redeemer as *Sidorshuk* or 'Little Isidore'.[18]

May 1942, brought an important addition to the devoted band in the Viktoriastrasse, not the redeemer himself but his John the Baptist. This was Milenti Zykov, an inconspicuous person with a rank no higher than that of Captain, but reputed to have been the Political Commissar

---

* According to Erich Dwinger (*General Wlassow*, p. 87), Trukhin had been a lieutenant of the Imperial Guard, to whom Kerensky had offered an appointment on the General Staff.

of a division or even of an army corps. Zykov had already prepared an extremely plausible memorandum on Soviet arms-production for Freytag-Loringhoven, then Chief of Intelligence to the Southern Army Group.* According to his story, Zykov was the son-in-law of the former Education Minister, the old guard Bolshevik Bubnov who had been liquidated in 1935. He had been deputy editor of *Isvestia* under Nikolai Bukharin, but after Bukharin's execution he had been exiled to Siberia till the outbreak of war. Zykov was therefore a man with strong motives for desertion and it was not clear whether he had genuinely been captured. It was also thought that his real rank had been much higher.**

Ten days after his arrival in the Viktoriastrasse, Zykov together with Kazantsev produced an elaborate draft for a Russian Liberation Army and for a Russian socialist government in alliance with Germany. The plan required a leader, that captured Russian marshal or general whose existence was still hypothetical. Partly because there was no such person in German hands, partly because Zykov was both a suspected Jew and an undoubted Political Commissar, whose existence had to be concealed from Heydrich's men if he was to be kept alive, the plan, which Grote and Dierksen submitted to Martin and Wedel, met with no immediate response. But Grote reported from the Viktoriastrasse to von Roenne at the office of Foreign Armies East, that 'the names of Rokossovski, Malinovski and *Vlasov* had come up repeatedly when discussing the new anti-Stalinist state with our Russians'.[19] This was on 7th June 1942. Five weeks later, as yet unknown to the Viktoriastrasse group, the third person of this triumvirate, the commander in chief of the captured Volkhov Army, was in German hands.

(b) The Discovery of General Vlasov

IT WILL NEVER be known whether, at the time of his capture by the Germans, Zykov knew something of Vlasov's plans and therefore included his name among the possible anti-Stalinist leaders. Zykov is no longer a witness, but there are certain features in the history of

* See p. 357
** George Fischer, op. cit., pp. 39–40. Dwinger (*General Wlassow*, p. 285), says that Zykov's mother was Sinaida Petrovna, a former friend of Lenin and a secret opponent of Stalin.

Vlasov's command of the doomed Volkhov Army, which are already suggestive of his future rôle.

In July 1942, Lieutenant General Andrei Andreievitch Vlasov was approaching the age of forty-two. He was a powerful, extremely tall and proportionately massive man with an intelligent, though somewhat expressionless face with high cheek-bones. In most photographs of Vlasov his features are masked by large and dark horn-rimmed spectacles. These photographs are less revealing than certain of the details in his life story, as published by his ADC, August Osokin in 1944.[20]

Vlasov was born on 1st September 1900 in the village of Lomakino in the *gouvernement* of Nizhni Novgorod, which was named Gorki after the revolution. Vlasov's father was little more than a smallholder and his own childhood and youth were spent in poverty. Yet the numerous Vlasov household qualified in the revolutionary vocabulary for the description of *Kulaks*. The great events of October 1917 found Vlasov studying for the priesthood in Nizhni Novgorod and renting part of a room off a cabdriver. It seems, however, that these circumstances did not drive the young student into the first enthusiasms of the revolution, for early in 1919 his career in the Red Army began as a conscript. But, within four months Vlasov obtained a commission and he fought the armies of Denikin and Wrangel as a company commander. In 1923 he decided to make soldiering his profession and tactical training his speciality. But it was not till 1930, when he was posted to an advanced school for instructors in Leningrad, that Vlasov decided to join the Communist Party.

Shortly afterwards, according to a conversation recollected by Captain Duerksen, Vlasov regretted that he had gone thus far. It was when he paid a visit to the village of his birth and beheld the ruin of the *Kulaks*, the class from which he had come.[21] Nevertheless Vlasov avoided military conspiracies. During the state trials of 1937–8 he was at Chungking, serving as military attaché with Chiang Kai Shek's government. From this he was recalled, according to one report, because of his refusal to make Marxist propaganda.[22] The real importance of this passage in Vlasov's life lies in the fact that, as a member of the diplomatic corps in a foreign country, he acquired the aptitude that he later displayed for the usages of Western society.

On his return from China, Vlasov reverted to his rôle as a training officer, distinguishing himself by his success with a very discredited division, the 99th. At the beginning of the war he commanded an army corps defending Lwow, then an army, the 37th, which fought a desperate retreat through Kiev. His next command was the 20th Army on the Moscow front, an army which drove the Germans out of Gshatsk and Volokolamsk and which earned Vlasov his promotion as Lieutenant General. Certain German admirers of Vlasov, such as Erich Dwinger and Juergen Thorwald, write as if Vlasov had now become a popular hero of the Soviet Union, the organizer of the legendary 'People's defence of Moscow' by the hastily enrolled factory militia.[23] Yet it is significant that no such claim was advanced in 1944 by Vlasov's official Russian biographer. In the Russian press the hero of the defence of Moscow was Marshal Zhukov and Vlasov was no better known than Zhukov's six other army commanders. Vlasov may have been the largest fish whom the Germans had yet landed in July 1942, but he was not a name to impress the Russian public. He was no Montgomery.[24]

Zykov indeed may have known that Vlasov was already in disgrace with Stalin, not on political but on strategic grounds. In the middle of January Stalin had ordered one of his many winter surprise attacks. The siege of Leningrad was to be relieved by means of a bold thrust by a whole army towards the rear of the German positions along the Volkhov river, north of Lake Ilmen. Vlasov was flown with Marshal Voroshilov to the headquarters of General Maretzkov, commanding the Leningrad Army Group. He was to be Maretzkov's deputy and to supervise the attack of Klykov's 2nd Shock Army.[25] Vlasov criticized the plan and Voroshilov duly informed Stalin. Vlasov's chief objection was that it would be impossible after the thaw of the early summer to get supplies across the formerly frozen marshes to an army west of the Volkhov. This turned out to be the truth. Stalin forbade the withdrawal of the 2nd Army and the thaw destroyed the last passage through the German lines. Klykov suffered a nervous breakdown and Vlasov took over the army command in person. He refused no less than four opportunities of escaping from the 'Kessel' by air, because, it would seem, his conduct in evacuating the heavy artillery, while there was still a way back to the main front, had been a direct disobedience. Consequently a message had reached Vlasov in the 'Kessel' from his wife in Moscow, indicating that his house had been searched by the NKVD.[26]

While it was apparently no longer safe for Vlasov to return to General Headquarters, it would seem that he had not yet made up his mind whether to perish with the surrounded army or give himself up to the Germans. The German High Command announced the capture of the 33,000 survivors of the 2nd Shock Army on 28th June, a minor item of news on the day when the great summer offensive of 1942 opened. But the survivors surrendered without their general who was not discovered for an entire fortnight. Vlasov had concealed his identity by changing uniforms with a dead staff officer and thereby spreading the report of his own death. The motive is by no means clear, for, if the intention was to escape to the Russian lines or to avoid identification as a prominent person, he would have chosen a private's uniform. Vlasov told Duerksen that, during this mysterious fortnight, he had meditated suicide, but, as he weakened with hunger, he became too disillusioned with his old cause to find this sacrifice worth while. He still made no attempt to reveal himself to the Germans, who ran him to earth in a cowshed, very emaciated and living with the devoted family servant whom his wife had sent to cook for him, a peasant woman, massive and vigorous who figures in some of the narratives as Dunia or Maria Voronova.[27]

From 38th Army Corps Headquarters at Novgorod Vlasov was conducted immediately to 18th Army Headquarters, where in a former Baltic baron's castle near Leningrad he was received with the honours of war by General Georg Lindemann.* The next destination of the future Russian liberator was a squalid unreformed Dulag at Loetzen in East Prussia, where he spent at least a fortnight without, it seems, storing up much resentment. At the end of July Vlasov was promoted to the special quarters for important officers, which were maintained by OKH at Vinnitsa. There on 3rd August he produced his first memorandum. It was signed jointly by Vlasov and the commander of a crack Guards division, Colonel Boiarsky, and it purported to represent the views of a number of captive officers. Little interest was shown by OKH, for at this moment of apparent German victory the memorandum stressed the immense strength on which Stalin could still draw. The memorandum declared that only a Russian movement could prevail against Stalin and it threatened that the movement would have to lean on England and the USA, if Germany produced no clear policy.[28]

To the *Ostpolitiker* this was the purest manna. Ribbentrop, still striving to preserve a stake in Russian policy, sent his oldest Russian

---

* Georg Lindemann was dismissed from the command of the Northern Army Group in June 1944. He should not be confused with Fritz Lindemann, head of the German artillery, who was shot during the following month while resisting arrest after the bomb plot.

hand, Gustav Hilger, to see Vlasov at Vinnitsa. More significantly von Roenne sent from Loetzen the obscure but persistent propagandist, who had drafted von Tresckow's first plan for a Russian Liberation Army. For the next two years Strik-Strikfeldt was destined never to be far from Vlasov's person. Vlasov was captivated by him at first sight. With the aid of Duerksen, who had reached Vinnitsa from the Viktoriastrasse, Strikfeldt composed an open letter in Vlasov's name, to be used in leaflet raids behind the Russian front. It was dated 10th September and it was distributed by Wehrmacht Propaganda IV, without the approval of Hasso von Wedel but thanks to the good offices of Gehlen and von Roenne. The Vlasov movement had been launched.

Vlasov was not yet ready to lend his name to an appeal for deserters to the Germans. The leaflet, which he signed, was addressed only to commanding officers and intelligence officers. It listed the crimes of the Stalin regime, it described the hopeless plight of the Russian intelligentsia and it urged revolt. Stalin, the leaflet declared, based all his hopes on British and American aid and on the launching of a second front. Paradoxically the leaflet then broke into the language of Stalin himself. The British and Americans would fight to the last Russian, they would make Stalin drag the chestnuts out of the fire for them. Then back again to the point of the leaflet, namely that the only course was to remove Stalin and conclude an honourable peace with Germany —just as easy as that.[29]

After the distribution of the leaflet, it was permissible to remove Vlasov, in the company of Strik-Strikfeldt, to the Viktoriastrasse villa with its atmosphere of exiles, glasses of tea and soul-searching gloom, something straight out of Tchekhov where a discussion could last four days. Grote set to work to convert Vlasov to the von Tresckow plan of September 1941. The Smolensk government, as proposed in that plan, should be headed by Vlasov himself. But Vlasov was not a politician. The constitution of the government, which was to overthrow Stalin, did not concern him very much, except that he wanted it neither Capitalist nor National Socialist. Vlasov was at first disturbed by the presence of emigré Russians like Kazantsev till he found that, like everyone else in this uniform age, the emigrés professed a brand of socialism. 'Funny sort of emigrés you are,' Vlasov once remarked to Kazantsev; 'more like *Komsomols*, I should say.'

In those days it was fashionable among *Ostpolitiker* to recall President Wilson's fourteen points for a New Europe, which were said to have accelerated the capitulation of Imperial Germany in 1918. Otto Braeutigam was not the only one to think that Russia could be undermined in the same way.[30] So Grote got to work on the new articles of freedom, numbering only thirteen to avoid plagiarism.[31] Vlasov was ready to sign, provided Hitler signed first, but he would not endorse a mere German propagandists' trick. Why could not Hitler sign? This forthright general, a prisoner and helpless, could not understand how there could be conflicts of policy within a dictatorial government—a government that was apparently anxious to use his services. But the weeks slipped past and Grote's repeated requests for a decision by Hitler came back with Keitel's refusal, scribbled in purple pencil in the margin. In the first half of November Wedel overcame his diffidence so much as to seek two personal interviews with Keitel, but he was told, 'any further propositions of this kind are finally and unequivocally forbidden'.[32]

To the staff of Wedel's department, who, after all, had the task of making propaganda for Germany and not the task of finding a new government for Russians, there was a way out of the impasse which had already been indicated in von Schenckendorff's memorandum of 18th March, namely a sham declaration of independence, a declaration worded in such a way that Hitler himself would be prepared to sign it for tactical reasons, knowing that he was not irredeemably committed by it. On 25th November Gehlen wrote a long memorandum on the employment of Russians in anti-Partisan warfare. In it he again recommended this sham declaration of independence, but added that it must be carefully worded, since the captive Russian generals, who might sign it, did not want to appear as traitors and mercenaries.[33]

But no one cared whether the captive generals signed it or not. Outside the offices of Stauffenberg and von Gehlen, the Vlasov declaration from Vinnitsa had been forgotten as a nine days wonder and the Viktoriastrasse group ruminated in almost complete isolation, a tolerated nest of cranks. In the Eastern Ministry Rosenberg, if he could be said to have a policy at all, was opposed to the idea of a Russian national leader, while Braeutigam, the sensible mentor, was only a half-way convert. Braeutigam did not think that a true counter-régime to Stalin was practicable. A dissident general, a sort of Russian de Gaulle, might, however, allay the discontent of the Slav parts of the occupied territory. It was a false analogy because the situations of Vlasov and De Gaulle were diametrically opposed to each other, except in one respect. On 25th October 1942, the Allies had not yet landed in North Africa and de Gaulle's position was still, as Vlasov's was intended to be by Gehlen and Braeutigam, a mere façade.[34]

It was the Military Rear Area Governors, of whom Schenckendorff had been the first, who demanded the use of this façade and with growing vehemence as a second winter of Partisan warfare loomed before them. Therefore they approached Rosenberg who was believed to command access to Hitler. Rosenberg for his part was prepared to meet the Military Governors, in spite of his inveterate bias against 'Great Russia', because he believed they might support him against Erich Koch.* He received them at his new office on Unter den Linden on 18th December 1942, not only the 'Koruecks' and their chiefs of staff, but also Stauffenberg and Altenstadt and the personalities of the *Hauptabteilung Politik*. The leading spokesman was Schenckendorff, in whose area the Partisan problem was now so severe that a new over-all command had been formed under a man who had been formerly under his orders, the SS General Erich von dem Bach-Zelewski.** Rosenberg was for the first time roused to the perils which beset the front with Stalingrad already cut off by the Russians. He went to the length of writing a memorandum for Hitler, describing the views that had been put forward and asking for an audience.[35]

Yet the conference resolved nothing on the subject of Russian autonomy or a Russian independent command. If none of the soldiers spoke out for a Ukrainian State on Rosenberg lines, neither did they advocate a Smolensk Committee or a recognition of Vlasov. Von Tresckow, the originator of that plan, now recommended with apparent indifference the setting up of a Russian Central Government or of several such governments for different areas. From the Caucasus Koestring's adjutant, Hans Herwarth von Bittenfeld, arrived straight from the stronghold of separatism, declaring surprisingly that Russia could be conquered only by Russians. In fact till the very end Koestring and his adjutant were not disposed to release the Caucasian troops to Vlasov.[36]

On 22nd December Hitler replied to Rosenberg's memorandum with sharp raps on the knuckles both for the Minister and the Military Government officers. Rosenberg had actually taken the report to Hitler in person after showing it to Jodl and Zeitzler. The rival chiefs of staff had been delighted with it. In Jodl's recollection it was the only

* See pp. 203, 205
** See pp. 236–7

occasion when the Eastern Ministry co-operated with the High Command of the Wehrmacht. But, said Jodl, Hitler merely pigeon-holed the report in his usual fashion.[37]*

It is conceivable that the memorandum might have had a better reception, had it been backed by the four Field Marshals commanding Army Groups in Russia, all of whom favoured a declaration that offered a real bait to the Soviet populations. But the Field Marshals again showed that timidity which had been so marked at the time of the Commissar Order. The action of von Kluge, two days before his own Rear Area Commander, Schenckendorff, took the lead at the conference, shows how little ripe were these men for any dramatic change. The background of this incident, which came very near to wrecking the Viktoriastrasse establishment, must be traced back to the first volunteer formations.

A Russian figure, as intriguing and in the outcome as important as Vlasov himself, was Grigori Nikolaievitch Zhilenkov. Party Secretary of a large Moscow district and then Political Commissar to the 24th Army, Zhilenkov was shot down while flying over the German front near Smolensk in August 1941. Although only thirty-two years of age and without military training, he had taken over the temporary leadership of the 24th Army in person. Equally resourceful was his conduct in destroying the incriminating insignia and papers of a Political Commissar, who could be shot at sight. Not till the following April was Zhilenkov's identity revealed to the Germans. For eight months he had been driving a lorry as a *Hiwi* and in November 1941, he drove into the very suburbs of Moscow, where he had been a party boss only a few months before.[38]

At Schloss Boyen, Zhilenkov impressed von Roenne by his forthright views on the strength of the internal opposition to Stalin. Being more opportunist by nature than Vlasov, he larded his pronouncements with a great deal of anti-Semitism in order to appeal to the Germans. Peter Kleist, who saw Zhilenkov at Nevel shortly afterwards, found this young man so smooth and ingratiating, so unlike a hard, fanatical Communist official, that he took him for a Paris Russian emigré.[39] Strange to say, this former high Political Commissar was first employed by the very Security Service, whose duty it was to destroy him. In Schellenberg's military intelligence department of the Security Office (bureau VI) there was a section called 'Zeppelin' which trained reliable Russian captives—after screening by the murder commandos—as

* See also p. 210

agents to be dropped behind the front. Zhilenkov was induced to join, but, owing to the shortage of aeroplanes, these Russian saboteurs were not called on to fulfil their mission. To keep them occupied, they were sent to Nevel, where they were formed into a battalion of ordinary infantry soldiers under the name of 'Druzhina'.* Against the advice of Schellenberg, Druzhina was used during the winter of 1942 for anti-Partisan operations on the Central front. The result was not very surprising. Ordered to remove a horde of captured Partisans to the wholesale butchery that waited them at the hands of their own SD colleagues, the Druzhina murdered all the German officers and NCOs who were attached to them and joined the Partisans. Colonel Gil-Rodionov, the commander of Druzhina, was flown out by the Partisans to Moscow and was decorated by Stalin.[40]

Zhilenkov was not involved. Since September 1942, he had been among the soul-searchers of the Viktoriastrasse but he was not left to scribble memoranda for long. On 14th October he was summoned together with Vlasov's earliest collaborator, Colonel Boiarsky, to Central Army Group Headquarters. Rudolf von Gersdorff wanted him to take command of an independent Russian infantry brigade, which had been expanded out of one of Schenckendorff's experimental volunteer battalions, known as *Graukopf* or *Osintorf*. Originally this battalion had been led by emigré officers of the old Imperial Russian Army, including the colonels, Sakharov and Kromiadi.[41] The arrangement had not been satisfactory and advantage was taken of von Kluge's orders for the reorganization of *Osintorf* by Gersdorff and Tresckow to make it a truly Russian Legion with Russian-style uniforms and the Russian title RNNA or Russian People's Army. *Osintorf* was not to be an anti-Partisan unit, but to take its place in the line.

Profiting from the failure of their much bigger project in the autumn of 1941, Gersdorff and Tresckow made their preparations quietly and waited till 16th December 1942, before presenting von Kluge with a brigade, all ready to take up position in Red Army style uniform. Kluge, who seems to have been maddeningly professional, inspected the Druzhina without saying a word. Then he ordered them to be dispersed among German units as *Hiwis*.[42]

The result was open mutiny. Confronted with the alternatives of obedience or court martial, Zhilenkov and Boiarsky declared that their men would defend themselves, if ordered to disarm. Had this been permitted to happen, there would have been open warfare between the

* See p. 20. *The Schellenberg Memoirs*, p. 316

Germans and their collaborators within twenty miles of the Red Army positions. Hitler would then have disarmed all the native volunteers on the eastern front and sent them to work in Germany. It took all the diplomacy of Gehlen, von Roenne and Tresckow to reach a compromise with von Kluge. The RNNA brigade was not disarmed but dispersed. They retained their Russian uniforms and remained in the rear areas to await favourable political developments. To prepare these developments Zhilenkov and Boiarsky were allowed to return to the Viktoriastrasse.[43]

The decision had been facilitated by the creation of the Inspectorate for Eastern Troops on the day before the mutiny. Keitel had been persuaded through the long devolution of Wagner, Stauffenberg, Gehlen and von Roenne, so that the unofficial battalions of volunteers on the Central Army Group front were now on the same footing as the National Legions, whose existence Hitler had recognized in April. Yet the new name *Osttruppen* was deliberately contemptuous, being chosen to avoid any suggestion of Russia or the Red Army, and to the Russians it recalled the *Ostarbeiter* or slave workers and the use of the word *Ost* in the speeches of men like Erich Koch. To the plotters in the Viktoriastrasse, however, unification even in this form spelt hope. It showed that the Stalingrad crisis had induced even Hitler and Keitel to make concessions. It dispelled the shadow of the Reinecke rules and the screening teams and it brought the volunteers a step nearer the status of German members of the Wehrmacht.*

Stauffenberg, Gehlen and von Roenne had scored a success, yet how limited it was can be seen from their failure to find an Inspector for the *Osttruppen*, who sympathized with their political plans. Men like Koestring, Schenckendorff and von Tresckow could not be spared. The choice fell on Heinz Hellmich, a divisional commander without a command, under whom von Roenne had served on the Moscow front. After failing to prevent a Russian thrust towards Gshatsk, directed by none other than Vlasov himself, Hellmich had joined the throng of disgraced commanders in December 1941 and had been relegated to a training post. He had had a Russian background, having escaped from a Siberian prisoner-of-war camp in 1919 and made his way to Riga, disguised as a Red Army soldier. Hellmich was rated as an expert, since he could speak some Russian and had served under the Weimar Republic as liaison officer with the Soviet military mission in Germany. Yet, in spite of such a typical *Ostpolitiker* background,

* See p. 308

Hellmich had no belief in the value of anti-Stalinist movements. His lack of faith was in part compensated by his choosing as his chief of staff, Colonel Freytag-Loringhoven, who had created the Cossack corps and who had previously served in Hellmich's 23rd Potsdam Division. This appointment, however, gave the *Osttruppen* office a separatist rather than a Russian nationalist bias; still more so the appointment by Stauffenberg of an intelligence officer for Hellmich in the person of Lieutenant Carl Michel. This romantic young man was essentially a champion of Ukrainian nationalism who, after the war, wrote a violently hostile account of Vlasov and his supporters. The hero of Michel's book is Stauffenberg, who is shown with some exaggeration as a downright opponent of Vlasov, but the unrealistic and sentimental views, attributed to Stauffenberg in this book, seem to be largely Michel's own. It is written in semi-fictional form but it contains accounts of real incidents which are of great value.[44]

Nine days after Rosenberg's conference with the Military Governors Vlasov signed the so-called Smolensk Committee Manifesto, which was based on Grote's thirteen points.[45] He signed it not from Smolensk but from a Berlin villa that was no more than a gilded prison-cell. With great patience Strik-Strikfeldt had persuaded Vlasov to sign without Hitler's endorsement. That is to say, Vlasov had put his name to promises which would be printed in leaflets and dropped in Russia, though he realized that the German government was not committed to them.

Vlasov had no reason to abandon his habitual gloom. Of what use were good intentions without guarantees? Of what use a blameless list of internal Russian reforms and a promise that Russia should belong to the New Europe without Bolshevism or Capitalism, if both remained unsigned by the arbiter of all things? Of what use was the manifesto of a captive Russian redeemer, who said not a single word concerning the freedom of Russia's subject peoples?

Vlasov was soon to know. Disguised in an ill-fitting civilian suit and overcoat and guarded by his gaolers, he was permitted early in 1943 to visit the officer-prisoner camps of Wuhlheide and Hammelburg. At Wuhlheide the seven Russian generals, whom Vlasov interviewed, had been made suspicious and frightened by German ill-treatment following successful Russian Party indoctrination in the past. At Hammelburg in Bavaria, the infamous Hammelburg where a Gestapo reign of terror had reduced life to a jungle, five intimidated generals, queueing for their soup at the cook-house door, professed themselves sympathetic to Vlasov but unwilling to stir.*

Keitel agreed that the fictitious 'Smolensk Committee' Manifesto should be dropped behind the Russian lines, but he made two conditions. On no account were the contents of the leaflet to be made known to the volunteers or to the population of the occupied areas. And he insisted that the document should be approved by Rosenberg. It might be thought that this was no serious obstacle, but separatism, as preached from Rosenberg's Ministry, had influential backers. Gerhard von Mende who looked after the Caucasus nationalities in the *Hauptabteilung Politik*, had the support of Koestring and Ewald von Kleist. Therefore, on 12th January 1943, when Rosenberg finally approved the draft, it was with the reservation that the leaflets were to be flown only to the 'Great Russian' area and that they were to be used only for military purposes.[46]

Millions of leaflets were dropped, but behind the scenes Captain Strik-Strikfeldt arranged through private contacts in the Luftwaffe that some of the flyers should lose their bearings and drop their leaflets on the wrong side of the line. Thus two things happened, one of them congenial to the official school of thought, the other less so. In the first place a fair number of Russians deserted to the Germans even in the black week of Stalingrad. In the second place the nature of the proclamation soon became known in German-occupied White Russia and particularly in Smolensk. It is interesting to record that in the subsequent inquest Keitel was not over-concerned about the misuse of the leaflets. While, four months later, it was Keitel who was to make trouble about 'Leaflet 13', on this occasion the objector was Rosenberg. But Rosenberg's futile protests at the insult to his national committees was not backed-up by Koestring and von Kleist. With the fall of Stalingrad and the certainty that the Wehrmacht would never approach the Caucasus again, national minorities no longer mattered. So there was no court of inquiry for Strik-Strikfeldt and his leaflet-droppers.

Under the influence of defensive warfare even Hitler had become indifferent to the colonialist concepts, that had once ruled his mind. On 8th February, five days after the surrender of Stalingrad, he at last granted Rosenberg's request for an interview and for the first time he did not cut the man short, when he brought up his everlasting committees for the Soviet minorities. State Secretary Paul Koerner reported to Goering that Hitler had permitted Rosenberg to submit

* See p. 93. Thorwald, pp. 171–8

proposals for Baltic autonomy, as well as for national committees in the Ukraine and on the Central Army Group front.[47] But Rosenberg was not going to fetch any chestnuts out of the fire for the rival government of the Wehrmacht in Russia. He proposed that the Russian Smolensk committee should be directed by a plenipotentiary from the Ministry and that Vlasov should be simply one Russian general among others serving on it.[48]

But, by dropping the Smolensk manifesto on the wrong side of the line, Strik-Strikfeldt had achieved more than Rosenberg supposed. The military government officers were electrified by its effects on the population and they demanded that this bogus proclamation be seriously implemented. Even Kluge had changed in the two months since he had been threatened with the rebellion of the RNNA brigade. Consequently Schenckendorff found it safe to invite Vlasov to Smolensk, expedient to bring the pretender to his capital. Although Keitel was subsequently to behave as if he had not authorized the Vlasov visits to Russia, he certainly did not interfere. So much had Stalingrad changed the face of things that, at the end of February, Keitel authorized an increase in the activity of Wehrmacht Propaganda IV, the tolerated cranks of the Viktoriastrasse. Under agreement with the Goebbels Ministry and the Gestapo, they were allowed to take over an army barracks at Dabendorf on the road from Berlin to Zossen. It was to be a school for Nazi propagandists, chosen from among the Soviet deserters. Trukhin and Zykov, who ran this establishment, were required to distribute great quantities of Nazi material, but they also introduced a conflicting propaganda of their own into the pamphlets and leaflets which were turned out at Dabendorf. It was the greatest victory yet achieved by Stauffenberg and the *Ostpolitiker* group. Furthermore, Keitel and Jodl never ceased to regret it.*

(c) The First Defeat of the Vlasov Movement

DRESSED IN A specially designed uniform, Vlasov left Berlin on 24th February 1943, for a three-weeks' tour of the Central Army Group rear area. At Loetzen, near Hitler's East Prussian headquarters, he was met by Schenckendorff's intelligence officer, Captain Schubert. From Loetzen to Smolensk they travelled on the ordinary leave train, but

* See p. 346

Vlasov was confined to his compartment during the traverse of the General Government of Poland and the *Reichskommissariat Ostland*. All this was changed in the military rear area. At Krasnibor across the Dnieper from Smolensk, Vlasov was allowed to shake hands with the huge undemonstrative von Kluge. At Mogilev, Schenckendorff went further and asked the pale captive to dinner and drank his health. But these courtesies were nothing to the freedom that Vlasov enjoyed for the first time, the freedom of addressing a Russian audience in Russia. In the ill-lit, icy cold theatre, the citizens of Smolensk could see with their own eyes and hear with their own ears the man whom the leaflets had made a hero. Yet the hall was half empty. Fear of the Partisans, fear of the German SS, fear of their neighbours, played its part. It took a bold opening by Vlasov to make them speak, but speak they did and the Smolensk *Rayonchef*, Nikitin, poured out all the doubts and disappointments of the anti-Stalinists. Such, it seems, was Schubert's impression of that singularly uncomfortable evening,[49] but in fact we know nothing of the general impression which Vlasov made on Smolensk. Already the Red Army was barely forty miles away, the town swarmed with Partisans and six months later the Iron Curtain descended on it well and truly.

The Occupation Powers had to take more notice of a speech which Vlasov made at Mogilev on 13th March, an embittered attack on every aspect of German occupation policy. He was speaking to Germans, both soldiers and civilians, and to them at least Vlasov made it unmistakably clear that he was not Hitler's puppet.[50] On his return to Berlin Vlasov repeated these observations in a memorandum which he wrote for Grote and Duerksen. He declared that the mass of Russians had lost faith in the Germans, in whom they saw only slave-masters and annexationists. It was a little better with the volunteer units whom he had inspected. Vlasov believed that they could be relied on to do their duty, if they were given a Russian committee. Today it was still possible to win them. Tomorrow it would be too late.[51]

The speeches at Mogilev and Brest-Litovsk—where Vlasov addressed 2,000 Russian prisoners of war—could not be concealed. They introduced conflict and publicity, new friends and new enemies, where for months there had been only neglect and contempt. Scarcely had Vlasov returned to Berlin when he received a new invitation. It was from Georg Lindemann, the commander of the 18th Army which was blockading Leningrad. Under the protection of this general, who had received him with honour after his capture, Vlasov was allowed again to address both Germans and Russians. At Pskov, Gatchina and Riga, Vlasov had complete liberty to address meetings and through Lindemann he was received by yet another Army Group Commander. It is true that Field Marshal Georg von Kuechler of the Nórthern Army Group was no 'Resistance General'. He had circulated the notorious Reichenau Order of October 1941, the Commissar Decree and every other murderous document that was sent him.* Yet even Kuechler had been persuaded that propaganda campaigns were valueless, if Vlasov was not given real military authority.

A still more striking sign of changed circumstances was the general but unofficial use of the Russian initials ROA to designate the troops that came under the *Osttruppen* office. It meant Russian Freedom Army and it was flattering to the volunteers, who, however, belonged to no kind of Russian Army at all, since no Russian commanded any unit above battalion strength and even these commanders were not under the orders of Vlasov, who did not even control the propaganda school at Dabendorf. In fact Vlasov had returned from his second Russian tour still a prisoner, even if the flat over the garage in the Viktoria-strasse had been changed for a villa in the Kiebitzweg, in the fashionable Dahlem quarter. He could move about, but his movements were haunted by a devoted though embarrassing watch-dog in the person of Lieutenant Sergei Frohlich, a repatriated Baltic German. Frohlich had attached himself to Vlasov not to spy on him but to serve a hero, a circumstance all the stranger because Frohlich belonged to the SD and had served in Schellenberg's military intelligence branch, helping to organize the Russian saboteur unit, 'Zeppelin'. Having been vetted and accepted by Strikfeldt, Frohlich proved a good acquisition. The new establishment at Dahlem possessed neither guards nor weapons. It was at the mercy of the Gestapo or of any government agency that chose to interfere. Frohlich, however, used his SD connections in Riga to smuggle firearms from the front and with them some vodka, cigarettes and bacon, so that the liberator could hold court.

Some domesticity of a distinctly Old Russian flavour returned to Vlasov's unhappy life. The massive peasant woman, Maria Voronova, who had shared his hardships in the Volkhov Kessel, appeared from a women's internment camp in Riga, loyal to her master but at the same time blindly devoted to Stalin. Vlasov used to say that she had been in

---

* See p. 113 Kuechler received a sentence of twenty years imprisonment at Nuremberg in 1948 but was released in February 1953 at the age of seventy-two.

contact with the Partisans, who had urged her to poison him.[52] In the Berlin of the Gestapo, the People's Court and the Party Bonzes, the situation had some piquancy. When this picturesque figure slammed the door in the presence of two German officers, Vlasov grimly observed, 'Excuse me, gentlemen, an *Untermensch*.' On many other occasions the correctness and formality that were expected in German military circles, were sadly lacking. In long periods of depression Vlasov drank heavily and there was an uninventoried German woman called Ilse, whom Vlasov described as his Catherine the Great.[53]

Scarcely had Vlasov returned from Russia to settle in this new establishment, when both his freedom of movement and the continuation of the activities of 'Wehrmacht Propaganda IV' were menaced with extinction. The Gestapo had hitherto held a watching brief and the *Ostpolitiker* had led a singularly protected existence. But on 17th April 1943, Himmler laid a complaint before Bormann which was submitted to Hitler. Keitel was at once ordered to investigate Vlasov's recent activities. It seems that, while addressing a staff-mess at Gatchina at the beginning of the month, Vlasov had used the following words.[54]

> The war will end. We shall liberate ourselves from Bolshevism and then we shall receive the Germans as our beloved guests in our own Leningrad, to which we shall restore its rightful historic name.

Von Wedel was obliged to inform Keitel that Vlasov had acknowledged using these words. They seem today not only without malice but excessively flattering to the Germans. But Vlasov was unaware that Hitler had repeatedly threatened to raze Leningrad to the ground and to give the site to the Finns. Keitel reacted to Wedel's report by sending a circular to the High Command, declaring that Vlasov's speeches and journeys had been unauthorized and that he was to be sent back to a prisoner-of-war camp. Hitler, the circular declared, did not want to hear of Vlasov's name again except in propaganda announcements which would require the use only of his name and not his person. Should Vlasov appear in public he must at once be handed over to the Gestapo and be made harmless.[55]

The timing of this *démarche* by Himmler was probably deliberate. Kurt Zeitzler, who had succeeded Franz Halder as Chief of Staff on the eastern front, had been converted by Wagner—or perhaps only half converted—to the necessity of a political offensive, if the forthcoming German attack on the Central Army Group front was to succeed. Wedel was authorized to launch this political offensive under the name, 'Aktion Silberstreif'. The text of a new leaflet, to be dropped behind the Russian lines, was drawn up by Grote in Wedel's office and by Heinz Herre in von Roenne's. It offered fair treatment to Red Army deserters. They could join the national legions if they were non-Russians. They could become *Ostarbeiter* or join the non-existent army, ROA, if they were Russians.[56]

To von Kluge's staff, who would have to conduct the great German offensive of 1943 this leaflet seemed most inadequate. Von Gersdorff not only demanded some promise of a Russian political future, but he persuaded von Kluge that Vlasov should be present at the front of operations. Gehlen's office put this proposition to Zeitzler but it was too late, for Zeitzler had already received Keitel's circular concerning Vlasov. He therefore signed 'leaflet No. 13', only in its harmless unamended form, though eighteen million copies were printed.[57]

It was already the end of April but now the last great German offensive on the eastern front, 'Operation Citadel' was postponed from 5th May to 5th July and, during these two months, the growing number of *Ostpolitiker* had time to look round and count their losses. And the first and most surprising discovery was that no one had gone to the Kiebitzweg to arrest Vlasov, in spite of the thunder of Jove. So on 14th May a meeting was arranged at Mauerwald between Schenckendorff, Tresckow, Gehlen, Gersdorff and von Altenstadt. They decided that, since Keitel was unapproachable, they could take advantage of the slowness in action of an unapproachable person. If Kluge's consent could be obtained, Tresckow and Gersdorff would set up Vlasov in a restricted self-government area behind the front, similar to that of Bronislav Kaminsky. Kluge not only agreed, but put the proposal in writing to Zeitzler on 22nd May.[58] In the meantime Wagner paid a visit to Braeutigam. Faithful to his belief that Rosenberg was a man who could influence Hitler, Wagner used Kluge's consent as a lever. Vlasov would be set up in territory, immediately adjoining Rosenberg's *Reichskommissariat Ostland*, if Rosenberg failed to get Hitler to sign a real declaration for the Soviet peoples.[59]

If Rosenberg was worried by this threat, he was much more worried by the prospect of having to make new proposals to Hitler. He agreed reluctantly that officials of the *Hauptabteilung Politik* should again meet the Rear Area Commanders, but the officials who attended the meeting at Mauerwald on 25th May, von Mende, Braeutigam and

Knueppfer were the very reverse of Vlasovites. If Thorwald's description is to be trusted, the spokesman of the Military governors was
Wagner himself. It is strange that this general should have insisted so
hotly that Rosenberg was the only man who could go behind Keitel
to Hitler. Wagner worked at Mauerwald and was required to see Hitler
at almost every daily *Lagebesprechung*, whereas Rosenberg's Ministry
was 450 miles away and was represented at Hitler's court by a mere
messenger-boy. Moreover, as recently as 19th May, Rosenberg had
experienced his greatest humiliation at Hitler's hands in the famous
confrontation with Erich Koch.*

Rosenberg of course reported only very perfunctorily on the outcome of this unwanted conference. He informed Keitel and Jodl that
he was ready to report to Hitler on the demand for a proclamation of
policy in the east, when required to do so. As we have already seen,
Rosenberg had arranged to spend most of the following month in the
Ukraine.**

The whole episode of this second approach to Rosenberg illustrates
the painful weakness of the Vlasov supporters, who were still confined
to Kluge's general staff, von Roenne's office and the original Viktoriastrasse group. The rest of the *Ostpolitiker*, who opposed the official
Party policy in Russia, were numerous but they were a house divided.
The weakest aspect of the Vlasovite position lay in the fact that, though
Stauffenberg and Gehlen had virtually created the *Osttruppen* Inspectorate, the so-called ROA army, they had not found a general of their
ideas to run it. At this time Freytag-Loringhoven offered his resignation as Hellmich's chief of staff. Gehlen replaced him with a man from
his own office, none other than that Major Heinz Herre whom we
encountered in the affair of the Russian prisoners at Stalino.*** Since
22nd April 1942, Herre had assisted von Roenne in the direction of the
special interrogation centre at Schloss-Boyen and he had been responsible for selecting some of the Russian personalities of the Viktoriastrasse. Herre, like Freytag-Loringhoven before him, was a Slavophil
and out of sympathy with the professional-soldier mentality of General
Hellmich, whom he regarded as 'the gravedigger of the volunteer
movement'.[60] And yet, after Himmler's *démarche* against Vlasov, it was
Hellmich who had to answer the new flood of complaints against the
volunteers.

For this purpose Hellmich was summoned at the end of April 1943,

* See pp. 209–10
** See p. 210. Thorwald, pp. 226–34
*** See p. 115

to report to Hitler's headquarters, then at Berchtesgaden. Hellmich delayed, hoping for advice from his mentor, Major Stauffenberg, who was in North Africa. But now came the news that Stauffenberg lay dangerously wounded after stepping on a mine. His return to office was problematic. So, without any briefing, Hellmich set off to be carpeted by Jodl, Warlimont and Himmler.

The little mission, composed of Hellmich, Freytag-Loringhoven and Michel, seems to have found Jodl surprisingly sympathetic and quite prepared to use his accessibility to Hitler to undo some of the effects of Himmler's *détente*. But the substantive complaints against the volunteers at this time were mainly concerned with the rebel Ukrainian militia in Volhynia and sprang from the political fears of the hated Erich Koch. Later on, when defections of the *Osttruppen* were reported from a critical sector of the front, Jodl changed his mind and boasted of the wisdom of shipping the volunteers out of Russia.[61]* Jodl's original benevolent feelings towards Hellmich's mission were not shared by his deputy. Warlimont wanted to shoot any 'political' volunteers who would not be disarmed—as if the anarchy in Volhynia and Polesia could be overcome this way. Michel claims that he then chimed in with a suggestion to mollify Warlimont. If such units must be decimated, it would be better that this should happen in battle against the enemy.[62]** But the original thought was not Michel's. It had already been incorporated in a memorandum of Hellmich's, dated 23rd March—a singular tribute to the unbewitched state of his mind.

> The stronger we are and the more the eastern peoples are bled white, the smaller will be the practical effect of their demands ... the volunteers must save German blood at the front and those unable to fight must be made to join the ranks of the labourers ... if in exceptional cases these auxiliaries fail, the fact can be used at the given time in order to weaken exaggerated demands, which may come from their ranks. For this reason failure is even desirable. It gives us the right to set limits to their political aims.[63]

In spite of Michel's starry-eyed admiration for his chief, Hellmich, the reader has only to turn to the end of the last chapter to see that this is precisely the attitude of which Heygendorff had complained and to combat which Gehlen and Stauffenberg had created the *Osttruppen*

* See p. 346
** See p. 247

Inspectorate. Hellmich could not therefore have been so estranged from the blood-drinking Warlimont as Michel pretends. *Soldat spricht zum Soldat*. Hellmich must have been relieved when Warlimont closed the interview by asking that no more volunteers be enlisted till Hitler had pronounced his decision. And that would be after the stabilization of the front in Russia.*

Hellmich owed all the trials of his visit to Berchtesgaden to the indiscretions of Vlasov and he had never liked the man. He had visited his former opponent, the victor of Gshatsk, in the Viktoriastrasse days and, in spite of much flattery from Vlasov, had come away with an adverse impression. On his way back from Berchtesgaden to Loetzen, Hellmich called on Strik-Strikfeldt in Berlin and demanded that the Vlasov propaganda be stopped forthwith. But the humble captain had little to fear from the Lieutenant General. Wehrmacht Propaganda IV came under OKW and not OKH and the Inspector of the *Osttruppen* had nothing to say in the matter. As a protest against both houses, Hellmich offered his resignation. Eight months were to pass before it was accepted.[64]

Hitler's decision, which Warlimont had promised Hellmich, was delayed for six or seven weeks, till 8th June, when the subject of the appeal for a liberation army was introduced by Keitel at an ordinary *Lagebesprechung*, of which the Minutes survived the war and were put in evidence at Nuremberg.** The only other persons present besides Zeitzler were Hitler's military adjutant, Colonel Rudolf Schmundt, and the official archivist, Colonel Scherff with his stenographer. Rosenberg, who should have presented his report, was in the Ukraine. Keitel proceeded to explain that the leaflet No. 13 had been prepared for distribution behind the enemy front, shorn of all references to ROA, the liberation army. The deserters were to be offered the alternatives only of civilian labour or *Hiwi* service at the front. Nevertheless 'implementation orders' had been issued by the *Osttruppen* office that the deserters could be transferred later to national units. Furthermore, there had been a dropping of unofficial Vlasovite leaflets, openly naming ROA.

---

* Michel, p. 143. The date of the interview with Warlimont is uncertain, but Michel makes it clear that it took place some days after Mussolini's departure from Berchtesgaden on 10th April. It should have taken place after Himmler's complaint to Keitel on the 17th.

** The Nuremberg Document, PS 1384, is abridged from a 22-page transcript, now in the library of World Jewish Congress in New York. Of all the many excerpts and translations that have been published, the fullest is the English version in George Fischer's *Soviet Opposition to Stalin*, pp. 176–87. The German version in *Vierteljahreshefte fuer Zeitgeschichte*, 1954, p. 312, is only a short extract.

Keitel must have received a shock when Hitler interjected, 'That's not so tragic either.' Thorwald and other Vlasovite writers have certainly exaggerated the drama of this conference, in which Hitler had scarcely an angry word to say about Vlasov. Anything, Hitler said, was permissible in propaganda, provided that it was not put into practice. To treat the national units seriously was to clutch at a straw like a drowning man. That too had been the action of Hitler's revered colleague in the Munich Putsch, Field Marshal Ludendorff, who had been urged to create the pro-German Polish legions of 1916. Thereby the Poles had acquired a half-million army, which they used for the liberation of Poland. And yet today Ludendorff's example was being followed by von Kluge.

I can tell Kluge and all the other gentlemen only one thing. I shall not create any Russian Army. That is a phantom of the first order. No one need instruct us that all we have to do is to create a Ukrainian State and then everything will be in order and then we shall acquire a million soldiers. We won't get one man that way, but we shall have perpetuated a singular madness. We shall have allowed our war aims to slip out of our hands and these have nothing to do with a Ukrainian State.

Under no circumstances must the volunteer units be delivered to a third party, a Russian who tells them, 'today you work with the Germans, but tomorrow you don't.' With his primitive logic Hitler argued that, if the volunteers acted against Russian interests, they would be dishonourable and worthless. If they served Russian interests, they would be dangerous to the Germans.

Hitler meandered on about the Rosenberg-Koch affair, which he had failed so egregiously to straighten out on 19th May, and it took Zeitzler some courage to get back to the terms of reference. With a view to saving the existing volunteer formations, he drew up a deliberate underestimate of their numbers. He declared that there was only one complete national regiment among the forty-seven battalions at the disposal of the Army Group Commanders and the Commander of the Reserve Army. All the rest were dispersed battalions. Out of 400,000 men, 60,000 were mere guard troops and 220,000 were still *Hiwis*. Outside Russia, on the other hand, there were a division of Cossacks training at Mlawa in Poland and the beginnings of a Turcoman division at Neuhammer in Silesia. Zeitzler was not in favour of creating any more such divisions and he was going to warn Hellmich.

Here Hitler interposed in the most agreeable manner that he was personally in favour of recruiting more Turkish-speaking units, 'when we get back to the Caucasus'.

It was left to Rudolf Schmundt to remind Hitler of the decision he was asked to make. He reminded him how Georg Lindemann of the 18th Army had kept the railways and the harvest workers protected from the Partisans with the aid of 47,000 *Hiwis*. They had served for 'bread and maintenance', but since Vlasov's visit to the 18th Army area, the *Hiwis* would expect the fulfilment of Vlasov's promises or they would sabotage the railways instead of serving them. To this Hitler reiterated dully that the decision to use Vlasov propaganda only on the Russian side of the front had been taken already. Keitel led him away from the subject and Hitler began a denunciation of von Kuechler's plan to enrol the Baltic nations in German units. Zeitzler riposted that the mixture of Germans and foreigners was showing good results in Niedermeyer's Turcoman division. So Schmundt's point about the *Hiwis* was missed and in two months Schmundt was completely vindicated, when Russian volunteer guard troops delivered the railway stations to the Partisans on the Central Army Group front.*

Finally, in reporting that Vlasov had been forbidden to conduct any propaganda activity on the German side of the front, Keitel asked whether ROA could still be named in propaganda for the other side. 'Yes,' said Hitler, 'there you can do anything'. And if the propaganda brought in any deserters, they could be sent to the coal mines where 50,000 new recruits or even 30,000 could perform wonders. Regretfully Hitler added, 'But one would have to treat them really correctly then'. For tactical reasons Zeitzler acclaimed the ominous proposal, declaring that in any case he could do little with the deserters, except fill some gaps among the *Hiwis*. At least Zeitzler knew now that the existing units would not be disbanded, for Keitel reminded him to provide Hitler with the terms of the new *Osttruppen* regulations, on which he was working. Supremely bored with the subject, Hitler affected not to notice this part of it. He murmured that perhaps he would get his top commanders together and tell them the things he had just said. Lammers could get something drafted out of the present Minutes.

Parturiunt montes! The blow had fallen and Hitler had decided against the *Ostpolitiker*, but what a decision! Tired, hesitant and lacking concentration, Hitler had left behind him a pitiful recording of what

* See p. 344

a dictator should not be. Zeitzler, however, had every reason to be pleased with the conference. He was free to publish the standard code of rules which would make the volunteers almost German soldiers. Freytag-Loringhoven had worked on it and then Heinz Herre. Now Stauffenberg, in hospital and swathed in bandages, urged its completion. To Herre the regulations '5000' and '8000' were mere *bonbons*, sugar candy to keep the baby quiet while its future was being discussed. Zeitzler, as a more professional soldier, perceived in them order and conformity to delight his soul. Two persons of equally good conduct could now at last get the same decoration. Differentials in leave and separation allowances would be a thing of the past. The marriage of Russian volunteers and Russian civilian workers no longer presented nightmarish complications for orderly room staffs.[65]

And what of Vlasov, who was forbidden to speak or publish on the German side of the line? Such were the gaps in totalitarian rule that he travelled that summer as far as Vienna and the Rhineland, held a greater court than ever before and sent his leading propagandists to Paris, while at Dabendorff the Vlasovites, Zykov and Trukhin, made a strange brew of the Nazi material with which they were supplied. That Vlasov was in disgrace was fairly generally known after 8th June and even the Allied press reported that he was about to be replaced by the Cossack, Krasnov.* In practice the Party Office of Martin Bormann forgot about Vlasov, so weak had been Hitler's ruling on 8th June, so lacking in any strong expressions which this antlike man could turn into a Party directive.

Since Bormann and other Party leaders—and Goebbels in particular —were silent, some civilians began to make their own propaganda for the Russian Liberation Army. On 10th March 1943, Goebbels had returned from his visit to Hitler at Vinnitsa, mortified by the rejection of his proposal for a 'Proclamation for the East'. He listened with rapt attention to the puppet Norwegian premier, Vidkun Quisling, who had known the Russia of the early revolution as one of Nansen's famine relief officers and who had married a Russian. Furthermore, Goebbels read Vlasov's report on his visit to Russia and 'it moved my heart-strings'.[66] But if Goebbels was henceforward a Vlasov man, it was in secret, whereas there were journalists, who sensing this, began to prepare the German public for a change.

One of Goebbels's visitors—almost certainly between 20th March and 9th April, where there is a gap in the *Diary*—was the frustrated

* See p. 295

Heinz Hellmich. Among the subjects discussed was the big illustrated brochure which Himmler distributed free from his 'SS schooling office', *Der Untermensch*. Hellmich described its ravaging effect on eastern workers and volunteers. Goebbels suggested that it might be possible, without offending Himmler, for his Ministry to buy up the remaining copies and distribute them in western Europe, where there were no Russians to read it. The omnipresence of this thing, which still embodied the spirit of the original 'Barbarossa' plan, meant quite a lot in the Germany of 1943.[67]

On my desk lies a battered copy, 'liberated' from a devastated German town in 1945. Fourteen inches by ten, it appears no less effective as publicity after seventeen years than it must have been in 1942. Sweetness and light, clean Aryan types in newly starched peasant costumes confront famine, squalor, bestiality and mass-murder, the former in perfect focus, the latter both literally and metaphorically over-exposed. The first page contains a passage on sub-humans from Himmler's only literary achievement, published in 1935. In the middle on the debit side there is an incongruous photograph of Epstein's Genesis, while Churchill and Roosevelt are depicted as Jewish types.[68]

Pasted on walls throughout Germany, *Der Untermensch* had its adversaries from the beginning. In March 1943, the editors of the glossy weekly Party magazine, *Das Reich*, brought out a companion piece, a special number full of photographs of handsome Soviet types under the caption, 'They bring us new allies'. Under pressure from Rosenberg, the issue was recalled and published without the offending article, but not till the early morning copies had reached the provinces.[69] In June a smaller though more daring gesture was made by Guenther Kaufmann, editor of the Hitler Youth quarterly, *Wille und Macht*, who produced a special number which included Vlasov's Smolensk manifesto, although this had been banned except for propaganda to the enemy. It was impossible to recall the edition, but Rosenberg persuaded Himmler, as head of the Police, to ban further printing. Kaufmann escaped the attentions of the Gestapo through a convenient calling-up order, which was procured by his friend, Carl Michel.[70]

Perhaps the most significant indication of a turn of the tide was the leading article in *Wille und Macht*, which was written by an SS man and special protégé of Himmler. Erich Dwinger had fought in the counter-revolutionary army of Admiral Kolchak in 1919 and on the side of General Franco in the Spanish Civil War. Himmler had designated this volatile Fascist romantic as the first SS war reporter in

Moscow. After serving under the police general, von dem Bach-Zelewski, Dwinger had been recalled as unreliable. But Dwinger was allowed to live peacefully on his farm in the Allgaeu, to continue writing his books and to receive Vlasov. Even his performance in the *Wille und Macht* magazine earned him no more than an order from Gottlob Berger to keep away from Berlin.[71]

Rather more serious was the memorandum of Professor Theodor Oberlaender, the so-called Lawrence of the Caucasus. It was the third memorandum from his pen, written in a Crimean village, to which Oberlaender had brought his mixed-nations 'Bergmann' battalion in the retreat from the Caucasus. Called 'Twenty propositions on the present situation', it was sent out in fifty copies. They were intended for every Army Group and Army Commander, as well as for Keitel, Jodl, Zeitzler, Himmler and Ribbentrop. At this hour (22nd June 1943) the professor maintained that it was not yet too late to neutralize Stalin's appeal for a patriotic front, which was to make every man a Partisan. Not only could Germany acquire an army 800,000 strong but even increase it. If the current policy in the east were changed, there was a last-minute chance to win all the peoples of Europe to fight Bolshevism.

The storm was created more by Oberlaender's address-list than by the heady, unrealistic, contents of his memorandum. Zeitzler ordered Heinz Herre, as Hellmich's new Chief of Staff, to destroy all the copies he could lay hands on. He regarded it as an attempt to undermine the hazy ruling he had received from Hitler on the 8th of the month. Keitel issued an order that Oberlaender should be relieved of the 'Bergmann' command and Himmler wrote to Hellmich that Oberlaender must be delivered to a concentration camp. This, as Himmler knew, was beyond his competence. Oberlaender was neither court-martialled nor cashiered.[72] The Wehrmacht protected him and he spent the rest of the war on the inactive reserve as a civilian. Today, Oberlaender is the Minister for Refugee Affairs in the Bonn government.

Hitler had suggested on 8th June that he might repeat his views on propaganda and collaboration to some of his top commanders. Possibly Keitel used the Oberlaender memorandum as a reminder, for Hitler kept his word. The surviving fragment of the long monologue, which he delivered on 1st July 1943, seems, however, to possess even less force than the earlier pronouncement. Hitler now used a new argument. If his soldiers were told that they were fighting not for conquest but in order to liberate Russians, why should they fight at all? As a simple soldier in the First World War, Hitler had believed, as his comrades had believed, that the soil of the Flanders battlefields would never be handed back to Belgium. That was the simple psychology of the soldier. Of course it was easy to say 'We shall create a completely independent Ukraine'. He could say that and not do it. But how to explain to the fighting man that all this was pure tactics? It just was not possible.[73]

CHAPTER ELEVEN

'A PHANTOM OF THE FIRST ORDER'

(a) The Eastern Troops sent West

WITH THE FIASCO of the last German offensive in the east which Hitler launched on 5th July 1943, the danger to the *Ostpolitiker* was not merely the loss of Vlasov and the Dabendorf propagandists. It was the loss of their troops as well. According to a recollection of Albert Speer, Hitler repeated his warning that the volunteers might be sent to the coalmines. This was at another *Lagebesprechung* on 8th July.[1] Hitler would deport from 150,000 to 200,000 Russian civilians to the German and French mining areas, if OKW failed to release that number of volunteers. With the failure of the offensive Hitler's language grew more threatening. At a meeting of the Central Planning Board in September, Speer reported that Hitler wanted to dissolve the eastern volunteers altogether, because the Army Groups seemed to him to be carrying a 'lot of ballast'. Speer understood that he was to meet Keitel and Zeitzler in order to determine the numbers that could be released.[2]

In the months of July and August the fate of the volunteers had hung precisely on their behaviour in the conditions of general retreat, which had begun to spread from the Central Army Group front to the Ukraine. North of the great Russian armoured drive to Kiev and the Dnieper, the exposed lateral railways had to be protected from Partisans who could count on a speedy link-up with the main Red Army. Very largely this duty fell on the guard battalions of ROA, some of which dated back to 1941 and the first plans of Tresckow and Schenckendorff. All the hopes of the *Ostpolitiker* were staked on these White Russian and Great Russian volunteers. But the patient work of the Dabendorf propagandists and the humane reforms of the *Osttruppen* office were alike nullified by the approach of the Red Army and Stalin's commissars. Moreover the dynamic personalities, who had created the volunteer units, were no longer on the spot. Early in the summer, Schenckendorff suffered a collapse, from which he did not recover, Tresckow went on sick leave between May and September while Kluge was injured on 12th October in a car smash which put him out of action for nine months.

On 17th August a security battalion of Russians, well provided with German weapons, seized a vital railway station and handed it over to the Partisans. In September there were several similar cases.[3] On the 14th of that month Himmler slipped in his word at the *Lagebesprechung*, which followed the fall of Briansk. He declared that, against Hitler's order, ROA units had been sent to the front. They had deserted and here was the result. This was not confirmed by Keitel who observed that, though there had been a report of the desertion of a volunteer unit, the Army Commander had not connected this with the breach in the front. But Hitler would listen no more. He would 'root out the plague spot'. The disarming of the ROA units must begin at once, even if force was needed. Within the next forty-eight hours Zeitzler must have the first 80,000 ready for dispatch to the French mining districts.[4]

Zeitzler passed on the orders to Hellmich abruptly and apparently without reluctance. Hellmich, appalled by the implications of a mass disarming at this critical moment, sent Herre to trace the report which had set off the explosion. Herre discovered that the troops who had gone over to the enemy consisted of no more than a Cossack company and part of a labour battalion, neither unit being fully armed or engaged in holding the line. What Himmler had heard was a hasty generalization, made by the army commander on this sector. So, primed with figures and percentages, Herre tried to stir Zeitzler. The affair of Leaflet No. 13 was a warning not to expect too much from this very professional soldier, whose bald head and round explosive face had earned him the name of 'Bullet-blitz'. Zeitzler, who had shown a genius for organizing supplies in armoured warfare in France and the Ukraine, was no lover of military politicians. But he was not a yes-man either. Though only a Major General, when called on to succeed Franz Halder in September 1942, he had quarrelled with Hitler within a few months over the decision to hold on to Stalingrad. But, away from battlefields Zeitzler was less likely to display this independence of spirit. There his inclination was to leave things to Keitel. 'So', said the 'Bullet-blitz', as Herre approached his desk, 'Subject, coalmining. Sit down but be brief.'[5]

After this unpropitious beginning Herre learnt that the danger had been exaggerated. Hitler would be content with 50,000 coalminers in all. Herre retorted that disbandment even on this scale would have terrible repercussions among loyal volunteers and workers. Zeitzler, in spite of his nick-name, was capable of listening. He agreed that Herre could have twenty-four hours in which to prepare a list of units, which could be disarmed without creating unrest. It was naturally a small list, but, though it comprised only 5,000 men, it was approved on 18th September at Hitler's next *Lagebesprechung*.

That this apparent victory should be followed by the almost complete removal of the volunteers from Russia cannot have been the surprise and disillusionment which Thorwald has described. Within a very few days, the Wehrmacht was in retreat on a front exceeding a thousand miles. Even among the political romantics, who believed that a crusade was still possible, some must have hesitated to expose 600,000 volunteers and their families to the fate that awaited Soviet traitors. In July Kluge had told Hitler that he could rely on 'the famous' Kaminsky' to burn the harvest and drive back the cattle before the Red Army. Yet by the end of September even the arch-collaborator had to deal with mutiny among his men. With difficulty the 'Kaminsky government' was moved back from Lokot to Lepel and this small remnant of the original volunteers was allowed to remain on occupied Russian territory.[6]

On 10th October 1943 Hitler issued the general orders for the removal of the volunteers from the eastern theatre of war.[7] Zeitzler did not conceal from Heinz Herre his relief that the *Osttruppen* problem had been shifted on to the shoulders of Alfred Jodl, a rival Chief of the General Staff. Zeitzler observed that Hellmich's office ought to find it a relief too, now that so many complaints were coming in. He was, moreover, confident that the gaps could be filled by the transfer of rear area troops from other fronts.[8] But Jodl, who found himself saddled with the operation, felt less light-hearted about it. If all these men, 600,000, perhaps 800,000, when all the local militia forces were included, were to be kept under arms, their loyalty could not just be taken for granted even if they were to be sent to places where there were no Russian forces to desert to. On 20th October Jodl demanded that 'Wehrmacht Propaganda IV' should obtain an open letter from Vlasov, explaining the purpose of the transfer of the volunteers to the west. Hitherto, Jodl had shown no signs of supporting Vlasov and one may surmise that he was trying to test how much influence over the volunteers Vlasov really possessed. Naturally Vlasov's reactions to the first news had been very violent. He made several demands to be re-interned and even von Grote reported that the efforts of Strik-Strikfeldt to win Vlasov over had failed.[9] As usual, Vlasov's policy was made for him over his head. An open letter was composed by Grote and Duerksen and published on 17th November in the Dabendorf Russian newspaper *Dobrovolets*. It promised the volunteers that their stay on the western front would be no more than a training and refreshing measure, that they were to return to the eastern front and fight for the recovery of their homeland.[10]

Jodl was to regret it. The printed sheets of the letter were hand-distributed by trained emissaries from Dabendorf. These alleged propagandists for the German cause spoke so freely that some of them had to be arrested by the Security Service on the 'Atlantic Wall'. Jodl quickly shifted his ground and forbade Vlasov to visit the western front in person. He denounced the Dabendorf school as a nest of enemies, perhaps with good reason, since members of the NTS Party, such as Kazantsev, had been talking of the advantage of being close to the Western Allies, with whom contact could be established when the continent was invaded.[11]

Thus Thorwald's narrative, but one may seriously doubt whether Jodl believed in the efficacy of the Vlasov letter. The hard-boiled cynic, who alone of the Nuremberg defendants retained his sense of humour in the dock, must have known better. As early as 7th November 1943, he revealed what he thought in a very long lecture, which he gave at Hitler's instance to an assembly of Gauleiters in Munich. It was a comprehensive review of the situation at the beginning of the fifth year of the war. Jodl described how a 'neurosis' had been created by the slogan 'Russia can only be beaten by Russians'. Such ideas had been encouraged at a time when victories were more or less continuous and as a result 160 battalions of eastern volunteers had been created. Now he was glad to say, there were only 100 and most of these were in the west.[12]

Nevertheless it was not thought necessary to disperse the fully mustered Pannwitz and Niedermeyer divisions. It was considered safe to keep them as entities on secondary fronts, since they were outside Russian territory at the time of Hitler's decision. Von Pannwitz's 1st Cossack division had actually been dispatched from Mlawa to Yugoslavia at the end of September.[13] There it grew into a corps, waging a sort of private war with Tito's Partisans of which Hitler could not complain, for no punches were pulled on either side in this combat between Slav and Slav. As to Niedermeyer's Turcoman division, the

162nd, it was allowed to proceed intact from Neuhammer to the Italian front. The division did not live up to the hopes voiced by Zeitzler on 8th June 1943.* Oskar von Niedermeyer was an unfortunate choice. He had gained a very spurious reputation as 'the German Lawrence' in the First World War through a ridiculous mission to Afghanistan.[14] His subsequent career was that of a political soldier, director of a secret arms purchasing commission in Russia and of an institute of military geography in Berlin. His career as a divisional commander ended soon after his arrival in Italy with his removal for insubordination, an experience which he was to repeat. However, under the first inspector of the National Legions, Ralph von Heygendorff, the very mixed division was restored to discipline and in the summer of 1944 it was in action at Bolsena, where the men of Central Asia in German uniform were said to have fought a Japanese regiment in American uniform. All this for a custom house in Danzig, like the Red Indians who tomahawked each other because Frederick the Great had entered Silesia.[15]

After the departure of the Cossacks a transit camp was set up at Mlawa in annexed Poland for the volunteers from Russia on their way to the west. By the middle of November hordes of soldiers, bringing with them numerous dependants, poured into Mlawa and no posting orders were issued to relieve the chaos till 12th December. It took five months for some seventy-two battalions to reach their positions on the west coast. In the meantime a third complete volunteer division was created from the Caucasian and Tartar legions for service in the south of France. With this exception, the volunteers in the west, among whom the Caucasians and Cossacks were still a majority, were kept in separated battalions, which were attached singly to German regiments. This precaution of Keitel's turned out to be no precaution. When the Russians realized the hopelessness of their position, the proximity of German units increased their capacity for mischief. A volunteer battalion at the mouth of the Somme, when told to lay a barbed-wire zone, stole the wire from the nearest German unit and shot at the men who tried to get it back.** Near Dax, Ulrich von Hassell met a veteran Baltic-German major, whose command included not only Cossacks but 'Free Indians'. He had served nineteen years in the old Russian Imperial Army. Before leaving the eastern front, many of his men had deserted to the Red Army, but some of them still sent him letters

---

* See p. 338
** Letter to the author from Ernest Pfau, Stuttgart.

through secret channels declaring that they were getting along famously.[16]

In this chaos, the old promoters of the liberation army plan struggled to preserve some shreds of an over-all purpose. At the end of the year 1943, Heinz Hellmich got his way at long last and was given the command of a German division. He was killed later in the defence of Cherbourg. A dynamic personality who could give the scattered phantoms of ROA some *ésprit de corps* was not to be discovered, though Stauffenberg concentrated on the problem. The terrible explosion had wrecked him neither morally nor physically, though he had lost an eye and a hand. He was now the deputy of General Olbricht, who dealt with the posting of officers from the Army Personnel Office in Berlin. In the end, Stauffenberg chose a pronounced Russophil, but certainly no Vlasovite. The 'wise Marabu', Ernst Koestring, was approaching seventy years of age and very quietly employed as inspector of Turki units with a desk in the Jaegerhohe Hotel near Mauerwald.[17] Stauffenberg could hardly have expected this old gentleman to be perpetually wandering up and down between the Pyrenees and the Texel, between Perpignan and Ventimiglia. It seems almost to have been a counsel of despair. Koestring himself told Heinz Herre that he had agreed to accept the post in order to oblige Keitel.

Once more there was a change in the status of the volunteers. Officially the appellation of ROA was not recognized, but at least they were now designated as volunteers and not as *Osttruppen*. At the beginning of 1944 the last traces of the *Untermensch* distinction disappeared. The volunteers could consort with whom they liked and marry whom they liked. If this was the work of Stauffenberg, it is to be remarked that he had not opposed their removal from Russia. The fact that Stauffenberg worked hard to protect the offices of Gehlen and Martin and that he strove to preserve some centralized control over the volunteers, has been interpreted in several ways. According to Mr Allen Dulles, an emissary of Stauffenberg's resistance circle, Adam Trott zu Solz, was sent to Switzerland about April 1944 to warn the Allies. In the event of their not recognizing an anti-Hitler government, Stauffenberg would use the Russian workers and volunteers in order to make common cause with Stalin.[18] That Stauffenberg was capable of a deal with Stalin was believed also by Hans Gisevius, who had a single brief conversation with him two months later.[19] Carl Michel, a more friendly witness who knew Stauffenberg very well, describes a nebulous plan by which the mass of Germans should combine with the four or five million Soviet subjects in Germany to keep the balance against *both Hitler and Stalin*. In December 1943, therefore, Stauffenberg wanted to keep as many Russian volunteers as possible in German training centres, which would become 'free market places' where Germans and Russians could make friends.[20] A singularly vain hope, for in 1945 when these 'Free market places' were actually occupied by Vlasov's troops, the very reverse occurred.

The balance of probability suggests that Stauffenberg kept his sympathy for the Soviet deserters, which dated from his experiences as a field commander in Russia, in 1941, in a separate compartment from his plans to overthrow Hitler. It is of course true that four members of Stauffenberg's conspiracy, who lost their lives after July 1944, had also been actively occupied with the plans for the deserters. They were Henning von Tresckow, von Roenne, Eduard Wagner and Freytag-Loringhoven. But it was no unnatural thing that liberalism towards the Russians should go with opposition to Hitler. It is incredible that Vlasov should have been considered as an agent in the plot. On 20th July 1944, the only high personality, who showed any interest in Vlasov as the commander of a Russian Army, was Himmler.

The fact is that at the time of the Allied invasion of Normandy the position of Vlasov and his supporters was even worse than it had been a year earlier, when Vlasov's visit to Russia had been denounced by Keitel. Vlasov could give no orders to the so-called ROA on the western front, though, from the start of the invasion, Allied commentators called them Vlasov soldiers. This mistake arose from the use of Vlasov's name in captured propaganda for the volunteers, some of it actually signed by Vlasov but most of it fabricated by 'Wehrmacht Propaganda IV'. Vlasov had not returned to a prisoner camp, as he had threatened to do in October 1943, but he was no longer allowed to travel and his residence was closely watched. When von Pannwitz's 1st Cossack division left Mlawa for the Balkan front, it was not Vlasov who was allowed to address them but the old White Guardist general, Piotr Krasnov.[21]

After 'D day', Vlasov could only watch impotently the destruction of the trained volunteer battalions. Yet amid their general failure and occasional disasters it was the battalions of White Russian or Great Russian structure which came out best, in particular two battalions under Colonel Buniachenko, a Vlasov man. This rough Ukrainian peasant had commanded a Red Army division in Vladivostok and had served on Marshal Timoshenko's staff. He was recalled to Berlin from

Normandy on 12th August and his reports did something at this critical moment to promote the Vlasovite cause.[22] By contrast, a considerable portion of the Caucasian and Asiatic volunteers mutinied or deserted. The greater part of the 'Stammdivision', which had been created from the National Legions, had to be disarmed during the retreat from the south of France to Belfort.[23] Koestring had to send out a field commander to rally together the scattered retreating units. Unhappily he chose his stormy protégé, Oskar von Niedermeyer, who had been in trouble already. With his Moscow background, Niedermeyer had little use for Caucasian or Asiatic troops. His reports became increasingly defeatist till finally he recommended complete disbandment. But at this moment Niedermeyer was arrested for some particularly gross insubordination and confined in the officers' remand prison at Torgau. Niedermeyer was never tried, but, after his liberation by the Russians, he made the further error of putting his experience at the service of the conquerors and as a result he has disappeared.[24]

After the Falaise encirclement and the abandonment of France and most of Belgium by the Germans, the remnants of the Russian volunteers in the west were put to work digging trenches on the German border. More than 30,000 had been captured by the Allies, perhaps a low proportion in relation to the total numbers. This was partly due to an accident. The Allied propagandists, who addressed the former Red Army men by wireless and loud speaker, assumed that their audience had been forced to serve with the Germans and that their country loved them still. Proudly they offered the deserters a speedy repatriation to Mother Russia.* On 24th June, Niedermeyer's Chief of Staff, Colonel Hansen, reported that some of the captured volunteers, who had been persuaded to work for the British and Americans, were covering up this mistake by broadcasting the news that volunteers who surrendered to the Allies would be sent to Canada.[25] In fact the Russian government successfully demanded their repatriation, which took place via Hull and Murmansk.

Hitler, as we now know, was not in the least interested in what happened to the volunteers. But after 20th July 1944, Himmler became Commander-in-Chief of the Reserve or Home Army and, as such, responsible for making up the losses in manpower at the fronts. The peculiar tragedy of the captured volunteers, who were surrendered to Russia, must have shown even Himmler that the volunteers had now nothing to gain by surrendering on any front whatsoever. The

* See p. 395

prospect of the unified deserters' command and the bogus Russian Liberation Army had at last something to commend it.

On 10th July, Vlasov's deputy Malyshkin was allowed to visit Niedermeyer's headquarters, where he found chaos and bewilderment. If Vlasov could learn nothing of the fate of the volunteers, neither could Koestring get any information. During the following weeks, while the volunteers made their way back to the western German border, Vlasov was virtually kept as Himmler's prisoner. But Vlasov was waiting not trial but promotion. The extraordinary truth is that Himmler, the exponent of the *Untermensch* theory, was about to create the Russian Liberation Army.

(b) Himmler and Vlasov

THROUGHOUT 1943 THE *Ostpolitiker* had one irreconcilable enemy—Himmler. On 17th April he had denounced Vlasov's Gatchina speech. On 14th September he had accused the volunteer units of causing a Russian break-through. If we are to credit Peter Kleist, on 17th August Himmler flew to the *Wolffsschanze* solely to inform Hitler that Ribbentrop had given Vlasov some support.[26] Presumably this was the occasion of Malyshkin's visit to Paris. It seems that Vlasov's deputy had spoken before an audience of Tsarist emigrés on the old theme of an integral and independent Russia—and the Gestapo had reported. But from the Salle Wagram to the Kiebitzweg villa Malyshkin was allowed to journey in peace. The blow did not fall, because even in the Gestapo and Security Service there were dissensions on *Ostpolitik*. Himmler's complaint to Hitler had no special sequel.[27]

Himmler, however, could not resist showing his delight at Hitler's decision to disperse the volunteers. He made two allusions to Vlasov; at Posen on 4th October before his police leaders and at Bad Schachen near the Swiss border on 14th October before a number of high army officers.[28] Himmler seems to have read from a prepared text, for many passages in the two speeches are identical. This very literal translation of part of the Bad Schachen speech will convey some idea of Himmler's verbose, lumbering, undistinguished style of oratory.

> I must here mention quite openly the name of Herr General Wlassow. Great hopes were based on this general Wlassow. The hopes were not so well grounded as many people supposed. I think we have been misled here by a false estimate of the Slavs.

Any Slav, any Russian general will start chattering in a yarn-spinning style, suitable for us Germans, when we get him to speak —if we appeal sufficiently to his vanity. . . .

So Herr Wlassow has made propaganda even in Germany— and this has so utterly astonished me—and he has, as I must now tell you, lectured us Germans many times in an utterly grotesque manner. And herein I see the greatest scandal. For the outer world we can make propaganda and apply whatsoever means we like . . . every means that exploits these savage peoples and brings it about that a Russian dies in place of a German is right. That is right before God and man and can be admitted. Here, however, something has happened that we did not want. Herr Wlassow has begun to hold forth with the overweening pride that is common to the Russian and the Slav. He has declared that Germany cannot conquer Russia. Russia can only be conquered by Russians. Observe, gentlemen, that this sentence is mortally dangerous. . . .

The morning, midday and evening prayer of the German Army ought to be this. We have overcome the enemy, we, the German infantry have overcome every enemy in the world. If then some Russian comes along, some deserter who was perhaps, the day before yesterday a butcher's boy and yesterday a general, created by Stalin, who now delivers lectures with the insolence of the Slav and inserts a sentence that Russia will only be conquered by Russians; if then all this occurs, I must tell you something. The man shows what sort of a swine he is by this sentence alone.*

Some of this, it may be said, was the mixture as before, the mixture as it was in the days of the 'Barbarossa' plan, for Himmler concluded both speeches with his usual phantasy of a German Reich, increased to 120 million Germanic inhabitants and with a frontier pushed at least 300 miles to the east. The language was far more intemperate than Hitler's in his two pronouncements on Vlasov, which he had made on 8th June and 1st July. Himmler had failed to keep abreast of the times, but in one respect he was ahead of them. His 120 million Germanic inhabitants were to be obtained by Germanizing suitable racial types. Although the Russians were a 'savage people', the retreating Wehrmacht were encouraged in Himmler's speech to bring back with them

* In the earlier speech, made at Posen, Himmler stated quite incorrectly that Vlasov had made public statements in Paris, Brussels and Berlin. In fact the only places where Vlasov had been permitted to speak in public were in the Military Rear Areas behind the Eastern front.

suitable children. It was a sign that among the SS élite the standard-
bearers of racialism were wavering. The Slav was no longer a sub-
human. He was human enough to be permitted the privilege of dying
in battle in place of a German.

Zeitzler had not mentioned to Hitler on 8th June, when he tried to
minimize the volunteer movement, that Himmler was training a
division of Ukrainians. As a matter of fact, Hitler was none the wiser
at the end of the war.[29] The fact was that, at the time of the Posen and
Bad Schachen speeches, several groups in the SS were trying to pick up
the threads which the Stauffenberg-Gehlen-von Roenne-group had let
drop. Within the incoherent overgrown structure of the SS, these groups
were striking out on their own against the policy of *Untermensch*.

Roughly the wartime SS organization could be divided into four
main heads. There was the Security Office, RSHA, which included
besides the Gestapo, the Criminal Police and Security Police and the
intelligence services of the SS, civilian and military. There was the SS
Leadership head office, SSFHA, which included the administrative
staff of the field divisions of the fighting SS and numerous expert
advisory bodies or *Leitstelle*. Then there was the office for the
strengthening of German nationhood (RKFDV) which included the
population resettlement agencies, VOMI and RUSHA and a number
of lunatic fringe agencies such as the *Lebensborn* and *Ahnenerbe* which
were devoted to racial purity. With a fourth main group, the WVHA
or economic administration of the SS (including concentration camps)
we are not concerned, but in all the first three main groups the same
shift of policy was taking place at the time of Himmler's two speeches.
The Pan-European anti-Bolshevik crusade was replacing pure naked
pan-Teutonism. In October 1943, there were already SS divisions of
Albanians and Bosnians, while new divisions were being recruited from
Estonians, Latvians and Ukrainians from Galicia.

In the RSHA organization Walter Schellenberg of Group VI had
recruited Russian special service units since 1941, while Ohlendorf of
Group III, the information service, had recruited Tartars during his
tour of duty as an extermination unit commander. At the head of
RSHA was Ernst Kaltenbrunner, by his very nature an exponent of
the *Untermensch* philosophy but not above using Russian collaborators
if they brought him power. At the High Leadership Office, SSFHA,
the key personality was, as we have already seen, Gottlob Berger, the
former village schoolmaster and gymnastics instructor.* Of all the SS

* See pp. 216–17

H.B.S.—M

leaders, Berger was the most valuable convert to the new outlook. Not a man of parts and really rather stupid and blustering, in spite of his ambitions and his incessant petty intrigues, Berger not only controlled the administration of the SS field divisions but, at the time of the Bad Schachen speech, he ran Rosenberg's *Hauptabteilung Politik* and he was reputed to have become the keeper of Himmler's conscience.

Berger had taken over the strongly separatist views of the *Hauptabteilung Politik* and he never abandoned them, even when the policy of the SS was supposed to be pro-Vlasov. He was, as has already been noticed, a not very pronounced Slav hater but he had approved the publication of the monstrous *Untermensch* brochure by the SS *Schulungsamt*, when he could have prevented it, and he had conducted a lively defence of the excesses of the notorious Dierlewanger regiment in Poland.[30] While Berger was a real enthusiast in the cause of the greater Teutonic sphere, his Russian interests were dictated by the purest opportunism. The very peculiar nature of Partisan warfare, as it had begun to develop in the first winter of the war, when White Russians and Ukrainians were found to be conducting a sort of civil war among themselves, had led Berger into the contradictions of a Slav SS. The Ukrainian police units, which had been created by Otto Waechter and Vladimir Kubiowych to fight the Polish Partisans in the Galician Carpathians, had been built up into an ill-equipped SS infantry division at the time of the Bad Schachen speech. It was also intended to make SS divisions out of Kaminsky's private army and other White Russian collaborationist bands. In Estonia and Latvia, where the population were prepared to resist a second entry of the Red Army with arms, it was Berger who persuaded Himmler to give them the arms, when Keitel and Jodl failed to concern themselves.

With Berger's easy acceptance of hard facts, theory was made to keep pace in the ideological departments of the SS. In 1940 it had been all Teutonism—a Teutonism that could be stretched to include Flemings and Burgundians as well as Danes and Norsemen. This was the period of the *Germanische Leitstelle* of the Swiss physician, Fritz Riedweg, a hot-air factory which got Himmler into great difficulties when it was a matter of post-war promises for collaborating Germanics. In October 1943, however, the dominant voice in the SS was the *Europaische Mittelstelle* of Colonel Sparmann, a collection of former Youth Movement enthusiasts who wanted to exclude no nation in Europe from the anti-Bolshevik crusade, provided that the Jews and Gypsies were killed off as usual. At the end of May 1944, the Sparmann group established another *Leitstelle* which was to be concerned with the peoples of the Soviet Union. The emphasis was to be on the Ukrainians, plenty of whom were still left behind the German lines in Galicia and Slovakia. The wounded SS officer whom Berger appointed, Lieutenant Fritz Arlt, had been concerned with Ukrainian groups in the newly established General Government of Poland as long ago as 1939–40, when such encouragements had to be concealed from Hitler as the signatory of the second Moscow pact.[31] The *Leitstelle Ost* of Fritz Arlt immediately became very useful to Rosenberg and Koestring but, though some approaches were made by Heinz Herre and the Vlasovites, Arlt was in conflict with them on almost all points and was destined to become a considerable nuisance.[32]

There was, however, a parallel and conflicting policy within the SS. Not long after his Bad Schachen speech Himmler ordered Ohlendorff's information service of the SD, a body famous for an objectivity which Himmler considered defeatism, to prepare a report on German policy in the event of Stalin's death. At first these political intelligencers were cautious, warning Himmler in very general terms that no benefit could be derived from Stalin's death, unless there was a change in the German attitude towards political warfare. Instead of exploding with rage, Himmler appointed a Russian expert. The choice was typical of Himmler. Woldemar von Radetzky was yet another racial German from Riga, who had been repatriated to Germany by the Russians as late as 1940. Officially an interpreter, he had in fact served as a Section Commander in an *Einsatzgruppe* and had been implicated in the extermination of the Jews of Zhitomir, for which he was sentenced at Nuremberg in 1948 to twenty years' imprisonment.[33] There is evidence that Radetzky took part in similar massacres at Kursk and Voronezh in June 1942.[34] Radetzky was nevertheless pardoned and liberated by the Americans in 1951. Such a record was inconsistent neither with American pardons nor with enthusiasm for Vlasov. Thus, in the first months of 1944 Radetzky and his SD comrade, Colonel Ehlich, continuously recommended Vlasov to Himmler.[35]

Here then we have two SS groups working on Himmler, Berger and Arlt in the direction of separate national committees, while Kaltenbrunner, Radetzky and Ehlich worked for Vlasov. Now there came a third group. On 27th April 1944, there fell into Himmler's hands the copy of a report, which had been prepared in the Wehrmacht Propaganda Department by von Grote and Duerksen. It showed that, in spite of all the delays and the pruning-down, the famous 'leaflet 13' had met with some success. In the summer of 1943 it was said to have brought in 13,000 Soviet deserters. But after that the numbers had been pitiful. In the first three months of 1944 there had been only 2,200 deserters. No realistic person could have expected anything better at a time when the Red Army had recovered the pre-1939 borders of the Soviet Union with every prospect of invading Germany a few months hence. But it pleased Himmler mightily to think that he could succeed where Wehrmacht propaganda officers had failed. The fighting SS had its own propaganda section, the battalion 'Kurt Eggers' which contained not only war-reporters but also ideological lecturers who were sent to the field units. Naturally the propaganda was now pan-European. The 'hordes of Asia', of whom there had once been mention in the orders of the day of Reichenau, Manstein and von Kuechler, were no longer even a figure of speech. Himmler wanted a new drive for Red Army deserters and these were the men to speak across the battle-front.

At the head of the Kurt Eggers Battalion was Colonel Gunter d'Alquen. He was thirty-four years of age and had been the editor of the SS Journal, *Das Schwarze Korps*, a cross between a school magazine and an unusually yellow Sunday paper. He was also the author of the official handbook, *Der SS*. D'Alquen was typical of the SS men who believed that they had a mission. The son of a well-to-do Essen merchant, he had been involved since his schooldays in the brawlings of the SA and had grown up, dedicated to the cause of golden youth; youth with a knuckle-duster and not too much independence of thought. For ten years he had been very close to Himmler, who needed competent scribblers as much as police chiefs, but discovered them less easily. According to Thorwald, d'Alquen claims that he first interested Himmler in propaganda for the Russians during a visit to the Arctic front in September 1943. As a consequence, he was permitted two months later to practice on the Leningrad front in the SS Corps area of Lieutenant General Felix Steiner, an earlier apostle of the pan-European crusade. D'Alquen became convinced of the importance of the Vlasov movement, but Himmler, who had been reluctant and suspicious from the beginning, sent him off to Italy in March 1944, to direct his radio propaganda towards the Polish Corps in the British 8th Army.

But about this time d'Alquen came in contact with Grote and Duerksen, whose report he forwarded to Himmler at the end of April. Himmler now recalled d'Alquen for a new propaganda drive on the

Russian front, the so-called 'Exercise Scorpion'. At last d'Alquen was to be allowed to name the Russian liberation movement and to make any promises he liked, so long as the name of Vlasov, the 'impudent butcher's boy' of the Bad Schachen speech, was left out of it. He was to proceed to Field Marshal Model's headquarters near Lwow, taking with him a hand-picked Russian general. D'Alquen chose Zhilenkov, the most opportunist and ambitious of the Vlasov circle, together with the enigmatic Zykov, who was now the editor of two Dabendorf news-sheets.

D'Alquen and Zhilenkov reached Model's headquarters on 26th June but without Zykov. It seems that Zykov had been summoned to the telephone in a shop next door to his suburban flat in Ransdorf, where two unknown civilians had spirited him away in a military motor-car towards Berlin. Thereafter he was seen no more. Those who have written about the Vlasov circle, Thorwald, Dwinger, Fischer and Dallin have competed in theories to explain this sinister event without finding anything wholly satisfactory. If at the last moment Himmler decided against employing an ex-political commissar and suspected Jew, there was no reason why Zykov should not have been re-interned without creating so much unnecessary suspicion and unrest among the Soviet collaborationists. Zykov must therefore have been accused of something which embarrassed too many parties for any kind of official inquiry or exposure to be feasible.

Himmler must at first have been ignorant of these accusations, since there actually exists a note from Himmler to d'Alquen, approving the employment of Zykov under the date, 14th June.[36] Both Thorwald and Dallin consider that Zykov was the victim of a feud inside the SS and here the murderous jealousy of Ernst Kaltenbrunner seems to fit in very well. But Berlin, which had become an underground troglodyte city, also abounded with agents of the Soviet NKVD and *Rasviedupr*, remnants of the famous *Rote Kapelle* network, who would have equal cause to murder the renegade 'Old Bolshevik' Zykov. It must also be considered that in this very month the Gestapo made quite a round-up of NTS leaders, including Baidalakov.[37] Many of the NTS people, Kazantsev in particular, favoured an approach to the Allies. Dwinger, who accompanied Malyshkin to Paris in the summer of 1943, together with Zykov, declares that Zykov interviewed a British agent.[38] This is not a reliable source, because Dwinger also invented a fictional visit of Vlasov himself, but the action is at least in keeping with Zykov's reputation. Whatever the truth, history has lost the one man who could perhaps have explained the mystery of Vlasov's behaviour in the Volkhov Kessel in June 1942.

In spite of this sinister beginning, d'Alquen claimed that the use of Zhilenkov's name on the Galician front had been effective beyond all expectation. In some eighteen days 4,500 Russian deserters crossed the lines. On the strength of these figures, d'Alquen tried to persuade Zhilenkov to take Vlasov's place as leader of the Soviet opposition, but Zhilenkov refused.[39] D'Alquen reported this to Himmler as a sign of the magic that Vlasov's name could still exercise over his leaders. Zhilenkov was more probably thinking of his own position, if the Reich were to collapse immediately. On 23rd June, the great Red Army offensive had started on the central front in White Russia. Panic and despair overwhelmed the Germans on a scale that had hitherto been exceeded only by the defeat of France in 1940 and by the first Soviet defeats in 1941. And on the night of 11th July the offensive that was to overwhelm Lwow and Polish Galicia, burst on Model's south Ukraine front. With difficulty d'Alquen managed to fly to Himmler at Salzburg. Finally at Himmler's headquarters in East Prussia, three days later, d'Alquen learnt that Hitler had given permission for Himmler to negotiate personally with Vlasov.[40]

So far d'Alquen's explanation. Mr Dallin analyses Himmler's change of attitude at greater length, discovering intrigues and counter-intrigues within the SS framework that make one's head spin. It does, however, seem that Kaltenbrunner's jealousy of practically everybody influenced Himmler's final decision as much as the persuasive d'Alquen. On the one hand Berger, who supported Rosenberg and separatism, was more powerful at Himmler's court than d'Alquen; on the other hand Berger was hated by Kaltenbrunner. For the sake of weakening Berger's influence, Kaltenbrunner was ready to listen to the pro-Vlasov arguments of his intelligence chief, Walter Schellenberg, though in reality he prefered the old *Untermensch* policy. The meaning of all this was that Himmler was induced to support Vlasov, but without sufficient co-operation among his own officials to give his support much meaning.

Only eleven months elapsed between the bitter abuse of Himmler's Bad Schachen speech and his courteous reception of Vlasov on 16th September 1944, but the drama of Himmler's change of mind has been over-played. From the very beginning, Vlasov and his followers had been shuttlecocks of this and that department and now they were shuttlecocks of departments within departments, subjects of disputes within disputes, the sport of all the amateur idea-merchants of the SS, so grotesquely named the 'state within a State'. Despite the hopes of the Russophile idealists, it could never have been otherwise. In June 1941, Hitler had a policy for the peoples of the Soviet Union, 'Slay them, enslave them, deport them, exploit them'. After the great retreats he had none. Hitler refused to make any positive pronouncement and in the absence of directions each little group made its own *Ostpolitik*, which it hoped would be recognized.

Carl Michel has advanced the theory that Himmler only decided to get the Vlasov movement into his own hands after the July bomb plot had persuaded him that Russian volunteers would have been used by the plotting generals.[41] But the timetable does not agree, in fact Himmler approached Hitler as early as 14th July and he was prepared to meet Vlasov on the day before the plot. It would seem that the plot delayed Himmler's decision rather than it advanced it, since it was not till 16th September that the postponed meeting took place.

The true significance of the bomb plot in the creation of a Russian Liberation Army lies in the fact that it made Himmler the Commander-in-Chief of the Reserve Army. On the night following the plot, Fritz Fromm was dismissed from this post. Later he was executed. Within a few hours of the explosion Himmler was already in Fromm's shoes. Now Fromm's Chief of Staff had been Stauffenberg himself and in the big shiny attaché case, that contained Stauffenberg's bomb, there was also a long report on new recruiting measures to replace the enormous losses of the Central Army Group. The manpower situation was so critical that whoever commanded the Reserve Army, whether Fromm or Himmler, had to reconsider the question of the Russian volunteers.

There were at least 800,000 of them serving with the Wehrmacht, but the western front had not received more than seventy-two battalions, and on the day of the bomb plot these were mostly dis-armed and employed as labour gangs. On 16th September, when Himmler at last met Vlasov, only a few battalions of eastern volunteers served in the line, apart from the two Cossack divisions fighting Tito's Partisans. Suspicion of the volunteers remained profound, for as late as November a battalion of Georgians tried to deliver Texel Island to the British.[42]

As Commander-in-Chief of the Reserve Army, Himmler could dispose of all the volunteers, but how was he to satisfy Hitler, whose suspicions and warnings had been justified ten times by the outward semblance of events? This alone accounts for Himmler's extreme caution.

Himmler cancelled his meeting with Vlasov on 19th July, preferring to keep him on ice till he could coax a straightforward decision out of Hitler. With surprising docility, Vlasov agreed to take a rest-cure at a nursing home, appointed by Himmler, a former monastery near Ruhpolding on the Bavarian Taubensee. Vlasov believed, when he left Berlin on 27th July, that it would be a matter of three weeks before Himmler resumed the interview. In fact there were seven weeks of doubt and despair. Erich Dwinger claims that he broke his parole at Seeg im Allgaeu in order to visit Vlasov in his monastery; that he found him in the depths of depression, demanding to be sent back to a prisoner camp and that he helped Vlasov draft an appeal to Guderian, the new Chief of Staff and successor to Zeitzler.[43] What is more certain is that Vlasov consoled himself with a love affair with the matron of the nursing home and that at the very end of the war he went through a form of marriage with her, assuming rightly or wrongly that his former wife had been executed as a hostage when the news of his treachery had reached Russia. Vlasov's second marriage provides not the least mystifying aspect of his career. Heidi Bielenberg was a lady who frequented SS circles. She had run her nursing home for the SS and she was a friend of the hero of Narva, the SS general, Felix Steiner. Yet she married an *Untermensch*.[44]

The meeting of 16th September 1944, took place in East Prussia in a room at 'Birkenwald', Himmler's headquarters on the Mauersee. Nearby was Angerburg, where three years ago Hitler had announced the destiny of occupied Russia. Hitler's own headquarters, the *Wolffs-schanze*, was twenty-five miles away and forty miles away was the Red Army. Vlasov was allowed to take with him Strik-Strikfeldt and Colonel Sakharov, an old Tsarist officer and former commander of the *Osintorf* Battalion;* but Strik-Strikfeldt was forbidden to take part in the conference, an intimation that the ball had now passed out of the hands of the Wehrmacht Propaganda Section. It was a prelude to Strikfeldt's official separation from Vlasov two months later. On Himmler's side the supporters were Gottlob Berger and Gunter d'Alquen. There was also the interpreter, a Baltic German called Dr Kroeger. He was a Security Service man, whom Kaltenbrunner had posted permanently in Arlt's office in order to find out what Berger was up to. Finally Ohlendorff's information service was represented by Colonel Ehlich.

The conversation lasted for six hours and included a luncheon. Both

* See p. 325

parties spoke with a most scrupulous politeness, calling each other
Herr Minister and Herr General. Himmler began very handsomely
indeed by apologizing for all the recent delays and obstacles and for
all the mistakes that had been made in the past. Vlasov in turn compli-
mented Himmler by calling that essence of mediocrity the strongest
man in Germany; but he spoilt the compliment by saying what a good
thing it was that the strongest man in Germany could talk with the
first Russian general to defeat a German Army. Such were the lengths
to which Vlasov went in order to avoid the part of a suppliant. He
demanded maliciously to know Himmler's opinion of his own book,
'*Der Untermensch*, that has impressed me so deeply'. Vlasov perhaps
did not realize what an art evasion had become among Nazi officials
till, blinking across his pince-nez, Himmler replied.[45]

> There are sub-humans in every nation. The difference between
> ourselves and your home-land is only that there the sub-humans
> possess the power, while here in Germany I have got them under
> lock and key. In the end your assistance will achieve this reversal
> of position in Russia too.

At this point Himmler put the direct question whether Vlasov had
any reason to believe that the Russian people would trust him. Vlasov
replied with a long criticism of the Germans, accusing them of falsely
estimating the Russian people. Stalin, he declared, had not believed that
the Germans would be so foolish as to conduct a war 'with arms alone'.
In September 1941, Stalin had told his High Command that his greatest
fear was that the Germans would adopt the Russian liberation thesis.
He had therefore proclaimed a patriotic war and had revived the
teaching of intense nationalism. Yet, in spite of Stalin's military
successes, it was not too late for Germany to do what Stalin most
feared. 'Herr Minister, I know that today I can end the war against
Stalin, if I can lead a shock army of men of my own country and
advance with them to Moscow. I could end this war by telephone,
because I would speak to my own friends fighting on the other side.'[46]
'I come not with empty hands', was Vlasov's refrain. The deliverance
of Russia from Stalinism by the Russian opposition must also be the
deliverance of Germany.

Surprisingly, d'Alquen reports that Himmler betrayed no irritation
at this rubbishy rodomontade. If any memories of Bad Schachen
surged to his brain, he suppressed them. Yet now the 'Russian
butcher's boy', who had had the impertinence to say that only Russians

could beat Russians, had gone a step further and declared that only
Russians could save Germany. With a gesture of changing the subject,
Himmler asked Vlasov for his views on the purely military side of the
situation. Vlasov thereupon criticized the pointless sacrifice of the
volunteers in the west, but he declared that he could still raise a
million soldiers from the prisoner-of-war camps and from the ranks
of the eastern workers. Himmler's reply was that of a man, who, when
asked to lend five pounds, offers half a crown. He declared that he had
Hitler's authority to make Vlasov Commander-in-Chief of an army
with the rank of Colonel General. Vlasov would have the power to
select his own officers up to the rank of colonel. On the other hand
there was a shortage of weapons and the eastern workers could not be
spared from German arms production. For the moment Himmler
could offer Vlasov no more than two divisions, formed from serving
volunteers.

Vlasov blinked this off. Bargain meant counter-bargain. He would
be content to start with even that, but the remnants of the various
national legions must be scraped together, the meddlesome national
committees and their sponsors must be made harmless. Self-government questions must be left till after victory. It might be that the
Ukraine and the Caucasus would then seek self-government within
the framework of the new European order, for which Himmler's
European SS had fought. It might be, but Stalin must be beaten first.
Vlasov proposed the immediate formation of a single national committee on a federalist basis. This would have disciplinary power over
all former Soviet subjects in the Reich, who would retain a recognized
Russian nationality.

The crux of the matter had been reached. Hitler was only interested
in foreign mercenary troops; he had not authorized Himmler to
negotiate for anything more than an insignificant Russian field command within the framework of the Wehrmacht. As to Berger, who kept
making vain signals to Himmler, he wanted no tampering with the
national committees which he had taken over from Rosenberg.
Himmler parried Vlasov's final proposal with his usual evasive skill.
He pointed out to Vlasov that personal responsibility for millions of
deported workers would not increase Vlasov's popularity among them.
Let him get on with his national committee and his army. Other
decisions could be sought from Hitler later.[47]

D'Alquen's recollection of this extraordinary conference occupies
fourteen pages of Thorwald's book and rightly so. It is the most

important of all Vlasov documents, revealing his true mind more than public speeches or manifestos, which were written for Vlasov by German and Russian propagandists. Himmler himself was enormously impressed with Vlasov, but no less suspicious than he had been before. He kept repeating to d'Alquen, 'But the man remains a Slav'.

The conference showed clearly the course events would take, the hostility of the national committees, the rage of Rosenberg, the in-difference of Himmler and behind this indifference the petty quarrels of the 'SS State', the shuffling of policy between Kaltenbrunner's court and Berger's. Although Kaltenbrunner favoured the overall leadership of Vlasov while Berger did not, it is curious that Kaltenbrunner delayed sending an announcement of the meeting to the German press. It has been suggested by Mr Alexander Dallin that Kaltenbrunner placed hopes in a so-called Russian peace mission in Stockholm, which had existed since the end of 1942. But, in September 1944, this mission had long been without signs of life. Probably it had never been any-thing but a *canard* to exercise the Western Allies. Moreover, jealousy of Ribbentrop had impelled Kaltenbrunner to oppose the Stockholm negotiation. His motive for suppressing the news of the Vlasov accord was perhaps simpler and more typical of the primitive mentality of the man. He just did not want the credit of the meeting to go to Berger.[48]

(c) The Prague Committee

HIMMLER HAD NOT got down to details at the Vlasov meeting. He had not even thought about them. It was left to Ernst Koestring, as Inspector of the *Osttruppen*, to arrange with Himmler the first of the transfers to the new Liberation Army. Koestring had to travel with Hans Herwarth from Mauerwald in East Prussia to the special train at Triberg in the Black Forest, where Himmler astonishingly exercised the function of Commander-in-Chief of the Upper Rhine Army Group, a lamentable episode in his career.[49] It became quite clear that Himmler knew little of the conflicts of the *Ostpolitiker*. He had failed to observe the results of Hitler's doctrine that there weren't any Russians, but only eastern peoples. He failed to see that this doctrine had made the Russians a tribe among Soviet tribes, possessing no hegemony. At the interview with Koestring on 2nd October 1944, Himmler is described by Thorwald as using these words.[50]

What does it mean if such and such a White Russian or Ukrainian
has his own troop, he is just the same a Russian. In other circumstances the fellow would seem to me just like some German
emigrant, who comes from Baden or Bavaria and declares that he
is no German, but a Badener or Bavarian, fighting for the freedom
of Baden or Bavaria. That's all nonsense. Only that fool Rosenberg has taught us such things. I want to know the number of *all*
these Russians.

Koestring said there were nearly a million and Himmler declared
that this was something terrifying which he had heard for the first
time. It meant two Army Groups. How many were pure Russians?
Koestring thought they accounted for nearly half the number, less
losses through the invasion of the west. Himmler made no attempt to
grapple with these new possibilities. He stuck to his first proposal,
one division to be ready by the beginning of 1945 and another to
follow. Hitler should decide the rest. Himmler was, however, prepared
to give Vlasov nominal authority over the remaining scattered volunteers without detaching them from the parent German units. Koestring
submitted this camouflage proposal to Keitel, to Jodl, to Zeitzler's
successor, Guderian. All refused to concern themselves about it.
Koestring perceived that Hitler had authorized nothing more than the
creation of the two divisions.

The news of the plan to create a Vlasov all-Russian government
travelled fast. It brought despair to the numerous official and unofficial
national committees of the minority races, vast races like the Ukrainians, White Russians and Georgians, little tribes like the Kalmucks,
Ossetes and Ingushes. As the protests arrived in Rosenberg's Political
Department, Berger began to intrigue for all the things that he had not
been allowed to mention at the Himmler-Vlasov meeting. In Galicia
Model's front had been stabilized before Cracow, so, under pretence of
maintaining contact with Ukrainian Partisan Groups behind the Red
Army front, Berger tried to create for the first time an official Ukrainian
National Committee. After forty months, the doctrine of Angerburg
and the policies of Erich Koch were to be reversed. In October, in the
face of tough opposition from Kaltenbrunner and his creature, 'Gestapo'
Mueller, Berger obtained the release of the Ukrainian nationalists in
Sachsenhausen concentration camp, among them Melnyk and Bandera.
The purpose was to supersede the pro-Vlasov Ukrainian committee
with a working union between OUN-M and OUN-B. The two

factions had not been a very harmonious party even behind the wires, but they could at least agree on a flat refusal to work with Vlasov.

Thus for a time there were two Ukrainian National Committees, opposing each other. The 500 members of the travelling circus, which Vlasov was to address in Prague on 14th November, included a pro-Vlasov Ukrainian delegation, among them members of the hand-picked city council of Kiev who had survived the rule of Erich Koch. But the remnants of the SS Galician Division and its political sponsors would have nothing to do with these Russianized people. Through the offices of Fritz Arlt and the *Leitstelle Ukraine* of Colonel Ludwig Wolff there was created a rival force to the Vlasov Army. These men built the Galician Division up to strength and began the creation of a still further SS Division, composed of east Ukrainians. With some difficulty a former Ukrainian general of the Polish Army was discovered.[51] Himmler, influenced by Kaltenbrunner against Berger, made a half-hearted attempt to support Vlasov and at one moment in February 1945, he attempted to reach a compromise by allowing the new general, Pavlo Shandruk, to run a Galician National Committee and division, while Vlasov took over the east Ukrainian Committee and division. Hitler, however, would have none of this and official recognition was given only to the Shandruk Committee, which was sponsored by the Rosenberg Ministry.* Vlasov had lost.

The influences at work on *Ostpolitik* had now become so inter-locked and tribal that it mattered not a scrap whether the Ukrainians were commanded by Pavlo Shandruk, who had been working as a cinema commissionaire in a little Polish town, or whether the com-mander was Vlasov. Yet there had been a time, when the Germans could have had a Ukrainian Army of several divisions, defending Ukrainian soil and marching beyond it.

In the light of the military situation in the autumn of 1944, the proposed proclamation of Vlasov as the shadow head of an anti-Stalinist State, seems today pathetically ludicrous. Yet it did not seem so to the protagonists. Rosenberg in particular, whose ministry was responsible for no territories any longer, felt more deeply wounded than if he had lost an empire. In actual fact Vlasov was to steal nothing from the Political Department, whose mosquito National Committees under the busy von Mende worked against him to the last, bolstered

---

* Dallin, p. 646. The command of the Ukrainian SS divisions was only turned over to Shandruk on 27th April 1945. The tactical leadership remained German. Armstrong, p. 184

by Arlt and his *Leitstelle Ost*. For Rosenberg, however, with his almost unique capacity for suffering, the climax was reached some six days after the Himmler-Vlasov meeting, when Lammers told him that Hitler was too busy to see him and advised him to consult 'The Reichsfuehrer SS'.[52] The result was that, on 12th October, after more than three years of the Eastern Ministry, Rosenberg sent Hitler his one and only offer of resignation. It was embedded in an exceptionally long memorandum, the often quoted Rosenberg Defence Document No. 14.

In this document Rosenberg assumed that there was some reality in the pompous farce of Himmler's recognition of Vlasov as the representative of all the peoples of Russia. He denounced the agreement as a revival of Great Russian ambitions and he enclosed the meticulous protests of every national committee from the Baltic to Turkestan. The only reply that Rosenberg ever received was a telegram from Lammers on 14th November, the morning of Vlasov's Prague conference. Rosenberg's resignation was neither accepted nor rejected. He was simply told that Hitler had entrusted his decisions on the Vlasov affair to Himmler and Ribbentrop, both of whom Rosenberg should consult.[53]

Rosenberg might have been a happier man, had he been able to see the meeting between Vlasov and the great overlord of the Main Security Office, RSHA, Ernst Kaltenbrunner. The intention was to reconcile Vlasov with the head of the Georgian National Committee, Mikhail Kedia. Under Heydrich the RSHA policy had been firmly separatist, but, now that Kaltenbrunner had become the sponsor of Vlasov, Kedia, the former protégé of Heydrich, was in downright opposition. Kaltenbrunner decided to bring Kedia and Vlasov together in a private house, because Vlasov refused to enter the hateful Gestapo Main Office. Kaltenbrunner brought his dark eminences of the Police State, Schellenberg and Ohlendorff, the intention being to intimidate Kedia, but at this awkward meeting Vlasov refused to accept any press-ganged supporters. Kaltenbrunner did not call in 'Gestapo Mueller' to arrest Kedia, for it would have been useless. The full circle of history had been completed. The most dreaded organization in Germany found itself completely nonplussed—by the *Untermensch*.[54]

Contrary to Kaltenbrunner's wish, the meeting of the Grand Committee for the Liberation of the Peoples of Russia (KONR), was held not in Potsdam but in Prague, an occupied Slav capital. The Protector of Bohemia, Karl Hermann Frank, had protested at the danger of this libertarian symbol and there is little doubt that Himmler and Kaltenbrunner shared Frank's fears.[55] Yet Vlasov was allowed his own way, both in the choice of site and in the nature of the programme to be announced. This excessive feather-bedding was less surprising than it looked. Hitler had not changed his mind since his policy statements of 8th June and 1st July 1943. Anything was permissible in pronouncements intended for 'the other side' and the antics that were to be performed in the Spanish Hall of the Hradcany Palace were for Russian consumption first and foremost. Even if there had been the least chance of victory over Russia in November 1944, Hitler would have had no use for KONR. Why should Hitler have insisted on keeping the whole structure of the useless and costly Eastern Ministry intact, if it were not for the purpose of restoring a German civil government to such territories as might be recovered? Strik-Strikfeldt, who refused to accept promotion from Captain to Colonel by entering the SS, and who was thereby forced to part with Vlasov after twenty-seven months' attachment, warned Vlasov of the true situation two days before the Prague meeting. Vlasov answered that he could not back out now and betray so many people who had staked their hopes on him. In the light of history, it would have been better for the twelfth-hour collaborators if Vlasov had abandoned them in November 1944, rather than in April 1945. But who can see present events as history will see them?[56]

The best indication of the essentially camouflaged nature of the Prague meeting and manifesto of 14th November was the absence of Hitler's ministers. Originally Himmler had intended to invite the Secretaries of State from the Ministries of Propaganda, Interior and Labour, as well as representatives of the Foreign Office and Wehrmacht. And perhaps, since the interview of 16th September, Vlasov expected the presence of Himmler. But Himmler contented himself with a congratulatory telegram and only the Foreign Office was represented. It had been intended to treat KONR as a sovereign government by sending Ribbentrop's Secretary of State, Steengracht von Moyland. This plan was abandoned and the Foreign Office was represented by two inconspicuous counsellors, both of them specialists on Russian collaboration. They were Werner Lorenz, who was really an SS man, and former head of the Resettlement Office, RUSHA, and the former Counsellor of the Moscow Embassy, Gustav Hilger, who had visited Vlasov at Vinnitsa in August 1942. An even more significant change was Kaltenbrunner's refusal to allow the delegates of the eastern workers and the prisoners of war to travel as free men. According to another Security Service official, Friedrich Buchardt, who had much to do with the back-stage arrangements, this was the work of Rosenberg. Von der Milwe of the Eastern Ministry went so far as to say that 'Rosenberg had opened Hitler's eyes'.[57]

The fact is that the pitiful tone of Rosenberg's protests to Lammers and Hitler was exaggerated. Hitler would not see him—had not seen him since November 1943—but Rosenberg knew that, if the thing could be thrashed out before Hitler, the balance of that hesitant dictator's opinion would have to come down on the side of separatism and not on the side of Vlasov. Rosenberg moreover was supported by Koestring in the Wehrmacht, by Taubert in Goebbels's Ministry, by Berger and Arlt in Himmler's own organization.[58] In that dreaded Kremlin in the Prinzalbrechtstrasse Kaltenbrunner could not ride the high horse for ever and in October he paid Rosenberg a personal visit in his evacuated office at Michelsdorff. Kaltenbrunner listened to Rosenberg's verbose warnings on revived Russian imperialism in contemptuous silence. But, after the meeting, Rosenberg was at last stimulated into risking a direct attack on Himmler. He proposed to send a memorandum to Hitler, complaining that the SS had exceeded their brief. Himmler took fright and cancelled the original invitations, whereas Rosenberg, the living emblem of colonial re-occupation, was at last allowed to send a representative to Prague in the person of the ubiquitous Braeutigam.[59]

The inaugural meeting of KONR on 14th November 1944, was a well-staged affair. A special train brought 500 delegates from Berlin, of whom forty-nine were chairmen of committees while many were eastern workers who had been dragged from labour camps by the Gestapo and provided with a suit of clothes. These submerged people, who possessed no civil rights whatever, had had forced on them a spurious committee under the chairmen, Gordenko and Janushevskaia.[60] Russian propagandist generals from Dabendorf and the Kiebitzweg were of course present in full force, as well as leading members of NTS—the same people who, quite recently, had languished in Sachsenhausen under suspicion of negotiating with the Allies. The Cossacks were represented by the generals, Balabin and Turkul, and there were numerous committees from such minority tribes as favoured federalism under Vlasov, including it was supposed the Kalmucks. But the Baltic States, White Russia and the Caucasian peoples produced no delegations.

As a document, the manifesto of KONR is interesting only as an exhibition of German camouflage. It welcomed German military help and it promised honourable peace with Germany, but, so far as policy was concerned, there was no mention of anything that savoured of Hitler or National Socialism.[61] Yet the document must have been submitted to Hitler. 'The curious thing', said Sherlock Holmes, 'was the behaviour of the dog at night time'; and Watson had replied that the dog had done nothing at night time. Had there been the remotest chance that this innocuous programme would be fulfilled by KONR even in a hundred square miles of the Soviet Union, Hitler would have stopped the manifesto. But there was no chance of fulfilment and the only purpose in giving the manifesto publicity was to persuade the anti-Communists of the world that Vlasov was not acting under compulsion. For this reason Vlasov was allowed to advocate a form of government, which in the western countries Hitler denounced as decadent, capitalistic and middle-class. Himmler had insisted on a preamble in which an attack was launched on the 'Powers of Imperialism, led by the plutocrats of England and the USA'. It did not alter the fact that Vlasov's fourteen points—that 1918 symbolism again—were a deliberate attempt to establish his democratic credentials with the Western Powers. And the dog had not barked.[62]

In the afternoon a reception in the Russian style was arranged for the delegates in the Czernin Palace. It went on well into the night. The host of this Dance of Death, Karl Frank, was destined for the hangman's noose like his principal guest. But Vlasov was lifted from his habitual gloom. He promised Herre that in the good times to come he should be military attaché in Moscow. And he sang some Cossack ballads with Ernst Koestring.* In Berlin the pantomime was repeated in the form of a reunion of round-eyed bewildered eastern workers in the flag-bedecked Europahaus near the now demolished Anhalter Railway Terminus. Russian prisoners of war were seen wandering about at large, as well as Orthodox Russian priests. On the platform Vlasov appeared with his generals. The theme was the unnatural union of Moscow with world capitalism, which hindered the natural union of Russia with Germany.[63] It was the last of the public appearances of KONR. Henceforward the quarrels of the Prague committee with the various separatist committees, its struggle to obtain arms, to assert control over its troops, finally to find a roof over its head in the

---

* Thorwald, p. 456. Dwinger, p. 319. Michel, however, denies that Koestring was there at all. He writes that Hans Herwarth, who was sent to observe for Koestring, reported that the whole thing was 'a cabaret entertainment'. Michel, pp. 253–6

fast shrinking Reich, became minor undertones of war, scarcely perceived by the harassed German public. The squalid and the tragic were thinly veiled in the patriotic junketings of the Hradcany Palace. In the real outcome, the fate of the Vlasov Army, they were not veiled at all.

CHAPTER TWELVE

FIRST AND LAST OF THE VLASOV ARMY

(a) KONR

THE UNENTHUSIASTIC TASK of creating the army of liberation was first tackled by Koestring a week before the Prague meeting. On 7th November he summoned Herre from the Italian front and gave him the duty of organizing the first Vlasov Division at the old training centre of Muensingen, west of Ulm in Wuerttemburg. There Herre prepared quarters for the first volunteer troops to be released to him by Himmler as Commander-in-Chief of the Reserve Army.

Himmler found it easiest to assign SS troops. The choice was not wide. Apart from the Galician Division, which had been mauled in action and which would not have accepted Vlasov in any case, there were only two undispersed bodies of SS volunteers from the Soviet Union, a so-called division and an independent brigade. The first was the 30th SS Division, 'Ruthenia', which had been formed by a Colonel Sigling from the White Russian anti-Partisan militia. The second available formation was none other than the private army of Bronislav Kaminsky, the former 'Tsar of Lokot', which had been incorporated in the SS in the spring of 1944.

No worse choice could have been made. The record of both formations was abominable. At Posen, on 3rd August, Himmler himself had rejoiced before a meeting of Gauleiters, because both Kaminsky's and Sigling's men had extricated themselves from the rout of the Central Army Group in new German uniforms, which they had pillaged from the stores.[1] As to Kaminsky's men, it had been intended at that time to send them to fight in Hungary, together with that equally shocking 'Independent Unit', the German convict brigade of Oskar Dierlewanger. The two brigades were fished out of eastern Poland and assembled at Neuhammer in Silesia, but the road to

Hungary was blocked by the outbreak of the Slovak rebellion. Gauleiter Bracht of Upper Silesia refused to burden the civilian rationing system with the appetites of the *Untermensch*, so here, among the lace curtains of the German Reich, Kaminsky's men resumed their ancient habit of living on the country. Hastily and discreetly Hitler dispatched both the Kaminsky and the Dierlewanger Brigades to Warsaw, where from 1st August to 3rd October the repression of the great rebellion was in the hands of von dem Bach-Zelewski, Himmler's Chief of Partisan Warfare. Slav mercenaries were notoriously never so ruthless as when fighting Slavs. Warsaw proved to be the downfall of Bronislav Kaminsky and the end of his army as a self-contained force. Smashed to rubble and terrorized though it was, Warsaw still contained riches, unknown in the Briansk forest, riches sufficient to drive Kaminsky's White Russians beyond all control.

Misconduct by SS units, a thing that had meant nothing to the High Command during the Warsaw Ghetto rebellion of 1943, was embarrassing when it took place under the eyes of front-line troops. Long after organized resistance had ceased in Warsaw, Kaminsky refused to give up looting and under Himmler's protection his men might well have continued to loot, rape and murder. But it happened that General Bor (Komorowski), the Polish rebel leader, had as a show rider been a friend of the jockey, Hermann Fegelein. As Himmler's adjutant to Hitler, Fegelein added the weight that tipped the balance against Kaminsky.* But Kaminsky avoided arrest and escaped to the Carpathians, to hide among pro-German Ukrainian Partisans south of Tarnow. Here he was ambushed and murdered by the Security Police of Colonel Bierkamp, the former expert on children's homes in the happy Caucasus. Early in November, Kaminsky's private army was entrained from Warsaw for Muensingen, unwilling to believe the official report that their leader had been murdered by Polish Partisans, fighting the Germans.[2]

To command the first Vlasov division, the 600th Division of the Wehrmacht, Hitler had designated the Ukrainian Colonel, Sergei Buniachenko, who had so distinguished himself in Normandy.** Buniachenko possessed both the cunning of the Ukrainian peasant and the ruthlessness of a Cossack mercenary leader. He had need of both, for the trains from Poland disgorged an appalling ragged regiment of the

---

* The actual circumstances have been disputed by different witnesses, including Guderian, Jodl and Bach-Zelewski. For a full discussion see Reitlinger, *The SS*, pp. 376–7
** See p. 349

armed and unarmed in every sort of uniform, the women loaded with jewellery, the officers only to be distinguished from the men by the possession of three or four wristwatches. On his arrival at Muensingen, Buniachenko gave them a quick look and drove away. By all appearances he had abandoned the task to Major Keiling, who acted as Herre's deputy. Keiling had commanded a Russian volunteer battery and he had seen the retreat of Kaminsky's private army from Lokot in September 1943, so he was not altogether unused to this sort of thing. He did his best, but two days later he was surprised when Buniachenko returned to Muensingen. Buniachenko dealt drastically with the private army; he dismissed all the Kaminsky officers and some of them he arrested.

The situation was less hopeless but still very shocking when Herre reached Muensingen from the Prague Conference. Deprived of every comfort through the indifference of German officials, civil and military, the Vlasov soldiers roamed the countryside in search of illicit liquor and Russian girls from the eastern worker camps. Reinforcements kept arriving, but not weapons, bedding, fuel or supplies. Nevertheless, by January the Sigling and Kaminsky units had been expanded through the addition of some prisoners of war to the 20,000 men requisite for a division. Herre could now proceed to Heuberg to prepare the second Vlasov division which was to be commanded by the newly-promoted Major General Zverev. It was also proposed to remove Vlasov's general staff from Dahlem to Heuberg, an operation which took nearly three weeks. The seven generals of the Kiebitzweg, who had once fitted comfortably into a single villa, had now acquired a headquarters personnel of 700. This of course was in a tradition of the Second World War, which was observed by both sides, who were still unaware that they were obeying Parkinson's Law.

At the same time the decision was taken to evacuate the KONR Government from Dahlem to Karlsbad, along with several collaborationist governments in exile who cluttered up the scanty accommodation of devastated Berlin. Even this meaningless act could not escape criticism. KONR could still attract anger and controversy in January and February 1945, though the end of the Reich seemed almost a matter of days. Rosenberg continued to denounce KONR as the kernel of a new Russian imperialism, while Himmler fussed over integrating the KONR army into the SS framework, together with his Ukrainian divisions. In the outcome, the two Vlasov divisions were not destined to receive SS badges or numbers, simply because it could be brought home even to Himmler that the SS runes were not the symbols to attract Russian recruits.[3]

Nevertheless, as an empty propaganda gesture, Hitler permitted the fiction to be announced on 28th January that the Vlasov troops were not part of the Wehrmacht, of which he was Commander-in-Chief, but under the orders of the sovereign KONR Government.[4] If Hitler was really aware that he had authorized this, he had gone back on his own decisions of June and July 1943, that no Russian general was to be in a position to use a propaganda device for his own advantage. The order was doubly disastrous. It absolved German agencies from seeing that the Vlasov divisions received their share of equipment and it absolved Buniachenko's conscience from taking the orders of German army commanders.

That Hitler knew anything about it seems unlikely from the glimpse we have of his views at the precise moment when Vlasov was declared an independent Allied commander. The *Lagebesprechung* for the evening of 27th January 1945, has survived in sixty-three printed pages.[5] Much of the two hours' discussion concerned the redrafting of discharged German officers for inferior tasks in the last desperate defence of the Reich. The idiocy and lack of trenchancy in this interminable argument, in which Hitler became involved with Goering, Burgdorf and Fegelein, has to be read to be believed. Vlasov came up early in the proceedings.[6] Hitler said gruffly that Vlasov was just nothing and he complained bitterly because the Vlasov troops were dressed like Germans. German generals did not understand these things. While the British dressed their Indian troops like natives, 'Herr Seeckt' had shown a total lack of sense of honour by selling German steel helmets to the Chinese. But Guderian wanted to know whether Buniachenko's division at Muensingen was to be brought to strength and Hitler curtly agreed. Fegelain then put in a word for his chief, Himmler, who wanted to retain both Vlasov divisions in the SS, but Hitler seemed to imply that this was not necessary, because, in spite of Goering's doubts, Vlasov would not desert. It was not the general but the men who would desert, because that was what had happened in France. Fegelein observed that, if they did so, the Russians would execute them. He had good information that the Red Army executed even Russian labourers. Fortified by this argument, Goering withdrew his opposition, as if that meant anything anyway. Six days later Vlasov was permitted to visit the much-deflated *Reichsmarschall* at Karinhall.

Later in the evening Hitler launched a similar attack on Pannwitz's Cossacks, who served in Yugoslavia, but both Guderian and Jodl assured him that these troops did *not* wear German uniform. They wore red fur caps and red breeches with silver stripes. Hitler was put in a good temper and was quite delighted when Burgdorf told him that Pannwitz reviewed his troops in this uniform, carrying a curved sword in front of him 'and looking quite mad'. After this brief burst of interest in the revival of fancy-dress soldiering, there was a difference of opinion on a more tragic matter. It was not known whether the families of the Cossacks had been overrun by the Red Army at Mlawa or whether they had been sent on to Belgrade. In fact they were at Tolmezzo in the Italian Dolomites. This ignorance concerning the volunteers persisted till the end, for at the last of all recorded Staff Conferences in March 1945, Hitler professed not to know of the existence of any Ukrainian SS Division.[8]

February 1945, saw the promotion of five of Vlasov's commanders to the German rank of Major General, as well as the mustering of the second KONR division, the 650th of the Wehrmacht, at Heuberg. The second division drew largely from volunteer units, which had been shipped back from Norway, and from newly-released prisoners of war. But the proposal to form three more KONR divisions from Pannwitz's Cossacks and from other Russian and Cossack formations in Austria and Slovenia was shelved, as Himmler had always meant it to be. At this moment there were less than 50,000 Vlasov soldiers. There were never any more, though there were 800,000 deserters in German uniform, while the prisoners of war and able-bodied male eastern workers in Germany must have numbered more than two million. For this failure there is a tendency among post-war German writers to blame only the indifference and the disorganization of the Nazi State in defeat. But the greatest of all sources of failure was the badness of the cause. The Dabendorf propagandists swarmed over the prisoner camps without success. The Vlasovite generals paid well-publicized visits, but, now that the policy of the Western Allies was known, the response was negligible. Cruel and unimaginative as it was, the Allied policy reaped dividends. If it had stopped the Russians deserting to the west, it had also stopped them bearing arms for the Germans.

As Commander-in-Chief of the reserve army, Himmler had been succeeded by Gottlob Berger, who remained hostile to all Vlasov's political pretensions. Yet, as an SS man, he had to find a remedy for the recruiting failure among the Russian prisoners. He wrote at the end of January that subversive elements among the prisoners, who resisted the recruitment of Vlasov troops, would be handed over to the SD.[9] In other words the original Commissar Order of 1941, which had never lapsed, was to be put into practice again. But the conditions, which had produced a reign of terror in the Russian camps in 1941, could not be re-created. A British officer prisoner, who had exceptional opportunities of observation at Stalag IV B at Muhlberg, writes as follows.

> The Germans always arranged for all prisoners' entertainments to be watched by their own men, and in the case of these Russian performances there were always a Vlasov captain and sergeant present. With a delightful sense of irony the Russian prisoners refused to have them in the audience and had made a little stage box of plywood at one side of the stage, which was lined with some crimson-dyed stuff simulating red velvet. The two Vlasov men used to come into the barracks with something between a pitiful swagger and a shamefaced slink and sit in the box. My friend would explain to me that a lot of double entendre was worked into the dialogue on the stage, references to mythical beings with two faces, certain people being given a lot of rope to play with, with which they would eventually hang themselves, and so on. The Vlasov men took all this with stony faces, occasionally covering up their embarrassment when the thrusts became too obvious, by lighting cigarettes, whereupon some comic character on the stage would come to the edge of the box and give a 'Bisto Kid' sniff at the smoke.[10]

But from Muensingen Major Keiling reported that Buniachenko's men, who listened to broadcasts from everywhere, were again putting their hopes in the west. It was a mystery to them that their training area had not been bombed by the British and Americans. One of Buniachenko's officers had spoken with a captured British airman at a Berlin railway station. From this Berlitz conversation he had concluded that the delivery of captured volunteers to the Soviet Union was only a temporary concession to Stalin and would cease at the end of the war. Then the Allies would be needing volunteers for the fight against Bolshevism.[11]

At the end of January the Russians crossed the Oder at Kuestrin, within forty miles of Berlin. Koestring was convinced that only a successful action at the front would stimulate the authorities into equipping the two KONR divisions. The Vlasov Army must win its spurs or sink into oblivion. On 7th February Herre was ordered to arrange the dispatch of a few anti-tank companies to the Oder front. Buniachenko resisted strongly and the detachment was made up from an independent volunteer battalion, which was stationed at Stettin. Rather astonishingly Himmler, as Commander-in-Chief of the Vistula Army Group, telegraphed Vlasov that the action had been a great success and later told Herre that Red Army men had actually deserted to this detachment, a proof that Russians could still defeat Stalin.[12] Vlasov's own ADC, Colonel Sakharov, who had been present at the Vlasov-Himmler meeting, had been in command.

The benevolent, though disbelieving, Ernst Koestring now decided that it was time for Vlasov to visit his troops and with some pomp and ceremony he brought him to Muensingen on 15th February. Here in a snow shower Vlasov reviewed the first KONR division and watched the disciplined march-past of a body of men that had been purged both of camp followers and of officers who sported three or four wristwatches. But during the days that he spent in Muensingen and Heuberg, Vlasov became more and more gloomy, more and more convinced of the realities of the situation. Herre encouraged Vlasov to believe that, by building up the KONR Army, he could create a bargaining force with the Western Allies. Herre pointed out that a successful action even on a lost front might persuade the Allies that the free Russians were a force to be reckoned with. Such was the dream-world, divorced from all realities, in which the German *Ostpolitiker* lived between 1941 and 1945.[13]

Determined to get the Vlasov troops into the news, Herre obtained an interview with Himmler at his headquarters in a wood at Prenzlau on 23rd February. At this time Himmler's Vistula Army was spread in a thin screen from the Oder south of Stettin to the neighbourhood of Danzig, a ridiculous elongated flank, which would have melted away had the Russians diverted their main attack, but which Hitler insisted on holding because Admiral Raeder needed Baltic submarine bases. Himmler had just attempted a so-called offensive at Arnswalde, which had evaporated miserably. Behind his bombast, Himmler was scared to death and on 19th he had already begun his famous contact with Count Bernadotte of Sweden.[14] Himmler was about to take to his bed and did not want to hear about the volunteers, nor listen to the crack-brained notions of this Russophile colonel. Within the past few days Hermann Fegelein, Himmler's adjutant at Hitler's headquarters, had reported to him that the Vlasov volunteers were deserting right and left and that they refused under any circumstances to serve on the eastern front.[15]

Indifferently Himmler consented that part of the Vlasov Division should be given a fair chance to distinguish itself on his front and not be left to fall into Red Army hands in some untenable fortress. He listened dully to Herre's record of unsatisfied hopes and unassuaged fears, but when Herre spoke of the Vlasov Army as a trump card, if only Germany could hold out till a breach occurred between the Western Allies and Russia, Himmler replied with more sense than he is usually credited with. 'That is a *cura posterior*.'[16]

It was none the less remarkable that, while Hitler boasted of the convicts, the deaf and dumb, the grandfathers and the schoolboys who had been thrown into the line by 'improvisers', like his old mad SA leaders, Petersdorff and von Pfeffer, Himmler should have been so indifferent about the Vlasov Army.[17] As usual, backstairs politics were playing their part. At this moment Vlasov was courted by the highest Party personalities. He was received by Goering, Ribbentrop and Goebbels. Yet Himmler did not see Vlasov a second time, because he feared to display his interest too openly. It was believed that Himmler's star was setting and that Bormann had procured his appointment as an Army Group Commander in order to ruin him.[18] Bormann, a private secretary, was now the most powerful man in Germany and one of the stupidest. Beyond keeping a dying Fuehrer absolutely isolated from a crumbling nation, he appears to have had no real plan. And he was still the Bormann who had been shocked by the great number of healthy babies in the Ukraine. So to keep an eye on the scheming *Ostpolitiker*, Bormann attached to KONR the unamiable figure of Paul Dargel, Erich Koch's former deputy.[19] It was fear of this watch-dog, rather than the antics of Rosenberg and the separatist committees, which caused the fanfares of the Prague Conference to die out in silence. Yet the KONR Government was now established on former Slav soil, even if the Gauleiter, Konrad Henlein, tried to expel it from the Richmond Hotel in Karlsbad. Any further moves in the direction of pan-Slavism were discountenanced by Himmler himself. There was for instance to have been a conference in Bratislava in February 1945. In this front-line town, representatives of all the satellite Slav governments, Croatia, Serbia, Slovakia and KONR, were to have met.[20]

It is easy to see why last-ditchers like Bormann were frightened of such a conference. They feared that the volunteers would desert them in order to create a third force among the Slavs in the south. Such a third force was ludicrous in Germany, where the eastern and western armies were moving in with such intense *élan* that they had no time to quarrel. It was rather different in the Balkans. From the Carpathians to the Adriatic, the satellite governments of Tiso, Szalasy, Nedic and Pavelic, were only pro-German because they were anti-Soviet. Had it been possible for the 800,000 Russians who could not go home to unite with all these elements, it would have added to the problems of the Red Army. It would have taken them as long to pacify the Balkans as it took to purge the Ukraine and Galicia of the bands of OUN. Only to a much smaller extent was there such a problem in the western Balkans, though for many months after the war Cossacks and Turcoman SS men roamed the mountains east of Trieste, together with the survivors of the Serbian Chetniks and Pavelic's Ustashe.[21]

That Vlasov was unable to cash in on this situation was largely the result of his own fatalism and inertia, but it may also have been the suspicion of Himmler that kept the two divisions in Germany till the very last moment. In Slovenia and Croatia, von Pannwitz was willing to surrender his Cossack Army Corps to Vlasov. If Vlasov had gone in person to the Balkan front, he would have been acclaimed by the Cossacks as their leader. He was acknowledged even by such Cossack separatists as the Ataman Domanov, who had recruited a militia in the Don territory in 1942. This conciliation was the work of an SS man, Odilo Globocnik, the Higher SS and Police Leader for Dalmatia and Trieste. Having employed several Cossack units in anti-Partisan operations, Globocnik went with them after the war when they took to the mountains. In June 1945, he was caught by a British patrol in the Karavanken Alps. Globocnik, the executioner of two million of the Jews of Poland, chose the alternative of cyanide. But in the SS this sort of activity had been no unusual combination with liberal *Ost-politik*.[22]

(b) Anabasis Without Hope

WHEN BUNIACHENKO FINALLY received his marching orders for the Oder front at the beginning of March 1945, he may have planned an escape to the south, but he received no lead from Vlasov, who was preoccupied with another aimless session of KONR at Karlsbad. At one meeting, on 27th February, a Cossack officer declared that 803 Cossacks of the Red Army had deserted to Pannwitz's Corps in the western Balkans, landing in stolen transport aeroplanes. The story could hardly have been true, and if it was intended to draw Vlasov to the south, it failed. Vlasov was full of the successes of his men on the eastern front. In marked contradiction was the gloomy speech of the former mayor of Kiev under Erich Koch, the ex-priest Leonti Forosti-visky, who is now a refugee in South America. Even this collabora-tionist of all collaborationists no longer hesitated to tell the Germans that they had betrayed the anti-Stalinist cause, that the twelfth hour had struck.[23]

Buniachenko refused to march without the permission of his own Commander-in-Chief, so Vlasov had to confirm Himmler's orders in person before the first division began its slow lumbering march with-out railway trains or motor transport across Wuerttemburg and Bavaria. For a fortnight the columns plodded on, joined frequently by fugitives from eastern worker or prisoner-of-war camps. The German commanders of the Labour Camps had to replace the barbed wire and withdraw the few liberties that had been accorded, in order to prevent further desertion. The eastern workers told their stories of long oppression to the volunteers, whose morale was not improved. Some 18,000 disgruntled and undisciplined men slouched through the heart of prosperous, unravaged rural Germany. Gauleiters, Kreisleiters and all the apparatus of Party rule were stirred to protest at this terrifying menace. Finally the march was halted in the Nuremberg region and an effort was made to obtain trains for the passage across Bohemia. It was not till 26th March that the division was reassembled at the training centre of Lieberose, north of Cottbus, near the Oder front.

The Vistula Army Group was commanded by Himmler's successor, Gotthard Heinrici. He was a by no means Nazi general, whose busi-ness-like lack of sympathy with the *Goetterdaemmerung* mentality of Hitler and Goebbels, may have saved tens of thousands of lives during Hitler's last days. Heinrici was the last person to believe any nonsense about Stalin being beaten by Russians in 1945. He listened to Major Schwenninger, the chief of staff of the 1st Vlasov Division, with incredulity. Then brusquely he decided that Himmler, who had sent this division to the Oder, must make up his mind what next to do with it. So Schwenninger had to look for Himmler, who was said to be in Berlin but was in fact in Hohenlychen Hospital. Himmler would not see him, but Gottlob Berger, who hung round the hospital like a faithful spaniel, knew a useful contact on the Oder front. He was Major General Hoelz, Chief of Staff to the 9th Army of General Busse.[24]

At the end of March, two regiments, composed of German officer cadets, had failed to recapture the Russian bridgehead at Erlenhof, south of Frankfurt on Oder. The place had consequently been strengthened with new defences and it appeared that the Russians would use it as a springboard for their great offensive. Both Hoelz and Busse were prepared to use the Vlasov troops, but Buniachenko was not easily persuaded to undertake a fresh assault. He believed that his men would be sacrificed in a useless blood-bath. Much time was spent by Busse in bargaining with his former enemy. Buniachenko demanded full artillery support. With all his air of drunkenness and brutality and despite the carefully fostered oriental device of non-comprehension, he showed an uncanny grasp of the tactical situation. But in the end Buniachenko agreed to make the assault on 13th April after only a brief artillery preparation.

Vlasov appeared in Lieberose on the 11th. He concealed his over-whelming pessimism and harangued the units, one by one, with all the eloquence he could muster. Even Heinrici was sufficiently won round to receive Vlasov in his mess.* But the attack on Erlenhof was an engagement which recalled some of the unwisest battles of the First World War. Without adequate artillery and with no tactical bombing force, the infantry was sent into an intact zone of barbed wire. Since there were absolutely no reserves behind them, the men straggled back, leaving hundreds of dead, and within four hours Buniachenko called off the attack.

That same night, returning from a visit to Koestring at Zossen, Schwenninger found Buniachenko leading his men back to the training centre at Lieberose. Buniachenko had decided to move south, to put the mountains between his division and the Red Army and to gain time in some war-area that was not yet threatened. Thus began a march of 300 miles from Lieberose to Prague with the Red Army from twenty to sixty miles from his route and the German High Command closely dogging his heels.

At first there was no difficulty. Heinrici was glad to be rid of him, while Jodl authorized the transfer of the division to the front in Czechoslovakia. But, on leaving the Army Group area, Buniachenko was ordered to give up his artillery. A long argument followed, in which Buniachenko demanded his artillery as firmly as the famous

---

* Fischer, p. 99, disbelieves Thorwald's story that Vlasov ever got to Lieberose.

Ten Thousand had demanded their breakfast after the battle of Cunaxa. In order to be rid of this nuisance Busse let the artillery go.

But now Schwenninger encountered fresh trouble. Buniachenko received an order to put his men at the disposal of the 275th Infantry Division as a reserve force, a reversion to the despised state of *Hiwis*. This division formed part of the Central Army Group of Field Marshal Schoerner, the most disliked officer in the German High Command. Buniachenko obeyed Jodl, but not Schoerner.[25] In great anxiety Schwenninger went off to the headquarters of the 5th Army Corps to explain the situation to Schoerner, who was due to arrive there. Schoerner, known affectionately as the Bloodhound or the 'Strength Through Fear' Field Marshal, was a formidable person. Just as many people retain a faith in the efficacy of pills, Schoerner believed in shooting officers. Even in 1958, attempts were still being made to bring him to judgment for some of his arbitrary executions[26] and he is at present serving a short sentence of imprisonment.

Schoerner lived up to his reputation. He told Schwenninger that he would have Buniachenko's 17,000 men machine-gunned from the air by a fighter squadron, if they failed to surrender their general for execution. But it was 14th April 1945. There was no fighter squadron available for Field Marshal Schoerner, who was on his way to Berlin for his last visit to Hitler in the Reich chancellery bunker.

For answer—and once again one is reminded of the Ten Thousand —Buniachenko formed his division into a strongpoint, protected with tanks, artillery and anti-aircraft weapons; all that had been obtained so grudgingly from German ordnance stores. As a gesture it was wasted. The Red Army had broken Schoerner's front between Muskau and Guben. Berlin was threatened from the north, east and south, and no one was interested in the mutiny of a Russian collaborator.

Orders came on the 16th that the Buniachenko Division should retire to Hoyerswerda, about twenty miles to the south towards the mountains of Sudetenland. That suited Buniachenko. A further order to retire to Radeburg near Dresden was obeyed, for it was still a step in the right direction. But when it came to entraining for an unknown destination in Bohemia, Buniachenko rebelled again. This entrainment aroused his suspicions. Why should Schoerner want it, when the Red Army was already barely twenty miles east of Radeburg? Buniachenko continued to march past Dresden, some thirty miles to the south, to the fantastic rocks of Bad Schandau in 'the Saxon Switzerland'. Here he was ordered to report to Schoerner, whose latest headquarters were quite close, but on the afternoon of the 24th he sent a staff officer to Schoerner to explain that he could not move on account of a motor accident. In the meantime he marched his men south across the Czech border and placed them up a mountain, the Hohenschneeburg west of Tetschen.*

Finally, on 27th April, two days after the Americans and the Russians had met at Torgau and three days before Hitler committed suicide, Mahommed decided to come to the mountain. The commander of a million men announced that he would land in person in a Fiesler Storsch machine on the Hohenschneeburg to meet the *Untermensch*. But at the last moment Schoerner changed his mind. The guard of honour and the military orchestra were turned out only to greet Schoerner's chief of staff, Major General von Natzmer. Buniachenko, who was dramatically swathed in bandages, agreed to entrain his men for Bruenn, north of Vienna. As soon as Natzmer had gone, Buniachenko changed the orders. He realized that Schoerner wanted to get his division where it could be re-equipped with new arms for the front. So the march south continued. On the afternoon of the 29th, Buniachenko's headquarters were at Kosojed, a bare forty miles from Prague. This time Schoerner really did visit the elusive sub-human person, close to Frederick the Great's battlefield of Lobositz. There was a show of cordiality. Buniachenko changed from a dirty white sleeveless shirt into his best uniform. The Bloodhound advanced, flourishing a bottle of vodka and a box of cigars, but Buniachenko could not resist reminding Schoerner that barely a fortnight had passed since the Field Marshal had a 'different treatment of my person in view'.[27] Getting down to brass tacks was not easy. Schoerner kept repeating, 'Will you fight with your division or will you not?' 'Naturally', said Buniachenko, but he would not bind himself as to when and where. Finally, Schoerner left, perfunctorily hoping that Buniachenko would get his men to Bruenn in his own way. It could not have mattered much to Schoerner behind all the bombast. Six days later he fled to the Americans, leaving his Army Group to escape the Russians as best they could.

Two days after Schoerner's visit, Vlasov arrived at Buniachenko's headquarters. For some days past, the division had been quietly getting rid of the few Germans attached to it, while Buniachenko had been receiving members of the Czech Gendarmerie and a few mysterious

* To be distinguished from Teschen, which Lloyd George believed to be in Mesopotamia.

civilians. Now he disclosed his plan to Vlasov. It was too late to think of reunion with the Cossacks and the Slav collaborationists in Slovenia and Croatia. There Tito was already master, while Pavelic, Nedic and Mihailovitch were mere shadow rulers. But here on the spot were the possibilities of a third force. No decision had been taken at Yalta to halt the American forces on the Czech border. It is known now that Stalin only insisted on this on 4th May, when Eisenhower informed Moscow that his troops were ready to take up position in Bohemia along the entire line of the Elbe and Moldau.[28]

Thus the Russian volunteers were not alone in believing that Bohemia was to be an American zone of occupation. Of course there were Czech Communists who were going to deliver the country to the Red Army, but, if the volunteers supported the legitimist faction of Benès and Masaryk and welcomed the Americans, they must obtain some recognition. Within a week Buniachenko believed he could get rid of every Communist and every German in Bohemia, if he had the help of Zverev's second Vlasov division, which, however, was as far away as Linz, 120 miles south of Prague.

At this point the news of Hitler's death arrived. To Vlasov it was no reinforcement of Buniachenko's argument. He had heard the news already and he believed that to desert the Germans at this stage was to show the world that the volunteers were simply adventurers who had betrayed both sides and deserved no mercy—an interpretation which was justified by the events that followed. Nevertheless, Vlasov would not forbid Buniachenko's enterprise. He simply declared that he would not stand in the way.[29]

Vlasov no longer speculated on the mercy of the Western Allies. He had made his attempt in that quarter and failed. The story goes back to 19th April, when Heuberg and Muensingen camps had to be evacuated suddenly in the face of the advancing Americans. The second Vlasov division, numbering together with Vlasov's general staff, reserve troops and training establishments, some 22,000 men, was forced to take the road for the eastern front. Without heavy weapons or defence from air attacks, with little but rifles and hand-weapons, this large force took the road to Fuerstenfeldbrueck, there to be entrained for Linz. It was expected that in Linz some equipment would be provided by Rendulic's Southern Army Group.

The march did not lead in the direction of Vlasov's loyal Cossacks and friendly Slav collaborators, but Vlasov had one trick left to play, an approach to the American generals Patch and Patton, whose armoured columns were plunging through south Germany, close on the heels of his own march. A hundred miles south-east of Muensingen lay the Alpine village of Seeg im Allgaeu on the Austrian border. Here Erich Dwinger, in disgrace with Himmler since his *Wille und Macht* article in 1943, lived in affluent calm on his Hedwigshof estate amid the cracks and fissures of the foundering Reich. Vlasov had heard that his old mentor, Strik-Strikfeldt, a disengaged man, was staying with Dwinger. On 24th April, five days after the departure of the second division from Muensingen, Vlasov appeared in the company of his generals at Hedwigshof.*

Apart from the 'Third Force' plan for a stand either in Slovenia or Bohemia, two new projects were discussed in Dwinger's house. The first was Dwinger's own. Twenty miles from Hedwigshof, near the town of Fuessen, was an internment camp for prominent foreigners, one of whom was Pierre Laval. Dwinger proposed that a party of volunteers should liberate the camp and take the prominent captives with them. The volunteer forces would then abandon their march to Linz and cut south into the Tyrol, where in an easily defensible position they could use their hostages to bargain with the Western Allies. Vlasov turned this down abruptly, though Dwinger declares that he was ready to liberate Fuessen himself with a car-load of Russians, promised him by Trukhin. Dwinger says that it was not till next day, when the SS had caught up with Vlasov's movements, that Trukhin gave up the project as too dangerous.[30]

Strange to say it was the head of the Security Office, Ernst Kaltenbrunner, so busily dogging Vlasov's footsteps, who now carried out this plan. A few days later he had the prominent captives, who had been evacuated south from various concentration camps, marched to the Tyrol with the intention of bargaining his own person against their lives. Gottlob Berger, however, piloted the captives to freedom unconditionally, a course which saved him from Kaltenbrunner's fate at the gallows.[31]

The second proposal came from Major General Aschenbrenner, a Luftwaffe officer who had been lent to Vlasov by Goering. Aschenbrenner proposed to send Strik-Strikfeldt, a fluent linguist, to the nearest US General Headquarters in the company of Vlasov's former deputy, Major General Malyshkin. They were to offer the surrender of the Vlasov forces against a guarantee that they would not be handed

---

* Thorwald (p. 522) says 19th April, which is barely possible. Dwinger himself (p. 422) gives the date as 24th April.

over to Russia. But that which happened next had all the painful qualities of the obvious and inevitable. While the second Vlasov division and a number of other Vlasov establishments continued marching east, Strik-Strikfeldt and Malyshkin drove north-west and within a matter of hours surrendered to an American detachment. They were taken to General Patch, commanding the 7th Army. Patch was ready to accept the surrender of the volunteers, but he could offer no conditions. These must be approved by Eisenhower, perhaps even by the White House. Strik-Strikfeldt and Malyshkin were informed that they could take this message back, but on various pretences they were detained by subordinate officers till finally they were told that they were no longer parliamentaries but prisoners. For Malyshkin it meant extradiction and the gallows. For Strik-Strikfeldt the bitterest disappointment of all.

Five or six days passed, Vlasov reached Linz and still no answer had come back.[32] In the meantime Aschenbrenner tried to send another agent, none other than Theodor Oberlaender, to General Patton commanding the US 3rd Army. Patton, who was more soft-hearted towards Nazi collaborators, actually permitted Oberlaender to return with the message that he would treat personally with Vlasov. It was not easy to convey this news to Vlasov in secret. After spending two days with his wife at the village of Reit im Winkel on the German side of the Austrian border, Vlasov reached Linz on the 29th. Even then, to avoid the eye of Dr Kroeger and his SD Staff, Aschenbrenner's message had to be passed to Vlasov in the lavatory by his faithful German guard from the Viktoriastrasse, Sergei Frohlich. Vlasov followed the instructions and saw Aschenbrenner next day at Spitzberg in the Bohmerwald, but now the mission of Strik-Strikfeldt and Malyshkin had been reported to Washington. Instructions had gone out that no bargains were to be made with Russian collaborators. Aschenbrenner had been told that Vlasov's mission would be fruitless.[33]

So it was that Vlasov played no part in the conference with Buniachenko on 1st May and in the drama that was enacted in Prague. Nor did the German liaison staff under Major Schwenninger. They found themselves arrested suddenly on the morning of 5th May at Suchomast in the south-western outskirts of Prague. There they learnt that a National Czech government had been declared and that Buniachenko had agreed with Czech emissaries to aid in the fight against both fascism and communism.[34]

That same afternoon, the Nationalists secured control of most of the city with the exception of the Hradcany and Czernin palaces and some German strongpoints in the suburbs. Only the police units of the SS, the most fanatical of the last-ditchers, resisted. More Germans would have done so, had they realized how savage the vengeance of the Czechs was to be. Next day, however, without any orders from Schoerner, who had already gone underground, some SS units penetrated the city and created a critical situation in the Hradcany quarter. Appeals to Buniachenko were sent over the Prague radio and finally, after disarming the last of their detached Germans, the first Vlasov division left Beroun on the morning of the 7th and moved into Prague. By five o'clock in the evening Buniachenko was master of Prague and Karl Frank, who had seen in KONR the danger of pan-slavism, was delivered by his former guests to the Czechs. He was hanged outside the Hradcany Palace a year later.

In the meantime Zverev's second Vlasov division, accompanied by Trukhin as Vlasov's chief of staff, had moved north from Linz and the Danube towards Prague, instead of towards the Russian front which was west of Vienna. On 4th May they held a line from Budweis to Strakonitz, nearly half-way from Linz to Prague. Only twenty miles behind them was an American Army Corps, but the foremost American detachments seemed to halt deliberately just inside the Czech border. On Herre's advice Zverev sent a deputation and next day he learnt that the American commander was prepared to accept the division as prisoners of the west,[35] provided they reached the required line within thirty-six hours.

Trukhin hesitated. There was no guarantee against delivery to the Soviet Union. And, while he hesitated, Boiarsky arrived with the news that Buniachenko was marching into Prague. Vlasov had sent Boiarsky to summon the second division to the aid of Buniachenko. Trukhin, knowing Vlasov's state of apathy and virtual collapse and knowing also Buniachenko's headstrong disposition, refused to believe that Vlasov had given the orders. He demanded a written order. At noon on the 6th, Boiarsky had not returned with the order, while alarming rumours of the insurrection in Prague were circulating. Only twenty-four hours remained in which to obey the American ultimatum. Trukhin decided to go to Prague himself.

Trukhin set off, taking with him only his driver and Romashkin, his adjutant. As they drew closer to Prague, they observed that the Red Partisans outnumbered the Czech nationalists. Finally at Pribram, forty miles south-west of Prague, having completed only half their journey, they ran into a road-block. The two Russians were arrested and taken into the orderly room of a Red Army parachute officer, who recognized them for what they were, having caught Boiarsky and his adjutant Shepavalov and hanged them on the spot on the previous day. Romashkin was rescued three days later, but Trukhin survived in captivity to face the gallows in Moscow after fifteen months.[36]

This ambush took place on 6th May, a full day before the centre of Prague had been conquered for the Nationalists. It was a portent. On the 8th, Buniachenko learnt of the Rheims capitulation, according to which the Americans would retire to the German border, leaving the Red Army to take over all Bohemia. The ultimatum to the second Vlasov division had now expired. Inconceivable chaos followed. Hordes of Schoerner's troops poured into Prague on their way to the American lines. The armistice terms, according to which the Czech nationalists agreed not to molest this march, were not recognized by the Communist Partisans, with whom fighting broke out again. In the meantime, all over Prague, the Vlasov portraits and banners were replaced by Stalin portraits and the hammer and sickle. Buniachenko had gambled and lost.

(c) Red Vengeance

EARLY ON THE morning of 9th May Buniachenko learnt that a Russian Commissar had been parachuted into Prague. He had delivered a message to Buniachenko's reconnaissance officer, expressing Stalin's sarcastic hope that the division would be brought back to the homeland. Buniachenko, who had withdrawn to Beroun on the previous day, avoided that temptation. An early-on-the-scene reporter, Ivan Peterman of the *Saturday Evening Post*, reported that General Vlasov and his men had melted away as mysteriously as they had come.[37] In fact it is uncertain whether Vlasov was ever in Prague at all. The National Council, which had summoned Buniachenko's aid was now taking orders from members of Benes's exiled government, who naturally wanted to do nothing to annoy the Red Army. They declared that Buniachenko must either move over to the Russian lines and surrender or vacate the country immediately.

It was an appalling march, German soldiers, SS men, German civilians and Russian volunteers kept close together, despite their mutual hate, for fear of the menacing Communist bands. In one village many of Buniachenko's officers were treacherously kidnapped at the luncheon table of the newly-elected mayor. Yet through a ludicrous accident Buniachenko's division was admitted across the American demarcation line on the night of the 10th. An American subaltern assumed it to be a Red Army division, which had pushed on through lack of information of Stalin's arrangements. Cheerfully he proposed that Buniachenko should lunch next day with the American corps commander. When the mistake was discovered, the division was ordered to lay down its arms, but the Americans saw to it that there was no interference from Red Partisans. The same thing had happened on the previous day to Vlasov himself, when he crossed the border with the smallest of personal staffs. A Soviet liaison officer had already appeared at the American Army Corps headquarters to demand the surrender of the deserters. Not only was this refused, but an American captain protected Vlasov from swarming Czech Partisans and hid him in a room in the castle of Schluesselberg in the Bohmerwald.*

On 12th May Vlasov was still without news of either of his divisions. The Americans evacuated Schluesselberg and pulled back to the final zone demarcation line. Vlasov's presence was still unknown to the Russian troops, whom he could see from the windows of the castle. The American captain enabled Vlasov to follow the march of the American division in civilian disguise, riding in a jeep which was escorted by Vlasov's German car. This contained his ADC and his typist. Barely three miles from Schluesselberg the car was stopped by a Russian motor column. The Russian commander mistook Vlasov for a German civilian in American custody and did not interfere. But calamity was always waiting for Vlasov. A Red Army soldier recognized him. The Americans in the jeep began to argue. This was their prisoner for whom they were responsible. Russian soldiers crowded round the Americans and the situation looked dangerous, when another American officer appeared. As soon as he learnt that the prisoner was not German but Russian, this officer gave his orders. There must be no international incidents. The jeep must continue its journey and its occupants must not interfere in disputes between Russians. So the car was abandoned. Vlasov was seen no more. Except for *Pravda*'s brief reference, in August 1946, to his trial and execution, he disappeared that afternoon from the stage of history.[38] Thus Thorwald's account, based on the narrative of Vlasov's woman secretary who escaped.[39]

* According to Dwinger, p. 372, the American officer was the town major of Pilsen.

A shadowy end to an unusually shadowy man. Dwinger and Thorwald have built Vlasov into a hero, but they have not painted a recognizable portrait of a living man. Yet Thorwald had the diaries and recollections of Strik-Strikfeldt and Heinz Herre, of Duerksen, von Grote, Kazantsev and Sergei Frohlich to draw on, men who saw Vlasov frequently, who could have known him intimately. What was it that eluded them all? The Russian de Gaulle was an expression that came easily to the lips of the *Ostpolitiker*, but, except for his great height, his air of melancholy, his solitude and his passionate sincerity, Vlasov had little in common with that greater and stronger man. Vlasov lacked the austerity of a dedicated leader. A frustrated being, a character from a Chekhov play, always on the way to Moscow, redeemed from desperate tiresomeness by an over-average appetite for women and strong drink, lovable nevertheless and easily winning the loyalty of strangers—but for what end?

If Vlasov's capture was a sly trick of fate, he lost nothing by it. He could not have escaped the fate that awaited his closest colleagues, even though some resisted their extradition for many months. The 15,000 men of Buniachenko's division remained at Birkendorf from the night of the 10th till the afternoon of 12th May. A number listened to the blandishments of Russian propaganda officers, who circulated through the bivouacs in spite of the American tanks which surrounded them. It was believed that those men, who had gone off with the propagandists, were shot or hanged out of hand within earshot. Most of the division waited for reports of Vlasov's supposed negotiations at the nearest American Army headquarters. Finally, when the Americans evacuated Birkendorf, Buniachenko was left to make his own decision. The American local commander was able to wash his hands of the matter, for the deliberate delivery of masses of Russians, according to a strict appeasement policy had not yet begun. Buniachenko had shown himself a resourceful commander, possessing the skill and cunning of a guerilla chief. His march from Lieberose to Prague was something remarkable in the annals of war. But even Buniachenko's *débrouillard* qualities could not master the present situation. He neglected to shave or to dress, he drank incessantly, he roamed his room like a caged beast. There was only one order that he could give. On being told that the area was to be given up to the Red Army, he absolved his men from their soldier's oath. They could go where they liked. But what could they expect in hostile, shattered Germany, foreigners and outlaws as they would be and unused for many years past to fend for

themselves individually? Most of the first Vlasov division waited for
the Red Army with resignation. Better a Siberian labour camp among
fellow Russians than to roam the Bavarian woods like a wolf. A few
resisted with concealed weapons, about 2,000 trekked into south
Germany, but most of them only delayed their extradition by a few
months. As to Buniachenko himself, the circumstances of his capture
and delivery to the Red Army are not known.[40]

The dissolution of the second Vlasov division, which lay eighty
miles south of Prague, followed a more complicated course. Vlasov's
Chief of Staff, Major General Meandrov, succeeded in getting the
American ultimatum prolonged till 9th May, but could not establish
contact with Zverev and the divisional front. As the acting deputy for
Vlasov, Meandrov therefore marched the reserve troops, the general
staff, and the Vlasov officer school into American custody at Krumau.
With them went Herre and Keiling. In the meantime Zverev remained
at Kaplitz, a good thirty miles into Bohemia, drinking and living with
his Russian mistress, completely indifferent to his own fate or the fate
of his men. On the initiative of its own officers, one regiment moved
back in time to be interned at Krumau. Zverev gave no further orders.
When his mistress took poison, he refused to part from her body. On
12th May, when the Red Army came for him, there was some shooting
in which Zverev was wounded, but he too, like Buniachenko and
Trukhin, lived to share Vlasov's fate in July 1946.[41] Most of the
division surrendered, though some parties made their way into
Bavaria to be interned with Meandrov's men at Landau.[42]

It was the fate of the Cossack and Turcoman divisions to surrender
to the British. Pannwitz's Cossacks had joined in the general retreat of
the German Balkan forces through Slovenia to Austria and at the end
of April they were fighting on the Drava river in the neighbourhood of
Celje. The news of Hitler's death created a cleavage between the plans of
the Cossack and the German officers—not that either could really be
called plans. The Cossack commanders thought of combining with the
Vlasov divisions as a Third Force, while Pannwitz, though not
opposed to this, put his faith in an agreement with the British. Early
in April he had sent a fruitless mission to the 8th Army in Italy under
the leadership of Count Schwartzenburg. The Cossack plan was
entrusted to a brigade commander, the Colonel Kononov who had
formed a Cossack battalion for the Germans in White Russia as early
as the winter of 1941.* On 5th May, on the eve of the march into

* See p. 309

Prague, Kononov saw Vlasov at Suchomast. It was the lowest ebb in Vlasov's life. He had no further interest in the plans of Meandrov or Buniachenko, but he performed the vain gesture of accepting the Cossack troops into his army. Kononov's vanity was gratified with the title of 'Field Ataman of All The Cossacks'. That was as much as the much-discussed plans for a Third Force ever amounted to.

Three days later, when the Corps were fighting west of Varazdin, an officer of Marshal Tito communicated the terms of the Rheims Armistice—by telephone. Pannwitz was now determined to hasten the march into Austria, shaking off fugitives, Partisans and obstructive German units who cluttered the road. Going ahead himself with a small staff, he arranged a surrender to the British 11th Armoured Division, who held the area between Klagenfurth and the border. The surrender took place on the 9th and 10th in parade order and perfect discipline and the two divisions were allotted an internment area between Klagenfurth and St Veit, where they could move about freely though disarmed.

It was a repetition of the same story. The British officers on the spot did not realize that this honourable internment meant delivery to the Soviet Union. There was no formal accord on the subject till 23rd May, when repatriation was discussed by special British and Russian delegates in Vienna. The British delegation ceded the more readily to Russian demands, because the Pannwitz corps were classed by the Russians as 'special units of the German SS Partisans'. This was the result of a double confusion. It had been intended to incorporate the Pannwitz corps into the SS as the 15th SS Cavalry Corps since Pannwitz had believed that he would get better equipment this way. In spite of a statement in Fischer's book on the authority of the SD man, Friedrich Buchardt,[43] the incorporation was never confirmed. The 15th SS Cavalry Corps is mentioned neither in General Hausser's book on the SS, nor in Ernst Kraetschmer's directory of SS heroes.[44] Except for the police units of the Ataman Domanov, who worked for the notorious Globocnik, it is unlikely that the Cossack command included 'special units' in the extermination group sense. There seems therefore to have been an element of injustice in an agreement which delivered men who had never used arms against the Russian nation. The aged generals, Shkuro and Krasnov, who were handed over in May 1945 and hanged in March 1947, had never been Soviet citizens, while it is difficult to see what grounds the Russians had for hanging Pannwitz, who had certainly not committed crimes on Russian territory.[45]

But one thing should be said in palliation of diatribes by German Vlasovite writers against the British and Americans. The final disposition of the Cossack deserters was at least no more ruthless than the kind of war they had been fighting for the past eighteen months. The German High Command considered that the Balkan Partisan front called for specially desperate units, such as convict regiments and even the 'Wirth Commando', which had managed the gas-chambers in Poland for two whole years.[46] It can be added too that British units were reluctant to carry out the duty of incarcerating the Cossacks prior to handing them over. A large proportion took the opportunity to escape. For at least another year there were opportunities of joining guerilla bands in Yugoslavia, though heaven knows where that led. It is unlikely that the number of deserters, Cossacks, Vlasov men, Ukrainian SS, militia and other categories, who submerged themselves in the general mass of Displaced Persons will ever be known, though Mr Fischer has worked out a very tentative figure of a quarter of a million.[47] One is even less likely to know what happened to the larger proportion of the deserters who let themselves be taken back to Russia. One may ask in vain how many were done to death, how many were kept in labour camps, how many were merely exiled.

Doubts have also been expressed as to the justice of handing over the Turkomen and Caucasians of the 162nd Division, men who had always regarded themselves as subjects of the Soviet Union rather than citizens. It is ironical to compare their fate with the treatment that was accorded the soldiers of the Indian Army who fought for the Japanese. The 162nd Division surrendered to the British near Padua under the capitulation of 2nd May. Many weeks later, those who had not escaped were entrained from Modena camp for Taranto, a distance of 700 miles, and then shipped with infinite trouble in Allied vessels for Odessa. On this long complicated journey there was an enormous number of suicides.[48] But the Indians, who had done precisely the same thing, marched in their Japanese uniforms in a great liberation parade in Delhi.

There was a small mitigation of the Turcoman tragedy. Heygendorff was a more resourceful commander and a better politician than Pannwitz, who was little more than a show rider who liked good horsemanship and ceremonial displays. He provided his men with certificates, showing that the bearers had been non-combatants, and he advised them to procure disguises in good time. Helplessness in a foreign country and Asiatic fatalism was, however, the deciding factor for most of them. And, as an anti-Partisan division, the men of central Asia had not made themselves loved by the Italians.

Others profited by legality. The first Ukrainian division was almost entirely spared, though it was landed in the same gigantic net in the Klagenfurth area as the Cossack divisions. The British authorities were persuaded by Pavlo Shandruk that his men were Polish subjects from Galicia. In reality the Galician character of the division had been changed since the new Ukrainian policy which followed the retreat from Lwow. At least half the division had been replaced with prisoners of war and deserters from the Soviet Ukrainian republic. Yet, after some hesitations, the entire division was interned at Rimini and eventually the Ukrainians found new homes.

It is easy but it is erroneous to sort out these variants of treatment in terms of black and white, of justice and injustice as in the works of Dwinger, Thorwald and Kleist. For their weakness in 1941, when they had served the Germans rather than die in heaps from hunger and typhus in the Dulags, hundreds of thousands of men faced a long prospect of misery in 1945. On the other hand thousands of members of the unspeakable collaborationist police units escaped delivery to the Soviet Union, simply because they could claim to be Galicians, Latvians or Lithuanians or pre-Revolution emigrés. They became prisoners of the Western Allies, then DPs, and finally citizens of foreign countries, where they live today, their atrocious past obliterated and forgotten. It is even possible to be too self-righteous over the Soviet practice of demanding the bodies of men who did not want to return, demanding them in order to use them as slaves or subjects without rights of citizenship. It is impossible, in a country which was never occupied by the Germans, to understand the 'liberation' mentality, the terrible hunt for victims and scapegoats in order to atone for years of frustration and indignity. One must picture the Red Army soldier, who had led for four years a life that was barely human, cut off from home and family and the most elementary comforts, and who now met hordes of his countrymen who had fought on the enemy's side. He had not seen the conditions in which nearly four million Russian prisoners had died in German hands, but he did see Russian prisoners in new German uniforms, well fed and by his own standards well looked after. Was it entirely un-European that he should run wild and that there should be cases of mass-shooting? Were things so much better among the older civilizations of the West?

One has only to compare the case of France, a country of only a quarter the population of the Soviet Union, a country which certainly did not provide 800,000 or a million soldiers for Germany, in fact nothing more than a few thousand collaborationist militia-men and about a thousand French volunteers for the SS. Yet, according to the statement issued by the Minister for Justice on 11th April 1952, 10,519 Frenchmen had been executed since the liberation, only 846 after legally recognized sentences. Prison sentences for collaboration had numbered 38,266 and 2,400 Frenchmen remained in prison seven years after the war.[49]

From the Allied point of view, the deliveries of Soviet subjects to the Soviet Union were inevitable, so long as the pursuit of victory and the promotion of peace after victory demanded a sacrifice of personal choice. As early as autumn, 1944, the Russians had insisted on their rights. In October and November some 10,000 Russians, volunteers and conscripted eastern workers, who had been captured in France, were shipped indiscriminately from Hull to Murmansk. It was given out in the Allied press that the returning wanderers were welcomed in Russia as heroes, but that did not prevent a number of Tartars and Kalmucks breaking out of the transit camp at Tranby Croft and roving the Lincolnshire countryside. So meticulous were the Russians on this article that the Government of General de Gaulle received a crisp diplomatic note because some of the deserters were sheltering in the French Resistance Movement.

Compliance with Russian demands became more questionable when so much time had elapsed that the Russian prisoners came to believe that they enjoyed Allied protection. The considerable numbers who followed Vlasov's deputy, Meandrov, were certainly in this position. Those who drifted from Bohemia into Bavaria were given an internment area at Landau, from which they could wander freely if they had the initiative to do so. Unfortunately they preferred to stick together, while Meandrov himself, an ardent NTS man and very much a political soldier, unwisely encouraged his officers to believe that the Allies would use their services soon against Stalin. After two years of indoctrination from Dabendorf on Goebbels's lines, it is not surprising that these Russians seized on the first signs of an inter-Allied rift. They were just a little premature, for today NTS and its members are tolerated in the USA as a by no means un-American activity. Not unnaturally, the Soviet Government protested vigorously at the activities round Landau. In September 1945, the surviving 3,000 Vlasov men were transferred by the Americans from Landau to a genuinely closed and guarded camp at Plattling near Regensburg, not far from the zone border.[50]

At Plattling those who had not been Soviet subjects in 1939 were placed on a special registry. It was an ominous sign, but the remainder, the great majority, were assured that there was no question of repatriation. It is possible that the terrible stories, recounted without citing any authority by Thorwald, Dwinger and Kleist, were exaggerated. There is, however, no question that in February 1946, the men were entrained across the zone border by force and that there were numerous suicides. Meandrov himself lived to be hanged in Moscow with Vlasov, Malyshkin, Zhilenkov, Trukhin, Zverev, Buniachenko and five others in July 1946. There was no publicized State trial. The sentence and execution were divulged in the curtest and most inconspicuous of paragraphs in *Pravda* on 2nd August, when the men had been dead several days.[51]

With Meandrov's costly error the last illusion of *Ostpolitik* perished. The house, built on sand, had finally foundered.

NOTES

An explanation of the initials in the footnote-references and of the method by which the various Nuremberg trials are cited will be found at the beginning of the bibliography on page 415.

Note INTRODUCTION

1. *IMT*, V, 347
2. Hitler, *Mein Kampf*, American edition, p. 966.
3. Ibid., p. 950
4. *IMT*, Document PS 386
5. *Nazi-Soviet Relations*, p. 324
6. B. H. Liddell-Hart, *The Other Side of the Hill*, p. 15
7. *Hitler's Table Talk*, p. 524
8. *IMT*, Document PS 294
9. Wallace Carroll, 'It takes a Russian to Beat Russians', *Life*, 19.12.49
10. *The Goebbels Diaries*, p. 92
11. *Nazi-Soviet Relations*, p. 333
12. J. Wheeler-Bennett, *Nemesis of Power*, p. 296
13. Juergen Thorwald, *Wen sie verderbern wollen*, p. 101
14. Peter Bamm, *Die Unsichtbaere Flagge*, p. 278

CHAPTER ONE

1. J. Wheeler-Bennett, *The Nemesis of Power*, p. 296
2. Gustav Hilger, *The Incompatible Allies*, p. 226
3. Ibid., p. 236
4. Wilhelm Hoettl, *The Secret Front*, pp. 83–87, pp. 168–71. Peter Kleist, *Zwischen Hitler und Stalin*, pp. 210–13
5. Hilger, p. 231
6. Ibid., p. 252
7. Ibid., p. 268
8. Ibid., p. 268
9. *Nazi-Soviet Relations*, p. 333
10. Ibid., p. 76. Hilger, p. 296
11. Ibid., p. 6
12. Ibid., pp. 12–15
13. Ibid., p. 39
14. Ibid., pp. 48–49
15. Ibid., pp. 50–53
16. Ibid., p. 60
17. Hilger, p. 300
18. Ibid., p. 203
19. *Nazi-Soviet Relations*, p. 75
20. Ibid., pp. 87–91
21. Hilger, p. 312
22. *Nazi-Soviet Relations*, p. 103
23. Hilger, p. 314
24. *Nazi-Soviet Relations*, p. 127
25. Ibid., pp. 131–4. Hilger, pp. 136–7
26. *Nazi-Soviet Relations*, p. 139
27. Ibid., p. 154
28. Ibid., p. 156
29. *IMT*, XV, p. 345

Note
30 *Nazi-Soviet Relations*, p. 158
31 Hellmuth Greiner, *Die Oberste Wehrmacht Fuehrung*, pp. 298–9
32 *IMT*, XV, p. 347
33 *Nazi-Soviet Relations*, pp. 167–8
34 Hermann Tescke, *Die Silbernen Spiegel*, p. 92
35 Greiner, p. 290
36 *Trials of War Criminals*, X, p. 492
37 *IMT*, XV, pp. 345–7
38 PS 3032 (Aff. Warlimont)
39 *IMT*, VI, p. 237
40 Chester Wilmot, *The Struggle for Europe*, p. 56
41 PS 3014 (Aff. Koestring)
42 *IMT*, VI, p. 240
43 Greiner, p. 295
44 *IMT*, XI, p. 12
45 *Trials of War Criminals*, X, pp. 1012–14. (Evidence Halder)
46 *IMT*, XI, p. 13
47 *Nazi-Soviet Relations*, p. 194
48 Ibid., p. 207
49 Ibid., p. 200
50 *Nuremberg Document*, PS 444
51 *Nazi-Soviet Relations*, p. 227
52 Ibid., p. 225
53 *Nazi-Soviet Relations*, p. 258
54 Greiner, p. 237
55 Tescke, op. cit., p. 109
56 *Nuremberg Document*, PS 446. *Nazi-Soviet Relations*, pp. 260–4
57 *Trials of War Criminals*, X, p. 1018
58 Ibid., X, p. 1037
59 *Nazi-Soviet Relations*, pp. 266–72
60 *IMT*, Document C 134
61 Greiner, p. 34
62 *IMT*, VI, p. 249, Tescke op. cit., p. 109
63 *Nuremberg Document* C 134
64 PS 872. Greiner, p. 235
65 *IMT*, XV, p. 348
66 Hilger, p. 235. *Nazi-Soviet Relations*, p. 318
67 *Nazi-Soviet Relations*, p. 291
68 Ibid., p. 285
69 Ibid., p. 301
70 Hilger, p. 236
71 *Nazi-Soviet Relations*, p. 137
72 Ibid., pp. 331–2
73 Ibid., p. 324
74 *Nuremberg Document*, PS 1157. IMT, pp. 245–6
75 *Nazi-Soviet Relations*, p. 340
76 *Nuremberg Document*, EC 126
77 Kalinov, *Soviet Marschaelle haben das Wort*, pp. 29–30
78 Hermann Tescke, p. 104
79 *IMT*, VI, pp. 154–62, XIX, p. 377
80 *Trials of War Criminals*, X, p. 952
81 *IMT*, VI, pp. 154–62, XIX, p. 377
82 *Count Ciano's Diary, 1939–43*, pp. 343, 354, 356 (English edition)
83 *Trials of War Criminals*, X, pp. 1005, 1046
84 *Nuremberg Document*, C 78
85 *IMT*, XI, p. 16
86 *Nazi-Soviet Relations*, p. 345
87 Ibid., pp. 352–5
88 Kalinov, op. cit., p. 32

CHAPTER TWO

Note

[1] *Nuremberg Document*, PS 798. *IMT*, I, p. 171
[2] Ibid., 321. *IMT*, XX, p. 351
[3] Greiner, p. 369
[4] *Trials of War Criminals*, X, p. 950
[5] *Nuremberg Document*, PS 2884 (Aff. Warlimont)
[6] *Trials of War Criminals*, X, p. 1103
[7] *Nuremberg Document*, PS 2884 (Aff. Warlimont)
[8] *Trials of War Criminals*, X, p. 950
[9] Ibid., X, p. 124
[10] *The Halder Diary*, 1.9.39, quoted by Telford Taylor, *The March of Conquest*, 1958, p. 57
[11] *IMT*, XXI, p. 32
[12] Ibid., p. 38
[13] *IMT*, XXI, p. 40
[14] *Trials of War Criminals*, X, p. 1265
[15] Ibid., p. 1084
[16] Ibid., p. 1091, *IMT*, XXI, 90
[17] Guenther Weisenborn, *Lautloses Aufstand*, p. 138. Fabian von Schlabrendorff, *Offiziere gegen Hitler*, p. 59
[18] Paul Leverkuehn, *The German Secret Service*, p. 34
[19] Major General Walter Donberger, '*V.2*', London, 1954
[20] *The Schellenberg Memoirs*, p. 123
[21] *Trials of War Criminals*, X, pp. 140, 1239–41. Document NOKW 2080
[22] *The Schellenberg Memoirs*, p. 211
[23] *Nuremberg Document*, PS 790 and PS 884
[24] *Trials of War Criminals*, X, pp. 1071–3
[25] Ibid., X, p. 1058
[26] Ibid., p. 1082
[27] *IMT*, XV, pp. 291–2. Document PS 884
[28] *Trials of War Criminals*, X, p. 27
[29] Ibid., pp. 124, 1057. Document NOKW 1076
[30] *The Answers of Ernst von Salomon*, p. 500, English edition, 1954
[31] *Trials of War Criminals*, X, pp. 1136–44
[32] Ibid., XI, p. 693
[33] *IMT*, Documents, C 50, PS 886
[34] *Nuremberg Document*, L 221
[35] Ibid., C 52
[36] *Trials of War Criminals*, X, pp. 1189–20, XI, p. 519
[37] Ibid., X, p. 1288
[38] Ibid., X, p. 228
[39] Ibid., XI, p. 588–9. Document NOKW 2672
[40] PS 3710 (Aff. Schellenberg, 26.11.45)
[41] *The Schellenberg Memoirs*, 1956, p. 214
[42] Schlabrendorff, *Offiziere gegen Hitler*, p. 51
[43] *Trials of War Criminals*, X, p. 1273
[44] Schlabrendorff, *Offiziere gegen Hitler*, p. 51. Documents NOKW 3146, PS 3047
[45] *IMT*, IV, p. 21 (Aff. Hans Roettiger)
[46] Karl Abshagen, *Canaris*, p. 200
[47] Ibid., p. 201
[48] *IMT*, I, pp. 280–2
[49] *Nuremberg Document*, PS 4060
[50] *Trials of War Criminals*, X, p. 253, XI, p. 648
[51] Erich Dwinger, *General Wlassow*, pp. 145–50
[52] *IMT*, I, p. 290
[53] *IMT*, III, pp. 203–4. Document PS 502

Note
[54] *IMT*, p. 74, Document EC 338
[55] *IMT*, XI, p. 33
[56] Ibid., XI, p. 74
[57] *Nuremberg Document*, R 98
[58] Schlabrendorff, op. cit., p. 65
[59] *The von Hassell Diaries*, p. 195. *Trials of War Criminals*, XI, pp. 551-2
[60] *Trials of War Criminals*, XI, p. 565
[61] Ibid., p. 277, Document NO 3422
[62] Ibid. Document NO 2653
[63] Ibid. Document, NO 2825
[64] Ibid. Documents, PS 084 and PS 1520
[65] *Trials of War Criminals*, XI, p. 26
[66] Thorwald, *Wen sie verderbern wollen*, pp. 171-8
[67] Ibid., pp. 202-3
[68] Nuremberg Trials Case XI, Transcript, p. 28562
[69] Alexander Dallin, op. cit., p. 427
[70] *Trials of War Criminals*, X, p. 1070 (Aff. Warlimont)
[71] Ibid., X, pp. 1088-9
[72] Ibid., X, p. 1098-1101
[73] *IMT*, XXI, p. 51
[74] *Nuremberg Document*, L 180
[75] *IMT*, XXI, p. 38
[76] *Trials of War Criminals*, X, 1906. NOKW 2096

CHAPTER THREE

[1] *IMT*, VII, p. 187
[2] *Trials of War Criminals*, XI, p. 42
[3] *Nuremberg Document*, PS 1201. Lecture by Erwin Mansfeld, 20.2.42
[4] *IMT*, XV, p. 361. Evidence Jodl
[5] *Trials of War Criminals*, X, p. 1196
[6] *IMT*, VII, p. 9
[7] *IMT*, IX, p. 142. Evidence Goering
[8] Hans Baur, p. 209
[9] *IMT*, VII, pp. 318-23
[10] *IMT*, VII, p. 336
[11] *Trials of War Criminals*, X, p. 132
[12] Ibid., XI, p. 31. Document NOKW 1651
[13] Ibid., XI, p. 57
[14] Ibid., XI, pp. 17-24
[15] Ibid., XI, pp. 584-6
[16] Ibid., X, p. 132
[17] R. T. Paget, *Manstein, his campaigns and his trial*, p. 136. Gerald Reitlinger, *The SS, Alibi of a Nation*, p. 148
[18] *IMT*, VII, p. 317, order dated 28.10.41
[19] *IMT*, VI, p. 313 (Aff. Kurt von Oesterreich)
[20] *Nuremberg Document*, PS 886. *Trials*, etc., XI, p. 1008
[21] *Trials of War Criminals*, X, p. 124
[22] *IMT*, I, p. 283. Evidence Lahousen
[23] *IMT*, affs. H and L
[24] *Nuremberg Document*, PS 1519
[25] Ibid., PS 1193
[26] Nuremberg Trials Case IX, Document NO 3157. Gerald Reitlinger, *The Final Solution*, p. 231n
[27] Ibid., NO 3159
[28] *IMT*, IV, p. 15. Document D 411
[29] *Nuremberg Document*, NOKW 663
[30] Ibid., NOKW 3411. *IMT*, XXI, p. 721, PS 4064

Note
[31] *The von Hassell Dairies*, p. 213
[32] Peter Bamm, *Die Unsichtbaere Flagge*, 1955, p. 74
[33] *Nuremberg Document*, EC 194. Alexander Dallin, *German Rule in Russia*, p. 411
[34] *IMT*, VII, p. 232
[35] *IMT*, PS 1517
[36] *Trials of War Criminals*, XI, p. 31. NOKW 1605
[37] Ibid., etc., XI, p. 264
[38] Thorwald, *Wen sie verderbern wollen*, pp. 47–52
[39] *IMT*, VI, p. 238
[40] Ibid., p. 327. Peter Bamm, *Die Unsichtbaere Flagge*, pp. 80–100
[41] *IMT*, XXI, p. 303
[42] *Nuremberg Document*, USSR 89, *IMT*, VII, p. 12
[43] Luedde—Neurath, *Regierung Doenitz*, p. 92
[44] Document D 225. *IMT*, VI, p. 304
[45] Document USSR 177. *IMT*, VI, p. 306
[46] Long extracts from Molotov's note in *IMT*, VI, pp. 302–6. Document USSR 51
[47] *Nuremberg Document*, PS 1201
[48] Ibid., PS 081
[49] *IMT*, XV, p. 123
[50] Erich Dwinger, *General Wlassow*, p. 169
[51] *The Goebbels Diaries*, p. 132
[52] *IMT*, VII, p. 10
[53] *Nuremberg Document*, PS 393
[54] *Trials of War Criminals*, X, p. 1090. NOKW 147
[55] *IMT*, XX, pp. 242–80
[56] Aff. von Oesterreich, *IMT*, XVI, p. 24
[57] Gerald Reitlinger, *The Final Solution*, pp. 145–6. Affidavit of Rudolf Hoess in *Nuremberg Document*, D 749
[58] *IMT*, VII, pp. 2–8. Document USSR 311

CHAPTER FOUR

[1] Rosenberg, *Letzte Aufzeichnungen*, 1955, p. 14. Ernst Dwinger, *General Wlassow*, p. 93
[2] *Memoirs of Alfred Rosenberg*, English text, pp. 14–18
[3] Rosenberg, *Letzte Aufzeichnungen*, p. 244
[4] Alan Bullock, *Hitler, a study in tyranny*, 1952, p. 71
[5] *Hitler's Table Talk*, p. 479
[6] *Memoirs of Alfred Rosenberg*, English text, p. 164
[7] Ernst Hanfstaengl, *Hitler, The Missing Years*, London, 1957, p. 196
[8] *IMT*, II, p. 74. XI, p. 385
[9] Braeutigam, *Ueberblick*, pp. 59, 25
[10] *Memoirs of Alfred Rosenberg*, English text, p. 180
[11] Max Weinreich, *Hitler's Professors*, pp. 98–99. Reitlinger *The Final Solution*, p. 80
[12] *IMT*, XII, p. 12
[13] PS 1017
[14] Braeutigam, p. 3
[15] Thorwald, p. 26
[16] Braeutigam, op. cit., p. 5
[17] PS 1058
[18] *IMT*, XII, pp. 13–14
[19] Kleist, *Zwischen Hitler und Stalin*, p. 141
[20] PS 1019
[21] Thorwald, p. 29, quoting Otto Braeutigam
[22] Braeutigam, p. 9. *Nuremberg Document*, PS 1030

Note
23 *Memoirs of Alfred Rosenberg*, English text, pp. 97, 142
24 Braeutigam, op. cit., p. 7
25 Ibid., p. 9
26 Kleist, p. 156.
27 Thorwald, p. 34
28 *IMT*, XII, p. 16
29 Braeutigam, p. 8. Dallin, op. cit., p. 85
30 *IMT*, XII, p. 15. Document L 221. Full text in *Hitler's Europe*, II, pp. 230–6
31 Braeutigam, p. 3
32 Kleist, p. 155
33 Hans Baur, p. 228
34 Ibid., pp. 206, 250
35 Kleist, p. 156
36 Braeutigam, p. 15
37 *Nuremberg Document*, L 180. Gerald Reitlinger, *The Final Solution*, **pp.**
     212–14
38 Dallin, p. 190
39 Braeutigam, p. 16
40 Kleist, p. 163
41 Ibid., p. 154
42 Kleist, p. 162
43 Toynbee, *Hitler's Europe*, I, p. 291
44 Ibid., pp. 124–5. *Nuremberg Document*, PS 1520
45 Kleist, p. 164
46 Rosenberg, *Letzte Aufzeichnungen*, p. 144
47 Kleist, p. 166
48 Dallin, p. 189
49 Kleist, pp. 167, 227
50 Dallin, p. 194
51 Paul Hausser, *Waffen SS im Einsatz*
52 Toynbee, *Hitler's Europe*, I, p. 571
53 PS 294
54 Reitlinger, *The Final Solution*, pp. 37, 40
55 PS 1520
56 Braeutigam, p. 79
57 Ibid., p. 80. Toynbee, *Hitler's Europe*, I, pp. 573–4
58 *Hitler's Table Talk*, p. 548
59 PS 1017
60 *The Kersten Memoirs*, pp. 173–5 (in the 1947 New York edition)
61 *Hitler's Table Talk*, p. 25
62 PS 1520. Toynbee, *Hitler's Europe*, I, p. 51
63 Eugene. M. Kulischer, *Displacement of Population in Europe*, p. 65. Braeu-
     tigam, p. 32
64 Kleist, p. 170
65 Dallin, p. 285
66 PS 1017
67 PS 1029
68 Reitlinger, *The Final Solution*, p. 210. Documents NO 5530 and 5538
69 Gerald Reitlinger, *The Doubts of Wilhelm Kube*, Wiener Library Bulletin,
     September and December 1950. *Hitler's Table Talk*, p. 176
70 *Aufbau*, New York, XII, NO 36, 1946, *affidavit of von dem Bach—Zelewski*.
     Von Oven, *Mit Goebbels bis zum Ende*, I, p. 113
71 Dallin, p. 217
72 Ibid., p. 223. Braeutigam, p. 16

CHAPTER FIVE

1 *Trials of War Criminals*, X, p. 124
2 W. E. D. Allen, *The Ukraine, a history*, p. 273

Note

[3] Toynbee, *Hitler's Europe*, I, p. 638
[4] Rosenberg, *Letzte Aufzeichnungen*, p. 214
[5] W. E. D. Allen, p. 338
[6] Thorwald, *Wen sie verderbern wollen*, p. 239
[7] Paul Leverkuehn, *German Military Intelligence*, pp. 158–9
[8] *Nazi-Soviet Relations*, p. 145
[9] Leverkuehn, p. 160
[10] *Nazi-Soviet Relations*, p. 107
[11] Leverkuehn, p. 163. *IMT*, VI, p. 252, affidavit Colonel Erwin Stolze
[12] Wiener Library Bulletin, 1950, No 4
[13] John A. Armstrong, *Ukrainian Nationalism*, pp. 66–68, 74
[14] Case IX, NO 2651, PS 3876
[15] Reitlinger, *The Final Solution*, pp. 227–30. Josef Tennenbaum, *In Search of a Lost People*, New York, 1948, p. 115. A. Silberschein, *Extermination des juifs en Pologne*, Geneva (stencil) 1945, No 8
[16] Text in Armstrong, pp. 79–80
[17] Leverkuehn, p. 164. Armstrong, p. 80
[18] Armstrong, p. 82. Dallin, p. 120
[19] Nuremberg Trials Case IX, transcript, pp. 930–9
[20] Armstrong, op. cit., pp. 85, 92–98
[21] Ibid., pp. 92, 102
[22] Ibid., pp. 116–17
[23] Document L 221 and see Chapter Four, p. 28
[24] Kleist, op. cit., p. 187
[25] Dallin, p. 128 (unpublished minute)
[26] Leverkuehn, *The German Secret Service*, p. 166
[27] *IMT*, XII, p. 108
[28] Dallin, pp. 118, 598
[29] Erich Kern, *Der Grosse Rausch*, p. 57
[30] *IMT*, VII, p. 177
[31] Braeutigam, p. 19
[32] *IMT*, VII, p. 281
[33] PS 196
[34] Reitlinger, *The Final Solution*, p. 413
[35] PS 3319
[36] Peter Bamm, *Die Unsichtbaere Flagge*, p. 240
[37] *IMT*, VI, pp. 282–3
[38] *The Ciano Diaries*, p. 385
[39] Filippo Anfluso, *Du Palais de Venise au Lac de Garde*, pp. 186–7
[40] Nuremberg Document, L 221
[41] Rosenberg, p. 213
[42] Kleist, p. 191. Erich Dwinger, *General Wlassow*, p. 28
[43] Leverkuehn, p. 166
[44] *Hitler's Table Talk*, p. 677
[45] PS 025. *IMT*, XV, p. 166
[46] PS 192, *IMT*, XII, p. 31
[47] Robert Waite, *Vanguard of Nazism*, p. 237
[48] Konrad Heiden, *Geschichte des Nationalsozialistische Partei*, Berlin, 1932, pp. 232–3. *Der Fuehrer*, Boston, 1944, p. 299
[49] Konrad Heiden, *Hitler, das Leben eines Diktators*, Zuerich, 1936, p. 260
[50] *Hitler's Table Talk*, p. 53 (26.6.42)
[51] Gisevius, *To the Bitter End*, p. 207
[52] *The Times*, 23.10.58
[53] Hjalmar Schacht, *My First Seventy-Six Years*, pp. 349–50. *IMT*, IV, p. 32
[54] Ulrich von Hassell, *Diaries*, English text, 1948, p. 219
[55] Walter Hagen, *Die geheime Front*, p. 13
[56] Gisevius, p. 208
[57] Schwerin von Krosigk, *Es geschah im Deutschland*, 1951, pp. 164–5
[58] Rosenberg, p. 213. Erich Koch, *Aufbau im Osten*

Note
59 Hilger, *The Incompatible Allies*, p. 268
60 *The von Hassell Diaries*, p. 218
61 Thorwald, *Wen sie verderbern wollen*, pp. 41–42
62 Kleist, p. 150
63 Thorwald, p. 75
64 PS 264, *IMT*, VII, p. 151
65 *Nuremberg Document*, L 221. A decree incorporating the 'Bezirk Bialystok' (Document NG 3480) is quoted by Dallin, p. 90
66 Kleist, op. cit., p. 150
67 *Nuremberg Document*, L 221
68 Braeutigam, *Ueberblick*, etc., p. 80
69 *Hitler's Table Talk*, p. 548
70 Braeutigam, p. 21. Dallin, pp. 253–6
71 Clifton Childe, in *Hitler's Europe*, I, p. 643
72 *The Goebbels Diaries*, p. 270
73 Dallin, pp. 263, 359
74 See the entries in Kienast, *Die Grossdeutsche Reichstag*, 1943
75 Kienast, p. 248
76 *Nuremberg Document*, L 221
77 Toynbee, *Hitler's Europe*, I, p. 634n.
78 Armstrong, p. 122
79 Braeutigam, p. 42. Armstrong, p. 220
80 Braeutigam, p. 34, quoted in Dallin, op. cit., p. 324
81 Unpublished document, NG 3513
82 *The Goebbels Diaries*, p. 149
83 Braeutigam, p. 32a
84 Ibid., p. 37
85 Gallin, pp. 327–9
86 Ibid., pp. 330–34
87 *Hitler's Europe*, I, pp. 37–40
88 Braeutigam, p. 37
89 *IMT*, XII, p. 87
90 PS 294
91 Dallin, p. 346. Kienast, *Die Grossdeutsche Reichstag*, 1943
92 *Hitler's Table Talk*, p. 68
93 Ibid., p. 38. For the Meyer-Hetling plan see No 2585, and *Hitler's Europe*, I, p. 84. A complete text, occupying 33 pages, was printed in *Vierteljahreshefte fuer Zeitgeschichte*, July 1958
94 PS 1743. *IMT*, VII, pp. 151–4
95 *Hitler's Table Talk*, 27.8.42, p. 665
96 Braeutigam, p. 44

CHAPTER SIX

1 PS 1517. Rosenberg Defence Document, 10
2 Braeutigam, p. 23
3 Kleist, p. 185
4 *The Goebbels Diaries*, p. 37
5 PS 032
6 PS 045
7 Rosenberg Defence Document, 36
8 *The Goebbels Diaries*, p. 149
9 PS 1520
10 NG 1329, Dallin, pp. 138–9
11 *Nuremberg Document*, PS 192, Dallin, p. 157
12 *Hitler's Table Talk*, p. 587
13 PS 660. Full German text, *Vierteljahreshefte fuer Zeitgeschichte*, 1957, No 2, p. 197

Note
[14] *Hitler's Table Talk*, p. 590
[15] *Nuremberg Document*, NG. 1878, quoted in Dallin, p. 457
[16] Rosenberg Defence Document. 36, *IMT*, XII, 56
[17] Rosenberg Defence Document, 14 (letter of 14.10.44)
[18] PS 042, *IMT*, XII, p. 56. Dallin, pp. 144, 457
[19] Braeutigam, p. 60
[20] No 2832, *Einsatzgruppen*, Daily report No 135
[21] Braeutigam, p. 61
[22] *IMT*, XII, p. 58
[23] PS 192
[24] Koch's Memorandum of 16.3.43 in Document PS 192
[25] Document USSR 170, *IMT*, IX, p. 324
[26] Erich Kern, *Der Grosse Rausch*, p. 108
[27] Memorandum of 25.10.42 in Document PS 294
[28] Rosenberg Defence Document, No 19
[29] PS 294. *IMT*, XII, p. 23
[30] Koch's Memorandum, 16.3.43. PS 192
[31] Kienast, *Die Grossdeutsche Reichstag*, 1943. The ensuing narrative is trans-
     lated from Juergen Thorwald, *Wen sie verderbern wollen*, pp. 178–80, and
     purports to be von der Milwe's own account
[32] *The Goebbels Diaries*, p. 182
[33] Hans Baur, *Ich flog Maechtige der Erde*, p. 222
[34] PS 1130. *IMT*, II, p. 290
[35] PS 192
[36] *IMT*, XII, p. 32, quoting PS 192
[37] PS 358
[38] Dallin, p. 000
[39] PS 032. (Tsuman file of *Nuremberg Documents*)
[40] Nuremberg Trials Case IX, Document No. 511
[41] *IMT*, XII, p. 33
[42] Dallin, pp. 160–2, principally quoting notes of Walter Hewel (NG 3288)
[43] *IMT*, XI, p. 123
[44] Dallin, p. 162. Case XI, Document NO 1809
[45] Carl Michel, *Ost und West*, pp. 108, 115
[46] Thorwald, p. 234
[47] Dallin, p. 362 (quoting unpublished Himmler file)
[48] Kleist, p. 183
[49] Rosenberg, *Letzte Aufzeichnungen*, p. 168
[50] Thorwald, p. 227
[51] Dallin, p. 163
[52] Thorwald, p. 238
[53] Rosenberg, p. 166
[54] Thorwald, p. 240
[55] *IMT*, XXI, p. 59
[56] *IMT*, XII, p. 56
[57] All the following details from Leyser's report will be found in the Documents
     PS 265–6
[58] PS 1384
[59] *IMT*, XII, p. 30
[60] Document NG 947, quoted in Dallin, p. 162n
[61] Braeutigam, p. 12a
[62] Dallin, p. 363
[63] Thorwald, p. 240
[64] Gerald Reitlinger, *The SS, Alibi of a Nation*, 1956, pp. 197–200
[65] Braeutigam, op. cit., p. 32a. Alexander Dallin, p. 172
[66] Braeutigam, op. cit., p. 33
[67] Kleist, p. 259
[68] Braeutigam, p. 76
[69] Ibid., p. 81

Note
70 Ibid., pp. 22, 22a
71 Documents EC 317, NO 007
72 PS 1702. *IMT*, II, p. 312
73 Toynbee, *Hitler's Europe*, I, p. 215
74 PS 054
75 PS 192
76 Carl Michel, *Ost und West*, pp. 152–4
77 Erich Kern, *Der Grosse Rausch*, p. 148
78 *The Times*, 27.9.47
79 Peter Bamm, *Die Unsichtbaere Flagge*, p. 286
80 Ibid., p. 240
81 *IMT*, VII, pp. 158–9
82 *IMT*, VII, p. 161
83 Hans Friessner, *Verratene Schlachten*, Hamburg, 1956, p. 27
84 Thorwald, *Es begann an die Weichsel*, p. 29.
85 PS 743. *IMT*, VII, p. 166
86 Kleist, p. 192
87 Thorwald, *Es begann an die Weichsel*, pp 165–8

CHAPTER SEVEN

1 Kleist, pp. 187, 190
2 Hermann Tescke, 1952, p. 181
3 *Nuremberg Document*, R. 130. *IMT*, VII, p. 211
4 Hermann Tescke, pp. 172–5. Fabian von Schlabrendorff, *The Revolt Against Hitler*, London, 1948, p. 79
5 *Nuremberg Document*, L 180
6 *IMT*, XI, pp. 70–1, PS 829
7 PS 2273
8 NG 140, Dallin, p. 40. Ulrich von Hassell, p. 176
9 Hans Baur, *Ich flog Maechtige der Erde*, p. 222
10 *The Goebbels Diaries*, p. 164
11 *Nuremberg Document*, No 2662
12 *Nuremberg Document*, No 2921. Reitlinger, *The SS, Alibi of a Nation*, p. 174
13 Report on the Manstein Trial, *Daily Telegraph*, 2.9.49
14 PS 3713. *IMT*, IV, pp. 20–21
15 Affidavit No 17. (Ernst Rode) *IMT*, IV, p. 22
16 *IMT*, VII, pp. 167–70
17 PS 447
18 NO 1611, Dallin, p. 211
19 *IMT*, IV, p. 26
20 PS 3712
21 Felix Gilbert, *Hitler Directs His War*, pp. 8, 14
22 PS 638, *IMT*, IX, p. 278
23 PS 1742, *IMT*, IX, p. 281
24 *IMT*, X, p. 307. Document D 729
25 Felix Gilbert, p. 9. *IMT*, XVI, p. 22
26 *Trials of War Criminals*, X, p. 1161, Document NOKW 2181
27 Ibid., X, p. 1168. NOKW 2961
28 Solomon M. Schwarz, *Jews in the Soviet Union*, p. 322
29 From a selection of despatches in the *Nuremberg Document*, PS 3943
30 PS 2280 and 3000
31 Document, quoted in report of Koch's trial, *Hanoversche Algemeine Zeitung*, 27.9.58
32 PS 3012, report of Colonel Christiansen, commanding *Einsatzgruppe D*
33 PS 1786, *IMT*, IV, p. 31
34 *Trials of War Criminals*, XI, 608–14. PS 2171
35 Dallin, p. 212, quoting NG 3228

Note
[36] R 135. *IMT*, IV, p. 16
[37] NO 2608
[38] R 124 and R 135
[39] NO 3028. Extracts will be found in Max Weinreich, *Hitler's Professors*
[40] NO 2607, PS 1475
[41] Dallin, op. cit., p. 219
[42] *IMT*, IV, p. 35
[43] Hans Baur, op. cit., p. 223
[44] See the maps in John Armstrong, *Ukrainian Nationalism*, p. 137
[45] Armstrong, pp. 99–100, 139
[46] Ibid., p. 147
[47] Ibid., p. 150
[48] PS 3712, Affidavit, Bach-Zelewski
[49] Armstrong, p. 177
[50] Ibid., p. 184
[51] Solomon M. Schwarz, *The Jews in the Soviet Union*, Syracuse, 1951, p. 200
[52] Ibid, p. 197
[53] *The Schellenberg Memoirs*, p. 311
[54] PS 3407
[55] Peter Bamm, *Die Unsichtbaere Flagge*, p. 205
[56] See the evidence at the Kharkov Trial, December 1943. *The People's Verdict*, London, 1944, p. 54
[57] *The Goebbels Diaries*, p. 74
[58] *Nuremberg Document* NO 3255
[59] Josef Tenenbaum, *In Search of a Lost People*, New York, 1950. Gerald Reitlinger, *The Final Solution*, p. 222–3
[60] PS 3259
[61] Schlabrendorff, *The Revolt Against Hitler*, p. 50
[62] *Trials of War Criminals*, X, p. 332. NOKW 1686
[63] PS 3319 and PS 1752. Max Weinreich, op. cit., pp. 223–33
[64] PS 3663, *IMT*, XII, p. 65. Braeutigam to Lohse, 18.12.41
[65] Karl Loewenstein, *Minsk, in Ghetto der deutschen Juden*, supplement to *Das Parlament*, 7.11.56, p. 717
[66] Reitlinger, *The Final Solution*, pp. 287–9. Wiener Library Bulletin, September and December 1950. *The Doubts of Wilhelm Kube*. Documents NO 2262 and No 4317
[67] George Fischer. *Soviet Opposition to Stalin*, pp. 188–93
[68] Wilfried von Oven, *Mit Goebbels bis zum Ende*. Vol. II, p. 257

CHAPTER EIGHT

[1] USSR 386, *IMT*, VII, pp. 231–2
[2] USSR 51/2, *IMT*, VII, 240
[3] Hans Baur, *Ich flog Maechtige der Ende*, p. 215
[4] PS 580 and PS 1201
[5] Evidence Albert Speer, *IMT*, XVII, p. 22
[6] *IMT*, XV, pp. 72–78
[7] *IMT*, XV, p. 81 and II, p. 240. PS 2974
[8] Rosenberg, *Letzte Aufzeichnungen*, p. 167
[9] *The Goebbels Diaries*, pp. 215 and 251
[10] Rosenberg, p. 166
[11] PS 1666, *IMT*, XV, p. 82
[12] *IMT*, XV, pp. 205, 227
[13] *IMT*, XV, p. 85
[14] Kleist, pp. 193–4
[15] PS 016, Memorandum of 20.4.42
[16] PS 025
[17] *IMT*, XV, p. 166

Note
[18] *IMT*, VII, p. 170
[19] PS 184
[20] *IMT*, VII, pp. 231–2
[21] PS 3040, *IMT*, II, p. 347
[22] *IMT*, XV, p. 87
[23] PS 1520
[24] *IMT*, XV, pp. 102–3
[25] PS 2241, *IMT*, II, 317
[26] *IMT*, XV, p. 103
[27] *Nuremberg Document* L 316 and PS 184
[28] PS 054. *IMT*, I, pp. 316–17
[29] *IMT*, XV, p. 104
[30] *IMT*, p. 121
[31] *Hitler's Table Talk*, pp. 650–1
[32] *IMT*, XV, p. 197. PS 3044
[33] PS 025. *IMT*, XV, p. 166
[34] PS 294
[35] *IMT*, pp. XV, 112, 198
[36] PS 017
[37] *IMT*, XV, p. 202
[38] *IMT*, III, p. 43. PS 654
[39] R 124, *IMT*, II, p. 335
[40] *IMT*, II, p. 296, Document L 61
[41] PS 1063. *IMT*, XV, pp. 117–18. *Trials of War Criminals*, V, p. 273
[42] *IMT*, XV, p. 168
[43] PS 018, *IMT*, XV, p. 100. Reitlinger, *The SS, Alibi of a Nation*, pp. 262–4
[44] S 182. *IMT*, XV, pp. 101–2
[45] PS 407–11, *IMT*, II, p. 349
[46] *The Goebbels Diaries*, p. 215
[47] Ibid., p. 231
[48] PS 019, *IMT*, II, p. 301
[49] PS 315
[50] PS 205, *IMT*, XV, p. 108
[51] Carl Michel, *Ost und West*, pp. 77–94
[52] PS 019. *IMT*, II, p. 301
[53] *IMT*, XV, p. 189
[54] *IMT*, Document S 84
[55] *IMT*, XV, p. 90
[56] *The Goebbels Diaries*, pp. 266–8
[57] Rudolf Sammler, *Goebbels, the Man Next to Hitler*, p. 156
[58] *IMT*, II, p. 302. PS 2280
[59] *IMT*, II, pp. 302, 311. PS 204 and 3000
[60] *IMT*, XVII, p. 87. PS 774
[61] Dallin, p. 434, quoting Document NO 022
[62] PS 266, *IMT*, II, p. 311
[63] R 124
[64] PS 3010. *IMT*, II, p. 303
[65] *Trials of War Criminals*, XI, pp. 608–14. Jenny Spritzer, *Ich War No 10291* Zurich, 1946
[66] Thorwald, *Wen sie verderben wollen*, p. 252
[67] Dallin, p. 449. PS 3040. *IMT*, XV, p. 128
[68] Braeutigam, p. 93
[69] PS 3819
[70] PS 1742. *IMT*, IX, p. 281
[71] NO 002, printed in *Nazi Conspiracy and Aggression*, Annexe B
[72] *Trials*, etc., Vol XI, pp. 574–5
[73] Dallin, p. 589. PS 345 and 117. *IMT*, XV, p. 111
[74] *IMT*, XII, p. 21–23
[75] PS 199, XV, p. 194

Note
[76] PS 200 and 345, *IMT*, XV, p. 111
[77] *IMT*, XII, p. 21
[78] Rosenberg, *Letzte Aufzeichnungen*, p. 239
[79] *IMT*, XV, pp. 111, 194
[80] Dallin, p. 451, Statistical Table
[81] Eberhardt Zeller, *Geist der Freiheit*, p. 177
[82] *Vierteljahreshefte fuer Zeitgeschichte*, No 4, p. 593
[83] Von Oven, *Mit Goebbels bis zum Ende*, Vol. II, p. 212
[84] George Fischer, p. 109
[85] *The Times*, 2.5.45
[86] Ibid., 29.6.45

CHAPTER NINE

[1] Memoranda of 2.4.41. Documents PS 1017 and 1019
[2] *Nuremberg Document* L 221
[3] Dallin, p. 134
[5] Kleist, p. 177
[6] Thorwald, *Wen sie verderbern wollen*, p. 71
[8] Thorwald, p. 122
[7] PS 084. Memorandum from Otto Braeutigam
[8] Thorwald, p. 122
[9] Ibid., p. 71
[10] PS 1520
[11] George Stewart, *The White Armies in Russia*, 1933, p. 28
[12] Ibid., p. 68
[13] Sir Percy Sykes, *A History of Persia*, Vol. II, p. 491–4
[14] *The Times*, 3.7.43
[15] Karl Abshagen, *Canaris, Weltburger und Patriot*, p. 224
[16] Thorwald, p. 116
[17] Ibid., p. 117
[18] Dallin, p. 300
[19] PS 3014 (Aff. Koestring)
[20] Thorwald, p. 107
[21] Carl Michel, *Ost und West*, p. 186
[22] Kleist, p. 178
[23] Peter Bamm, pp. 175, 189
[24] Kleist, p. 178. Kurt von Tippelskirch, *Geschichte des zweiten Weltkrieges*, p. 285
[25] Dallin, p. 240
[26] Kienast, *Die Grossdeutsche Reichstag*, 1943
[27] Thorwald, p.111
[28] *Nuremberg Document*, L 221
[29] Kleist, pp. 178–9
[30] Thorwald, p. 111
[31] Dallin, p. 240
[32] *IMT*, VII, pp. 155–6. *The People's Verdict*, London, 1944, p. 8. (Krasnodar Trial 14.7.43)
[33] *IMT*, VII, p. 97
[34] *IMT*, VII, p. 336. Reitlinger, *The Final Solution*, p. 243
[35] Dallin, p. 247
[36] Erich Kern, *Der Grosse Rausch*, p. 97
[37] Peter Bamm, p. 205
[38] Dallin, p. 246
[39] Thorwald, pp. 114–15
[40] Ibid., p. 130
[41] Thorwald, p. 123. Braeutigam, pp. 96–97
[42] Thorwald, p. 119

Note
43 Ibid., p. 134
44 *The Times*, 12.2.57
45 Kleist, p. 205
46 Thorwald, p. 120. Braeutigam, p. 86
47 PS 477
48 Thorwald, p. 122
49 Ibid., pp. 123–6

CHAPTER TEN

1 Thorwald, *Wen sie verderbern wollen*, pp. 70–80, 250, 565
2 Kleist, p. 200. Dallin, p. 526
3 Thorwald, p. 80
4 *Die Silbernen Spiegel*, p. 181
5 *The Schellenberg Memoirs*, English edition. Thorwald, p. 441. For Himmler's opinion of Kaminsky see his second Posen speech in *Vierteljahreshefte fuer Zeitgeschichte*, 1954.2
6 Hermann von Tescke, p. 31
7 Thorwald, p. 82
8 Evidence Bazilevsky, *IMT*, XVII, pp. 256–62
9 Dallin, p. 529
10 PS 695
11 Thorwald, pp. 178–88
12 PS 1685, Dallin, p. 519
13 *The Goebbels Diaries*, pp. 44, 119
14 Albrecht, op. cit., p. 196
15 Thorwald, p. 54
16 Ibid., p. 94
17 Fischer, pp. 20, 9, 679
18 Thorwald, p. 103
19 Ibid., pp. 94–104
20 Fischer, pp. 166–75
21 Thorwald, p. 142
22 Erich Dwinger, p. 73
23 Thorwald, p. 383
24 George Fischer, pp. 30–32
25 Dwinger, p. 56
26 Dwinger, p. 57. Thorwald, p. 140
27 Thorwald, p. 140–5, Dwinger, p. 58
28 Dallin, p. 555n
29 Thorwald, pp. 150–2. Fischer, p. 33
30 Thorwald, p. 159
31 PS 294
32 Thorwald, p. 159
33 Dallin, p. 546
34 PS 196
35 Thorwald, pp. 182–3
36 Dallin, pp. 153, 547, 561, 643
37 *IMT*, XV, pp. 313, 379
38 Thorwald, p. 60
39 Kleist, pp. 200–201
40 Kleist, p. 201. Schellenberg, p. 317. Fischer, p. 43
41 Fischer, p. 43
42 Thorwald, p. 167
43 Ibid., p. 163–71
44 Carl Michel, *Ost und West*, p. 49
45 Thorwald, pp. 127–8, Michel, pp. 49–60
46 Thorwald, p. 189

Note
47 Dallin, pp. 563–5
48 Ibid., p. 565
49 Thorwald, pp. 197–9
50 Dallin, p. 567
51 Thorwald, p. 211
52 Ibid., p. 276–7
53 Ibid., p. 258
54 Ibid., p. 218
55 Ibid., pp. 219–20
56 Dallin, p. 570–1
57 Thorwald, p. 223
58 *Nuremberg Document* NOKW 3521 in Alexander Dallin, op. cit., p. 573
59 Thorwald, p. 228
60 Carl Michel, p. 173. Thorwald, p. 225
61 Carl Michel, p. 149
62 Ibid., p. 154
63 Dallin, p. 537. Fischer, pp. 45–47
64 Michel, p. 142–73
65 Thorwald, pp. 246–54
66 *The Goebbels Diaries*, pp. 196, 216, 254, 271
67 Michel, p. 116
68 *Der Untermensch*, edited by the *Schulungsamt* of the SS head office and published by Nordland Verlag, n.d.
69 Michel, pp. 106–7
70 Thorwald, pp. 249–63
71 Ibid., p. 260. Dallin, p. 512. Dwinger, pp. 180, 248
72 Thorwald, pp. 241–3. Dallin, p. 514
73 PS 739. Full German text in *Vierteljahreshefte fuer Zeitgeschichte*, Munich, 1954, pp. 309–12

CHAPTER ELEVEN

1 Aff. Albert Speer, PS 3720
2 *IMT*, II, pp. 355–6. Document R 124
3 Hermann Tescke, *Die Silbernen Spiegel*, pp. 195, 197
4 Thorwald, p. 284
5 Ibid., p. 291
6 Felix Gilbert, *Hitler Directs His War*, p. 65
7 Dallin, p. 582
8 Thorwald, p. 298
9 Ibid., p. 302
10 Fischer, p. 54
11 Thorwald, p. 308
12 Document L 178 (in Nuremberg Trial series, XXXVII, 63). Evidence Jodl in *IMT*, XV, p. 288. *Hitler's Europe*, I, p. 228
13 Thorwald, p. 211
14 Sir Percy Sykes, *A History of Persia*, 1921, II, p. 449
15 Thorwald, pp. 313–6
16 *The von Hassell Diaries*, p. 290
17 Thorwald, p. 331
18 Allen Dulles, *Germany's Underground*, New York, 1947, p. 137
19 Hans Gisevius, *To the Bitter End*, pp. 501–4
20 Michel, pp. 183–4
21 Thorwald, p. 311
22 Thorwald, p. 398. Dallin, p. 614n
23 Thorwald, pp. 395, 402
24 Ibid., pp. 404–5
25 Ibid., p. 397

Notes
[26] Kleist, p. 259
[27] Thorwald, pp. 269–70
[28] For the two Himmler speeches: see *Nuremberg Document* PS 1919 for the
    Posen speech and L 70 for the Bad Schachen speech. Best printed German
    version, Thorwald, p. 304. Also Fischer, p. 73, and Dallin, p. 593
[29] Felix Gilbert, *Hitler Directs His War*, pp. 147–9
[30] Reitlinger, *The SS, Alibi of a Nation*, 1956, p. 157
[31] John A. Armstrong, *Ukrainian Nationalism*, 1939–45, p. 49
[32] Thorwald, pp. 328–40. Arlt is now a Lecturer at the Institute of German
    Industry in Cologne
[33] Nuremberg Trials Case IX, Transcript, p. 6864
[34] *The People's Verdict*, London, 1944, p. 100 (Kharkov Trial)
[35] Dallin, pp. 603, 615
[36] Ibid., p. 605
[37] Thorwald, p. 42. Fischer, p. 79
[38] Dwinger, p. 213
[39] Thorwald, p. 363
[40] Ibid., pp. 336–8
[41] Carl Michel, op. cit., pp. 251–3
[42] Thorwald, pp. 463–4
[43] Dwinger, p. 293
[44] Thorwald, pp. 376–7
[45] Ibid., p. 383
[46] Ibid., p. 385
[47] Ibid., pp. 380–94
[48] Dallin, pp. 619–20. Peter Kleist, op. cit., pp. 252–3
[49] Reitlinger, *The SS, Alibi of a Nation*, pp. 394–9
[50] Thorwald, p. 409
[51] Armstrong, pp. 180–6. Thorwald, pp. 342–3. Fischer, p. 207
[52] Dallin, p. 627
[53] No 3125, quoted in Dallin, p. 632. Thorwald, p. 426
[54] Thorwald, pp. 422–3
[55] Ibid., p. 425
[56] Ibid., p. 428
[57] Kleist, p. 224. Dallin, p. 635
[58] Fischer, p. 81
[59] Thorwald, pp. 426–7. Buchardt MS, quoted by Fischer, p. 85
[60] Dwinger, p. 315
[61] Full text in Fischer, pp. 194–200
[62] Buchardt MS, quoted in Dallin, p. 633
[63] Michel, p. 256

CHAPTER TWELVE

[1] Reitlinger, *The SS, Alibi of a Nation*, p. 376
[2] Thorwald, pp. 439–41
[3] Ibid., pp. 467–8. Dallin, pp. 640–4
[4] Text in Fischer, pp. 94–95
[5] PS 3786, full version in German text of Nuremberg Trial, XXXIII, pp.
    81–144
[6] Ibid., pp. 103–5
[7] Dallin, p. 649
[8] Felix Gilbert, *Hitler Directs His War*, p. 147
[9] Nuremberg Trials Case XI, Judgment, Transcript 28401
[10] Communication to the author from Mr Roland Gant
[11] Thorwald, p. 469
[12] Thorwald, p. 480. Fischer, p. 211. The boast was repeated by Vlasov at
    Karlsbad sixteen days later

Note
[13] Thorwald, p. 477
[14] Reitlinger, op. cit., pp. 404–7
[15] Nuremberg Trials Case XI, Transcript, p. 28402
[16] Thorwald, p. 483
[17] Felix Gilbert, *Hitler Directs His War*, p. 134
[18] Reitlinger, *The SS*, p. 408
[19] Dallin, p. 648
[20] Ibid., pp. 652–3
[21] *The Times*, 19.5.45. Some Vlasov men were identified as far East as Teschen in Upper Silesia, *Daily Telegraph*, 19.10.45
[22] Dallin, p. 656. Thorwald, p. 418. Reitlinger, *The Final Solution*, p. 481
[23] Thorwald, p. 486
[24] Ibid., pp. 488–92
[25] Ibid., p. 500
[26] Reitlinger, *The SS*, p. 384. *The Times*, 5.8.58
[27] Thorwald, p. 500
[28] Ibid., p. 538
[29] Ibid., pp. 532–5
[30] Ibid., p. 522 Dwinger, pp. 342–52
[31] Various accounts in Payne-Best, *The Venlo Incident*, Hjalmar Schacht, *My First Seventy-Six Years*
[32] Thorwald, pp. 525–9
[33] Ibid., pp. 529–31
[34] Ibid., p. 536
[35] Ibid., pp. 554–5
[36] Ibid., p. 558
[37] Fischer, p. 102
[38] Thorwald, pp. 544–51
[39] There are two slightly differing accounts in Fischer, pp. 115–16
[40] Thorwald, pp. 551–4
[41] Ibid., pp. 563–4
[42] Fischer, p. 116
[43] Ibid., p. 49
[44] Paul Hausser, *Waffen SS im Einsatz*. Ernst Kraetschmer, *Die Ritterkreuztraeger der Waffen SS*
[45] Thorwald, pp. 564–72
[46] Reitlinger, *The Final Solution*, p. 125n
[47] Fischer, pp. 108–112
[48] Thorwald, pp. 572–4
[49] *The Times*, 12.4.52
[50] Fischer, p. 116
[51] Ibid., p. 120

BIBLIOGRAPHY

IN WRITING A book of this kind, the current practice is to fill a third of every page with a sort of biblical commentary in the smallest of print, abounding with cryptic initials and with names that are not to be found in the index. This practice both impresses university examiners and puts reviewers in their place, besides comforting the reader with the thought that he has mastered a learned work.

I should have liked well to dispense with all this apparatus, had it been possible to do so. Unfortunately, while the footnotes have been reduced to a minimum, on most pages the cryptic initials remain. This is because the sources consist largely of German documents and these are only available for consultation in the printed or stencilled extracts which were prepared for the Nuremberg war trials. The initials offer the only means of simple reference to the sources. They can be explained briefly.

Where a document was used in the first Nuremberg trial, the International Military Tribunal trial or IMT, the fact is denoted by the initials PS (the great majority), EC, S, L, R and USSR. Where the document was used in the twelve later trials, which were conducted by the American Nuremberg Tribunal, it bears the initials, NG, NO or NOKW. Where excerpts were read in court during examination and cross-examination of witnesses, the presentation and the replies will be found in the printed court transcripts. The transcript of the International Nuremberg Trials is quoted under the initials IMT and the volume and page numbers follow the London (HM Stationery Office) text, *Trial of the German Major War Criminals*, in twenty-three volumes, 1946–51. In the case of the twelve later Nuremberg trials, excerpts from the evidence are quoted mostly from the published text, known as *Trials of War Criminals* and published in Washington in fourteen volumes in 1951–3. This series, however, contains only an extremely abridged selection of documents and court transcripts.

As regards access to documents, this is simple in the case of the IMT trial. Extracts will be found, printed in the original German text, in the forty-two volume edition of the trial which was printed in Nuremberg by the American occupation authorities under the same title as the shorter London edition. The initial headings PS, S, L, EC and USSR will be found on the binding of the volumes. A rather less complete selection will be found printed in English in the eleven-volume Washington series, which bears the title, *Nazi Conspiracy and Aggression*. It must be emphasized that in very many cases only relevant portions of the documents have been printed.

In the case of the NO, NG and NOKW documents which are cited in the footnotes, consultation is not such a simple matter. Where the extracts have been printed in the Washington series, *Trials of War Criminals*, the page and volume references are given. In most cases, however, photostats or stencil copies have been used and these must be sought in such document centres as the Foreign Office Library, Library of Congress, Institut fuer Zeitgeschichte or Centre de documentation juive contemporaine.

As regards published works on the Germans in Russia, some very important studies have appeared in the past seven years, notably those of Otto Braeutigam, Juergen Thorwald, Peter Kleist, George Fischer, John A. Armstrong and Alexander Dallin, to all of which the present work is considerably indebted. On the other hand only one leading figure has left his memoirs and these, the *Letzte Aufzeichnungen* of Alfred Rosenberg, are, save for a few indiscretions and some revealing passages, a mountain of useless litter. Specialized studies of the Germans in Russia add up to a very short list and some of them are of indifferent value, Thorwald's book, *Wen sie verderben wollen*, is a magnificent and indispensable piece of reporting, which suffers only from the author's determination to make all his material equally dramatic and readable. In this book, as in Dwinger's book and Michel's, the Thucydidaean device of the personal dialogue is often used to make the story more lively. It goes without saying that this reduces the value of the work as a source book, in spite of the enormous numbers of protagonists whom Thorwald interviewed or who wrote their stories for him. Thorwald, therefore, requires the use of companion studies. The most judicious seems to me that of Mr George Fischer, who lowers the reader to the ground gently from some of Thorwald's romantic peaks. Two other German authors, who cover the same ground, took some part in the events, but the position of Erich Dwinger and Carl Michel was hardly that of experts or practical men. Their books, which have been quoted far more sparingly, are interesting as displaying the outlook of polemists for rival causes. Objective they are certainly not.

On the other hand one actively concerned person has produced a brilliant critique of German policies—and so objective as to have the value of an original document. It is unfortunate that Otto Braeutigam's *Ueberblick* is very short and distributed only in stencilled copies. A colleague, Peter Kleist, has also left his memoirs but these are much more sardonic in tone and more in the nature of a personal vindication. Kleist is a brilliant observer and to him I owe a string of witty stories which lighten the monotony of the scene. The Americans, Armstrong and Dallin, seem to me to offer less than Braeutigam and Kleist, in spite of their long years of arduous research, their painstaking interrogations of survivors and their knowledge of Slavonic tongues. Both authors devote a great deal of space to newspaper polemics by small political groups of Russians or Ukrainians who collaborated with the Germans against Stalin. Most of these groups were and are inconceivably obscure—and fortunately they are likely to remain so. Thus Mr Armstrong fails to make the divided aims of his Ukrainian politicians at all lucid, while Mr Dallin sees the conflicts of German bureaucracy from so many different facets that the resultant vistas recall the mirror-lined hotel lifts that added fascination to an Edwardian childhood. The pioneering work of these two authors is nevertheless prodigious and absolutely indispensable to the student.

The second and longer list includes books which are only partly concerned with the occupation of Russia. Thus Hermann Tescke, Peter Bamm and Erich Kern give glimpses of the soldiers' point of view. *Hitler's Table Talk* and the *Goebbels Diary* afford all too rare glimpses of German policy at the highest level—or rather its absence. Gisevius, Allen Dulles and Ulrich von Hassell shed a faint and dubious light on the links between *Ostpolitik* and the Resistance circle. Schellenberg, Abshagen and Leverkuehn illustrate the rôle of the German Intelligence services. Hilger's book and the Halder Diary complete the document sequence for the preliminary invasion plans, which can be studied in the State Department publication, *Nazi-Soviet Relations.* Other books and articles reveal only a relevant detail here and there.

Abshagen, Karl — *Canaris*, translated by Alan Houghton-Brodrick. London, 1956.

Albrecht, Karl — *Sie aber werden der Welt zerstoeren.* Munich, 1954.

Allen, W. E. D. — *The Ukraine, a history.* Cambridge, 1940.

Anfuso, Filippo — *Du palais de Venise au lac de Garde.* Paris, 1949.

Armstrong, John A. — *Ukrainian Nationalism, 1939–1945.* New York, 1955.

Bamm, Peter (Kurt Emmrich) — *Die unsichtbaere Flagge.* Munich, 1952.

Baur, Flugkapitaen Hans — *Ich flog Maechtige der Erde.* Kempten im Allgaeu, 1956.

Braeutigam, Otto — *Ueberblick ueber die besetzten Ostgebiete waehrend des 2. Weltkrieges.* (Stencil) Tuebingen, 1954.

Ciano, Count Galeazzo — *Ciano's Diary, 1939–1943.* London, 1947.

Dallin, Alexander — *German Rule in Russia, 1941–1945.* London, 1957.

Dulles, Allen — *Germany's Underground.* New York, 1947.

Dwinger, Erich — *General Wlassow, ein Tragoedie unserer Zeit.* Ueberlingen, 1951.

Fischer, George — *Soviet Opposition to Stalin, a case study of World War II.* Harvard, 1952.

Friessner, Generaloberst A. D. Hans — *Verratene Schlachten.* Hamburg, 1956.

Gilbert, Felix — *Hitler Directs His War.* New York, 1950.

Gisevius, Hans Berndt — *To the Bitter End.* London, 1948.

Goebbels, Josef — *The Goebbels Diaries*, edited by Louis Lochner. London, 1948.

Greiner, Helmuth — *Die Oberste Wehrmachtfuehrung, 1939–43.* Wiesbaden, 1952.

Hagen Walter (Wilhelm Hoettl) — *Die geheime Front.* Linz, 1950.

Halder, Franz — *Tagebuch, 1939–1942.* Stencil copy, 1947 (available at Wiener Library, London).

Hassell, Ulrich von — *The von Hassell Diaries, 1938–1944.* London, 1948.

Hilger, Gustav and Alfred G. Meyer	*The Incompatible Allies*, a memoir history of German-Soviet relations. New York, 1953.
Himmler, Heinrich (edited by)	*Der Untermensch*. Berlin, 1942. For speeches, see *Nuremberg Documents*, PS 1919 and L 70. Also, *Vierteljahreshefte fuer Zeitgeschichte*. Munich, Vol. 4, 1953.
Hitler, Adolf	*Mein Kampf, 1925 and 1926*. Quoted in English version, Reynal and Hitchcock, New York, 1939. *Hitler's Table Talk, 1941–1944*. London, 1953.
Institute of International Affairs	*Chronology of the Second World War*. London, 1947.
Kalinow, Kyrill D.	*Sowiet Marschaelle haben das Wort*. Hamburg, 1950.
Kern, Erich	*Der Grosse Rausch, Russlandfeldzug, 1941–45*. Zuerich, 1948.
Kersten, Felix	*The Kersten Memoirs* (Totenkopf und Treue). London, 1956.
Kienast, E.	*Der Grossdeutsche Reichstag, 1943*.
Kleist, Peter	*Zwischen Hitler und Stalin*. Bonn, 1950.
Koch, Erich	*Aufbau im Osten*. Breslau, 1934.
Kuehl, Robert L.	*RKFDV*, German resettlement and population policy, 1939–45. Harvard, 1957.
Leverkuehn, Paul	*German Military Intelligence*. London, 1954.
Liddell-Hart, B. H.	*The Other Side of the Hill*. London, 1948.
Lowenstein, Karl	*Minsk, im Lager der deutschen Juden*. Supplement, *Das Parlament* 7.11.56.
Luther, Michel	*Die Krim unter deutscher Besatzung im zweiten Weltkrieg*. Berlin, 1956.
Manstein, Erich von	*Verlorene Siege*. Bonn, 1955.
Michel, Carl	*Ost und West, der Ruf Stauffenbergs*. Zuerich, 1947.
Nazi-Soviet Relations (1939–41)	Edited by James Sontag and James Stuart Beddie. Washington, 1948.
Nazi Conspiracy and Aggression	Eleven volumes. Washington, 1947–9. (See observations on Nuremberg trial documents).
Oven, Wilfried von	*Mit Goebbels bis zum Ende*. Two vols. Buenos Ayres, 1949.
Red Cross Committee	Report of the International Committee of the Red Cross, 1939–47. Vol III, relief activities. Geneva, 1948.
Reitlinger, Gerald	*The Final Solution*, the attempt to exterminate the Jews of Europe, 1939–45. London, 1953. *The SS, Alibi of a*

	Nation. London, 1956. *The Doubts of Wilhelm Kube.* (Wiener Library Bulletin, September and December, 1950.)
Rosenberg, Alfred	*Letzte Aufzeichnungen, Ideale und Idole der Nazionalsozialistischen Revolution.* Goettingen, 1955.
Schellenberg, Walter	*The Schellenberg Memoirs,* edited by Louis Hagen. London, 1956.
Schlabrendorff, Fabian von	*Offiziere gegen Hitler.* Zuerich, 1946.
Schwarz, Solomon M.	*The Jews of the Soviet Union.* Syracuse, 1952.
Tescke, Hermann	*Die silbernen Spiegel.* Heidelberg, 1952.
Tippelskirch, Kurt von	*Geschichte des zweiten Weltkrieges.* Bonn, 1951.
Thorwald, Juergen	*Wen sie verderben wollen. Bericht des grossen Verrats.* Stuttgart, 1952.
Toynbee, Arnold and Veronica (edited by)	*Hitler's Europe,* 2 vols. Oxford, 1954.
Weinreich, Max	*Hitler's Professors.* New York, 1946.
Wheeler-Bennett, J. W.	*The Nemesis of Europe, The German Army in Politics, 1919–45.* London, 1953.
Wilmot, Chester	*The Struggle for Europe.* London, 1952.
Zeller, Eberhard	*Geist der Freiheit.* Munich, 1953.

APPENDIX I

Comparative chronological tables of the German Occupation of Russia and subsequent fighting on the Eastern Front, June 1941–May 1945.

Military Events	Civil Government Events	German-sponsored Russian Liberation Movements
JUNE 1941 22.6.41. Soviet Union invaded. 24.6.41. Vilna and Kaunas taken. 30.6.41. Lwow taken.	**JUNE 1941** 14.6.41. Hitler on 'abandoning' the usual restraints of warfare. 29.6.41. Hitler defines Goering's independence of action in Russia.	**JUNE 1941** Roland and Nachtigall Ukrainian battalions serve under German Abwehr.
JULY 1941 1.7.41. Riga captured. 16.7.41. Smolensk and Pskov areas reached. 11.7.41. Encirclements claimed at Minsk and Bialystok.	**JULY 1941** 12.7.41. Stalin's appeal to the conquered areas. 16.7.41. Hitler at Angerburg announces civil government areas. 25.7.41. Civil government in the north as far as the Dvina river.	**JULY 1941** 2–11.7.41. The so-called Stetsko Ukrainian government in Lwow.
AUGUST 1941 5.8.41. Defeat of Budenny offensive in Ukraine. 14.8.41. Smolensk taken. 20.8.41. Germans surrounding Leningrad. 28.8.41. Reval and Dniepropetrovsk fall.	**AUGUST 1941** 19.8.41. Hitler confirms Rumanian occupation of Ukraine as far as the Bug. 25.8.41. Civil government established in Volhynia and Zhitomir under Erich Koch.	**AUGUST 1941** Mass arrests of pro-Bandera Partisans in western Soviet Ukraine.

SEPTEMBER 1941 12.9.41. Chernigov taken. 19.9.41. Kiev taken. 26.9.41. 655,000 prisoners on Southern Army Group front.	**SEPTEMBER 1941** 29.9.41. Greatest massacre of Jews in Kiev. 29.9.41. Hitler announces no preferential treatment for Ukraine. 'Policy by postponement. No alternative to collective farms'. 25.9.41. Hitler refuses to rescind the Commissar Order.	**SEPTEMBER 1941** A Ukrainian republic or Sich established by Borovets in Polesia with Wehrmacht connivance. Hitler receives Russian collaborationist manifesto from Smolensk.
OCTOBER 1941 2.10.41. Opening of the Moscow offensive. 8.10.41. Orel taken. 13.10.41. Briansk and Viasma taken. 16.10.41. Rumanians take Odessa. 24.10.41. Kharkov taken. 29.10.41. Germans in Crimea and seventy-five miles from Moscow.	**OCTOBER 1941** Backe in the Ukraine. Reports against plans for decollectivization. 10.10.41. Reichenau order of the day against fraternization in the Ukraine.	**OCTOBER 1941** First Russian anti-Partisan units created with connivance of Generals Schenckendorff and Rudolf Schmidt in White Russia. Von Tresckow's plan for a Russian volunteer army.
NOVEMBER 1941 25.11.41. Turn of the tide on Moscow front. 28.11.41. Von Kleist in retreat from Rostov. Most of Crimea taken.	**NOVEMBER 1941** 8.11.41. Goering re-issues the instructions in the 'Green File' forbidding decollectivization. Goering announces that military and civil prisoners from Russia will work in Germany.	**NOVEMBER 1941** Von Bock forwards Tresckow's plan to Hitler's headquarters during the battle for Moscow. First volunteer units from Soviet Moslem nationalities.
DECEMBER 1941 11.12.41. Hitler announces winter campaign for Moscow is over. 19.12.41. Hitler takes over as commander-in-chief Russia.	**DECEMBER 1941** 16.12.41. Hitler receives decollectivization plan of Economic Staff East.	**DECEMBER 1941** Hitler finally rejects Tresckow's plan for a Russian volunteer army.
JANUARY 1942 19.1.42. Russians retake Mozhaisk on Moscow front.	**JANUARY 1942** 29.1.42. Conflict between Rosenberg and Koch over restoration of religion in Ukraine.	**JANUARY 1942**

Military Events	Civil Government Events	German-sponsored Russian Liberation Movements
FEBRUARY 1942 23.2.42. Russian offensive in White Russia recaptures Dorogobuzh. Von Busch encircled at Staraya Russa. Partisan conspiracy in Minsk.	FEBRUARY 1942 8.2.42. Speer succeeds Todt as Minister for Armaments. 20.2.42. 627,000 Russian workers to be sent to Germany. 26.2.42. Agrarian decree published, progressive decollectivization. Measures against OUN nationalists in Kiev.	FEBRUARY 1942 24.2.42. Stalin declaration; 'not at war with the German people but with Fascism'. 25.2.42. Braeutigam memorandum attacking German occupation policy.
MARCH 1942 15.3.42. Hitler promises Russian 'annihilation' in the summer. Sporadic Russian attacks on central and northern fronts.	MARCH 1942 24.3.42. Amended rules on treatment of prisoners of war. 16.3.42. Rosenberg protests at Koch's policy in Ukraine. 21.3.42. Sauckel takes over as plenipotentiary for labour recruitment.	MARCH 1942 18.3.42. Schenckendorff's memorandum on use of Russian volunteers. Russian collaborationist centre established by Wehrmacht Propaganda, Section IV.
APRIL 1942 18.4.42. Von Leeb replaced on northern front by von Kuechler. Vlasov's 2nd Shock Army cut off by the thaw.	APRIL 1942	APRIL 1942 20.4.42. OKW sanctions formation of Caucasian and Turki national legions.
MAY 1942 13.5.42. Russian offensive at Kharkov countered by Germans on 19th.	MAY 1942 Rosenberg visits Ostland; disagreements with Lohse. Ribbentrop forbidden to interfere in Russian policy.	MAY 1942 The Soviet Party officials Zhilenkov and Zykov working for Wehrmacht Propaganda, IV.

JUNE 1942	JUNE 1942 Memorandum for Hitler drawn up in the Eastern Ministry, so-called *Grosse Denkschrift*. Sauckel in Smolensk. Army leaders criticize labour conscription.	JUNE 1942 10–25.6.42. Successful German action to rectify front at Kharkov. 28.6.42. Opening of German Caucasus offensive at Kursk.
JULY 1942 Mid-July, Vlasov surrenders on Volkhov front. Cossacks of the Don recruited by Army Group B.	JULY 1942 Hitler at Vinnitsa. 23.7.42. Bormann's 'eight principles for civil government in the east.'	JULY 1942 4.7.42. Germans reach Don river. 24.7.42. Germans capture Rostov and enter Kuban territory.
AUGUST 1942 SS recruiting legionaries in Estonia and Latvia. 3.8.42. First Vlasov manifesto.	AUGUST 1942 6.8.42. Goering's food production conference calls attention to Partisan menace. 10.8.42. Ernst Koestring, military governor, Kuban-Caucasus.	AUGUST 1942 8.8.42. Germans capture Krasnodar and Maikop. 13.8.42. Reach Caucasus foothills. 26.8.42. Furthest SE penetration at Mozdok.
SEPTEMBER 1942 10.9.42. First Vlasov airborne leaflet distributed. Vlasov kept in Berlin. 8.9.42. Native governments in Caucasus recognized by OKW.	SEPTEMBER 1942 3.9.42. Hitler decides that some Ukrainians can be Germanized. He demands half a million Ukrainian domestic servants.	SEPTEMBER 1942 5.9.42. Novorossiisk taken. 16.9.42. Germans in outskirts of Stalingrad. 23.9.42. First Russian counter-attack in Stalingrad region.
OCTOBER 1942 25.10.42. Braeutigam memorial demanding a political declaration for occupied Russia.	OCTOBER 1942 3.10.42. Ukraine to produce 450,000 armament workers. 28.10.42. Koch bans technical schools in Ukraine.	OCTOBER 1942 Halder superseded by Zeitzler. Stalemate at Stalingrad. German Caucasus offensive resumed at Nalchik on 29.8.42.

Military Events	Civil Government Events	German-sponsored Russian Liberation Movements
NOVEMBER 1942 24.11.42. Stalingrad cut off by Russian counter-offensive. In White Russia Germans withdraw to within forty miles of Smolensk.	NOVEMBER 1942 10.11.42. Hitler confirms limited autonomy for the Cossacks.	NOVEMBER 1942 25.11.42. Gehlen recommends a sham declaration of independence. Vlasov under pressure to sign.
DECEMBER 1942 29.12.42. Stalingrad doomed by German loss of Kotelnikovo.	DECEMBER 1942 Joint recommendations of Rosenberg and the military governors turned down by Hitler. Koch sends to Berlin butter from Ukraine.	DECEMBER 1942 15.12.42. Inspectorate of all eastern troops set up. 24.12.42. Vlasov signs 'Smolensk manifesto'.
JANUARY 1943 Gradual German evacuation of the Caucasus and Don fronts. Stalingrad and the 6th Army 100 miles behind the front.	JANUARY 1943 New industrial policy in Ukraine. Dnieperstroi dam repaired. All mines and factories to restart work.	JANUARY 1943 Westward trek of collaborationist tribes from the Cossack steppes and the Caucasus. Rosenberg sanctions Smolensk manifesto.
FEBRUARY 1943 2.2.43. Capitulation of Stalingrad army, Fall of Kursk 8.2.43, Rostov 14.2.43, Kharkov 16.2.43. Donetz basin lost.	FEBRUARY 1943 Labour deportation to Reich stops through lack of transport. 23.2.43. Rosenberg fails to re-open technical schools in Ukraine. Hitler turns down autonomy plan for the Baltic States.	FEBRUARY 1943 The Smolensk manifesto circulated on both sides of the front. 24.2.43. Vlasov begins his first tour of occupied Russia. Dabendorff school established for Russian collaborationists.

MARCH 1943	MARCH 1943	MARCH 1943
8.3.43. Opening of last successful German counter-offensive in the east. 15.3.43. Germans re-occupy Kharkov. Kuban front withdrawn.	Heldengreif commission combing out German civil government personnel. 16.3.43. Koch's memorial against Rosenberg. Labour deportation resumed.	Vlasov criticizes German policy at Mogilev and Brest. Eastern volunteers now number 800,000.
APRIL 1943	**APRIL 1943**	**APRIL 1943**
Almost a complete lull on the Russian front. Hitler receives his wilting satellite leaders. 19.4.43. Goebbels publishes the Katyn revelations.	Rosenberg accuses Koch of the Tsuman forest scandal. UPA controlling large parts of Volhynia. 16.4.43. Better treatment announced for eastern workers. Sauckel in Russia seeking a million workers in four months.	SS Galician division planned. Vlasov visits northern front. Eastern volunteers receive ROA badge. Keitel bans Vlasov's activities. Leaflet No. 13 held up.
MAY 1943	**MAY 1943**	**MAY 1943**
Lull on the Russian front continues. The German offensive 'Operation Citadel', postponed. Fierce anti-Partisan campaign in western White Russia.	19.5.43. Hitler decides between Rosenberg and Koch. The latter now virtually independent. Sauckel labour programme breaking down everywhere. White Russia written off.	Rosenberg backs out of the plan for a Proclamation for the East after conference 25.5.43. Pannwitz Cossack corps formed.
JUNE 1943	**JUNE 1943**	**JUNE 1943**
General lull on eastern front but 'Operation Cortbus' concluded against Partisans and Kovpak begins his raid to the Carpathians.	Second Agrarian decree abolishing collective farms. 2.6.43. Rosenberg visits the Ukraine. Complaints of Leyser and von Kleist. Koch again opposes opening the technical schools.	8.6.43. Hitler rejects a genuine proclamation of Russian independence, but tolerates an improvement of the volunteer status. 2.6.43. Storm over Oberlaenders 'twenty propositions'.
JULY 1943	**JULY 1943**	**JULY 1943**
5.7.43. 'Operation Citadel' opened in Kursk sector. 15.7.43. Failure of 'Citadel'. Russians open offensive at Orel.	Koch continues to resist the restoration of private land-ownership in the Ukraine. Gottlob Berger, Himmler's chief of staff, invited to direct Rosenberg's Political Department.	1.7.43. Hitler reaffirms his opposition to Russian liberation. Transfer of volunteers to the mines advocated by Speer.

Military Events	Civil Government Events	German-sponsored Russian Liberation Movements
AUGUST 1943 Russians recapture Orel on 4.8.43, Kharkov on 23.8.43 and Taganrog on 30.8.43. Germans moving back to Dnieper line.	AUGUST 1943 17.8.43. Sauckel orders conscription of boys of sixteen in Ukraine. Return of Kovpak from his raid, leaving most of western Ukraine in hands of nationalists.	AUGUST 1943 Numerous desertions of volunteer anti-Partisan units reported in the threatened sectors.
SEPTEMBER 1943 8.9.43. Stalin announces recapture of entire Donetz basin. Briansk retaken 17.9.43; Chernigov 21.9.43; Poltava 23.9.43, Smolensk 25.9.43, Kremenchug 29.9.43.	SEPTEMBER 1943 7.9.43. Scorched Earth order for the Ukraine published by Himmler and Goering. Koch informed that Hitler regards the private property decree as a dead letter.	SEPTEMBER 1943 14.9.43. Hitler wants to send all the volunteers to the coalmines. Decision postponed. Kaminsky government evacuated from Lokot.
OCTOBER 1943 7.10.43. Nevel retaken and Dnieper crossed. Zaporozhe retaken 14.10.43; Melitopol 23.10.43, Dniepropetrovsk 25.10.43.	OCTOBER 1943 Deportation to concentration camps from Vitebsk. Children rounded up on Leningrad front. von Gottberg, Generalkommissar, White Russia.	OCTOBER 1943 10.10.43. Hitler orders removal of all volunteers from occupied Russia. von Pannwitz's Cossacks in Yugoslavia; Turcoman division in Italy. Himmler's two denunciations of Vlasov.
NOVEMBER 1943 1.11.43. Germans in Crimea cut off. 6.11.43. Kiev retaken; 13.11.43, Zhitomir taken on 13th but lost five days later. Russians take Cherkassy 20.11.43, Gomel 26.11.43.	NOVEMBER 1943 13.11.43. Rosenberg's last interview with Hitler. Autonomy for the Baltic States again refused. Retreating Wehrmacht pillage Zhitomir. Ukrainian nationalists shooting Germans in Rowné.	NOVEMBER 1943 Chaotic conditions among volunteers transferred west. Himmler asks for SD reports on possible Russian alternatives to Stalin. D'Alquen conducts SS broadcasts to Russians.

DECEMBER 1943 Koestring succeeds Hellmich as inspector of eastern troops, now known as volunteers. New conditions of service on a parity with Germans.	**DECEMBER 1943** Rosenberg demands that the Wehrmacht hand over control of the Economic Staff East. Arrest of the OUN leaders, Borovets and Bandera.	**DECEMBER 1943** 26.12.43. Russian offensive west of Kiev produces break-through. End of the 'orderly retreat'. Russians in Zhitomir again 31.12.43.
JANUARY 1944 Caucasian parent division created for service in France. Stauffenberg wants to keep volunteers in German training centres.	**JANUARY 1944** Litzmann installs virtual autonomy in Estonia in defiance of Lohse. Gottberg appoints National Council in White Russia. *Reichskommissariat* Ukraine almost non-existent.	**JANUARY 1944** Russians take Berdichev 5.1.44, reach old Polish border next day. New Russian offensive in north frees Leningrad blockade 27.1.44.
FEBRUARY 1944 Baltic SS divisions in defence of Narva line.	**FEBRUARY 1944** Eastern workers' *Ost* badge exchanged for national armlets.	**FEBRUARY 1944** 4.1.44. Russians reach Narva river line in Estonia and occupy Luck and Rowné next day. Practically all *Reichskommissariat* Ukraine in Russian hands by end of month.
MARCH 1944 Vlasov forbidden to visit volunteer units in France. Arrest of members of Dabendorff propaganda school.	**MARCH 1944** Wehrmacht ordered to collect Russian boys during their retreat to serve as auxiliaries.	**MARCH 1944** 9.3.44. Russians enter Galicia, take Kherson 13.3.44. Reach Dniester river 19.3.44.
APRIL 1944 Himmler, interested in a repetition of 'leaflet 13', recalls d'Alquen from Italy for a new Russian propaganda drive.	**APRIL 1944** Rosenberg continues to fight for the control of the Economic Staff East, in the remaining territory of White Russia, Latvia and Lithuania.	**APRIL 1944** 2.4.44. Russians cross Pruth river into Rumania and on 8th reach Czechoslovak border; on 10.4.44 take Odessa and by end of the month all Crimea, except Sevastopol.

Military Events	Civil Government Events	German-sponsored Russian Liberation Movements
MAY 1944 9.5.44. Russians retake Sevastopol. Of the pre-1939 Soviet Union only the area east of Minsk left in German hands.	MAY 1944 Koch without a territory. Gottberg in Minsk, virtually independent of Lohse in Riga.	MAY 1944 Himmler sanctions a *Leitstelle* for Russian collaborators under Fritz Arlt.
JUNE 1944 Last Red Army offensive on Russian soil opens 23.6.44; takes Vitebsk 25.6.44, Mogilev 28.6.44, Bobruisk 29.6.44.	JUNE 1944 So-called national council meets in Minsk shortly before Russian offensive.	JUNE 1944 First Russian volunteers captured in Normandy. Two battalions under Buniachenko put up a fight.
JULY 1944 Russians take Minsk 3.7.44, Kovel 6.7.44, Vilna 13.7.44. Galician offensive opens on the 16th. By end of the month Red Army close to Riga, Kovno, Warsaw, take Lwow 27.7.44.	JULY 1944 *Aktion Heu.* Decision on 11.7.44 to send children aged ten upwards from the retreat-front to Germany.	JULY 1944 20.7.44. Suicide of the pro-Vlasov officers, Freytag-Loringhoven, von Roenne, Wagner after the failure of the bomb plot. Himmler defers his support of Vlasov, but permits Zhilenkov to visit Galician front.
AUGUST 1944 1.8.44. Baltic States cut off from East Prussia. 23.8.44. Rumanians go over to Russian side. 24.8.44. Slovakia rebels against Germany. 29.8.44. Russians in Bucharest.	AUGUST 1944 Litzmann organizes defence of remains of Estonian territory. Lohse deserts his post in Riga.	AUGUST 1944 Remains of eastern volunteer units in the west disarmed and turned into labour-force. Pending Hitler's decision Himmler keeps Vlasov on ice at Ruhpolding. Turcoman division in action on Italian front. Galician SS division depleted in action at Tarnopol.

Comparative Chronological Tables (after evacuation of Soviet Union)

Military Events	German-sponsored Liberation Movements
SEPTEMBER 1944 6.9.44. Russians reach Yugoslav border. 9.9.44. Bulgaria capitulates. 10.9.44. Finland capitulates. 21.9.44. Russians take Reval and occupy all Estonia by end of the month.	**SEPTEMBER 1944** Himmler sees Vlasov 16.9.44, and agrees to a Vlasov Army limited to two divisions. Russian volunteers removed from Warsaw on complaint of OKW. Kaminsky murdered in Galicia.
OCTOBER 1944 10.10.44. The Baltic pocket finally sealed off by land from Germany. 15.10.44. Germans prevent Hungarian armistice with Russia. 20.10.44. Russians reach Adriatic.	**OCTOBER 1944** 2.10.44. Lukewarm response of OKW to Koestring's demand for equipment for Vlasov army. Berger obtains release of Ukrainian nationalists Melnyk, Bandera, Borovets, Stetsko, etc. 12.10.44. Rosenberg's offer of resignation.
NOVEMBER 1944 Complete lull on Baltic, Polish and Carpathian fronts, but continued Russian advance in Hungary and Yugoslavia.	**NOVEMBER 1944** 14.11.44. Meeting in Prague of Vlasov's Grand Committee for the Liberation of Russia, KONR. 7.11.44. Formation of first Vlasov division begun at Muesningen.
DECEMBER 1944 Almost complete stalemate in the east. Russians advance slowly in Hungary. Budapest besieged 24.12.44.	**DECEMBER 1944** Berger and Rosenberg planning a Ukrainian army, rival to Vlasov and KONR.

Military Events	German-sponsored Liberation Movements
JANUARY 1945 11.1.45. Russian offensive across Vistula opens. Fall of Warsaw. 22.1.45. East Prussia cut off by second Russian thrust to the Baltic. Russians reach the Oder. 27.1.45. Germans abandon Lithuania, retaining only a pocket in Latvia.	**JANUARY 1945** Formation of second Vlasov division begun at Heuberg. KONR government recognized by Hitler 28.1.45. Its seat removed from Dahlem to Karlsbad in Bohemia. 27.1.45. Minutes of Hitler's staff conference show complete oblivion of Vlasov movement.
FEBRUARY 1945 Russians occupy most of the Oder-Neisse line, leaving Koenigsberg and Danzig besieged. Capitulation of Budapest completed 12.2.45.	**FEBRUARY 1945** Ukrainian national committee and army under Pavlo Shandruk recognized. 12.2.45. One Vlasov battalion in action near Stettin. Koestring demands further commitments. Collaborationist conference at Bratislava cancelled.
MARCH 1945 12.3.45. Russian bridgehead at Kuestrin on Oder 30.3.45. Russians take Danzig. 6–13.3.45. German attempt to relieve Budapest, the last German offensive fails. 30.3.45. Russians enter Austria.	**MARCH 1945** Beginning of March, first Vlasov division ordered to the Oder front. Reaches Oder front 26.3.45.
APRIL 1945 Russians take Koenigsberg 9.4.45, take Vienna 13.5.45. Last Russian offensive starts 19.4.45, across the Oder. Outskirts of Berlin reached 23.4.45. Link-up with Americans at Torgau on Elbe 25.4.45. Stettin and Bruenn fall 26.4.45. Russians near Reich Chancellery 30.4.45, death of Hitler.	**APRIL 1945** 13.4.45. First Vlasov division fails to take Russian Oder bridgehead and under Buniachenko begins a march to Prague in defiance of orders. 19.4.45. Vlasov's staff and second division leave Heuberg for Linz. 26.4.45. Vlasov's envoys fail to obtain guarantees from General Patch of US 7th Army. Vlasov in Bohemia with Buniachenko at end of the month.

MAY 1945

2.5.45. Capitulation of Berlin.

3.5.45. Americans enter Bohemia. German plenipotentiaries at Rheims

5.5.45.

8.5.45. Operations cease at 11 pm. Same day Germans capitulate to nationalist committee in Prague.

10.5.45. Russians in Prague.

23.5.45. Arrest of the Doenitz government.

MAY 1945

5-7.5.45. First Vlasov division invited by Czech nationalists into Prague to secure complete German capitulation.

10.5.45. First Vlasov division accepted across US demarcation line.

12.5.45. Vlasov falls into Russian hands. Buniachenko disbands his men. Most of second division fall into Russian hands in Bohemia, same day.

23.5.45. Anglo-Russian accord in Vienna, by which all Cossack and most Ukrainian forces in Austria are handed over to USSR. Last mass-delivery of Russian collaborators at Plattling, February 1946. Execution of Vlasov and his collaborators announced in Moscow, 2nd August 1946.

APPENDIX II

Alphabetical list and short description of the principal characters in this book.

Altenstadt, Colonel Schmidt von	Head of Military Government section, OKW.
Anfuso, Filippo	Italian ambassador in Germany. Accompanied Mussolini to Ukraine, 1941.
Arlt, Colonel Fritz, SS	Head of *Leitstelle Ost* at the SS Main Office, 1943–5. Champion of Russian minorities.
Aschenbrenner, Major General	Luftwaffe attaché to Vlasov's Army, 1945.
Astakhov, Georgei	Russian Councillor of Embassy, Berlin, 1938–41.
Antonescu, Marshal Ion	Rumanian Premier, 1939–44. Executed, June, 1946.
Bahazy, Volodimir	German appointed mayor of Kiev. Executed, February 1942.
Bach-Zelewski, General Erich von dem, SS	Chief of anti-Partisan warfare, Russian front, from October 1942. Nuremberg prosecution witness, living.
Backe, Herbert	German Minister of food and agriculture, joint head of Economic Staff East from 1941. Committed suicide, 1947.
Baidalakov, Viktor	Leader of Russian emigré party, NTS or solidarists.
Bandera, Captain Stepan	Founder (1939) of secessionist Ukrainian Nationalist group, OUN-B or Benderovce. Interned by Germans, 1941–4. Now living in south Germany.
Bazilevsky, Boris	Deputy mayor of Smolensk under German military government. Nuremberg prosecution witness, 1946.
Berger, General Gottlob, SS	Head of SS Main Leadership Office from 1938. Head of Rosenberg's Political Department from June 1943. Released from prison, 1951.
Bicherakhov, Colonel	Cossack civil war leader living in Berlin during the war.
Bielenberg, Heidi	Matron of SS convalescent home, married to Vlasov at end of the war.

Bierkamp, Colonel SS	Commander of an extermination unit in the Kuban-Caucasus, 1942. Head of Security Police, Cracow, 1944. Fate unknown.
Blagovestchensky, Major General Ivan	Vlasovite officer, hanged in Moscow, August 1946.
Blaskowitz, Colonel General Johannes	Military governor, Poland, 1939. Committed suicide, Nuremberg Prison, 1948.
Bock, Field Marshal Fedor von	Commander-in-Chief, Central Army Group, 1941–2. Killed in an air raid, 1945.
Boiarsky, Major General Vladimir	Vlasovite officer, former Red Army Guards Colonel. Hanged in Moscow, August 1946.
'Bor, General' (Colonel Komarowski)	Leader of the Warsaw rebellion, 1944.
Bormann, Martin	Head of the Nazi Party Office after the flight of Rudolf Hess (1941). Hitler's private secretary and chief mentor. Presumed to have been killed in the battle of Berlin, 2nd May 1945.
Borovets, Taras	Leader (1941–4) of the Ukrainian nationalist force, UPA and head of the so-called Sich or Republic of Polesia under the German occupation. Living in Germany.
Braemer, General Walter Friedrich	Military plenipotentiary in the civil government *Ostland*, 1941–5.
Braeutigam, Otto	Deputy head of the Political Department in the Eastern Ministry, 1941–5. Reinstated in the Eastern section of the Bonn Foreign Office after a brief suspension in January 1956.
Brauchitsch, Field Marshal Walter von	Commander-in-Chief on the Russian front till December 1941. Died in a British camp at Muensterlager, 1948.
Buchardt, Major Friedrich, SS	Security Service (SD) officer in liaison with Vlasov 'government'.
Buerckel, Josef	Gauleiter of Palatinate and Saarland from 1939. Committed suicide, November 1944.
Buniachenko, Major General Sergei	Vlasovite officer from 1942. Commanded first Vlasov division, 1944–5. Hanged in Moscow, August 1946.
Busse, Infantry General	Commander-in-Chief, 9th Army on the Oder front, 1945.

Canaris, Admiral Wilhelm — Head of the German Intelligence Service, *Abwehr* 1935–44. Executed at Flossenbuerg Concentration Camp, April 1945.

Chokai, Mustafa — Member of a German Turcoman national committee, died of typhus, 1941.

Ciano, Count Galeazzo — Italian Foreign Minister till 1943. Executed at Verona.

Crantz, Major Carl — Chief of Press section, Rosenberg Ministry till 1943.

d'Alquen, Major General Gunter, SS — Commander of SS propaganda battalion, 'Kurt Eggers'. From end of 1944 chief of Wehrmacht propaganda. Fined 60,000 marks by a Berlin Denazification court, July 1955.

Dargel, Paul — Deputy to Erich Koch as *Reichskommissar* Ukraine, 1941–44. Then Bormann's liaison officer with Vlasov Army.

Dierlewanger, Major General Oskar, SS — Commander Dierlewanger regiment (later brigade) of convict SS men. Anti-Partisan commander, disappeared 1945.

Duerksen, Captain Eugen — Promoter of Vlasov movement, member of section IV of the Wehrmacht Propaganda Department.

Dwinger, Eduard Erich — Journalist, employed on Himmler's staff. Ardent supporter of Vlasov, sent into retirement, 1943.

Dekanosov, Vladimir — Russian Ambassador to Berlin, 1938–41.

Ehlich, Colonel Hans, SS — Chief of 'Nationalities section' of the Security Service (SD). Helped draw up Himmler-Vlasov accord.

Eberstein, Lieutenant General Friedrich von, SS — Higher SS and Police commander, Bavaria. Implicated in 1941 in executions of Russian prisoners of war. Nuremberg defence witness.

Eichorn, Field Marshal Hermann — Commander-in-Chief in Ukraine, 1918. Murdered by Bolshevik agents.

Eicke, Lieutenant General Theodor, SS — Commander, SS Totenkopf division, from 1940. Killed in action, March 1943.

Fegelein, General Hermann, SS — Commander SS Cavalry division 'Florian Geyer' 1941–3. Hitler's liaison officer with the SS from April 1943. Executed by Hitler's orders, 29th April 1945.

Forostivsky, Leonti — German-appointed mayor of Kiev, 1942–3. Now living in Argentina.

Frank, Hans	*Reichskommissar* for the 'Generale Gouvernement' of Poland, October 1939–January 1945. Hanged at Nuremberg, October 1946.
Frank, Karl Hermann	German 'Protector' of Bohemia, 1943–5. Hanged in Prague, 1946.
Freytag-Loringhoven, Colonel Wessel von	Intelligence officer, Army Group B, 1942. Chief of Staff to Inspector, Eastern Troops, December 1942, to July 1944. Committed suicide, 20th July 1944.
Friderici, General Erich	Military plenipotentiary, Bohemia, 1939–45, except for a few months in 1943 when he commanded Southern Army Group Rear Area, Kharkov.
Frauenfeldt, Alfred	Viennese playwright. *Generalkommissar*, Taurida, 1942–3. Intended for Crimea.
Gehlen, Major General Reinhard	Head of the German intelligence section, 'Foreign Armies, East', 1941–45. Said to have worked since the war for the US Intelligence Service in Germany.
Gersdorff, Major General Rudolf von	Chief of Intelligence to Central Army Group, 1941–3, associate of von Tresckow.
Globocnik, Lieutenant General Odilo, SS	Higher SS and Police Leader, Lublin, 1939–43, and Trieste-Dalmatia, 1943–5. Vlasov supporter. Committed suicide in Carinthia, June 1945.
Goebbels, Josef	Reich Minister for propaganda and Gauleiter of Berlin. From August 1944, plenipotentiary for Total War. Committed suicide, 1st May 1945.
Goering, Hermann	*Reichsmarschall* or senior member of the armed forces. Head of the German Air Force. *Reichskommissar* for the Four-Year-Plan. Dismissed from his offices, April 1945. Committed suicide, Nuremberg, 15th October 1946.
Gottberg, Major General Hans von, SS	Settlement commissioner, Prague, 1939. Higher SS and Police Leader, Minsk, 1941–3. *Generalkommissar*, White Russia, 1943–4; said to have been killed in action, 1945.
Grote, Major Nikolaus von	Section chief in Wehrmacht Propaganda Department. Early promoter of Vlasov movement.
Gutterer, Leopold	Under-secretary in Goebbels's Ministry. Concerned in drafting new charter for eastern workers, April 1943.

Guttkelch, Dr — Head of ZAVO, Central Warfare Office for eastern workers in the Rosenberg Ministry.

Hellmich, Lieutenant General Heinz — Inspector of eastern troops, December 1942 to December 1943. Killed near Cherbourg, June 1944.

Halder, Colonel General Franz — Chief of Staff of the Wehrmacht, 1938–42. Dismissed by Hitler, September 1942. Imprisoned as a suspect after the July plot, 1944. Now seventy-nine years old, 1959.

Heinrici, Colonel General Gotthard — Commander-in-Chief, Vistula Army Group, March–May 1945.

Herre, Colonel Heinz — Chief of Staff to Hellmich and Koestring as inspectors of the eastern troops. Part-creator of the Vlasov Army.

Herwarth von Bittenfeld, Colonel Hans — Adjutant to Ernst Koestring as Military Governor, Kuban-Caucasus, 1942, and as Inspector, eastern troops, 1943–5. At present German ambassador to London.

Heydrich, General Reinhardt, SS — Head of the Security Police and Security Service (Sipo and SD) known after the outbreak of war as RSHA. Killed in Prague, May 1942.

Heygendorff, Lieutenant General Ralph von — Inspector of the eastern 'legions', September 1942. Commander, 162nd Turcoman Division, 1943–5.

Hewel, Walter — Foreign Office chief of liaison at Hitler's headquarters, throughout the war. Killed while trying to escape from Berlin, 2nd May 1945.

Hilger, Gustav — German Councillor of Embassy, Moscow, till 1941. Later served on Ribbentrop's Russia Committee.

Himmler, Heinrich — Reichsfuehrer of the SS and Head of the German Police. After 20th July 1944, commanded the replacement forces (Ersatzheer) as well as the Upper Rhine and Vistula Army Groups. Committed suicide, 23rd May 1945.

Hitler, Adolf (1889–1945) — Reich Chancellor (1933), Head of the German State (1934), Commander-in-Chief of the armed forces (1938), Commander-in-Chief in Russia (December 1941). Committed suicide, 30th April 1945.

Hoepner, Colonel General Erich	Commanded 4th Armoured Group 1941–2. Dismissed from the army by Hitler, 8th January 1942. Executed for his part in the bomb plot, 8th August 1944.
Jaeckeln, Lieutenant General Franz, SS	Higher SS and Police Leader, Ukraine, 1941, *Ostland*, 1941–3. Thereafter SS corps commander. Hanged by the Russians in Riga, 1946.
Jodl, Colonel General Alfred	Chief of the Operations Section of the High Command (OKW) from 1938. Hanged, Nuremberg, October 1946.
Kaltenbrunner, General Ernst, SS	Head of Main Security Office (RSHA) from March 1943. Hanged, Nuremberg, October 1946.
Kaminsky, Major General Bronislav, SS	Head of self-government area Lokot, 1941–3. Commander of SS Kaminsky brigade, 1943–4. Murdered in Galicia by the SD, October 1944.
Kaufmann, Guenter	Editor of Hitler Youth magazine, *Wille und Macht*, polemist for Vlasov, 1943.
Kayum Khan, Veli	Head of Turkestan National Committee, 1941–5. Said to be living in Germany.
Kazantsev, Alexei	Russian emigré official of Wehrmacht Propaganda Department, Section IV. Member of solidarist party, NTS. Living in Germany.
Keiling, Major Siegfried	German liaison officer with Vlasov Army.
Keitel, Field Marshal Wilhelm	Chief of High Command of the Wehrmacht (OKW), from February 1938 to May 1945. Hanged, Nuremberg, October 1946.
Kinkelin, Dr Major, SS	Referent for Ukraine in Rosenberg's 'Political department'.
Khedia, Micha	Head of Georgian national committee in Berlin. Opponent of Vlasov movement.
Kleist, General Field Marshal Ewald von	Commander-in-Chief of Army Group B in Caucasus and Ukraine, 1942–3. Died in Russian prison camp, October 1954.
Kleist, Peter	Referent *Ostland* in Rosenberg's Political department. Champion of Baltic self-government.
Kluge, General Field Marshal Guenther von	Commander-in-Chief Central Army Group, December 1941 to November 1943. Committed suicide in France, August 1944.

Koch, Erich — Gauleiter, East Prussia 1928–45. *Reichskommissar* Ukraine, September 1941 to April 1944. Extradited to Poland 1950. In Mokatow prison (1959). Sentence of death not carried out.

Koch, Professor Hans — *Abwehr* officer in Lwow and Ukraine, 1941.

Kononov, Major General — Russian Cossack deserter who served with the Pannwitz Cossack Corps. Hanged in Russia, 1947.

Koeppen, Dr Werner — Rosenberg's representative at Hitler's Field Headquarters in East Prussia.

Koerner, Paul — State Secretary to Goering as head of the Four-Year-Plan Office. Released, December 1951 from Landsberg prison.

Koerner, Colonel Hellmut, SS — Chief of agricultural affairs in Koch's Ukraine administration.

Koestring, General Ernst — German military attache in Moscow till 1941. Military Governor, Kuban-Caucasus, September 1942–February 1943. Inspector of eastern troops, December 1943–May 1945. Living, aged eighty-three.

Konovalets, Eugen — Ukrainian nationalist leader during the civil war, 1918–21. Murdered, 1939.

Kovpak, Major General Sidor — Ukrainian leader in the civil war on the Bolshevik side. Head of the Ukrainian Red Army Partisans in 1942–3 and hero of the famous raid to the Carpathians.

Krasnov, General Piotr — Former Cossack civil war leader who worked for the Germans in 1941–5. Said to have been hanged in Russia, 1947 after extradition by the Allies.

Krebs, Colonel General Hans — Acting military attaché, Moscow, 1941. Last Chief of Staff of the Wehrmacht, 1945. Committed suicide, Berlin, 2nd May 1945.

Kroeger, Brigadier General Erhard, SS — Former repatriation commissioner, employed by Kaltenbrunner to observe Vlasov's movements.

Krosigk, Colonel von — Chief of Staff to General von Roques as Rear Area Commander, Southern Army, Group, 1941–2.

Kube, Wilhelm — Gauleiter, Brandenburg-Grenzland, 1933–6. *Generalkommissar*, White Russia, 1941–3, assassinated in Minsk, 23rd September 1943.

Kubiovych, Professor Volodimir	Head of Ukrainian central committee Cracow, 1939–44 under Governor Frank. Vice-president, Ukrainian National Committee, 1945.
Kuechler, Field Marshal Georg von	Commander-in-Chief, Northern Army Group, January 1942–August 1944. Vlasov supporter. Released from Landsberg prison, 1953.
Lahousen, Brigadier General Erwin von	Staff officer of Canaris's *Abwehr*. Nuremberg prosecution witness, 1945.
Lammers, Hans	Chief of the Reich Chancellery, 1933–45. Released from Landsberg prison, December 1951.
Leeb, Field Marshal Wilhelm Ritter von	Commander-in-Chief, Northern Army Group, June 1941–April 1942. Released from internment, 1948. Died May 1956.
Leibbrandt, Georg	Head of the Political Department in the Eastern Ministry, July 1941–June 1943. Charged in Germany as a war criminal, January 1950. Not brought to trial.
Ley, Robert	Head of organization 'Arbeits front' which replaced the German Trade Unions in 1933. Committed suicide at Mondorf, 1945.
Leyser, Ernst	*Generalkommissar*, Zhitomir, September 1941 to October 1943, under Erich Koch.
Lindemann, Colonel General Hans	Commander-in-Chief, 18th Army, 1941–3. Supporter of Vlasov.
Litvinov, Maxim	Russian Foreign Minister, dismissed, 3rd May 1939.
Lohse, Hinrich	Gauleiter, Schleswig-Holstein, 1933–41. *Reichskommissar, Ostland*, July 1941–September 1944. Released from prison, 1951.
Lorenz, General Werner, SS	Head of resettlement office, RUSHA. Foreign Office plenipotentiary to Vlasov, October 1944. Released from Landsberg prison, 1955.
Maë, Dr Hjalmar	Leader of the Estonian National Socialists. Head of German picked National Council, 1941–4.
Magunia, Waldemar	*Generalkommissar*, Kiev, under Erich Koch from February 1942 to September 1943.

Malyshkin, Major General Vassili — Vlasov's plenipotentiary with the Allies at the end of the war. Hanged in Moscow, August 1946.

Mal'zev, Major General Vladimir — Vlasovite officer, hanged in Moscow, August 1946.

Manstein, Field Marshal Erich von — Commander, 11th Army, 1941–2. Southern Army Group, 1943–4. Released from Werl prison, 1952.

Markull, Friedrich — Head of legal section in Eastern Ministry.

Martin, Colonel Hans — Head of section IV, Wehrmacht Propaganda Department.

Matsuoka, Yosuke — Japanese Foreign Minister who concluded a non-aggression pact with Russia in 1941.

Meandrov, Colonel Vassili — Chief of Staff, 2nd Vlasov Division, 1945. Hanged in Moscow, August 1946.

Melnyk, Andrei — Head of Ukrainian exile nationalist group, OUN-M, interned by Germans in 1944 for some months. Now lives in Luxembourg.

Mende, Professor Gerhard von — Head of section 'Caucasian nationalities' in the Eastern Ministry. Now in Bonn Refugees Ministry.

Meyer-Hetling, Professor Konrad — Expert on racial resettlement, employed by Hitler at the SS main office. Acquitted at Nuremberg, 1947.

Meyer-Mader, Colonel — Commander of Turkish-speaking special unit in 1941–2 and later director of training for the Caucasian legions.

Meyer, Alfred — Gauleiter of Westphalia. Deputy to Rosenberg as head of the Eastern Ministry 1941–5. Committed suicide, 1945.

Mikoyan, Anastas — Soviet commissar for Foreign Trade in 1939, a post which he retains today.

Michel, Captain Carl — Intelligence officer to Hellmich and Koestring as inspectors of the Eastern Troops. Friend of Stauffenberg. Anti-Vlasovite.

Milwe, Anatol von der — Referent for cultural affairs in Eastern Ministry.

Molotov, Viacheslav — Russian Foreign Minister, appointed, May 1939. Now ambassador to Mongolian Republic.

Moltke, James Hellmuth von — Expert on international law, employed by the *Abwehr* in 1941. Executed after the July plot, 1944.

Mussolini, Benito — *Duce* or leader of the Italian State, 1922–43. Murdered, April 1945.

Mueller, Lieutenant General Eugen — Quartermaster General, 1939–41. General for Special Assignments, 1941–2.

Mueller, General Heinrich, SS — Head of the Gestapo (RSHA, section IV) from 1935 to 1945. Disappeared during battle of Berlin, April 1945.

Mueller, Lieutenant General Vincenz — Deputy commander, 4th Armoured Group, captured June 1944. Nuremberg prosecution witness.

Natzmer, Major General von — Chief of Staff to Field Marshal Schoerner, April 1945.

Neubacher, Hermann — Goering's economic plenipotentiary for south-east Europe. Intended in 1942 for the Caucasus.

Nickel, Siegfried — Referent on Youth Movement affairs in the Eastern Ministry.

Niedermeyer, Lieutenant General Oskar von — Commander Turcoman Division, 1943. Deputy inspector, Eastern Volunteers on western front, 1944. Imprisoned for insubordination. Has disappeared since the war in Russian captivity.

Oberlaender, Major Theodor — Commanded 'Bergmann' Caucasian battalion till June 1943, when he was dismissed for a critical manifesto. At present Minister for Refugee Affairs, Bonn.

Ohlendorff, Major General Otto, SS — Commanded extermination unit, *Einsatzgruppe D*, 1941–2. Head of Amt III, RSHA (the SD) 1938–45. Hanged at Landsberg, June 1951.

Oster, Major General Hans — Chief of Staff to Admiral Canaris in the *Abwehr*. Executed, April 1945.

Ostrovsky, Professor Rodoslav — Head of German-appointed White Russian National Committee, 1944–5.

Paltzo, Joachim — Chief of propaganda to Erich Koch in the Ukraine, 1941–4.

Pannwitz, Lieutenant General Hellmuth von — Commanded Cossack Cavalry Corps on Balkan front, 1944–5. Extradited to Russia and hanged, 1947.

Paulus, Field Marshal Friedrich — Surrendered with remains of his 6th Army at Stalingrad, February 1943. Broadcast for Moscow Free Germany committee. Nuremberg prosecution witness. Returned to East Germany, October 1953.

Petlyura, Simon — Ukrainian nationalist leader during civil war, 1918–21. Murdered in Paris, 1926.

Peuckert, Staatsrat — Deputy to Fritz Sauckel as plenipotentiary for labour recruitment.

Pruetzmann, Lieutenant General Hans, SS — Higher SS and Police Leader, Ukraine, 1941–4. Founder of 'Werwulf' organization. Committed suicide, May 1945.

Quisling Vidkun — German puppet premier of Norway, 1940–5. Famine relief official in Russia after First World War. Strong Vlasov supporter. Hanged, 1946.

Radetzky, Colonel Woldemar von, SS — Extermination group commander. Adviser to Himmler on Russian volunteer affairs, 1944. Released from Landsberg prison, 1951.

Reichenau, Field Marshal Walter von — Commanded 6th Army and Southern Army Group. Died mysteriously, 17th January 1942.

Reinecke, Lieutenant General Hermann — Head of AWA, the general Wehrmacht office, and chief of prisoner-of-war affairs, 1938–44. Released from Landsberg prison, 1957.

Reinhardt, Colonel General Hans — Commanded 3rd Panzer Army, 1942–4. Involved in deportation and other charges. Released from Landsberg prison, autumn, 1952.

Ribbentrop, Joachim — German Foreign Minister, 1938–45. Hanged, Nuremberg, October 1946.

Riecke, Hans Joachim — State secretary, Ministry of food and agriculture. Backe's deputy on Economic Staff East. Nuremberg witness, 1945.

Riedweg, Major Fritz, SS — Head of *Germanische Leitstelle* at SS Main Office. Pioneer of European SS movement.

Roques, Colonel General Karl von — Rear Area Commander to Northern Army till October 1941, then Southern Army Group, Ukraine till autumn, 1942. Died in Landsberg prison, Christmas day, 1949, aged seventy years.

Roenne, Colonel Alexis von — On staff of section Foreign Armies East till 1943, then Foreign Armies West. Committed suicide in France after July 1944 plot.

Rundstedt, Field Marshal Gerd von — Commanded Southern Army Group, Ukraine, till December 1941. Trial cancelled by British government in 1949 on account of illness, died 1953, aged seventy-eight years.

Sakharov, Colonel Igor	Russian emigré. ADC to Vlasov and commander of a Russian volunteer battalion. Not extradited.
Sauckel, Fritz	Gauleiter of Thuringia. General plenipotentiary for labour recruitment, April 1942 to April 1945. Hanged at Nuremberg, October 1946.
Schellenberg, Major General Walter, SS	Head of foreign intelligence section of SD, 1939–44. Head of *Abwehr*, 1944–5. Released from Landsberg, 1949, died 1952.
Schenckendorff, Lieutenant General Count von	Rear Area commander, Central Army Group, died of heart failure, summer, 1943. Strong Russian liberation supporter.
Schickedanz, Arno	Former editor, *Voelkische Beobachter*. Nominated *Reichskommissar*, Kuban-Caucasus, July 1941, but never served. Committed suicide, 1945.
Schiller, Otto	Former commercial attaché, Moscow. Consultant on land distribution for Economic Staff, East.
Schlabrendorff, Major Fabian von	Intelligence officer at von Kluge's headquarters, intimate with Tresckow and Gersdorff.
Schmidt, Colonel General Rudolf	Commander-in-Chief, 2nd Panzer Army, 1941–2. Originator of Russian collaborationist units.
Schmundt, Lieutenant General Rudolf	Hitler's military adjutant with OKW, 1938–44. Died of injuries after July 1944, bomb plot.
Schnurre, Karl	Commercial counsellor for Eastern Europe, Foreign Office, 1939–41.
Schoerner, Field Marshal Ferdinand	Commanded Southern Army Group, 1944–5. Sentenced, July 1958, four-and-a-half years imprisonment for illegal execution orders (after twelve years captivity in Russia).
Schulenburg, Werner von der	German ambassador to Moscow, 1935–41. Then member of Ribbentrop's Russia committee. Executed after the July plot, 1944.
Schwenninger, Major Helmut	German liaison officer, attached to 1st Vlasov Division in 1945.
Seeckt, Colonel General Hans von	Commander-in-Chief German Army, 1920–6. Signatory of Seeckt-Tukhachevski protocols. Died, 1936.

Seraphim, Professor Peter Heinz — Referent in Ukraine, 1942, for Wehrmacht Armament Office.

Shandruk, Major General Paul — Head of Ukrainian National Committee of 1945. Now living in Germany.

Sheptytski, Archbishop Andrei — Metropolitan of the western Ukrainian Uniate Catholic Church. Died in Lwow, 1944.

Sigling, Lieutenant Colonel, SS — Creator of White Russian anti-Partisan brigade, 1944, nucleus of 1st Vlasov Division.

Skoropadsky, Hetman Paul — Head of the German sponsored Ukrainian State in 1918. Living in Germany during Second World War.

Sparmann, Colonel Eugen, SS — Former resettlement official. Founded, 1943, *Leitstelle Europa* at SS main office.

Speer, Albert — Minister of armaments and munitions from February 1942. Serving twenty year sentence at Spandau (1959).

Stalin (Dzugashvili) Generalissimo Josef — De facto head of the Russian State between 1941 and 1954 as chairman of the Council of People's commissars (in addition to his position since 1927 of secretary of the Communist Party).

Stahlecker, Brigadier General Franz, SS — Commander of *Einsatzgruppe A*. Killed by Partisans, March 1942.

Stauffenberg, Colonel Claus von — Chief of organization section, OKW. Later Chief of Staff to Olbricht and Fromm in Reserve Army. Executed after failure of his plot, 20th July 1944.

Steiner, Colonel General Felix, SS — Commander of Army Corps defending Narva, 1944.

Stetsko, Jaroslav. — Member of Ukrainian movement, OUN-B, who tried to form a government in Lwow, July 1941. Interned by Germans, now reported to live in Hamburg.

Strik-Strikfeldt, Captain Wilfried — Member of Wehrmacht Propaganda Department, Section IV. Vlasov's German ADC, August 1942 to October 1944.

Taubert, Eberhardt — Chief of Russian section, Ministry for Propaganda.

Tresckow, Major General Henning von — Chief of Staff to Central Army Group till summer, 1943. Father of the Russian volunteer movement. Committed suicide, 1944, after July plot.

Trukhin, Major General Fedor — Leading propagandist of Vlasov movement. Captured by Partisans in Bohemia. Hanged, Moscow, August 1946.

Trott zu Solz, Adam — Foreign Office and *Abwehr* official, executed after July plot, 1944.

Tukhachevski, Mikail Marshal of the Red Army — Russian Chief of Staff, executed, 12th July 1937.

Vlasov, General Andrei — Commander of 2nd Russian Shock Army, who surrendered in July 1942. Head of German-sponsored anti-Stalinist government and army, KONR, 1944–5. Hanged in Moscow, August 1946.

Voloshin, Father Augustin — Head of the so-called Carpato-Ukraine government, 1939.

Waechter, Lieutenant General Gustaf Adolf, SS — Governor of Galicia under Hans Frank. Sponsored a Ukrainian committee and SS field division. Said to have died incognito in a monastery in Rome, September 1949.

Wagner, Artillery General Eduard — Quartermaster General of the forces in Russia. Committed suicide after the July plot, 1944.

Warlimont, Lieutenant General Walter — Head of the section 'territorial defence' in the operations department, OKW, and deputy to Jodl. Strong opponent of pro-Russian movements. Released from Landsberg prison, 1957.

Wedel, Major General Hasso von — Head of Wehrmacht Propaganda Department till July 1944.

Weizsaecker, Baron Ernst von — Secretary of State in Foreign Office and Ribbentrop's deputy till April 1943. Released from prison, 1949, died 1951.

Zeitzler, Lieutenant General Kurt — Chief of general staff in Russia, September 1942–July 1944. Still living.

Zhilenkov, Major General Georgei — Former Communist Party official and Political Commissar. Vlasovite officer. Hanged, Moscow, August 1946.

Zimmermann, Job — Chief of propaganda section in Rosenberg Ministry.

Zverev, Major General Georgei — Commander of 2nd Vlasov Division, 1945. Hanged, Moscow, August 1946.

Zykov, Milenti — Former Communist Party official and journalist. Director of propaganda for Vlasov. Mysteriously murdered, July 1944.

APPENDIX III
(See Chapter Three)

Russian and German Casualties

IN CHAPTER THREE mention is made of a German estimate of close on four million Red Army soldiers who died *after* their surrender and while in German hands. The figure is derived from a document which was headed 'information on the survival of the Russian prisoners of war' and which was captured among the files of General Reinecke's AWA office. Dated 1st May 1944, the text will be found on page 427 of Alexander Dallin's *German Rule in Russia*. Since the document was compiled a full year before the capitulation of Germany, Mr Dallin tries to complete the picture from other sources. Certain German files, which he fails to specify but which he calls 'more authoritative but still incomplete', show that at least another 200,000 Red Army soldiers surrendered in the last twelve months of the war and that the Reinecke list underestimated the matter, since the final count of prisoners was 5,754,000. On this basis the count on 1st May 1944, must have been at least five-and-a-half millions and not 5,160,000 as stated.

At that time only 1,053,000 of these men remained alive in German hands as prisoners of war, though an additional 818,000 had been 'released to civilian or military status'. It follows that at least 3,700,000 were missing. Furthermore, since 178,000 of the men who were classed as prisoners were unfit for labour, a large proportion of this additional number must have succumbed to the conditions of camp life in the last year of the war. The 3,700,000, who were already missing in May 1944, were for the most part dead. This is unquestionable since the Reinecke list gives the following enumerations. On the camp registers 1,918,000 deaths had been recorded. A further 473,000 had been *exterminated* while in the custody of OKW in Germany and Poland; 273,000 had died or disappeared while in transit and 495,000 had been *exterminated* or had died in transit or were merely unaccounted for while in the Wehrmacht's custody in occupied Russia. This left a mere 67,000 who were believed to have escaped. Perhaps the most shocking feature of the list is its casualness. On the long marches to the rear-zones those who were shot dead, those who died by the way and those who bolted, were lumped together in one figure (see page 98). The final results were exhibited without shame. Of five-and-a-half million captives who might have been working for Germany in May 1944, there were left 818,000 working or serving in uniform outside the camps and 875,000 working inside.

At any rate these figures can be regarded as roughly established. The same does not hold good for the other casualties of the war in Russia, of whose enormous scale the Reinecke list offers a hint. According to the Nuremberg witness, General von dem Bach-Zelewski, Himmler predicted to a select audience in March 1941, that Russia would have to lose thirty million people. Long after the trial, Bach-Zelewski explained that Himmler had not meant a planned extermination but the probable cost to Russia of a German invasion (IMT, IV, 36 and Hildegard Springer, *das Schwert auf der Waage*, Heidelberg, 1953, page 95). Quite recently the publication of the Soviet population census for 1959 has been interpreted in the English press as vindicating Himmler's prediction and even exceeding it. The population of the Soviet Union in January 1959, was 208,826,000. In January 1939, it had been in the region of 170 millions, but to this figure must be added the population of territories which did not then form part of the Soviet Union. It is apparently assumed that twenty millions must be added in respect of these territories which consist of Latvia, Lithuania and Estonia, besides former Polish parts of White Russia and the Ukraine, Ruthenia which had been formerly Czechoslovak, Bukovina and Bessarabia which had formerly been Rumanian.

Assuming a real population in 1939 of 190 millions, *The Times* (11.5.59) concluded that after twenty years this greater Soviet Union should have had more like 250 million inhabitants than 209 million. Even Himmler had not foreseen that Russia's population growth would be retarded by forty millions, still less had he foreseen that, in spite of this retardation, Russia twenty years hence would be more powerful and prosperous than ever in her history. These statistical inferences must, however, be regarded with caution, if not with suspicion. Even if the subsequently annexed territories represented a population of twenty millions in 1939 (which is doubtful) it is likely that quite half of it shifted further west with the retreat of the German armies. A population which rose from 180 millions to 209 millions in twenty years would still have increased at a rate of 0·80 per cent per annum, a rate higher than that of any Western country and in fact equal to the increase of the Soviet population between 1932 and 1939, completely peaceful years in which the population of the original territory rose from 161 to 170 millions. One may for instance contrast the increase of population of England and Wales between 1911 and 1951, which ran at 0·60 per cent per annum.

It is, however, asserted in the same *Times* article that the population of the Soviet Union is now increasing at the rate of three-and-a-half millions a year or 1·75 per cent. If this is the case, then we have a rate of increase more than double that of 1932–9. If this tremendous fecundity has been going on for some years, it may conceal equally tremendous losses in 1941–5. Including in his estimate eight million military casualties, *The Times* statistician estimates a loss in the war-years of thirty millions, partly through excess-deaths but also through diminished births.

Here, however, we have two entirely separate causes for the temporary decline in the population of the Soviet Union. The first cause is death at the hands of the enemy. The second cause is a peculiarity of Soviet social organization. Among the Western Allies the war stimulated a rise in the birth-rate, whereas in the Soviet Union the birth-rate declined because family life was far more disrupted. Between sixteen and twenty million men were called up to serve up to six years on end without a day's home leave.

Even the wives of men who were not called up for military service were often separated from them in factories or temporary homes thousands of miles apart. The loss in births from these causes cannot be counted as war casualties.

As to the real war casualties, it may be thought that a clue is offered in the statement of the Central Soviet Statistical Board that today females exceed males by more than twenty millions, an excess which occurs only among subjects born before 1927. It may be inferred from this that twenty million men of the war-service generation failed to return. This is hardly borne out in an examination of probabilities, which may lead to the conclusion that much of the twenty million female surplus is due to demographic conditions long native to the Soviet Union. There is no Soviet official estimate of the war-dead nor are there any reliable indications. On 22nd June 1944, for instance, Stalin declared in a speech commemorating the third anniversary of the war that 5,300,000 Red Army men were dead, missing or prisoners. This was a manifest understatement since more than this number had surrendered to the Germans. The Russians of course claimed that the Germans falsified their figures, but even Reinecke's office could hardly have regarded the loss of over three million prisoners as a matter for boasting. The real figure was, therefore, much higher than Stalin cared to admit. But how much higher? To build up a tentative estimate one must start with the comparative German losses, but here again Reinecke's lists stop short. Casualties on the Russian front can be traced to 30th November 1944, when they stood at 1,419,000 identified as dead, 907,000 regarded as missing. Since the Russians did not report the names of men in captivity as a general rule, it is impossible to ascertain how many of these 907,000 were alive in Russian prisoner-of-war camps. The Soviet High Command claimed in May 1945 that they held 3,180,000 German prisoners. This offers no clue, because it is well known that most of these surrendered in the last few days of the war or shortly afterwards. (*The Times*, 13.3.57.) It is estimated that, all in all, over three million German soldiers died on active service, irrespective of those who failed to return from Russia. The losses on the eastern front could hardly have been less than two-and-threequarter millions.

The Russians lost many more men than the Germans in actual fighting. Between November 1942, and May 1945, they were almost continuously the attackers and Russian methods of attack were always wasteful. Three-and-a-half to four millions, killed or died of wounds, seems a fair estimate. The destruction of the prisoners in German hands might well bring the total to something nearer eight millions than seven millions. To these must be added the civilians, who were executed or killed in action in the course of Partisan operations, and these might well be numbered at a quarter of a million, if the German Security Service reports on individual actions are a safe guide. Then there are the Jews of the Soviet Union who were deliberately massacred. In *The Final Solution* I have endeavoured to show that, in spite of many poetic estimates, the real number was probably in the region of 750,000. There are also deaths, due to the hardships of the German occupation, a most intangible figure. It is possible that these hardships did not greatly effect the populations of the three Baltic States nor the peasant population as a whole. The great sufferers were the urban inhabitants of the Ukraine, for whom the German distribution system made no provision in the first winter of the war (see page 102). Indeed they were deliberately written-off till the summer of 1942, when efforts were made to revive industry, as well as to recruit labour for the German farms and factories. This writing-off might well have cost a million lives. Even the Russian efforts to preserve the active labour force by hurried evacuation in the face of the enemy must have been costly in lives, while the re-occupation of the country after the enemy had practised a scorched earth policy may have been as destructive as the first winter of the war. On all three counts a civilian death roll of three millions is not impossible. Thus, all in all, the Soviet Union may have lost twelve million subjects.

On the German side one must add what would appear to be a loss of 1,200,000 men, who failed to return from Russia, (*The Times*, 13.3.57) to the figures of the war-dead. Should one add a million for German civilians who disappeared during the flight to the West before the advancing Red Army and during the forcible repatriations which were conducted by Poland and Czechoslovakia? If so the German losses in the eastern theatre alone may have reached five millions.

Adopting the test of comparative population increases, Germany has paid for her dreams of conquest far more dearly than her chief victim. In 1956 the two Germanys had a population of 68,174,000. The small number of Germans who remained behind in the territory annexed by Poland, would hardly have raised the figure beyond sixty-nine millions. This was actually less than the population of 'Versailles Germany' at the time that Hitler came to power and only four millions more than the population of the Kaiser's Germany in 1910, which, however, included two million Poles and nearly two million inhabitants of Alsace-Lorraine. This means that between 1910 and 1956 the number of Germans has increased only from sixty-one millions to sixty-nine millions or barely 13 per cent, a fact which becomes more impressive when it is remembered that in 1910 the increase was reputed to be running at the rate of 1 per cent per year. The quest for *Lebensraum* through war has solved the problem by removing the necessity for *Lebensraum* altogether, a solution more appropriate to ants than to men. To this solution Hitler's war contributed far more than the Kaiser's. With a possible seventeen million deaths shared between Germany and Russia, Hitler's adventure, which began on 22nd June 1941, has proved the mostly costly ordeal by battle in the whole of human history.

INDEX

Thrace, 56
Thuringia, 263
Tiflis, 139
Tighina, 172
Timoshenko, Marshal, 296
Tippelskirch, General Kurt von, 81
Tito, Marshal, 245, 346, 392
Tolbukhin, Marshal, 27
Tolmezzo, 304, 375
Torgau, 350, 383
Tranby Croft Camp, 395
Transdniestria, 171, 173
Transylvania, cession of, 171
Tresckow, Lt. Gen. Henning von, 73, 91,
    311, 321, 323, 333, 396
Trott zu Solz, Adam, 348
Trukhin, Maj. Gen. Feodor, 93, 316, 329,
    339, 385, 387–8, 396
Tsuman forest, 207–8, 247
Tukhachevski, Marshal, 26, 38
Turcoman Division, 304, 307, 337, 347,
    391–3
Turkestan, 134–5, 293
Turkey, 109, 292
Turnu Severin conference, 48
Tver, 134, 155
Tyrol, last stand plans, 383
Tyrol South, resettlement, 153, 185

Uiberreither, Gauleiter, 211
Ukraine, Carpathian, 61
Ukraine, famine, 1934, 39, 162
Ukraine, German independence plan, 45,
    134–5, 164–5, 364–5
Ukraine, nationalism, 21, 30, 160–71
Ukrainian police units, 221, 247, 335
Ukrainian refugees, 284, 393
Uman, 103–4, 164, 173–4
United Nations Declaration, 250
Unruh, General von, 148
Untermensch pamphlet, 26, 340, 351, 361
UPA forces, 169, 221, 246–8
Urals, 51

Vaccination, 201–2
Veltheim, Lieutenant von, 310
Versailles Treaty, 13
Viasma, 103, 235
Vienna award, 1940, 48, 52
Vienna pact, 1941, 60
Viktoriastrasse group, 315, 321
Vilna, 280
Vinnitsa, GHQ, 168–9, 212, 214, 244,
    270, 274, 297, 320, 339
Vitebsk, 156, 240, 278
Vlasov, Lt. Gen. Andrei, 25, 29, 256, 279,
    283, 295, 317–21, 327, 329–32, 338–9,
    345, 349, 351–2, 355, 360–2, 365, 379,
    383–7, 389–90, 392, 396

Voelkische Beobachter, 131
Volga Cossacks, 291
Volga Germans, 89, 142
Volhynia-Podolia, 45, 187, 207, 221, 246–9
Volkov Kessel, 319–20, 358
Volksdeutsche, 45, 112, 153
Volkssturm units, 224
Volokolamsk, 319
Voloshin, Father, 164
VOMI office, 153, 186
Voronezh, 295, 355
Voronova, Dunia, 320, 331
Voroshilov, Marshal, 38, 319
Vucoopspilka association, 189

Waechter, Otto, 170, 247
Wagner, General Eduard, 71, 74–76, 78,
    83, 108, 115, 117, 171, 182, 210, 240–1,
    292, 294, 296–300, 333, 349
Walkuere Signal, 283
Wansee conference, 255
Warlimont, General Walter von, 50, 77–
    81, 108, 170–1, 221, 240–1, 247, 277–80,
    335
War losses, 446–9
Warsaw rebellion, 29, 305, 311, 372
Warsaw trial, 1958 (Erich Koch), 226–7
Weber-Krohse, 181
Wedel, Colonel Hasso von, 81, 116, 314,
    322, 332–3
Wehrkreis VII, 107–8
Wehrmacht propaganda section, 116, 165,
    308, 313, 332, 345, 349, 355–6, 360
Weimar, 264, 273
Weimar Republic and Russia, 35
Weiss, Major, 309
Weizsaecker, Ernst von, 25, 53
Wetzel, Erwin, 255
White Russia plan, 134
White Russian General-Kommissariat,
    155–60, 234, 243, 251, 281–3
White Russian SS troops, 159
Wilhelm II, Kaiser, 13
Wille und Macht, 340
Windau, 43
Wirth Commando, 393
Wirth, Josef, 55
Wolff, Colonel Ludwig, 365
Wolfsschanze, Hitler's GHQ, 144, 224, 315,
    351
Women's Labour Service, 266
Wuhlheide camp, 327
Wuppertal, 177
Wustrow, 316

Yalta conference, 384
Yankoi, 168